MW01129211

# Fundamentals of Transfer Pricing

# Fundamentals of Transfer Pricing

## A Practical Guide

Edited by

Michael Lang
Giammarco Cottani
Raffaele Petruzzi
Alfred Storck

Institute for Austrian and
International Tax Law Vienna
WU Transfer Pricing Center

**L&P**

**LUDOVICI PICCONE & PARTNERS**

*Published by:*
Kluwer Law International B.V.
PO Box 316
2400 AH Alphen aan den Rijn
The Netherlands
E-mail: international-sales@wolterskluwer.com
Website: lrus.wolterskluwer.com

*Sold and distributed in North, Central and South America by:*
Wolters Kluwer Legal & Regulatory U.S.
7201 McKinney Circle
Frederick, MD 21704
United States of America
Email: customer.service@wolterskluwer.com

*Sold and distributed in all other countries by:*
Air Business Subscriptions
Rockwood House
Haywards Heath
West Sussex
RH16 3DH
United Kingdom
Email: international-customerservice@wolterskluwer.com

*Printed on acid-free paper.*

ISBN 978-90-411-8994-3

e-Book: ISBN 978-90-411-9021-5
web-PDF: ISBN 978-90-411-9022-2

Printed in the United Kingdom.

# Editors

**Prof. Dr DDr. h.c. Michael Lang** is the head of the Institute for Austrian and International Tax Law of WU (Vienna University of Economics and Business) and Academic Director of both the LLM Programme in International Tax Law and the Doctoral Programme in International Business Taxation (DIBT) of this university. He is the President of the Austrian Branch of the International Fiscal Association (IFA) and has been visiting professor at Georgetown University, New York University, Sorbonne, Bocconi, Peking University (PKU), University of New South Wales (Sydney), and others.

**Dr Giammarco Cottani, LLM**, is partner at L&P- Ludovici Piccone & Partners, Italian tax law firm. He coordinates the transfer pricing practice, with regards to both prevention and resolution of domestic and international disputes and the assistance in complex audits of large multinational enterprise groups. Until August 2015, he acted as Advisor on International Tax to the Central Assessment Director of Italy Revenue Agency. In this role, he focused on international tax issues related to large multinational groups and SMEs, with a specific focus on transfer pricing issues. He was one of the delegates for Italy involved in the OECD BEPS project. Before joining the Agency, he worked as a Transfer Pricing Advisor in the Tax Treaty and Transfer Pricing Unit of the OECD, where he was involved in the introduction of the new Chapter IX of the OECD Transfer Pricing Guidelines concerning business restructurings. Giammarco has served as a Member of the Sub-Committee Group of the United Nations in charge of the Draft of the Practical Manual on Transfer Pricing for Developing Countries and he has been the Delegate for Italy on a number of OECD Working Parties. Giammarco is a member of the faculty of the International Tax Center of the University of Leiden far transfer pricing. He was the National Reporter for Italy during the 2011 IFA Congress on the topic of cross-border business restructurings. He regularly lectures in postgraduate courses in international taxation (with a specific focus on transfer pricing) both in Europe and the Americas. He is currently involved in a number of technical assistance projects for tax administrations in several LATAM countries on behalf of international and regional organizations. He received his degree in Law from LUISS Rome University in 2003, an LLM in European and International Taxation from the European Tax

College (Tilburg and Leuven) in 2005, and a PhD in Corporate Taxation from LUISS Rome University in 2009.

**Dr Raffaele Petruzzi**, LLM, is the Managing Director of the WU Transfer Pricing Center at the Institute for Austrian and International Tax Law at WU (Vienna University of Economics and Business) and an international tax advisor specializing in international corporate taxation and transfer pricing at L&P Global (Vienna, Austria) and at L&P – Ludovici Piccone & Partners, Italian tax law firm. Since 2007, Raffaele has gained extensive experience in dealing with topics related to international corporate taxation and transfer pricing, both from a professional and an academic perspective. From the professional perspective, he has gained relevant experience in advising clients on specific topics (e.g., international tax issues and transfer pricing issues related to services, permanent establishments, financing, business restructuring, intangibles, and indirect taxes), international tax and transfer pricing risk management and compliance, drafting and reviewing intra-group agreements, optimizing international tax structures, as well as implementing mechanisms of dispute avoidance (e.g., rulings and APAs) and dispute resolution (e.g., MAPs and arbitrations). From the academic perspective, he is a frequent speaker in international conferences and lecturer of numerous courses (in Europe, Asia, and Latin America), as well as author of many publications on international tax and transfer pricing topics. Moreover, he regularly cooperates with professionals in advisory, the business community, governments and international organizations (e.g., OECD, United Nations, World Bank Group, European Union). Inter alia, he has gained experience in providing assistance on tax policy issues, capacity building for tax administrations, and advising governments on projects related to fight against tax evasion. Finally, amongst others, he is a member of the United Nations Subcommittee on Article 9 (Associated enterprises: Transfer Pricing), of the International Fiscal Association (IFA), and of Transfer Pricing Economists for Development (TPED). Raffaele holds a Master of Science degree in Business Administration and Law (major: Corporate Taxation) at Bocconi University (Italy), a Master of Laws degree (LLM) in International Tax Law at WU, and a PhD in International Business Taxation at WU.

**Prof. Dr Alfred Storck** is co-chair of the board of directors of the WU Transfer Pricing Center at the Institute for Austrian and International Tax Law at Vienna University of Economics and Business (WU) and, since April 2009, has been a visiting professor at the same Institute. The focus of his research and teaching activities are international business taxation and transfer pricing. From 2009 until January 2015, Alfred Storck was teaching as Honorary Professor for Company Taxation and Managerial Finance at the Institute of Accounting, Controlling and Auditing (ACA) at the University of St. Gallen Switzerland. Before his activities at both universities, Alfred Storck held various executive positions in a large multinational company headquartered in Switzerland. Alfred Storck is acting as co-editor of the journal 'Transfer Pricing International' and is appointed as arbitrator in transfer pricing disputes.

# Contributors

**Dr Sven Bremer** has over twenty years of expertise in international tax issues, especially corporate restructurings, financing and transfer pricing. Prior to joining Siemens, he worked for Big4 companies in Germany and the United States with focus on international tax issues, specifically inbound/outbound investments, merger and acquisitions and cross-border strategies. In 2005, he joined Siemens AG as Global Head of Transfer Pricing and formed an international transfer pricing team. There, his areas of expertise regard all areas of transfer pricing including planning, global documentation, intellectual property structuring, intercompany financing, as well as risk and controversy management (especially, audit defence, joint audit within the EU, APA and numerous MAPs). Sven Bremer is a regular speaker at seminars and conferences and writes frequently on transfer pricing and international tax topics. He lectures in transfer pricing at IBFD in Amsterdam and at the Vienna University of Economics and Business. Sven Bremer graduated in taxation, audit and company law from the Ludwigs-Maximilian-University in Munich (1993). He wrote a dissertation on Holding Companies in Europe at the University in Eichstaett/Ingolstadt for which he received his PhD, with honors, in 1996. He is a certified tax advisor (Steuerberater) at the Munich Tax Advisor Bar. *Sven has contributed to Chapter 7 of this volume*

**Melinda Brown** is a senior transfer pricing advisor at the OECD's Centre for Tax Policy and Administration (CTPA). She was heavily involved in the development of transfer pricing guidance under the BEPS Action Plan and now has a leading role in the post-BEPS transfer pricing work at the OECD. Melinda also works closely with non-OECD economies and is a member of the UN Subcommittee on Transfer Pricing. In 2016, Melinda took over the OECD leadership of the international tax Toolkits for low-income countries, a joint initiative of the OECD, IMF, World Bank Group, and the UN. *Melinda has contributed to Chapter 3 of this volume*

**Svitlana Buriak** is a teaching and research associate at the Institute for Austrian and International Tax Law at WU (Vienna University of Economics and Business) cooperating with the WU Transfer Pricing Center. Svitlana has also gained practical experience in corporate taxation and transfer pricing while working at Tax Law and

Investment Law Department of ILF Law Firm, Kyiv (Ukraine). *Svitlana has contributed to Chapter 5 of this volume.*

**Eter Burkadze** is a Senior Tax Analyst at PVH Europe BV since November 2017. Before she worked at Ludovici Piccone & Partners (from December 2015 till October 2017), a leading Italian tax law firm based in Milan, Italy. Eter has also worked at the Georgian Tax Administration (from July 2012 till October 2015) and at the Advisory Group of Prime Minister of Georgia in Fiscal Issues (from July 2011 till July 2012). Eter is specialized in international tax and transfer pricing matters. She holds an LLM in International Tax Law from Leiden University and MA in Economics from International School of Economics at Tbilisi State University. *Eter has contributed to Chapter 6 of this volume.*

**Ian Cremer** joined the WCO in February 2009 and is a Senior Technical Officer in the Valuation sub-Directorate, Tariff and Trade Affairs Directorate. Ian previously worked in HM Customs and Excise and HM Revenue and Customs in a number of areas including excise and inland Customs as well as VAT enforcement and Origin. He was the UK delegate to the EC Customs Code Committee (Customs Valuation Section) and WCO Technical Committee on Customs Valuation. From 2005 to 2008, Ian was the Chairperson of the Technical Committee. He has conducted valuation workshops in many developing countries, delivered presentations, and participated in major international conferences and is co-author of the WCO's current valuation training modules. *Ian has contributed to Chapter 13 of this volume.*

**Pietro Piccone Ferrarotti** is partner at L&P – Ludovici Piccone & Partners, Italian tax law firm. Pietro has more than twenty years of experience in the areas of tax controversy and litigation. He gained significant experience in advising domestic and foreign clients in complex tax audits, pre-litigation and judicial settlements, and defence before tax courts and the Court of Cassation. His work ranges from legal services in relation to reviews, audits, disputes and litigation to strategic and legal advice on major transactions in Italy and abroad. *Pietro has contributed to Chapter 6 of this volume.*

**Sébastien Gonnet** is a Vice President in the Global Transfer Pricing Practice at NERA Economic Consulting. Based in Paris, he specializes in the areas of transfer pricing, intellectual property, and valuation. For a number of years, he has advised multinational companies in transfer pricing system design and implementation, business restructurings, and intellectual property and business valuation primarily in Europe, but also in China, in a range of industries including industrial and retail clients as well as financial institutions. He also acts as an expert economist in advance pricing agreements and tax audits in Europe and China. Sébastien is a frequent lecturer and has authored many publications on the economics of transfer pricing. He is also a frequent speaker at transfer pricing, intellectual property, and valuation conferences and training workshops and has presented to tax authorities in Europe and China. He is listed in International Tax Review's World's Leading Transfer Pricing Advisors by

Expert Guide. Mr Gonnet is the founder and President of Transfer Pricing Economists for Development (TPED – www.tped.eu), a Paris-based think-tank aimed at promoting the development and sharing of business economics knowledge in transfer pricing as an enabler of development of emerging economies and developing countries. Before joining NERA Economic Consulting, Sébastien Gonnet was an economist at KPMG. He holds a Master of Science in Management from HEC, Paris (Ecole des Hautes Etudes Commerciales) and a Master of Science in International Taxation from Paris II Law University. *Sebastien has contributed to Chapter 4 of this volume.*

**Raphael Holzinger** LLM, LLM (WU), MSc (WU), LLB (WU), BSc (WU) is currently enrolled in the Doctoral Programme in Business Law at WU, and works as a research and teaching fellow at the Institute for Austrian and International Tax Law at WU. Prior to his PhD studies Raphael received a BSc and a MSc in Business Administration and a LLB and a LLM in Business Law from WU and received another postgraduate LLM in Tax Law and Accounting from University of Vienna. Besides his academic activities Raphael works in tax consultancy and is specialized on business tax, international tax and transfer pricing topics. *Raphael has contributed to Chapter 8 of this volume.*

**Benson Lim** is currently has been employed as the Technical Attaché in the Valuation Sub-Directorate, Tariff and Trade Affairs Directorate, at the World Customs Organization (WCO) since 2016. Prior to this, Benson worked at Singapore Customs from 2001 to 2016 where he spent twelve years working in the Valuation Unit. Additionally, he gained experience working at the Customs checkpoints and in the Compliance Division investigating minor technical offences. *Benson has contributed to Chapter 13 of this volume.*

**Paolo Ludovici** founded L&P – Ludovici Piccone & Partners, Italian tax law firm in November 2014. He advises on all areas of tax law encompassing all domestic and cross-border tax matters. His expertise includes domestic and international corporate reorganizations, M&A and structured finance transactions, tax planning for high net-worth individuals and trusts. He often acts as an expert in criminal and tax proceedings. He is consistently ranked by the most reputed independent researchers as a leading tax professional. He regularly speaks at tax conferences and lectures in post-graduate specialization courses. He is a member of the Tax and Legal Committee of Italian Private Equity and Venture Capital Association (AIFI) as well as of the Legal Committee of the Italian Private Banking Association (AIPB). He is full member STEP (Society of Trust and Estate Practitioners) Italy. *Paolo has contributed to Chapter 11 of this volume.*

**Guillaume Madelpuech** holds a MBA from the ESSEC Business School and a MSc in Economics from the Paris Dauphine University. He is a Principal within NERA Economic Consulting in Paris. He is an economist with more than ten years of experience in transfer pricing, including in particular intangible valuation, business structuring, option realistically available analysis, transfer pricing policy design and litigation. Mr Madelpuech has conducted a number of transfer pricing projects for multinationals in a wide range of industries, including high-tech, consumer goods, automotive, luxury goods, financial services, health care, real estate, media and entertainment, and energy. He is a regular contributor to the OECD and a frequent contributor to journals and trade publications. Prior to joining NERA, Mr Madelpuech was an economist with EY, in both Paris and in New York City, in the transfer pricing and valuation groups. *Guillaume has contributed to Chapter 4 of this volume.*

**Alexandra Miladinovic** received an LLM and LLB in Business Law as well as a BSc in Business Administration, from WU (Vienna University of Economics and Business). She works as a research and teaching associate at the Institute for Austrian and International Tax Law, WU. *Alexandra has contributed to Chapter 14 of this volume.*

**Marco Orlandi** is part of the transfer pricing unit at L&P – Ludovici Piccone & Partners, Italian tax law firm. His main areas of expertise are transfer pricing and international tax law. He worked as a tax officer for the Italian tax authorities where he focused on risk analysis and tax audits of large taxpayers. In 2015, he was appointed as an expert, delegated for Italy, within the Project Tax Inspectors Without Borders promoted by the OECD and UNPD and, in 2013, was involved in a joint audit pilot project between the Land of Bavaria's tax administration and the Italian Revenue Agency. *Marco has contributed to Chapter 3 of this volume.*

**Claire (Xue) Peng** is a Research and Teaching Associate at the Transfer Pricing Center at the Institute for Austrian and International Tax Law at WU (Vienna University of Economics and Business). She graduated from the Leiden University with an adv. LLM degree and worked at Deloitte Malta afterwards at the cross-border tax department. She is currently pursuing a PhD degree in Business Law from WU. Besides, she is writing on her PhD thesis in the area of transfer pricing. *Claire has contributed to Chapter 6 and 9 of this volume.*

**Sayee Prasanna** is a Research and Teaching Associate in the WU Transfer Pricing Center at the Institute for Austrian and International Tax Law at WU (Vienna University of Economics and Business). Sayee has worked extensively as an international tax and transfer pricing consultant with EY India. His experiences include global transfer pricing documentation, transfer pricing audit defence at various appellate forums, advance pricing agreement processes, and advisory projects for multinational companies. Sayee is a Doctoral Candidate in Economics and Social Sciences at the WU (Vienna University of Economics and Business). *Sayee has contributed to Chapters 1, 2 and 12 of this volume.*

**Stig Sollund** is the Director General for International Tax at the Tax Law Department, Ministry of Finance, Norway. He is currently the co-coordinator of the UN Subcommittee working on enhancing and keeping the TP Manual updated. Mr Sollund is the delegate to the OECD Committee on Fiscal Affairs and the Inclusive Framework on BEPS (and the Bureau/Steering Group of same) and Working Party No. 6 and its Bureau. He was a member of the United Nations Committee of Experts on International

Cooperation in Tax Matters 2005–2017 and coordinator of its Subcommittee on Transfer Pricing that developed the Transfer Pricing Manual for developing countries. He has also served as a deputy judge and practiced tax law in the private sector, most recently as a partner of Bugge, Arentz-Hansen and Rasmussen (BA-HR) law firm, Oslo. He has held various positions at the Norwegian Ministry of Finance since 1980 where his areas of work have included legislation on business taxation, special tax regimes for petroleum production, hydro power and shipping, transfer pricing, and negotiator of tax treaties. Mr Sollund holds a law degree from the University of Oslo that he obtained in 1975. He has served as Chairman, International Fiscal Association, Norwegian Branch, and Editor, Norwegian Tax Journal 'Skatterett'. *Stig has contributed to Chapter 1 of this volume.*

**Marco Striato** is an international tax advisor at L&P – Ludovici Piccone & Partners, Italian tax law firm. His main areas of expertise include transfer pricing, valuation, and international tax law. He has gained extensive experience in dealing with topics related to transfer pricing in a range of industries including industrial and retail clients as well as financial institutions. Before joining L&P, he worked as a transfer pricing specialist with PwC Tax and Legal Services and, prior to that, as a financial analyst. Marco holds a Master of Science in Law and Business Administration from Bocconi University, Milan (Italy) and graduated cum laude. He also attended postgraduate courses in the area of international taxation and corporate finance at Peking University in Beijing (China), WU University of Economics and Business in Vienna (Austria), and American University in Dubai (UAE). He is an Italian certified public accountant. *Marco has contributed to Chapter 5 of this volume.*

**Dr Rita Szudoczky** is an assistant professor at the Institute for Austrian and International Tax law, WU. She has written her PhD thesis on the relationships between different sources of EU law in the field of taxation including the relationship between the EU State aid rules and the fundamental freedoms. Her PhD thesis was published in the IBFD's Doctoral Series and was granted the Sorbonne Tax Law Thesis Award in 2014 and the European State Aid Law Quarterly (EStAL) PhD Thesis Award in 2016. She has written several contributions and commentaries on issues of EU fiscal State aid and spoken at numerous conferences related to this subject. *Rita has contributed to Chapter 14 of this volume.*

**Zahira Quattrocchi** is Tax Director at CNH Group, Italy. Zahira has held several leading positions in tax functions with multinational companies and specializes multi-country restructuring programs. Zahira holds a Diploma in Tax Administration and Controlling at SDA Bocconi, Italy and a Law degree from Università degli Studi di Palermo, Italy. *Zahira has contributed to Chapter 12 of this volume.*

# Table of Contents

Table of Contents

# List of Figures

# List of Tables

# Preface

A rapidly integrating global economy with increasing digital content in multinational enterprises (MNE) poses unique challenges to fiscal administrations and multinational enterprises. Questions have been raised about the adequacy of international tax law for addressing the new forms of integrated businesses and ensuring compliance with various legal and tax positions that are adopted by countries. As a consequence of the landmark Base Erosion and Profit Shifting (BEPS) project undertaken by the OECD, specific action plans (primarily Actions 4, 7, 8, 9, 10, and 13) have had varying influence on the way that multinational enterprises and tax administrations approach transfer pricing. The role of transfer pricing, both as a challenge and a solution, has come under the spotlight. Considering the significant tax implications and the risk of double taxation that accompanies transfer pricing, the importance of understanding and applying the fundamental principles of transfer pricing becomes crucial.

In order to streamline the approaches to an arm's length analysis across various tax jurisdictions, organizations such as the OECD, EU, UN, World Bank, and IMF along with specific tax jurisdictions have continuously issued guidelines and jointly worked to create common forums and guidance for harmonizing transfer pricing policies. The OECD has, over the years, substantially updated its Transfer Pricing Guidelines since its early adoption in 1995, most recently and notably in July 2017, incorporating the outcomes of the BEPS project. The European Union and its Joint Transfer Pricing Forum continue to actively discuss frameworks and tools for tackling the challenges of transfer pricing and the digital economy while continuing to work on an EU-wide unified tax concept. The United States (US) introduced significant tax reforms at the end of 2017 embracing, to some extent, the territoriality principle and with features impacting transfer pricing. Emerging economies such as Brazil, China, India, and Mexico, while faced with problems specific to their respective tax jurisdictions and their integration into the global economy, have continued to devote significant resources to modernize and simplify transfer pricing approaches, particularly under the guidance provided by the UN.

Considering this environment, this book is the outcome of continuous joint efforts from the WU Transfer Pricing Center at the Institute for Austrian and International Tax Law at WU (Vienna University of Economics and Business) and the international tax firm L&P – Ludovici Piccone & Partners. Furthermore, the book also reflects on the experiences from the annual advanced transfer pricing courses and the conferences undertaken by the WU Transfer Pricing Center. The book, titled *Fundamentals of Transfer Pricing*, aims to capture the concepts of transfer pricing and present the fundamental principles. Existing books and literature on this topic are observed to be either highly specialized or dealing with specific topics of international tax law and tax treaties which affords an opportunity for dedicated work that bridges both the conceptual framework and practical issues arising in transfer pricing. Therefore, this book aims to bridge those gaps by providing theoretical and practical knowledge on transfer pricing topics for both graduate and postgraduate studies as well as professionals working on transfer pricing matters on a daily basis. To achieve this, the book encompasses contributions from various authors including policy makers, practitioners, and academics who have extensive experience in this field. Further, this book is also used as a reference tool in the Advanced Transfer Pricing Courses organized by the WU Transfer Pricing Center.

This book benefits from the expertise of renowned policy makers, academics, and practitioners for developing a beneficial instrument for individuals with different background knowledge. Each contribution contains a good mix of theoretical understanding and practical examples, i.e., case studies and references to key case law. Given the importance and global influence of the OECD's and the UN's guidance on transfer pricing matters, each chapter takes into account their approach when analysing the related topics. Additionally, this book encapsulates selected country practices when it is relevant. The wide range of transfer pricing topics covered in this publication are divided into general topics and specific topics that are structured as follows:

Part I: General Topics

    I.   Introduction to transfer pricing
    II.   Accurate Delineation and Recognition of Actual Transactions: Comparability Analysis
    III.   Transfer Pricing Methods (Part I): Traditional Transaction Methods
    IV.   Transfer Pricing Methods (Part II): Transactional Profit Methods
    V.   Administrative Approaches to Avoiding/Minimizing Transfer Pricing Disputes
    VI.   Administrative Approaches to Resolving Transfer Pricing Disputes
    VII.   Transfer Pricing Documentation: Master File, Country File and Country-by-Country Reporting

Part II: Specific Topics

    VIII.   Attribution of Profits to Permanent Establishments
    IX.   Transfer Pricing and Intra-group Services
    X.   Transfer Pricing and Intra-group Financial Transactions
    XI.   Transfer Pricing and Intangibles

XII. Transfer Pricing, Supply Chain Management and Business Restructurings

XIII. Transfer Pricing and Customs Valuation

XIV. Transfer Pricing and EU State Aid

Considering the evolving nature of transfer pricing in the specific topics mentioned above, this book will be periodically updated in order to provide up-to-date guidance to its first publication.

The editors would like to express their sincere thanks to the authors who made it possible to provide this ambitious work. In this context, thanks goes to Claire (Xue) Peng and Sayee Prasanna for their invaluable efforts and support in coordinating the various contributions. Many thanks are forwarded to Kluwer Law International BV for supporting and cooperating with this publication project. Last, but not least, the editors would like to thank Renée Pestuka for her precious support during the publication process and Jenny Hill for providing linguistic support to the authors during the publishing process.

*Prof. Dr DDr. hc. Michael Lang*
*Dr Giammarco Cottani, LLM*
*Dr Raffaele Petruzzi, LLM*
*Prof. Dr Alfred Storck*

Part I    General Topics

# CHAPTER 1

# Introduction to Transfer Pricing

## 1  INTRODUCTION

Transfer pricing is arguably the most relevant and challenging topic in international taxation. The number of countries with effective documentation rules has increased more than twentyfold from a mere four countries[1] in 1994 to over 100 jurisdictions in 2018. It is important to first understand that, from a technical standpoint, transfer pricing is the by-product of the existence of multinational enterprises (hereinafter: MNEs), i.e., the simple fact that entities part of the same group enter into commercial or financial relations with each other require the application of transfer pricing provisions. In recent years, however, the outrage in the way that MNEs have mismanaged their tax affairs gave transfer pricing a somewhat pejorative meaning, leading some commentators to begin talking about transfer mispricing as a proxy to refer to schemes aimed at allowing corporations to avoid paying their fair share of taxes. The annual amount of tax revenue losses due to 'mispricing' of transfer prices has been estimated by Global Financial Integrity in Washington to be several hundred billion dollars.[2] In the United States alone, USD 60 billion of tax revenues is lost every year.[3] The Base Erosion and Profit Shifting (BEPS) project attempted to clarify the accurate meaning of what is the exact purpose of transfer pricing rules, leading to the creation of a spectrum where the two extremes lie, respectively, with (i) proper allocation of taxable income and (ii) transfer mispricing. The tool to move within this spectrum is the proper application of the arm's length principle.

    Increased interest on transfer pricing topics stems mainly from the fact that recent decades have seen extensive changes in international trade. Globalization has been constantly changing international businesses and the way in which transactions are performed. Many companies decide to carry on their business in different jurisdictions through subsidiaries or permanent establishments (hereinafter: PEs),[4] thus creating an extensive network of related entities. Moreover, more than 60% of the current

---

1. EY Survey 2007, source: https://www.ub.unibas.ch/digi/a125/sachdok/2012/BAU_1_5682903 _2007_2008.pdf, p. 8 (last accessed on 30 October 2018). Effective indicates that either the country has specific legislation or regulations requiring transfer pricing documentation or other guidance strongly suggests that transfer pricing documentation should be in place.
2. Tax Justice Network, 'Transfer Pricing', available at http://www.taxjustice.net/topics/corporate -tax/transfer-pricing/ (visited on 2 Jan. 2015).
3. Clausing, K.A., 'Should Tax Policy Target Multinational Firm Headquarters?', *National Tax Journal* 63 (December 2010), pp. 741–763.
4. In accordance with Art. 5(1) of the OECD Model Tax Convention on Income and on Capital, the term 'permanent establishment' means a fixed place of business through which the business of an enterprise is wholly or partly carried on.

worldwide business transactions are performed within MNEs,[5] meaning that intra-group relations are of major importance for the functioning of the entire economy.

In order for MNEs to comply with transfer pricing legislation, the economic returns of each subsidiary and PE should be aligned with their value creation. This, however, is not an easy task and generates many relevant issues. As a result, the application of transfer pricing legislation is currently one of the most difficult tasks that taxpayers and tax administrations around the world must face, as it requires MNEs to have complete consistency between the form (i.e., the contractual terms) of an intra-group transaction and its real economic substance.

This chapter will provide an introduction to transfer pricing. Section 2 outlines the key fundamentals of transfer pricing, section 3 will highlight the relevance and reputational impact of the topic, section 4 will introduce the arm's length principle, section 5 will provide an overview of the application of the arm's length principle and, finally, section 6 will illustrate the consequences of a transaction not being in accordance with the arm's length principle. As a general premise, most of the concepts introduced in this chapter will be further developed in detail in the following chapters of this book.

## 2   WHAT IS TRANSFER PRICING?

From an economic, business, and accounting perspective, transfer prices can be commonly referred to as the prices that are charged by individual entities (or departments) for property or services that are supplied to one another within MNEs (hereinafter also referred to as 'group(s)'). The setting of these prices (i.e., 'transfer pricing') is typically an issue that is relevant for the accounting and controlling departments of each entity operating within a group, as it defines, inter alia, the business results (profitability) of the various group operations. Arguably, transfer pricing used in this respect may be characterized as an assessment tool of the performance of the various cost centres, investment centres, and revenue centres of MNEs.

---

**Example**

Company A, located in State X, is the parent company of ABC group, and Company B, located in State Y, is a subsidiary of the same group. Company B needs to receive a service from Company A. Company A and Company B will need to define a transfer price for such service provided intra-group. This transfer price will be relevant for the accounting and controlling departments of both companies.

---

5. OECD, 'OECD Insights – Debate the Issues', OECD Insights (http://oecdinsights.org/2012/03/2 6/price-fixing/), 26 Mar. 2012.

However, for many years, transfer pricing has become increasingly relevant in the tax environment. This is primarily because a group has a certain amount of discretion in determining how to allocate expenses and returns to its subsidiaries and PEs located in different countries. This is for management accounting and reporting purposes (i.e., subsidiaries and PEs may be accounted for as stand-alone businesses, or they may be integrated into larger business segments or geographies). However, for tax purposes, only the statutory returns of the group's local entities and PEs are relevant as they are the starting point for calculating the tax liability in the specific country in which the entities and PEs are operating. Otherwise stated, the profitability (and the related tax liability) of subsidiaries and PEs belonging to a group highly depends on the conditions (including prices) in which these subsidiaries and PEs exchange goods and services with other entities of their group. Therefore, altering these conditions in order to reduce the profitability of subsidiaries and PEs located in high tax jurisdictions and to increase the profitability of subsidiaries and PEs located in low tax jurisdictions will reduce the tax burden (therefore, increasing the net – i.e., after tax – profits) of the overall group. This phenomenon is one of the main elements of so-called 'profit shifting' which typically occurs – from a transfer pricing standpoint – in the event that the local entities and PEs reporting their profits do not perform the functions, do not assume risks, and/or do not own the assets leading to value-creation (and associated profitability).

**Example**

Company A, located in State X (a low-tax country), is the parent company of ABC group and Company B, located in State Y (a high-tax country), is a subsidiary of the same group. Company B needs to receive a service from Company A. Company A and Company B might set the price for this service at a very high amount in order to increase the taxable profits in State X and decrease them in State Y. In this case, this intra-group transaction might generate profit shifting from State Y to State X.

In order to counter such a phenomenon, countries around the world have introduced so-called 'transfer pricing provisions' in their domestic tax systems that are commonly defined as the particular skill sets in tax laws that determine the income allocation for tax purposes between the respective entities of groups.

**Example (continues from previous example)**

In order to prevent the profit shifting from State Y to State X, State Y can introduce transfer pricing rules in its national legislation. Based on these rules, the transaction between Company A and Company B, for tax purposes, might be subject to review by the tax administration of State Y.

Based on most of these rules, transactions between entities and PEs of the same group (i.e., 'related entities') should be settled 'at arm's length' for tax purposes. The terms and conditions of transactions between related entities (i.e., intra-group transactions) are defined within contracts in the case of subsidiaries and 'dealings' in the case of PEs. These should be accorded with those applied to similar transactions between separate and independent entities ('unrelated entities') in similar circumstances.

---

**Example (continues from previous example)**

During the review to Company B's tax returns by the tax administration of State Y, the latter concludes that the terms and conditions of transactions agreed upon by Company A and Company B for the intra-group service are not at arm's length. Therefore, based on State Y's transfer pricing rules, the tax administration of State Y can adjust the tax profits of Company B in order to reflect what would have been the tax profits that would have been generated by the application of the arm's length terms and conditions.

---

## 3 THE RELEVANCE AND REPUTATIONAL IMPACT OF TRANSFER PRICING

The major shift that occurred with the overall perception of transfer pricing is the fact that it moved from being a topic discussed mainly within the tax departments of MNEs to a significant issue with respect to which managers must report to their corporate boardrooms. For example, if ABC Group is subject to a general tax audit leading to a major transfer pricing adjustment, the primary concern of top management will be to avoid that such an event makes the headlines in mainstream media. Such a defensive approach is justified by the fact that, should the latter (risky) scenario for the MNE materialize, its overall value (in terms of market capitalization or goodwill) may be negatively affected. Such a concern by taxpayers is confirmed by anecdotal evidence.[6] Based on a relevant study,[7] *'thirty percent of tax directors in parent firms worldwide identify transfer pricing as their most important tax issue'* (Figure 1.1).

---

6. *See*, for example, Tax Justice Network, *Transfer Pricing*, available at http://www.taxjustice.net/ topics/corporate-tax/transfer-pricing/ (visited on 22 Jun. 2016).
7. Ernst&Young, 2010 Global Transfer Pricing Survey: Addressing the challenges of globalization, Ernst&Young (2010).

*Figure 1.1   Significance of Transfer Pricing*

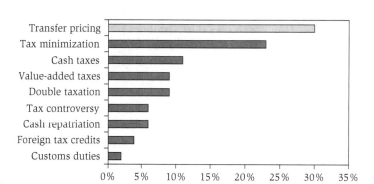

Moreover, another study has shown that '57% of tax administrators identified transfer pricing as their top risk focus'.[8] The graphics below respectively depict the frequency with which transfer pricing policies were examined by a tax authority during an tax audit in FY 2009–2013 (Figure 1.2),[9] the percentages of tax examinations resulting in an adjustment in FY 2009–2013 (Figure 1.3),[10] and the frequency with which penalties were imposed on the adjustment in FY 2009–2013 (Figure 1.4).[11]

*Figure 1.2   Frequency of Transfer Pricing Audits*

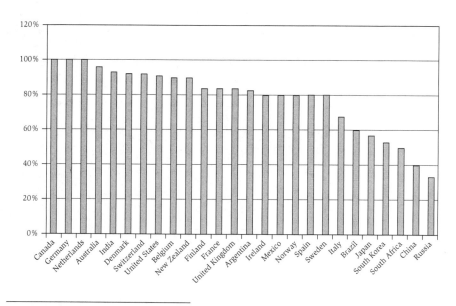

---

8.   EY, 2013 Global Transfer Pricing Survey: Navigating the choppy waters of international tax', *EY* (2013).
9.   Data derived by the authors from *Ibid.*
10.   *Ibid.*
11.   *Ibid.*

*Figure 1.3    Transfer Pricing Adjustments Across Tax Jurisdictions*

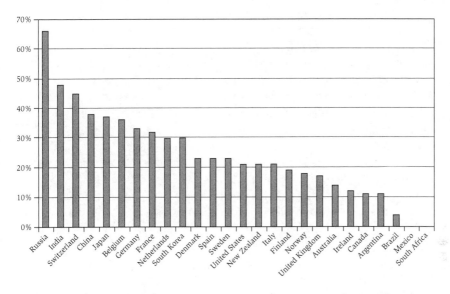

*Figure 1.4    Frequency of Penalties in Transfer Pricing*

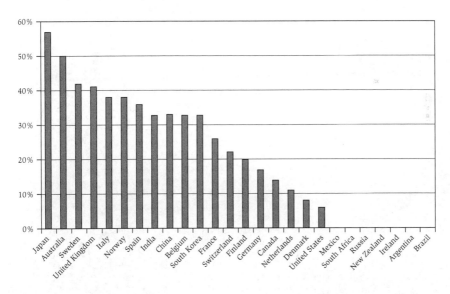

Various reasons have been contributing to this phenomenon. First of all, the recent financial crisis and global recession in the aftermaths of 2008, on the one hand, have reduced the profitability of many groups (and their subsidiaries and PEs) and, on the other hand, have incited governments around the world to increase their scrutiny of 'taxpayers' bills' as they seek to maintain or increase their tax revenues.

Moreover, another objective difficulty with transfer pricing provisions lies in the application of the arm's length principle. In this respect, there are increasing complexities around the application of the arm's length principle. It is based on the working hypothesis of having enterprises be a part of the same MNE but acting as if they were independent and is also reliant on identifying independent third party transactions. Therefore, it is sharply boosting the relevance of tax controversy (in terms of both the number of cases and the amount of tax liabilities/revenues involved) around the world on transfer pricing topics and the related issue of attribution of profits to PEs. Nowadays, court cases involving the most substantial amounts of tax liabilities are related to these topics.

As a result, transfer pricing topics have been attracting the attention of not only taxpayers and tax administrations but also media, civil society, and non-governmental organizations around the world.[12] Inquiries into the tax and transfer pricing practices of household names such as Amazon, Google, Starbucks and others[13] have been featured in the mainstream media, and tax policies concerning international transactions, aggressive tax planning, and tax avoidance have become an issue of extensive national and international debate.

Therefore, for the taxpayers, the costs of not complying with the relevant transfer pricing legislations include not only additional taxes together with related penalties and interest but also a considerable amount of costs related to reputational losses. On the other side, for the tax administrations, revenue losses due to the manipulation and the misuse of the transfer pricing systems that are implemented in their own countries also have considerable value.[14]

Finally, the relevance of transfer pricing topics has also been emphasized by the work of many international and regional organizations around the world. In this context, the BEPS Project initiated by the OECD under the mandate of the G20 leaders[15]

---

12. OECD, 'Addressing Base Erosion and Profit Shifting', *OECD Publishing* (2013).
13. World Time 2012; The Guardian 2012.
14. *See*, for example, Bartelsman, E.J., Beetsma, R.M., 'Why Pay More? Corporate Tax Avoidance Through Transfer Pricing in OECD Countries', *Journal of Public Economics* 87 (2003), pp. 2225–2252; Clausing, K.A., 'Tax Motivated Transfer Pricing and US Intrafirm Trade Prices', *Journal of Public Economics* 87 (2003), pp. 2207–2223; Clausing, K.A., 'The Revenue Effects of Multinational Firm Income Shifting', *Tax Notes* (28 Mar. 2011), pp. 1580–1586; Dharmapala, D., Riedel, N., 'Earnings Shocks and Tax-Motivated Income-Shifting: Evidence from European Multinationals', *Journal of Public Economics* 97 (January 2013), pp. 95–107; McDonald, M. (2008), 'Income Shifting from Transfer Pricing: Further Evidence from Tax Return Data', Office of Tax Analysis, OTA Technical Working Paper 2 (July 2008); McIntyre, R.S., Gardner, M., Wilkins, R.J., Phillips, R., 'Corporate Taxpayers and Corporate Tax Dodgers', *Citizens for Tax Justice with the Institute on Taxation and Economic Policy* (November 2011).
15. OECD, 'Addressing Base Erosion and Profit Shifting', *OECD Publishing* (2013).

and considered by many parties as the most comprehensive and far-reaching work on international taxation in recent history has highlighted the relevance of transfer pricing topics.[16]

## 4  THE ARM'S LENGTH PRINCIPLE

As mentioned in the previous section, the current transfer pricing provision of basically all countries around the world[17] are based on the utilization of the arm's length principle as the fundamental criterion for allocating business income between associated enterprises that are resident for tax purposes in different countries. This principle, which originated many years ago, requires that the nature of a transaction between related entities be in accordance with the nature of a comparable transaction between unrelated entities in similar circumstances.

In order to provide guidance to taxpayers and tax administrations on how the arm's length principle should be determined, the OECD began developing its Transfer Pricing Guidelines ('OECD Guidelines') in 1995[18] based on the work already published in two reports in 1979[19] and 1993.[20] However, notwithstanding the considerable amount of work by the OECD in this area, the assessment of the arm's length principle is still characterized by a significant degree of complexity[21] that generates substantial uncertainty and numerous areas of concern in the application of the transfer pricing rules in all countries around the globe.

### 4.1  A Brief History of the Arm's Length Principle

The origins of transfer pricing rules date back to 1915 when the UK Commissioners[22] were awarded the power to charge non-resident persons with further income taxes.

---

16. Indeed, the BEPS project has been focusing, for one-third, entirely to transfer pricing topics (*see* Actions 8, 9, 10 and 13). Moreover, many other parts of the project (*see* Actions 1, 4, 5, 7, 12, 14, and 15) embed the analysis of many relevant transfer pricing considerations.
17. With some significant exceptions, such as Brazil which is already making joint efforts for convergence with the OECD principles. Source: http://www.oecd.org/ctp/transfer-pricing/oecd-and-brazil-launch-project-to-examine-differences-in-cross-border-tax-rules.htm (last accessed on 4 Jun. 2018).
18. OECD, OECD Transfer Pricing Guidelines for Multinational Enterprises and Tax Administrations (Paris: OECD, 1995); OECD, OECD Transfer Pricing Guidelines for Multinational Enterprises and Tax Administrations (Paris: OECD, 1999); OECD, OECD Transfer Pricing Guidelines for Multinational Enterprises and Tax Administrations (Paris: OECD, 2009); OECD, OECD Transfer Pricing Guidelines for Multinational Enterprises and Tax Administrations (Paris: OECD, 2010); OECD, OECD Transfer Pricing Guidelines for Multinational Enterprises and Tax Administrations (Paris: OECD, 2017) (collectively 'OECD Guidelines').
19. *Transfer Pricing and Multinational Enterprises*, OECD, 1979.
20. *Intercompany Transfer Pricing Regulations under US Section 482 Temporary and proposed regulations*, Committee of Fiscal Affairs, OECD, 1993 Paris.
21. Collier, R.S. and Andrus, J.L., 'Transfer Pricing and the Arm's Length Principle After BEPS', Oxford University Press 2017, pp. 246–247.
22. Petruzzi, R., *The Arm's Length Principle: Between Legal Fiction and Economic Reality*, in (eds) Lang, M., Storck, A. and Petruzzi, R., 'Transfer Pricing in a Post-BEPS World', Kluwer Law International, Vienna, 2016.

This could occur when, based on the 'close connection' and 'substantial control' with resident persons, 'the course of business between those persons [could] be so arranged, and [was] so arranged, that the business done by the resident in pursuance of his connection with the non-resident [produced] to the resident either no profits or less than the ordinary profits which might [have been] expected to arise from that business'.[23] Two years later, the tax administration of the United States[24] was provided with the authority to consolidate the accounts of two or more related trades or businesses 'whenever necessary to more equitably determine the invested capital or taxable income'.[25] These regulations subsequently led to the draft of the first transfer pricing rules that afforded the United States Commissioner with the authorization to consolidate the accounts of affiliated corporations 'for the purpose of making an accurate distribution or apportionment of gains, profits, income, deductions, or capital between or among such related trades or business'.[26] This would assist in tackling the international tax avoidance opportunities that were available to MNEs.[27]

In the meantime, the Committee of Technical Experts, nominated in 1922 by the League of Nations to analyse issues related to double taxation and tax evasion, produced the first Draft Model Convention for the Prevention of Double Taxation and Evasion in 1927.[28] In this report, the concept of 'permanent establishment' was introduced in order to allocate the taxing rights related to double taxation of business income. According to this concept, business income should have been taxed in the contracting State in which a permanent establishment including, among others, 'affiliated companies' was established. Consequently, whenever an enterprise had permanent establishments in both contracting States, such income should have been apportioned based on a separate accounting approach. Nevertheless, when separate accounting was not available, no method of apportionment was identified, and the determination of such an apportionment was left to the agreement between the competent authorities of the contracting States.

The separate accounting approach was abandoned in the 1928 Model Convention for the Prevention of Double Taxation and Evasion,[29] and the method of apportionment of always being defined by an agreement between competent authorities was enacted. A decision on the method of apportionment was not made due to the committee's lack of time to address the issue more closely.[30] Nonetheless, the General Meeting

---

23. See s. 31 of the Finance (No. 2) Act of 1915 [quotation slightly amended by the author].
24. The Internal Revenue Service (IRS).
25. See Regulation 41, Arts 77–78, promulgated under the War Revenue Act of 1917.
26. Revenue Act of 1921, Ch. 136, s. 240(d), 42 Stat. 260 (1921) (re-enacted in Revenue Act of 1924, Ch. 234, s. 240(d), 43 Stat. 288 (1924), and Revenue Act of 1926, Ch. 27, s. 240(f), 44 Stat. 46 (1926)).
27. Avi-Yonah, R.S., 'The Rise and Fall of Arm's Length: A Study in the Evolution of U.S. International Taxation', Finance and Tax Law Review 9 (2006), pp. 310 et seq.
28. League of Nations, Report on Double Taxation and Tax Evasion, presented by the Committee of Technical Experts on Double Taxation and Tax Evasion, C.216.M.85, London, 12 Apr. 1927.
29. League of Nations, Report on Double Taxation and Tax Evasion, presented by the Committee of Technical Experts on Double Taxation and Tax Evasion, C.562.M.85, London, 31 Oct. 1928. In this Model, reference to 'affiliated companies' was deleted.
30. Wittendorff, J., Transfer Pricing and the Arm's Length Principle in International Tax Law (Kluwer Law International, The Netherlands, 2010), p. 88.

unanimously suggested creating a standing fiscal committee dealing, *inter alia*, with the question of the taxation of business income.[31] This question was discussed in a first report by the American economist Thomas S. Adams,[32] however, the result of this report was that the problem was characterized with more complexity than originally believed.[33]

In this context, in 1933, the arm's length principle was suggested as being the most appropriate method to allocate taxable rights related to business income between different countries. The American lawyer Mitchell B. Carroll, appointed by the Fiscal Committee to internationally analyse the rules adopted to allocate business income, had referred to the arm's length principle introduced for the first time in the United States report to the League of Nations on income allocation in 1932.[34] This method was favoured by most countries at that time.[35]

Based on the Carroll Report, the arm's length principle was included in Article 3 and Article 5 of the 1933 Draft Convention on the Allocation of Business Income between States for the Purpose of Taxation[36] as the preferred method for allocating income to permanent establishments and between associated companies. Since that moment,[37] it has been the preferred method for allocating business income between head offices and permanent establishments and also between associated companies both in the OECD Model Tax Convention on Income and on Capital (hereinafter 'OECD Model') and in the United Nations Model Double Taxation Convention between Developed and Developing Countries (hereinafter 'UN Model') and the basic principle embedded in all transfer pricing rules around the world.

## 4.2   The Legal Framework to the Arm's Length Principle

The primary statement of the arm's length principle is found in Article 9(1) of both the OECD Model and the UN Model:

Where

  a) an enterprise of a Contracting State participates directly or indirectly in the management, control or capital of an enterprise of the other Contracting State, or

---

31. *Ibid.*
32. League of Nations, *Fiscal Committee: Report to the Council on the Work of the Committee – First Session*, C.340.M.140.1930.II, Geneva, 31 May 1930.
33. Wittendorff, J., *Transfer Pricing and the Arm's Length Principle in International Tax Law* (Kluwer Law International, The Netherlands, 2010), p. 89.
34. League of Nations, *Taxation of Foreign and National Enterprises: Vol. I*, C.73.M.38.1932.II.A, Geneva, 1932; Carroll, M.B., *Global Perspectives of an International Tax Lawyer* (Exposition Press, New York, 1978), p. 34.
35. League of Nations, *Taxation of Foreign and National Enterprises: Vol. IV, Methods of Allocating Taxable Income*, C.425(b).M.217(b).1933.II.A, Geneva, 1933.
36. League of Nations, *Fiscal Committee: Report to the Council on the Work of thee Fourth Session of the Committee*, C.399.M.204.1933.II.A, Geneva, 26 Jun. 1933.
37. The first tax treaty including the arm's length principle was the United States-France Tax Treaty negotiated in 1930 and signed in 1932.

b) the same persons participate directly or indirectly in the management, control or capital of an enterprise of a Contracting State and an enterprise of the other Contracting State,

and in either case conditions are made or imposed between the two enterprises in their commercial or financial relations which differ from those which would be made between independent enterprises, then any profits which would, but for those conditions, have accrued to one of the enterprises, but, by reason of those conditions, have not so accrued, may be included in the profits of that enterprise and taxed accordingly.

This article incites numerous questions that must be resolved by interpretation both at a national and at an international level.[38] The wording of Article 9(1) does not clearly encapsulate its purpose as being exclusively directed to the prevention of economic double taxation.[39] In general terms, the main purpose of Article 9 is the avoidance or limitation of the economic double taxation deriving from adjustments to income tax bases resulting from national transfer pricing rules.[40] Additionally, numerous authors have ascertained the following additional purposes that this article aims to achieve:[41]

– The 'fair' allocation of taxing rights between the contracting States;[42]
– The establishing of a criterion for determining if domestic rules restricting the deduction of payments to persons residing in the other contracting State are compatible with Article 24(4) OECD Model;
– The definition of the term 'associated enterprises' under other provisions of the double tax treaty preventing the abuse of the tax treaties.

Moreover, it has been argued[43] that one of the primary purposes of Article 9 is the prevention of tax avoidance. Nevertheless, such a purpose did not find a unanimous consensus within the literature, and its relevance continues to be controversial.

When analysing the specific elements of this principle, it is evident that its subjective scope is defined by 'related enterprises', broadly defined as: 'a) an enterprise of a Contracting State participates directly or indirectly in the management, control or capital of an enterprise of the other Contracting State, or b) the same persons participate directly or indirectly in the management, control or capital of an enterprise of a Contracting State and an enterprise of the other Contracting State'. Countries interpret this requirement in a different way whereby referring, in some cases, to

38. Wittendorff, J., *Transfer Pricing and the Arm's Length Principle in International Tax Law* (Kluwer Law International, The Netherlands, 2010), pp. 112–145; Baker, P., *Double Taxation Conventions*, 3rd Edition (Sweet & Maxwell, the United Kingdom, 2013).
39. *Supra* n. 22.
40. OECD, *OECD MC Commentary to Article 25*, para. 11; Wittendorff, J., *Transfer Pricing and the Arm's Length Principle in International Tax Law* (Kluwer Law International, The Netherlands, 2010), pp. 145, 148–150.
41. Wittendorff, J., *Transfer Pricing and the Arm's Length Principle in International Tax Law* (Kluwer Law International, The Netherlands, 2010), p. 112.
42. OECD, *OECD Transfer Pricing Guidelines for Multinational Enterprises and Tax Administrations* (Paris: OECD, 2010), para. 7 (Preface).
43. *Ibid.*

requirements that are more defined (e.g., a certain participation in the capital) while, in other cases, to requirements that are more flexible (e.g., de facto control).

The objective scope of the principle is 'profits', hence clarifying that not only prices but the entire conditions in the commercial or financial relations between the related enterprises should respect the principle.

The arm's length principle is based on three fundamental pillars: the separate entity approach, the relevance of contractual arrangements, and the comparability analysis.[44] These three pillars, fundamental for interpreting the arm's length principle, were established as legal fictions to allocate business income between different countries. However, the interpretation of these pillars has been amended throughout the years in order to reflect the economic reality of a transaction.[45]

Based on the first pillar (i.e., the separate entity approach), two parts of a single enterprise or two enterprises belonging to the same group of companies should be treated as separate legal entities pursuing their own interests.

---

**Example**

Company A, located in State X, is the parent company of ABC group, and Company B, located in State Y, is a subsidiary of the same group. Company B needs external financial resources which it obtains from a third-party bank. Company B must pay 100 bps interest rate on this loan, and the loan is guaranteed by Company A. Company A's credit rating is AAA while Company B's stand-alone credit rating is BB and, on the market, the interest rate for an AAA loan is 100 bps while the interest rate for a BB loan is 600 bps. If the pure separate entity approach is considered to be relevant, Company B should most probably need to pay Company A a guarantee fee that is determined as the difference between its stand-alone interest rate (600 bps) and the interest rate charged by the bank (100 bps), i.e., 500 bps. However, if the separate entity approach is deviated, i.e., Company B is not considered completely as a stand-alone entity, and the guarantee fee could be in an amount between 0 and 500 bps (depending on how strong the impact is of the 'implicit support' deriving from belonging to the ABC group).

---

Based on the second pillar (i.e., the relevance of contractual arrangements), the analysis of the 'legal arrangements' between the different enterprises (or 'dealings' in the case of permanent establishments) should be based on the legal structure adopted by the related entities involved in the transaction.

---

44. *Supra* n. 23.
45. *Ibid.*

15

**Example**

Company A, located in State X, is the parent company of ABC group, and Company B, located in State Y, is a subsidiary of the same group. Company A and Company B have entered into an intra-group service agreement whereby Company A should provide management services to Company B, and Company B should pay a service fee to Company A. In the course of an audit in State Y, the tax auditor determines that Company B receives the same (i.e., identical) management services from a third-party service provider. If the relevance of contractual arrangements is applied without any doubt, Company B will be able to deduct the management fees paid to Company A. However, if some elements of doubt are included in the relevance of contractual arrangements, there might be circumstances under which Company B would not be able to deduct the management fees.

Based on the third pillar (i.e., the comparability of the transaction), the assessment of the arm's length nature of the transaction should be performed by a 'comparison' of 'conditions made or imposed' between non-independent enterprises and those between independent enterprises.

**Example**

Company A, located in State X, is the parent company of ABC group, and Company B, located in State Y, is a subsidiary of the same group. Company A provides Company B with the right to use a specific patent developed in Country X that Company B needs for its manufacturing process. Company B partially (but significantly) contributes to the development of the patent. Some information is available on license agreements on similar patents concluded in the market between independent entities. If the comparability of the transaction is applied *strictu sensu*, the most appropriate transfer pricing method to use in order to determine the arm's length royalty that Company B should pay to Company A could be the CUP method. However, if the comparability of the transaction is applied with more flexibility, the transactional profit split method might well be applied in this case. To this end, key issues to be considered will be, for example, how comparable are the license agreements in the market and how significant is the contribution of Company B to the development of the patent.

Article 9 does not create any taxing rights but rather limits those established under the national law of the various countries. Therefore, the legal basis for the application of transfer pricing rules (and the interpretation of the arm's length principle) resides with each countries' legislation that might differ from each other.

In order to align the various understanding on the application of transfer pricing rules and the interpretation of the arm's length principle, the OECD began working on a document in the 1970s that would extensively deal with these topics. The first results of this work were reproduced in the OECD 1979 Report[46] and resulted in the first OECD Guidelines in 1995. These guidelines were subsequently modified in 1999, 2009, 2010, and 2017. The OECD Guidelines, though not being legally binding (i.e., having a 'soft law' character since they are mere 'recommendations' provided by the OECD Council), are a valid source of reference in applying transfer pricing rules and interpreting the arm's length principle for various reasons. First of all, they are drafted by the tax administrations of the OECD Member States and approved by the OECD Committee on Fiscal Affairs and the OECD Council. Second, they derive a strong relevance from Articles 31–33 of the Vienna Convention on the Law of Treaties.[47] Finally, numerous courts around the globe have often used them to interpret issues referring to specific transfer pricing cases.

However, the relevance of the OECD Guidelines for non-OECD Member States is still highly disputed. Moreover, in order to provide developing countries' tax authorities with guidance that is more practical and easier to read, the UN issued its United Nations Practical Manual on Transfer Pricing for Developing Countries (hereinafter 'UN Manual') in 2013[48] which was revised in 2017.[49] The UN Manual was made more responsive to issues in developing countries, particularly in the backdrop of the OECD BEPS Project. The UN Manual substantially addresses issues surrounding practical implementation of the arm's length principle in developing countries along with country specific practices.

## 4.3 An Alternative to the Arm's Length Principle: The Global Formulary Apportionment[50]

As previously mentioned, the current transfer pricing rules of all countries around the world are based on the utilization of the arm's length principle as the fundamental criterion for allocating business income between different countries. This principle has been selected as being the relevant one (and thus far is the only principle used for these purposes) due to its numerous advantages such as the following:

(a) Equal treatment of related and unrelated transactions
(b) Allowance of commercial flexibility for specific business circumstances
(c) Prevention of phenomena of tax avoidance and/or aggressive tax planning
(d) Avoidance of double taxation and of less-than-single taxation
(e) Fair and balanced allocation of taxing powers between different States
(f) Stability and certainty of law
(g) Overcome issues related to cross-border transactions

---

46. OECD, *Transfer Pricing and Multinational Enterprises* (Paris: OECD, 1979).
47. UN, *Vienna Convention On The Law Of Treaties*, (Vienna 23 May 1969).
48. UN, *United Nations Practical Manual on Transfer Pricing for Developing Countries* (New York: 2013).
49. *Ibid.*, (New York: 2017).
50. *Supra* n. 22, pp. 282–293.

      – Compatibility with tax treaties
      – Compatibility with EU law
(h) Enforceability
(i) Allowance of a coordinated approach
(j) Avoidance of conflicts between different kinds of rules

However, the arm's length principle is perceived to be difficult to implement, therefore, generating a substantial administrative burden on both taxpayers and tax administrations.

In order to attempt to overcome these difficulties, the most commonly known alternative to this principle is the implementation of a system based on a global formulary apportionment. Based on this system, the profits of an MNE would be split between different countries by: a) defining a common taxable base and b) splitting this taxable base using a formula and taking into account various production factors (e.g., revenues, assets, and human capital). This system, perceived as being able to be simplified in its implementation (hence, overcoming the abovementioned administrative burden on taxpayers and tax administrations) nevertheless embeds numerous areas of concern such as the following:

– Difficulties in reaching a general consensus on the common profits and formula to be used
– Inflexibility in accounting for specific characteristics of single entities
– Difficulties in granting an efficient implementation
– High political and administrative complexity
– Subjectivity in defining the global formula
– Negative distortions deriving from exchange rate movements
– High compliance costs and data requirements
– Substantive valuation issues related to all of the relevant factors to allocate a taxable base within the MNE group (especially in the so-called 'phase-in')
– Questions about the relevance of imposing withholding taxes on cross-border payments
– Difficulties in administrating the relationships between both the group members that are included and those that are excluded in the formulary apportionment.

For these purposes, a system based on a global formulary apportionment has never been introduced on an international level to allocate business income between different countries, and the arm's length principle still remains the only applied principle.

## 5 THE APPLICATION OF THE ARM'S LENGTH PRINCIPLE

The process leading to application of the arm's length principle should comply with the following fundamental steps:

- Step 1: The identification of the commercial or financial relations
- Step 2: The recognition of the accurately delineated transaction undertaken
- Step 3: The selection of the most appropriate transfer pricing method
- Step 4: The application of the most appropriate transfer pricing method.

## 5.1 Step 1: The Identification of the Commercial or Financial Relations[51]

The process leading to the accurate delineation of the actual transaction undertaken begins with the identification of the commercial or financial relations between the related entities in a transaction. This process requires a preliminary understanding of the industry sector in which the MNE operates as well as of the factors affecting the performance of any business operating in that sector.

Subsequently, the role of each related entity in the specific transaction should be defined, and the commercial or financial relations between them should be ascertained based on the understanding of the following key 'economically relevant characteristics' or 'comparability factors':

(a) *Contractual terms of the transaction*: written contracts act as a starting point for understanding the intent behind the related entities entering into trans- actions. A typical contract captures the roles, responsibilities, functions, risks, assets, obligations, rights, and terms of the transactions. However, at times, the written contracts may not provide sufficient information or the actual conduct of the parties to the transaction could vary significantly from the written agreement. In such cases, the characteristic substance of the transaction based on the actual conduct of the parties takes precedence over and above the contract in writing.

(b) *Functional analysis*: under independent circumstances, the compensation for products transferred or services provided between related entities are commensurate with the functions undertaken, risks assumed, and assets deployed by the respective entities. Therefore, it is imperative to perform a detailed analysis of critical functions, key assets that are deployed, and the assumption of economically significant risks. Additionally, such an analysis should be 'including how those functions relate to the wider generation of value by the MNE group to which the parties belong, the circumstances surrounding the transaction, and industry practices',[52] hence confirming the above-mentioned relevance of the performance of a thoughtful global value chain analysis of the MNE. The functional analysis is considered crucial in determining the functional profile of the transacting entities in order to accurately delineate the transactions. In this context, the analysis of the relevant risks that are undertaken by each transacting entity, the inherent

---

51. *See* 2017 OECD Guidelines, Ch. I, s. D1. For further details on this topic, *see* Ch. 2 in this book.
52. OECD, *OECD Transfer Pricing Guidelines for Multinational Enterprises and Tax Administrations* (Paris: OECD, 2010), para. 1.36 (Ch. I).

19

risks in conducting the business activities by each entity, and the allocation of risks between the entities will be crucial. The financial capacity to assume the risks and the degree of control over the risks exercised by each entity ultimately plays a role in determining the risk profile of each entity. The indicative steps established in the OECD Guidelines could be followed in determining such risk profile:[53]

(i)   Identification of specific, economically significant risks which includes identifying, for example, strategic risks, such as risks emerging from changes in an external environment, technology, and political environment; operational risks that arise during execution and conduct of business; financial risks due to an entity's ability to manage liquidity, cash flow, and creditworthiness; and hazard risks owing to external events such as natural disasters.

(ii)  Analysis of the contractual allocation of the economically significant risks by verifying how these specific risks have been contractually assumed between the parties to the transaction.

(iii) Performance of a detailed functional analysis to understand the conduct of parties, i.e., how the parties to the contract share the specific economically significant risks and who are the parties assuming control over risk management functions. Additionally, observations on the parties' role in bearing the consequences of business outcomes that determines the financial capacity to assume the risks.

(iv)  Assessment of whether the actual conduct of the transacting parties (Step 3) is in accordance with the contractual assumption of risks (Step 2).

(v)   If, in Step 4, it is ascertained that the financial capacity to assume the risks and control over the risks (Step 3) is in line with the contractual assumption of risks (Step 2), Step 6 can be performed. If, instead, it is ascertained in Step 4 that the financial capacity to assume the risks and control over the risks (Step 3) does not accord with the contractual assumption of risks (Step 2), then the risks should be allocated between the parties based on the actual conduct (Step 3).

(vi)  The accurately delineated transaction is priced considering the financial consequences of the risks assumed and re-allocated (whenever necessary) and appropriate compensation, in line with the functions and risks assumed, is warranted. Based on the above process, it is expected that the entity assuming greater risks would be entitled to higher returns.

(c) *Characteristics of property or services*: the characteristics of property transferred or services provided also play a relevant role. In the case of tangible property, criteria such as physical attributes, quality, volume, and reliability

---

53. *Ibid.*, paras 1.60–1.106 (Ch. I).

are essential. In the case of intangible transfers, the form of transfers, type of intangible, duration, and degree of legal protection and the potential benefits of the intangible are ascertained.

(d) *Economic circumstances*: the markets in which the parties operate have relevant effects. For example, market forces, competitiveness, business cycle of the industry *vis-à-vis* the parties to the transaction, and the geographical markets are relevant criteria to consider.

(e) *Business strategies*: the business strategies pursued by the parties including the degree of innovation, product portfolio, and market penetration strategies that are adopted need to be ascertained.

The above analysis will lead to the accurate delineation of the actual transaction undertaken by the related parties.

---

**Example**

Company A, located in State X, is the parent company of ABC group, and Company B, located in State Y, is a subsidiary of the same group. Company A provides goods to Company B. Based on the contractual arrangements between Company A and Company B, the goods will be paid for by Company B in State X's local currency (which is different than State Y's local currency). Therefore, based on the analysis of the contractual arrangements, Company B is attributed with the currency risk embedded into the intra-group transaction. However, based on the identification of the commercial or financial relations, Company A has the financial capacity to assume the currency risk and the control over such risk. Therefore, the accurate delineation of the actual transaction undertaken by Company A and Company B will lead to the attribution of the profits or losses connected to the materialization of the currency risk to Company A.

---

## 5.2 Step 2: The Recognition of the Accurately Delineated Transaction Undertaken[54]

After the above Step 1, leading to the the accurate delineation of the actual transaction undertaken by the means of the identification of the commercial or financial relations, it will be necessary to determine whether independent enterprises under comparable economic circumstances would and could perform the accurately delineated transaction that is identified. The underlying principle in an arm's length analysis is that independent enterprises operate in a rational manner by considering options that are realistically available before concluding the transactions.

In specific and exceptional circumstances, an accurately delineated transaction could be disregarded if the intra-group arrangements when viewed in totality differ

---

54. *See* 2017 OECD Guidelines, Ch. I, s. D2. For further details on this topic, *see* Ch. 2 in this book.

from those that would have been adopted by independent enterprises behaving in a commercially rational manner in comparable circumstances thereby preventing determination of a mutually acceptable price by taking into account their options that are realistically available.

---

**Example**

Company A, located in State X, is the parent company of ABC group, and Company B, located in State Y, is a subsidiary of the same group. Company A provides a service to Company B. Based on the analysis of the recognition of the accurately delineated transaction undertaken, Company B does not need the service provided by Company A. Therefore, the result is that Company A and Company B have not behaved in a commercially rational manner based on the specific circumstances. Consequently, the tax administration might exceptionally disregard the transaction between Company A and Company B.

---

In this process, the taxable profits of the enterprises that are involved in the transaction are subjected to adjustments. This is in order to reflect commercially rational arrangements under similar economic circumstances, i.e., the transaction being replaced by an alternative transaction that is determined to be rational or the possibility that the transaction could be negated based on an appropriate analysis to warrant such a negation.

Moreover, MNEs could undertake transactions that are unique to their business circumstances, and such occurrences may not be common among independent enterprises. Failure to recognize a transaction merely due to the lack of comparable economic circumstances or due to the absence of a similar arrangement between independent parties does not provide valid grounds to disregard an otherwise valid transaction. A key point is to verify if the MNE as a whole would be in the least favourable position if not for the tax benefits had it not entered into the transaction which indicates a lack of rationality in entering into such a transaction.

## 5.3 Step 3: The Selection of the Most Appropriate Transfer Pricing Method[55]

Once a transaction has been accurately delineated and recognized, it will be necessary to select the most appropriate transfer pricing method in order to determine the arm's length remuneration for the transaction. In this process, the following five methods that are commonly prescribed are categorized into: (a) traditional transactional methods and (b) transactional profit methods.

---

55. *See* 2017 OECD Guidelines, Ch. II, part I. For further details on this topic, *see* Ch. 3 in this book.

| Traditional Transaction Methods | Transactional Profit Methods |
|---|---|
| Comparable Uncontrolled Price (CUP) Method | Transactional Net Margin Method (TNMM) |
| Resale Price Method (RPM) | Transactional Profit Split Method (TPSM) |
| Cost Plus Method (CPM) | |

The typical process for selecting the most appropriate method takes into account the following factors:

- Strengths and weaknesses of each method
- Appropriateness of the method that is considered in view of the nature of the controlled transaction based on the functional profile of the parties
- Availability of reliable information (in particular on uncontrolled comparable transactions) that is necessary to apply the selected method and/or other methods
- The degree of comparability between controlled and uncontrolled transactions including the reliability of comparability adjustments that may be required to eliminate material differences between them[56]

All the above-mentioned five methods have the same degree of relevance. Therefore, the most appropriate method should be applied, based on the specific circumstances of the case. However, traditional transaction methods are considered as being more direct for establishing the arm's length nature of transactions. Since it is relatively straightforward to identify reasons for differences in prices between controlled and uncontrolled transactions under the traditional transaction method, it is suggested that the traditional transaction method be preferred over the transactional profits method when both are applicable with the same level of reliability. Also, should more than one traditional transaction method be applicable with the same level of reliability to a given situation, the CUP Method is to be given preference.

In the event of non-availability of reliable information regarding uncontrolled transactions such as the details of gross margin that are essential for undertaking an analysis under the RPM or the CPM, the traditional transaction methods are inapplicable and the transactional profit methods are considered more appropriate.[57]

However, transactional profit methods cannot be applied merely due to the non-availability of information for the application of traditional transaction methods. Adequate consideration is to be given to traditional transaction methods before resorting to the use of transactional profit methods based on the criteria prescribed. It is worth highlighting that all methods (both traditional transactional methods and transactional profit methods) should be in accordance with Article 9 of the OECD and

---

56. OECD, *OECD Transfer Pricing Guidelines for Multinational Enterprises and Tax Administrations* (Paris: OECD, 2010), para. 2.2 (Ch. II).
57. OECD, *OECD Transfer Pricing Guidelines for Multinational Enterprises and Tax Administrations* (Paris: OECD, 2010), paras 2.3–2.11 (Ch. II).

UN Models. In general, it will be better to apply to right method using the wrong comparables than the wrong method using the right comparables.

Additionally, methods other than the above-prescribed methods could be adopted for the purpose of the arm's length test. However, the reasons as to why the prescribed methods were inapplicable and why a method other than the prescribed methods is considered more appropriate need to be established.

In situations when the arm's length result could be derived by using more than one of the prescribed methods, it is suggested that the one method that is considered more appropriate be used. However, the use of multiple methods could be provided as evidence for meeting the arm's length result when the situation warrants the same.

## 5.4   Step 4: The Application of the Most Appropriate Transfer Pricing Method[58]

After defining the most appropriate transfer pricing method based on the accurately delineated and recognized transaction, this method will be applied.

### 5.4.1   Traditional Transaction Methods

#### 5.4.1.1   Comparable Uncontrolled Price Method

Based on the comparable uncontrolled price (CUP) method, a comparison is performed of the price charged or paid for property transferred or services rendered in a comparable uncontrollable transaction or a number of such transactions. Such a price is adjusted to account for differences, if any, between the transaction and the comparable uncontrolled transaction or between enterprises entering into such transactions, which affects the prices. The adjusted price is assumed to be the arm's length price for the property transferred or services provided as part of the transaction.

The criteria for comparability between an uncontrolled and controlled transaction is satisfied if: (a) no differences exist that could materially affect the price in the open market and (b) reasonably accurate adjustments could be made to the prices to achieve closer comparability. If these two conditions are satisfied, then the CUP method is considered the most appropriate methodology.

The practical challenges in applying the CUP method could be the lack of availability of appropriate information on comparable transactions or the inability to undertake reasonable adjustments to the comparable transactions that are identified.

The CUP method is typically applicable in the case of commodity transactions wherein the comparable prices are obtained based on price quotes that are obtained from government agencies that are transparent statistical agencies that publish information on commodity indices in the public domain. In using such prices, adequate consideration is provided to the nature of commodity, volume discounts, date of

---

58. *See* 2017 OECD Guidelines, Ch. II, parts II–III. For further details on this topic, *see* Chs 3 and 4 in this book.

transactions, insurance terms, terms of delivery, currency of trade etc. Moreover, the CUP method is often used in pricing financial transactions.

### 5.4.1.2    Resale Price Method

Based on the resale price method (RPM), the price at which the products or services are purchased or obtained by an entity from its related entity and resold or provided to an unrelated entity is identified. Such a resale price is reduced by the amount of a normal gross profit margin accruing to the entity or to an unrelated entity from the purchase and resale of similar goods or obtaining and providing similar services in a comparable uncontrolled transaction. The price so defined is further reduced by the expenses incurred by the entity in connection with the purchase products such as customs duty, etc.

This price is adjusted to take into account the functional and other differences including those in accounting policies, between the controlled transaction and the comparable uncontrolled transaction, or between the entity entering into such transactions that could materially affect the amount of gross profit margin in the open market. The adjusted price thus determined is considered the arm's length price in respect of the purchase of the goods or obtaining of the service by the entity from the related entity.

The RPM is particularly applied in cases when product differences are not relevant, for example, reseller/distributor and marketing activities.

### 5.4.1.3    Cost Plus Method

Based on the cost plus method (CPM), the direct costs and indirect costs of production that are incurred by the tested entity regarding property transferred or services provided to a related entity are determined. The amount of normal gross profit markup to such costs (computed according to the same accounting norms) arising from the transfer or provision of the same or similar property or services by the entity or by an unrelated entity in a comparable uncontrolled transaction is determined.

The normal gross profit markup is adjusted to take into account functional and other differences, if any, between the tested transaction and the comparable uncontrolled transaction or between the entities entering into such transactions that could materially affect such profit markup in the open market. The direct and indirect costs of production that are incurred by the entity in the tested transaction are marked up by the adjusted gross profit margin defined as described above.

The sum thus arrived at is considered to be the arm's length price in relation to the supply of the goods or provision of services.

The CPM is particularly applied in cases when tested transactions involve services or semi-finished goods/contract manufacturer/fully fledged manufacturer.

### 5.4.2  *Transactional Profit Methods*

#### 5.4.2.1  *Transactional Net Margin Method*

Based on the transactional net margin method (TNMM), the net profit margin realized by the tested entity from the tested transaction is computed in relation to costs incurred, sales effected, assets employed, or regarding any other relevant base. The net profit margin realised by the tested entity or by an unrelated entity from a comparable uncontrolled transaction is computed according to the same base. It is adjusted to take into account the differences, if any, between the tested transaction and the comparable uncontrolled transaction or between the entities entering into such transactions that could materially affect the amount of net profit margin in the open market.

The net profit margin thus computed is established to be the same as the net profit margin arising from the tested transaction. The net profit margin is then taken into account to arrive at the arm's length price in relation to the tested transaction.

The TNMM is particularly applied in cases when significant product or functional differences occur.

#### 5.4.2.2  *Transactional Profit Split Method*

Based on the transactional profit split method (TPSM), the combined net profits of the related entities arising from the tested transaction in which the entities are engaged are determined. The relative contribution made by each related entity to the earning of such combined net profit is then evaluated on the basis of the functions performed, assets employed, and risks assumed by each entity. It is also evaluated on the basis of reliable external market data which indicates how such a contribution would be evaluated by unrelated entities performing comparable functions, employing comparable assets, and assuming comparable risks in similar circumstances.

The combined net profit is then split amongst the entities in proportion to their relative contribution. The profit thus apportioned to the entity is taken into account to arrive at the arm's length price in relation to the tested transaction.

Also, it is possible that the combined net profit may, in the first instance, be partially allocated to each entity in order to provide it with a basic return that is appropriate for the type of tested transaction in which it is engaged (with reference to market returns that are achieved for similar types of transactions by unrelated entities). Thereafter, the residual net profit may be split amongst the entities in proportion to their relative contribution. In such a case, the aggregate of the net profit that is allocated to each entity for providing it with a basic return and the residual net profit apportioned on the basis of the relative contribution of each entity shall be considered as the net profit arising from the tested transaction and allocated to that entity.

The TPSM is particularly applied primarily in cases when the tested transaction involves the transfer of unique intangibles or in multiple tested transactions that are so interrelated that they cannot be evaluated separately for the purpose of determining the arm's length price of each single transaction.

## 6 THE CONSEQUENCES OF A TRANSACTION NOT IN LINE WITH THE ARM'S LENGTH PRINCIPLE

### 6.1 Primary Adjustments

When an intra-group transaction is determined to not be in accordance with the arm's length principle, tax administrations can adjust the taxable profits that are generated by such a transaction in order to bring them to the level of the arm's length taxable profits. This adjustment, referred to as the 'primary adjustment', should find its legal basis in the national transfer pricing legislation of a country and is not limited by the application of any double tax treaty embedding Article 9(1) in line with the OECD and UN Models.

---

**Example**

Company A allows its wholly owned overseas subsidiary, Company B, to use certain equipment at no charge. Based on an audit examination by the tax administrators of Company B, the tax administration assessing Company A determines that the arm's length charge for the use of the equipment is EUR 50,000.

For the year under assessment, EUR 50,000 of income is allocated by the tax administration from Company B to Company A (i.e., the primary adjustment) to reflect an arm's length charge for the use of the equipment. Therefore, the primary adjustment increases Company A's taxable income for the relevant assessment year by EUR 50,000.

---

A primary adjustment will generate an economic double taxation (in the event of transactions between two related companies) or a juridical double taxation (in the case of transactions between a head office and its PE). Therefore, once the tax administrations of a country have made a primary adjustment to the taxable profits of their taxpayer, the tax administrations of the second country should correspondingly reduce the taxable profits of their own taxpayer in order to eliminate such double taxation. This adjustment is called 'corresponding adjustment' and should find its legal basis either in the national transfer pricing legislation of a country or in any existing double tax treaty embedding Article 9(2) and/or Article 25 in line with the OECD and UN Models.

A corresponding adjustment may be made either by recalculating the taxable profits using the price as revised in the first country (most commonly used) or by letting the calculation remain and giving the taxpayer relief against its own taxes that were paid for the additional tax charged as a consequence of the primary adjustment.[59]

---

59. OECD TPG, para. 4.34.

> **Example**
>
> In the above example, let us consider Company A's country of residence to be State A and that of Company B to be State B.
>
> Consequent to the primary adjustment made in State A, if State B considers the adjustment to be 'justified both in principle and in regards to the amount,'[60] then a relief to the effect of additional taxes paid in State A (arising due to the increase in income of EUR 50,000 in State A) is to be provided.

Corresponding adjustments, in the absence of a binding arbitration procedure (e.g., in line with Article 25(5) of the OECD Model) are not mandatory.[61] Moreover, some timing issues might be raised when making primary and corresponding adjustments.[62]

Another type of adjustment to the taxable profits of a taxpayer is known as 'compensating adjustment'. Based on this adjustment, a taxpayer might be allowed to report a transfer price for tax purposes that is different than the one actually charged and, therefore, would be allowed to record the difference between the arm's length price and the actual price recorded in its books and records.[63] However, this kind of adjustment is not recognized by most countries.

> **Example**
>
> Company A identifies the arm's length price to be higher than the actual transaction price (in this case EUR 0) in the amount of € 50,000 and accordingly files its return of income reflecting the arm's length price. Company A's actions are based on the rationale that the arm's length price for the transfer of equipment were not identifiable at the time of the actual transfer and were subsequently acknowledged and identified at the time of filing the annual tax return.
>
> However, the filing position is not accepted by State A being an OECD member country based on the principle that tax return should reflect only actual transaction values.

## 6.2 Secondary Adjustments

A primary adjustment in one country may trigger not only a corresponding adjustment in the second country but also a secondary adjustment in the first country. Indeed, a primary adjustment implies an assessment of extra tax profits in the first country that

60. OECD, *Transfer Pricing, Corresponding Adjustments and The Mutual Agreement Procedure*, 1 Oct. 1984.
61. OECD TPG, para. 4.35.
62. *Ibid.*, para. 4.36.
63. *Ibid.*, paras 4.38–4.39.

results in a misalignment between the actual profits (i.e., the profits shown in the financial statements) and the tax profits. In order to balance this misalignment, some countries' legislations might assert the existence of a constructive transaction whereby the excess profits resulting from the primary adjustment are considered as having been transferred from the assessed taxpayer in some other form and taxed accordingly.

The scope of these constructive transactions is to prevent tax avoidance. In fact, a taxpayer in one country might make an excessive (hence, non-arm's length) payment for the receipt of goods or services to a related company in another country in order to avoid the withholding taxes that would have been levied if that payment would have been, for example, a distribution of profits (typically subject to withholding taxes).

These constructive transactions might take the form of constructive dividends, constructive equity contributions, or constructive loans and could trigger the levying of related withholding taxes (on the related dividends or interest payments) by the country making the primary adjustment.

---

**Example**

In the above example, Company B also received a loan of EUR 100,000 from Company A on which it is required to pay 7% interest per annum (EUR 7,000). Upon examination, the company determined that the arm's length interest rate should have been 5% per annum (EUR 5,000). Therefore, Company B determines that it has paid excessive interest of EUR 2,000 to its Company A. Company B, therefore, is required to make a TP adjustment to increase its taxable income by EUR 2,000 in order to account for the excessive interest expense. This will be the primary adjustment.

Further, a secondary adjustment will result in the creation of a deemed dividend in lieu of the amount of EUR 2,000 which will accordingly be subject to dividend tax.

---

The juridical double taxation related to such withholding taxes might be reduced by means of unilateral measures by the second country (e.g., by means of providing a foreign tax credit) or by internationally agreed measures (e.g., by means of providing relief from the withholding taxes or a related credit under the relevant double tax treaty between the first and the second country).

## 6.3 Penalties and Interests

Penalties adopted by tax administrations could be categorized as civil or criminal by nature. Criminal penalties are directed towards significant fraud where the burden of proof rests with the tax administration to prove the charges whereas civil penalties are more routine and frequent in day-to-day tax audits.[64] For transfer pricing audits, civil

---

64. *Ibid.*, para. 4.20.

penalties are levied based on provisions of respective domestic law typically due to reasons such as a delay in the filing of returns of income, an understatement of tax liability based on wilful intent,[65] or failure to provide transfer pricing documentation.[66] The quantum of penalty is based on the nature of compliance failure. Also, different tax jurisdictions could have different means to penalise MNEs for this. This could be in the form of what are termed as 'penalties', 'additional tax' or 'interest' that involve time value of money. Regardless of the forms of punitive actions, the underlying intent of tax administrations in exercising penal provisions remains the same.[67]

Considering the complexity of transfer pricing problems and the quantum of transfer pricing adjustments to taxable incomes, the imposition of a penalty by tax administrations could result in significant impact to the tax position of MNEs.[68] Further, transfer pricing penalties invariably involve two or more tax jurisdictions and, therefore, different rates of penalties in different jurisdictions could potentially trigger tax arbitrage incentives wherein there could be a situation that income is deliberately overstated in one jurisdiction in contravention to Article 9 of the OECD and UN Model.[69]

Therefore, implementation of penalties require consistent application of domestic laws that could encourage compliance by MNEs.[70] Countries are expected to maintain the penalties in proportion to the degree of tax offence based on a tax system aligned with the following considerations:[71]

– When transactions are understated by a certain amount due to error(s) committed in good faith rather than wilful negligence or a concerted intent to evade tax, the penalty could be designed to be less punitive. For example, when tax administrators are convinced that appropriate documentation has been prepared and transfer pricing adjustments to the income is only a result of varying interpretation of the transfer pricing position of the tax administration, the penalties are expected to be relatively lower.[72]
– When a taxpayer demonstrates having taken reasonable efforts to align transactions with the arm's length principle, then the penalty could be designed according to the degree of that effort.[73] For example, when the taxpayer is able to demonstrate that access to data was not possible and, consequently, a particular transfer pricing method could not be applied, then evidence of such practical constraints should to be considered in determining the penalty.

65. *Ibid.*, para. 4.21.
66. UN TP Manual, para, C.2.4.3.1.
67. OECD TPG, para. 4.22.
68. Lohse,T., Riedel, N., *Do Transfer Pricing Laws Limit International Income Shifting? Evidence from European Multinationals.* CESifo, Working Paper No. 4404, p. 14 (September 2013).
69. OECD TPG, para. 4.26.
70. Mehafdi, M., 'The Ethics of Transfer Pricing', *Journal of Business Ethics*, pp. 365–382, (Kluwer: Netherlands).
71. OECD TPG, para. 5.39.
72. UN TP Manual, p. 410.
73. OECD TPG, para. 5.42.

- When considering a situation whereby the Mutual Agreement Procedure (MAP) is sought, payment of an outstanding penalty should not be more burdensome to taxpayers than it would have otherwise been under a normal course of domestic litigation.[74] Therefore, competent authorities are to provide due attention to situations involving penalty.

In most situations, for transfer pricing penalties, documentation plays a key role in defending tax positions and determining whether the burden of proof rests with the taxpayer or tax authorities. In summary, countries are expected to design penalty systems that encourage documentation by MNEs.

## 6.4 Burden of Proof

The burden of proof in tax litigation refers to the necessity of affirmatively proving the truth of facts alleged by a litigant on a preponderance of evidence.[75] The question of whether the burden of proof rests with the tax administration[76] or the taxpayer[77] could vary depending on the provisions of domestic laws in each country.[78] The characteristic features of both regimes are summarized comparatively below:

| Tax Administration[79] | Taxpayer[80] |
| --- | --- |
| Taxpayer may not have any legal obligation to establish the arm's length nature of transactions and the tax administration makes the prima facie demonstration as to why the transfer prices are not at arm's length. | When the taxpayer demonstrates reasonable efforts to establish the adherence to arm's length criteria, tax administrations may not have the liberty to determine an adjustment to arm's length prices not based in law by ignoring the arm's length principle. |
| A taxpayer could be asked to furnish necessary information to the tax administration based on request on the basis that the tax administration could establish the need for making an adjustment to arm's length prices. In the absence of furnishing information, the tax administration could determine the arm's length price based on its assumptions. | Generally, the burden of proof placed on a taxpayer could be shifted legally or de facto to the tax administration in such cases. However, if the taxpayer fails to demonstrate that reasonable efforts have been taken, the actions of the tax administrations may be upheld. |

---

74. UN TP Manual, para. C.2.4.3.7., p. 411.
75. OECD TPG, para. 5.42, p. 364.
76. UN TP Manual: examples include Germany, France, Netherlands, Japan, *paras B.8.6.10–B.8.6.13.*
77. UN TP Manual: examples include Australia, Brazil, Canada, India, South Africa and the United States, *paras B.8.6.4–B.8.6.9.*
78. OECD TPG, para. 4.11.
79. *Ibid.*, para 4.12.
80. *Ibid.*, para 4.13.

The effect of diverging principles of law between countries with regard to the burden of proof could lead to double taxation.[81] In a case when the burden of proof is on the tax administration examining the controlled transaction, the tax administration could determine or re-determine the arm's length price, and such a price could be accepted by the taxpayer. However, the tax administration in the corresponding jurisdiction to the transaction may contradict with the position which could lead to complexities in resolving the standoff. Also, the taxpayer in the second jurisdiction and the tax administration in the first jurisdiction could deviate from the arm's length principle which leads to the question of which parties have complied with the actual arm's length criteria.

Further, in the situation discussed above, when the burden of proof is considered as the guiding behaviour to verify whether the taxpayer has complied with the arm's length criteria, a taxpayer in one jurisdiction (a subsidiary) may not be in a position to provide information about the transaction with the taxpayer in a second jurisdiction (parent company). This will result in the tax administration making an adjustment to transfer prices based on the extent of information available. The corresponding parent company may also not be obligated by domestic law to prove the arm's length nature of the transaction to its tax administration which will lead to conflicts between the two tax administrations.[82]

Considering the above complexities inherent in transfer pricing disputes, taxpayers and tax administrations are expected to tread responsibly on the issue of burden of proof and not consider it as the sole guiding behaviour for verifying deviations from the arm's length principle. Therefore, under the MAP or dispute resolution processes, the tax jurisdiction that proposes the primary adjustment to the transfer price bears the burden of demonstrating to the other State that the adjustment 'is justified both in principle and as regards the amount'.[83] In all conflicting situations, both competent authorities are expected to take a cooperative approach to resolve disputes.

## 7  CONCLUSIONS

This chapter has discussed the fundamental concept of transfer pricing and its relevance in the backdrop of an international tax system. Transfer pricing has been centred around the arm's length principle. The initial sections have demonstrated how this principle, originally conceived as a legal fiction to allocate business income among different jurisdictions, has soon developed into an economic principle reflecting the economic reality of the transactions.[84] Global formulary apportionment, as an alternative to the arm's length principle, was evaluated, and it was concluded that, based on practical evidence, the approach, as an alternative has never gained global acceptance

---

81. *Ibid.*, para 4.14.
82. *Ibid.*, para. 4.15.
83. *Ibid.*, para. 4.17.
84. *Supra* n. 23, p. 29.

despite some merits put forth by international tax experts. Therefore, the arm's length principle continues to be the driving principle in a transfer pricing analysis

The application of the arm's length principle is achieved by means of a four-step process commencing with the identification of commercial and financial relations, recognition of accurately delineated transactions, choice of transfer pricing methodology, and application of methodology that is adopted. The chapter then provides a brief overview of the methods and resultant arm's length prices obtained by using such methodologies.

Finally, the chapter enumerates the consequences of transactions that are not aligned with the arm's length principle and the consequent types of adjustments that could be imputed by tax administrations. The role of the burden of proof in the event of a transfer pricing dispute is briefly addressed. Overall, this chapter provides an overview for the detailed discussions on each of the above topics.

CHAPTER 2

# Accurate Delineation and Recognition of Actual Transactions: Comparability Analysis

35

# 1 INTRODUCTION

The assessment of the arm's length nature of an intra-group transaction requires that the terms and conditions of the transaction between the related parties ('tested transaction') are similar to those that would have been entered into by independent parties. This would imply the performance of the following four-step analysis:[1]

- Step 1: Identification of the commercial or financial relations
- Step 2: Recognition of the accurately delineated transaction undertaken
- Step 3: Selection of the most appropriate transfer pricing method
- Step 4: Application of the most appropriate transfer pricing method.

This chapter will provide more details on the first two steps of the analysis. The result of the application of the first two steps of the analysis will ultimately provide an

---

1. *See* Ch. 1.

answer on whether any compensation for the tested transaction can be chargeable/deductible. This analysis is of outmost importance, as described in section 2.

In order to provide guidance on this relevant topic, both the OECD Guidelines and the UN Manual have included some terminology. Under both documents, in general, the arm's length nature of a transaction should be assessed by referencing the 'transaction actually undertaken by the associated enterprises as it has been structured by them'.[2] However, in some 'exceptional circumstances', tax administrations may adjust the structure of an intra-group transaction and the conditions agreed upon by the related parties. This process leads to the recognition of the accurately delineated transaction undertaken as described in section 3.

Moreover, since the application of the arm's length principle is fundamentally based on a comparison of the conditions in a controlled transaction with those that would have been made had the parties been independent and undertaking a comparable transaction under comparable circumstances, this chapter will also present the process of performing a comparability analysis in section 4.

## 2   THE IDENTIFICATION OF THE COMMERCIAL OR FINANCIAL RELATIONS

The identification of the commercial and financial relations is instrumental to two fundamental aims in a transfer pricing analysis:[3]

(i)   To identify the commercial or financial relations between the associated enterprises and the conditions and economically relevant circumstances attached to those relations in order to ensure that the controlled transaction is accurately delineated.

(ii)  To compare that the conditions and the economically relevant circumstances of the controlled transaction are accurately delineated with the conditions and the economically relevant circumstances of comparable transactions between independent enterprises.

This section will focus on the first of the abovementioned aims while the second aim will be analysed in section 4.

The result of the application of the first two steps of the analysis will ultimately provide an answer on whether any compensation for the tested transaction can be chargeable/deductible. This analysis is of outmost importance. Indeed, without the performance of this analysis, an entity could feasibly deduct expenses that would not have incurred at arm's length. Therefore, the risk of corporate tax base erosion in the country of the entity paying for the tested transaction would radically increase.

---

2. Paragraph 1.64, 2010 OECD Guidelines; para. 5.4.9.1, 2013 UN Manual.
3. *See* 2017 OECD TPG, *supra* para. 1.33.

**Example**

Company A, a resident in Country X, and Company B, a resident in Country Y, belong to the Group ABC. Country X's and Country Y's nominal tax rates are 50% and 5%, respectively. Although Company A does not require any service, the Group ABC decides that Company A should pay Company B some fees for intra-group services. In this way, Company A will be able to deduct the service fees at the nominal tax rate of 50% while Company B will be taxed on those service fees at the nominal tax rate of 5%.

However, the incorrect performance of this analysis (whereby either a tested transaction that should be chargeable is ascertained to not be chargeable or a tested transaction that should not be chargeable is determined to be chargeable) could increase the risk of double taxation or less-than-single taxation in the country of the entity paying for the tested transaction.

**Example**

Company A, a resident in Country X, and Company B, a resident in Country Y, belong to the Group ABC. Company B has provided an intra-group service to Company A. This intra-group service should be chargeable. However, Country X's tax administration incorrectly ascertains that the intra-group service should not be chargeable. As a result, Company A will not be able to deduct the service fees related to the service while, at the same time, Company B will be taxed on the service fees received from it. Ultimately, economic double taxation will arise.

**Example**

Company A, a resident in Country X, and Company B, a resident in Country Y, belong to the Group ABC. Company B has provided an intra-group service to Company A. This intra-group service should not be chargeable. However, Country X's tax administration incorrectly ascertains that it should be chargeable. As a result, Company A will be able to deduct the service fees related to the service while, at the same time, Company B might be able to avoid taxation on the service fees received from it by proving to Country Y's tax administration that the intra-group service should not be chargeable. Ultimately, less-than-single taxation will arise.

The process of identifying the commercial or financial relations between the associated enterprises and the conditions and economically relevant circumstances commences with a broad based understanding of the industry sector in which the MNE Group operates and the various factors that influence the performance of the sector as a whole.[4] The process then continues with an analysis of the MNE Group itself, the ownership structure, and the commercial and financial relationships based on the transactional flow between individual enterprises that require fulfilling the arm's length criteria. The process of identifying the commercial or financial relations between the associated enterprises will result in providing an accurate delineation of the actual transaction that is undertaken between the associated enterprises.

The 1995 OECD TPG[5] first provided various constituents for successful identification of the commercial and financial relations. It contained detailed provisions on comparability wherein a mix of five factors of comparability analysis were identified. These factors were also recognized by other tax jurisdictions such as the US[6] and continue to be the foundations on which the process of identifying the commercial and financial relations rests:[7]

(1) Contractual terms
(2) Functional analysis
(3) Characteristics of property or services
(4) Economic circumstances
(5) Business strategies.

It is also critical to note that the interplay of these factors have undergone changes over a period of time indicating a change to the approach of a comparability analysis in an effort to improve the process (Figure 2.1).

*Figure 2.1   Comparability Factors*[8]

| Historical process | Current process |
| --- | --- |
| *Characteristics of property or services* | *Contractual terms* |
| Functional analysis | Functional analysis |
| *Contractual terms* | *Characteristics of property or services* |
| Economic circumstances | Economic circumstances |
| Business strategies | Business strategies |

---

4. *Ibid.*, para. 1.34.
5. *See* OECD, *Transfer Pricing Guidelines for Multinational Enterprises and Tax Administrations*, (Paris: OECD Publishing, 1995).
6. *See* US Treas. Reg. s. 1.482-1(d)(1).
7. *See* 1995 OECD TPG, *supra* n. 13, at paras 1.19–1.35.
8. *See* Gao, J., Beats.,S; *Recent Developments on Comparability Analysis in Transfer Pricing*, Recent Developments in Transfer Pricing, 2017, Kluwer Tax Law (Vienna: 2018) (*Forthcoming*).

The beginning point for accurately delineating is the evaluation of controlled transactions that are undertaken between related parties. For this purpose, the written inter-group contracts between the transacting parties are the basis for a traditional transfer pricing analysis. However, the coverage of a sound arm's length analysis has expanded considerably to include an evaluation of the economic substance of the transaction. This expanded approach requires taxpayers to ascertain economically relevant characteristics of a transaction.[9] Once obtained, these characteristics help in determining whether the commercial and financial relations of the transacting parties are performed under conditions that could differ from those that would have been agreed upon in an uncontrolled transaction under comparable circumstances.

## 2.1 Contractual Terms of the Transaction

One of the five economically relevant characteristics (or comparability factors) presented in the OECD TPG to accurately delineate the actual transaction is the contractual terms of the transaction.[10] MNEs use informal arrangements, tacit understandings, etc. to operate with 'relational contracts'.[11] Therefore, an analysis of contractual relations functions as a starting point to the process of a comparability analysis.

An analysis of contracts is associated with the larger arm's length principle since transactions between independent enterprises are typically based on divergence of interest. i.e.: (i) that contractual terms are concluded based on each individual's rational preferences, (ii) the contracting parties will hold each other liable for consequences of deviation from the contract, and (iii) any modification to the contract will be permitted by the parties if it is mutually beneficial. Since associated enterprises could deviate or act in concert, material differences between the contractual terms and actual conduct determine the factual substance and accurately delineate the actual transaction.[12]

### 2.1.1 Identification of Written Terms

Legal clauses define the functions undertaken and risks assumed by the transacting parties depending on the manner in which the contract is composed. Without an established contract, the actual conduct of parties is left open to interpretations, leading to potential disputes.

This has been further emphasized by the OECD:

*[w]here a transaction has been formalised by the associated enterprises through written contractual agreements, those agreements provide the starting point for*

---

9.  *See* 2017 OECD para. 1.35, p. 44.
10. *See* 2017 OECD TPG, para. 1.37.
11. *See* Rauterberg, *Contracting Within the Firm, Columbia Law School* (4 May 2005).
12. *See* OECD TPG 1.46.

*delineating the transaction between them and how the responsibilities, risks, and anticipated outcomes arising from their interaction were intended to be divided at the time of entering into the contract.*[13]

Contractual agreements are critical in evaluating the facts and circumstances underlying a taxpayer's intra-group transactions and form the basis for much of the functional, legal, and economic analyses that support a taxpayer's transfer pricing positions. Therefore, it becomes critical to ensure that the intended substance of the arrangement is reflected in the contractual language as much as possible.[14]

---

**Example**

Company P, legally owning a manufacturing technology, provides an exclusive license to Company B to manufacture goods by entering into a legally binding contract. The agreement captures the roles and responsibilities of the parties to the contract.

Further, based on a group transfer pricing policy, Company B and Company A agree on a cost plus 10% remuneration for the activities undertaken by Company B. The contractual agreement includes an appropriate pricing clause explicitly stating the remuneration model adopted by the two companies and also capturing the components of costs on which the mark up is applicable.

Additionally, the agreement includes details of currency of payment, tenure of the contract, collection period, etc. which are factors to be considered in the comparability analysis.

---

### 2.1.2 Evaluate Intentions of the Parties

It is recognised that the actual conduct of the parties could vary from what is documented in the contract, and also the information contained may not be sufficient for understanding the circumstances of entering into the transaction, leading to a lack of basis for undertaking a comparability analysis.[15] This is primarily due to the intent of entering into a transaction which may not be fully understood in the contract[16] while tax administrators aim to comprehend the intent from the contract.[17] In this regard, the OECD has recognized the need to take into account the principles of contract interpretation.[18]

---

13. *See* OECD, BEPS Actions 8–10 Final Reports, *supra* para. 1.42.
14. *See* Sharon, A, *Drafting Intercompany Agreements with an Eye on Transfer Pricing*, International Tax, Bloomberg BNA, 28 Nov. 2012.
15. *See* OECD 2017, *supra* para. 1.43.
16. *See* Pichhadze, A., *Exposing Unaddressed Issues in the OECD's BEPS Project: What About the Roles and Implications of Contract Interpretation Law and Private International Law in the Transfer Pricing Arm's Length Comparability Analysis?* World Tax J.1 (2015), at 99, 131–132, Journals IBFD.
17. *See* Canadian Supreme Court in the case of *Manulife Bank of Canada v. Conlin* (1996), para. 79.
18. *See* 2017 OECD TPG, *supra* para. 1.43.

**Example[19]**

Company X, a manufacturer that has functional currency in US dollars sells to Company Y, an associated distributor in another country having functional currency in euros. The written contract states that Company Y assumes all exchange rate risks arising from the transaction. If, however, the price for the goods is charged by the manufacturer to the distributor in euros, the currency of the Company Y, then the actual conduct is not in accordance with the intention of the contractual arrangement.

### 2.1.3 Analysis of Substance

#### 2.1.3.1 Source of Evidence

When the actual conduct of the parties is not consistent with economically significant terms that are evident from the contract, further analysis is required in order to identify the actual transaction. In doing so, it is critical to analyse how third-party enterprises could have determined the contractual terms under similar circumstances.[20] If material differences between contractual terms and the conduct of the associated enterprises in their relations with one another exist, the functions actually performed, assets used, and risks actually assumed in relation to the contractual terms should ultimately determine the factual substance and accordingly accurately delineate the actual transaction.[21] The information from written contracts should be clarified and supplemented by considering the evidence of the commercial or financial relations provided by the other four comparability factors.[22]

**Example[23]**

Company X is the parent company while Company Y is a wholly-owned subsidiary of Company A and acts as an agent for Company A's branded products that have been newly launched in Company B's local market. The agency contract between Company A and Company B is silent about any marketing and advertising activities that are required to be undertaken by Company B.

Based on an analysis, it is identified that Company B incurred significant expenses for creating awareness about the product locally. Further, based on evidence provided by the conduct of the parties, it could be concluded that the

---

19. *Ibid.*, para. 1.89.
20. *Ibid.*, para. 1.46.
21. *Ibid.*, para. 1.47.
22. *Ibid.*, para. 1.42.
23. *Ibid.*, para. 1.33.

written contract did not reflect the full extent of the commercial or financial relations between the parties. Beyond the terms contained in the written contract, the extent of Company B's awareness campaigns is to be ascertained.

### 2.1.3.2 Control and Financial Capacity to Undertake Functions and Risks

In situations when the parties to the contract do not have the capacity to perform a particular function even if the written contract ordains the role, the actual transaction should be determined only based on an evaluation of the conduct of parties. If the actual functions performed, assets used, and risks assumed by the parties are not in accordance with the written contract, the transaction is determined based on the conduct and not on the written terms.

---

**Example[24]**

Parent Company A manufactures products sold by subsidiary Company B according to a licensed agreement. External customers prefer Company B as a joint contracting party along with Company A for administrative convenience while the fee is paid to Company A. Though Company A has given a license to Company B, the control of risks and output of Company B continue to be undertaken by Company A. Therefore, the conduct overrides the contractual assumption of functions, risks, and assets.

---

In summary, an analysis of contracts helps to delineate in the following circumstances:

(a) When transactions remain unidentified from what is reported or are deducible from the contract due to conduct;

(b) Characteristics of a transaction that are economically relevant are inconsistent with the written contract between the associated enterprises, therefore, requiring a recharacterization of the transaction;

(c) When no written terms exist in the first place, the actual transaction is deduced from the actual conduct that is identified by the economically relevant characteristics of the transaction.

### 2.1.4 Role of Aggregation of Transactions in Contracts

Analysing contracts for the purposes of delineation helps to identify if a contract contains a number of elements including leases, sales, and licenses all packaged into

---

24. *Ibid.,* para. 1.48.

one deal.[25] Upon delineation of a transaction, an evaluation is required to determine if a transaction-by-transaction approach is suitable for further comparability analysis stages. If separate transactions are intrinsically linked and continuous, then an aggregation of the transactions is more appropriate. However, accurate delineation of the separate transactions is still necessary and, the question of aggregation of disaggregation comes into focus only upon recognition of the transaction. Functional analysis

The analysis of the contractual terms is followed by the identification of the functions performed, assets used, and risks assumed specifically for the tested transaction. This functional analysis process determines whether a given uncontrolled transaction is relevant for comparison purposes to the related party transaction that is being examined. It examines the specific economic activities that are inherent in the transactions that are being compared. In this manner, a functional analysis acts as a filter for eliminating uncontrolled transactions that are not comparable from a transfer pricing analysis.[26]

Additionally, such an analysis should be 'including how those functions relate to the wider generation of value by the MNE group to which the parties belong, the circumstances surrounding the transaction, and industry practices'.[27] In this context, the performance of a comprehensive global value chain analysis of the MNE will be fundamental.[28] From a transfer pricing perspective, the following steps of a value chain analysis should be relevant:[29]

(1) Mapping out a generic value chain for the industry.
(2) Mapping out an MNE's value chain.
(3) Comparing the generic value chain to an MNE's value chain and analysing the differences that may explain why an MNE has a competitive advantage over its competitors.
(4) Distinguishing between an MNE's main functions and its support functions.
(5) Identifying and understanding which of the MNE's main functions are critical to the success of the organization (i.e., a critical success factor).
(6) Identifying and understanding which activities performed by an MNE add value to the goods and services it produces that may distinguish the MNE from its competitors, i.e., value-adding activities.
(7) Understanding and confirming how the various functions across the value chain are split by the MNE between the various legal entities in the group.

---

25. *See* United Nations, *Practical Manual on Transfer Pricing for Developing Countries* (New York: United Nations, 2013), para. B.2.3.1.
26. US IRS Reg. 1.482.
27. OECD, *OECD Transfer Pricing Guidelines for Multinational Enterprises and Tax Administrations* (Paris: OECD, 2010), para. 1.36 (Ch. I).
28. *See* 2017 UN TPM, A3.5.1.
29. *Ibid.*

## 2.1.5   Functions Performed

The analysis of functions that is performed involves tracing the flow of products or services at various stages from the conceptualization to their final sales. The typical components of a functional analysis for transactions involving tangible goods include understanding and documenting the roles of the parties that undertake the following in the transaction flow:[30]

- Research and development;
- Product design and engineering;
- Manufacturing, production and process engineering;
- Product fabrication, extraction, and assembly;
- Purchasing and materials management;
- Marketing and distribution functions including inventory management, warranty administration, and advertising activities;
- Technological developments and marketing analytics;[31]
- Transportation and warehousing; and
- Managerial, legal, accounting and finance, credit and collection, training, and personnel management services.

Generally, the analysis is two-sided, i.e., involving both the transacting parties, and captures the relative strength of each party performing the stated function.

---

**Example[32]**

Company B manufactures food products with support from Company A. Company A provides its expertise on market development and undertakes the product development including food technology, composition, and knowhow. Company A also executes the quality control of the manufactured goods. Company B undertakes limited market development functions and has its inhouse R&D team to support Company A. After a detailed analysis, the functional profile of Company A and Company B is summarized as below:

| Intensity of Functions | Company A | Company B |
|---|---|---|
| Market Development | X | XXX |
| Product Development | XXX | X |
| Manufacturing | None | XXX |
| Quality Control | XXX | X |
| Corporate Strategy | XXX | X |

---

30. US IRS Reg. 1.482.
31. *See* 2017 UN TPM B.2.3.2.14.
32. *See* 2017 OECD TPG, *supra* para. 1.48.

| Intensity of Functions | Company A | Company B |
|---|---|---|
| Finance, treasury, legal | XXX | X |
| Human Resource Management | X | XXX |

### 2.1.6 Assets Used

Tangible as well as intangible assets that are utilised in the course of an international transaction or transferred between associated enterprises must be ascertained. Capital assets that are employed such as plant and equipment, intangible assets, financial assets, etc. and their relative usage by the transacting entities also need to be evaluated.[33] An industry analysis (refer to section 4.1.1) determines the level of assets in an industry. In the case of capital intensive industries, the employment of a capital asset such as property, plant, and equipment play a significant role in determining the comparability.

Intangibles for transfer pricing purposes are broader in scope than what is recognized as intangible assets for accounting purposes.[34] Therefore, 'intangible' is intended to address something that is not a physical asset or a financial asset that is capable of being owned or controlled for use in commercial activities and whose use or transfer would be compensated had it occurred in a transaction between independent parties in comparable circumstances.[35] Intangibles could be further classified as 'hard' and 'soft' intangibles, 'marketing' and 'trade' intangibles, 'routine' and 'non-routine' intangibles from a transfer pricing perspective.[36] For details on transfer pricing aspects of intangibles, refer to Chapter 11.

List of tangible and intangible assets (not limited to) requiring consideration are as follows:[37]

| Tangible Assets | Intangible Assets |
|---|---|
| – Land and buildings;<br>– Plant and machinery;<br>– R&D equipment;<br>– Office equipment;<br>– Furniture and fixtures;<br>– Vehicles; | – Patents<br>– Know-how and trade secrets<br>– Trademarks, tradenames and brands<br>– Rights under contracts and government licenses<br>– Licenses and similar limited rights in intangibles |

---

33. *See* 2017 UN TPM, B.2.3.2.20.
34. *See* 2017 OECD TPG, *supra* para. 6.7.
35. *Ibid.*, para. 6.6.
36. *Ibid.*, para. 6.15.
37. *See* 2017 UN TPM, B.2.3.2.22.

| Tangible Assets | Intangible Assets |
| --- | --- |
| – Computers; and<br>– Testing equipment. | – Goodwill and ongoing concern value<br>– Group synergies<br>– Market specific characteristics |

---

**Example[38] (Cont.)**

Company B holds a significant number of plants and machines, fixed installations such as warehouses, and premises for the manufacture and distribution of finished products. The technological know-how for Company B's operations are end-to-end provided by Company A. Company B undertakes certain awareness campaigns and customized marketing efforts, establishing certain marketing intangibles apart from the brand already owned legally by Company A. Considering the above, the intensity of risk on brand and technology is attributed.

| Intensity of Assets | Company A | Company B |
| --- | --- | --- |
| Tangible assets | | XXX |
| Intangible assests Technological | XXX | None |
| Trademark | XX | X |

---

### 2.1.7 Risks Assumed

A transfer pricing analysis should involve the identification of risks and subsequently attribute them to the entity that assumes the identified risks. A risk analysis follows the functional and asset analysis, and they cannot be isolated from one another. This analysis results in the identification of the relevant risks and to their allocation, irrespective of which party is responsible in the contract for them, to the parties to the parties that have: (a) the control over such risks and (b) the financial capacity to assume such risks.[39] Control over a specific risk in a transaction focuses on the decision-making of the parties to the transaction in relation to the specific risk arising from the transaction. It is also to be noted that other parties in an MNE's organizational structure could be involved in establishing general policies that are relevant for the assumption and control of the specific risks that are identified in a transaction without such policy-setting itself stipulating decision making.[40]

---

38. *See* 2017 OECD TPG, *supra* para. 1.48.
39. *See* 2017 UN TPM, B.2.3.2.17.
40. *See* 2017 OECD TPG, *supra* para. 1.76.

### 2.1.7.1  Overview of the Risk Framework

For the purpose of evaluating, the following broad parameters could be considered:[41]

- The capability to make decisions to assume, discontinue or decline a risk-bearing opportunity together *'with the actual performance'* [emphasis added] of that decision-making function (i.e., who makes the decisions and performs the functions related to the risk); and
- The capability to make decisions on whether and how to respond to the risk-bearing opportunity together *'with the actual performance'* [emphasis added] of that decision-making function (i.e., who makes the decisions and performs the related functions responding to risk).

The role of the value generated by the MNE groups as a whole, the interplay of functions performed, and the relative contributions of the co-creation of value facilitates understanding the functional profile.[42]

It is also critical to note that, while one party could perform multiple functions, it is the economic significance of the functions in terms of frequency, nature, and value that is to be given importance.[43] The identification of capabilities also helps in determining options that are realistically available to the party before entering into the transaction, demonstrating the rationale adopted by the transacting parties in making the transaction decision.[44]

### 2.1.7.2  The Six-Step Process

The functional analysis remains incomplete without a detailed analysis of material risks that are assumed by parties to the transaction(s) under review. For this purpose, the functional analysis of risk in the TPD 2017 is broken down to a six-step process:[45]

(1) *Step 1:* Identify economically significant risks with specificity
(2) *Step 2:* Contractual assumption of risk
(3) *Step 3:* Functional analysis in relation to risk
(4) *Step 4:* Interpreting steps 1–3
(5) *Step 5:* Allocation of risk
(6) *Step 6:* Pricing of the transaction, taking account of the consequences of risk allocation

---

41. *Ibid.*, para. 1.65.
42. *Ibid.*, para. 1.51.
43. *Ibid.*, para. 1.51.
44. *Ibid.*, para. 1.52.
45. *Ibid.*, paras 1.56–1.70.

While the process is prescribed consistently by the OECD and the UN, several individual tax jurisdictions have adopted a similar process for risk framework.[46] The steps are diagrammatically represented in Figure 2.2.

*Figure 2.2   Risk Recognition Framework*[47]

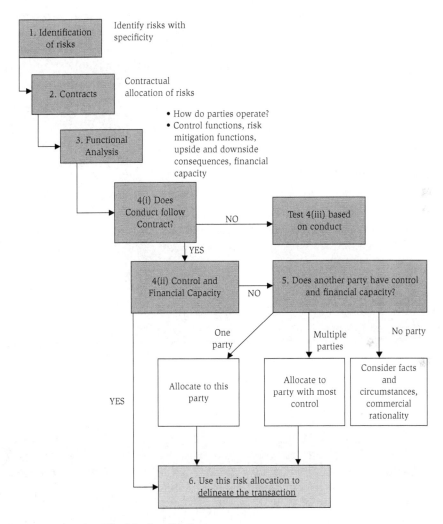

The process is described in detail below:

46. *See* Source: http://www.hmrc.gov.uk/gds/intm/attachments/flowchart-re-accurate-delinea tion.docx (last accessed 3 Mar. 2018).
47. *See* 2017 UN TPM, *supra.* p. 88.

## Step 1: Identify economically significant risks with specificity

For MNEs, risk is associated with opportunities for returns and not only disadvantageous implications. Risk taking is a means by which MNEs aim to achieve or maximize profits.[48] The first step is to identify such risks that should be considered in the course of a transfer pricing analysis. However, the emphasis here is to identify those risks that are 'economically significant' and not merely make an exhaustive record of risks.[49] Broadly, risks are inclusive of but not limited to: (a) strategic risk or marketplace risks arising out of the external environment, (b) infrastructure or operational risks arising out of the execution of business, (c) financial risks such as liquidity and handling cash-flow, (d) transactional risks including pricing and payment risks, and (e) hazard risks due to accidents or natural disasters.[50]

The direct relevance of identifying such risks is in the context of potential comparables that are identified and whether they bear the same level and management of risks.[51] Further details on the comparability process is provided in section 4.

## Step 2: Contractual assumption of risk

The next step is to return back to the contract (considered in section 2.1) to take into account the contractual risk setting for the specific risks that are identified in connection with the transaction. As stated previously, the mere pricing arrangements that are visible in the contractual agreement would not be sufficient for deciding about the actual conduct.[52]

In the case of tax audits, evidence (*ex ante*) regarding the conduct (or execution of contractual obligations) plays a significant role in a transfer pricing analysis. The certainty of business outcomes of the MNE group also determines whether a contractual assumption of risk actually exists in reality (including ex post reallocation of risk).[53] The role of risk mitigation strategies that are evident from the concluded contract is also to be taken into consideration.

## Step 3: Functional analysis in relation to risk

The role of each of the transacting enterprises with regard to the following questions becomes important under Step 3.[54] The party that performs risk management functions will be reviewed under two functional components, i.e., the control over risk functions and risk mitigation functions. Further, the entity that bears upside or downside consequences of risk outcomes and has the financial capacity to assume the specific risk determines the risk allocation matrix.

Therefore, the capacity to make decisions with regard to a risk-bearing opportunity along with the actual execution of this ability to make decisions determines the

---

48. *See* 2017 OECD TPG, *supra* para. 1.70.
49. *Ibid.*, para. 1.71.
50. *Ibid.*, para. 1.72.
51. *Ibid.*, para. 1.73.
52. *Ibid.*, para. 1.81.
53. *Ibid.*, para. 1.78.
54. *Ibid.*, para. 1.82.

actual risk profile. Also, parties performing mitigation activities in connection with the risk need not necessarily assume control over such a risk. It is also possible to outsource the day-to-day risk mitigation but not the functions associated with the control over risk. The role of financial capacity[55] to access funding options, liquidation, and ability to bear the cost of mitigation of risks and to bear the consequence of risk materialization is evaluated in this process.

Having control over a risk and having the financial capacity to assume the risk must both be fulfilled in order to allocate the risk to a particular contracting entity while the earlier guidance indicated that assuming either of the risks would qualify a particular enterprise to assume the risk. The same is diagrammatically illustrated in Figure 2.3.[56]

*Figure 2.3   Risk Recognition Process*

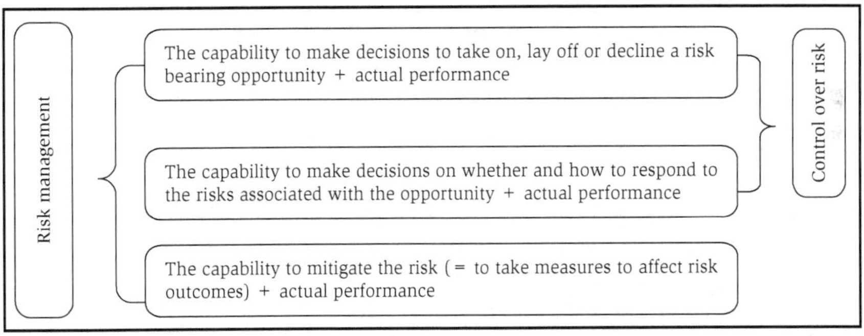

### Step 4: Interpreting steps 1–3

After collecting the information from Steps 1 to 3, the next step is to interpret that information,[57] specifically, to determine: (i) whether the associated enterprises follow the contractual terms and (ii) whether the party assuming risk, as analysed under (i), exercises control over the risk and has the financial capacity to assume it.

When both of the above conditions are satisfied, no further analysis is necessary. However, when differences between contractual terms related to economically significant risk and the conduct of the parties exist, the conduct of parties in fulfilling contractual obligations is considered as the best evidence of risk assumption. It is evaluated separately whether the party controls the risk and also has the financial capacity to assume it. If it does, the analysis can directly proceed to the final step (Step 6). If it does not, the analysis continues with an intermediary Step 5.

---

55. *Ibid.*, para. 1.64.
56. *See* Gao, J., Baets.,S; *Recent Developments on Comparability Analysis in Transfer Pricing*, Recent Developments in Transfer Pricing, 2017, Kluwer Tax Law (Vienna: 2018) *(Forthcoming)*.
57. *See* 2017 OECD TPG, *supra* para. 1.86.

### Step 5: Allocation of risk

If it is identified under Step 4 that the entity contractually assuming the risk does not exercise control over it or does not have the financial capacity to assume it, then effort is taken to re-allocate the risks to the parties that actually control the risk and have the financial capacity or, in cases when there is a sharing of risks, the relative share of exercising the most control is recognized.[58] While methodology to accurately allocate or demarcate the risks is still a question of attribution, as a general practice, the intensity of risks could be recorded by the taxpayers at this stage before concluding the pricing in order to obtain a reasonably accurate position.[59]

---

**Example[60]**

Company P operates a garment manufacturing facility and enters into a contract with Company Q for manufacturing that includes design and specifications and quality control standards provided by Company Q. Based on an assessment before purchases, if Company P meets the quality control standards established by Q, the latter will indemnify for any warranty or compensation claims that may arise from the sale to end customers thereby mitigating Company P's risk. The products will be sold in Company Q's brand name, and Company Q bears the reputation risk of any damages. Company Q takes title to goods and bears the inventory risk arising from the sale activity. The currency of the manufactured sale from Company P to Company Q is USD, which is the local currency of Company Q. Therefore, the risk of foreign exchange fluctuation is borne by Company P. Company Q and P do not assume any credit and collection risk for the internal transfer of the sale of manufactured goods. However, Company Q assumes the collection risk for the sale to external customers.

An illustrative assignment of risks for the above fact pattern is provided below:

| Intensity of Risks | Company P | Company Q |
|---|---|---|
| Master risk | None | XX |
| Product liability risk | X | XXX |
| Technology risk | X | XXX |
| Credit risk | None | XXX |
| Inventory risk | XX | XX |
| Foreign currency risk | XX | None |

---

Step 6: Pricing of the transaction taking account of the consequences of risk allocation

---

58. *Ibid.,* para. 1.98.
59. *See* 2017 UN TPM, *supra.* p. 100.
60. *Ibid.,* para. B.2.3.2.36.

The final step is to price the accurately delineated transaction. The pricing is made on the basis of the assumption that the risk should be compensated with an appropriate anticipated return. In this regard, a contracting entity that is assuming risks and undertaking risk mitigation support will be entitled to greater anticipated remuneration than a taxpayer that only assumes a risk or only mitigates but does not do both.[61] The pricing is based on the TP Methods in relation to the comparability analysis discussed in sections 4.2.1 and 4.3.1 of this chapter. For detailed reading on TP Methods and applicability, refer to Chapters 3 and 4.

## 2.2 Characteristics of Property or Services

Comparisons between uncontrolled and controlled transactions on the characteristics specific to the property that is transferred or services involved in the intra-group transaction would be beneficial for determining the comparability of controlled and uncontrolled transactions. Characteristics that require being identified include:[62]

- In the case of tangible property, the physical features, quality, reliability, and availability of volume and supply;
- In the case of services, the nature, and extent of such services; and
- In the case of intangible property, the form of the transaction, i.e., licensing arrangement, type of property, degree of protection, duration, and future anticipated benefits from the intangible would need to be ascertained.[63]

The suitability of a specific transfer pricing method and comparability adjustments that could be necessary depends on the characteristics of property or services. For methods based on gross or net profit indicators, functional similarities take precedence over product similarities. For more information on the suitability of methods and the comparability factors that play a significant role, refer to sections 4.2.1 and 4.3.1. For detailed reading on TP Methods and applicability, refer to Chapters 3 and 4.

---

**Example**[64]

Company P undertakes the sale of coffee beans that are imported from associated enterprise Q for sale to third parties. For the purpose of a comparability analysis, key characteristic properties of the transaction include evaluation of the following:

- Whether the coffee beans are branded and comparable transactions included unbranded (potential) comparables
- Delivery terms (CIF/FOB)

---

61. *See* 2017 OECD TPG, *supra* para. 1.100.
62. *Ibid.*, para. 1.33.
63. *Ibid.*, para. 1.108.
64. *See* 2017. UN TPM, *supra* para. B.2.3.2.36.

> – The effect of the differences in volume on price
> – Product differences such as changes to aroma, coffee grade, and extraction location
> – The technology involved in types of coffee bean processing
>
> In undertaking the comparability analysis, it is to be evaluated if reasonably accurate adjustments could be effected for the above differences.

While the scope of comparability is generally extended to include products of broad categories (or of similar nature, exhibiting similar characteristics), the level of differences would determine the reliability of the comparable information.

## 2.3 Economic Circumstances

Economic circumstances that aid in determining market comparability include the following:[65]

- Geographic location and the size of the markets;
- the extent of competition in the markets and the relative competitive positions of the buyers and sellers; the availability (and risk thereof) of substitute goods and services;
- the levels of supply and demand in the market as a whole and in particular regions, if relevant;
- consumer purchasing power;
- the nature and extent of government regulation of the market;
- costs of production including the costs of land, labour, and capital; transport costs; the level of the market (e.g., retail or wholesale); the date and time of the transactions;

Further, businesses operate based on cycles (e.g., economic,[66] business,[67] or product[68] cycles), therefore, this is one of the economic circumstances that should be identified. The use of multiple year data in a comparability analysis is justified by the existence of economic cycles. Also, for cases where similar controlled transactions are performed by the same MNE group in several countries with homogeneous circumstances, the MNE could rely on a multiple-country comparability analysis to support its transfer pricing policy towards this group of countries. For further information, refer to section 4.

---

65. *See* United Nations: *Working Draft of UN Comparability Analysis*, (New York:2011).
66. *See* Sage, A., Mass, N., *Economic Cycles: An Analysis of Underlying Causes, IEEE Systems, Man, and Cybernetics Society*, pp. 302–302 (1977).
67. *See* Schumpeter, J. *Business Cycles – A Theoretical, Historical and Statistical Analysis of the Capitalist Process*, McGraw-Hill, (New York: 1939).
68. *See* Finger, J.M., *A New View of the Product Cycle Theory, Review of World Economics*, Volume 111/1, pp. 79–99, Springer Publications (1975).

## 2.4 Business Strategies

The traditional role of business strategies in a comparability analysis were limited[69] to situations such as: (a) the supplier waiving payment from a customer 'in temporary difficulties in order to preserve a potentially valuable outlet for his goods'[70] and (b) sellers temporarily lowering prices as part of a market penetration or start-up strategy.[71] New strategies such as market penetration[72], blue-ocean,[73] merger-acquisition,[74] or digital transformation[75] have had increasing impact.

From a strategic perspective, business strategies could be classified as follows:[76]

- Market penetration strategy;
- Market expansion strategy; or
- Market maintenance strategy.

While the above strategies are legitimate and recognized based on commercial rationale, taxpayers are expected to define a timeframe for pursuing such strategies and accordingly evidence them, particularly in the cases of perennial losses. The costs arising from pursuing such strategies requires allocation between associated enterprises from a transfer pricing perspective. For example, on market penetration as a business strategy, refer to the example provided in section 5.1.

In circumstances when an MNE group launches its products in a new market incurs substantial set up costs due to which the margins of the initial years are low due to low capacity, the taxpayer must undertake the necessary adjustments on under-utilization and start-up costs.[77] More information on the economic adjustments that are applicable to a taxpayer's circumstances is provided in section 5. Another factor to consider is whether the nature of the relationship between the contracting parties is consistent with the taxpayer bearing the costs of the business strategy.[78] The timing issues play a significant role as business strategies may or may not be aligned to expected outcomes, therefore, warranting a TP adjustment. The presence of domestic

---

69. *See* Gao, J., Baets, S; *Recent Developments on Comparability Analysis in Transfer Pricing*, Recent Developments in Transfer Pricing, 2017, Kluwer Tax Law (Vienna: 2018) (*Forthcoming*).
70. *See* OECD, *Transfer Pricing and Multinational Enterprises* (Paris: OECD Publishing, 1979), para. 40.
71. *See* OECD 1979, para. 43.
72. Market penetration is the key performance metric for a business growth strategy stemming from the Ansoff Matrix (Richardson, M., & Evans, C. (2007). H. Igor Ansoff first devised and published The Ansoff Matrix in the Harvard Business Review in 1957, titled '*Strategies for Diversification*'.
73. Blue Ocean Strategy is a marketing theory from a book published in 2005 that was written by W. Chan Kim and Renée Mauborgne, professors at INSEAD and co-directors of the INSEAD Blue Ocean Strategy Institute.
74. *See* Cartwright, Susan; Schoenberg, Richard, '*Thirty Years of Mergers and Acquisitions Research: Recent Advances and Future Opportunities*'. British Journal of Management. 17 (S1): S1–S5. (2006).
75. *See* Matt, Christian & Hess, Thomas & Benlian, Alexander. Digital Transformation Strategies. Business & Information Systems Engineering. 57. 339–343. (2015).
76. UN TPM para. B.2.3.2.63.
77. *See Amdocs Business Services Pvt. Ltd. v. DCIT* – ITA No. 1412/PN/2011.
78. *See* 2017 OECD TPG, *supra.* p. 76.

regulations to permit a reassessment for the duration of such a business strategy often becomes a challenge that leads to increased scrutiny of the strategies at the stage of the initial assessment itself. It should also be noted that tax authorities and taxpayers could have the benefit of hindsight between the transaction, the preparation of transfer pricing documentation, and the conduct of actual audit, leading to potential disputes. For a detailed discussion on *Administrative Approaches to Avoiding/Minimizing Transfer Pricing Disputes,* refer to Chapter 5.

Furthermore, it could occur that unusually intensive marketing and advertising efforts often accompany market penetration or market share expansion strategies. While the OECD has stated that adequate consideration is required to be provided in order to test the reasonableness of the circumstances as part of the comparability, the view adopted by tax administrators diverges, particularly in developing countries.[79]

## 3   THE RECOGNITION OF THE ACCURATELY DELINEATED TRANSACTION UNDERTAKEN

The topic of recognition of the accurate transaction has gained significance in recent times due to several disputes[80] surrounding the topic. It addresses whether the transaction was correctly characterized and reported in the first place. Non-recognition refers to a situation when tax authorities modify the nature of transactions based on an analysis of the actual conduct of the parties, ideally after having performed the steps mentioned in the previous section. Tax authorities are expected to recognize controlled transactions unless under exceptional circumstances. Such non-recognition powers are often pointed out as conflicting with domestic laws of various countries[81] and could also result in double-taxation.[82]

The argument regarding the non-recognition of transactions by tax administrators stems from the apprehension that, without a provision for non-recognition, taxpayers would be permitted to freely design economic structures that ultimately resulted in violating arm's length structure requirements.[83] The concept of fundamental economic attributes of arrangements between unrelated parties and the concept of commercial rationality has been the basis[84] for arguments for non-recognition. In this regard, the 2017 OECD Guidelines and the 2017 UN Manual specify the circumstance under which a transaction could be disregarded (not recognized);[85] when similar

---

79. *See* Maruti Suzuki Ltd [TS-212-ITAT-2013(DEL)-TP].
80. *See* KHO 2017:145 (Finland).
81. *See* Pichhadze, A., *The Non-recognition and Recharacterisation of Contracts in Transfer Pricing: Exposing the Tensions with Private Contract Law,* New Zealand Journal of Taxation Law and Policy, (New York: December 2017).
82. *See* 2017 OECD TPG, *supra* para. 1.122.
83. *See* OECD Discussion Draft, para. 87 – https://www.oecd.org/ctp/transfer-pricing/discussion-draft-actions-8-9-10-chapter-1-TP-Guidelines-risk-recharacterisation-special-measures.pdf.
84. *See* 1995 and 2010 OECD TPG, *supra.*
85. *See* 2017 OECD TPG, *supra* para 1.123–1.125. The 2010 OECD Guidelines and the 2013 UN Manual identified the following two situations for a non-recognition of the accurate transaction:

   – When the economic substance of the transaction differs from its form.

uncontrolled transactions could be ascertained between independent enterprises under comparable economic circumstances, i.e., when all economically relevant characteristics are the same as those under which the tested transaction occurs other than that the parties are associated enterprises.

To this end, the mere absence of a comparable transaction does not warrant a total disregarding of the transactions. It is clarified that the key question is not the mere presence or absence of similar transactions but, instead, the commercial rationality as to whether independent organizations would have entered into a similar transaction under comparable circumstances.

---

**Example[86]**

Company X, a manufacturer, holds substantial inventory and fixed installations. The commercial properties are situated in a zone that is prone to frequent flooding. External insurers experience significant uncertainty over the exposure to large claims in the area where insurance is not common. Company Y, an associated enterprise, provides insurance to Company X and an annual premium representing 80% of the value of the inventory, property, and contents of Company X. Considering this fact pattern, Company X has entered into a commercially irrational transaction since the transaction is uncommon in comparable circumstances and either relocation or not insuring may be more attractive realistic alternatives. Since the transaction is commercially irrational, there is not a price that is acceptable to both X and Y from their individual perspectives.

---

In the event of recharacterization by the tax administrators, the replacement structure should be guided by the economically relevant characteristics including the functions performed, assets used, and risks assumed of the commercial or financial relations of the associated enterprises. These facts aid in narrowing the range of potential replacement structures to the structure most consistent with the facts of the taxpayer's case.

---

**Example[87]**

Company A, a pharma subsidiary, proposes to undertake extensive R&D functions and develop significant intangibles. Company A plans to provide unlimited rights to Company B, an associated enterprise, along with future intangibles that may arise. Since valuation of these proposed intangibles is not feasible at this

---

- When arrangements between the related parties involved in the transaction differ from those that would have been made between commercially rational independent enterprises, and the actual structure of the transaction hinders tax administrations from determining an appropriate transfer price.

86. *See* 2017. OECD TPG, *supra* para. 1.126.
87. *Ibid.*, para. 1.127.

> stage, the proposed transaction between Company A and B is commercially irrational.

In summary, while tax administrators are provided with guiding pointers that permit non-recognition and recharacterization of existing transactions, the identification of the risks and steps to recharacterize transactions could be difficult to apply, especially in certain industries such as financial services,[88] since the attribution of risks and consequent return remains a practical challenge.

## 4   COMPARABILITY ANALYSIS

The most significant disputes in any transfer pricing litigation are based on the practical conduct of a comparability analysis and often instigated by the differences in approach towards criteria for comparability. The potential fundamental disagreement begins with the identification of the transaction as emphasized in sections 2 and 3 and later develops into disputes on characterization and valuation. Once the transaction has been accurately delineated and recognized, conducting a comparability analysis is commenced.

Historically, the 1979 OECD Report of the OECD Committee on Fiscal Affairs – Transfer Pricing and Multinational Enterprises did not contain detailed guidance on the comparability analysis but only a general guidance on the approach to an arm's length analysis. After incremental updates to its publication in 1995, a major significant update on the comparability standards of the OECD TPG occurred in 2010.[89]

The OECD and the UN provide guidance for performing a nine-step process.[90] However, the OECD cautions that the approach suggested is only guidance. The actual conduct should depend on specific facts and circumstances, and this approach in itself would not guarantee that the outcome would be the most suitable arm's length benchmark.[91] This process is detailed in Table 2.1.

*Table 2.1   The Nine-Step Process to Comparability Analysis*

| | |
|---|---|
| 1 | Determination of years to be covered. |
| 2 | Broad-based analysis of the taxpayer's circumstances. |

---

88. *See* Plunkett Jt., R.W., Yohanna, B, Green, B., *Risk and Recharacterisation – Does it Make Sense in a Financial Services Context?*, International Tax Review, 4 Aug. 2015.
89. *See* Gao, J., Baets.,S; *Recent Developments on Comparability Analysis in Transfer Pricing*, Recent Developments in Transfer Pricing, 2017, Kluwer Tax Law (Vienna: 2018) (*Forthcoming*).
90. *See* 2017 OECD TPG, *supra* para. 3.4.
91. *Ibid.*, para. 3.5.

3   Understanding the controlled transaction(s) under examination, based in particular on a functional analysis, in order to choose the tested party (when needed), the most appropriate transfer pricing method for the circumstances of the case, the financial indicator that will be tested (in the case of a transactional profit method), and to identify the significant comparability factors that should be taken into account.

4   Review of existing internal comparables, if any.

5   Determination of available sources of information on external comparables when such external comparables are needed taking into account their relative reliability.

6   Selection of the most appropriate transfer pricing method and, depending on the method, determination of the relevant financial indicator (e.g., determination of the relevant net profit indicator in case of a transactional net margin method).

7   Identification of potential comparables: determining the key characteristics to be met by any uncontrolled transaction in order to be regarded as potentially comparable based on the relevant factors identified in 3 and in accordance with the five comparability factors (characteristics of property and services, functional analysis, contractual arrangements, economic circumstances, and business strategies).

8   Determination of and making comparability adjustments where appropriate.

9   Interpretation and use of data collected, determination of the arm's length remuneration.

## 4.1   The Benchmarking Process of Comparability Analysis

The end-to-end process of a typical comparability analysis requires a consistent application of the analytical approach beginning with accurately delineating the transaction, selecting the appropriate transfer pricing method, reviewing potential comparables and forming a conclusive result on the arm's length nature of the controlled transaction that is identified that is in accordance with Article 9 of the OECD Model Tax Convention.[92] A key aspect to consider in performing the process is to not take linear approach to arriving at the results but to repeat the steps (specifically Step 5 to 7) whenever necessary to refine the process and improve the results. Also, it is essential that the ultimate objective of undertaking the comparability analysis is always kept in mind during every stage of the process.

### 4.1.1   Determination of Years to Be Covered

Taxpayers use the data that is available at the time the transfer prices are established which means in terms of benchmarking data from previous years. The OECD recognizes the influence of information from past years while undertaking the analysis.[93] For

---

92. *See* Article 9, OECD: *Model Convention With Respect To Taxes On Income And On Capital*, (Paris: 2014).
93. *See* 2017 OECD TPG, *supra*.

instance, multiple year data is used for traditional methods when the CUP method is not applied. Generally, data from previous years can be utilized to obtain a comprehensive understanding of the facts and circumstances of a transaction when a transactional profit method is applied.[94]

Domestic regulations also generally permit the use of multiple year data depending on the extent of 'complete and accurate' information being available for the tax year under review and when the effects of business cycles and product life cycles are known.

In this context, the assumptions underlying the determination of the transfer price and the comparable results are typically reviewed at the end of a fiscal year. Adjustments may be considered if the taxpayer employs the same set of comparability criteria at the end of a fiscal year that was applied at the outset and documents the underlying logic of the adjustment so that tax authorities may verify the reasonableness of this adjustment (in practice called 'true-up').

In recent times, controversies surrounding timing issues with regard to and interplay of the year of data come into focus with dispute resolution mechanisms such as APA/MAPs and the use of transfer pricing for customs valuation... For detailed discussions on this topic, refer to Chapter 6 on dispute resolution and Chapter 13 on transfer pricing and customs valuation.

### 4.1.2  Analysis of Taxpayer's Circumstances

A 'broad-based analysis' that accounts for the MNE group's industry, competition, economic and regulatory factors, and other elements that affect the taxpayer and its environment[95] in combination with the transaction forms the foremost step. This information could be gathered from sources such as annual reports, product brochures, news articles, research reports prepared by independent agencies, management letters, and internal reports that indicate the circumstances.[96]

### 4.1.3  Understanding the Controlled Transaction and Choice of Tested Party

In order to understand the controlled transaction, it is essential to understand what qualifies as one from a transfer pricing perspective. A controlled transaction is simply a transaction between two (or more) enterprises that are 'associated enterprises' with respect to each other. While domestic laws could provide diverging interpretations on the thresholds of what qualifies as being controlled, a widely used understanding of a controlled transaction is:[97]

---

94. *Ibid.*, para. 1.49.
95. *Ibid.*, para. 3.70.
96. *See* 2017 UN TPM, *supra* para. B.2.3.13 p. 70.
97. *See* Source: https://transferpricingasia.com/what-is-tp/controlled-transaction/ (last accessed on 10 Mar. 2018).

(i) An enterprise participates directly or indirectly in the management, control, or capital of another enterprise or,

(ii) The same persons participate directly or indirectly in the management, control, or capital of two enterprises.

Further, in a controlled transaction, one of the parties being a 'tested party' is defined as the one to which a transfer pricing method can be applied in the most reliable manner and for which the most reliable comparable can be found, i.e., it will most often be the one that has the less complex functional analysis.[98] The conditions to be evaluated in selecting the tested party are concisely shown below:

(1) Available of reliable and accurate data for comparison
(2) Least Complex (relatively, amongst the parties to the transaction)[99]
(3) Data available can be used with minimal adjustments.

In the context of TP Methods, when applying a cost plus, resale price, or transactional net margin method, it is necessary to select the party to the transaction for which a financial indicator (mark-up on costs, gross margin, or net profit indicator) is tested. The choice of the tested party should be consistent with the functional analysis of the transaction. Specifically, one-sided methods (e.g., cost plus, resale price, or transactional net margin method) may require only examining a financial indicator or profit level indicator for one of the tested parties and, therefore, information pertaining to the controlled transaction only from the domestic taxpayer perspective could be necessary. However, information on foreign enterprises could be necessary for tax administrators when other methods are deployed.[100] From developing countries' perspectives, the choice of the tested party has, in the past, heavily hinged on the sufficiency of comparable data and acceptance of the foreign tested party by tax administrators for an arm's length analysis.[101]

The role of country-by-country reports and master files that capture information on non-tested parties are expected to have significant influence in future tax audits, particularly the potential influence of the selection of the tested party and the methodology by taxpayers could undergo a change. Further information about the new documentation requirements is provided in Chapter 7.

## 4.2 Undertaking the Comparability Analysis

The controlled enterprises have the flexibility to select the methodology that is suitable for demonstrating the arm's length nature of transactions. As part of the process, a

---

98. *See* 2017 OECD TPG, *supra* para. 3.18.
99. *See* General Motor India Pvt. Ltd [ITA nos. 3096/AHD/2010 and 3308/AHD/2011] (2 Aug. 2013).
100. *See* 2017 OECD TPG, *supra* para. 3.24.
101. *See* 2017 UN TPM, *supra* para. B2.3.3.

comparable uncontrolled transaction is considered for determining the arm's length price. An uncontrolled transaction is between two independent parties that is comparable to the controlled transaction under examination. It can be either a comparable transaction between one party to the controlled transaction and an independent party ('internal comparable') or between two independent enterprises, neither of which is a party to the controlled transaction ('external comparable').[102] While internal and external comparables have their respective pros and cons, the general preference in practice is to review the presence and appropriateness of internal comparables before venturing to take efforts in identification of external comparables.

### 4.2.1   Review of Internal Comparables

An analysis of internal financial information may be easier and more reliable as it depends on internal data based on similar accounting standards. Further, it is presumably more complete and cost effective *vis-á-vis* external comparable searches. Internal comparables typically include:

- Transaction by either party to the controlled transaction
- Transactions only the party being examined
- Transactions by only the tested party
- Transactions by any other member of the MNE group

While internal comparables are considered very reliable if they are suitably available, it is also observed that internal comparables could suffer from the propensity of being overly scrutinized as the information that is available could lead to clear demarcation of uncontrolled and controlled transactions based on the five factors of comparability while, for external comparables, the same similar differences could be ignored.[103] Further, it is critical for internal comparables to be put through the test of the same five comparability factors and their ability to be subjected to reliable economic adjustments.[104]

Sources of internal comparables, depending on the type of method to be applied could be considered (see Table 2.2).[105]

---

102. *See* 2017 OECD TPG, *supra* para. 3.24.
103. *See* OECD Draft: *General Preference for Internal Comparables, OECD Conference,* November 2008, Paris Source: http://www.oecd.org/tax/transfer-pricing/41695089.pdf.
104. *See* 2017 OECD TPG, *supra* para. 3.28.
105. OECD, *Working Paper 6.*

*Table 2.2    Internal Comparables: Applicable Scenarios*

| Traditional Transactional Methods | Transactional Profit Methods |
|---|---|
| – Purchase/sale of the same products or services to third-parties can occur but in different markets or under different business strategies. <br> – Commission rates or trade discount structure in distribution agreements with unrelated parties. <br> – Manufacturing agreements (outsourcing all or part of the manufacturing process) to third parties. | – **PSM:** Joint ventures or strategic alliance agreements for the percentage profit split applicable to the relative contributions of the parties. Also, in some respects, the CUTs for licensing intangibles is a profit split that is translated into a share of the revenue (i.e., royalty based on sales). <br> – **TNMM:** If CUTs exist that indicate the net margin earned in an uncontrolled transaction, then it likely that gross margin data (or to calculate an appropriate commission or gross margin that would achieve the net margin result) is available to apply a modified RPM or Cost Plus method |

### 4.2.2    Determination of Sources for Identification of External Comparables

In general, the search for external market information for the purpose of arm's length could be considered as an articulation of the traditional market approach to valuation. [106] External search for finding uncontrolled transactions similar to taxpayer's circumstances could be considered as a process of elimination of the least similar comparables.[107] 'To be comparable means that none of the differences (if any) between the situations being compared could materially affect the condition being examined in the methodology (e.g., price or margin), or that reasonably accurate adjustments can be made to eliminate the effect of any such differences'.[108]

Inherently, tax policy makers have taken an approach that the use of external data offers a more realistic picture. Historically, this is observed from both the 1968 US Regulations and the OECD's 1979 Report which were based on the assumption that, by and large, actual comparables in the marketplace could be found. Accordingly, they prioritized the use of transfer pricing methodologies that were based on the market approach to valuation (e.g., the CUP method). Therefore, the use of external data is considered as producing the most reliable objective indication of the arm's length

---

106. *See* Y. Brauner (2008), *Value in the Eye of the Beholder: The Valuation of Intangibles for Transfer Pricing Purposes*, 28 Va. Tax Rev. 79, p. 104.
107. *See* 2010 UN TPM, *supra* para. 3.2.
108. *See* IRS Treasury Regulations, s. 1.482-1(d)(2). Regarding the option of conducting comparability adjustments, these are adjustments 'made to the conditions of the uncontrolled transaction in order to eliminate the effects of material differences which exist between them and the controlled transaction'.

price.[109] However, over the subsequent years, several doubts have arisen on the validity of the arm's length principle being dependent on external market information which is inherently subject to bias.[110] With increasing difficulty of identifying comparable information, there have been several calls for rethinking the approach to the arm's length analysis.[111]

Nevertheless, several sources of information that can be used to identify potential external comparables have been recognized. These are broadly categorised as commercial databases, foreign comparables, and information undisclosed to taxpayers.[112] The three categories of sources are analysed in Table 2.3.[113]

*Table 2.3    Comparative Analysis of Sources of Data*

| Source | Usage | Pros and Cons |
| --- | --- | --- |
| **Databases** | The most common source of information are commercial databases developed by independent developers who compile financial information electronically to enable statistical analytics. | – Cost effective source and reliable, depending on the nature of databases<br>– Better quantity of information thereby making the analysis robust<br>– All countries may not have the capacity to maintain such information and quality of databases (methodology of compilation of data) is susceptible. |
| **Foreign comparable information** | In the absence of reliable or robust databases, overseas databases containing reliable information could be considered | – Offers an alternative to lack of comparable information<br>– Market differences and geographical criteria are under greater scrutiny by tax administrators.<br>– Accounting differences could influence comparability |
| **Undisclosed information** | Tax administrators could have access to information not available in public domain or in the procession of the taxpayer that could be used. | Data could be aggregated and allocation (segmental profits and costs) comparable to the transaction(s) under tested segment could be a challenge |

109. *See* Pichhadze, A, *The Arm's Length Comparable in Transfer Pricing: A Search for an 'Actual' or a 'Hypothetical' Transaction?*, IBFD, 2016.
110. *See* K. Sadiq, *The Fundamental Failing of the Traditional Transfer Pricing Regime – Applying the Arm's Length Standard to Multinational Banks based on a Comparability Analysis*, Bull. Intl. Taxn. 2 (2004), IBFD.
111. R.S. Avi-Yonah & I. Benshalom, *Formulary Apportionment – Myths and Prospects: Promoting Better International Tax Policies by Utilizing the Misunderstood and Under-Theorized Formulary Alternative*, 3 World Tax J. (2011), p. 376, Journals IBFD, p. 377.
112. *See* 2017 OECD TPG, *supra* para. 3.29.
113. *Ibid.*, para. 3.30–3.38.

In summary, at this stage, the choice of source of data should be driven purely by the objective approach to achieve maximum comparability, and the result of the functional analysis should be constantly referred to before concluding on the uncontrolled transaction identified from either categories, i.e., internal or external sources. Further information on the decision on comparables is provided in section 4.4.

## 4.3 Review and Determination of Most Appropriate TP Method and Financial Indicators

Chapter 2 of the 2017 OECD TPG deals with the selection of TP methods for arm's length in detail. The selection of the most appropriate TP method depends on the facts and circumstances of each case based on factors considered in the steps thus far. The fundamentals of these methods have been addressed in Chapter 1 of this book. This section will further detail the application of TP Methods in the context of a comparability analysis and detail the role of Profit Level Indicators (PLIs) in the analysis. For detailed reading on TP Methods and applicability, refer to Chapters 3 and 4.

### 4.3.1 Synopsis of Comparability Considerations for Choice of TP Method

Choice of methods from a comparability analysis perspective is discussed in Table 2.4.

Table 2.4   Choice of Methods from a Comparability Analysis Perspective

| TP Method | Examination of Suitability under Comparability Analysis |
| --- | --- |
| Traditional Transaction Methods | |
| **CUP** | – Similarity in nature of assets or services concerning the transactions between unrelated parties to the assets or services of the foreign-related transaction shall be found.<br>– Typical examples include quoted price in commodity transactions[114] when either internal or external comparables could be considered. The comparable prices however, should carry the ability to be adjusted, if warranted. |
| **RPM** | – Similarity of functions takes precedence.[115] However, when making comparisons for purposes of the resale price method, fewer adjustments are normally needed to account for product differences than under the CUP method.<br>– Minor product differences are less likely to have as much of an effect on profit margins as they do on price on profit margins as they do on price.[116] |

114. *Ibid.*, para. 2.24.
115. *Ibid.*, para. 2.34.
116. *Ibid.*, para. 2.29.

| TP Method | Examination of Suitability under Comparability Analysis |
|---|---|
| *Traditional Transaction Methods* | |
| **CPM** | – Similarity of functions takes precedence. Similar to the comparability approach towards RPM, fewer adjustments may be necessary to account for product differences under the cost plus method than the CUP method, and it may be appropriate to give more weight to other factors of comparability and potential to carry further adjustments to the comparable prices would be necessary.<br>– Another key factor to consider under the CPM is the cost-base on which the comparable markup is applied.[117] Use of different cost bases, in effect, distorts comparability. |
| *Transactional Profits Method* | |
| **TNMM** | – Similarity of functions takes precedence under TNMM.<br>– Net profit indicators are less adversely affected by product differences and, therefore, provide greater opportunity for comparability in practice. Considerations on profit level indicators are discussed separately below.<br>– The use of TNMM is also triggered by the lack of applicability of CUP or RPM which require more distinctive and strict conditions for being suitable. |
| **PSM** | – Identification of comparable transaction could be a challenge given the individuality and uniqueness of the intangible properties.<br>– In the absence of comparable data, a contribution analysis is to be considered[118] whereby the use of external market data in the profit split analysis is used in ascertaining the value.[119] Existence of Comparable PSM information in case of pricing royalty licenses are increasingly under consideration.[120]<br>– However, it has been observed that the use of comparable data in transactional PSM is not addressed comprehensively in the OECD TPG, UN TPM, nor the US IRS Regulations.[121] |
| *Other Methods* | |
| **Sixth Method** | – The use of a sixth method has been in practice in specific tax jurisdictions in developing countries in circumstances when there is simply inadequate comparable data or potential comparables that are selected may have material differences that could not be resolved by means of adjustments.<br>– While this method has been considered as a variance of CUP, to use market data, the basic principles of a comparability analysis remains the same with regard to the applicability of this method. |

---

117. *Ibid.*, para. 2.50.
118. *See OECD Public Discussion Draft, BEPS Action 10, Revised Guidance on Profit Split Method*, para. 39 (Paris: 2017).
119. *Ibid.*, para. 53 (Paris: 2017).
120. *See* R.P Rozek & G.G Korenko, *Transfer Prices for Intangible Property Embodied in Products with Extraordinary Profit Potential*, BNA Tax Notes International, (October 1999).
121. *See* Gonnet, S, *Recent Developments on the Profit Split Method*, Global Transfer Pricing Developments (Vienna 2018) *(Forthcoming)*.

### 4.3.2  Profit Level Indicators

A profit level indicator ('PLI') is a measure of a company's profitability that is used to compare comparables with the tested party. The ideal PLI contains a numerator that is economically caused by the variable in the denominator.[122]

In practice, one may use any profitability ratio that enables comparison of the profit resulting from the intra-group transactions. Typically, a profit level indicator may express profitability in relation to: (i) sales, (ii) costs or expenses, or (iii) assets.

The choice of the appropriate ratio is considered keeping in mind the functional characterization and the nature of business of the tested party that is chosen. The choice is also to be reviewed depending on the nature of comparables that are finalized and the reliability of information that is available.[123] For example, if the tested party is a distributor, depending on other facts and circumstances of the analysis, *operating profit/sales* could be considered as an ideal ratio as it measures the return as a percentage of sales achieved, which is the main function and responsibility of a distributor. If the tested party belongs to the manufacturer involving significant capital assets, *return on capital employed (ROCE)* could be considered. Some of the PLIs that are used in a comparability analysis are listed in Table 2.5.

*Table 2.5   Indicative List of Common PLIs[124]*

| List of PLIs | |
|---|---|
| Return on assets (ROA) | operating profit divided by the operating assets (normally, only tangible assets) |
| Return on capital employed (ROCE) | operating profit divided by the capital that is employed which usually computes as the total assets minus cash and investments |
| Operating margin (OM) | operating profit divided by sales |
| Gross margin (GM) | gross profit divided by sales |
| Berry Ratio | gross profit divided by operating expenses |
| Return on total cost (ROTC) | operating profit divided by total costs |
| Return on cost of goods sold | gross profit divided by cost of goods sold |

Out of the above PLIs, (i) operating margin, (ii) Berry Ratio, and (iii) return on capital employed (ROCE) are most used in practice.[125] The use of net profit indicators and other popular indicators are discussed below:

---

122. *See* Reichert, T., Hutchinson, E., Suhler, D., *Capital Intensity and Margins, A Method for Analysing Financial Comparability with Application to Distributors*, White Paper Series, Economic Partners LLC, 2013-02.
123. *See* 2017 OECD TPG, *supra* para. 2.82.
124. *See* 2017 UN TPM, *supra* para. B.3.3.7.1.
125. *Ibid.*, para. B.3.3.7.3.

Composition of net profits

The use of net profit indicators potentially introduce a greater element of volatility into the determination of transfer prices for two reasons:[126]

(1) Net profit indicators can be influenced by factors that do not have an effect on gross margins and prices due to the presence of operating expenses.
(2) In the traditional transaction methods, the effect of factors such as competitive position may not be eliminated while the same can be eliminated in traditional transaction methods by considering criteria such as product comparability.

Only those items that: (a) directly or indirectly relate to the controlled transaction at hand and (b) are of an operating nature should be taken into account in the determination of the net profit indicator for the application of TNMM. Costs that do not contribute to the controlled transaction such as extraordinary expenses and non-operating expenses (in the case of non-financial institutions, this would be interest expenses) should be excluded from the composition of costs in order to arrive at a profit value that is comparable. Accounting treatment of depreciation, amortization, stock options, and pension costs are to be carefully considered in carrying out the analysis.[127] Also, start-up costs that are preliminary in nature may be excluded depending on the facts and circumstances of the tested party's economic circumstances (see Table 2.6).[128]

*Table 2.6   Illustrative Example of a Profit Ratio Computation*

| *Case 1: Manufacturer* | *Case 2: Captive Service Provider* | *Reference* |
| --- | --- | --- |
| Income* from sale of products to third party customers | Income* from provision of services to AE | A |
| Less: Financial and non-routine income | Less: Financial and non-routine income | B |
| **Cost of Goods Sold (A-B)** | **Cost of Services (A-B)** | **C = A – B** |
| Less: Expenses* related to the purchases from AEs | Less: Expenses* related to provision of services to AEs | D |
| Less: Financial, extra-ordinary expenses, non-recurring expenses such as sale of fixed assets, preliminary expenses and taxes | Less: Financial** and extra-ordinary expenses, non-recurring expenses such as sale of fixed assets, preliminary expenses and taxes | E |
| Operating Expenses | Operating Expenses | F = D + E |
| **Operating Net Profit** | **Operating Net Profit** | **G = C - F** |

126. *See* 2017 OECD TPG, *supra* para. 2.76.
127. *Ibid.*, para. 2.90.
128. *Ibid.*, para. 2.91.

| Case 1: Manufacturer | Case 2: Captive Service Provider | Reference |
|---|---|---|
| Arm's length profit as percentage of assets, sales costs or capital employed, as appropriate to facts and circumstances | Arm's length profit as percentage of assets, sales costs or capital employed, as appropriate to facts and circumstances | G as a percentage of chosen denominator |

*excluding third-party segment income and expenses, if any[129]
** Depending on the facts of whether the services are in connection with financial services

With regard to the weighting of the net profits discussed above under Case 1 and Case 2, the following considerations are made:[130]

> Divided by Sales: For cases when net profit is divided by sales, the sales figure in the denominator restricts itself to the value that is relevant to the controlled transactions (related-party activity). In this regard, additional importance should also be provided to treatment of net foreign exchange gains/losses and rebates/discounts. The treatment is dependent on the accounting standards. While discounts/rebates could be deducted from the sales revenue or expenses, foreign exchange gains or losses should be treated consistently between tested party and comparable companies.
>
> Divided by Cost: For cases when net profit is divided by costs, an appropriate level of segmentation is required to exclude costs (third-party) that relate to other activities or transactions and materially affect comparability with uncontrolled transactions. In this aspect, the treatment of pass-through costs[131] to which no profit element can be allocated is to be carefully considered considering that the information on such costs incurred by comparable companies may not be available in the public domain which leads to distortion of comparability.
>
> Further, the use of budgeted costs or actual costs as the base for calculation of the PLI depends on facts and circumstances. Concerns have been raised that the use of actual costs does not provide any incentive to the tested party to closely monitor the costs (especially under a routine-cost plus method). In this context, it is recommended to carefully compare the behaviour of the parties to the transactions to situations involving independent arrangements. The use of budgeted costs also entails pitfalls such as actual costs overrunning the budgets, leading to unforeseen results.
>
> Divided by Assets: The use of assets as a base is predominant in certain manufacturing or other asset intensive financial services circumstances.

---

129. *See* Furtun, M.E., Mert-Beydilli, N,., Saito, Y., *Information Overlooked: When Segment Reporting Can Enhance Reliability of a Transfer Pricing Analysis*, Tax Management Transfer Pricing Report, Vol. 23 No. 11, 10/2/2014.
130. OECD paras 2.96–2.105.
131. *See* Li & Fung.

Here, operating assets typically include tangible operating fixed assets including land and buildings, plant and equipment, operating intangible assets used in the business such as patents and know-how, and working capital assets such as inventory and trade receivables (less trade payables). The choice of whether to consider book value or market value of assets have respective consequences, for example, use of book value for a comparable with ongoing depreciation against a tested party having fully depreciated assets whereas the use of market value could lead to differences in valuation outcomes. Also, in relation to intangibles, the process of valuation itself could be complex.

Use of Berry Ratio:[132]

The Berry ratio[133] has been the subject of numerous articles. It is seldom used in practice due to its complexities and litigated history.[134] Largely viewed as a variant of the cost plus method, it can have quite a significant impact on the profitability of a tested party compared to the operating margin.[135] Therefore, great caution is advised in deciding whether to apply the Berry ratio in practice. Primarily, in order for it to be applicable, the following conditions must be satisfied:[136]

(1) the value of the functions performed in the controlled transaction (taking into account assets used and risks assumed) is proportional to the operating expenses;

(2) the value of the functions performed in the controlled transaction (taking into account assets used and risks assumed) is not materially affected by the value of the products distributed, i.e., it is not proportional to sales; and

(3) the taxpayer does not perform any other significant function in the controlled transactions that should be remunerated using another method or financial indicator.

The US IRS APA Study Guide suggests caution in using the Berry ratio to compare companies with low operating expense/sales[137] to companies with higher operating

---

132. The Berry ratio existed as a PLI for transfer pricing services at the end of the 1960s and early 1970s. It is named in honour of Dr Charles Berry, then professor of economics at Princeton University, who was sought by the US Internal Revenue Service (IRS) and Justice Department to evaluate the economic circumstances underlying a dispute in the DuPont Case.

133. *See* 2017 OECD TPG, *supra* para. 2.106; *See* 2017 UN TPM, *supra* para. 6.3.7.

134. US: Ct. Cl., 17 Oct. 1979, *E.I. DuPont de Nemours & Co. v. United States*, 608 F.2d 445 (Ct. Cl. 1979).

135. Dorward, R., *When Could the Berry Ratio Be Used in Transfer Pricing Analyses? International Transfer Pricing* Journal, 2016 (Volume 23), No. 4, Vol. 3. (19 Jul. 2016).

136. *See* 2017 OECD TPG, *supra* para. 2.107.

137. US: Internal Revenue Service, APA Study Guide (1999), available at http://www.irs.gov/pub /irsapa/apa_study_guide_.pdf.

expense/sales ratios. To this extent, if the Berry Ratio is considered, the benchmarking analysis should accordingly consider a modified search strategy for such differences.

## 4.4 Identification of Potential Comparables

In order to ensure a sufficient degree of objectivity, it is important that the process to identify comparable companies is to be transparent, systematic, and verifiable.[138] In this regard, the process could be undertaken as 'additive' or 'deductive'. The additive approach could be a simple compilation of identified industry peers who are competitors to the taxpayer and subsequently proceed to transactions that are comparable to the taxpayer's circumstances. The additive approach could also have internal comparables that are readily identified. Whether internal or external, the additive approach involves verification of whether an existing potential comparable is actually comparable. The deductive approach in this process begins with an industry or sector-wide search for similar companies. In practice, the 'deductive' approach is typically initiated with a search in a database and an application of several filtration criteria to arrive at the final set of comparables. It is recommended that, in this deductive process, the following five step process could also be considered in order to ensure that the process is scientific:[139] The entire process is considered a search strategy as the step-by-step process forms the core of deriving the arm's length results:

(1) examination of the five comparability factors for the controlled transaction;
(2) development of comparable search or 'screening' criteria;
(3) approach to identifying potential comparables;
(4) initial identification and screening of comparables; and
(5) secondary screening, verification, and selection of comparable.

The overall search strategy is diagrammatically represented in Figure 2.4.

---

138. *See* 2017 OECD TPG, *supra* para. 3.41.
139. *See* 2017 UN TPM B2.3.4.8.

*Figure 2.4    Summary of Search Strategy*[140]

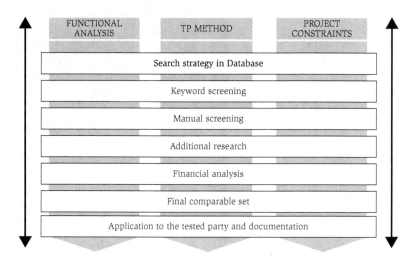

For this purpose, several qualitative and quantitative criteria could be used. An indicative list of such criteria are provided below.[141] The filters could be considered based on the facts and circumstances of each case.

- Independence and ownership criteria, i.e., threshold based rejection of companies with significant comparable companies[142]
- Date of incorporation
- Industry via Industry codes or textual search[143]
- Availability of financial accounting information[144]
- Size criteria in terms of Sales, Assets, or Number of Employees
- Intangible-related criteria such as ratio of Net Value of Intangibles/Total Net Assets Value or ratio of Research and Development (R&D)/Sales
- Export sales (Foreign Sales/Total Sales)
- Inventories in absolute or relative value
- Criteria to exclude third parties such as start-up companies, bankrupted companies, etc. when such peculiar situations are obviously not appropriate comparisons.

---

140. Grambusch, L., Frotscher, J, *Benchmarking Manufacturing and Distribution Activities* (2017: Vienna).
141. *See* 2017 OECD TPG, *supra* para. 3.43.
142. For example, Bureau van Dijk data bases use the BvD Independence indicator that can be used to identify independent companies. BvD Independence Indicators are noted as A, B, C, D, and U with further qualifications.
143. The codes are defined by the local statistical authority, e.g., EuroStat for EU member countries; in the US, the US SIC code is broadly used; in Europe the NACE Rev. 2 code.
144. Issues such as local GAAP versus IFRS are to be evaluated depending on the database.

The above 'deductive' approach is also more reproducible, transparent, cross-verifiable, and could be reviewed for the selection process[145]. However, the quality of the outcome of a 'deductive' approach is entirely dependent on the quality of databases. This can be a practical limitation in countries where the reliability and usefulness of databases in comparability analyses are questionable. For further discussion on issues surrounding a comparability analysis, refer to section 4.7.

Other sources of information based on business mix, product line, geographic market, functional mix, and ownership information on the first-round selection of potential comparables are listed below:[146]

(a) Government sources: many governments and regulatory agencies maintain databases on several industries. Such sources can be located on the agency's Internet websites;

(b) Trade institutions and organizations: these institutions or organizations will often maintain databases and research reports and/or hold files with data on potential comparables. Generally, these institutions or organizations would be:
   - Chambers of commerce;
   - Trade and professional organizations;
   - Embassies, consulates or trade missions; or
   - International organizations (e.g., the United Nations, the Organisation for Economic Co-operation and Development, the World Bank, the International Monetary Fund).

## 4.5 Comparability Adjustments

In the practical conduct of a comparability analysis, the comparables that are identified could often be non-comparable to begin with. In many cases, without undertaking necessary comparability adjustments, the arm's length prices can never be arrived at. Even in broadly comparable circumstances, the prices of uncontrolled transactions may require an adjustment to reflect lower intensity of certain operating costs such as sales and marketing expenses that are often associated with intra-group transactions.[147] However, there is no presumption that comparability adjustments are always needed or will always improve comparability or its reliability.[148]

Invariably, challenges are often observed with regard to the volume or operational scale, risks, or geographic differences. However, there has been extensive work

---

145. *See* 2017 OECD TPG, *supra* para. 3.44.
146. *See* 2017 UN TPM, *supra* para. B.2.3.4.43.
147. *See* Starkov, V., *Adjusting Uncontrolled Profit-Based Benchmarks for Differences in Operating Expense Structure*, Tax Planning and International Transfer Pricing Journal, BNA International, August 2008.
148. *See* 2017 OECD TPG, *supra* paras 3.47 and 3.52.

undertaken to minimize differences due to working capital and[149] capacity utilization, leaving open the applicability of adjustments to different facts and circumstances. In the absence of granular guidance from international organizations or numerical thresholds that are prescribed that demand adjustments, the following questions could be considered when performing the analysis to verify the need for adjustments.

Reliability: Is the result of the comparability analysis before undertaking the adjustments reliable enough to conclude the arm's length analysis?

Materiality: Is there 'material impact' to the arm's length result and, if so, what would be the variance in outcome between a pre-adjustment and post-adjustment scenario?

(1) Accuracy: How accurately can the adjustments be applied? If the result becomes an approximation of ALP, then the strength of the entire comparability analysis is undermined.
(2) Documentation: Can the adjustments be documented sufficiently, or would the exercise be theoretical?

The above questions only provide a qualitative direction to make comparability adjustments and cannot be considered as a rule of thumb. Some of the typical comparability adjustments that are undertaken in practice are as follows:

(A) Accounting adjustments: Taxpayers face practical issues with respect to a comparability analysis when accounting standards of the compared enterprises are potentially different.
   (i) Classification differences: Similar expense or revenue items could be classified differently between two potentially comparable companies.
   (ii) Intangibles: The presence of elective accounting rules could result in affording the opportunity for companies to either capitalise R&D Costs or the method of depreciation or to amortise goodwill or intangibles which lead to significant differences in comparable outcomes. (Refer to Chapter 11 for detailed discussion on intangibles).
   (iii) Database issues: Simple issues could arise from the way financial information is recognised and categorized by databases. This issue is protracted when data are taken from multiple sources and leads to inconsistencies. A verification of actual financial statements and not relying on only databases is essential in practice.
(B) Balance sheet adjustments: A key source of discrepancy between the tested party and comparables is the impact of balance sheet items on profitability. Asset intensity adjustments[150] to account for differences in inventory,

---

149. *Ibid., Supra* Annexure III.
150. *See* US: TC, 22 Sep. 1992, *Westreco Inc. v. Commissioner,* TCM 1992-561 (1992).

accounts receivables, payables, interest rate, etc. have become more common. The use of asset based adjustments based on 'imputed interest'.[151]

(C) Other: Adjustments for equipment failure, inefficiencies in manufacturing processes, new equipment introduction, differences in contractual terms of an arrangement surrounding payment cycles[152], lack of comparable data[153], and adjustments due to different levels of risks[154] (e.g., between a risk-mitigated tested party and variable risk taking comparables) and growth[155] have been used for achieving improved comparability. However, adjustments for differences in functions and risk have been difficult to adopt on a widespread basis due to variances in application.[156] Also, though the use of foreign comparables with appropriate adjustments such as differences in the cost of capital has been considered, it has yet to gain widespread acceptance.[157] Further, differences in ready markets, business strategies employed, the regulatory system in place, buyer behaviour, bargaining power of the entities, and risks associated with operating in a particular market leads to geographical differences that are to be adjusted.[158] In the absence of reliable adjustments for recognized issues such as location savings, the traditional approaches for identifying comparables has resulted in an unfavourable outcome.[159] However, the applicability of geographical risk adjustments have often been met with resistance from tax administrators.[160]

## 4.6 Interpretation and Use of Data Collected

The summation of the process undertaken lies in interpreting the results of the arm's length analysis. In some cases, the arm's length result is a single figure (e.g.,

---

151. *See* Silva,E., *The Fallacy of Asset-Based Adjustments to Profits*, BNA Bloomberg Transfer Pricing, Vol. 12, No. 15, p. 703 (12 Oct. 2003).
152. *See* Saito, Y., Furtun, M.E., *Rethinking Terms of Trade Adjustments in Transfer Pricing: An Argument for a More Reliable Benchmarking Analysis*, BNA Bloomberg Transfer Pricing Report, Vol. 23, (27 Nov. 2014).
153. *See* Starkov,V, Gonnet,S., Pletz, A., Maitra, M., *Comparability Adjustments: In the Absence of Suitable Local Comparables in Emerging and Developing Economies – Case Studies*, BNA Bloomberg Transfer Pricing Report, (25 Mar. 2014).
154. *See* Westreco (1992).
155. *See* ITAT (Delhi), 2 Nov. 2007, *Mentor Graphics v. Deputy Commissioner of Income Tax*, ITA 1969/D/2006.
156. *See Indian Tribunal in Philips Software Centre (2008) paras 4.69 and 4.70; ITAT Delhi, 2011, Motorola Solutions India (P) Limited v. ACIT, ITA 5637/Del/2011.*
157. *See* Starkov,V., Maitra, M, Li, A., *Comparability Adjustments in the Absence of Suitable Local Comparables in Emerging and Developing Economies*, Transfer Pricing International Journal, Bloomberg BNA, Vol. 16, No. 15 (May 2015).
158. *See* Muyyaa, E., *Transfer Pricing Comparability Adjustments: The Pursuit of 'Exact' Comparables*, International Transfer Pricing Journal, IBFD, 2014, pp. 347–355.
159. *See* Silva, E., *'Pygmalion' Comparables: Why Data from the 'Center' Does Not Apply for the 'Periphery'*, BNA Tax, Vol. 23, No. 22.
160. *See* TC, 2008, *GlaxoSmithKline Inc. v. The Queen*, 2008 TCC 324 (2008); FR: CAA Versailles, 5 May 2009, Société Man Camions et Bus, 08-2411, 3ech., DF 41, 8 Oct. 2009, comm. 500.

price or margin), however, in others, there is a range of results. Depending on the number of results forming the range, statistical tools that take account of central tendency to narrow the range (e.g., the interquartile range or other percentiles) are used for interpreting the outcome.

In the process of an audit, if the price of the controlled transaction falls beyond the designated range, an adjustment is warranted. To calculate the differences, measures such as median, the mean, or weighted averages, etc. (which fall within the arm's length range) are considered. However, it is also to be noted that statistical (confidence or tolerance) intervals and the use of inter-quartile range (IQR) in practice may not be completely reliable.[161] The IQR has been a subject of debate in statistical literature,[162] and even using the IQR could lead to potential litigation.[163]

Further, extreme results in the arm's length outcome demand intensive scrutiny on the reliability of the comparables. Extreme results that skew the arm's length range could be due to genuine business circumstances such as potential comparables experiencing super-normal profit years or prolonged loss-making situations. It is generally viewed that no rational company would experience prolonged losses and, therefore, such companies warrant removal from the comparable set.

It is critical to note that the results typically provide a preliminary view of the arm's length outcome, and efforts are to be taken to revisit the comparables considering the numerical output. Any anomalies that can be associated with the basic five factors of comparability analysis should be resolved by reconsidering the inclusion of comparables that cause the anomaly.

## 4.7 Issues in Comparability Analysis

Over the years, the comparability analysis has become a question of soundness in technique where specific factors about the enterprise as well as a general understanding of other factors such as the market in which the enterprise operates has become necessary. Along with the growth of the science of the comparability analysis, the complexities of businesses have simultaneously increased with vertical integration and ever changing business models leading to difficulties in understanding the controlled transactions and accurately delineating transactions which is the basis on which the entire comparability analysis rests.

### 4.7.1 Capacity Issues

Despite several advancements in technology and work in this area, the lack of available information for identifying comparables continues to be an area requiring considerable improvement. The lack of availability of comparables could be due to the following reasons:

---

161. *See* Gerald Hahn & William Meeker, *Statistical Intervals* (John Wiley, 1991).
162. *See* David Hoaglin, Frederick Mosteller, and John Tukey, *Understanding Robust and Exploratory Data Analysis* (John Wiley, 1983).
163. Silva, E., Arm's Length Range – Most Reliable Measure, RoyatyStat Blog, (20 Mar. 2016).

- Different accounting and reporting requirements in different jurisdictions making it difficult to enable easier comparability
- Time required and cost of obtaining such information making it difficult for relatively smaller firms (subject to transfer pricing provisions) to undertake the analysis independently

### 4.7.2 Timing Issues

Timing issues in comparability are arising due to differences between the time of origin, collection, and production of information on comparability factors and comparable uncontrolled transactions that are used in a comparability analysis.[164] Timing of origin arises as TP documentation is expected to be maintained contemporaneously while comparable information may not be available to obtain the complete arm's length result at the time of a transaction or preparation of the document.[165] Due to this, taxpayers take efforts to demonstrate that the best efforts have been taken at the time of collection of available information (*ex ante* basis). In certain circumstances, taxpayers test whether the actual outcome of controlled transactions were consistent with arm's length requirements at year-end (*ex post*) just for compliance purposes. To compound these issues, the task of valuing highly uncertain events continues to be a challenge. In such situations, it is expected that tax administrators and taxpayers are to resolve potential issues by viewing how independent enterprises would have faced similar uncertainties in valuation.[166]

Further, the benefit of hindsight often plays a critical role for providing a wholesome analysis. Even in cases when the data of subsequent tax years could help in establishing the movement of business cycles, the ability to use the data could be restricted.[167] On a related note, the use of multiple year data, though not necessary, helps in establishing a holistic business picture. However, attention is to be paid for ensuring that a similar time period is considered for comparable companies to ensure consistency in results.

## 4.8  Other Key Comparability Parameters

### 4.8.1  Losses[168]

Tax administrators are particularly concerned about associated enterprises experiencing persistent losses while the overall MNE group still continues to have a profitable outcome. Genuine losses that are commercial in nature, such as the initial outlay at start-up stages, economic conditions, inefficiencies etc., are permissible. However

---

164. *See* 2017 OECD TPG, *supra* para. 3.67.
165. *Ibid.*, para. 5.27.
166. *Ibid.*, para. 3.73.
167. *Ibid.*, para. 3.74.
168. *Ibid.*, para. 1.129–1.131.

independent enterprises that are operating in comparable circumstances may not continue to make indefinite losses. This anomaly provides cause for tax administrators to question whether controlled transactions are directly linked to the losses and if the loss making associated enterprise is being adequately compensated as per the transfer pricing model adopted by the MNE group.

In circumstances when the reasons are commercially induced, such as the nature of product differences causing losses to one enterprise while selling better in another market, and result in a profitable outcome in the corresponding associated enterprise, the compensation paid to the loss making enterprise by its associated enterprise is expected to be similar to that independent enterprise operating in comparable circumstances. Product differences between MNEs are also driven by business strategies adopted by each MNE group.

---

**Example[169]**

Company A, a distributor, decreases the prices of its products to suffer temporary incurring losses as part of its market penetration to increase its share of an existing market and dissuade competitors. Company B, an associated enterprise, manufactures the goods imported by Company A for distribution locally.

The prices are lower than market prices only for a reasonable period of time with the specific objective of improving profits in the longer term. However, if Company A continues to keep its prices artificially lower than the market price beyond a reasonable period, a transfer pricing adjustment could be warranted. Further, tax administrations may not accept low prices as arm's length prices unless independent enterprises could be expected to have determined prices in a comparable manner.

---

While there could be a number of causes for losses, the most common recognized circumstances include:[170]

- Scale of operations;
- Product failure or product line failure;
- Loss making history within the entity and within the MNE group; or
- Losses due to natural disasters.

### 4.8.2  The Effect of Government Policies[171]

Government interventions in the economy such as price controls, interest rates, interest limitations, intra-group services, payment of royalties, subsidies to particular

---

169. *Ibid.*, para. B.2.3.2.36.
170. *See* 2017. UN TPM, *supra* para. B.2.4.5.3.
171. *See* 2017 OECD TPG *Supra* para. 1.132–1.138.

sectors, foreign exchange regulations, anti-dumping duties, and exchange controls could render an otherwise comparable transaction to be non-comparable. If the conditions are common across an industry or a comparable group of companies, then such differences could be neutralized by default.

The impact of government policies on the pricing of product/service prices could vary between associated enterprises when such costs may or may not be passed on to the intra-group customer. However, independent enterprises may withhold the burden of such policy impacts on its pricing and are more likely to pass on the burden to end-customers. Further, a country could prevent the payment of an amount that is owed by one associated enterprise to another or that would be charged by one associated enterprise to another in an arm's length arrangement.

---

**Example(s)**[172]

For a transfer of interest payment being blocked by a country, an associated enterprise located in a counter party country may or may not treat the income to have been received, or the borrower's country may treat the expenses as not being incurred. Treaties may specifically address the approaches that are available to the treaty partners when such circumstances exist.

---

Further, independent enterprises may not engage in a transaction that is subject to government interventions, and a comparable transaction may not be available for a controlled transaction. In this regard, the following possibilities and challenges are possible:

(i) Notionally treat the payment as having been made between the associated enterprises based on the rationale that an independent enterprise would have demanded such a payment. The receiver of such a payment is considered to be a service provider.

(ii) Alternatively, the income and the relevant expenses of the taxpayer could be deferred subject to the country's acceptance, i.e., if the deduction is claimed by an AE in one jurisdiction, a corresponding addition to the income is expected in another jurisdiction.

### 4.8.3 Customs Valuation

Taxpayers could have competing incentives to specify intra-group import prices in such a way that a low price is beneficial for customs purposes; a low price leading to lower duties while a higher price would increase the deductible costs in the importing country. The interplay of customs and transfer pricing has also led to customs

---

172. *See* 2017. UN TPM, *supra* para. B.2.3.2.36.

authorities favouring upward adjustments to transfer prices accompanied by revisions to customs value under the transaction value method.[173]

Cost savings attributable to operating in a particular market or, otherwise stated, 'location savings' result in geographical differences in a comparability analysis. For the purpose of comparability, it is to be ascertained first whether a location savings exists. If applicable, the amount of any location savings and the benefit arising out of such savings for the associated enterprise is determined. When location savings are not fully passed on to independent customers or suppliers, the savings is allocated in accordance with how independent enterprises would have performed this. The comparability analysis in such situations is centred on identifying comparable transactions in similar geographical markets and independent enterprises engaged in similar activities, bearing similar functions, assuming risks, and deploying assets that result in the savings. Location savings could generally arise due to the following:[174]

- Labour costs;
- Raw material costs;
- Transportation costs;
- Rent;
- Training costs;
- Subsidies;
- Incentives including tax exemptions; and
- Infrastructure costs.

In cases when reasonably reliable local market comparables cannot be identified, comparability adjustments related to features of the local market could be necessary. Market advantages or disadvantages may affect the arm's length prices of goods that are transferred or services that are provided between associated enterprises and hence need to be considered in a comparability analysis, particularly involving a low cost jurisdiction. Further details on location specific advantages in undertaking business restructuring transactions is provided in Chapter 12.

### 4.8.4 Assembled Workforce[175]

Some businesses are successful in building a skilled workforce which could differentiate its position in the market. Such factors should ordinarily be taken into account in a transfer pricing comparability analysis.

173. *See* Petruzzi R, Prasanna P, CJEU: Restricting the Interplay of Transfer Pricing and Customs Valuation, Transfer Pricing International, January 2018.
174. *See* UN TPM para. B.2.3.2.51.
175. *See* OECD TPG, para. 1.152.

**Example(s)**

Company A, a payment technology company, develops a niche workforce over a period of time that enables it to command a premium for its service prices. Company A is considered as being a comparable for a taxpayer operating in a similar industry. However, the taxpayer will be expected to make appropriate comparability adjustments according to differences in employee skill levels.

The most complex aspects of an assembled workforce occurs in business restructuring transactions and require a comparability analysis to evaluate its arm's length nature. The assembled workforce that is transferred between enterprises due to restructuring requires being valued and the forgoing entity is expected to be compensated for the loss of skill which could translate into a profit potential.[176] However, it is to be noted that not all secondments or employee transfers are encompassed under the ambit of this expectation. Transfer of such employees for the transfer of knowledge or technology is to be analysed based on principles of evaluating and conducting a comparability analysis of an intangible transaction. Refer to Chapter 11 for further details.

### 4.8.5  Group Synergies[177]

Under specific circumstances, entities of MNE groups transacting with each other could generate synergies that independent organizations may not be able to achieve. Synergies could also be negative depending on the scale of operations or forced adoption of certain technologies on a group wide basis when certain entities of the group may not have the functional capabilities for such technologies. Whether such synergistic benefits are incidental or create substantial savings due to deliberated and concerted group actions requires evaluation.

**Example(s)**

A group takes clearly defined actions to centralize procurement functions group wide and gains substantially from volume discounts. The products that are procured are then sold to group entities. At this stage, the transfer price that is charged to group entities is expected to reflect the benefits due to volume discounts.

The benefits arising from synergies are to be identified and shared between group members. In cases when group synergies are recognized, appropriate comparability adjustments could be warranted.

---

176. Microsoft Case, *Israel v. Getko*, July 2017.
177. OECD TPG 1.157–1.163.

## 4.9 Work of International Organizations

Considering the issues highlighted above, international organizations have taken efforts to provide continuous guidance to help bridge historic as well as evolving gaps.

### 4.9.1 Revisiting the Evolution of the OECD TPG and UN TPM

The OECD has been on the forefront of evolving transfer pricing guidance and released its first guidance in 1979.[178] The next update came in 1995[179] which was subsequently significantly revised in the 2010 update.[180] On 10 July 2017, the OECD released its next update which has strengthened the guidance on the application of the ALP and standards of comparability. With regard to comparability, the important change has been the effort from transitioning (section D1) from *'Comparability analysis'* to *'Identifying the commercial or financial relations'*.

The United Nations published the first edition of TPM in 2013[181] consistent with the principles of the OECD TPG. This manual was updated in 2017[182] and provided revised guidance including a comparability analysis in the aftermath of the OECD BEPS Project.

While the principles emanating from the OECD TPGs and UN TPMs have been discussed in the previous sections of this chapter, this section focusses on the contributions of other international organizations to the guidance literature. The International Monitory Fund (IMF), United Nations (UN), the World Bank Group (WBG), and the OECD developed the *Toolkit for Low Income Countries*[183] through its Platform for Collaboration on Tax (PCT) that was constituted in 2016[184] and focused on comparability issues specific to developing countries. Recognizing that the issues surrounding comparability are not limited to only developing countries, the EU Joint Transfer Pricing Forum (EU JTPF) has issued guidance on issues that are specific to the EU. First, the work of the EU JTPF is discussed in the following section and proceeded by the work of the PCT and the WBG.

### 4.9.2 European Union Joint Transfer Pricing Forum

The EU JTPF is an expert group that supports the European Commission (EC) on TP matters. Apart from working to resolve comparability related issues, the EU JTPF

178. *See* 1979 OECD TPG, *supra.*
179. OECD, *Transfer Pricing Guidelines for Multinational Enterprises and Tax Administrations* (Paris: OECD Publishing, 1995).
180. *Ibid.,* (Paris: OECD Publishing, 2010).
181. United Nations, *Practical Manual on Transfer Pricing for Developing Countries* (2013).
182. *Ibid.,* (2017).
183. *See* World Bank, *A Toolkit for Addressing Difficulties in Accessing Comparables Data for Transfer Pricing Analyses. Platform for Collaboration on Tax.* Washington, D.C.: World Bank Group (June 2017).
184. Established in April 2016, *see* http://www.worldbank.org/en/programs/platform-for-tax-collaboration (last accessed on 27 Dec. 2017).

focusses on topics such as the use of the transactional profit split method (PSM) in the EU, use of economic valuation techniques for transfer pricing in the EU, and Multilateral Controls in the EU to improve the double taxation dispute resolution there.[185] For the purpose of this section, only the work of EU JTPF on comparability is discussed.

First, the EU JTPF finalized and approved the *Report on Use of Comparables in EU*.[186] The report established best practices and pragmatic solutions by issuing various recommendations for both taxpayers and tax administrations in the EU and aimed at increasing in practice the objectivity and transparency of comparable searches for transfer pricing analyses.[187]

The JTPF recognizes that key aspects of a comparability analysis: (a) accurate delineation of the transactions and (b) the search for comparables are equally critical and that the success of step (a) would determine the reliability of (b) and not vice versa.[188]

Further, the report emphasizes the need for documenting the steps of the comparables search and keeping in mind that the search should still be proportionate but with a focus on quality, transparency, and consistency.[189] The JTPF makes recommendations to increase the validity of the search process by:[190]

- Documenting the search and screening criteria, rejection criteria, and adjustments made;
- A broad range of sources is useful and adds value in refining the comparables search;
- Transparency and proportionality when judgment is used;
- Explaining the choice of the deductive approach or additive approach and why the approach is appropriate;
- Mentioning the financial data of the comparables and its sources;
- Maintaining the document supporting the search.

The detailed steps to be undertaken in identifying comparables bases on an external search process is detailed in Figure 2.5.

---

185. *See* Source: https://ec.europa.eu/taxation_customs/business/company-tax/transfer-pricing-eu-context/joint-transfer-pricing-forum_en (last visited on: 12 Mar. 2017).
186. EC (June 2016), doc. JTPF/007/FINAL/2016/EN, Source: https://ec.europa.eu/taxation_customs/sites/taxation/files/jtpf0072017encomps.pdf.
187. *See* Petruzzi, R., *Global Transfer Pricing Developments*, in: Lang, M., Storck, A. & Petruzzi, R. (eds), *Transfer Pricing Developments around the World* (Vienna: Kluwer, 2017).
188. *See Supra.* p. 3.
189. *Ibid.*, para. 8.
190. *Ibid.*, para. 11.

*Figure 2.5    EU JTPF Approach*

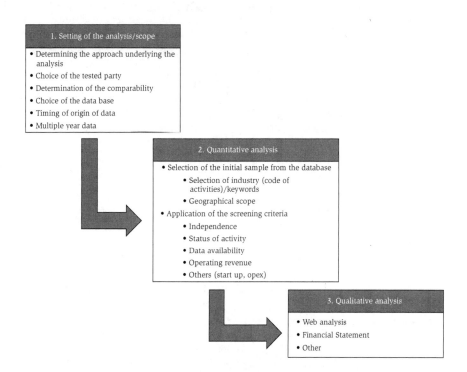

Further, the EU JTPF has expressed further interest in working on unexplored aspects of economic adjustments mentioned in section 4.5 to provide the exact definition, reasonableness and, if considered reasonable, their functioning and the aspects to be considered for their application and reliability.[191]

Finally, in accordance with the OECD approach, the EU JTPF concludes that companies must take a strategic approach to pan-European comparable sets[192] involving a representation of all major geographic markets. Companies should not, however, always assume that the pan-European approach will or will not be feasible for them. Depending on the level of vertical integration in industries, specific regulations, facts, and circumstances should determine the use of a pan.EU comparable set.[193]

---

191. *Ibid.,* p. 13.
192. *Ibid.,* p. 14.
193. *See* Connor, J., Europe as One Market – Update on Transfer Pricing, FinanceMagazine.com, October 2006; Source: http://www.finance-magazine.com/display_article.php?i = 6826& (last accessed 13 Mar. 2018).

**EC State-aid investigations[194]**

The role of a comparability analysis in the EC State aid transfer pricing cases is significant. The EC has, in effect, begun to address the comparability analysis by discussing 'what should have been subjected to tax'. The EC does not fully delve into discussions on what its expectations on comparable uncontrolled circumstances are, leaving the disputes open. However, with the cases attaining finality, as evidenced from the Amazon Case,[195] the EC has pointed out errors in the identification of comparable transactions (under the CUP analysis for benchmarking intangibles). The EC has also referred to why certain transactions such as a 'Licence Fee' in the facts and circumstances of the cases were erroneously benchmarked based on non-comparable factors. Therefore, the role of the comparability analysis in prominent EU State-aid litigation is significant. For a detailed analysis of State-aid rulings and the Amazon Case, refer to Chapter 14.

### 4.9.3 Platform for Collaboration on Tax

The PCT, constituted in 2016, seeks to intensify the harmonization of tax policy aspects between international organizations. On 24 January 2017, the PCT issued a discussion draft for public consultation and later, on 22 June 2017, it released the comments received on it.[196] Guidance on 'Addressing Difficulties in Accessing Comparables Data on Transfer Pricing Analyses' specifically addresses the ways that low-income countries can overcome the issue of lack of comparable data or of market prices for goods and services transferred within MNEs.

    The guidance presents an alternative paradigm that, in cases when local comparables to the tested party are scarce or unavailable, data from other geographic markets can be considered as the OECD TPG or UN TPM does not preclude its usage. The guidance states that, in some cases, the geographic market may be less relevant than other characteristics, meaning that the most reliable comparables that are available are those from a foreign market.[197]

---

194. EC Decision SA.38373, State aid implemented by Ireland to Apple (Aug. 30, 2016), not published on O.J. L 187, 1-110 – 19 July 2017; EC Decision SA.38375, State aid which Luxembourg granted to Fiat (Oct. 21, 2015), O.J. L 351, 1-67 (Dec. 22, 2016); EC Decision SA.38944; EC Decision SA.38374, State aid implemented by the Netherlands to Starbucks (Oct. 21, 2015), O.J., L 83, 38–115 (29 March 2017); EC Decision SA.37667, Excess profit exemption in Belgium – Art. 185§2 b) CIR92 (Jan. 11, 2016), O.J. L 260, 61–103 (Sep. 27, 2016; EC Decision SA 38373, State aid implemented by Ireland to Apple (Aug. 30, 2016), OJ L 187, 1-110 – 19 July 2017, recital 255.
195. See EC Decision, On State Aid SA.38944 (2014/C) (ex 2014/NN) implemented by Luxembourg to Amazon Source: http://ec.europa.eu/competition/state_aid/cases/254685/254685_196618 1_890_2.pdf.
196. *See* Petruzzi, R., Prasanna., S., *Global Transfer Pricing Developments*, in: Lang, M., Storck, A. & Petruzzi, R. (eds), *Transfer Pricing Developments Around the World* (Vienna: Kluwer, 2018) – *Forthcoming.*
197. *Supra* p. 40.

While the guidance does not provide complete solutions to the issues, the work of the PCT could be considered as the first steps for a greater number of sustainable long-term solutions or long-term solutions that are more sustainable to developing country constraints in the future.

### 4.9.4  World Bank

The World Bank Group published a transfer pricing handbook in 2016, specifically, 'Transfer Pricing and Developing Economies: A Handbook for Policy Makers and Practitioners' (WBG Handbook).[198] While the WBG Handbook does not provide additional or other guidance on the ALP and comparability than what is available under the OECD TPG or the UN Manual, it gives guidance on how to design and implement transfer pricing legislation.[199]

Chapter 4 of the WBG Handbook addresses comparability and largely converges with the OECD TPG and UN TPM approaches to comparability. While the WBG Handbook does not comment on how to arrive to the lasting solution (e.g., reporting requirements, regional access to databases), some alternative solutions that are provided are listed in Table 2.7.[200]

*Table 2.7    Alternative Solutions[201]*

| Solution or Alternative Approaches | Advantages | Disadvantages |
| --- | --- | --- |
| Use of foreign comparables (i.e., use of comparables from other geographic markets) | Widens the pool of potential comparables | – Access to databases containing foreign comparables may not be available or can be expensive<br>– Complex (and somewhat arbitrary) comparability adjustments may be required |
| Use of comparables from other industries or with different functional profiles | Widens the pool of potential comparables | – Requires that comparables exist for which differences that materially affect the condition being examined can be appropriately adjusted for<br>– Complex (and somewhat arbitrary) comparability adjustments may be required |

198. *See* World Bank Group, *Transfer Pricing and Developing Economies: A Handbook for Policy Makers and Practitioners*, at pp. 143–151.
199. *Supra (Petruzzi, R)*.
200. *Supra (Beats, S.)*.
201. *Supra* N179, pp. 144–145.

| Solution or Alternative Approaches | Advantages | Disadvantages |
|---|---|---|
| Safe harbours (with fixed margins) | – Safe harbours can increase certainty for both taxpayers and the tax administration and can increase administrative efficiency<br>– No reliance on comparables information required – Design can draw on administrative data, which is readily available | – Where safe harbours are unilateral, there is a risk of economic double taxation (if not optional) or foregone revenues<br>– Scope for safe harbours may be limited (i.e., generally used for low-value adding services, small loans, etc.) |
| Rebuttable fixed margins | – Simple to administer<br>– No reliance on comparables (except for initial determination of margins)<br>– Certainty | – Similar to safe harbors: Risk of double taxation; limited scope<br>– Complacent tax administration may ignore arguments for rebuttal |
| Advance pricing arrangements | – Can provide a solution where no comparables are available<br>– Provides certainty for taxpayer and the tax administration<br>– Bilateral or multilateral advance pricing arrangements can limit instances of economic double taxation | – Arrangement should be based on the arm's length principle, which generally requires comparables<br>– Can be resource-intensive for the tax administration<br>– Unilateral advance pricing agreements do not prevent economic double taxation<br>– Needs capacity and skilled staff |
| Use of internal rates of return | Provides a solution when no comparables are available | – Relies upon subjective assumptions<br>– Rate of return can be influenced by a range of different factors other than transfer prices |
| Lower independence requirements for uncontrolled transactions | Widens the pool of potential comparables | Transactions between associated parties may be influenced by those parties' transfer pricing policies |
| Use of secret comparables | Greater availability of information for the tax administration | – Not equitable as information cannot generally be disclosed to taxpayers, hence taxpayer is unable to defend its position |

| Solution or Alternative Approaches | Advantages | Disadvantages |
|---|---|---|
| | | – Information cannot generally be disclosed in mutual agreement procedures hence may lead to cases of unrelieved economic double taxation |
| Use of customs valuations | Access to vast amounts of transactional data | – Generally, information required to conduct a comparability analysis is unavailable<br>– Customs valuation methods and transfer pricing operate differently and have different objectives<br>– Only limited transactions types are dutiable |
| Use of industry average returns | Greater availability of information | – Limited information as to composition of industry average hence cannot assess comparability<br>– Industry averages generally include data from controlled transactions |

## 5  CONCLUSIONS

This chapter has provided a detailed description of the processes leading to the identification of the commercial or financial relations as well as recognizing when an accurately delineated transaction has occurred. Moreover, the comparability analysis based on best practices and adopted by various international guidance has been illustrated. The 2017 TPG has provided emphasis on the heightened need for accurately delineating a transaction in order to have a more reliable end result. The use of a one-sided analysis is set to change more with the availability of information about the MNE group as a whole due to Country-by-country reporting (refer to Chapter 7 for a detailed discussion) thereby providing an opportunity to both tax administrators and taxpayers to reconsider the way the comparability analysis is performed. At the same time, the availability of information could lead to new uncertainties and potential disputes that have never been seen before (refer to Chapters 5 and 6 for a detailed discussion on dispute avoidance and dispute resolution).

Therefore, the efforts for dispute avoidance and dispute resolution will continue to be under focus. Measures to make safe-harbour rules (refer to Chapter 9 for a detailed discussion on safe-harbour rules) more connected with taxpayer expectations could be expected, especially from a developing country perspective, when the volume of disputes surrounding routine issues on comparability are far more than that of developed countries. In this regard, the UN will seek to provide further technical assistance and capacity building for strengthening member countries' practices in comparability searches, technology, and knowledge on the comparability analysis.

Further, international organizations are expected to work more cohesively as evidenced by the emergence of PCT in recent years. Efforts are already underway to resolve divergences in various guidance that is now available for both tax practioners and taxpayers. To a certain extent, it has been recognized that the abundance of guidance has led to new forms of misconceptions for legislators and taxpayers, requiring international organizations to quickly resolve such discrepancies.

The challenges faced by developed countries are different and yet are many. Identification and delineation of transactions, specifically with potential restructurings within a highly integrated business holding significant intangibles that feature among significant IP holding jurisdictions, continues to be a grey area requiring concerted efforts (refer to Chapters 11 and 12 for detailed discussions on intangibles and business restructuring aspects). The Pan-EU comparability analysis remains an area of dispute, and prominent EU State-aid rulings have been centred on issues with respect to comparability. To add to existing complexities in the developed world, an increasing drive for digitalization demands more innovations in the very principles of the comparability analysis which could ultimately determine the survival of the arm's length principle itself.

Also, the role of technology as we see it today in the form of electronic databases and tools could undergo significant changes in the future both in terms of reliability and the scale of collection of data. Most importantly, digitization of transfer pricing as a science could result in the entire comparability analysis process being operated in automated or simulated environments where arm's length scenarios could be tested and analysed more quickly, accurately, and conveniently.

# CHAPTER 3

# Transfer Pricing Methods (Part I): Traditional Transaction Methods

## 1 INTRODUCTION

The choice and the proper application of a transfer pricing method represent one of the most critical aspects for MNEs for determining the transfer pricing policy of the group. Indeed, tax authorities scrutinize both the selection of the method and its application in order to determine whether prices that were charged in controlled transactions reflect arm's length conditions. Moreover, the implementation of a specific transfer pricing policy also has practical implications as MNEs should ensure that their internal procedures that are aimed at aligning transfer prices to the arm's length value are properly shared within the organization to ensure their consistent and coherent application as well as being monitored in a timely fashion. The OECD Guidelines [1] and the UN Manual [2] describe five methodologies that are classified respectively into traditional transaction methods and transactional profit methods and are aimed at either setting or testing the conditions of a controlled transaction. The scope of this chapter is to provide a general overview of the traditional methods both from a theoretical and a practical perspective, specifically, the comparable uncontrolled price method (CUP method) in section 2, the resale price method (RPM) in section 3, and the cost plus method (CPM) in section 4.

## 1.1 Transfer Pricing Methods

The OECD Guidelines and the UN Manual recognize five methods or 'methodologies' that can be used to determine whether the conditions established in transactions between associated companies are consistent with the arm's length principle. [3] The methodologies are divided into two categories: the traditional transaction methods and the transactional profit methods. The first category consists of the CUP method, the RPM, and the CPM. The second category includes the transactional net margin method (TNMM) and the transactional profit split method (TPSM). As a general introduction to traditional and transactional profit methods, it can be stated that, in order to test or establish the arm's length conditions relating to the controlled transactions, the CUP method compares prices, the RPM compares gross margins, the CPM compares gross profit markups on costs, the TNMM compares net margins and, lastly, the TPSM compares the allocation of profits between the parties.

A further important distinction is that some of these methods are one-sided while others are two-sided. As the name implies, one-sided methods apply to one party of the controlled transaction and tests the results against those derived by independent enterprises engaged in comparable transactions. The 'tested party' should be the party with the less complex functional profile. [4] As a result of applying a one-sided method, the other party will be entitled to any remaining actual profit from the transaction(s) concerned (however, note that this remaining amount may, in fact, be positive, zero, or even negative). Two-sided methods, however, are effectively applied to both parties in the controlled transaction; they determine either an arm's length price to be used by each party or an allocation of relevant profits from the transaction(s) between the parties.

---

1. Chapter II of the 2017 OECD Guidelines.
2. B.3. of the 2017 UN Manual.
3. Paragraph 2.1 of the 2017 OECD Guidelines.
4. Paragraph 3.18 of the 2017 OECD Guidelines. The tested party is usually the simplest party of the transaction because it is more likely to identify reliable comparables with respect to which perform the analysis.

All transfer pricing methods may be used to establish or to test the transfer prices that are charged between associated companies for the transfer of property (in whatever form) or the provision of services. It is frequently observed in practice that MNEs establish their transfer prices by adopting a method [5] that is practical to apply in its day-to-day activities, periodically testing the outcome with one or more of the OECD recognized methods, and making adjustments when necessary.

---

**Example**

Company A, a tax resident in Country A, is engaged in the production and distribution of scanners for the banking sector. Concerning the manufacturing process, Company A is responsible for all of the R&D associated with the scanners as well as the design and planning activities. Other phases of the manufacturing process, including procurement and assembly, are performed by unrelated contract manufacturers that are also located in Country A. Provided they meet the contracted specifications, Company A purchases 100% of the scanners produced on its behalf by the unrelated contract manufacturers and subsequently markets and distributes them to unrelated customers around the world.

In year T1, Company A purchases 100% of the shares of Company B, a resident of Country B. Company B is an assembler of technical equipment. Country B is a developing country where the cost of labour is low (significantly lower than in Country A), and there is a high degree of competition from similar companies engaged in assembly activities. From year T1, Company B is converted into an assembler of scanners. Company A undertakes the procurement of the raw materials and components that are required for the assembly process by Company B. Company B then makes the scanners under contract from and to the specifications provided by Company A which then purchases 100% of the contracted scanners. As the scanners assembled by Company B are identical to those produced by the unrelated manufacturers, for the sake of simplicity, the MNE group applies the same price list to the scanners supplied by Company B to Company A as that used by Company A to remunerate its unrelated Country A contract manufacturers. However, establishing the controlled prices by adopting the same prices that are charged in uncontrolled transactions (i.e., similar to applying a CUP method) may not produce a result that is compliant with the arm's length principle in this case. In particular, regarding the assembly of scanners by Company B, the procurement activities are performed by Company A while, in the uncontrolled transactions, the unrelated manufacturers are responsible for this function. Moreover, the economic conditions in which the

---

5. For example, the method applied may be a simplified or fixed approach to calculating transfer prices, or a method which superficially resembles an OECD method, but which is not applied in a manner consistent with the arm's length principle.

associated Company B operates are significantly different from the conditions of the uncontrolled '...transactions as the economic circumstances, including the cost of labour that has a major impact on this assembly process, are significantly different. Therefore, the method used by the MNE group for establishing prices must be tested to determine whether it produces outcomes that comply with the arm's length principle. This can be accomplished by comparing those outcomes against those that result from applying the OECD recognized method, which is most appropriate method under the circumstances. Assuming that is possible to identify comparables, independent companies operating in comparable circumstances and performing comparable functions to those performed by Company B (taking into account the assets used and risks assumed by each), it may be possible to apply the TNMM to verify whether prices in the controlled transactions are arm's length.

Assume, in this case, that it is determined that the TNMM is the most appropriate method, and a return on the total costs of the assembler is the most appropriate profit level indicator for determining an arm's length outcome. Assume further that an analysis of comparable independent assemblers shows that an arm's length return on total costs (ROTC) [6] is 20%. Table 3.1 shows how to test and, if necessary, adjust the controlled prices such that they satisfy the arm's length principle.

*Table 3.1   Profit and Loss Account of Company B at 31 December Year T1*

| A | Sales | 1,000 |
|---|---|---|
| B | Cost of goods sold | 500 |
| C | Other costs (including cost of labour) | 100 |
| $D = B + C$ | Total Costs | 600 |
| $E = A\text{-}D$ | Net Operating Profit | 400 |
| $F = D/E$ | ROTC | 67% |
| G | Arm's length ROTC | 20% |
| $H = D*G$ | Net Operating Profit at arm's length | 120 |
| $I = H\text{-}E$ | Year-end Adjustment | -280 |
| $L = A\text{-}I$ | Adjusted sales | 720 |

As indicated in the profit and loss account shown above, in year T1, Company B realized an ROTC equal to 67% while the arm's length ROTC is 20%, meaning that the prices established were not at arm's length. In order to remedy this, those prices must be adjusted such that the ROTC earned in the controlled transaction

---

6. ROTC = Total Costs/Net Operating Profit.

> equals the arm's length value. Company B could affect this adjustment by issuing a credit note or refund of 280 to Company A. [7] These adjusted amounts should then be used as the basis of the tax return filings of Company A and Company B.

Although the five methods described by the OECD Guidelines are not intended to encompass all of the possible ways of determining or verifying whether controlled transactions result in outcomes that are at arm's length, they are 'widely accepted by national authorities'. [8] MNEs are free to apply other methods that they deem more appropriate to establish prices 'provided those prices satisfy the arm's length principle'. [9] However, in this case, the taxpayer must demonstrate that the OECD recognized methods 'were regarded as less appropriate or non-workable in the circumstances of the case' and provide the reason why the other method was regarded as providing a better solution. [10] In practice, such 'other methods' tend to be confined to applications where they are used to set transfer prices and are then supported by recognized methods that are applied to test the compliance of those methods with the arm's length principle. Table 3.2 provides a brief description of the OECD recognized methods.

*Table 3.2   Summary of the OECD Recognized Methods*

| Traditional Methods | Comparable Uncontrolled Price Method (CUP) | The CUP method is a two-sided method that compares the price charged for property or services transferred in a controlled transaction to the price charged for comparable property or services in an uncontrolled transaction under comparable circumstances. [11] |
| --- | --- | --- |
| | Resale price Method (RPM) | The RPM is a one-sided method which compares the gross margin earned by an associated reseller with the gross margin achieved by independent resellers from comparable uncontrolled transactions. |
| | Cost plus Method (CPM) | The CPM is a one-sided method which compares the gross markup added to the direct costs incurred by a manufacturer or a service provider in a controlled transaction to the gross markup achieved by an independent manufacturer or service provider in comparable uncontrolled transactions. |

---

7. Note that domestic law requirements vary on the need to adjust actual transfer prices or to simply make adjustments to outcomes for tax purposes.
8. Paragraph B1.5.12 of the 2017 UN Manual.
9. Paragraph 2.9 of the 2017 OECD Guidelines.
10. *Ibid.*

| | | |
|---|---|---|
| Transactional Methods | Transaction Net Margin Method (TNMM) | This method compares the net profit margin (i.e., after direct and operating expenses are deducted) relative to an appropriate base realized from the controlled transaction(s) with the net margin realized by independent parties in comparable, uncontrolled transactions. |
| | Transactional Profit Split Method (TPSM) | The TPSM first determines the relevant profits from one or more transactions between two associated companies and splits these profits between the parties on an arm's length basis. |
| Other Methods | Other methods are applicable only when they can be shown to be more appropriate than OECD recognized methods. Taxpayers must demonstrate that the alternative method is consistent with the arm's length principle. | |

## 1.2 Selection of the Method

The OECD Guidelines and the UN manual require that the transfer pricing method to be selected in a particular case must be the one that is the 'most appropriate method'. [12] Similarly, the US Treasury Regulations require the application of the so-called 'best-method rule'. [13] The selection of the most appropriate method is a vital step in a transfer pricing analysis since there is generally a much greater risk of error or unreliable results from the application of an inappropriate method than from applying the correct method with imperfect comparables. [14] Even though the OECD Guidelines, as they read from 2010 onwards, do not establish a hierarchy of methods, they do express a preference for the application of the traditional methods when all other things are equal. In particular, when a traditional method and a transactional profit method 'can be applied in an equally reliable manner, the traditional transaction method is preferable to the transactional profit method' as they 'are regarded as the most direct means of establishing' the arm's length outcome of a transaction. [15] The profit split method, in particular, has long been regarded as a method of last resort by many despite the explicit absence of a hierarchy of methods in the OECD Guidelines from 2010 forward. However, recent initiatives of the OECD suggest a rebalancing with more guidance being provided on the transactional profit split method. [16] At the same time, a number of stakeholders, in particular from non-governmental organizations, advocate for the

---

12. Paragraph 2.2 of the OECD Guidelines, or para. B 2.1.2.1 of the 2017 UN Manual.
13. US Treasury Regulations section 1.482 -1 (c)(1).
14. *See* the example in Part II of 'A Toolkit for Addressing Difficulties in Accessing Comparables Data for Transfer Pricing Analyses' published by the Platform for Collaboration on Tax (2017).
15. Paragraph 2.3 of the OECD Guidelines.
16. *See*, in particular, the ongoing work of the OECD with the application of the TPSM, the refinement of which was outlined in the BEPS Actions 10 Final Report and further refined with the publication on 22 Jun. 2017 of the revised discussion draft 'Revised Guidance on Profit Split' on the very application of the latter method. The document is available at http://www.oecd.org/ctp/transfer-pricing/Revised-guidance-on-profit-splits-2017.pdf.

TPSM to be given explicit priority, especially for developing countries. [17] Notwithstanding this, the OECD response thus far has maintained a strict neutrality on methods and continues to advocate for the most appropriate method rather than returning to any type of hierarchy of methods.

In order to select the most appropriate method, several factors must be taken into account among which the functional analysis that is aimed at understanding the nature of the transactions is the most important. [18] In particular, functional analysis helps to accurately delineate or define the transaction particularly in terms of:

- Understanding who does what which subsequently helps to identify the activities that are performed by each party to the transaction and in what capacity;
- Identifying the responsibilities of each party, especially regarding the economically significant risks, and who controls, bears, and assumes those risks for the purposes of the transfer pricing analysis;
- Identifying the key assets that are used including any unique and valuable intangible assets such as trademarks, patents, know-how, etc.

The functional analysis must be considered in the context of the industry and business environment in which the controlled transactions occur. For example, consideration should be given as to what comprises the key value drivers in the industry as well as the value proposition of the multinational enterprise group in the sector. This contextual information, for example, will help to determine which functions, assets, and risks are the most economically significant in relationship to a transaction.

The functional analysis will also help in:

- Determining whether a change in the functional profile over time of the parties involved in the controlled transactions requires a modification to the method applied or the selection of another;
- Determining whether any adjustments are necessary in order to apply the method in a reliable manner.

---

17. *See, ex multis*, the comments of the BEPS Monitoring Group (BMG) to the White Paper on Transfer Pricing Documentation (related to country-by-country Reporting) where it has been stated, in highlighting the advantages of profit-based methods for developing countries and overall in promoting transparency, that 'Arm's length pricing is just one method of ensuring that a multinational corporation has made an appropriate apportionment of its taxable profits between the various states in which it operates. There are, of course, others available and as members of the BMG have argued previously:

    *Consolidated accounts are also necessary to apply the "profit-split" method, which is already allowed within the current OECD guidelines. Under this method, the total profits of an MNC are allocated to different jurisdictions according to so-called "allocation keys" – clear and concrete criteria defined on a case-by-case basis by the parties concerned.'*
    The document is available at https://www.oecd.org/ctp/transfer-pricing/BEPS-Monitoring-Group.pdf.

18. Paragraph B 3.1.2.2 of the 2017 UN Manual.

Once the functional analysis is performed, the other main factors to take into account are the strengths and weaknesses that are inherent in each method and the availability of uncontrolled comparable transactions data that is needed in order to apply the method reliably.

Table 3.3 summarizes the key factors to be taken into account when selecting the most appropriate method.

*Table 3.3   Summary of the Key Factors to Take into Account When Selecting the Method*

| Functional Analysis | |
| --- | --- |
| Functions performed | Identification of the activities performed by the enterprises involved in the transactions. For example, manufacturing activities, distribution activities, R&D activities, etc. In this phase, it is also important to understand which activities are key to value creation within the group as a whole. [19] In this regard, the context within which the business operates the industry and commercial environment and the group's business strategies must be taken into account. |
| Risks | Identification of the risks borne by the parties to the transactions. Examples of risks commonly undertaken are: financial risks (currency, interest rate, funding risks, etc.), credit and collection risks (trading credit risk, commercial credit risk), operational risks (systems failure risk), inventory risks, R&D risks, environmental and other regulatory risks, market risks and product risks (product liability risk, warranty risks, and costs and contract enforceability). In this phase, it is also important to understand not only where risks have been contractually allocated but also to test whether this party also exercises control over the key decisions relating to that risk and has sufficient financial capacity to assume it. Without both of these elements, the risk would need to be allocated to another party for the purposes of the transfer pricing analysis. [20] |

19. Paragraph 1.51 of the 2017 OECD Guidelines.
20. While the OECD Guidelines do not give priority to the control requirement over the requirement for financial capacity, in cases when the contractual allocation and bearing of the risk do not align with these factors, the risk may be reallocated to the party which exercises the 'most control' over the key decisions relating to the risk. Exercising control, in this context, relates to the capability and the actual making of key decisions in relationship to the risk and the business opportunity that it represents. While 'most control' is not expressly defined in the Guidelines, it is likely to refer to the party with the most significant influence on such key decisions. Note, however, that this party must still meet the requirement for financial capacity as this is effectively a threshold test. *See* para. 1.98. Situations where no party both exercises control and has financial capacity are described as 'not likely to occur in transactions between third parties' (para. 1.99) and thus should be subject to 'rigorous analysis'.

| *Functional Analysis* | |
| --- | --- |
| Assets used | Among the assets, it is important to consider both tangible assets (property, plant and equipment, etc.) and intangible assets (patents, trademarks, other marketing intangibles, and know-how, etc.). |
| **Other factors** | |
| Strengths and weaknesses of each method | Each method has inherent strengths and weaknesses that have to be carefully evaluated when selecting the most appropriate method to the transaction. |
| Availability of reliable information on uncontrolled transactions | There may be cases when there is no reliable information on uncontrolled transactions that would be required for the application of the most appropriate method. In such cases, a number of practical solutions may be adopted such as broadening the search, for example, to comparables in different industries or geographic markets.[21] The key in this aspect is to ensure the uncontrolled transactions are still sufficiently comparable to the transactions under review in terms of their economically significant characteristics such as the functional analysis and/or economic circumstances. |

## 2  COMPARABLE UNCONTROLLED PRICE METHOD

### 2.1  What Is It?

The CUP method compares the price charged for the goods that are transferred or for the services that are provided in a controlled transaction to the price that is charged for similar goods that are transferred or similar services that are provided in an uncontrolled transaction under comparable circumstances. [22] The CUP method may also be used to determine the arm's length price for the use of an intangible asset (e.g., a royalty) or to identify the correct price in financial transactions (e.g., interest rate, commissions, etc.).

The CUP method can be applied based on internal comparable transactions (*see* Figure 3.1) or external comparable transactions (*see* Figure 3.2) depending on the information that is available.

---

21. Paragraph B 3.1.2.9 of the 2017 UN Manual.
22. Paragraph 2.13 of the 2017 OECD Guidelines.

*Figure 3.1 Application of the CUP Method Based on Internal Comparable Transactions*

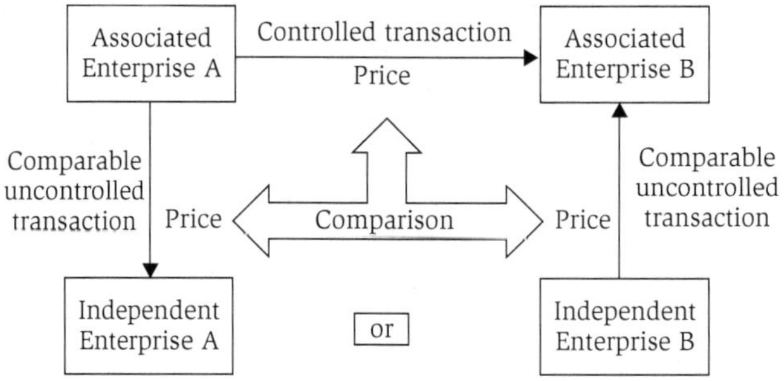


*Figure 3.2 Application of the CUP Method Based on External Comparable Transactions*

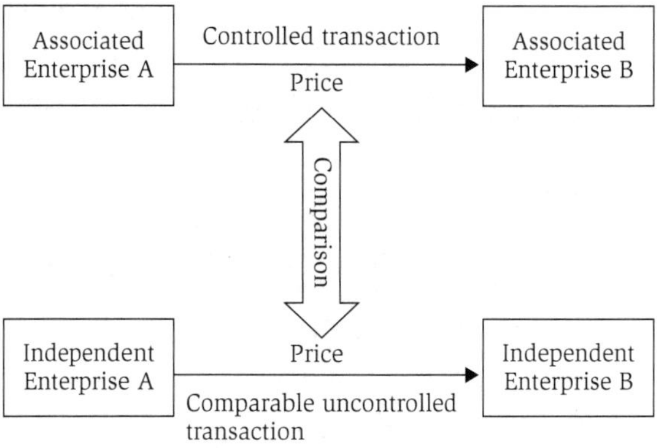


**Example**

Associated Company A, a resident of Country A, produces high purity aluminum ingots, a product that it sells to its associate, Company B, a resident of Country B. Company B uses the aluminum ingots to produce aluminum products for unrelated buyers in the automotive and construction industries.

During the same period, Company A also sells similar quantities of identical aluminum ingots to unrelated buyers in Country B. An analysis of the economically relevant characteristics of these uncontrolled transactions shows that they are comparable to the transactions between Company A and Company B that are under review. In some cases, there are material differences between the transactions, e.g., differing trade or shipping terms, but reliable adjustments can be made to account for these. In this case, it is possible to apply the CUP method by comparing the prices charged in the controlled transactions with those in the uncontrolled transactions.

Note that, for commodities such as aluminum, it may also be possible to apply the CUP method by reference to quoted prices on a recognized commodities exchange such as the London Metal Exchange or the Shanghai Futures Exchange. 23 When there are differences between the specifications or conditions relating to the quoted price and the tested transaction, adjustments may be required.

---

**Example**

Associated Company A, located in Country A, operates in the food industry and developed several techniques for producing sauces that are protected by registered patents. Associated Company A is also responsible for producing and distributing sauces in Country A. Associated Company B, a tax resident in Country B, is responsible for producing and distributing the sauces in Country B by using the recipes that were developed and owned by Company A. Company A does not license the patents to third parties nor does Company B buy similar licenses from third parties. Therefore, it is not possible to use internal transactions to determine the arm's length price of the patents licensed from Company A to Company B. However, through the use of a commercial database, it is possible to identify some comparable transactions where a company licenses similar patented techniques to unrelated parties for producing food products. As a result, the controlled transaction could be tested by comparing the price charged between Company A and Company B with the range of prices, representing the range of market values, charged in the uncontrolled transactions that are identified.

---

## 2.2  When to Use It?

When reliable comparables are available, the CUP method is the most direct means of testing whether prices charged in a controlled transaction are at arm's length. However, the CUP method can also be a difficult method to apply in practice as it requires a very high level of comparability. [24] While all of the comparability factors need to be considered, the characteristics of the property or service and the economic circumstances of the transaction are often particularly important when applying the CUP method. Indeed, even minor differences in either of these comparability factors may have a substantial impact in the prices that are compared. [25] As a result, the CUP method is generally applicable only when the products that are transferred or the

---

23. Paragraphs 2.18–2.22 of the 2017 OECD Guidelines.
24. Paragraph 1.40 of the 2017 OECD Guidelines.
25. Paragraph 2.15 of the 2017 OECD Guidelines.

services that are rendered in a controlled transaction are identical or very similar to the products transferred or the services rendered in uncontrolled transactions. This is also valid when the economic circumstances (e.g., the market in which the transaction occurs) are the same or very similar or, alternatively, reliable adjustments can be made to account for any material differences. For example, adjustments for the following factors are commonly seen:

- Volumes: Volume discounts are common between independent buyers and sellers in the open market. These allow a purchaser to buy additional goods at a reduced price and sellers or manufacturers to increase sales. The comparability analysis should consider the volumes of the controlled and uncontrolled transactions and, if necessary, adjustments should be made when differences in volume would have a material effect on prices.
- Minor differences in characteristics of the property or services: Minor variations in the characteristics of the property or services that have a material effect on pricing may be adjusted when there is reliable information available to do so. For example, Company A, located in country A, purchases copper concentrate from a related party smelter in Country B. It also buys copper concentrate from an independent smelter located in Country C. The copper concentrate from the related smelter contains 33% copper while that from the independent smelter contains only 31% copper. In other respects, the concentrates are of similar quality with neither containing material amounts of precious metals or deleterious elements. A review of the other comparability factors ascertains that there are no other material differences between the transactions. In this case, an internal CUP may be applied to determine the price of the concentrate, however, an adjustment should be made to reflect the greater copper content of the controlled transaction.
- Contractual terms: Assume that associated Company A supplies its products to both a related party and to an unrelated party. All of the comparability factors are sufficiently comparable except that the unrelated company has longer credit terms than the related company. This means that the unrelated company is implicitly being provided with financing for a longer period by Company A relative to the related company. This implicit difference in financing should be reflected in the prices that are charged to the unrelated company and to the related company.

In contrast, it is not usually possible to perform reliable adjustments in the following cases:

- Differences in the use or application of unique and valuable intangibles: Company A is engaged in the manufacturing of refrigerators. Company A also developed two trademarks: Freezer and Freeze Premium. The first is attached to the products that are positioned in the low range segment of the market and are sold at a less expensive price. These refrigerators are sold through an independent distributor in Country B. The second is used for the refrigerators that are positioned at the top of the market and are more expensive. These refrigerators are sold through a related marketer/distributor in Country B. From a technical standpoint, the two types of refrigerators are virtually identical. However, there is a significant difference in the marketing strategy that is adopted by the group which positions the refrigerators in two different segments of the market. This strategy is used by businesses to access different parts of the market and thereby sell more products and/or achieve higher margins on products from customers who are less sensitive to prices. Although the products are essentially the same, it will be impossible to adjust for the effect of the trademark on the price. A method other than the CUP method is likely to be the most appropriate method in this case.

– Fundamental differences in product characteristics: When the products that are transferred in the controlled transactions are significantly different from the product that is sold in the uncontrolled transaction, it may not be possible to make a reliable adjustment to eliminate such a difference.

In practice, the CUP method is most likely to be applicable when internal comparable transactions exist, and there are no differences in the product characteristics that may affect prices or reasonable adjustments may be made to eliminate such differences. Indeed, 'In such a case, all relevant information on the uncontrolled transactions is available and it is, therefore, probable that all material differences between controlled and uncontrolled transactions will be identified.' [26]

Aside from situations where an internal comparable is available, the CUP method is often determined to be the most appropriate method for pricing commodities and is also frequently used for financial transactions (interest) and transactions for the use of intangibles (royalties). In each of these cases, external comparable data is more likely to be available and, from these, arm's length prices may be determined.

## 2.3 How to Use It

---

**Example**

Company A is a tax resident in Country A and is the parent company of a group engaged in the production and the distribution of socks. Associated Company B is a contract manufacturer located in Country B that produces two types of socks, i.e., X and Y, and sells them to Company A. Company A also purchases socks from four unrelated manufacturers located in Country B. Those unrelated manufacturers produce four types of socks: X, Y, Z, and V. Considering that the circumstances of the controlled and the uncontrolled transactions are substantially the same and that there are no material differences that may affect the prices, it is possible to compare the prices that are charged in the controlled transaction for product X and Y with the prices that are charged in the

---

26. Paragraph B 3.2.4.4 of the 2017 UN Manual.

uncontrolled transactions for the same products. The analysis that is performed shows that Company B charges 0.50 for model X and 0.70 for model Y.

Table 3.4 shows the unrelated parties charge the following prices for the two types of socks:

*Table 3.4   Prices Charged By Unrelated Manufacturers*

| Unrelated Companies | X – Prices | Y – Prices |
|---|---|---|
| UCOA | 0.40 | 0.65 |
| UCOB | 0.45 | 0.68 |
| UCOC | 0.56 | 0.72 |
| UCOD | 0.59 | 0.75 |

The uncontrolled prices shown in the table above represent the arm's length range of prices compared with the prices charged in the controlled transaction. Considering that the prices charged in the controlled transaction (0.50 for product X and 0.70 for product Y) fall within the arm's length range that is identified, they are considered as being consistent with the arm's length principle.

**Example**

The facts are the same as in the example in section 1.1 except that, in year T1, Company A establishes a related contract manufacturer in Country C, a developing country where the cost of labour is significantly lower than in Country B. The market for contract manufacturers of textiles and garments in Country C is competitive. The cost of labour represents one of the principal expenses of the sock manufacturing process as it requires a significant amount of manual work. As a result, the cost structure of the manufacturers that are located in Country C is significantly different from the cost structure of the related manufacturer located in Country B. Furthermore, Company A undertakes the procurement function on behalf of its related contract manufacturer in Country C.

The costs of production may be an important part of the economic circumstances of the transaction when performing a comparability analysis. Furthermore, in this case, there is a material difference in the functional analysis relating to the uncontrolled and uncontrolled transactions.

Therefore, in this case, the CUP method cannot be reliably applied even if there are uncontrolled transactions involving the products that are physically identical.[27] Instead, a CPM or TNMM may be found to be the most appropriate method in this case to test whether the gross or net margins earned by the related manufacturer are at arm's length.

---

**Example**

Company A is a tax resident in Country A and its associated Company B is a tax resident in Country B. Company C, located in Country B, is an independent enterprise. Company A sells Product X to Company B in a controlled transaction at a price of 55 per unit (excluding transportation costs) while the price charged to Company C for the same product is 65 per unit including transportation. The only difference that is identified between the controlled transaction and the uncontrolled transaction is in the shipping terms (i.e., which party is responsible for bearing the transportation costs). An analysis of the transportation costs ascertains that this additional element is valued at an amount equal to 5 per unit). This difference in contract terms has a material impact on the price. Therefore, a comparability adjustment is required. To do so, the price in the uncontrolled transaction is reduced by 5 to exclude the transportation costs: 65-5 = 60. The price charged in the controlled transaction (55 per unit) is less than the adjusted price in the comparable uncontrolled transaction (60 per unit), indicating that the price in the controlled transaction is not consistent with the arm's length principle.

---

## 2.4 Critical Aspects

The primary weakness of the CUP method consists of the difficulty in locating transactions that are sufficiently comparable considering the strict comparability requirements that must be observed. For instance, the cases described in the previous examples may exist when MNEs have a supply chain made up of both comparable related and unrelated suppliers or service providers or of related and unrelated customers. Even when related and unrelated suppliers or customers exist, it is often not possible to identify internal comparable transactions because MNEs often do not transact with independent suppliers or customers in the same manner that they do with associates, and those differences may materially affect the prices that would be expected for the property or service concerned. For example, taking into account the structure of the Alpha Group shown below, the primary difficulties that can be typically encountered in applying the CUP method are discussed in Figure 3.3.

---

27. Paragraph 1.110 of the 2017 OECD Guidelines.

Figure 3.3   Alpha Group Structure

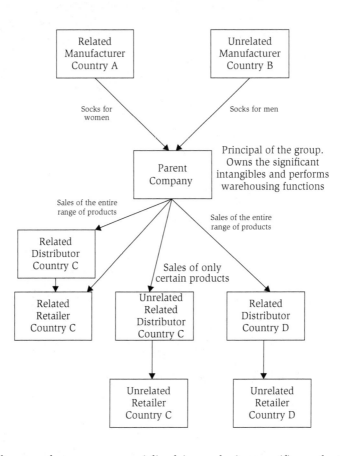

- The manufacturers are specialized in producing specific products. Related Manufacturer A produces only socks for women while the unrelated company, Manufacturer B, specializes in socks for men. Socks for men and women command different prices in the market. Consequently, the products are not comparable, and the CUP method cannot be applied;
- A related distributor in Country C distributes the entire range of the group's products but no other brands. Meanwhile, the unrelated distributor in Country C is a multi-brand distributor but only carries certain lines that are produced by the group. As a result of these differences, the related distributor also has a different functional profile in terms of its sales of the group's products including a significantly more intensive marketing effort relative to the unrelated multi-brand distributor. Therefore, the CUP method will not be the most appropriate method in this case since the differences between the transactions can be expected to materially impact upon the price, and reliable adjustments for these differences cannot be identified.

- It is also unlikely that the controlled sales between the related distributor in Country C and the related retailer can be directly compared to the uncontrolled sales between the related distributor in Country D and its independent retailer using a CUP method. If the economic conditions of the transactions are sufficiently similar such that they have no material effect on the price and there are no material differences in the other economically relevant characteristics of the transactions, then the CUP method can be used.
- It is also unlikely that the controlled sales between the related distributor in Country C and the related retailer can be directly compared to the uncontrolled sales between the related distributor in Country D and its independent retailer using a CUP method. If the economic conditions of the transactions are sufficiently similar such that they have no material effect on the price and there are no material differences in the other economically relevant characteristics of the transactions, then the CUP method can be used.

## 3 RESALE PRICE METHOD

### 3.1 What Is It

The RPM consists of comparing the resale margin that a purchaser of property in a controlled transaction earns from reselling that property in an uncontrolled transaction with the resale margin that is earned in comparable uncontrolled purchase and resale transactions. The resale price margin represents the amount that the reseller would seek in order to cover its selling and other operating expenses and make an appropriate profit taking into account the functions performed, assets used, and risks assumed. [28]

In order to identify the margin earned, the starting point of the analysis in applying the RPM is the price charged by the associated company to the unrelated party. This price must then be reduced by an appropriate margin to obtain the arm's length price (*see* Figure 3.4).

---

28. Paragraph 2.21 of the 2017 OECD Guidelines.

*Figure 3.4   Application of Resale Price Method*

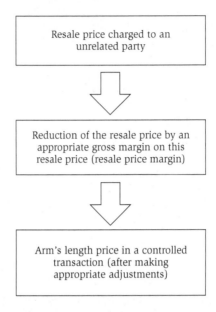

In particular, under this method, the resale price margin can be calculated with the following formula:

$$\text{Resale Price Margin} = \frac{\text{Sales Price} - \text{Direct and Indirect Costs}}{\text{Sales Price}}$$

The arm's length price can be calculated with the following formula:

$$\text{Arm's length price} = \text{Sales Price} \times (1 - \text{Resale Price Margin})$$

As the RPM is a one-sided method, a tested party needs to be selected to apply it. Guidance on the selection of a tested party is provided in Chapter II of this book. The tested party will generally be the less complex of the parties to the transaction (if not, the RPM is unlikely to be the most appropriate method) (*see* Figures 3.5 and 3.6).

*Figure 3.5   Application of the RPM Method Based on Internal Comparable Transactions*

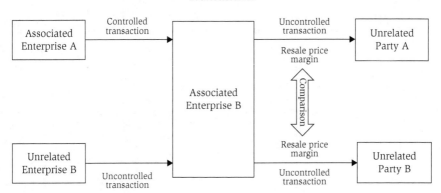

*Figure 3.6   Application of the RPM Method Based on External Comparable Transactions*

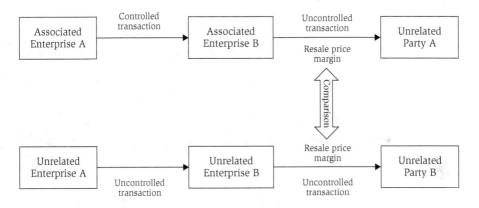

## 3.2   When to Use It

The RPM may be a suitable method in cases where one of the parties performs ordinary distribution and selling functions and adds relatively little value to the goods. [29] Minor differences in characteristics of goods and services may have a lesser impact on resale price margins than on the actual prices as the gross profits represent the compensation for performing specific functions and bearing certain risks. While prices may vary significantly based on minor differences in the physical characteristics of the product, resale price margins that are largely based on the functions, assets, and risks involved in on-selling the goods are much less impacted by such physical differences. As a result, the RPM may be applicable in situations where the CUP method cannot be applied.

---

29. Paraagraph 2.35 of the 2017 OECD Guidelines.

The RPM is also used to establish or test transfer prices for related party purchases of property by an entity with limited value-adding activities (Figure 3.7). The tested entity's resale price margin is benchmarked by comparing it to the resale price margins that are earned by comparable, uncontrolled entities engaged in comparable transactions.

*Figure 3.7   Resale Price Method*

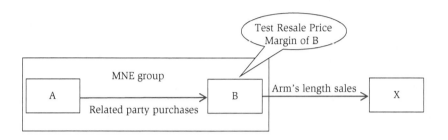

The RPM may be determined to be the most appropriate in cases when:

- Internal comparable transactions exist. The CUP method is not applicable, for example, due to differences in a product's characteristics (which cannot be adjusted for) that have a material impact on the price;
- Related party purchases of goods when the reseller's value-adding activities are limited and they do not contribute valuable or unique intangible assets or assume substantial risks.

---

**Example**

A distributor purchases and resells two models of the tablet PadX: the first with a storage amount of 32GB and the second with 128GB. The distributor is performing exactly the same functions in distributing the two models of the tablet, and his gross remuneration is not affected by the product difference. In contrast, the price of the two tablets cannot be compared as the different amounts of storage have an impact on prices. Table 3.5 illustrates this.

*Table 3.5   Summary of the Case*

|   |   | *32GB* | *128GB* |
|---|---|---|---|
| A | Sales price | 140 | 168 |
| B | Resale price margin or Gross margin | 40% | 40% |

---

| | | | |
|---|---|---|---|
| C = A*B | Gross profit | 56 | 67 |
| D = A-C | Cost of goods sold | 84 | 101 |

Although the distributor performs the same functions (taking into account the assets used and risks assumed) and earns the same gross margin in distributing the two different models, consumers would take into account the different storage amounts and would be willing to pay more for the tablet with the greater storage capacity. This example also shows that:

- It is not always necessary to calculate the gross margin on a product-by-product basis as it will often be sufficient to calculate the gross margin earned over a range of products for which it is appropriate to aggregate; [30] and
- In order to determine whether the RPM is the most appropriate method, the comparability factors other than product characteristics, particularly the functional analysis and economic circumstances, must be carefully considered, etc.

Indeed, the RPM is very sensitive to differences in the functional analysis, and the comparability analysis must verify whether there are material differences between the controlled and the uncontrolled transactions in this regard. Particularly when applying an external comparable, it is important to analyse the expenses accounted for below the gross margin line as these usually reflect the type and the intensity of the functions performed and the risks assumed by the reseller.

**Example**

Assume that an associated distributor purchases goods for 60 and sells them for 100, earning a gross margin equal to 40. Also assume that the distributor incurs a substantial amount of marketing expenses for promoting the brand owned by the parent company. Because of the high operating expenses, the distributor sustains a net operating loss. The P&L account of the distributor is shown in Table 3.6.

*Table 3.6   Summary of the Case*

| | | |
|---|---|---|
| A | Sales | 100 |
| B | Cost of goods sold | 60 |
| C = A-B | Gross profit | 40 |

---

30. Paragraph 6.2.8.3. of the 2017 UN Manual.

| | | |
|---|---|---|
| D = C/A | Resale price or Gross margin % | 40% |
| E | Marketing expenses | 45 |
| F | General expenses | 5 |
| G = C-E-F | Operating margin | -10 |

Also assume that there are no internal comparable transactions, and a set of independent distributors is identified that are selling similar products through the use of commercial databases and operating under similar economic circumstances (e.g., the same geographic area). From the analyses of the financial statements of the independent distributors, it is determined that, on average, the level of marketing expenses incurred by those distributors is 5% of sales while the associated distributor incurs an amount of marketing expenses equal to 45% of sales. This significantly greater amount of marketing expenses of the associated distributor might reflect the fact that it is performing additional marketing activities. The functional analysis would need to consider the extent of these activities and the capacity in which they are undertaken in order to determine whether they should be characterized as a marketing service that is for the benefit of the parent company, [31] activities which are intended to develop or create an intangible, or something else. Considering these differences, the RPM cannot be reliably applied to test the results of the distributor since its functional profile is significantly different relative to those of the uncontrolled distributors found in the database. As a result, either another method would need to be selected, or it may be determined that it is possible to define the excess marketing activities as a separate transaction for which additional remuneration should be provided (e.g., though segmenting the accounts and providing for a cost plus reward for the excess marketing activities).

Alternatively, it may be possible to search for uncontrolled distributors with levels of marketing intensity that are similar to the tested party. However, the greater the value added by the seller, the more difficult it will be to determine an appropriate resale margin as it will generally be difficult to identify independent comparable resellers in such a case.

In applying the RPM, a method based on a comparison of gross margins, it is crucial that costs are accounted in a similar manner between the tested party and the proposed comparables. There is often significant flexibility in the accounting standards such that amounts whi ch are of an economically similar nature may be accounted for differently, e.g., included in the cost of goods sold by one entity (and thus included in the gross margin) and as operating expenses by another (and thus not included in the gross margin). Such differences may be exacerbated when comparing typical accounting practices between different industries. This is a further reason why the RPM is often

---

31. That should be separately remunerated or valuated together with the distribution transaction in case of portfolio strategies.

thought to be unreliable if the potential comparables are from a different industry or deal in products that are unrelated to those of the tested party.

## 3.3 How to Use It

This section provides a series of examples, and main facts follow the first example.

---

**Example**

Company A is a tax resident in Country A and its associated Company B is a tax resident in Country B. Company B is a distributor that, after buying product X at a price of 84 per unit from Company A, resells it to independent parties at a price of 140 per unit. Company B does not modify or otherwise add any substantial value to the product. A comparability search using commercial databases and a subsequent analysis reveals four independent resellers performing similar functions (taking into account the assets used and risks assumed) of engaging in comparable uncontrolled transactions under similar economic circumstances that made the following resale price margins in the corresponding year:
- Independent reseller C: resale price margin of 35%;
- Independent reseller D: resale price margin of 38%;
- Independent reseller E: resale price margin of 43%;
- Independent reseller F: resale price margin of 45%;

Assume that the available information regarding all four comparable companies is sufficient for concluding that there are no material differences between the controlled transactions and comparable uncontrolled transactions that could materially affect the gross margins such that the full range of results represents a valid arm's length range of gross margins. Considering that the resale price margin in the controlled transaction (i.e., 40% = (140-84)/140) falls within this arm's length range, it can be concluded that the prices charged in the controlled transaction are consistent with the arm's length principle.

---

**Example**

The facts are the same as the first example except that the independent resale price margins are the following:
- Independent reseller C: resale price margin of 49%;
- Independent reseller D: resale price margin of 46%;
- Independent reseller E: resale price margin of 44%;
- Independent reseller F: resale price margin of 42%;

In this case, the gross margin earned by the associated distributor falls outside of the arm's length range. In order to be compliant with the arm's length principle, the gross margin must be increased such that it is within the arm's length range. Assuming that 42% (the nearest point in the range) is adopted, the purchase price has to be decreased to 81 per unit.

---

**Example**

The facts are the same as the first example except that some independent distributors may include promotional expenses such as rebates and customer bonuses as either COGS or negative amounts of sales while the associated distributor treats those costs that are below the gross profit line as operating expenses. In such case, it is not possible to make reliable adjustments to eliminate the effect of these potential differences on the gross margins since the detailed financial data of the independent distributors are not available. As a result, the RPM cannot be reliably applied in the case at stake. Note that a TNMM, which tests net margins and thus would account for costs both above and below the gross profit line, applied analogously to the RPM may be applicable. *See* Chapter IV of this book.

---

**Example**

The facts are the same as in the first example except that the independent distributor developed and promoted its own trademark which is attached to the goods purchased from Company A. Although the products are similar, in this case, it will be difficult to determine the effect of the trademark and associated promotional activities on the gross margin. Therefore, the RPM cannot be reliably applied, and another method should be adopted.

---

## 3.4   Critical Aspects

The main critical aspects in applying the RPM are:

- difficulties in finding comparable data with respect to gross profit margins. When there are no internal comparable transactions, it may be difficult to find reliable gross margin data due to variations in industry and accounting practices;
- even when it is possible to identify external comparable transactions, caution should be exercised in comparing transactions of companies that adopt different accounting standards. When this is the case, appropriate adjustments should be made where possible in order to ensure a sufficient degree of comparability between the controlled and the uncontrolled transactions.

For these reasons, the RPM is most commonly applied to the transactions of resellers that do not add significant value and for which internal comparables data is available.

## 4   COST PLUS METHOD

### 4.1   What Is It

The CPM method determines whether the prices charged in a transaction between related parties are in accordance with the arm's length principle by comparing the gross markup realized by unrelated parties in comparable transactions. To this end, the arm's length price for the related party is equal to the cost borne by the latter for producing the property or providing the service involved in the transaction plus an appropriate profit markup.

In order to apply this method reliably, good comparability between the functions performed, assets used, and risks assumed in the controlled and uncontrolled transactions is important (Figure 3.8).

*Figure 3.8   Application of the CPM Method*

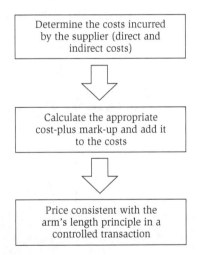

Cost plus markup is computed with the following formula:

$$\text{Cost Plus Markup} = \frac{\text{Selling Price} - \text{Direct and Indirect Costs}}{\text{Direct and Indirect Costs}}$$

The arm's length price can be computed with the formula below:

**Arm's – length Price = Direct and Indirect Costs × (1 + Cost plus markup)**

When applying the CPM, a tested party must be selected. Guidance on the selection of a tested party is provided in Chapter II of this book. The tested party, when applying the CPM, will be the party for which the markup on costs that are directly and indirectly incurred in the supply of goods or services is compared to the markup on costs directly or indirectly incurred in the supply of goods and services in a comparable uncontrolled transaction.

Once a tested party has been selected, the CPM can be applied based on internal or external comparable(s) (Figures 3.9 and 3.10).

*Figure 3.9   Application of the CPM Based on Internal Comparable Transactions*

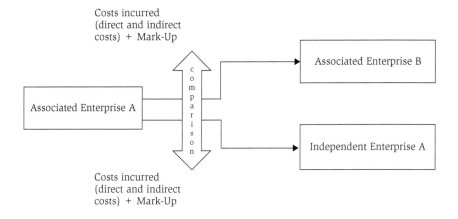

*Figure 3.10    Application of the CPM Based on External Comparable Transactions*

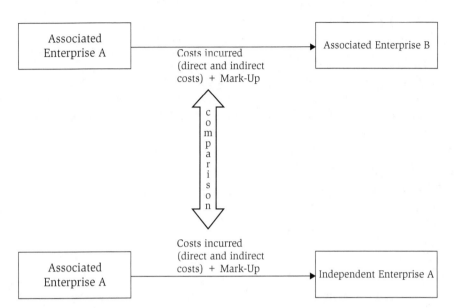

An uncontrolled transaction is comparable to a controlled transaction when applying the CPM if there are no differences between the transactions being compared that materially affect the gross profit markup or if reasonably accurate adjustments can be performed to adjust for the effect of such differences. [32] As with the RPM, this method is less affected by differences in the characteristics of the products than the CUP method because it evaluates the arm's length nature of the transactions by examining the remuneration of the tested party for the functions performed, assets used, and risks assumed. However, product characteristics must be analysed carefully as significant product differences often lead to differences in the functions performed, assets used, and risks assumed by the parties. These differences will often subsequently result in differences in the gross margin that an independent party would expect to earn from its transactions and, therefore, the transactions will not be comparable unless a reliable adjustment can be made to take these differences into account.

---

**Example**

Company A is a contract manufacturer engaged in assembling power generators. The assembly process is relatively simple and involves putting together four components on-site. Company A purchases the components from unrelated suppliers and produces two models of generators: X1 and X2. These products are identical except for one component, the engine; the X1 generator has a diesel

---

32. Paragraph 1.40 of the 2017 OECD TPG.

engine, and the X2 generator has a gas engine. X1 generators are sold to a related company while X2 generators are sold to an unrelated company. Similar quantities of each of the generators are sold. As shown in Table 3.7, in this case, the CUP method cannot be applied as the different type of engine that is mounted has a significant impact on the price. However, the functions performed, assets used, and risks assumed in assembling the X1 and X2 generators are very similar as the different type of engine does not have any impact on the production process. Therefore, it may be the case that the CPM method may be the most appropriate in this case and can be applied by comparing the cost plus markup charged in the controlled transaction with the cost plus markup charged in the uncontrolled transaction.

*Table 3.7    Summary of the Case*

|  |  | X1 | X2 |
|---|---|---|---|
| A | Component 1 | 15 | 15 |
| B | Component 2 | 20 | 20 |
| C | Component 3 | 25 | 25 |
| D | Engine | 100 | 150 |
| E | Other production expenses | 50 | 50 |
| $F = A + B + CPMD + E$ | Cost of goods sold | 210 | 260 |
| G | Cost plus markup % | 40% | 40% |
| $H = F*G$ | Cost plus markup | 84 | 104 |
| $I = F + H$ | Price | 294 | 364 |

When applying the CPM, two broad categories of costs and expenses of an enterprise are taken into account and marked up. These categories are:

- *Direct costs* – Costs that are incurred specifically for producing a product or rendering a service such as the cost of raw materials or the cost of employees.
- *Indirect costs* – Costs of producing a product or service which, although closely related to the production process, may be common to several products or services (e.g., the costs of a repair department that services equipment used to produce different products).

A third category of accounting costs are not marked up when applying a CPM: overheads or operating expenses. These costs, recorded below the gross profit line, cannot be directly or indirectly related to the product and include supervisory, general, and administrative expenses.

A CPM marks up only the direct and indirect costs of production in order to arrive at an arm's length sales price. In contrast, a net margin analysis (*see* Chapter IV on TNMM) applied on a basis that is analogous to a cost plus would also markup operating expenses. When the CPM is applied by reference to external comparables, for example, those identified through the use of commercial databases, caution must be taken to ensure consistent measurement of economically equivalent costs as direct, indirect, and operating costs may be accounted for in different ways between entities. [33]

When determining the appropriate costs to be taken into account, specific attention should be paid to ensure that both a comparable markup and a comparable cost basis are being used. That is, the cost base in the comparable uncontrolled transaction(s) must be the same (or at least very similar to) the cost base in the controlled transaction(s). This will require consideration of any differences in the accounting treatment of expenses which will necessitate particular attention when different accounting standards are being applied.

There must be an appropriate (internal) allocation of costs by the tested party. The tested party may be providing numerous different products or services to various parties. In this regard, when these products involve different counterparties or different functions, assets, and risks, it is important to ensure that these costs are appropriately allocated to the relevant goods or services that are the subject of the controlled transaction(s).

## 4.2  When to Use It

The CPM is commonly used for setting or testing inter-company prices in transactions involving the sale of tangible property or the provision of services when the related party manufacturer or the related service provider performs limited value-adding functions. The assets used and risks assumed must also be taken into account.

The CPM is also used to establish or test transfer prices for related party sales of property or services by an entity with limited value-adding activities. The tested entity's markup on its arm's length purchases or other inputs is benchmarked by comparing it to the markups achieved by comparable, uncontrolled entities that are engaged in comparable transactions (Figure 3.11).

*Figure 3.11    Cost Plus Method*

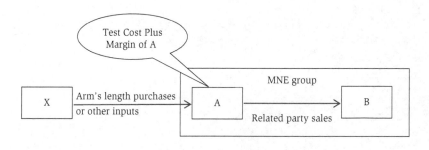

---

33. Paragraph B. 3.2.15.3 of the 2017 UN Manual.

Unless it is possible to identify comparable internal transactions, the CPM is usually not a suitable method when the related contract manufacturer or the related service provider owns unique and valuable intangibles or makes unique and valuable contributions. In this case, it will be very difficult to find reliable uncontrolled comparables.

The CPM may be determined to be the most appropriate in cases when:

- Internal comparable transactions exist, however, the CUP method is not applicable, for example, due to differences in product characteristics (which cannot be adjusted for) that have a material impact on the price;
- Related party sales of goods when the manufacturer's value-adding activities are limited and it does not contribute valuable or unique intangible assets or assume substantial risks, e.g., contract manufacturing or toll manufacturing;
- Related party provision of services whereby the provider does not contribute any valuable unique assets and does not assume substantial risks.

---

**Example**

Company A is a full-fledged manufacturer engaged in the production of scanners for the banking sector. Company A also performs R&D activities in addition to the ordinary manufacturing operations (procurement, scheduling, assembling, etc.). It owns several registered patents and the trademarks that are used in the development and marketing of the specific products. The scanners are produced in Country A and distributed only in Country B through a related distributor that is responsible for exclusively distributing the scanners to clients in Country B and providing after sale services. In this case, the CPM cannot be reliably applied to test the margins achieved by Company A as it is, by far, the more complex party of the two. Company A has a variety of interrelated functions and uses unique and valuable intangibles. This means that it is highly improbable that a reliable uncontrolled comparable will be found. It would likely be easier to identify uncontrolled companies located in Country B that are performing ordinary distribution functions and operating under similar economic circumstances as the related distributor. In this case, therefore, an RPM or a TNMM using a resale price analogue is likely to provide a more appropriate solution as each of these methods verify the intra-group prices by selecting the distributor as the tested party and testing its gross or net margin.

---

### 4.3 How to Use It

The CPM focuses on the profit markup charged by an entity on an appropriate cost basis. That markup on costs would represent the compensation earned by the entity for its value-adding activities (i.e., its functions, assets, and risks). For example, when the

CPM is applied to a contract manufacturer, the markup on costs would represent compensation for the entity for: (i) its performance of manufacturing services; (ii) its investment in its operating assets; and (iii) the limited risk it has assumed in connection with its contract manufacturing activities. Under the CPM, comparability is primarily dependent upon the similarity of: (i) the extent and value of the functions performed; (ii) the value and types of assets employed; and (iii) the business and economic risks assumed. The CPM is less dependent on the similarity of the services provided or the goods produced.

**Example**

Company A is engaged in the production and distribution of clothing. It owns the key intellectual property and is responsible for all of the key entrepreneurial functions. It also assumes the economically significant risks related to both the manufacturing transactions and the distribution transactions (meaning that it must also exercise key control decisions associated with those risks). The clothing is produced by a related entity, Company B. Company B uses the manufacturing processes developed by Company A to fill orders it receives from Company A. Company B assumes the risks associated with managing the manufacturing process. The functional analysis confirms that Company B is a contract manufacturer. It applies routine processes to meet defined orders for the manufacture of products designed by their customer. It assumes no risks related to the success of the products in the market, only those in relation to its ability to manufacture products to the agreed specifications and quality for the agreed price. It is determined that the CPM is the most appropriate method in this case. Company B represents the least complex party of the controlled transaction. Moreover, Company B also has a number of other contracts to produce apparel for independent customers under very similar conditions to those which apply with Company A. The manufacturing functions performed, assets used, and risks assumed by Company B in producing clothing for Company A are comparable to those involved in producing apparel for these unrelated parties.

*Table 3.8  Summary of the Case*

| Company B's Transactions with Company A | |
|---|---|
| Sales | 100 |
| Cost of goods sold | 60 |
| Other production costs | 10 |
| Gross margin | 30 |
| Cost plus margin % | 43% |
| Company B's transactions with Unrelated Company X | |
| Sales | 110 |
| Cost of goods sold | 65 |

| | |
|---|---|
| Other production costs | 10 |
| Gross margin | 35 |
| Cost plus margin % | 47% |
| *Company B's transaction with Unrelated Company Y* | |
| Sales | 110 |
| Cost of goods sold | 66 |
| Other production costs | 10 |
| Gross margin | 34 |
| Cost plus margin % | 45% |
| *Company B's transactions with Unrelated Company Z* | |
| Sales | 90 |
| Cost of goods sold | 54 |
| Other production costs | 10 |
| Gross margin | 26 |
| Cost plus margin % | 41% |

The different margins achieved by Company B in its uncontrolled transactions are due to minor differences in the ability of the unrelated companies to negotiate prices.

In this case, the cost plus margins earned in the comparable uncontrolled transactions by Company B can be used to benchmark an arm's length return for Company B's transactions with Company A. The range of the arm's length cost plus margins values represented ranges from a minimum of 41% to a maximum of 47%. Since the cost plus margin charged by Company B to Company A (43%) falls within the arm's length range, the intra-group prices are considered at arm's length. From that, it can also be concluded that the arm's length price for the products sold by Company B to Company A is at arm's length.

**Example**

The facts are the same as the previous example except that the related company, Company A, has different payment terms compared to those offered to unrelated Companies X, Y, and Z. Specifically, Company A is allowed up to 180 days to pay for its purchases from Company B while Companies X, Y, and Z are given only ninety days. In general, this type of material difference in payment terms may warrant an adjustment. The rationale is that a company with more (less) days payable is implicitly being provided more (less) financing by its suppliers. This implicit difference in financing cost should be reflected in differences between the cost of goods sold of the controlled transaction company and the cost of goods sold of the uncontrolled transactions. Depending on the circumstances, similar material differences in other working capital items (accounts receivable and inventories) may also be appropriate.

**Example**

The facts are the same as the previous example except that Company B contracts exclusively with Company A. Moreover, it is not possible to identify external comparable transactions as the commercial database does not provide any information with respect to the cost plus margins earned by independent parties in the geographic area where Company B is located. Assuming that it is not possible to extend the search to other geographical areas because the different economic conditions would affect the comparison, the CPM cannot be applied reliably. However, it may be possible that the TNMM may be the most appropriate method, and an arm's length return for Company B could be determined based on a comparison of its net profits relative to its total costs to those of comparable contract manufacturers. See Section xxx.

## 4.4 Critical Aspects

The main critical aspects of the CPM method include:

- The CPM method relies on the availability of reliable data of cost plus margins from uncontrolled comparable transactions.
- Accounting disclosures and consistency between what is included in the cost base are essential.
- The CPM method will only be the most appropriate method when the tested party has limited value-adding such that there is a strong correlation between its input or production costs and the arm's length price for its products or services.
- Since the method is based on actual costs, it cannot account for differences in the efficiency of the tested party relative to the comparables. (Note, however, that this may also be an issue for other methods such as the RSM and TNMM.).

## 5 CONCLUSIONS

This chapter has illustrated how to select and apply the transfer pricing methods described by the OECD Guidelines and the UN Manual from both a theoretical and a practical standpoint. In particular, section 1 emphasizes the importance of selecting the most appropriate method for the case in order to establish the arm's length prices to be charged in the controlled transactions. To do so, it is vital to accurately delineate the transactions in order to identify which are the most economically significant factors that must be taken into account in the selection process. Aside from the functional

123

analysis, other factors such as the availability of data and information have to be carefully evaluated as they may be relevant for determining the reliable application of the method that is selected.

Sections 2 to 4 describe the primary features of the traditional methods as well as the respective strengths and weakness. These paragraphs also provide a number of practical applications that are taken from actual cases that were addressed by the authors either during their academic work or in the practice in defending or assisting taxpayers. These cases demonstrate that, although the CUP method is defined as the most reliable method, its application is very limited and confined to only certain types of transactions in practice such as those involving commodities or financial instruments. The RPM and CPM are one-sided methods that have a wider application. The first is especially useful for testing simple distribution functions, and the second is generally utilized in the area of intra-group services or manufacturing operations.

CHAPTER 4
# Transfer Pricing Methods (Part II): Transactional Profit Methods

## 1  INTRODUCTION

Transactional Profit Methods 'examine the profits that arise from particular transactions among associated enterprises'.[1] They comprise the Transactional Net Margin Method (TNMM, in section 2) and the Transactional Profit Split Method (TPSM, in section 3). This chapter also discusses other valuation methods (in section 4).

## 2  TRANSACTIONAL NET MARGIN METHOD

### 2.1  What Is It?

The TNMM is arguably the transfer pricing method that is most widely employed by taxpayers and tax administrations around the world today. It is often used as the

---

1. Paragraph 2.62, 2017 OECD Guidelines:

> The 2017 UN Manual particularly addresses the transactional profit methods in B.3.3:
>
> > These methods differ from traditional methods in that the analysis is not necessarily based on particular comparable uncontrolled transactions involving identical or perhaps even broadly comparable products.
> >
> > Often, and depending on the facts and circumstances, the analysis is based on the net return (the earnings determined before interest and tax and extraordinary items, i.e. EBIT) realized by various companies engaged in a particular line of business (that is, a series of transactions that are appropriate to be aggregated). (*See* para. B.3.3.1.2., 2017 UN Manual).
> >
> > It is rare that enterprises use transactional profit methods to actually determine their prices. However, the profit resulting from a controlled transaction might be quite a good signal to establish whether the transaction was affected by conditions that differ from those that would have been made by independent enterprises in otherwise comparable circumstances. (*See* Para B.3.3.1.3., 2017 UN Manual).

default method for transfer pricing. The method is discussed in Chapter II, Part III.B of the OECD Guidelines.[2]

This method consists of setting and/or testing the transfer price of an intra-group transaction based on the net profit that the 'tested party' to the transaction, typically being the party with less complex and more routine activities, earns with respect to this particular intra-group transaction. 'The transactional net margin method examines the net profit relative to an appropriate base (e.g., costs, sales, assets) that a taxpayer realises from a controlled transaction.'[3]

In the TNMM, the transfer price is established by reference to the net profit made by only one party to the transaction. It is then assumed that, as long this profit is at arm's length, the 'residual' profit retained by the other party is to be considered at arm's length as well. As such, it is different from the TPSM (section 3) or the other methods (section 4), as it is a one-sided method.

The TNMM is used in various contexts, notably for setting and/or testing the price of transactions involving products or services. It is used less frequently in the context of transactions that are more complex, such as the ones involving intangibles.

In practice, the TNMM relies on a comparable company search (section 2.3.3). While the application of the TNMM involves the search for external comparables in public databases in most cases, its application may also involve the search for external evidence of net margins outside of public databases. For instance, if a group has similar transactions with external parties as those that are tested, it may be relevant to search for the net margins realized in those transactions in order to assess the target net margin that the tested party should be earning; this is a different application of the TNMM than the typical application involving searching in databases.

## 2.2   When to Use It?

In practical terms, the TNMM is generally the most appropriate method:

(a) In case external price data points are not available, i.e., the CUP method (*See* Chapter III) is not applicable; and

(b) The function which is tested is benchmarkable. To determine whether a function is benchmarkable, it should be determined, for instance, whether:
   – a comparable product or service can be found in the marketplace at the same market level;[4]
   – it could be realistically considered by the MNE to outsource the activity under review to a third party; and
   – the activity under review does not have a material impact on the MNE's overall value creation process or it does not manage the MNE's core risks.

---

2. Paragraphs 2.64–2.113, 2017 OECD Guidelines.
3. Paragraph 2.64, 2017 OECD Guidelines.
4. To be noted, the concept of comparability is at the core of the TNMM. We will only briefly discuss comparability in the TNMM in section 3.3 below. The concept is discussed in detail in Chapter 2.

It is worth noting that the CPM or RPM (*See* Chapter III) have similarities with the TNMM insofar that they may be all used in the absence of the CUP method. They assume the tested party to be benchmarkable, and they necessitate a comparables company search. The major difference is that the CPM and the RPM involve setting/ testing transfer prices based on the gross margin indicators of comparable companies (as opposed to the net margin in the case of the TNMM) which requires a significantly stronger comparability between the tested party and the comparables. Gross margins data are also more rarely available in databases (though increasingly) and are subject to accounting differences between country rules and accounting standards.

## 2.3 How to Use It?

According to the practical experience in interpreting the OECD Guidelines, it is suggested to follow a three-step procedure in the application of the TNMM. The first step is the delineation of the transaction. The second step is the determination of the net profit level indicator (net PLI), and lastly is the determination of an arm's length range of PLI value for the case at hand often through a comparable company search. These three steps are further described hereinafter together with (i) advanced applications of the TNMM and (ii) how to operate a TNMM-based transfer pricing system.

### 2.3.1 *Delineation of the Transaction*

Transaction delineation makes reference to a segmentation of a company's activity into several business segments (business lines) aiming to correspond to an intra-group transaction (or a relevant aggregation thereof) which make commercial sense and would enable understanding and pricing the relationships between the parties.

As such, the concept of aggregation of the intra-group transactions in order to reliably apply the TNMM is key as per the provisions of the OECD Guidelines:

> As a matter of principle, only those items that (a) directly or indirectly relate to the controlled transaction at hand and (b) are of an operating nature should be taken into account in the determination of the net profit indicator for the application of the transactional net margin method.[5]
>
> Costs and revenues that are not related to the controlled transaction under review should be excluded where they materially affect comparability with uncontrolled transactions. An appropriate level of segmentation of the taxpayer's financial data is needed when determining or testing the net profit it earns from a controlled transaction (or from transactions that are appropriately aggregated according to the guidance at paragraphs 3.9–3.12). Therefore, it would be inappropriate to apply the transactional net margin method on a company-wide basis if the company engages in a variety of different controlled transactions that cannot be appropriately compared on an aggregate basis with those of an independent enterprise.[6]

---

5. Paragraph 2.83, 2017 OECD Guidelines.
6. Paragraph 2.84, 2017 OECD Guidelines.

In practice, if the company operates several types of businesses, for instance, an autonomous business (in which no intra-group dealing occurs) and an intra-group business, then a segmented profit and loss statement (P&L) is likely to be required. Conversely, in the event that there are similar sets of intra-group transactions between two transacting parties (for instance, product transactions), these transactions should not be disaggregated for the purpose of the application of the TNMM but, on the contrary, they should be aggregated. This means that the target net margin of one party to the transaction involved in the application of the TNMM will be determined based on all of the similar transactions and not based on each individual transaction. In this context, the preparation of a segmented P&L is usually a complex exercise, in particular the allocation of operating expenses such as selling, general and administrative expenses (SG&As).

### 2.3.2   Definition of the Net PLI

The selection of a net PLI is discussed in the OECD Guidelines in paragraphs 2.82–2.108. A net PLI is a ratio of (i) the net profit for the activity that is appropriately segmented[7] divided by (ii) an appropriate financial metric.[8]

Considering the OECD guidance, the following net PLI may be distinguished:

- Net cost plus (NCP[9]): i.e., net operating profits divided by the fully loaded costs related to the activity (i.e., all costs between sales and EBIT including, for instance, the indirect costs related to support functions). Operating profit is used as opposed to net profit because the net profit is impacted by both extraordinary and financial items. Extraordinary items are, by definition, non-recurring and specific to one company in particular and, as such, do not represent a normal pace of business which is what is looked for in TNMM analyses. Financial items represent the very nature of the financing choices of a company and, therefore, are specific as well depending on the choices of capital structures.
- Return on sales (ROS): i.e., net operating profits divided by the sales.

The NCP is often used in the context of service provision/manufacturing while the ROS is used in the case of distribution to third parties.

The selection of a PLI should be grounded on:

- an understanding of the tested party's role and responsibility in the total value chain of the group,
- the type of financial items that this tested party is in a position to influence and can be held responsible for, and
- the intra-group dealings that the tested party is involved with.

---

7. Paragraphs 2.83–2.91, 2017 OECD Guidelines.
8. Paragraphs 2.92–2.105, 2017 OECD Guidelines.
9. Return on Total Costs is often used.

Companies within a group that operate as cost centres are responsible for producing a product or a service within budget limits are generally responsible for cost optimization and quality but not for sales/revenues. The profitability of such cost centres is well tested using a NCP as costs are the primary items for which they are responsible. This is even more valid when all (or most of) the costs within their P&L consist of external costs that are not influenced by any intra-group dealings.

Companies within a group that operate as revenue or distribution centres are responsible for sales maximisation and are responsible for sales/revenues origination. The profitability of such revenue centres is well tested using a ROS as revenues are the main items for which they are responsible. This is even more true when all (or most of) the revenues within their P&L consist of external revenues that are not influenced by any intra-group dealings.

Both the NCP and ROS are PLIs are based on the P&L (not the balance sheet) and are arithmetically associated.[10] However, the selection of one PLI over another should be done cautiously as well as being justified and documented.

While, in practice, the TNMM is most commonly used with an NCP or ROS, other net PLIs may be considered as well such as:

- Return on assets (ROA[11]): i.e., operating profits divided by the value of the assets (market value or, in another, more common variant, book value) operated in the context of the tested activity. It is sometimes used *'where assets (rather than costs or sales) are a better indicator of the valued added by the tested party'*.[12] This net PLI, for instance, may be used in the case of asset-intensive industries (e.g., real estate or financial services).
- Return on capital employed (ROCE): i.e., Earnings Before Interest and Tax (EBIT) / Capital Employed as a financial ratio that measures a company's profitability and the efficiency with which its capital is employed.
- Berry ratio: i.e., gross profits to operating expenses.[13] It is sometimes used *'where a taxpayer purchases goods from an associated enterprise and on-sells them to other associated enterprises'*.[14] In practice, the Berry ratio equals to 1 plus a return applied to the sole operating expenses. The Berry ratio provides a measure of profit only by reference to the operating expenses of a company excluding the costs of goods sold (COGS).

ROA and ROCE can be relevant PLIs in asset-intensive industries. These are the financial ratios that the companies communicate on publicly in their annual reports and utilize as internal indicators to assess their performance. In a transfer pricing context, these ratios have been less frequently used in Europe than the NCP or ROS for the following reasons:

---

10. As a matter of fact, ROS and NCP can be associated arithmetically:NCP = ROS / (1 – ROS)ROS = NCP / (1 + NCP).
11. Also called 'Return on Capital Employed' or 'ROCE'.
12. Paragraph 2.103, 2017 OECD Guidelines.
13. That is, costs booked between the gross profit and the operating profit.
14. Paragraph 2.108, 2017 OECD Guidelines.

- The denominator (assets or capital employed) is not a straightforward measure; what is observed is the balance sheet book value information – which book value may be close to or far from the market value (depending, for instance, on whether the company has re-evaluated its assets as part of an acquisition or for other reasons).
- The 'age' of the assets is a key determinant of the total value of the assets. When these ratios apply to capital-intensive industries, the extent to which they are depreciated matters significantly in the total weight of the assets in comparison to other indicators. When using the ROA and ROCE, adjustments need to be performed to cope with differences between the age of the assets of comparables and the age of the assets of the tested party.

It is worth noting that the OECD does not provide an exhaustive list of PLIs. As a general rule, it states that the denominator should be *'reasonably independent from controlled transactions'*[15] and *'capable of being measured in a reliable and consistent manner at the level of the taxpayer's controlled transactions and of the comparable uncontrolled transactions'.*[16] As such, the OECD refers to *'floor area of retail points, weight of products transported, number of employees, time, distance'.*[17] For instance, as per the OECD, *'for financial activities where the making and receiving of advances constitutes the ordinary business of the taxpayer, it will generally be appropriate to consider the effect of interest and amounts in the nature of interest when determining the NPI'.*[18]

### 2.3.3 Determining an Arm's Length Return

The most important step – and most time-consuming – in a TNMM analysis is determining the appropriate value for the net PLI by reference to the financial results of comparable independent companies.

The section below presents the generic process in five steps for the application of the TNMM following a comparable company search that was performed on a public database (*see* Figure 4.1). Such public databases include Bureau Van Dijk's Orbis,[19] Factset, or Compustat.[20] As per Figure 4.1, a comparable search should be an iterative process. In this regard, the work of the EU JTPF on comparables outlines in detail a possible practical approach for undertaking comparable searches.[21]

---

15. Paragraph 2.94, 2017 OECD Guidelines.
16. Paragraph 2.95, 2017 OECD Guidelines.
17. Paragraph 2.105, 2017 OECD Guidelines.
18. Paragraph 2.89, 2017 OECD Guidelines.
19. Orbis is a worldwide database. It subsumes regional databases such as Amadeus (Europe), Oriana (Asia-Pacific), and a number of jurisdiction-specific databases.
20. In particular for North-American searches.
21. EU JTPF Report on the use of comparables in the EU, June 2016 DOC: JTPF/007/2016/REV/EN, accessible at https://ec.europa.eu/taxation_customs/sites/taxation/files/jtpf0072016reven comparablesreport_.pdf.

*Figure 4.1   Five-Step Process to Determine the Arm's Length Value for the Net PLI*

### 2.3.3.1   Defining the Scope of the Search

The TNMM involves the definition of screenings to identify the companies that are most comparable within the database. Before entering into this process, it is necessary to identify the profile of comparable companies that will be searched for. This should be grounded on the understanding of the industry structure and the type of company profiles within it that may qualify as being involved in the benchmarked activity. On some occasions, the industry analysis will suggest that it will likely be difficult to identify companies within a specific industry segment, for instance, in that event that these companies are no longer operating in a certain geographic zone or in the case that these companies have been vertically integrated by large MNEs and, therefore, no longer qualify as being independent.

In the absence of such a profiling of comparable companies, it may be that the search process and results are less reliable and the outcome of the search more aleatory: comparables will likely not form a homogeneous group within an industry segment.

Usually, the scope of the search may be further outlined in a dedicated section of the search write-up which will serve as a foundation for the application of the comparability criteria in the search strategy and the manual review below.

### 2.3.3.2   Defining the Search Strategy

The first step in the analysis is to define a search strategy (i.e., an automated query on the search engine database). Typically, this search shall entail a logical combination of different screenings to ensure that only relevant active independent companies in the selected geography with available data are selected. A turnover threshold is usually considered as well in order to exclude too small companies.

The most important steps would be the steps related to the actual activity that is being sought. This is usually reflected through the consideration of one of several industry codes (e.g., SIC, NACE). Industry NACE codes can be used in combination with keywords (inclusion or rejection keywords) that are related to the description of the activity.

Typically, a search strategy would encompass the following steps:

- Business scope: The business activities of the tested party may be the primary field of interest. It is often approached by selecting one or several Industry

Codes. A number of practitioners also use inclusion or rejection keywords based on the activity test description to refine their set.

- Independence: Only entities without intra-group transactions should be taken as a reference point.[22] Otherwise, the results of these entities could reflect non arm's length situations. In practice, most search strategies, therefore, only seek to identify 'independent' companies, as – for example, in Orbis – shown below:

> Companies where a single shareholder holds more than 50%[23] direct or total ownership (except companies owned by a private person) were excluded. Companies owning subsidiaries at 50% or more of ownership, and without available consolidated accounts, were also excluded.

Competitors or peers of the taxpayer generally fail to be relevant comparables under the TNMM as they usually encompass much wider functions than the normally narrower set of functions involved in the intra-group transactions.

- Geography: It is common to restrict the search to territories with an economic environment (macro-economic environment, industry structure, maturity of the tested party's industry locally) that is comparable to the tested party's. Comparable searches are typically done on a local/country basis or regional basis, provided that the OECD encourages a comparability of 'economic circumstances' between the market(s) in which the tested party operates and the markets of the comparable companies.

Practical experience shows that most practitioners usually consider either the Pan-European, North-American, or Pan-Asian areas.

Comparable company searches for tested parties in emerging countries is a sub-field of its own. For instance, the toolkit published by the Platform for Collaboration on Tax (PTC) a joint initiative of the International Monetary Fund (IMF), the OECD, United Nations, and the World Bank Group (WBG) on addressing the ways that developing countries can overcome a lack of data on 'comparables' or the market prices for goods and services transferred between members of multinational corporations can be referred to.[24]

---

22. Even though the OECD points out in para. 2.11 of the 2017 OECD Guidelines that 'evidence from enterprises engaged in controlled transactions with associated enterprises may be useful in understanding the transaction under review or as a pointer to further investigation'.
23. The percentage threshold for independence varies by local legislation.
24. Platform for Collaboration on Tax, A Toolkit for Addressing Difficulties in Accessing Comparables Data for Transfer Pricing Analyses, available at http://www.oecd.org/tax/toolkit-on-comparability-and-mineral-pricing.pdf. For more discussions on this topic, also *see* S. Gonnet, V. Starkov, and M. Maitra, 'Comparability Adjustments in the Absence of Suitable Local Comparables in Emerging and Developing Economies,' Transfer Pricing International Journal, July 2013; V. Starkov, S. Gonnet, A. Pletz, and M. Maitra, 'Comparability Adjustments in the Absence

– Availability of financial data: Often, additional criteria related to financial data (e.g., availability of financial data over a certain period, etc.) are also considered.

Practically speaking, the number of companies under review after quantitative screenings often ranges from one hundred to several hundred companies.

### 2.3.3.3 Manual Review

The characteristics of the potentially comparable companies are then to be reviewed in detail to check their comparability. The manual review of the companies is on a case-by-case basis. This step usually includes an examination of the websites of the companies in order to ascertain their appropriateness in terms of comparability.

The main reasons for rejections are usually: (1) differences in functions performed, (2) differences in products/industry, (3) lack of independence, and (4) insufficient information.

Based on practical experience, the number of companies at the completion of the manual review often ranges from four or five (sometimes less) to fifteen or twenty.

### 2.3.3.4 Adjustments

The use of the TNMM may require a number of adjustments. Comparability adjustments[25] are discussed in paragraphs 3.47–3.54 of the 2017 OECD Guidelines.

The most common adjustment in the TNMM is the working capital adjustment, which is described in an Annex to Chapter III of the 2017 OECD Guidelines. However, many other adjustments exist.

Other types of adjustments are devised and used, but they should be used *'if (and only if) they are expected to increase the reliability of the results'*[26] and *'the need to perform numerous or substantial adjustments to key comparability factors may indicate that the third party transactions are in fact not sufficiently comparable.'*[27]

---

of Suitable Local Comparables in Emerging and Developing Economies – Case Studies,' Transfer Pricing International Journal, March 2014; V. Starkov, M. Maitra, and A. Li, 'Comparability Adjustments in the Absence of Suitable Local Comparables in Emerging and Developing Economies – Adjustment for Risk,' Transfer Pricing International Journal, May 2015; V. Starkov, S. Gonnet, and G. Madelpuech Comments by NERA Economic Consulting on the Draft Toolkit for Addressing Difficulties in Accessing Comparables Data for Transfer Pricing Analyses.

25. For a literature review of comparability adjustments in transfer pricing please refer to: M. Petutschnig and S. Chroustovsky, 'Comparability Adjustments A Literature Review' (October 1, 2018). WU International Taxation Research Paper Series No. 2018-08. Available at SSRN: https://ssrn.com/abstract = 3266107.
26. Paragraph 3.50, 2017 OECD Guidelines.
27. Paragraph 3.51, 2017 OECD Guidelines.

*2.3.3.5   Interpreting the Results*

The OECD discusses the ways to establish an arm's length range in paragraphs 3.55–3.66 and 3.75–3.79. It particularly states that '*where the range comprises results of relatively equal and high reliability, it could be argued that any point in the range satisfies the arm's length principle.*'[28]

Yet, in practice, practitioners typically consider an interquartile range of results for determining an arm's length range, which is also suggested by the OECD.[29] The interquartile range is the range of observations comprised between the 25th and 75th percentile of the sample (i.e., for a sample with 100 observations, taking out the first and the last 25 and keeping the remaining 50).

This range often uses multiple year data (often either three or five years, possibly weighted by the sales or costs of the comparables in the set) in order to increase the reliability of the analysis. As there is a time lag in the publication of data, it is common that the tested year (for instance, 2016) will be documented using data from previous years (for instance 2013–2015), as more recent data would not be available.

## 2.3.4   Advanced Applications

Section 2.3.3 has described the typical process for determining an arm's length range based on a comparable company search by using a public database. This section, on the other hand, discusses the advanced application of the TNMM without relying on a public database.

While, in most cases, the application of the TNMM in practice involves the search for external comparables in public databases, the application of a TNMM may also involve the search for external evidence of net margins outside public databases. For instance, if the MNE has similar dealings with external parties than the ones tested, it may be relevant to search for the net margins for such external parties in order to assess the target net margin that the tested party should earn. This is a different application of the TNMM compared to the typical application involving a search in public databases.

However, challenges may arise when using the advanced application of the TNMM. The first difficulty is that, generally there are fewer comparables available by using this approach than a typical search in public databases. Second, the selection of comparables may appear to be random and arbitrary compared to a process of objectively screening all comparables within a defined perimeter. Lastly, yet importantly, adequate financial data may not be available for the companies that the MNE

---

28. Paragraph 3.62, 2017 OECD Guidelines.
29. Paragraph 3.57, 2017 OECD Guidelines.

has dealings with. However, internal comparables usually present a substantially higher level of comparability than external comparables, which is an advantage of using the advanced method.

### 2.3.5 Operating a TNMM-Based Transfer Pricing System

The TNMM may be used both as a price setting (i.e., ex-ante) and a price testing (i.e., ex-post) method.

In most cases, the TNMM is used as a price testing method, notably in compliant documentation reports. Such reports do not necessarily discuss and justify in detail how individual prices are determined but rather demonstrate that the actual operating profits of the selected tested parties fall within an interquartile range of PLIs of comparable companies.

The TNMM is also utilized for price setting, however, prices in this case are not based directly on the application of the TNMM; the TNMM provides a measure of profits that allows prices to be set (for instance, by adding certain costs to that measure of profits, which is often referred to as the net cost plus method).

---

**Example**

The case study below illustrates the challenges related to the implementation of a TNMM-based system. The facts of the case are:

(a) The Chinese plant of a leading industrial company manufactures products for the Group and sells its production to distributors which are responsible for the sales budget process and placing orders.

(b) The transfer pricing policy of the Group relies on a TNMM with the net cost as the profit level indicator and a 10% margin resulting from benchmarking studies.

(c) In the sales budget process, the distributors make an estimation of orders for the following year of 10,000 units. The 10,000 units serve as a basis for the Chinese plant to determine the unit price by taking into account its projected costs and the transfer pricing policy agreed upon with the distributors. Figure 4.2 provides details about the unit price determination.

---

*Figure 4.2    The Determination of the Unit Price*

| Plant P&L | Budget |
|---|---|
| Volumes | 10000 |
| Transfer Price (per unit) | 0.011 |
| Revenues | 110 |
| Cost of Goods | 35 |
| OPEX – variable | 40 |
| OPEX – fixed | 25 |
| Operating Profit | 10 |
| Return on Total Costs | 10% |

(d) In the above budget process, the Chinese plant targets 10% of its cost base of 100 (Cost of Goods 35 plus Operating Expenses 65 which include OPEX – variable 40 and OPEX – fixed 25), meaning that the target operating profit is 10. In order for the plant to reach 10 operating profit, it needs revenues of 110 which necessitates a transfer price of 0.011 given volumes of 10000 (110/10000).

(e) In the course of the reforecasting in the following year, it appears that the orders placed by the distributors are expected to be 40% lower than expected (6000 units instead of 10000). This decrease in orders leads to the following options:

  – Option 1: the 0.011 unit price is considered at arm's length and has been agreed upon between the parties in a one-year agreement. It was based on the application of a TNMM and, therefore, can be considered at arm's length. Applying the 0.011 unit price leads to the following financial equilibrium for the plant: 1) revenues of the plant are decreasing accordingly down to 66 (6000*0.011); 2) total costs of the plant decrease as well (as lower volumes lead to lower Cost of Goods – for instance, raw materials and also lower variable costs). Still, the amount of costs does not decrease to the same extent as revenues (70 instead of 100 – a decrease of 30%, while the revenues decrease by 40%). As a result, the plant incurs a loss of 5.7, which is equal to a -5.7% operating margin. Figure 4.3 provides the P&L of the plant under this Option 1.

*Figure 4.3   P&L of the Chinese Plant under Option 1*

| Plant P&L | Option 1 - Lower volumes/reforecasting |
|---|---|
| Volume | 6000 |
| Transfer Price (per unit) | 0.011 |
| Revenues | 66 |
| Cost of Goods | 21 |
| OPEX – variable | 24 |
| OPEX – fixed | 25 |
| Operating Profit | (4) |
| Return on Total Costs | –5.7% |

– Option 2: the 10% markup on total costs is considered at arm's length and has been agreed upon between the parties in a one-year agreement. It was based on the application of a TNMM and, therefore, can be considered at arm's length. Applying the 10% markup on total costs leads to the following financial equilibrium for the plant: the revised unit price as part of the reforecasting is calculated to leave a 10% markup (equal to a positive operating profit of 7) on the plant's revised cost base (70). In order for the plant to reach 7 of operating profit, it needs revenues of 77, which necessitates a transfer price of 0.013 given volumes of 6000 (77/6000). Figure 4.4 provides the P&L of the plant under this Option 2.

*Figure 4.4   P&L of the Chinese Plant under Option 2*

| Plant P&L | Option 2 - Lower volumes/reforecasting |
|---|---|
| Volume | 6000 |
| Transfer Price (per unit) | 0.013 |
| Revenues | 77 |
| Cost of Goods | 21 |
| OPEX – variable | 24 |
| OPEX – fixed | 25 |
| Operating Profit | 7 |
| Return on Total Costs | 10% |

Both Option 1 and Option 2 appear to be fair applications of the TNMM, however, they lead to totally different outcomes.

The purpose of this case study is not to comment on which option, Option 1 or Option 2, is more indicative of what independent parties would have negotiated at arm's length conditions but rather to demonstrate that, even when a method has been selected (TNMM in this case), when a PLI has been selected (net cost plus, in this case), and when a benchmarking study provides an indication of the arm's length level of margin (10% in this case), the implementation of such a method necessitates caution and a comprehensive understanding of the financial and commercial relationships of the parties in the specific case at hand and an evaluation of how third parties would have behaved in similar circumstances. In such a case, it is presumable that parties would have agreed in advance on the conditions under which the price would be renegotiable depending on changes of order/volumes placements by distributors.

## 2.4   Critical Aspects

As a conclusion, based on practical experience, the three most common pitfalls in applying the TNMM would be those indicated below:

– Is the TNMM indeed the most appropriate method?
    As outlined in section 2.2, the TNMM may not be an appropriate method in all circumstances. In particular, if an activity comparable to that undertaken by

the group company may not be reliably found in the marketplace because the group company possesses unique intangibles, for instance, then the TNMM may not be the most appropriate method.

– Is it correctly applied in terms of scope?

The TNMM commands the use of the costs and revenues (typically a segmented P&L) only related to the tested activity.

– Are the 'comparables' comparable?

The quality of the comparable data is (as with the other methods) at the cornerstone of the TNMM.

# 3  TRANSACTIONAL PROFIT SPLIT METHOD[30]

## 3.1  What Is It?

### 3.1.1  Definition

The TPSM is described in Chapter II, Part III.C of the OECD Guidelines.[31]

According to the OECD, '[t]he transactional profit split method seeks to establish arm's length outcomes or test reported outcomes for controlled transactions in order to approximate the results that would have been achieved between independent enterprises engaging in a comparable transaction or transactions. The method first identifies the profits to be split from the controlled transactions the relevant profits and then splits them between the associated enterprises on an economically valid basis that approximates the division of profits that would have been agreed at arm's length. As is the case with all transfer pricing methods, the aim is to ensure that profits of the associated enterprises are aligned with the value of their contributions.'[32] (emphasis added)

### 3.1.2  Contribution and Residual Analysis

The OECD identifies two types of TPSMs, i.e., the contribution analysis and the residual analysis.

---

30. S. Gonnet, 'Recent Developments in the Profit Split Method – Application of the Method', in *Transfer Pricing Developments Around The World 2018*, edited by M. Lang, A. Storck and R. Petruzzi (Wolters Kluwer, 2018; S. Gonnet, 'Recent Developments in the Profit Split Method – Circumstances of Application of the Method', in *Transfer Pricing Developments Around The World 2017*, edited by M. Lang, A. Storck and R. Petruzzi (Wolters Kluwer, 2017).

31. At the time of this writing, the latest document issued by the OECD on the Transactional Profit Split Method is the Revised Guidance on the Application of the Transactional Profit Split Method, June 2018 (the '2018 Guidance'). This document was approved by the Inclusive Framework on BEPS on 4 June 2018 and prepared for publication in the OECD Guidelines by the OECD Secretariat. For an overview of the development of the Profit Split Method, *see* Petruzzi & X. Peng, The Profit Split Method: Historical Evolution and BEPS Insights, Transfer Pricing International 1 (2/2017), pp. 44–54.

32. Paragraph 2.114, 2018 Guidance.

**Contribution analysis**

Under a contribution analysis, the relevant profits, which are the total profits from the controlled transactions under examination, are divided between the associated enterprises in order to arrive at a reasonable approximation of the division of profits that independent enterprises would have achieved from engaging in comparable transactions.[33]

**Residual analyses**

As discussed further, thereafter, whether it is based on external or internal data, the application of the Contribution PSM involves challenges considering the absence – in most cases – of reliable techniques to split the total profits.

This explains why a second type of TPSM has been more widely used in past years and will likely continue being used in future years: the Residual Profit Split Method. The reason for its success is that it mitigates some of the intrinsic uncertainties related the use of the Contribution PSM.

A residual analysis is appropriate when the contributions of the parties can be separated into two categories and analysed in two stages (*see* Figure 4.5):

(1) the first step relates to the contributions that can be reliably benchmarked:
   – Typically simpler, 'routine' contributions for which reliable comparables can be found.
   – Ordinarily, this initial remuneration would be determined by applying one of the traditional transaction methods
(2) the second step concerns the allocation of the residual profit among the parties. It will be based on the relative value of the contributions which may be unique and valuable and/or are attributable to a high level of integration or the shared assumption of economically significant risks of parties in the same way as in the application of the contribution analysis outlined above in respect of Contribution PSM.[34]

Based on the practical experience, the RPSM is less likely to yield extreme results even if the determination of the split factor remains difficult.

## 3.2 When to Use It?

The OECD provides that the TPSM should not be considered as the most appropriate method in all situations by stating that *'the selection of the 'most appropriate' method should take into account the relative appropriateness and reliability of the selected method as compared to other methods which could be used'*.[35]

---

33. Paragraph 2.150, 2018 Guidance.
34. Paragraph 2.152, 2018 Guidance.
35. Paragraph 2.118, 2018 Guidance.

More specifically, the OECD identifies three situations when the TPSM is most likely to be the most appropriate method: (1) unique and valuable contributions, (2) highly integrated business operations, and (3) shared assumption of economically significant risks or a separate assumption of closely related risks. Historically, only the first two situations were within the scope according to the 2010 OECD Guidelines.[36]

**Unique and Valuable Contributions**

'[The TPSM offers] a solution for cases where both parties to a transaction make unique and valuable contributions (e.g., contribute unique and valuable intangibles) to the transaction:

– *In such a case independent parties might effectively share the profits of the transaction in proportion to their respective contributions, making a two-sided method more appropriate.*
– *Furthermore, since those contributions are 'unique' and 'valuable' there will be no reliable comparables information which could be used to price the entirety of the transaction in a more reliable way, through the application of another method.'[37]*

**Highly integrated business operations**

'[The TPSM] can also provide a solution for highly integrated operations in cases for which a one-sided method would not be appropriate.'[38] It is also worth mentioning that '[w]here the contributions are highly inter-related or inter-dependent upon each other, the evaluation of the respective contributions of the parties may need to be done holistically.'[39]

**Shared assumption of economically significant risks or separate assumption of closely related risks**

'Where there is a high degree of uncertainty for each of the parties in relation to a transaction, (for example in transactions involving the shared assumption of economically significant risks by all parties), the flexibility of the [TPSM] can allow for the determination of arm's-length profits for each party that vary with the actual outcomes of the risks associated with the transaction.'[40]

In particular, a lack of comparables is not enough to command the use of the TPSM. Yet, the absence of such comparables may point to the fact that the TPSM is indeed the most appropriate transfer pricing method for the case. 'In general, it will tend to be the case that the presence of factors indicating that a [TPSM] is the most appropriate method will correspond to an absence of factors indicating that an alternative transfer pricing method one which relies entirely on comparables is the most

---

36. Paragraph 2.109, 2010 OECD Guidelines.
37. Paragraph 2.119, 2018 Guidance.
38. Paragraph 2.120, 2018 Guidance.
39. Paragraph 2.138, 2018 Guidance.
40. Paragraph 2.121, 2018 Guidance.

*appropriate method. ... [I]f information on reliable comparable uncontrolled transactions is available to price the transaction in its entirety, it is less likely that the transactional profit split method will be the most appropriate method. However, a lack of comparables alone is insufficient to warrant the use of a transactional profit split.*[41]

In brief, if the TPSM is not supported by the facts and circumstances; its application in inappropriate circumstances will likely provide unreasonable results. Even in the event that comparables data are scarce, other methods that more heavily rely on comparables may still be the most reliable provided that proper adjustments can be performed.

## 3.3 How to Use It?

### 3.3.1 Understanding the Nature of the Transaction

Like with the application of any transfer pricing method, the selection and application of the TPSM must be grounded on an understanding of the nature of the accurately delineated controlled transaction.[42] As an example in practice, a tool often used in the Functional analysis (FAR) to reveal the group's value creation process is called the Value Chain Analysis (VCA). Both the FAR and the VCA are relevant for obtaining what the OECD refers to as a 'broad based understanding'[43] of the economics of the MNE Group.

As discussed in publications,[44] the VCA is a fundamental tool for understanding value creation within an MNE, for qualifying contributions of the various MNE's entities to value creation, and for structuring (and ultimately quantifying) the financial and commercial relationships between group entities with regard to the respective contributions of transacting parties enlightened by the VCA. The VCA, therefore, is not another approach for applying the TPSM but, instead, include the initial steps to be performed before determining the type of financial and commercial relationships that parties should enter into and delineating the transactions that are the reflection of those relationships.

Using a tool such as the VCA does not mean that the TPSM is the most appropriate method for the case by default. However, when the TPSM is ultimately selected as a transfer pricing method, the VCA certainly helps for understanding the parties' unique contributions and/or the assumption of economically significant risks in the value chain.

---

41. Paragraph 2.143, 2018 Guidance.
42. Paragraph 2.125 and s. C.2.2, 2018 Guidance.
43. Paragraph 1.34, 2017 OECD Guidelines.
44. S. Gonnet, Risks Redefined in Transfer Pricing Post-BEPS, in: M. Lang, A. Storck & R. Petruzzi (eds), Transfer Pricing in a Post-BEPS World (Vienna: Kluwer, 2016), pp. 33–59.

### 3.3.2   Typology of TPSMs

The critical step is the determination of the 'profit splitting factor'.[45] It is discussed in more detail hereinafter.

The profit splitting factor is the factor effectively relied upon to attribute the arm's length share of the total or profit to the various parties. The OECD lists as examples, in particular, asset-based factors[46] and costs-based factors.[47]

As described in Chapter 2, a VCA is a powerful tool for qualitatively assessing the respective contribution of transacting parties in the context of a specific transaction. The Value Chain Analysis informs about the contribution of the parties, it can therefore be particularly helpful in the consideration of the determination of profit splitting factors, even though it does not necessarily provide a direct estimation of the contribution of the various activities (or value drivers) without further analyses.

The quantification of the VCA requires the use of economic methods and is likely to provide reliable results only to the extent that such quantification is grounded on economics. Some illustrations are provided below of approaches for the purpose of the determination of the contribution of the parties and, as such, the determination of the profit splitting factor.

#### 3.3.2.1   Comparable Profit Split Method

The most direct manner to obtain the above-mentioned approximation is to rely on comparable data: how, in similar circumstances, third parties would have split the profits resulting from the transaction. This sharing of profits may be obtained when the MNE has similar transactions with third parties (as with group entities) and when financial information of the independent parties is available.

This approach also qualifies as the Comparable Profit Split Method (CPSM), which is specified in US Regulations per se (not specifically in the OECD Guidelines – even if the OECD Guidelines describe all of the parameters of the application of the method without specifically quoting it as 'CPSM'). The US Regulations provide the following definition that, '[u]nder [the CPSM], each uncontrolled taxpayer's percentage of the combined operating profit or loss is used to allocate the combined operating profit or loss of the relevant business activity'.[48]

The OECD specifies that,

> One possible approach is to split the relevant profits based on the division of profits that actually is observed in comparable uncontrolled transactions.

---

45. Section C.5.1, 2018 Guidance.
46. Paragraphs 2.179-2.180, 2018 Guidance.
47. Paragraphs 2.181-2.183, 2018 Guidance.
48. US Treasury Regs s. 1.482-6(c)(2)(i).

External market data can be relevant in the profit split analysis to assess the value of contributions that each associated enterprise makes to the transactions. In effect, the assumption is that independent parties would have split relevant profits in proportion to the value of their respective contributions to the generation of profit in the transaction.[49]

This approach relates to the CUP because the starting point is a relationship between the company and a third party. Instead of using the price (for a goods/services transactions) or the royalty percentage (for a license) concluded with the third party, the CPSM uses the sharing of profits that result from the transaction for the purpose of setting the internal transactions. The underlying assumption is that prices and/or royalties may be more sensitive to differences of comparability while the sharing of profits resulting from an arm's length negotiation may be less so.[50]

---

**Example**

Group A has an arrangement with a third party, Party B. An appropriate analysis shows that, under this arrangement, A and B share the jointly created or combined profits at 70% for A and 30% for B. Then, within A, two parties, A1 and A2, have an intra-group arrangement that is comparable to the arrangement between A and B, and A1 is considered comparable to A and A2 is considered comparable to B, in this respect. As such, in this example, the CPSM would conclude that the intra-group arrangement between A1 and A2 is at arm's length if the allocation of the jointly created or combined profit between A1 and A2 is 70% for A1 and 30% for A2.

---

In Figure 4.5, the respective share of profits of the buyer and seller within the taxpayer are determined based on the share of profits that the comparable buyer and seller achieve in similar transactions.

---

49. Paragraph 2.167 and 2.168, 2018 Guidance.
50. For a more practical and detailed overview of the CPSM, *see* 1999 article by former NERA experts Dr Richard P. Rozek and George G. Korenko, where economic studies have demonstrated the economic rationale for using the CPSM for blockbuster in the pharmaceutical industry in particular; Richard P. Rozek and George G. Korenko, Transfer Prices for the Intangible Property Embodied in Products With Extraordinary Profit Potentials, Tax Notes International, Vol. 19, No. 16, 18 Oct. 1999.

*Figure 4.5   CPSM*

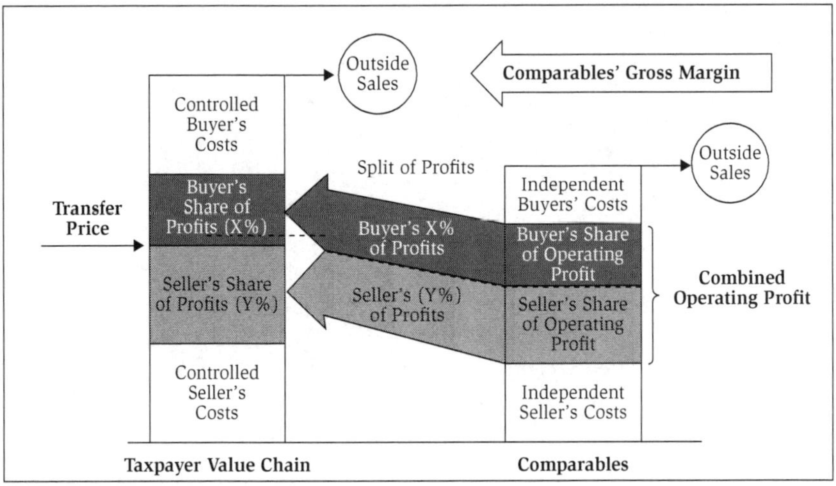

Based on practical experience, the CPSM can be considered as being a reliable transfer pricing method. Nevertheless, it requires available financial information on both sides of the transactions. In transaction with third parties, it is rarely the case that the third party discloses its own financial information, notably the profits that it makes in relation to the contract. In the absence of such information, the method cannot apply. Industries which involve the greatest number of contractual agreements with third parties are the best candidates for this method.

### 3.3.2.2   Entrepreneurial Investment Based TPSM

As part of a TPSM, the contribution of the parties can be derived from an evaluation of the investments made by each party to intangibles creation and/or value-added activities.

The underlying assumption is that the respective contribution of the parties can be assessed based on the investments each party has made in relation to intangibles building, taking into account that such investment may not yield an immediate benefit (e.g., due to gestation lag, notably for R&D spending) or have a long life duration.

As such, using capitalized costs is not equivalent to comparing the yearly investments that are made by each party. The profit splitting factor of year Y is derived from the intangible-building investments that are not only incurred in year Y but also those incurred in previous years. This reflects the fact that, in reality, an intangible-building investment will generate return not only the year it was incurred but also for a certain period of time.[51]

### 3.3.2.3 Compensation Based TPSM

An alternative to using the full costs of intangibles-building is to employ salary cost investments of the key staff that are involved in that activity. This may be particularly beneficial in contexts of an individuals' business where people are the core of value creation and can be held responsible for most risks (including strategic risks).

It can be contended that compensation payments reflect arm's length dealings between employers and employees which may be reflective of the value created by individual employees. As such, compensation-based profit splits may be used in certain circumstances.

Based on practical experience, this technique is most appropriate in situations when a limited number of individuals may be clearly identified as those individuals constituting the intangible-building functions. As such, it may be typically adapted to situations in the financial services industries (e.g., asset management, etc.).[52]

### 3.3.2.4 Other

There is not an exhaustive list of approaches for determining the contribution of parties and the profit splitting factor because the contribution of the parties relates to unique and valuable activities at the origin of the development of intangibles. Therefore, the most suitable approach must be determined by considering the facts and circumstances of the case and also in regard to data and information availability.

### 3.3.3 Key Aspects of the Use of TPSM

As evidenced earlier, even the TNMM, often presented as potentially the less complex TP method, involves challenges when the method is implemented in practice. This is obviously all the more true for the TPSM as it is a relatively complex method to implement.

In this respect, there are two critical aspects of the implementation of the TPSM which are also emphasized by the OECD. One aspect is that the TPSM is, as are all of the other methods, a transactional method. Therefore, the method should be on a

---

51. For a more detailed overview of the Capitalized Investments TPSM, *see* Harlow N. Higinbotham, The Profit Split Method: Effective Application for Precision and Administrability, BNA Tax Management Transfer Pricing Special Report. Vol. 5, No. 11 Report No. 24 2 Oct. 1996.
52. For further discussion, readers may refer to NERA presentation 'Transfer Pricing Challenge Designing the 'Perfect' Profit Split' by Emmanuel Llinares, Nihan Mert-Beydilli, Vladimir Starkov, National Association for Business Economics Transfer Pricing Symposium 21–23 Jul. 2015, Washington.

transactional basis and not on a company wide basis (unless the transaction in scope of the application of the TPSM covers the whole company).[53]

The other aspect is that the TPSM, in fact, has two variants.[54] The OECD introduces a relevant distinction between the TPSM based on actual profits and the TPSM based on anticipated profits:

> [i]f each party shares the assumption of economically significant risks or separately assumes inter-related, economically significant risks and a [TPSM] is considered to be the most appropriate method, [then] it is likely that a split of actual profits, rather than anticipated profits, will be warranted, since those actual profits (...) will reflect the playing out of the risks of each party.[55]

Under the TPSM of anticipated profits, the price of a transaction is established by reference to the share of profits that the parties expect to generate from that transaction; however, such parties do not contemporaneously share the risks related to the specific transaction in the same manner as the TPSM of actual profits. In most cases, transacting parties incur different types of risks (for instance, the licensor has incurred development risks while the licensee incurs market and operational risks) and not at the same time (early stage risks for one party, later stage risks for the other party). As a general rule, the analysis of whether or not parties actually share economically significant risks should be performed according to Chapter I, Section D of the 2017 OECD Guidelines in the context of transactions that are accurately delineated.

As pointed out previously, the TPSM is not a final recourse methodology. In transfer pricing, it is generally not straightforward to identify reliable comparables and, therefore, it may be tempting – both for taxpayers and tax authorities – to disregard methods involving the search for comparable third-party relationships and rely on some forms of profit apportionment between the parties. The OECD, however, has expressed a preference for searching for comparables and using the TPSM only when the facts and circumstances justify it.[56]

### 3.3.4. Operating a TPSM-based Transfer Pricing System

Similar to all other transfer pricing methods, the TPSM may be used as a price setting (i.e., ex-ante) and a price testing method (i.e., ex-post).

---

**Example**

The case study below illustrates the application of the TPSM for price setting. The facts of the case are:

---

53. Paragraph 2.114, 2018 Guidance.
54. S. Gonnet, Risks Redefined in Transfer Pricing Post-BEPS, in: M. Lang, A. Storck & R. Petruzzi (eds.), Transfer Pricing in a Post-BEPS World (Vienna: Kluwer, 2016).
55. Paragraph 2.142, 2018 Guidance.
56. Paragraph 2.128, 2018 Guidance.

(a) Affiliates A and B are project companies. They sell projects to clients that include products and services (design, engineering, production, and installation)

(b) Affiliate A and Affiliate B are jointly responsible for
- the response to tenders
- the subsequent operation of the contract (if won) and
- project management.

(c) Affiliate B contracts with the client and books sales while Affiliate A provides products and services (including design) to Affiliate B.

The first step would consist of determining the expected joint profits of A and B in relationship to Project X (*see* Figure 4.6).

*Figure 4.6   Expected Joint Profits of Affiliate A and B*

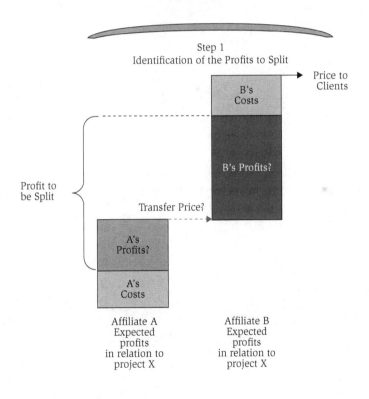

The second step would consist of determining the expected remuneration for the simple functions by benchmarking with functionally comparable and independent companies (*see* Figure 4.7).

*Figure 4.7   Expected Routine Returns on the Simple Functions*

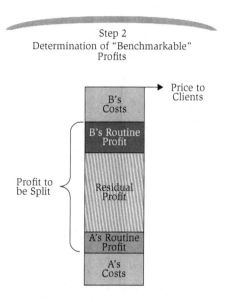

The third step would consist of determining the transfer price on the basis of an arm's length expected split of profits (*see* Figure 4.8). The residual profit (or loss) is allocated between the related parties based on the 'residual capital' associated with, for example, investments to develop, enhance, and maintain the value of key activities (e.g., design, engineering, and project management).

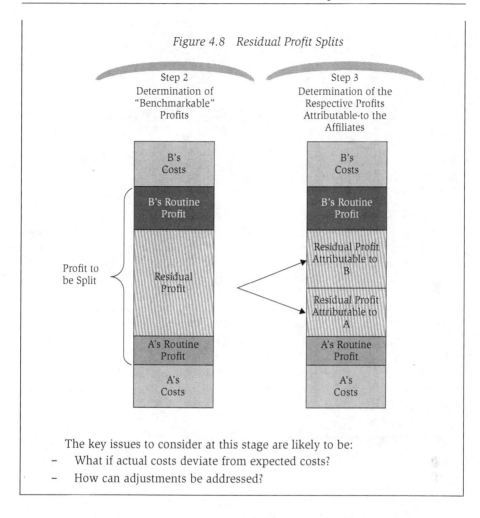

Figure 4.8   Residual Profit Splits

The key issues to consider at this stage are likely to be:
- What if actual costs deviate from expected costs?
- How can adjustments be addressed?

## 4   OTHER METHODS

### 4.1   Overview

The OECD Guidelines explicitly acknowledge the possibility of applying methods other than those outlined in the Guidelines.

> MNE groups retain the freedom to apply methods not described in these Guidelines (hereafter 'other methods') to establish prices provided those prices satisfy the arm's length principle in accordance with these Guidelines. Such other methods should however not be used in substitution for OECD-recognised methods where the latter are more appropriate to the facts and circumstances of the case. In cases where other methods are used, their selection should be supported by an explanation of why OECD-recognised methods were regarded as less appropriate or

non-workable in the circumstances of the case and of the reason why the selected other method was regarded as providing a better solution.[57]

Any method should be permitted where its application is agreeable to the members of the MNE group involved with the transaction or transactions to which the methodology applies and also to the tax administrations in the jurisdictions of all those members.[58]

As a matter of fact, a number of other methods exist including, but not limited to, the following items.

– Certain methods referred to by practitioners as 'non-OECD methods' are used by certain tax administrations, in particular in emerging countries. This would be the case of the so-called 'sixth method' which is applied among South-American administrations regarding commodities transactions.[59]

– A number of other pricing or valuation methods exist that were developed beyond the realm of the transfer pricing field. Certain aspects of some of these methods are discussed in Chapter VI, D.2.6.3 of the 2017 OECD Guidelines.

This section aims at providing an overview of valuation methods, mainly used to assess the price of asset transactions taking place in an intra-group context (as opposed to intra-group flows). The section also discussed the concept of option realistically available (ORA) which may not qualify as a method per se but as a framework which may often particularly be helpful in transfer pricing analyses. The non-OECD methods, such as the so-called 'sixth method', are not discussed in this section.

This section will notably cover the intricacy between OECD methods, valuation techniques, and ORAs:

– Valuation techniques relate to valuation of assets specifically. However, these techniques are/should be often deeply rooted in OECD transfer pricing methods. This is particularly the case for the Discounted Cash Flow (DCF) method and its variants (e.g., Relief from Royalty) that rely primarily upon estimates related to flows, which are often derived by using the CUP or TNMM method to define the profit component.

– Similarly, the application of ORAs relies in practice on the consideration of a combination of valuation techniques and/or OECD Transfer Pricing Methods.

---

57. Paragraph 2.9, 2017 OECD Guidelines. Please note that it could be contended that this paragraph relates only to 'price setting' methods. Conversely, it could be set forward that the overall context of this paragraph suggests that it also applies to 'price testing' methods.
58. Paragraph 2.11, 2017 OECD Guidelines.
59. For more details on this topic, see Ch. 3 of this book.

## 4.2  Valuation Techniques

The OECD has referred to valuation techniques more specifically in the context of valuations of intangibles (Chapter VI). This discussion primarily relates to valuation of intangibles as assets, in case for instance of a transfer between two companies within the same Group (Table 4.1).

### 4.2.1  Overview

'[V]aluation techniques may be used by taxpayers and tax administrations as a part of one of the five OECD transfer pricing methods described in Chapter II, or as a tool that can be usefully applied in identifying an arm's length price.'[60]

'[T]he application of income based valuation techniques, especially valuation techniques premised on the calculation of the discounted value of projected future income streams or cash flows derived from the exploitation of the intangible being valued, may be particularly useful when properly applied.'[61]

'[I]t is necessary to apply such techniques in a manner that is consistent with the arm's length principle and the principles of these Guidelines.'[62]

*Table 4.1   Commonly-Used Valuation Methods for the Evaluation of Intangible Assets*

| Valuation Method | | Remarks |
|---|---|---|
| Replacement cost approach | | Used only in certain specific circumstances |
| Comparable transaction method | | Rarely used due to lack of data – market for intangibles is not liquid |
| Discounted Cash Flow | Relief from royalty | Cash flows or intangible revenues are highly transfer pricing dependent |
| | Excess earnings method | Popular among valuation practitioners for accounting purposes; relies heavily on balance sheet data |
| | Real Options | Used in high uncertainty situations; a sophisticated DCF primarily used for some technology related intangibles |

---

60. Paragraph 6.153, 2017 OECD Guidelines.
61. *Ibid.*
62. Paragraph 6.154, 2017 OECD Guidelines.

The DCF method is one of the most common methods in valuation. It relies on the assumption that the value of an asset is equal to the net present value of all anticipated future cash flows. The discount rate used in the model particularly reflects the risk attached to these future cash flows. It is often used in combination with the Capital Asset Pricing Model (CAPM) which provides that, in a number of situations, the appropriate discount rate may derive from the Weighted Average Cost of Capital (WACC) of the company.

The task of discussing in detail the most common valuation techniques exceeds the scope of the book.[63] Towards this point, the OECD Guidelines refrain from attempting to comprehensively survey these techniques:

> It is not the intention of these Guidelines to set out a comprehensive summary of the valuation techniques utilised by valuation professionals. Similarly, it is not the intention of these Guidelines to endorse or reject one or more sets of valuation standards utilised by valuation or accounting professionals or to describe in detail or specifically endorse one or more specific valuation techniques or methods as being especially suitable for use in a transfer pricing analysis.[64]

At this stage, it is worth emphasizing that the valuation for accounting purposes (e.g., purchase price allocation in acquisition cases) may not always, as a general rule, be appropriate for transfer pricing purposes:

> Caution should [...] be exercised in accepting valuations performed for accounting purposes as necessarily reflecting arm's length prices or values for transfer pricing purposes without a thorough examination of the underlying assumptions. In particular, valuations of intangibles contained in purchase price allocations performed for accounting purposes are not determinative for transfer pricing purposes and should be utilised in a transfer pricing analysis with caution and careful consideration of the underlying assumptions.[65]

The determination of the arm's length value for intangibles is a realm of its own that is regulated by transfer pricing principles and possibly distinct, in certain aspects, from the usual standards observed in valuation for accounting purposes.

### 4.2.2 Critical Parameters

Yet, in the Guidelines, the OECD discusses five critical parameters of such valuation techniques:

---

63. One may, for instance, refer to the (non-transfer pricing related) handbook 'Investment Valuation: Tools and Techniques for Determining the Value of Any Asset' by Dr Aswath Damodaran, and the (transfer pricing related) discussion paper on the use of economic valuation techniques in transfer pricing by the EU JTPF/012/2016/EN, EU Joint Transfer Pricing Forum Discussion Paper on the Use of Economic Valuation Techniques in Transfer Pricing, available at: https://ec.europa.eu/taxation_customs/business/company-tax/transfer-pricing-eu-context/joint-transfer-pricing-forum/eu-joint-transfer-pricing-forum-meeting-20-october-2016_en.
64. Paragraph 6.156, 2017 OECD Guidelines.
65. Paragraph 6.155, 2017 OECD Guidelines.

(1) Accuracy of financial projections:[66] The accuracy of the future projections relies on many factors. For instance, it would depend on the purpose for which projections have been stated (in particular, projections for business planning purposes are generally more reliable than those prepared for tax purposes). The projections' reliability also depends on the time span they cover, on whether or not the underlying intangibles have a track of financial records determined by market mechanisms, and on the prospects of future development costs.

(2) Assumptions regarding growth rates:[67] In predicting future cash flows, it is reasonable to examine the past record of financial performances of the industry or the company itself.

(3) Discount rates:[68] There is no universal method for determining the rate on the basis of which future cash flows are actualized. The appropriate method would account for the riskiness of the intangible and the time value of money.

(4) Useful life of intangibles and terminal values:[69] In estimating the useful life of an intangible, it is essential to take into account the industry's technical change rate, as well as the intangible's nature, and legal protection. In the event that the intangible can contribute to the development of potential new products, a terminal value accounting for this contribution should be evaluated.

(5) Assumptions regarding taxes:[70] Taxes should be taken into consideration in that they affect the future cash flows generated by the intangible. Taxes on the transfer themselves should be included in the evaluation process as well.

## 4.3 Options Realistically Available

### 4.3.1 OECD Definition

Options that are realistically available may not qualify as an OECD transfer pricing method per se, however, it is unarguably a critical concept or framework for transfer pricing:

> All methods that apply the arm's-length principle can be tied to the concept that independent enterprises consider the options realistically available to them and in comparing one option to another they consider any differences between the options that would significantly affect their value.[71]

As a matter of fact, according to the postulates of economic theory, economic agents make their decisions in order to maximize their values. The OECD Guidelines –

---

66. Chapter VI, D.2.6.4.1, the 2017 OECD Guidelines.
67. Chapter VI, D.2.6.4.2, the 2017 OECD Guidelines.
68. Chapter VI, D.2.6.4.3, the 2017 OECD Guidelines.
69. Chapter VI, D.2.6.4.4, the 2017 OECD Guidelines.
70. Chapter VI, D.2.6.4.5, the 2017 OECD Guidelines.
71. Paragraph 1.40, the 2017 OECD Guidelines.

in accordance with mainstream economic and financial theory – suggest that this value should be the net present value of the options.

> It is economically neutral to take on [one option or the other] as long as the net present value of both options are equal.[72]
> Independent enterprises, when evaluating the terms of a potential transaction, will compare the transaction to the other options realistically available to them, and they will only enter into the transaction if they see no alternative that offers a clearly more attractive opportunity to meet their commercial objectives. In other words, independent enterprises would only enter into a transaction if it is not expected to make them worse off than their next best option.[73]

ORAs can be associated with other concepts such as the concept of Best Alternative to a Negotiated Agreement (BATNA) stemming from negotiation theory.

> The most common operational definition of power in most experimental studies of negotiation and power is the BATNA – The Best Alternative to a Negotiation Agreement (Fisher and Ury, 1981). As its name states, the BATNA represents the most positive, desirable and valuable alternative that a negotiator may choose if the current negotiation does not result in agreement. [It is] likely to continue to be the primary operational definition of power in the domain of negotiation.[74]

### 4.3.2 The Usefulness of the Concept

As such, the concept of ORA may be very beneficial in at least two situations, i.e., accurately delineating intra-group transactions and valuing complex intra-group transactions.

#### 4.3.2.1 Delineating Accurately Intra-group Transactions

The ORA is a holistic tool that is utilized at the level of the (individual) company in its entirety. As such, it may be used as a test to determine whether the transactions have been accurately delineated or whether an alternative delineation – under an ORA – would be more appropriate.

> [I]dentifying the economically relevant characteristics of the transaction is essential in accurately delineating the controlled transaction and in revealing the range of characteristics taken into account by the parties to the transaction in reaching the conclusion that the transaction adopted offers a clearly more attractive opportunity to meet commercial objectives than alternative options realistically available.[75]

---

72. Paragraph 1.79, 2017 OECD Guidelines. The full text of this quote is that '[i]t is economically neutral to take on (or lay off) risk in return for higher (or lower) anticipated nominal income as long as the net present value of both options are equal'.
73. Paragraph 1.38, 2017 OECD Guidelines.
74. Handbook of Research on Negotiation, Olekalns, Mara and Wendi L. Adair (eds), Edward Elgar Publishing, 2013, Canada, pp. 135–136.
75. Paragraph 1.38, 2017 OECD Guidelines.

*4.3.2.2.   Valuing Complex Intra-group Transactions*

Based on practical experience, ORAs may provide a very solid framework for approaching complex transactions. This may be particularly the case, for instance, in the event of business restructurings.

> In order to determine whether at arm's length the restructuring itself would give rise to a form of compensation, it is essential to understand the restructuring, including the changes that have taken place, how they have affected the functional analysis of the parties, what the business reasons for and the anticipated benefits from the restructuring were, and what options would have been realistically available to the parties.[76]

Business restructurings often entail the – de jure or de facto – transfer of a combination of rights or intangibles, the definition of which may sometimes be difficult. The holistic framework of the ORA usually offers – in principle – an opportunity to mirror the outcome of arm's length negotiations between independent parties, factoring in all of the aspects – economic or legal – of the case.

### 4.3.3   ORAs in Practice

The practical use of the ORAs can be complex, and it is not the intention of this chapter to discuss them comprehensively.

In practice, the ORAs allow the construction of a bargaining range, i.e., for a given transaction, the range of values comprises what the minimum price is that the seller would be willing to accept for the transfer of the asset/right and the maximum price the purchaser would be willing to accept for same. Each bound of the range would result from the respective ORAs of the parties outside of the intra-group transaction. The rationale is that a seller would not sell at arm's length to its group counterpart if it can obtain a higher price from another party outside of the negotiation and, vice versa, a purchaser would not buy at arm's length from its group counterpart if it can obtain a lower price from another party outside of the negotiation.

The in-depth use of ORAs often entails the construction of counterfactual scenarios.

At this step, only a range – possibly quite wide – is obtained. In theory, parties may agree at arm's length on any point in this range. Sometimes, practitioners need to further determine a point estimate of the arm's length price for the transaction.

Based on practical experience, there is some opportunity for debate among practitioners on the best way to determine a point estimate from the bargaining range. Some economic theories suggest that, at this stage, only the negotiation capabilities (in

---

76. Paragraph 9.42, 2017 OECD Guidelines.

terms of skills or the ability to maintain a bargaining position for an extended period of time) of the parties should affect the positioning of the point estimate within the range.[77]

In practice, it is common that taxpayers consider that the likeliest outcome of an arm's length negotiation would be the midpoint of the bargaining range.

## 5 CONCLUSIONS

Transactional profit methods are at the cornerstone of the practical application of the arm's length principle. Still, these methods involve an indirect setting of arm's length prices as they relate to margins as opposed to prices.

While the TNMM may be perceived as being less difficult to apply than the PSM, it still involves challenges in its application as illustrated by the case studies of this chapter. The application of the TNMM has also been subject to a number of tax audits by tax administrations around the world, notably in relation to the choice of comparables. The TPSM is a more complex method; it applies in a more limited number of circumstances, and its application involves economic analyses. Both methods will likely remain in the future key tools for applying the arm's length principle both by MNEs and tax administrations.

---

77. To be noted, in a seminal article, Rubinstein proposed a model of quantifying with the advantage of being less pressed for time, i.e., having a discount factor closer to 1 than that of the other party. For more details, *see* Ariel Rubinstein, *Perfect Equilibrium in a Bargaining Model*, Econometrica 50 (1), pp. 97–109.

# CHAPTER 5

# Administrative Approaches to Avoiding/Minimizing Transfer Pricing Disputes

# 1 INTRODUCTION

In the day-to-day practice of multinational enterprises (MNEs), the application of transfer pricing rules by tax authorities of different jurisdictions may lead to economic double taxation. It should not come out as a surprise then that the number of disputes are increasing between taxpayers and tax administrations on such a complex topic. Against this background, although a vast majority of jurisdictions have agreed to allocate the taxing rights that are applicable to cross-border activities of MNEs according to the arm's length principle,[1] there is neither a unified nor an accurate mechanism on how to determine the conditions (including the pricing) of intra-group cross-border transactions. Hence, tax authorities are sovereign in their fiscal jurisdiction to apply the transfer pricing regulations in accordance with their experience and practice.

---

1. Article 9, OECD (2017), *Model Tax Convention on Income and on Capital: Condensed Version 2017*, OECD Publishing, Paris, https://doi.org/10.1787/mtc_cond-2017-en.

At the same time, recent developments within the international tax policy arena show that countries are increasingly willing to cooperate to enhance their economic relationships as well as administrative cooperation and promote the development of trade and business relations between two or more States. Accordingly, it is not surprising that transfer pricing became a major field for cooperation and creation of mechanisms to balance the allocation of a taxable base among the jurisdictions in accordance with the economic activity performed in each State.

The OECD BEPS Project devoted a significant part of its work on the development of transfer pricing rules, which was finalized by the publication of the Final Reports on Actions 8–10 (the 'final BEPS Reports').[2] The outcome of the final BEPS Reports were translated in the July 2017 publication of the Transfer Pricing Guidelines (the 'new TP Guidelines').

One of the important directions of the OECD work is related to resolving the conflicts and mismatches between tax administrations of different countries that arise out of transfer pricing issues. Nevertheless, both tax administrations as well as MNEs found a point of convergence in understanding that, due to the technicality of the issues and the magnitude of the amounts potentially at stake, transfer pricing issues should be – to the maximum extent possible – *prevented* (or, at worse, mitigated) to avoid any risks of disputes and conflicts as well as long and complex dispute resolution procedures such as the Mutual Agreement Procedure (MAP) and arbitration. As confirmed by the Final Report on Action 14 of the BEPS project, international dispute resolution instruments proved to be costly and time inefficient as well as cumbersome for taxpayers.

For the sake of limiting the analysis solely to transfer pricing issues, it is important to first draw a distinction between dispute *prevention* (specifically, advance pricing agreements or 'APA') and dispute *resolution* instruments (namely, mutual agreement procedures or the 'MAP'). While the latter category addresses the situations and searches for solutions when instances of international double taxation dispute have already occurred, the concept of dispute prevention aims at anticipating confrontational situations between taxpayers and tax administrations revolving around the proper application of the arm's length principle. For example, assume the following scenario: a non-European group is envisaging a business restructuring involving the distribution layer of its supply chain. As a result of the restructuring, all of the European distribution entities of the group will be converted from a fully-fledged into a limited risk distributor model. In this respect, this type of reorganization may imply a reduction of the operating margins linked with the shift of certain risks and functions. These types of intra-group transactions often end up under the scrutiny of the tax administrations. As a result, it is better to disclose the transfer pricing considerations that accompany such reorganizations upfront by making use of dispute prevention mechanisms rather than discussing in the confrontational environment of a transfer

---

2. OECD (2015), *Aligning Transfer Pricing Outcomes with Value Creation, Actions 8–10 – 2015 Final Reports*, OECD/G20 Base Erosion and Profit Shifting Project, OECD Publishing, Paris, http://dx. doi.org/10.1787/9789264241244-en.

pricing audit. Hence, the dispute prevention mechanisms discussed in this chapter attempt to avoid or minimize the disputes between tax authorities and taxpayers in future periods.

The primary legislative framework contemplating the use of dispute prevention measures responds to the guidelines adopted at the international (OECD, UN, and EU) level. The instrument that is most commonly thought of is the Advance Pricing Arrangements, however, audit enforcement tools such as those of the: (i) Simultaneous Tax Examinations and (ii) Joint Audits in practice may generate the same beneficial effects. The additional tool ensuring the predictability of legal environments for taxpayers and the prevention of disputes within one jurisdiction is safe harbours.

This chapter focuses extensively on all of the essential elements of all of the mentioned mechanisms, specifically, Advance Pricing Arrangements (section 2), Simultaneous Tax Examinations and Joint Audits (section 3), and Safe Harbours (section 4). Every section is divided into four sub-sections addressing: *(i)* the concept of every mechanism, *(ii)* their procedural aspects, *(iii)* the advantages and disadvantages of every tool, and *(iv)* some outlook and recommendations for the application of dispute prevention mechanisms.

## 2   ADVANCE PRICING AGREEMENTS

### 2.1   What Are They and Do They Work?

The legal instrument of the Advanced Pricing Agreement (or Arrangement) (APA) has been examined extensively within the literature of publications by international organizations. In particular, the most relevant contributions to the clarification of the concept of the APA may be found in the following official documents:

- The 1999 OECD Guidelines for Conducting Advance Pricing Arrangements under the Mutual Agreement Procedure;
- The 2007 European Commission Guidelines for Advance Pricing Agreement within the EU.
   Moreover, this concept was to large extent mirrored in the domestic
- The 2017 OECD TPG;
- The 2017 UN Practical Manual on Transfer Pricing for Developing Counties;

The OECD TPG define an APA as '*an arrangement that determines, in advance of controlled transactions, an appropriate set of criteria for the determination of the transfer pricing for those transactions over a fixed period of time*'.[3] Stated otherwise, an APA may be deemed similar to a contractual arrangement with the major difference being that, while one of the parties is the private taxpayer, the other is the public body represented by the tax administration.

---

3. Paragraph 4.123, OECD (2017), *OECD Transfer Pricing Guidelines for Multinational Enterprises and Tax Administrations 2017*, OECD Publishing, Paris https://doi.org/10.1787/tpg-2017-en (hereinafter – 2017 OECD TP Guidelines).

The UN Manual on Transfer Pricing for Developing countries does not explicitly provide the definition of what is meant by an APA. However, it determines that an APA '*provide(s) for agreement on a transfer pricing methodology for future years*'[4] while it can also refer to previous years.

The European Commission establishes that an APA is an agreement between tax administrations encompassing an appropriate set of criteria for the determination of the transfer pricing for certain controlled transactions between taxpayers over a fixed period of time.[5]

The analysis of the definitions stated above primarily allows a distinction of specific features of an APA (the particularities of each element are discussed in the following section in more detail):

- The agreement must be concluded between a taxpayer and tax administration(s).
- The subject of the agreement is the methodology for the determination of the transfer price (i.e., concrete set of criteria).
- The scope of the agreement extends to the certain controlled transactions.
- The agreement has a time framework and extends its force to a certain specified period in the future and upon a certain provision in the past.

To sum up all of the elements, an Advance Pricing Agreement (APA) can be defined as a domestic law instrument akin to a contract between private parties, which is entered into between a taxpayer (and his foreign associated entities, if applicable), on the one side, and the tax authority in the jurisdiction of a taxpayer (and tax authorities in the jurisdictions of associated entities, if applicable), on the other side. The APA has, as one of its main features, the inclusion of the so-called 'critical assumptions', i.e., the identification of appropriate criteria for the pricing of a set of transactions between the taxpayer and his related parties over a fixed period of time in the future or over past periods.

### 2.1.1 Distinguishing the APA from Some Dispute Prevention and Resolution Mechanisms

The APA is a tool for the *prevention* of disputes between tax authorities and taxpayers. Such instruments are intended to supplement the administrative, judicial, and treaty mechanism for resolving transfer pricing disputes.[6] From a practical standpoint, and

---

4. UN (2017), *UN Practical Manual Transfer Pricing for Developing Countries*, New York. http://www.un.org/esa/ffd/wp-content/uploads/2017/04/Manual-TP-2017.pdf (hereinafter – 2017 UN TP Manuel).
5. Paragraph 2.4. (13), Communication from the Commission to the Council, the European Parliament and the European Economic and Social Committee on the work of the EU Joint Transfer Pricing Forum in the field of dispute avoidance and resolution procedures and on Guidelines for Advance Pricing Agreements within the EU {SEC(2007) 246} /* COM/2007/0071 final, https://eur-lex.europa.eu/legal-content/EN/TXT/?uri = CELEX%3A52007DC0071 (hereinafter – EU Commission Guidelines).
6. 2017 OECD TP Guidelines, at para. 4.134 at p. 214.

due to the increased scrutiny of transfer pricing arrangements by tax administrations around the world, the use of APA as a tool to mitigate upfront any transfer pricing challenge is becoming increasingly popular. APAs should be distinguished from the ordinary, treaty-based, dispute resolution mechanisms, such as the Mutual Agreement Procedures (MAP). As previously stated, the primary feature of an APA is the prevention of disputes in the future periods, and not *only* in regards to the past activities.

The process of concluding an APA is different than the **MAP** process. Table 5.1 illustrates the conceptual differences in the two concepts.

*Table 5.1    The Differences Between APAs and MAPs*

| | Advanced Pricing Arrangement | Mutual Agreement Procedure |
|---|---|---|
| Initiation of the process | Voluntary initiation by a taxpayer | Initiation by a taxpayer, with subsequent input by the competent authorities of the tax administrations involved in the dispute |
| Parties actively involved | Taxpayer plays an active role in the procedure (e.g., submission of documentation, participation to meetings) – from a technical standpoint, also MAP can follow the same path insofar as its opening is required to activate the APA (e.g., in the context of bilateral or multilateral APAs). | The process is held by tax authorities. Taxpayer is generally not involved in the active development of the MAP, unless it is expressly required to do so. |
| Timing | The process begins before the dispute to prevent it | The process attempts to resolve the already ongoing dispute arose at the single country level. |
| Covered transactions | Determination of the methodology applicable to future and, upon the agreement, to past transactions | Determination of the methodology applicable only to past transactions |
| Outcome of the process | The agreement on methodology preferable for taxpayer and tax authority (-ies). A taxpayer has the right not to sign the agreement with unsatisfactory outcome. | The outcome depends solely on decision of two or several tax authorities. Taxpayer must comply. |

At the same time, APAs, to some extent, differ from **private rulings**[7] as they are more traditional for some tax jurisdictions. While the private rulings tend to address the issues of a legal nature based on the presented factual background, which may not be questioned by tax authorities, in the APA procedure, the facts themselves are the focus of extensive examination.[8] Moreover, private rulings usually refer to the individual transactions while the APA provides the possibility to encompass a set of transactions or all cross-border transactions of a specific taxpayer. Finally, the private ruling is always issued and in force in one jurisdiction whereas the process of APAs, depending on the national legal framework and readiness for international cooperation, may operate on a multilateral basis.

### 2.1.2   Types of APAs and Their Advantages and Disadvantages

Depending on the number of parties representing the tax administration involved in the APA process, there are three types of these agreements, and namely: (i) unilateral, (ii) bilateral, and (iii) multilateral.

A **Unilateral** APA is one entered into between a taxpayer and the tax administration of the country where it is subject to taxation. In contrast, a **bilateral** APA involves three parties: the taxpayers and its associated entity (-ies), the tax administration of the home country, and the tax administration belonging to the fiscal jurisdiction of a taxpayer's associated entity. A **Multilateral** APA, however, is arranged between the taxpayers, the tax administration of the home country, and more than one foreign tax administration.

The advantage of a **unilateral** APA is in its less complexity compared to other types of APAs. This type of APA is limited to one fiscal jurisdiction and, therefore, pursues different fiscal interests and does not require the tax administration to coordinate its decision with any other jurisdictions where the associated entities of taxpayers are located. However, this advantage is gravely disproportional to the disadvantages of this type compared to *bilateral* and *multilateral* APAs. The unilateral APA is legally binding only within one jurisdiction. The jurisdiction of the associated entity has no obligation to accept the methodology agreed to by the unilateral APA in another jurisdiction. Therefore, even though the unilateral APA minimises the risk of disputes in one State, it does not guarantee to the taxpayer that the transfer prices in his controlled transactions will not be challenged in the second jurisdiction. The taxpayer would still tend to refer to a MAP procedure to resolve the arising dispute in the second jurisdiction. However, the critical issue in this aspect is whether the particular tax authority will be willing to cooperate to resolve the dispute by the MAP when there is a legally binding APA in force.

At the same time, **bilateral** and **multilateral** APAs are initially coordinated and agreed upon between the tax authorities of two or more jurisdictions, respectively, and have a legally binding effect for all of the tax administrations that are involved. The

---

7. A private ruling is a written decision by tax authorities, in response to a taxpayer's request for guidance on unusual circumstances or complex questions about their specific tax situation.
8. 2017 OECD TP Guidelines, at para. 4.143 at p. 216.

irrevocable advantage of the bilateral and multilateral APA processes is that they essentially incorporate the mutual agreement procedure into the stage when there is no dispute yet at stake. Hence, contrary to the traditional concept of a MAP, the tax authorities should bilaterally or multilaterally cooperate in advance in establishing the satisfactory transfer pricing methodology by commonly evaluating the relevant factual basis of the transactions. Hence, these types of APAs ensure a much lower chance of risk of economic double taxation of the controlled transactions.

Both the OECD and the UN expressed their support for the last two instruments. The OECD contends that '*the bilateral approach is far more likely to ensure that the arrangements will reduce the risk of double taxation, will be equitable to all tax administrations and taxpayers involved, and will provide a greater certainty to the taxpayers concerned*'.[9] The UN TP Manual emphasizes the same concerns that are mentioned in the previous section, arguing that '*to the extent there is advance agreement on key transfer pricing issues neither country faces the prospect of refunding taxes already collected*'.[10] The Guidelines of the European Commission, taking into account the specifics of the EU market, in principle, refer only to bilateral and multilateral APAs as effective tools for the mitigation of administrative burdens and ensuring certainty for taxpayers.[11]

### 2.1.3 APA Programmes

In 2014, the OECD completed the Base Erosion and Profit Shifting Project (BEPS). In its Action 14, the OECD recognized the bilateral APA Programmes as non-binding practice for ensuring the timely, effective, and efficient resolution of treaty-related disputes as well as providing a greater level of certainty in both treaty partner jurisdictions, lowering the likelihood of double taxation and proactive prevention of transfer pricing disputes.[12]

Transfer pricing problems and adjustments could be recognized as a 'global tax war' for tax revenues between the jurisdictions.[13] In this war, the taxpayers play a losing game and suffer a burdensome level of scrutiny, penalties, and formal obligations in order to comply with the transfer pricing requirements of the tax administrations of different jurisdictions.

To prevent the distortion of trade, boost the economic growth of countries, and economic cooperation between the States, many tax administrations tend to adopt the APA programmes as one of the tools of cooperation and to minimise the risk of conflicts in the international transfer pricing arena. The APA Programmes, in principle, refer to bilateral and multilateral applications.

9. *Ibid.*, at para. 4.141 at p. 216.
10. 2017 UN TP Manual, at para. C.4.4.2.4.
11. EU Commission Guidelines, *supra* n. 5.
12. Action 14, BEPS Project 2017 OECD TP Guidelines, at para. 4.134 at p. 214.
13. Calderón Carrero, J. M. (1998). Advance Pricing Agreements: a Global Analysis, Kluwer Law International at p. 18.

**Example**

The Australian Tax Office recognizes the APA Programme as an important part of their insurance programme. India launched its APA Programme in 2012, and Ireland's bilateral APA Programme was effective from 1 July 2016. Many other jurisdictions have also followed the same idea for developing their economic transfer pricing cooperation

### 2.1.4 Regulatory Prerequisites for APAs

Since 1999 when the OECD published Guidelines for Conducting Advance Pricing Arrangements under the Mutual Agreement Procedure, many jurisdictions have already experienced the effect of APAs and, hence, implemented the provisions on APAs in their domestic legislation. At this time, even more countries have adopted the respective provisions in their domestic legislation.[14] Especially proactive jurisdictions also issued the Guidelines for their taxpayers which clarified all of the stages of the process beginning from the application by a taxpayer to the effective supervision of the finalized APA.

Therefore, a taxpayer who plans to initiate the APA procedure must first consider whether the possibility to conclude an APA is provided by national legislation. Moreover, national legal frameworks often include additional technicalities over their APA procedure.

Some jurisdictions, however, have not implemented the APA procedure into their national tax legislation. Therefore, the question arises as to whether a taxpayer in such jurisdictions may rely on any other provisions to obtain the advantages of the APA instrument. When countries lack the explicit option for APA arrangements in their domestic legislation, the APA procedure may be considered, in principle, if the tax treaties of the country contain a clause regarding a mutual agreement procedure similar to Article 25 of the OECD Model Tax Convention which underlines the Mutual Agreement Procedure.[15] However, in this case, only a bilateral APA procedure may be possible.

The OECD reflects that, generally, the competent authorities should be allowed to conclude an APA.[16] Paragraph 3 of Article 25 of the 2017 OECD Model Convention reads as follows:

> *The competent authorities of the Contracting States shall endeavour to resolve by mutual agreement any difficulties or doubts arising as to the interpretation or application of the Convention. They may also consult together for the elimination of double taxation in cases not provided for in the Convention.*[17]

---

14. *See*, The Report of DLA Piper, *APA and MAP Country Guide 2017: Managing uncertainties in the new tax environment,* https://www.lexology.com/library/detail.aspx?g = 3ac3ce27-3e76-4423-a3a6-c5245cf6d3cd.
15. OECD TP Guidelines, at para. 4.152, at p. 219.
16. *Ibid.*
17. Paragraph 3 of Article 25 of the 2017 OECD Model Convention.

In this regard, the OECD emphasizes that Article 25 should have a broad scope to resolve the difficulties of a *'general nature'* arising out of the application of the treaties under the OECD Model Convention. Therefore, the APA might be useful for allocating taxable profits, issues with permanent establishments and brand operations under Article 7 of the OECD Model, and difficulties with determination of the arm's length price in transactions between associated entities according to Article 9 of the Convention.

Therefore, the legal prerequisites for the application of an APA are found in the domestic legislation of the particular jurisdictions and their tax treaties.

### 2.1.5  Goals for Concluding APAs and Mutual Expectations in Cooperation

An APA is a beneficial tool for both taxpayers and tax authorities. Each party entering into an agreement pursues its purposes and objectives and has expectations for a cooperative procedure.

**A taxpayer** initiating the APA procedure aims to **ensure the certainty and stability** of business planning, to **prevent costly and time-inefficient disputes** with a tax administration, to **avoid the economic double taxation** resulting from different assessments of transfer pricing by tax authorities, and to **minimize the reputational risks** connected with tax non-compliance.

A taxpayer may consider an APA especially but not exclusively in the following situations:

- when the controlled transactions of a taxpayer are significant in size and complexity;
- when a taxpayer faces recurring TP adjustments or litigation;
- when a taxpayer's applicable transfer pricing methodology has a definite risk of opposition by tax authorities;
- when there is well-developed cooperation between the fiscal jurisdictions of associated entities;
- when the advantages of an APA overshadow other more cumbersome dispute prevention and resolution mechanisms.

At the same time, **the tax authorities** would also be willing to cooperate in a transfer pricing APA process because of the range of advantages of APAs compared to other tools. APAs prevent a tax administration from being involved in long disputes and reimbursement of taxes paid if the tax authorities are not successful in the dispute. At the same time, the APA process might be beneficial for solving the issue of the lack of information or the consequent misinterpretation of the factual basis of transactions between the taxpayer and tax authorities in the contracting States as well as for enhancing the development of economic cooperation between them.

Referring to this issue, the Australian Taxation Office, for example, emphasizes the following expectations for the behaviour of the parties involved:

- all parties will cooperate fully with each other, including undertaking open and ongoing dialogue in the development of the APA;
- each APA request will be treated on its merits according to its own facts;
- each party will act transparently, in particular, each party will disclose all relevant and material facts;
- each party will provide prompt and complete replies to any reasonable queries.

The US, the EU, and other countries analyse the effectiveness of the APA Programmes and the number of agreements that are concluded on a yearly basis. Among the EU jurisdictions, the most active are Luxembourg, Belgium, the Netherlands, and Italy. The statistics address the number of applications filed, the total number of unilateral and bilateral agreements, and the number of applications that have been approved, withdrawn, and rejected.[18]

## 2.2 Procedural Aspects

The entire APA process can be distinguished into the five stages illustrated in Figure 5.1.

*Figure 5.1 The APA Process*

The procedural aspects of APAs are regulated by domestic law. This section aims to provide the overview of the general tendencies of the practices in different countries. However, every jurisdiction may provide its own rules which, in some aspects, may deviate from the information provided below.

## 2.2.1 *Pre-filing Consultation*[19]

In principle, tax authorities encourage taxpayers to arrange a pre-filing meeting before the formal APA application. At this stage, a taxpayer or his agent may contact the tax

---

18. EU (2015) Statistics on APAs in the EU at the End of 2015, EU Joint Transfer Pricing Forum, Meeting of 20 October 2016, https://ec.europa.eu/taxation_customs/sites/taxation/files/jtpf01 52016enapa.pdf; and US (2017), Announcement and Report Concerning Advance Pricing Agreements, 27 Mar. 2017, https://www.irs.gov/pub/irs-utl/2016_apma_statutory_report.pdf.
19. C2. paras 29–33 p. 408, Annex to 2017 OECD TP Guidelines.

authorities to discuss any issues that they have in relation to the APA application on an informal basis; an informal discussion aims to enhance the efficiency of the APA process.

In particular, at the pre-filing consultation, tax authorities are willing to pre-evaluate the appropriateness of the APA for a particular case and the likelihood of success of the APA agreement as well as to determine the formal requirements for admissibility of the APA application and the scope of information that the taxpayer might be required to provide for the APA process.[20]

**For taxpayers,** a pre-filing consultation is an opportunity to obtain detailed information on the APA procedure, to discuss the concerns on disclosure and confidentiality of data, and to understand the position of tax authorities and their willingness for further cooperation. In addition, a taxpayer can avoid the payment of the fees for the formal APA application if they realize during the pre-filing consultation that the case is not appropriate for an APA.

Nevertheless, regardless of the outcome of the pre-filing consultation, taxpayers must provide the tax authorities with some information about their activities already at this stage. This information might include the parties involved in the controlled transactions, the transactions and period to be covered, the proposed transfer pricing methodology, any existing inquiries from the tax authorities abroad,[21] any rollback, and the countries to be involved.[22] In order to have an efficient discussion, taxpayers typically provide a Memorandum for discussion outlining the mentioned topics for discussion.[23]

At the same time, the international guidance offers taxpayers an opportunity for a preliminary meeting to be conducted on a named or anonymous basis.[24] However, the scope of information on the transactions and activity must be sufficient to have a meaningful conversation with tax authorities. The form of the meeting primarily depends on domestic custom and practice. For example, the Irish Tax and Customs Revenue in its Bilateral Advance Pricing Agreement Guidelines *'strongly recommends that APA pre-filing meetings are conducted on a named basis. Recognizing international guidance that preliminary discussions may be conducted on an anonymous basis, Revenue would be prepared, on an exceptional basis, to consider conducting pre-filing meetings on an anonymous basis. However, Revenue will not admit a taxpayer into the APA programme until the identity of the taxpayer is known'.*

**For tax authorities,** a pre-filing consultation is useful for avoiding unnecessary work if it is clear that the case is inappropriate for an APA. The tax authorities, at the preliminary stage, may also exchange the information and positions not only with taxpayers but also with other tax administrations that are involved to determine

---

20. For example, the extent of any functional analysis of affiliated enterprises; identification, selection and adjustment of comparables, and the need for and the scope of market, industry, and geographic analyses.
21. https://www.revenue.ie/en/companies-and-charities/documents/apa-programme-guidelines. pdf, at p. 40 para. 11.
22. The EU Guidelines, *supra* n. 5.
23. Paragraph 32, Annex to 2017 OECD TP Guidelines.
24. *Ibid.*

whether the bilateral or multilateral cooperation is visible in order to mutually agree on transfer pricing issues for a specific taxpayer.

### 2.2.2 Formal APA Application

If the case was found to be suitable for an APA with the pre-filing consultation, then a taxpayer may proceed with filing a formal APA application.

A formal application of an APA should be made to a **competent authority** in the jurisdiction of a taxpayer. If a taxpayer requests a bilateral or multilateral APA, then that individual is also responsible for submitting the APA applications to all of the relevant tax authorities that are intending on being involved in the process. Moreover, the tax authorities may request submission of the copies of all of the documentation supplied by a foreign associated entity to a foreign tax treaty partner.

The **period** for the APA application is prescribed by domestic law, i.e., *'before the beginning of the first accounting period to be covered by the APA'*,[25] *'before the first day of the previous year relevant to the first assessment year which the application seeks to cover'*,[26] *'within the timeframe agreed to at the early engagement meeting(s) and/or as set out in the agreed APA case plan(s)'*.[27] In principle, formal application should be made as early as possible in relation to the periods intended to be covered by the APA and shortly after any informal approach.[28] When the APA regulations provide different timeframes in different jurisdictions, a taxpayer is responsible to ensure that all of the applications are submitted in time.

Many jurisdictions also require the payment of a **fee for a formal APA application**. The amount of such a fee is contained in domestic law and varies from jurisdiction to jurisdiction.

The **content** of the application should consist of all of the information on the facts and circumstances of the relevant controlled transactions that are stated in the APA application. The domestic regulations on an APA may require a taxpayer to submit a detailed proposal for the APA, the form and content of which is ideally prescribed at the preliminary meeting.[29] For example, at the preliminary meeting, the competent tax authority and taxpayer may agree that the letter has to specify the functional analysis of associated entities; identification, selection and adjustment of comparables; market, industry, and geographic analyses; etc. in the formal application.[30] The table below provides an exemplary scope of information to be disclosed to tax authorities in a

---

25. Irish Tax and Customs, *Bilateral Advance Pricing Agreement Guidelines,* Revenue Operational Manual, September 2016, https://www.revenue.ie/en/companies-and-charities/documents/apa-programme-guidelines.pdf.
26. Indian Income Tax Department, *Advance Pricing Agreement Guidance with FAQs*, Taxpayers Information series - 43, https://www.incometaxindia.gov.in/booklets%20%20pamphlets/advance-pricing-agreement-guidance-with-faqs-(tpi-43).pdf.
27. Australian Taxation Office, Guidance on Advance Pricing Arrangements, https://www.ato.gov.au/Business/International-tax-for-business/In-detail/Advance-pricing-arrangements/.
28. EU Guidelines, *supra* n. 5, at para. 26.
29. Paragraph 34 p. 482, to 2017 OECD TP Guidelines.
30. *Ibid.*

formal APA application,[31] which is not exhaustive by any means. Nevertheless, a concrete scope of information to be disclosed significantly depends on the specific facts of every particular case and the complexity of the transfer pricing analysis.

Typical information might include
- The transactions, products, businesses, or arrangements covered by the proposal.
- The associated entities and jurisdictions involved in the APA process.
- The world-wide organizational structure and functional analysis of the associated entities.
- A description of the proposed transfer pricing methodology and applicable comparables.
- The arm's length conditions relevant to the cross border dealing(s).
- The factors and critical assumptions significant for validity of the proposed methodology.
- The accounting periods or tax years to be covered.
- A general description of market conditions of industry and geographical specifics.
- Any other information relevant to the circumstances of the case and requested by tax authorities.

Tax authorities must confirm the acceptance of the APA application or the statement of rejection of acceptance of application with a specification of reasons for denial in the period of time prescribed by domestic rules. The letter of acceptance confirms that the tax authorities will precede with the next stage – the evaluation of the application that is received.

### 2.2.3 Evaluation and Negotiation of APA

Evaluation and negotiation are two different stages that are appropriate to conduct partly together. In this regard, the OECD suggests that '*a balanced approach should be adopted to ensure that the evaluation takes place as quickly as possible and the negotiation begins as soon as possible*'.[32]

**Evaluation** is a process of critical analysis by tax authorities of the information provided in the formal APA application. The domestic legislation generally provides a period following the acceptance of the APA application for tax authorities to critically examine the proposals submitted by a taxpayer and to determine their position in the

---

31. The OECD also has designed the exemplary list of information to be provided which can be found in Annex at p. 483.
32. Paragraph 29, Annex to 2017 OECD TP Guidelines.

case. If two or more tax administrations are involved, the competent authorities have to contact each other as soon as possible to design a timetable for evaluation and negation of the APA.

At this stage, revenue authorities may be entitled to seek any additional clarification related to factual circumstances, transfer pricing methodology, etc., organize a joint meeting with the representatives of both tax administrations and with a taxpayer, visit and conduct interviews with the personnel of the involved entities within the boundaries of fiscal jurisdiction, etc. All of the information provided to one tax administration should also be provided to the other tax administrations that are involved.

---

**Outcome of the evaluation stage of APA procedure**

As a result of the evaluation phase, the tax authorities must form their position on the transfer pricing methodology, comparables, APA essential terms (e.g., rollbacks), critical assumptions and, ultimately, the appropriate arm's length pricing (range) for the transaction(s) or arrangement. The tax authorities may issue a position paper including the outcomes of the evaluation that, in general, is subject to confidentiality under domestic law or respective tax treaty(s).

---

As soon as the tax authorities complete the evaluation of APA application, the parties can proceed to the following stage of **negotiation.** In the case of a *unilateral* APA application, the tax authorities should inform a taxpayer within the period prescribed by domestic legislation about their position in the case. In the event of any controversies, a taxpayer has to submit, generally in writing, any objections and must formulate arguments for and against the specific issues covered by a position of the tax authorities. If disparities are not resolved, taxpayers and tax authorities may agree on a formal meeting to negotiate the critical areas.

In the case of *bilateral and multilateral* APAs, following the evaluation process, tax authorities are expected to enter into formal negotiation and exchange of information with foreign competent tax authorities. When appropriate, a negotiation process typically begins from the exchange of the position papers between tax treaty contracting jurisdictions. The purpose of negotiation is to resolve any differences in tax authorities' positions in two jurisdictions. A taxpayer may or may not be a part of this process.

### 2.2.4    Formal Agreement of an APA

As soon as the competent tax authorities of tax treaty contracting States reach consensus on the terms of the APA, they must notify the taxpayer in writing on the agreed terms and conditions. If the taxpayer has any objections against the terms of the APA that is agreed upon between tax administrations, that individual can request for further consultation with the tax authorities on the possible modifications to the APA arrangements.

The APA should consist of all of the information that is essential for determining transfer pricing implications for a taxpayer and all of the conditions agreed by the taxpayer and tax authorities. In particular, a typical APA agreement includes the following provisions:[33]

### 2.2.4.1   The Parties to the Agreement

The APA must include the information on a taxpayer entering into the agreement and its foreign related parties in order to establish the relationship between them. Moreover, the APA also has to include the name(s) of the tax authority concluding the agreement, i.e., the tax authority of the country where the taxpayer is located and, in some cases, foreign tax authorities of the States where the Associated Enterprises (AEs) of the taxpayer are located.

### 2.2.4.2   Controlled Transactions Covered

The APA can cover all of the transfer pricing issues of the taxpayer, or its scope may be limited to particular transactions specified by the taxpayer in its APA application. Moreover, subject to a mutual agreement, the scope of the APA may be limited to transactions on which taxpayer and tax authorities have successfully reached agreement.

At the same time, some countries would tend to be flexible in the APA process addressing the scope of the controlled transactions and, as a consequence, extend it beyond the activities specified in the APA application.[34] The reason for that is that it might be difficult to evaluate some transactions separately from other controlled activities. Moreover, APAs might also include an agreement on non-transfer pricing issues when 'these other issues are sufficiently clearly connected to the underlying transfer pricing issues'[35] in order to ensure that mutual agreement is achieved on the respective conditions, and they will neither be a subject for further dispute nor the reason for revocation of the APA.

### 2.2.4.3   Transfer Pricing Methodology

Transfer pricing methodology is a key element of an APA agreement. The agreement should provide a fully detailed description of the chosen methodology. The APA must prove that the transfer pricing method is applicable to covered controlled transactions and the methodologies for its application based on, for example, functional analysis, comparability analysis, value chain analysis, etc. The method agreed upon by the

---

33. See, for example, H.M. Revenue and Customs, Advance Pricing Agreement between Taxpayer and H.M. Revenue and Customs, Sample Agreement, http://www.transferpricing.com/pdf/SP 2-10annex2.pdf.
34. Paragraph 36, Annex to 2017 OECD TP Guidelines.
35. Ibid.

parties should be accepted by all of the associated entities involved and should be recognized as permissible by both (or more) tax authorities.

The OECD Guidelines emphasize that, in the case of associated enterprises, the selected methodology should also respect the guidance on the application of the arm's length principle embedded in Article 9 of the OECD Model Tax Convention.[36]

### 2.2.4.4   The Arm's Length Price

In specific cases, the parties to an APA may agree on a concrete arm's length price or range of prices. However, more frequently, the tax authorities would tend to agree on less specific terms of the APA as predictions of absolute future profits may seem to be less plausible.[37] In this regard, the range of arm's length prices in conjunction with appropriate critical assumptions is a more reliable tool to predict future results and compliance with the arm's length principle.

### 2.2.4.5   Critical Assumptions

The other essential element of an APA is critical assumptions. **Critical assumptions** may be defined as a set of factual circumstances and economic conditions in which their continued existence indicates the validity of the transfer pricing methodology and arm's length range and price determined by the APAs. These assumptions may refer to business, industry and economic conditions, strategy, the structure of a particular MNE, and other criteria.

The critical assumptions are important as APAs rely heavily on the predictions about the future and presence of some business and economic conditions. At the same time, in the rapidly changing world of business and the economy, long-term predictions are not appropriate during the time in which the APA is legally enforceable. Therefore, the critical assumptions indicate the circumstances that influence transfer pricing and, hence, require its modification. Such an option of modification is beneficial for both the taxpayer and tax authorities as a taxpayer would be willing to have their transfer prices reflect the ongoing economic conditions, and tax authorities would be willing to receive a respective share of profits.

The EU Guidance on APAs additionally provides the following recommendation for its Member States to design the scope of critical assumptions:

> Critical assumptions should be tailored to the individual circumstances of the taxpayer, the particular commercial environment, the methodology and the type of transactions covered. … Critical assumptions should not be drawn so tightly that certainty provided by the APA is jeopardised but should encompass as wide a variation of the underlying facts as those involved in the APA feel comfortable with.[38]

---

36. Paragraph 41, Annex to 2017 OECD TP Guidelines.
37. 2017 OECD TP Guidelines, para. 4.138.
38. EU Commission Guidelines, *supra* n. 5, at paras 97–98.

Taxpayers have an obligation to inform their tax administrations if critical assumptions are not met over the lifecycle of the APA. The following table provides the exemplary list of assumptions prescribed by the OECD in its 1999 Guidance on an APA.[39]

Critical assumptions might include:
- Assumptions about the relevant domestic tax law and treaty provisions;
- Assumptions about tariffs, duties, import restrictions, and government regulations;
- Assumptions about economic conditions, market share, market conditions, end-selling price, and sales volume;
- Assumptions about the nature of the functions and risks of the enterprises involved in the transactions;
- Assumptions about exchange rates, interest rates, credit rating, and capital structure.
- Assumptions about management or financial accounting and classification of income and expenses; and
- Assumptions about the enterprises that will operate in each jurisdiction and the form in which they will do so.

### 2.2.4.6   Duration of APAs and Rollbacks

The APA should prescribe the time period in which it is legally effective. The period, on the one hand, must be long enough to ensure certainty for the taxpayer and set-off the advantages of the APA with the administrative and business resources spent for its conclusion. However, the period cannot be too long due to the predictions about long periods and the future risk being disproportionally inaccurate.

On average, an APA lasts for three to five years. Practice has shown that developed countries with a more stable economic and business environment would be willing to conclude an APA for five years whereas developing countries are recommended by the UN to sign an APA for a shorter term, at least three years. Some developing countries do not have any practice in APAs, and the concept of an APA for their jurisdictions is not familiar at all. Therefore, the shorter terms will ensure that both tax authorities and taxpayers test this instrument, hence, slowly developing trust with each other.

Also, APAs may provide a **rollback of the APA,** i.e., an extension of coverage of the APA to the previous *filed* tax years not included within its initial scope.[40] BEPS Action 14 stresses that the countries with bilateral APA programmes should include a

---

39. OECD (1999), *Annex: Guidelines for Conducting Advance Pricing Arrangements under the Mutual Agreement Procedure ('MAP APAs')*, http://www.oecd.org/tax/transfer-pricing/3800839 2.pdf.
40. 2017 OECD TP Guidelines, at para. 4.147.

rollback condition to APAs.[41] A rollback should be considered by the parties to the agreement when it has the capacity to resolve or minimise the risks of disputes in regards to the previous periods.[42] Moreover, a rollback is desirable when the facts and circumstances of the earlier transactions do not differ from those covered by APAs.

### 2.2.4.7   Other Conditions of APA

Other conditions of APAs may address the annual reporting requirements, conditions for revocation of the agreement by tax authorities, protection of business information provided by a taxpayer, and confidentiality as well as other conditions.

### 2.2.5   Monitoring and Compliance Stage

The OECD describes two ways of monitoring the compliance of a taxpayer with the APA conditions. A first monitoring tool requires submitting annual reports that confirm that the terms and conditions of APA are satisfied and that critical assumptions are relevant. The second instrument is conducting annual audits of covered entities, however, without re-evaluating transfer pricing methodology.[43]

The **annual compliance reports** and annual tax returns must be submitted by the taxpayer in the form and period provided by domestic law on the APA procedure. The information to be included in the annual compliance report may contain the following:

- an analysis of compliance with the APA including the data and calculations demonstrating the results of the application of arm's length methodology;
- relevance (breach) of any critical assumptions;
- the information on any compensating adjustments made to comply with the arm's length range according to the APA;
- the information on any modifications (revocation, renew, cancellation etc.) of an APA made by the tax authorities of the other contracting jurisdiction.

A concluded APA also does not prevent tax authorities from **auditing** the activities of the taxpayers who are parties to an APA agreement. In regards to the scope of transaction covered by APA, an audit is generally limited only to ensuring compliance with its terms and conditions. The tax authorities would tend to monitor the validity of all of the factors and information specified particularly in annual compliance reports.

---

41. OECD (2015), *Making Dispute Resolution Mechanisms More Effective, Action 14 – 2015 Final Report*, OECD/G20 Base Erosion and Profit Shifting Project, OECD Publishing, Paris, https://doi.org/10.1787/9789264241633-en.
42. EU Commission Guidelines, *supra* n 5.
43. OECD TP Guidelines, Chapter IV (F), Advance Pricing Arrangements.

## 2.3 Advantages and Disadvantages of APAs

### 2.3.1 Advantages of APAs

For **taxpayers, an** APA substantially enhances *certainty and predictability* of tax treatment over the time of legal enforceability of an agreement. Moreover, bilateral and multilateral APAs can reduce or substantially *eliminate the risk of juridical and economic double taxation.* The mutual agreement procedure under an APA process might be more time efficient compared to a traditional MAP as a dispute resolution mechanism. Moreover, APAs may reduce the costs of compliance with transfer pricing regulations over the period of the APA. Additionally, transfer pricing methodology is not subject to an annual audit.

APAs are assisting MNEs in strengthening their *reputation as a tax-compliant* company. Moreover, APAs help to build long, trusting relationships with tax authorities in the atmosphere of cooperation and not confrontation. This cooperation is especially important for effective long term business planning as the APA can be prolonged or renewed.

**For tax administrations,** the APA precludes time- and cost consuming litigation or arbitration. In principle, they could feasibly reduce the amount of resources spent for annual examination of cross-border operations of MNEs. The APA process balances the disproportionality of information about a taxpayer and, hence, allows the tax authorities to find a more appropriate scheme of compliance both for taxpayers and tax authorities. Moreover, during the APA procedure, taxpayers themselves may provide the comparables for their transactions, perform a detailed functional analysis of their cross-border activities, and actively assist tax administrations in its evaluation.

Furthermore, bilateral or multilateral APA programmes have strong potential for building effective cooperation between the tax administrations, exchanging of information, and promoting the jurisdiction as tax-friendly and cooperation-friendly.

**Both for taxpayers and tax administrations,** APAs provide an opportunity to communicate and consult in a non-adversarial spirit and environment which might stimulate the flow and exchange of information, looking for the compromises, and more objective evaluation of data and circumstances of every particular case.[44]

### 2.3.2 Disadvantages of APAs

At the same time, **a taxpayer** may face some disadvantages that are specific to APAs. The first concern is related to different types of APAs. In particular, *unilateral* APAs do not ensure the elimination of double economic and juridical taxation for taxpayers. In this regard, bilateral and multilateral APAs are more beneficial for these purposes. Moreover, the filing of an APA application might be *costly* and, therefore, a taxpayer has to balance the resources required to conclude an APA and expected outcomes from the process.

---

44. 2017 OECD TP Guidelines, at para. 4.154.

A different concern is related to the exchange of *information* in the APA process. The tax authorities might more closely examine the transactions and data of a taxpayer than they would for a regular annual tax examination. Furthermore, a taxpayer may be worried about the confidentiality of this information. Therefore, an APA should always include a clause of confidentiality of business related data of a taxpayer.

The provision of extra information is also a critical issue for a taxpayer when the APA *application is rejected*. '*Embarking on the APA procedure could increase the risk of an investigation into the taxpayer's past, present and future tax returns.*'[45] A taxpayer might be worried that the provided information in the APA application could be used against him in tax audits of his past and future activities. Addressing this concern, the OECD recommends that countries ensure the prohibition of information obtained in the APA process in further tax examinations though the effectiveness of such a prohibition is questionable.

**Tax authorities** might also experience the drawbacks of an APA procedure. Many companies experience continual changes, e.g., in business structures – acquisitions, divestments, restructuring; changing business environment – growth in electronic trade, new/changing products, etc.[46] The *changing business environment* requires the tax authorities to be especially careful in their predictions by formulating appropriate and reasonable critical assumptions in APA agreements.

Moreover, tax authorities must be extremely cautious when determining an appropriate arm's length range for pricing transactions and critical assumptions that influence this range in bilateral and multilateral APAs as taxpayers may abuse this range with the means of the mechanism of *corresponding adjustments*. Therefore, the determined arrangement should be clearly aligned with the arm's length principle. At the level of the European Union, the lack of the correlation between a determined pricing range and the arm's length range causes the additional risk of infringement of the EU state aid prohibition.

Finally, the scope of *administrative resources* that are required for ensuring compliance with the transfer pricing rules will not necessarily be reduced due to the network of APAs arranged on the domestic, bilateral, and multilateral levels. Tax authorities will still have to examine the compliance with the terms and conditions of APAs in the annual tax audits. Moreover, separate resources are needed to participate in the APA process on a continual basis, for example, an APA department.

## 2.4    Outlook and Recommendations

The overview of the concept of an APA allows concluding that this mechanism might be an effective tool to prevent disputes between taxpayers and tax authorities. Additionally, APA cooperation is beneficial for both taxpayers and tax administrations.

---

45. *Ibid.*
46. J. Elliott, 'Transfer Pricing: Lessons from Australia', Discussion Papers in the Department of Management, nos 97–135 (University of Southampton, 1997), p. 17.

Taxpayers and tax administrations should be mindful of possible hidden obstacles and hindrances during the process and thus professionally enter into the APA process to derive the maximum of benefits out of it. In particular, the following elements have to be considered:

- *Unilateral versus bilateral and multilateral APAs. Taxpayers* should cautiously select the type of APA applied for taking into account all of the benefits and drawbacks of each of them as well as the relations between the jurisdictions of associated entities. *Tax authorities* should develop APA programmes and build stable relations with other jurisdictions to strengthen the position of the entities in world business activities.
- *Legal basis for an APA.* In order to ensure certainty for taxpayers and efficiency of the process, countries are recommended to adopt the regulations on an APA in their domestic legislation or to design guidelines on all of the essential elements of the process.
- *Formal Agreement of an APA.* In the formal agreement, both the taxpayers and the tax authorities have to clearly define all of the terms and conditions of the agreements, avoid any ambiguities and complexities, and consult each other on any uncertainties arising during the process. The parties to the agreement are recommended to discuss all of the concerns in a preliminary consultation and address them in an APA agreement including the scope of critical assumptions, data confidentiality and prohibition of the usage of data outside the APA process, conditions for revocation and renewal of the APA, etc.
- *Monitoring the compliance of an APA.* Monitoring of compliance should not be so overly cumbersome for taxpayers and tax authorities that it eliminates all of the benefits of the APA. For taxpayers, entering into an APA should undermine voluntary compliance with its conditions.

## 3   CURRENT EXPERIENCE WITH INTERNATIONAL CO-OPERATION: SIMULTANEOUS AND JOINT TAX EXAMINATION

Due to the rising global dimension of taxation, the increasing number of cross-border transactions and, consequently, of tax disputes, cooperation between tax administrations is increasingly important.[47] As mentioned in the context of an APA, international coordinated regulations have begun to address these issues taking into account the need for avoiding and minimizing disputes between taxpayers and tax administrations. Among the different approaches available and in addition to the APA procedure,

---

47. OECD, *The Changing Tax Compliance Environment and the Role of Audit*, 29 Sep. 2017 (2017), p. 79.

current experience with international cooperation shows that cross-border audits can be valuable tools for a number of reasons.[48] Within this framework, simultaneous tax examinations (STEs) and joint audits (JAs) are, by far, the most innovative tools that, with some degree of difference, bring auditors from the relevant tax administrations to the same table in order to cooperate for the purpose of a tax investigation.

Notwithstanding the encouraging results of the first pilot projects delivered at the international level, many questions still remain unanswered, and several items should be considered for further improving these instruments. In particular, the legal and practical features of STEs and JAs, as described in the following section, constitutes the key elements that define their applicability in real cases. These forms of mutual assistance may, in fact, encounter critical issues that could limit their applicability and the positive outcomes of their processes.

## 3.1 What Are They, and Do They Work?

When an international tax risk emerges (typically in a matter of transfer pricing, tax residency and permanent establishment determinations, structures and aggressive planning schemes, restructuring, cost allocation agreements, hybrid instruments, and VAT fraud),[49] there are several possibilities for the cross-border exchange of information to apply (Figure 5.2).

*Figure 5.2    Approaches for Cross-Border Exchange of Information for Tax Purposes[50]*

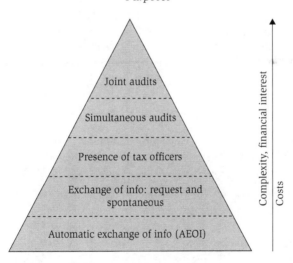

---

48. *Ibid.*
49. OECD, *Transfer Pricing Guidelines for Multinational Enterprises and Tax Administrators*, Committee on Fiscal Affairs, OECD, Paris (2017), para. 4.87.
50. OECD, *The Changing Tax Compliance Environment and the Role of Audit*, 29 Sep. 2017 (2017), p. 81.

181

As illustrated in Figure 5.2, in addition to the traditional exchange of information (in the form of automatic, on request, or spontaneous exchange), STEs and JAs can be applied for more complex situations when other tools appear to be insufficient and a more intense form of cooperation seems to be requested. From a transfer pricing perspective, this situation is quite common: frequently, during transfer pricing audits, tax inspectors and MNEs interpret the same situation differently even though both may bring supportive and valid arguments in favour of their positions. These scenarios usually involve the comparability on internal/external comparables, the nature or the substance of a transaction, the ownership of IPs, etc.

Regarding the selection of the most appropriate tool, as indicated in the figure above, tax administrations shall rely on three main characteristics:[51]

- *Complexity of the situation*: in several cases (e.g., interpositions of tax havens, aggressive planning & TP-driven structures, etc.), a unilateral approach to a tax audit could limit the scope of the analysis. For this reason, tax administrations shall evaluate the opportunities that are offered by bilateral/ multilateral approaches that entail a different intensity of cross-border exchange of information;
- *Financial interest*: the relevance and the amount of the potential risk to be assessed clearly influence the selection of the tool used for the exchange of information;
- *Costs*: all measures that avoid time consuming and expensive procedures (e.g., the MAP) for taxpayers and tax authorities are welcomed. Costs constitute a relevant driver in the selection of the most appropriate approach for the cross-border exchange of information.

### 3.1.1 Definition of STEs

STEs are defined in Part A of the OECD *Model Agreement for the Undertaking of Simultaneous Tax Examinations*[52] (**OECD Model Agreement**) as '*an arrangement between two or more Parties to examine* **simultaneously** *and* **independently**, *each on its own territory, the tax affairs of (a) taxpayer(s) in which they have a common or related interest, with a view to exchanging any relevant information which they so obtain*'.

---

**Example 1**

A common STEs scenario comprises two tax treaty partners, A and B, located in countries A and B, respectively, that have a common or related interest in the proper income tax reporting of MNE Z operating in the A and B countries. The idea is that A and B agree to conduct two simultaneous and separate

---

51. Van der Hel-van Dijk, E.C.J.M (2016), *Joint Audits: Chance or Threat?*, Journal of Tax Assurance, Netherlands.
52. OECD, *Model agreement for the undertaking of simultaneous tax Examinations*, (1992).

examinations on Z's accounts and intend to exchange relevant information that they unilaterally obtain.

### 3.1.2 Definition of JAs

JAs are defined in Chapter 1 of the OECD *Joint Audit Report*[53] as '*two or more countries* **joining together** *to form a* **single audit** *team to examine an issue(s) / transaction(s) of one or more related taxable persons (both legal entities and individuals) with cross-border business activities, perhaps including cross-border transactions involving related affiliated companies organized in the participating countries, and in which the countries have a common or complementary interest; where the taxpayer jointly makes presentations and shares information with the countries, and the team includes Competent Authority representatives from each country*'.

---

**Example 2**

A common JA scenario comprises two tax treaty partners, A and B, located in countries A and B, respectively, that have a common or complementary interest in the proper income tax reporting of MNE Z operating in the A and B countries. The idea is that A and B could work as one team rather than conducting two separate examinations on Z's accounts. In theory, all requests for information from Z would be issued simultaneously by A and B, following their own domestic rules and procedures, and then analysed and discussed by the tax authorities under the provisions of the Information Exchange article in their bilateral tax treaty.

---

### 3.1.3 Legal Basis of STEs and JAs

The term '*joint audit*' as well as '*simultaneous tax examination*' are not legal terms, however, they have been used in practice for tax purposes to express the idea that two or more tax administrations work together. Notwithstanding best practises, when these innovative tools must be applied, a legal framework based on which different tax administration could cooperate must first be defined. In particular, it is necessary to identify the legal basis to support: (i) the exchange of information and (ii) the specific type of mutual assistance in tax matters that go beyond a mere exchange of information:

    (i) Legal framework for exchange of information

---

53. OECD, *Joint Audit Report*, (2010).

A legal framework for the exchange of information, as reported by the OECD,[54] can be found in the network of bilateral/multilateral tax treaties as a form of mutual assistance for tax purposes, in particular:

- – are within the scope of the exchange of information provision based on Article 26 of the OECD Model Tax Convention; or
- – may be based and facilitated on bilateral information exchange agreements ('*Tax Information Exchange Agreements or TIEA*'); or
- – may be authorized under Article 8 of the joint Council of Europe and *OECD Convention on Mutual Administrative Assistance in Tax Matters*; or
- – may be based on the *Council Directive 2011/16/EU of 15 February 2011 on administrative cooperation in the field of taxation and repealing Directive 77/799/EEC* of 19 December 1977 (*European Union Mutual Assistance Directive*); or
- – may be authorized under Article 12 of the *Nordic Convention on Mutual Assistance in Tax Matters*; or
- – may be authorized under Article 5 of the *CIAT Model Agreement on the Exchange of Tax Information*; or

(ii) Legal frameworks for STEs and JAs

- – Tax examination abroad which entails that the representatives of the competent authority from one State are allowed to be present in the territory of the other State may be based on Article 6 of the *Model Agreement on Exchange of Information in Tax Matters*[55] or Article 9 of the *Convention on Mutual Administrative Assistance*;[56]
- – A legal foundation for a simultaneous tax examination is provided in Article 8 of the *Convention on Mutual Administrative Assistance*[57] and its *Commentary*. EC Regulation 1798/2003 regulates a number of specific issues in the field of indirect taxes;
- – International tax audits may occur under the aforementioned international legal framework although national legislations may have an impact on the procedures. Moreover, in addition to legal constraints, different administrative cultures and strategies for engaging with taxpayers may also limit the extent of cooperation that can be achieved. Possible legal and/or practical constraints may also be addressed with an agreement between the tax administrations involved and the taxpayers. The relevant tax administrations frequently execute working

---

54. OECD, *Joint Audit Participants Guide,* (2010).
55. *See* the Commentary to Article 6 of the OECD, *Model Agreement on Exchange of Information in Tax Matters.*
56. *See* Article 9 of the OECD and Council of Europe, *The Multilateral Convention on Mutual Administrative Assistance in Tax Matters: Amended by the 2010 Protocol,* OECD Publishing (2011).
57. *See* Article 8 of the OECD and Council of Europe, *The Multilateral Convention on Mutual Administrative Assistance in Tax Matters: Amended by the 2010 Protocol,* OECD Publishing (2011).

arrangements in order to define objectives, engagement, and practical procedures for the purpose of their international cooperation. A legal foundation under domestic law usually takes relevance in defining such working arrangements, the responsibilities, and communication rules between the parties.

---

**Example 3[58]**

During the pilot project between Germany and the Netherlands in 2013, domestic law provisions determined the inclusion of certain additional steps in the JA process. In particular, as reported by the Netherlands Tax and Customs Administration and the German Federal Ministry of Finance, the JA required that all companies were asked to give their consent prior to the pilot. A notification procedure was, in fact, required under the Netherlands' domestic law before initiating the exchange of information to foreign countries (i.e., foreign tax authorities).

---

### 3.1.4 JAs vis-à-vis STEs

As reported by the OECD, both JAs and STEs comprise an integrated and advanced exchange of information, although JAs appear to be the most appropriate for the most complex situation that requires the most intense form of cooperation. STEs, in fact, have a less integrated approach by the relevant tax administrations into the investigation because, in practice, they entail a separate approach with an advanced exchange of information.

As *per* definition, a JA is different from an STE where two or more countries join together to conduct a single audit with all of the countries receiving the same information and presentations from the taxpayer. Thus, tax administrations share the information and statements simultaneously and come together to the same conclusion. In the case of an STE, tax administrations conduct a separate audit and then exchange the information on the results. In the case of discrepancies, the MAP and corresponding adjustments follow. Consequently, JAs could be considered as an extensive tool that, in some way, incorporate a typical MAP process in the audit process.

Although a sound legal basis does not exist, STEs seem to be acceptable from a broader range of countries compared to JAs. Under certain domestic laws, auditors may, in fact, conduct audits only on the territory where they are certified to do so. In this sense, STEs have a better chance to survive as they do not infringe on State sovereignty in tax matters.

---

58. *Netherlands Tax and Customs Administration,* Germany, Federal Ministry of Finance (2017).

## 3.2 Procedural Aspects

The procedural aspects of STEs and JAs rely on the step-processes that are identified, respectively, by the OECD in the *'Manual on the Implementation of Exchange of Information for Tax Purposes. Module on Conducting Simultaneous Tax Examinations'* and in the *'Joint Audit Participant Guide'*. The step-processes are quite the same although a JA *vis-à-vis* an STE entails a more intense form of cooperation that also results in a partially different procedure.

Below, the step-processes for STEs and JAs are described beginning with the guidance provided by the OECD.

### 3.2.1 Selecting, Conducting and Concluding a STE[59]

The OECD provides for the purpose of selecting, conducting, and concluding a STE with a ten-step process. In particular:

#### Initial case selection

Tax administrations individually consider suitable cases for an STE. In preforming this exercise, normally, the number and the complexity of cases proposed by the simultaneous tax examination coordinators should take into account tax administration resource constraints and other factors that may reduce the tax administrations' ability to conduct the audits.

Selection criteria include:

– indication of substantial non-compliance with local legislation;
– the economic performance does not reflect appropriate profits;
– indication of consistent long-term losses;
– indication of little or no tax paid over a relevant timeframe.

#### Agreement on suitable cases

Agreement is reached by the relevant tax administrations based on the initial case selection. Usually, tax administrations agree on suitable cases after matching their own list of cases that are considered being suitable for an STE. In this regard, the simultaneous tax examination coordinator may seek to obtain any information that it requires in order to reach a decision either under its domestic laws or under the provisions of the appropriate exchange of information.

#### Conduct preliminary examinations

Prior to holding the initial planning meeting between the designated representatives, the auditors should perform a comprehensive review of the financial statements and the income tax return with an in-depth analysis of the MNE's organization.

---

59. OECD, *Manual on the Implementation of Exchange of Information for Tax Purposes – Module on Conducting Simultaneous Tax Examinations*, 23 Jan. 2006 (2006), p. 9.

### Contact the taxpayers

Taxpayers are contacted and informed about the STE. The formal rules of the individual countries that are governing taxpayer(s) notification of the audit must naturally be observed. Some countries, as reported by the OECD, require that taxpayers who have been selected for an audit be given sufficient notice of the examination.

### Initial planning meeting

A kick-off meeting for designated representatives to define their engagement procedures, coordination strategies, etc. is planned. This meeting should be held before the individual countries commence the actual audit of the selected case.

### Meetings and interviews with taxpayers

As indicated by the OECD, during the preliminary meeting between the taxpayer and the auditors, the designated representative should inform the taxpayer about the simultaneous tax examination, including advice about how information will be exchanged among the relevant tax administrations and the legal basis (or bases) for doing so. A number of pieces of information and data should be requested by the tax auditors depending on the case (e.g., history, description of the accounting/reporting system, official documents, TP policies, records, and other info).

### Further examinations

An STE examination occurs after the meetings and interview with the taxpayers. During this phase, potential double taxation issues may arise and, for the purpose of minimizing tax disputes, the taxpayers will be able to present a request for the opening of the mutual agreement procedure at an earlier stage while the representatives of the competent authorities will be able to gather additional factual evidences for those tax adjustments for which the mutual agreement procedure may be requested.

### Finalization of case

If either country concludes that it is no longer beneficial to continue the simultaneous tax examination, it should withdraw by notifying the other country (or countries) in writing as soon as possible after making that decision.

A meeting shall be held in order to attempt to agree on a common position regarding the taxpayer(s) with respect to the areas subjected to simultaneous tax examination for which there is a concurrence between legislation in the various countries.

### Final report prepared

At the conclusion of the simultaneous tax examination, the designated representative should produce and share a comprehensive report containing a summary of the results that are achieved and an evaluation of the procedures that were implemented to achieve these results.

## Process Improvements implemented

Recommended process improvements are implemented by the simultaneous tax examinations coordinator.

### 3.2.2 Selecting, Conducting and Concluding a JA[60]

The OECD provides for the purpose of selecting, conducting and concluding a JA the following step process:

### Introduction

The JA Teams may begin the JA based on the JA plan. The location of the joint audit will be flexible based on the circumstances surrounding the taxpayer's situation.

### Audit Structure

In general, the steps to follow during the auditing process can be defined as follows:

- *Risk assessment*: Usually, auditors collect all of the available information about targeted taxpayers from different internal and external sources, including results from risk analyses, before the planning meeting. In the planning meeting, the JA Team(s) should evaluate and update the gathered information taking into account the information obtained from each other.
- *Audit planning*: Based on the agreed-upon JA plan, the JA Team members will ensure that all essential areas, transactions, and taxes are identified and that the audit is conducted in a timely and efficient manner. The audit plan must be sufficiently flexible to allow for changes during the audit process that result from the information forwarded by other Participating Countries or from the taxpayer.
- *Audit performance*: In this stage, the JA Team jointly requests and gathers audit information. This stage is usually complicated for a number of reasons including the communication between audit teams, the preparation of audit progress reports, and the need for flexibility for unforeseen circumstances or potential divergences from the JA plan.

### Conclusion

The final stages of a JA are the production of the final audit reports, the final meeting with the taxpayer, and the JA Agreement. The final meeting with the taxpayer is after the JA Teams from the Participating Countries have met, discussed, and finalized their prospective audit reports.

---

60. OECD, *Joint Audit Participants Guide*, (2010).

## 3.3 Advantages and Disadvantages

### 3.3.1 Advantages of STEs and JAs

Due to their common nature (i.e., advanced approaches for cross-border exchange of information for tax purposes), STEs and JAs share common advantages while their specific disadvantages usually determine the best suitable approach to be applied in the case at stake.

The advantages, described in Table 5.2, basically include the access to and sharing of information; the prevention of long, expensive arbitration procedures; and the ensuring of certainty and predictability of the outcome for both taxpayers and tax administrations.

*Table 5.2   Advantages of STEs and JAs*

| | | STEs | JAs |
|---|---|---|---|
| 1. | Clarify complex scenarios | Access to information in Other jurisdiction | Direct Access to Information (i.e., *one team- one audit)* |
| 2. | Improve the adequacy of data | Exchange of information | |
| 3. | Speed-up the resolution of issues | The possibility to solve the issues simultaneously | Tax administrations should come to a single outcome during the process |
| 4. | Better understanding of the big picture *(e.g., validate local assumptions, finding internal comparables)* | Two-sided analysis based on an advanced exchange of relevant information | One input-one output process based on a single audit team that analyses the entire scenario |
| 5. | Reduce compliance costs (e.g., *advisory/internal personnel costs)* | Money-saving process for companies | |
| 6. | Engagement to reach a result | If a reassessment is made, both countries involved should endeavour to reach a result that avoids double taxation | |
| 7. | Reduce possibilities of double economic taxation | Although STEs may lead to different outcomes of audits in two jurisdictions | Strong commitment considering the unique outcome of the audit |
| 8. | Minimize risk of tax disputes | | |
| 9. | Minimize/facilitate MAP | MAP/Corresponding adjustments follow STEs | MAP/Corresponding adjustment as a part of JAs |
| 10. | Corresponding adjustment may be made in an early stage | | |

### 3.3.2 *Disadvantages of STEs and JAs*

The disadvantages of the procedures can be classified taking into account a three-step process shared by STEs and JAs, i.e.: (1) legal basis, (2) process execution, and (3) results (Table 5.3).

*Table 5.3    Disadvantages of STEs and JAs*

| | | STEs | JAs |
|---|---|---|---|
| 1. | Legal basis | – | Principle of territoriality limits the discretion of tax inspectors to conduct an audit in different jurisdiction |
| | | Taxpayers cannot voluntarily enter into an STE/JA | |
| 2. | Process execution | Audit processes among countries may not be harmonized | |
| | | Language barriers and differences in the skills of auditors from different countries might be an issue | |
| | | – | Difficulties in forming a team and in cooperation |
| 3. | Results | May lead to different outcomes of audits in two jurisdictions | – |
| | | The outcome reached is not binding for tax administrations in years not covered by the joint audit | |
| | | Different accounting standards and national legislation | |

## 3.4    Outlook and Recommendations

Notwithstanding that the first pilot projects (e.g., 2013–2015 JA between Italy and Germany) appear to provide encouraging results, many questions still remain unanswered, and several items should be considered for further improving STEs and JAs in the future:

(a) **Voluntary application**. The opportunity to apply for an STE or JA should be granted to taxpayers. Thresholds and/or other quantitative/qualitative criteria should be considered in a first stage to render these tools to be as effective as possible. Moreover, the selection of relevant countries to be covered by the STE/JA should primarily consider the interest of tax administrations but also the interest of MNEs.

(b) **Legal basis**. A sound legal basis should be established. In this regard, an MLI may support the introduction of STEs and JAs in local legislations.

(c) **Standardization**. These tools must be accepted globally. This result may be achieved by embedding STEs and JAs in local legislations or by translating the results of these innovative tools into international practises that are more common, i.e., simplified APAs that incorporate the results of STEs/JAs could be straightforward both in the perspective of tax administration and MNEs.

(d) **Consolidation**. The positive results achieved during the pilot projects have to be consolidated notwithstanding the strong commitment that usually characterises start-up phases. It is also necessary to consider that the pilot cases have not generally been selected for the high level of complexity but for the reliability to achieve a result between tax administrations and to prove that the innovative tool works.

(e) **Beyond national legislation**. Lack of alignment between tax administrations should be avoided. Coherence and coordination shall be respected beyond national boundaries in regards to:
   – Audit approaches and timetable;
   – Engagement and communications rules;
   – Periods under investigation;
   – TP practice and Audit/Quality standards;
   – Language and skills required by the representatives of the tax administrations that are involved.

Despite these few suggestions for improvement, it is perhaps worth re-examining the innovation and the effectiveness of these tools in the matter of avoiding and minimizing transfer pricing disputes. STEs and JAs can, in fact, alleviate the difficulties experienced by both taxpayers and tax administrations when approaching transfer pricing and could constitute a real game-changer in the relationship between these two.

## 4 SAFE HARBOURS

### 4.1 What Are They, and Do They Work?

#### 4.1.1 Setting the Framework: The Definition and Distinguishing Features of Safe Harbours

A **safe harbour** is an administrative simplification which is, in principal, optional for taxpayers and permits the determination of transfer prices using a pre-established method. A safe harbour in a transfer pricing regime is a provision that applies to a defined category of taxpayers or transactions that relieves eligible taxpayers from certain obligations otherwise imposed by a country's general transfer pricing rules.[61] Basically, a safe harbour substitutes simpler obligations for those under the general transfer pricing regime.

Considering the aforementioned, it is evident that safe harbour rules can be a valuable option to prevent or minimize transfer pricing disputes. In the event that a safe harbour is applied, potential disputes may regard only the election and reporting requirements, i.e., tax administrations must ensure that taxpayers have met specific eligibility conditions and complied with the safe harbour provision. This means that minimal procedures to audit transfer prices will be required by tax administrations and a relatively standardized and simplified approach to cover inter-company transactions for MNEs.

A multi-country analysis of existing transfer pricing simplification measures[62] presents that safe harbours can work for manufacturing, outsourcing, non-core services, and inter-company financing. Basically, the appropriateness of safe harbours can be expected when there is a low transfer pricing risk, and the negotiation of these simplified measures is performed on a bilateral or multilateral basis.

---

**Example**

Current experience with safe harbour rules include:
- a 7.5% markup on inter-company services in **Australia**. A similar measure has been granted in New Zealand;
- a safe harbour for interest charged in inter-company loans granted by **Swiss** tax administrations. The safe harbour rule provides different rates for loans financed through equity and loans financed through debt. The taxpayer can prove that the arm's length amount varies from the safe harbour;
- a safe harbour for inter-company financing in the **US** where taxpayers are allowed to use the US Government AFR ('Applicable Federal Rate') which is published by the IRS every month as a reference rate;
- the 'Maquiladora' rule that effects **Mexican** subsidiaries of foreign companies involved in manufacturing activities. Under this alternative, the maquiladora company agrees to declare a minimum taxable income, whichever results are higher from comparing a 6.9% on the value of assets and 6.5% of the costs and expenses related to the manufacturing operation;
- a 5% markup on low-value adding intra-group services has been granted by **India**'s Central Board of Direct Taxes. Moreover, as reviewed in 2018, a margin for software development services and IT enabled services have been established at 17%–18% depending upon the value of transactions

---

61. OECD, *Transfer Pricing Guidelines 2017, Revised Section E on Safe Harbours in Chapter IV*, para. 4.95–4.132.
62. OECD, Report on *Multi-country analysis of existing transfer pricing simplification measures*, 2011.

(earlier, the margins ranged from 20%–22%). The revised margins for knowledge process outsourcing services are now fixed between 18–24%, depending upon the value of transactions and employee costs in relation to operating expenses (earlier, a single margin of 25% applied). For contract research and development services, the margin has been reduced significantly, dropping from 30% to 24%.

- a relief for **Brazilian** companies from preparing a study to demonstrate the legality of transfer prices in the event that less than 5% of revenue are with related parties. Safe harbours are also provided for import and export transactions as well as transactions involving commodities, etc.

## 4.2 Procedural Aspects

From a procedural standpoint, for purposes of establishing and implementing safe harbour rules, tax administrations must determine the following critical elements:

- the qualifying person: eligible taxpayers entitled to apply for the simplified regime provided by the safe harbour rules;
- the qualifying transactions: the controlled transaction(s) that will be accepted by the relevant tax administration(s) to be covered by safe harbours;
- the taxable income: the income (e.g., price charged/paid, cost pool, etc.) subject to taxation under the specific rules provided by the safe harbour;
- the election and reporting requirement: tax administrations have to ensure that taxpayers have met specific eligibility conditions and complied with the safe harbour provisions.

---

**Example 4**

Key-elements and details relevant for defining and negotiating safe harbour rules on a bilateral or multilateral basis
When approaching the development of safe harbours on a bilateral or multilateral basis, the following elements may be of relevance:
- Criteria required for qualifying enterprises (e.g., functions/assets/risks required or disallowed, categories of entities included or excluded per se from the safe harbour provision, etc.)
- Description of the qualifying transaction;
- Definition of the arm's length range/compensation;
- The time span considered for the purpose of applicability of the safe harbour provision;
- Statement that the bilateral/multilateral arrangement is binding between the tax administration involved upon the fulfilment of eligibility conditions by the taxpayers;

---

- Definition of reporting and documentation requirements to be maintained by the qualified enterprises;
- Reporting and monitoring procedures to be applied by tax administrations both in regard to the application and the review of the safe harbour
  provision;
- A mechanism for resolving disputes that may arise in applying the safe
  harbour provision.

## 4.3   Advantages and Disadvantages

### 4.3.1   Advantages of Safe Harbours

For **taxpayers,** safe harbour rules can be an attractive option mainly for avoiding/
minimizing transfer pricing disputes.[63] Basically, when a safe harbour rule is utilized,
there is more certainty for taxpayers that transfer pricing will be accepted by tax
administrations as well as fewer burdensome compliance obligations and costs during
the performance of the transfer pricing analysis. The possibility to establish tax
obligations without applying complex and burdensome rules,[64] such as transfer pricing
methodologies, constitutes the key element of safe harbour rules which explain their
current application in different tax jurisdictions.

Moreover, transfer pricing safe harbours might, in some cases, contribute to
solving the issue of the valuation of supplies of services for the purposes of applying
withholding taxes or VAT as well as supporting potential custom duties issues.

For **tax administrations,** safe harbour rules may help to focus their limited
resources on areas with the most significant transfer pricing risk while increasing their
efficiency, responsiveness, and the possibilities to grant taxpayers with much-desired
certainty. The availability of safe harbour rules, in fact, provides tax administrations
the opportunity to reduce time-consuming risk analyses and tax audits provided that
the safe harbour rules are well-designed, their outcomes are in accordance with the
arm's length principle, and their application has been carefully evaluated based on the
facts and circumstances of the specific case. In developing countries, they could also
constitute a first legal framework that would allow tax auditors to practise in the field
of transfer pricing.

In addition to the aforementioned advantages, tax administrations should, in
implementing safe harbour rules, also consider that these instruments can help boost
foreign direct investment and may improve equity among taxpayers. Indeed, they help
to ensure that all taxpayers placed in similar situations are subject to the same
treatment, which is not always the case in the context of tax audits or negotiated
agreements between businesses and tax administrations.

A detailed summary of safe harbour's advantages from the perspective of both
taxpayers and tax administrations is provided in Table 5.4.

---

63. OECD, *Comments for EOCD on Transfer Pricing and Safe Harbours.*
64. OECD, *Transfer Pricing Guidelines, Revised Section E on Safe Harbours in Chapter IV,* para. 4.95.

*Table 5.4    Advantages of Safe Harbours*

| | Taxpayers | Tax Administrations |
|---|---|---|
| 1. | Simplified approach, i.e., alternative to general transfer pricing rules | Simplified approach allows tax administration to focus on high risk transactions/taxpayers |
| 2. | Lower burdensome compliance | Greater administrative simplicity |
| 3. | More certainty that transfer prices will be accepted by tax administrations | Minimal procedure to audit transfer prices under safe harbour regime |
| 4. | Avoid/minimize transfer pricing disputes | Fewer number of disputes, audits, and MAPs |
| 5. | Potential tax planning opportunity | |
| 6. | MAP available in case of double taxation | |

### 4.3.2    Disadvantages of Safe Harbours

The simplified approach provided by safe harbour rules has been applied several times in practise in many advanced countries as well as those still developing. Although current experience with safe harbours shows that they can be valuable, a number of disadvantages should be considered before engaging in implementing such an approach into local legislation.

In particular, tax administrations (and taxpayers) should be aware of the following potential disadvantages of safe harbours:

- they may lead to results that are not in accordance with the arm's length principle;[65]
- unilateral safe harbour rules may create a risk of double taxation or double non taxation. This is because it should be recognized that a safe harbour provision does not bind or limit any tax administration in any way other than the tax administration that adopted the safe harbour;
- potentially opens avenues for inappropriate tax planning;[66]
- may raise issues of equity and uniformity;
- may be arbitrary in nature.

---

65. As reported by the United Nations *Practical Manual on Transfer Pricing for Developing Countries* (2017), para. B.8.8.7. '*on the issue of the practical application of safe harbour regimes, the experience of the Republic of Korea represents a relevant example. Before joining the OECD, the Republic of Korea's national tax authority, the National Tax Service (NTS), employed a so-called "standard offer-commission rate" for import and export business taxation. Under this scheme, the NTS used a standard offer commission rate based on a survey of actual commission rates. This was available as a last resort under its ruling only in cases where other methods for identifying the arm's length rate were inapplicable in determining commission rates charged by a foreign party. The NTS finally repealed this ruling as it considered the ruling to be contrary to the arm's length principle'.*
66. United Nations *Practical Manual on Transfer Pricing for Developing Countries* (2017), para. B.8.8.5.

A detailed summary of safe harbour's disadvantages from the perspective of both taxpayers and tax administrations is provided in Table 5.5.

*Table 5.5   Disadvantages of Safe Harbours*

|  | Taxpayers | Tax Administrations |
|---|---|---|
| 1. | Safe harbours may be available only for a certain category of transactions/taxpayers | High risk detail setting process |
| 2. | Divergence from the arm's length principle | |
| 3. | Risk of double taxation (in the case that the simplified approach unilaterally granted to a taxpayer is not accepted by other country/ies involved) | Risk of double non taxation (in the case of unilateral safe harbour rules) and tax planning opportunities |
| 4. | Competitive/trade/investment discrimination/distortions | |
| 5. | Safe harbour rules may be subject to relevant review by tax administration | Necessary monitored going-forward approach |

## 4.4   Outlook and Recommendations

Transfer pricing compliance and administration is often complex, time consuming, and expensive.[67] Due to the increasing number of cross-border transactions and, consequently, tax disputes, properly designed safe harbour provisions that are applied in appropriate circumstances can help to relieve some of these burdens and provide taxpayers with greater certainty.[68] Among the possible solutions to minimize and/or eliminate transfer pricing disputes, safe harbour rules may, in fact, help taxpayers and tax administration since, if accepted (i.e., the taxpayer has satisfied the eligibility conditions of and complied with the safe harbour provisions), no tax audit will be performed and no disputes will arise.[69]

When examining the current international experiences with safe harbour rules, it is recommended to apply these instruments when the benefits outweigh the problems raised by such provisions. In particular, they can be a valuable solution when small taxpayers and less complex transactions are involved and when safe harbours can be negotiated on a bilateral or multilateral basis. Among the businesses surveyed, they consider that improving transfer pricing tax certainty for many undertakings is important even when transfer pricing is not an obstacle per se to investment. In this way, a majority of businesses would welcome the implementation of an optional and

---

67. OECD, *Transfer Pricing Guidelines, Revised Section E on Safe Harbours in Chapter IV*, para. 4.95.
68. *Ibid.*, para. 4.108.
69. OECD, *Comments for EOCD on Transfer Pricing and Safe Harbours*.

rebuttable safe harbour that would apply to low-risk or low value-added activities that do not involve the development or use of intangibles.

Notwithstanding the disadvantages, safe harbours seem to provide administrative simplifications that decrease the compliance required by MNEs and may help tax administrations to focus on high risk transactions and taxpayers as well as, in the case of developing countries,[70] to begin building capabilities and a first basic legal framework for transfer pricing purposes.

## 5 CONCLUSIONS

This chapter has illustrated, from both a theoretical and a practical standpoint, the most effective administrative approaches that are available for avoiding or minimising transfer pricing disputes. In particular, section 2 describes the Advanced Pricing Agreements that allow taxpayers and tax administrations to agree on the selection of an appropriate criteria for pricing a set of transactions over a fixed period of time. Distinguished features of the APAs, their differences from MAPs, and their procedural aspects have been carefully evaluated as they may determine the positive outcomes of this instrument.

Section 3 describe simultaneous tax examinations and joint audits which are, by far, the most innovative tools that, with some degree of difference, bring auditors from the relevant tax administrations to the same table in order to cooperate for the purpose of a tax investigation. As well as the APAs, STEs and JAs represent valuable options for avoiding and minimizing transfer pricing disputes. This section outlines the specific features of these two instruments together with an in-depth analysis of the advantages and disadvantages and a number of practical applications that are taken from actual cases that were addressed by the authors either during their academic work or in the practice of assisting taxpayers.

In addition, section 4 presents another tool which may avoid or minimize transfer pricing disputes, i.e., safe harbours. These administrative simplifications have been extensively described, and a number of current experiences in developing and developed countries have also been provided.

Although several disadvantages and issues may arise from the application of the aforementioned tools, the cases and the practical experience in dealing with transfer pricing disputes demonstrate that APAs, cross-border audits, and safe harbours can be valuable since they provide more certainty and encourage cooperation between taxpayers and tax administrations.

---

70. United Nations *Practical Manual on Transfer Pricing for Developing Countries* (2017), para. B.8.8.2.

# CHAPTER 6

# Administrative Approach to Resolving Transfer Pricing Disputes

# 1  INTRODUCTION

The volume of international tax disputes is rising at a startling speed and resolving them might take many years. As a result, the inventory of those that are unresolved is accumulating astonishingly every year. According to statistics disclosed by the OECD, at the end of 2015, the total of the mutual agreement procedure (MAP) inventory of OECD member countries was 6,176, representing an increase of 13.76% compared to the year 2014.[1] It has also been observed that a significant number of MAP cases involve transfer pricing disputes. In the US, all of the open MAP cases are transfer pricing disputes.[2] In Canada, a large percentage of the MAP inventory consists of transfer pricing cases: 88.94% in 2013, 90.27% in 2014, and 88.97% in 2015.[3] Resolving these international tax disputes is of urgent significance, otherwise, double taxation will arise and create considerable hindrances to international trade and global economic growth.

Indeed, the enhancement of the dispute resolution mechanisms is on the top agenda of many countries around the world. Significant developments on the MAP and arbitration occur at the level of the OECD and the EU. They have responded to the concern that the introduction of measures developed in the BEPS project as an overhaul in the international tax law field may lead to uncertainties and unintended double taxation with Action 14. It is devised as a minimum standard to ensure a timely resolution of the international double taxation cases and the effective implementation of the decisions reached during the MAP negotiations. Furthermore, the Multilateral Instrument (MLI) aiming at implementing the outcomes of the BEPS project in the existing bilateral tax treaties, in particular, includes separate sections on Improving the Dispute Resolution and on Arbitration. In the context of the EU, a significant development is the adoption of the EU Arbitration Directive[4] on 10 October 2017.[5] It is based

---

1. *See* the OECD MAP statistics: http://www.oecd.org/tax/dispute/map-statistics-2015.htm.
2. *See* the US MAP statistics: http://www.oecd.org/tax/dispute/map-statistics-2015.htm.
3. *See* the Canadian MAP Program Report: https://www.canada.ca/content/dam/cra-arc/migration /cra-arc/tx/nnrsdnts/cmp/mp_rprt_2012-2013-eng.pdf, https://www.canada.ca/content/dam/ cra-arc/migration/cra-arc/tx/nnrsdnts/cmp/mp_rprt_2013-2014-eng.pdf, https://www.canada. ca/content/dam/cra-arc/migration/cra-arc/tx/nnrsdnts/cmp/mp_rprt_2014-2015-eng.pdf.
4. 2016/0338 (CNS): Council Directive on Double Taxation Dispute Resolution Mechanisms in the European Union, 9806/17, 2 Oct. 2017.
5. For more details, *see*: https://ec.europa.eu/taxation_customs/business/company-tax/resoluti on-double-taxation-disputes_en_en.

on the EU Arbitration Convention (90/436/EEC)[6] which contains a clause on the mandatory binding arbitration mechanism; however, its application is only limited to cases related to transfer pricing and permanent establishments (PEs). The newly adopted Directive has a broader scope and includes the enforcement blocks to address the deficiencies of the Arbitration Convention.

When a tax dispute arises, taxpayers may use the domestic dispute resolution resources such as administrative appeals and court proceedings and/or international dispute resolution mechanisms such as the MAP and arbitration. This chapter focuses on international dispute resolution mechanisms, i.e., the MAP (section 2), and arbitration (section 3). It also provides an analysis of their interplays with domestic remedies. Each section first identifies the advantages and disadvantages of these mechanisms and then discusses their procedural aspects in relationship to these procedures. Lastly, it identifies the issues related to these dispute resolution processes and examines possible solutions in this regard.

## 2  MUTUAL AGREEMENT PROCEDURE

According to the MAP statistics published by the OECD,[7] the top five countries where MAP processes have been initiated are the United States, Germany, France, Belgium, and Switzerland. The same countries had the largest number of the inventory of MAP cases by the end of 2014. The huge number of the inventory of MAP cases indicates that the resolution of international tax disputes through MAP is time consuming and, in certain instances, the contracting states cannot arrive at a solution that is acceptable to both of them. Despite the MAP being a bilateral dispute resolution mechanism available to MNEs to fight against the international double taxation (both juridical and economic double taxation), it may not always be an effective tool for providing double taxation relief to taxpayers.

Section 2 of this chapter is structured as follows: (i) it provides a definition of the MAP and an analysis whether it actually works in practice; (ii) it investigates the advantages and disadvantages of the MAP process; (iii) it describes the procedural aspects of the MAP; and (iv) it identifies the issues and provides possible solutions.

### 2.1  What Is It and Does It Work?

In accordance to common understanding, MAP is an '*[a]dministrative procedure provided for in tax treaties for resolving difficulties arising out of their application. The procedure is most commonly used in regards of double taxation that are not clearly resolved by the treaty (e.g. as regards allocation of head office expenses, arm's length allocation of profits between associated enterprises, etc.)*'.[8]

---

6. 90/436/EEC: Convention on the Elimination of Double Taxation in Connection with the Adjustment of Profits of Associated Enterprises, L 225/10.
7. *See* the OECD MAP statistics: http://www.oecd.org/tax/dispute/map-statistics-2015.htm.
8. IBFD, *International Tax Glossary*, sixth revised edition (Amsterdam: IBFD, 2009).

The MAP is a dispute resolution mechanism made available under the bilateral tax treaty to resolve disputes and interpretative questions arising under the treaty. Depending on which model convention the applicable bilateral tax treaty recourses to, the legal basis for the use of the MAP corresponds to either Article 25 of the OECD Model Convention or Article 25 of the UN Model Convention. It is important to be aware of the differences that exist with respect to the MAP process under the OECD Model Convention, the UN Model Convention, and the applicable bilateral tax treaty. As per Article 25 of the OECD Model Convention (also the UN Model Convention) the MAP process can be activated when: (1) the taxation is considered to be 'not in accordance with the provisions' of the Convention;[9] (2) doubts or difficulties exist in the interpretation and application of the Convention;[10] or (3) the competent authorities[11] would like to consult with each other in cases not expressly provided for in the Convention in order to ensure taxpayer relief from double taxation.[12] As per Article 25(1) of the OECD Model Convention, the MAP can be initiated when the taxpayer considers that the actions of the contracting state results or will result in taxation not in accordance with the provisions of the OECD Model Convention (Figure 6.1). Typical examples where MNEs apply for the MAP processes are related to transfer pricing cases. For example, where a contracting state adjusts the price of the goods sold (or purchased) or the services rendered (or received) in a transaction between associated enterprises (i.e., in cases of primary transfer pricing adjustments); or where the contracting states dispute the amount of the profits attributable to the PE.[13] Article 25 (1) of the OECD Model Convention also prescribes that the taxpayer must file the MAP request within three years from the first notification of the action resulting in taxation that is not in accordance with the provisions of the Convention. If a taxpayer is unable to meet the deadline specified in the applicable bilateral tax treaty, which varies case-by-case, the competent authority may deny taxpayers' access to the MAP. In order to activate the MAP process, the taxpayer may submit the request to the competent authority of either the contracting state or the state of nationality in accordance with BEPS Action 14.[14]

---

9.  OECD Model Convention, at Article 25(1); UN Model Convention, at Article 25(1).
10. *Ibid.*, Article 25(3).
11. The sixth revised edition of IBFD's International Tax Glossary defines the Competent Authority as an *'entity responsible for resolving disputes and questions of tax treaty interpretation'*.
12. OECD Model Convention, at Article 25(3); UN Model Convention, at Article 25(3).
13. OECD, *Manual on Effective Mutual Agreement Procedures (MEMAP)* February 2007 Version, at pp. 12–13.
14. OECD (2015), Making Dispute Resolution Mechanisms More Effective, Action 14 - 2015 Final Report, OECD Publishing, Paris. Accessible at: http://dx.doi.org/10.1787/9789264241633-en.

*Figure 6.1   Procedure of Initiating MAP under Article 25 of the OECD MC*

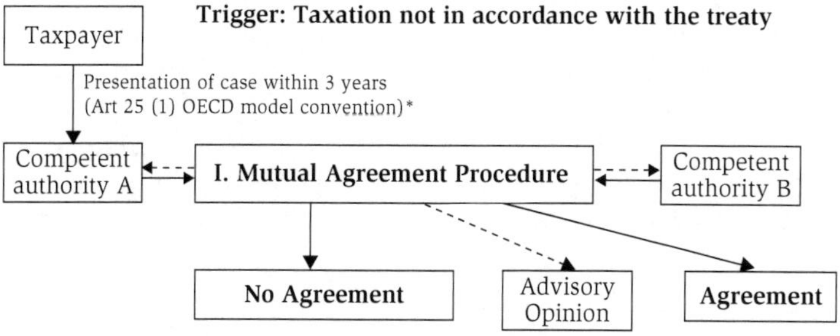

*A complaint does not bar domestic legal proceedings.

Pursuant to Article 25(2) of the OECD Model Convention, the competent authority that receives the MAP request shall assess whether the objection of the taxpayer is justified. If so, that individual should first attempt to resolve the case unilaterally. However, if that competent authority fails to resolve the matter by using domestic resources, it will communicate with the other competent authority and initiate the MAP process. However, the competent authorities, as a rule, generally only 'endeavour' to solve the case, meaning that the MAP as a treaty-based remedy is not a mandatory dispute resolution tool.

Article 25(3) of the OECD Model Convention authorizes the competent authorities to resolve the issues with respect to the interpretation and application of the bilateral tax treaties.[15] This provision addresses the issues of a general nature that concern or might concern a particular category of taxpayers rather than a specific taxpayer's case.[16] For example, it can be used to complete or clarify a term that has been incompletely or ambiguously explained in a tax treaty.[17] The competent authorities can also resolve any difficulties arising from the amendments made to the domestic legislation of one of the contracting states.[18]

The second sentence of Article 25(3) of the OECD Model Convention enables the competent authorities to deal with the cases of international double taxation that do not fall within the scope of the OECD Model Convention.[19] Thus, the mentioned provision ensures that the competent authorities consult with each other in order to eliminate any double taxation, even for situations not provided for by the bilateral tax treaty. An example of double taxation that is not addressed by the OECD Model Convention is a

---

15. OECD, *Commentaries on Model Tax Convention*, Article 25, at para. 50.
16. *Ibid.*
17. *Ibid.*, para. 52.
18. *Ibid.*
19. *Ibid.*, para. 55.

case of when a tax resident of a third country has PEs in two contracting states, and these contracting states disagree with the amount of profits attributable respectively to the PEs located in their tax jurisdictions.[20]

The OECD recognizes that the competent authorities of certain countries might be prevented from resolving cases not explicitly or at least implicitly provided for in the bilateral tax treaty.[21] For example, Brazil, Thailand, Tunisia, and Ukraine reserve their position on the second sentence of Article 25(3) of the OECD Model Convention.[22] The reason for the reservation is that, under their domestic laws, these countries do not have the authority to eliminate double taxation when not provided for in the bilateral tax treaty.

---

**Example**

A Co, a tax resident in Country A, is a parent company of an MNE group producing and distributing coffee and coffee machines. A Co manufactures the mentioned products and sells them to the group's local distributors who distribute those products in their respective territories. B Co is a company tax resident in Country B and a member of the same MNE group as A Co. In order to distribute the products in Country B, A Co sells them to B Co, and the latter is responsible for the distribution. The tax administration of Country B audited B Co and adjusted the price of the products purchased. As per the Country B's tax administration, the purchase price paid by B Co to A Co was higher than the arm's length price of those products. In case at stake two scenarios leading to double taxation are possible. First, the Competent Authority of Country A may refuse to make a corresponding adjustment and hold that the original price of the product is arm's length. Second, based on its interpretation of the arm's length principle the Competent Authority of Country A might make a corresponding adjustment that only partially amends the initial price of the product. Where one of the mentioned two situations occur, the MNE group suffers economic double taxation. A solution to this could be that B Co applies to the Competent Authority of Country B for the MAP based on the bilateral tax treaty concluded between Country A and Country B. In the course of the MAP negotiations, the Competent Authorities of Country A and Country B could reach an agreement on the arm's length price and eliminate the double taxation.

---

In addition, Article 25(5) of the OECD Model Convention contains an arbitration procedure. If the competent authorities cannot resolve the issue within two years, the process may become eligible for arbitration at the request of the taxpayer. However, Article 25B(5) of the UN Model Convention prescribes that, if the competent authorities

---

20. *Ibid.*
21. *Ibid.*
22. Kees van Raad, *Materials on International TP and EU Tax Law*, fourteenth edition (International Tax Center Leiden, 2014) (Vol. 1), para. 3, at p. 553.

cannot reach an agreement on the case within three years, the competent authority of either contracting State can decide whether or not to send the case to arbitration.

One of the significant features of the MAP is that the discussions take place between the relevant competent authorities. More specifically, MAP is a government-to-government administrative procedure and taxpayers do not directly participate. In practice, the role of taxpayers is to provide the competent authorities with complete and accurate information required to resolve the case, to present their opinion on the case, and to assist the competent authorities with finding and comprehending the case facts.[23]

In addition to the (standard) MAP process, some competent authorities allow taxpayers' requests for an accelerated MAP (sometimes referred to as a bilateral APA). The standard MAP process normally targets a tax event that occurred in previous years, i.e., a specified adjustment of income, while an accelerated MAP enables assistance on the same issue that occurs in following years. However, request for or an access to the accelerated MAP does not ensure that taxpayers are free from a tax audit on the issues addressed by the mentioned procedure.[24]

Once a request for an accelerated MAP is submitted, the competent authority would need to internally evaluate and determine whether or not the application of an accelerated MAP is suitable for the case under consideration. Once the case is accepted, the competent authority will consult with the foreign competent authority under the MAP process endeavouring to resolve the case.

The application of the provisions of Article 25 of the OECD Model Convention to transfer pricing double taxation cases is very important, as the transfer pricing adjustments represent the most significant source of international tax disputes. However, sometimes, taxpayers may not need to seek assistance through Article 25 in the transfer pricing cases as Article 9(2) may also provide protection. Article 9(2) of the OECD Model Convention provides a sound legal basis for corresponding adjustments that remove double taxation arising from the primary transfer pricing adjustments. The OECD Commentary on Article 25 emphasizes that bilateral tax treaties signed before 1977 do not include Article 9(2) of the OECD Model Convention. However, the OECD considers that, when the contracting states included Article 9(1) of the OECD Model Convention in their bilateral treaties, they intended to cover the cases of economic double taxation as well.[25] This position is taken by numerous countries.[26]

---

**Example**

A Co, a tax resident in Country A, is a parent company of an MNE group producing and distributing coffee and coffee machines. A Co manufactures the mentioned products and sells them to the group's local distributors who distribute those products in their respective territories. B Co is a company tax resident in Country B and a member of the same MNE group as A Co. In order to distribute

---

23. *See* OECD *MEMAP*, at pp. 23–24.
24. *Ibid.*, at p. 43.
25. OECD, *Commentaries on Model Tax Convention*, Article 25, at para. 11.
26. For example, Austria.

the products in Country B, A Co sells them to B Co, and the latter is responsible for the distribution. The tax administration of Country B audited B Co and adjusted its profitability. As per the Country B tax administration, the purchase price paid by B Co to A Co was higher than the arm's length price of those products. After examining the case, the competent authorities of Country A agreed that the adjustment made by Country B reflected the arm's length price. The competent authorities of Country A then applied Article 9(2) under the bilateral tax treaty concluded between Country A and Country B and made the corresponding adjustment to the amount adjusted by Country B. As a result, there was no double taxation and no need to initiate the MAP.

## 2.2 Advantages and Disadvantages

### 2.2.1 In General

The most significant advantage of the MAP process is the possibility of obtaining double taxation relief. In particular, the MAP grants taxpayers a right to discuss the double taxation issue with the relevant competent authorities and to subsequently resolve the case. Depending on how broad the respective treaty language is (e.g., with the inclusion of the second sentence of Article 25(3)), the bilateral tax treaty may well provide protection beyond the specific treaty matters. Another reason to apply for MAP is the high level of confidentiality that the MAP process ensures, as it is a discussion between the competent authorities. In particular, all of the information obtained or generated during the MAP process is fully protected by the confidentiality provision of the applicable tax treaty, i.e., Article 26 of the OECD Model Convention on exchange of information and also that of domestic legislation of the countries in question.[27] However, a number of scholars consider the non-transparency of the MAP procedure as problematic, due to the fact that the outcome of one specific MAP case is normally not going to be considered by tax authorities when assessing other similar cases. Additional advantage of the MAP process is that it is less expensive compared to existing alternatives, such as litigation. Very few countries require filing fees in practice.[28] In certain cases, for example, the accelerated MAP, the resolution reached under MAP negotiations on the same issues may be applicable for future years.

Despite being a favourable dispute resolution tool, MAP assistance is available only where the applicable bilateral tax treaty contains an article similar to Article 25 of the OECD Model Convention or the UN Model Convention.

As regards the disadvantages of the MAP process, it has the following major shortcomings:

---

27. See OECD *MEMAP*, at p. 16.
28. See the OECD MAP profiles at http://www.oecd.org/tax/dispute/country-map-profiles.htm.

- taxpayers do not have a right to participate in the discussions between the competent authorities;
- the MAP procedure is time-consuming and lengthy; and,
- MAP negotiation does not always lead to the elimination of the double taxation.

The above-mentioned flaws in the MAP process are discussed in detail in sections 2.2.2–2.2.4 of this chapter.

## 2.2.2   Taxpayers' Participation in the MAP Negotiations

MAP discussions between the competent authorities are government-to-government processes in which there is generally no direct involvement of a taxpayer. As a result, the complaints often arising from taxpayers are that a specific MAP case is non-transparent as they have no clearly defined rights about their ongoing involvement in the process after it is initiated. Also, MAP is sometimes time consuming, as the taxpayers do not have means to accelerate the process prior to the arbitration.[29]

Normally, taxpayers are only allowed to provide the information regarding the facts and circumstances of the case and present their views on the dispute without participating in the discussion between the competent authorities. During the course of the MAP process, it is of particular importance that the information received by the two competent authorities is not conflicting. The cooperation and support from taxpayers with the MAP process is indeed instrumental for enabling the competent authorities to reach a fair outcome and to resolve the case in an effective and efficient manner.

In certain situations, taxpayers may be invited to make a presentation before the competent authorities in order to ensure that the facts of the case are consistently understood. The OECD's Manual on Effective Mutual Agreement Procedures (MEMAP) recommends that countries implement a practice where the taxpayer would be eligible to present a case to both of the contracting states.[30] Such presentations might not be made for all of the MAP cases; however, in certain complex cases such as transfer pricing issues, the presentations of the taxpayers can possibly provide clarification to the competent authorities with respect to the facts and circumstances of the case and, therefore, might be of great significance in resolving the double taxation.

As taxpayers do not have a right to attend the meetings of the competent authorities and witness the discussions between them, the MEMAP recommends that the competent authorities debrief the taxpayer after each substantial discussion or after a conclusion of an important file for the purposes of transparency.[31] Such debriefings can take the form of, e.g., a telephone call.[32] The competent authorities are not obligated to provide taxpayers with detailed information; only a summary of the

---

29. J.S. Wilkie, Article 25: Mutual Agreement Procedure – Global Tax Treaty Commentaries, Global Tax Treaty Commentaries IBFD, at section 1.1.2.5.
30. *See* OECD *MEMAP,* at p. 24.
31. *Ibid.,* p. 30.
32. *Ibid.*

meeting without full disclosure is sufficient.[33] Such a summary should assist the taxpayer in understanding why that particular result has been achieved.[34] To a large extent, it provides assurance to taxpayers that the resolution reached by competent authorities is not an outcome of 'horse-trading'.

The limited participation of the taxpayer in the MAP negotiations represents a significant imperfection of the entire process. That is why the OECD recommends that the competent authorities involve taxpayers in the procedure to a certain extent.

### 2.2.3 MAP Procedure is Time Consuming

The amount of time required to complete a MAP case ranges from two to three years in practice and will vary according to the complexity of the case under consideration. In this respect, it is important to mention that the MEMAP provides best-in-class timelines for a typical MAP process.[35] The mentioned timelines may be extended or shortened depending on the facts and circumstances of a particular case. In general, competent authorities can communicate face-to-face to improve the efficiency of the MAP and subsequently reduce the time required to reach consensus. However, it should be emphasized that face-to-face communication does not always decrease the amount of time that is required to arrive at a solution that is acceptable to both of the parties involved in the MAP. Particularly, in some cases, the negotiations between the competent authorities could feasibly last more than two years or more than the timeframe agreed upon by the contracting states in the double tax treaty. Normally, the mentioned problem might arise in very complex situations. In such cases, the MEMAP advises the competent authorities to review the case, determine the reasons for the delay, and agree on an approach to be taken in order to efficiently solve it.[36]

---

**Example[37]**

Many countries do not have model timeframes for the steps to be completed by the competent authorities of those countries from the receipt of a MAP request to its resolution. Such countries include, e.g., Austria, Brazil, Chile, Costa Rica, Czech Republic, Denmark, Finland, Greece, Hungary, Iceland, India, Indonesia, Israel, Japan, Korea, Latvia, Luxembourg, Mexico, Norway, Portugal, Russia, Slovak Republic, Slovenia, South Africa, Spain, Sweden, Switzerland, Turkey, and the United Kingdom.

---

One of the minimum standards introduced under OECD BEPS Action 14 is a commitment to a timely resolution of an MAP case. The average timeframe to resolve

---

33. *Ibid.*
34. *Ibid.*
35. *Ibid.*, at pp. 45–46.
36. *Ibid.*, at p. 32.
37. *See* the OECD MAP profiles at http://www.oecd.org/tax/dispute/country-map-profiles.htm.

a case under the mentioned process is determined to be twenty-fourth months.[38] The MAP statistics will be used to monitor whether the countries meet this minimum standard.[39]

### 2.2.4 MAP Negotiations Might Fail

The most significant weakness of the MAP mechanism is that the competent authorities do not have an obligation to resolve the double taxation. As per Article 25(2) of the OECD Model Convention, the competent authorities:

> shall endeavor, if the objection appears to it to be justified and if it is not itself able to arrive at a satisfactory solution, to resolve the case by mutual agreement with the competent authority of the other contracting state...[40]

Therefore, even though the case might be successfully admitted[41] to the MAP process, negotiations between the competent authorities might not lead to an agreement, thus, leaving the double taxation unresolved.

It is also important to be aware that the MAP process may not be available for a case to which a solution is already provided in the appeal settlement or the court of one of the contracting states. The appeal settlement and court decision that are occurring involve the interaction between the taxpayer and the tax authority of that contracting state. However, it does not reflect the interest of the other contracting state. In principle, the competent authority of the other contracting state is not bound by the decision given by a foreign court or a foreign appeal settlement. Therefore, it is highly likely that double taxation will remain, where the other contracting state does not consider arm's length to make an appropriate corresponding adjustment.

However, such situations are addressed under minimum standard 1 of BEPS Action 14. The mentioned standard emphasizes that the treaty obligation, especially with respect to the dispute resolution under the MAP mechanism, shall be implemented in good faith and in a timely manner.[42] Consequently, in the post-BEPS world, countries are under the obligation to resolve the dispute resolution cases in a timely manner.

### 2.3 Procedural Aspects

It is important to emphasize that neither the OECD Model Convention nor the OECD Commentaries have established detailed rules as to the form in which the taxpayers can apply for the MAP process. The competent authorities are authorized to prescribe the

---

38. OECD. *Making Dispute Resolution Mechanisms More Effective*, (Paris: 2015), at p. 15.
39. *Ibid.*, pp. 15–16.
40. OECD Model Convention, at Article 25(2).
41. The issues with regards to the limited access to the MAP mechanism are discussed in section 2.3 of this chapter.
42. OECD. *Making Dispute Resolution Mechanisms More Effective*, (Paris: 2015), at p. 13.

special rules and procedures in this respect under their domestic legislation.[43] The OECD Commentary states that, when no special rules and procedures are adopted, the taxpayers can submit the objections in the context of a MAP process in the same way they present the objections regarding taxes that are under consideration to tax authorities of the contracting states.[44]

The requirements established in Article 25(1) of the OECD Model Convention shall be satisfied in order for the MAP request to be admitted. In particular, the MAP request must be presented within three years from the moment taxpayer considers that the actions of one or both contracting states result or will result in a taxation that is not in accordance with the applicable double tax treaty.[45] Therefore, MAP may be initiated at a very early stage based upon the mere likelihood of taxation that is not in accordance with the applicable tax treaty, and it is not required that the mentioned action or actions already resulted in double taxation. According to previous wording, MAP request may be presented to the Competent Authority of the taxpayer's state of residence or nationality.[46] However, it is important to point out that OECD BEPS Action 14 introduced an option to allow taxpayers to present a case to either of the contracting states under consideration.[47] When the contracting state does not provide taxpayers with such an option, it shall introduce a bilateral notification mechanism in order to inform the other contracting state that it does not consider the admitted MAP case to be justified.[48]

In accordance to the OECD Commentaries, the time limit of three years is specified to prevent taxpayers from presenting late objections to the administration.[49] However, this limit is to be understood as a minimum notice period, and contracting states are free to agree on a longer period in their double taxation treaties.[50] The mentioned period begins from the act of taxation itself such as by a notice of tax assessment for the collection or levy of taxes.[51] Article 25(1) of the OECD Model Convention permits a taxpayer to present a case as soon as it considers that taxation will result in taxation not in accordance with the provisions of the OECD Model Convention. Therefore, in some cases, taxpayers will have the right to initiate the MAP before the three-year time limitation begins.[52] In certain cases, the OECD also recommends that jurisdictions suspend the three-year period during the course of domestic law proceedings.[53]

The MAP procedure can be split into two different stages. In the first stage, the taxpayer presents its objections to the Competent Authority. The MAP request shall be

---

43. OECD, *Commentaries on Model Tax Convention*, Article 25, at para. 16.
44. *Ibid.*
45. *Ibid.*
46. OECD Model Convention, at Article 25(1).
47. OECD. *Making Dispute Resolution Mechanisms More Effective*, (Paris: 2015), at p. 22.
48. *Ibid.*
49. OECD, *Commentaries on Model Tax Convention*, Art. 25, at para. 20.
50. *Ibid.*, para. 20.
51. *Ibid.*, para. 21.
52. *Ibid.*
53. *Ibid.*, at para. 25.

submitted to the relevant Competent Authority of the contracting state.[54] At this time, MAP takes place exclusively at the level of a taxpayer and the Competent Authority to which the objection was presented.[55] When the Competent Authority reaches a conclusion that taxpayer's objection is justified, it is obliged under the bilateral tax treaty to take action to eliminate the double taxation. Before opening the MAP discussion, the Competent Authority shall consider whether it can itself provide such relief to the taxpayer. Where the Competent Authority concludes that the double taxation is an outcome of the activities undertaken in the state of the Competent Authority it shall provide the taxpayer relief as promptly as possible.[56] Generally, in such situations, the issues can be resolved without activating the MAP process.[57] However, when the Competent Authority determines after the examination of the issue that the double taxation is caused by the activities of the other contracting state, it shall activate the MAP.[58]

In the second stage, the contracting states shall enter into negotiations for the purpose of eliminating the double taxation. However, as already indicated, the contracting states do not have an obligation to resolve the issue in accordance with the current Article 25 of the OECD Model Convention. When the competent authorities manage to arrive at a solution that is acceptable to both of them, the second sentence of Article 25(2) of the OECD Model Convention requires the implementation of the agreement reached through the negotiations notwithstanding the time limits existing under the domestic legislation of the contracting states. It is necessary to mention that several countries have had reservations regarding this second sentence of the mentioned article. The issues in relationship to the limitations on the implementation of the MAP decision that is reached are addressed in OECD BEPS Action 14.[59]

---

**Example**

Many of the OECD member countries have publicly available rules, guidance, and procedures on how a taxpayer can access the MAP process. Such rules and guidance also include a list of documents and information to be submitted in order for a taxpayer's request to be accepted for assistance within the MAP framework. Countries that have such guidance publicly available include Australia, Austria, Belgium, Canada, China, Denmark, Estonia, Finland, France, Germany, Hungary, India,[60] Indonesia, Ireland, Israel, Italy, Japan, Korea,

---

54. *Ibid.*, at para. 7.
55. *Ibid.*, at para. 31.
56. *Ibid.*, at para. 32.
57. *Ibid.*
58. *Ibid.*, at para. 33.
59. OECD. *Making Dispute Resolution Mechanisms More Effective*, (Paris: 2015), at p. 26.
60. The rules of the Indian income tax law (1962) is publicly available, but there is no detailed guidance yet. However, a guidance consistent with the recommendations of OECD BEPS Final Report on Action 14 will soon be available.

Latvia, Mexico, the Netherlands, New Zealand, Slovenia, South Africa, Spain, Sweden, Switzerland, Turkey, the United Kingdom, and the United States.[61]

### 2.3.1  Interaction of Domestic Legislation with the MAP

The domestic legislations of some jurisdictions may conflict with the MAP process. Such conflicts intensify the inefficiencies of the mentioned dispute resolution mechanism. The major issues arising during the application of the MAP mechanism are as follows:

- taxpayers may not be entitled to access the MAP process when the case is already settled under an audit settlement mechanism or adjudicated in a court;
- access to the MAP might be limited as a consequence of the domestic anti-abuse provisions;
- interest and penalties may not fall within the scope of the MAP mechanism;
- taxes could still be collected even though the issue continues to be discussed within the framework of a MAP; and,
- the decision reached under the MAP negotiations might not be effectively implemented due to the domestic time limitations.

The sections below provide additional information that is more detailed with respect to these issues.

#### 2.3.1.1  MAP and Domestic Resolution Mechanism

Some countries do not allow taxpayers to access the MAP when the issue has already been addressed by an audit settlement agreement between a tax administration and a taxpayer. An overview of the country dispute resolution profiles demonstrates that the majority of the countries listed therein allow taxpayers to access the MAP mechanism even when the dispute is already covered by an audit settlement mechanism; however, there are some exceptions.[62] For example, Mexico limits access to the MAP process when the taxpayer voluntarily requests a statutory dispute settlement mechanism.[63] Turkey considers audit settlement as an administrative remedy, and taxpayers are eligible to select between the mentioned mechanism and the MAP.[64] However, if a settlement agreement is not achieved, Turkey permits taxpayers to continue litigation in court or with the MAP.[65] Country legislations depriving taxpayers a right to pursue a dispute through a MAP once it has been addressed by an audit settlement agreement could possibly lead to a situation where the double taxation is only partially eliminated. Such partial removal of double taxation might be due to the fact that an audit

---

61. *See* the OECD MAP profiles at http://www.oecd.org/tax/dispute/country-map-profiles.htm.
62. *Ibid.*
63. *Ibid.*
64. *Ibid.*
65. *Ibid.*

settlement does not completely eliminate double taxation and, as a consequence of domestic legislation, a taxpayer is not allowed to discuss the issue with the Competent Authority of the other contracting state in order to obtain relief from the remaining double taxation.

The OECD BEPS Action 14 Final Report addresses this issue. In particular, one of the minimum standards provides that countries should allow taxpayers to access MAP process even when the case has been addressed under the audit settlement. However, the mentioned standard allows countries to limit the access to the MAP process when such a dispute settlement procedure is separate from the audit functions, and taxpayers can only proceed to that procedure upon their request. Countries must notify their treaty partners about it and shall address this issue in their published MAP guidance.[66]

Furthermore, pursuing a court proceeding should not of itself constitute an obstruction to the access of the MAP process under Article 25 of the OECD Model Convention. Indeed, the OECD Model Convention provides the taxpayer a right to apply for an MAP to the relevant Competent Authority irrespective of whether the taxpayer has made a claim or commenced litigation under the domestic law of that contracting state.[67] However, if the case has been finally adjudicated by a court in that contracting state, depending on domestic law, the competent authority cannot easily reach a resolution departing from the domestic court decision.[68]

### 2.3.1.2 MAP and Domestic Anti-abuse Provisions

Jurisdictions take different views on whether to allow access to MAP when the transactions subject to dispute fall within the scope of domestic anti-abuse provisions. On the one hand, there are countries that do not allow taxpayers to access MAP in such circumstances. On the other hand, there are also countries admitting such cases to MAP, however, they limit themselves to forwarding the case to the other Competent Authority for any relief that it may provide. As per the OECD, simple fact that tax is charged by means of applying domestic anti-avoidance provisions cannot justify a rule preventing a taxpayer to access MAP in the absence of a specific limitation in a bilateral tax treaty.[69]

In this respect, it may be of interest to analyse whether the domestic anti-avoidance laws conflict with a country's obligations under a tax treaty. Some bilateral tax treaties may explicitly allow for domestic anti-avoidance provisions and, as a result, the application of the anti-avoidance provision may not necessarily violate it. However, even in such bilateral tax treaties, mere assertion that a domestic anti-avoidance provision is applicable to a specific case does not justify the denial of taxpayers' access to the MAP. In cases where there is no explicit allowance in the bilateral tax treaty, it would be important to check whether a particular domestic anti-avoidance law is operating consistently with the convention as per Article 1 of the OECD Model

---

66. OECD. *Making Dispute Resolution Mechanisms More Effective,* (Paris: 2015), at p. 19.
67. *Ibid.*
68. OECD, *Commentaries on Model Tax Convention*, Art. 25, at para. 35.
69. *Ibid.*

Convention.[70] Briefly, in the absence of a special provision, there is no general rule in the OECD Model Convention that denies access to a MAP based on perceived abuse. However, when the issue concerns a serious violation of domestic law and, as a consequence, significant penalties, the contracting states might wish to deny a taxpayer's access to a MAP.[71]

---

**Example[72]**

Australia considers the double taxation arising from the application of domestic anti-abuse rules to be beyond the scope of MAP. Canada accepts the request for MAP even when the adjustment is made by the application of the domestic anti-avoidance provision. However, it limits itself only to discussions that seek relief from the other contracting state regarding the double taxation. According to the French legislation, if an issue is subject to serious penalties and this is also confirmed by the court decision, it is not eligible for relief under the MAP mechanism. As regards Portugal and Slovenia, they allow a taxpayer to access MAP if the domestic anti-avoidance provisions are considered to be in conflict with the applicable double tax treaty. In accordance to Latvian law, where the case is covered by the domestic anti-abuse provisions, it is eligible for relief only within the framework of the Arbitration Convention. Japan will not reject a taxpayer's request for MAP solely based on the fact that the transaction falls within the scope of domestic anti-avoidance provisions.

---

In this regard, OECD BEPS Action 14 as one of the minimum standards provides that countries should not limit the access to a MAP in cases where the taxpayer and the tax administration disagree on the fact that the treaty anti-abuse provisions are met or that the domestic anti-abuse rules are in conflict with the bilateral tax treaty.[73] Instead, jurisdictions should accept MAP requests and inform other contracting states about the issue. It is good practice for a contracting state applying domestic anti-avoidance rules to inform the other contracting state about the issue even if it does not intend to provide any relief from double taxation. In such cases, the other contracting state may possibly be willing to remove the double taxation.

### 2.3.1.3   MAP and Interest and Penalties

A taxpayer might effectively experience double taxation even in cases when the underlying double taxation is removed under a MAP process if the countries involved in the negotiations have different perspectives on the interest and penalties applicable to the tax liability. Whilst some countries waive the interest and penalties in cases

---

70. *See* OECD MEMAP, at p. 22.
71. *Ibid.*
72. *See* the OECD MAP profiles at http://www.oecd.org/tax/dispute/country-map-profiles.htm.
73. OECD. *Making Dispute Resolution Mechanisms More Effective,* (Paris: 2015), at p. 14.

where the issue is resolved under MAP, others consider that the interest and penalties do not fall within the scope of a MAP. Therefore, when such asymmetry exists between the opinions of the countries engaged in the negotiations, double taxation can effectively remain even when the competent authorities arrive at a solution.

As per the OECD recommendation, when interest and penalties are not considered to be taxes that are included in the applicable double tax treaty, they should not be applied in a manner that nullifies taxpayer's benefits from the bilateral tax treaty.[74] For example, a contracting state shall not introduce a requirement regarding the payment of outstanding interest and penalties that is more onerous for the taxpayer in the context of a MAP.[75] An overview of the dispute resolution profiles of the countries available on the website of the OECD indicates that almost half of the countries consider that interest and penalties resulting from the adjustment made pursuant to a MAP cannot be waived or regarded as part of the MAP.[76]

---

**Example[77]**

Australian double tax treaties specifically exclude penalties and interest from the definition of tax and, therefore, those amounts are not eligible for double tax relief.[78] Moreover, in Australia, interest and penalties begin to accrue when a tax liability becomes due and payable under the relevant Australian law.[79] However, when the collection of taxes is deferred until the completion of the MAP procedure, the policy of the Australian Tax Office (ATO) is to remit the interest on that liability.[80] Moreover, France considers that interest and penalties do not fall within the scope of a MAP. Whilst France charges interest on the tax liability, it does not pay back the interest on taxes to the taxpayer when it performs a corresponding adjustment.[81] In some countries such as Czech Republic, Indonesia, Japan, South Africa, Turkey and the United Kingdom, the amount of interest and penalties are associated with the tax liability; therefore, MAP agreement also impacts the amount of interest and penalties that are applicable to that tax liability. As per German domestic legislation, interest claims are connected to the adjustment and, consequently, when the adjustment is repealed, corresponding interest claims are also repealed or reduced. Countries including Belgium, Iceland, Ireland, and Israel utilize a case-by-case approach in this respect. They do not have a specific rule in accordance to which they will waive interest and penalty applicable to the tax liability or when they have an obligation to discuss them in the framework of the MAP procedure. Denmark addresses the issue of interest and penalties only in certain non-transfer pricing cases. As for the Netherlands, its tax treaty policy aims to include a provision that

---

74. OECD, *Commentaries on Model Tax Convention*, Article 25, at para. 49.
75. *Ibid.*
76. *See* the OECD MAP profiles at http://www.oecd.org/tax/dispute/country-map-profiles.htm.
77. *Ibid.*
78. *Ibid.*
79. *Ibid.*
80. *Ibid.*
81. *Ibid.*

deals with the interest charges and refunds in relation to MAP. So far, it has included such a provision in the double tax treaties with Albania, Bahrain, Barbados, Ethiopia, Ghana, Poland, Slovenia, Switzerland, Uganda, and the United Arab Emirates. The Netherlands also entered into the Competent Authority Agreement with France and the United States that, *inter alia*, regulates the matters of interest charges and refunds as part of the MAP process.[82]

OECD BEPS Action 14 addresses the issue related to interest and penalties. In particular, the OECD recommends that countries provide guidance in this regard in their public MAP guidance. It further provides that the OECD intends to introduce amendments to the OECD Commentary in the next update of the OECD Model Convention in order to address these matters.[83]

**Example**

A Co, a tax resident in Country A, is the parent company of an MNE group producing and distributing coffee and coffee machines. A Co manufactures the mentioned products and sells them to the MNE group's local distributors who distribute those products in their respective territories. B Co is a company tax resident in Country B and a member of the same MNE group as A Co. In order to distribute the products in Country B, A Co sells them to B Co, and the latter is responsible for the distribution. The tax administration of Country B audited B Co and adjusted its profitability. As per the Country B tax administration, the purchase price paid by B Co to A Co was higher than the arm's length price of those products. Therefore, the Country B tax administration made a tax assessment that ultimately also resulted in penalties and interest on the outstanding tax liability. B Co applied for a MAP to the Competent Authority of Country B. In the course of the MAP negotiations, the competent authorities of Country A and Country B reached an agreement. In particular, the Country A's tax administration agreed to make a corresponding adjustment and, consequently, to decrease the profits of A Co in order to eliminate the double taxation. However, Country A agreed to refund only the taxes paid by A Co. The policy of Country A is not to pay interest on tax refunds. Therefore, even though the competent authorities achieved the agreement under the MAP, the taxpayer is still effectively double taxed. Country A only receives a tax refund while Country B must pay the penalties and interest in addition to the taxes due.

---

82. *Ibid.*
83. OECD. *Making Dispute Resolution Mechanisms More Effective,* (Paris: 2015), at p. 37.

## 2.3.1.4   MAP and Suspension of Tax Collection

In some states MAP cannot be initiated unless and until the payment of the total amount or the part of the taxes that are under dispute is due. Such a requirement could feasibly place cash flow burdens on taxpayers, especially when the negotiation process between the tax administrations is lengthy before arriving at a solution that is acceptable to both of the parties involved in MAP negotiations. The OECD recognizes that the perspectives of states might differ concerning the payment of outstanding taxes. In particular, some countries consider this liability to be a procedural matter that is not governed by Article 25 of the OECD Model Convention and, therefore, it does not contradict with the mentioned article.[84] However, other countries hold a different view, contending that this additional requirement is not consistent with Article 25.[85] Moreover, according to the OECD, no matter the approach taken, jurisdictions should recognize that Article 25 of the OECD Model Convention should be understood in the context of the object and purpose of the Convention, i.e., the avoidance of double taxation and prevention of fiscal evasion.[86] The OECD is of the opinion that the payment of taxes should not be a prerequisite to initiate the MAP process, where such requirement does not apply to the initiation of the domestic legal remedies.[87]

The OECD considers the suspension of tax collection to be a desirable tax policy[88], as the tax administration will be required to pay back to the taxpayer those taxes, where the objection of the latter is justified. The collection of taxes as a condition for accessing the MAP process can also be onerous for taxpayers due to the following reasons: (i) the time value of money; (ii) imposition of cash-flow burdens on taxpayers; and, (iii) delays in the resolution of good-faith cases.[89] For instance, even if a MAP ultimately removes double taxation, a requirement to pay taxes in order to activate MAP imposes a permanent cost on taxpayers in terms of time value of the money especially when the interest policies of the contracting states do not compensate taxpayers for such costs.[90] Thus, it could plausibly lead to a situation where MAP cannot achieve the goal of fully eliminating the burden of double taxation on the taxpayers.[91] Moreover, the imposition of a cash-flow burden on taxpayers is not consistent with the goal to eliminate barriers to cross-border trade and investment.[92] Further, the OECD contemplates that, when a jurisdiction requires the payment of outstanding tax liability as a precondition to initiate a MAP, it should have a system in place to refund interest on any underlying amount of tax to be returned to the taxpayer when a MAP agreement is reached between the competent authorities.[93]

---

84. OECD, *Commentaries on Model Tax Convention*, Article 25, at para. 46.
85. *Ibid.*
86. *Ibid.*, para. 47.
87. *Ibid.*
88. *Ibid.*, para. 48.
89. *Ibid.*
90. *Ibid.*
91. *Ibid.*
92. *Ibid.*
93. *Ibid.*

**Example[94]**

In some countries, collection of taxes cannot be suspended during the period MAP is pending. Many countries suspend the collection of taxes only upon taxpayer's request, and it is not directly connected with the dispute resolution through MAP. Countries requiring a request for a suspension include jurisdictions such as Austria, Czech Republic, Germany, Sweden, Iceland, and the United Kingdom.[95] Others, such as Portugal and Israel; also offer such relief as long as the taxpayer provides a guarantee. Ireland requires the taxpayer to make an appeal against the tax assessment and pay the undisputed amount of the taxes; otherwise, taxes will be collected. Regarding India, it provides relief from tax collection if there is a bilateral agreement or Memorandum of Understanding with India and another jurisdiction providing for such a suspension. Korea will not collect taxes if such a deferral of taxes is also provided for by the other treaty partner. The opinion of the ATO is that they may allow suspension of collection as they consider that tax collection would impose a burden of temporary double taxation on the taxpayer. Some other countries, such as Turkey, suspend the collection of taxes only in cases where the taxpayer goes through the litigation process.

In accordance to OECD BEPS Action 14, best practice would be to suspend the collection of taxes during the period when the MAP case is pending. The OECD provides that such a suspension should at least be available to the taxpayers under the same conditions as applicable during domestic administrative or judicial proceedings.[96]

### 2.3.1.5  MAP and Statutory Limitation Period

The OECD clarifies in sentence 2 in paragraph 2 of Article 25 that the MAP agreements shall be implemented notwithstanding the domestic time limits as contained. However, a number of countries have reserved their positions on this point. The OECD also recommends that the existing obstacles to execute the MAP agreement should generally be built into the terms of the tax treaty.[97] In addition, when the changes in the domestic legislation impact the implementation of such agreements, a contracting state amending the legislation should inform another contracting state about it.[98]

---

94. *See* the OECD MAP profiles at http://www.oecd.org/tax/dispute/country-map-profiles.htm.
95. *Ibid.*
96. OECD. *Making Dispute Resolution Mechanisms More Effective,* (Paris: 2015), at p. 31.
97. OECD, *Commentaries on Model Tax Convention*, Article 25, at para. 29.
98. *Ibid.*

**Example**[99]

Some States such as Chile, Greece, Ireland, Italy, Mexico, Poland, Portugal, and Switzerland have reservations on the second sentence of Article 25 paragraph 2 of OECD Model Convention.[100] These countries contemplate that the implementation of reliefs and refunds obtained under MAP agreement should be linked with the domestic time limits. Some other jurisdictions execute MAP agreements even if the statutory limitation period is over only in cases where the applicable double tax treaty provides for it, i.e., the relevant double tax treaty includes the second sentence of Article 25 (2) of the OECD Model Convention. For example, the mentioned approach is used by South Africa, Spain, and the United States.[101]

For those countries with reservations, their domestic legislations contain a statutory limitation after which those countries are not eligible to make any adjustment to the profits declared by taxpayers. As a consequence, such limitations create a significant problem for taxpayers especially when a tax administration initiates a tax audit just before the statutory limitation date. In this case, taxpayers may not effectively be able to benefit from the bilateral dispute resolution mechanism. Alternatively, in cases when an MAP agreement is achieved after the statutory limitation period, the domestic laws of those countries will limit the implementation of such MAP agreement.

OECD BEPS Action 14 recommends that jurisdictions include the second sentence of paragraph 2 of Article 25 of the OECD Model Convention in their bilateral tax treaties as a minimum standard 3.3. It further provides that, when the jurisdiction cannot include the mentioned sentence in its bilateral tax treaties as an alternative, it should include a provision in the bilateral treaties limiting the time during which it can make an adjustment under Article 9(1) and Article 7(2) of the OECD Model Convention.[102]

**Example**

A Co, a tax resident in Country A, is a parent company of an MNE group manufacturing and distributing pharmaceutical products. A Co manufactures the products and sells them to local distributors of the group in order for them to distribute the products in their respective territory. B Co is a company tax resident in Country B and member of the same MNE group as A Co. In order to distribute the products in Country B, A Co sells them to B Co, and the latter is responsible for distribution. Country B has a domestic statutory limitation of six years. Therefore, once the statutory limitation period is over, the tax administration of Country B cannot make any adjustment to the profits declared by companies. In Year 5, the tax administration of Country B audits B Co and

---

99. *See* the OECD MAP profiles at http://www.oecd.org/tax/dispute/country-map-profiles.htm.
100. OECD, *Commentaries on Model Tax Convention*, Article 25, at para. 98.
101. *See* the OECD MAP profiles at http://www.oecd.org/tax/dispute/country-map-profiles.htm.
102. OECD. *Making Dispute Resolution Mechanisms More Effective*, (Paris: 2015), at p. 26.

upwardly adjusts its profitability, stating that the price paid by B Co to A Co for the pharmaceutical products was not at arm's length. As Country B has a six-year statutory limitation rule, only one year is available for the entire procedure, i.e., (i) to make an application for a MAP; (ii) to accept the case to a MAP; and, (iii) to solve the issue under dispute. Such a stringent timeline could feasibly lead to a situation where the double taxation is not eliminated or is only partially eliminated.

### 2.3.2 MAP and Domestically Available Remedies

While the majority of the jurisdictions prefer to only handle the issue either under the MAP process or under the domestic remedy, a number of jurisdictions address the dispute simultaneously with MAP and domestically available dispute resolution mechanisms. A reason why countries allow pursuance of the double taxation issue either by utilizing one of the mentioned remedies could be to avoid the duplication of effort.

Another reason for selecting such an approach is that, in some countries, the competent authorities are bound by administrative appeals or court decisions. Therefore, in certain countries, taxpayers have to choose among the available dispute resolution mechanisms as they cannot simultaneously pursue an issue under domestic and bilateral dispute resolution mechanisms. The MEMAP recommends that the competent authorities make their positions public with respect to court decisions, especially when they are considered to be bound by a court's decisions.[103] The MEMAP also suggests explaining the legal basis for such an approach.[104] It is important to emphasize that, when the competent authority cannot provide relief from double taxation solely due to a binding court decision, it should not reasonably expect the other Competent Authority to remove it.[105]

According to the OECD, domestic law does not justify a failure to meet treaty obligations even if the law is a constitutional law.[106] This general principle is reflected in Article 27 of the Vienna Convention on the Law of Treaties.[107] The OECD provides that, when a Competent Authority relies on the domestic law impediment and does not grant the taxpayer a right to initiate the MAP, it should inform the other Competent Authority about it and explain the legal basis of its position.[108] The OECD also provides that taxpayers are entitled to present a case to the appropriate Competent Authority whether or not they have made a claim or initiated litigations under the domestic law of the relevant State.[109] The Competent Authority to which the request was submitted

---

103. *See* OECD MEMAP, at p. 33.
104. *Ibid.*
105. *Ibid.*
106. OECD, *Commentaries on Model Tax Convention*, Article 25, at para. 27.
107. *Ibid.*
108. *Ibid.*
109. *Ibid.*, para. 34.

should not wait for the final decision and decide whether the request is eligible for the MAP mechanism.[110] In general, the OECD is of the opinion that the application for a MAP should not be rejected without a 'good reason'.[111]

The overview of the dispute resolution profiles of countries indicates that the majority of the countries that allow dealing with a dispute with both bilateral and domestic remedies will do so unless a binding court decision exists. That is, in most cases, the competent authorities are bound by court decisions. Therefore, the competent authorities initiating negotiations with the other competent authorities might not be able to implement MAP decisions if their domestic court decided the case in another way.

---

**Example[112]**

Ireland accepts a MAP request even if judicial or administrative proceedings are ongoing with respect to this case. However, in such circumstances, the taxpayer is requested to suspend the litigation under domestic legal remedies while the outcome of the MAP is pending. If the taxpayer does not agree to do so, the Competent Authority will delay MAP negotiations pending the outcome of these proceedings. A similar position is taken by Spain i.e., when the taxpayer activates both domestic and bilateral dispute resolution mechanisms, the judicial or administrative proceedings shall be suspended until the MAP is concluded. In some jurisdictions such as Costa Rica, Estonia, Korea, and Poland, taxpayers can apply for the MAP as long as there is no binding court decision. In Turkey, they do not allow the taxpayers to be involved in a MAP and administrative or judicial proceedings together. Thus, if a taxpayer wishes to access a MAP, it is obligated to withdraw from the judicial process. In Belgium, MAP is available to taxpayers irrespective of the judicial or administrative remedies. Thus, MAP and domestic remedies exist independently of each other and can be simultaneously launched in parallel. The same approach is also shared by Denmark. Regarding Japan, it does not reject a case solely based on the fact that the taxpayer applied for the domestically available judicial or administrative remedies.

---

**Example[113]**

In some jurisdictions, taxpayers are eligible to apply for a MAP when the court has rendered its decision, however, in such cases, the competent authorities of those countries limit the negotiations to the explanation of the facts to the other competent authorities as they are legally bound by their court decisions. Such an approach is taken by Austria, Canada, Czech Republic, Ireland, Israel, and New

---

110. *Ibid.*
111. *Ibid.*
112. *See* the OECD MAP profiles at http://www.oecd.org/tax/dispute/country-map-profiles.htm.
113. *Ibid.*

221

Zealand. Domestic laws of some countries take different approaches with respect to court and administrative decisions. In these countries, the competent authorities are bound by the courts' decisions while administrative decisions can be overridden. Therefore, those countries provide MAP assistance to the taxpayer only in the case of administrative decisions. States taking this approach include Indonesia, Portugal, South Africa, and Spain. Australia provides MAP assistance to the taxpayer as long as the double taxation still remains after administrative or judicial decisions but only to the extent of such double taxation. In Chile, MAP assistance is available to the event the new information is provided that was not available when an administrative or a court decision was rendered. Other countries such as Hungary, Iceland, and Slovenia do not provide assistance under a MAP when an administrative or court decision has already been made.

OECD BEPS Action 14 provides that countries should include an explanation on the relationship of the domestic and bilateral dispute resolution mechanisms in their published MAP guidance.[114] In particular, the mentioned guidance should state whether the countries are bound by the administrative and judicial remedies.[115]

### 2.3.3 Elimination of the Economic Double Taxation

Countries have different opinions on whether or not economic double taxation arising through the application of Article 9(1) of the OECD Model Convention falls within the scope of the MAP. While a certain number of double tax treaties include a provision requiring the contracting states to perform a corresponding adjustment provided that specific requirements are met, other double tax treaties do not contain such a provision.[116] Therefore, it is a matter of discussion whether countries are still obligated to provide relief from economic double taxation in the absence of an article similar to Article 9(2) of the OECD Model Convention. It is worth noting that the OECD is in favour of resolving economic double taxation with a MAP even in cases when a paragraph similar to Article 9(2) of the OECD Model Convention is lacking in the applicable double tax treaty.

As pointed out above, jurisdictions have differing views on whether or not economic double taxation is covered by the bilateral tax treaties. In particular, some jurisdictions consider that economic double taxation conflicts with the spirit of the OECD Model Convention while others do not share this view.[117]

114. Certain countries have publicly available information regarding the relationship between administrative and judicial remedies and the MAP process. These countries include Australia, Austria, Canada, France, Germany, Hungary, Indonesia, Ireland, Iceland, Italy, Korea, the Netherlands, New Zealand, Slovenia, Spain, Sweden, Switzerland, Turkey, the United Kingdom, and the United States.
115. OECD. *Making Dispute Resolution Mechanisms More Effective*, (Paris: 2015), at pp. 32–33.
116. OECD Model Convention, at Article 9(2).
117. OECD, *Commentaries on Model Tax Convention*, Article 25, at para. 12.

**Example**[118]

A number of countries such as Czech Republic, Brazil, Thailand, and Vietnam reserve a right not to insert Article 9 (2) of the OECD Model Convention in their double tax treaties. Hungary, Slovenia, Azerbaijan, Malaysia, and Serbia reserve a right to clarify Article 9 (2) in order to make a corresponding adjustment only in cases where those adjustments are justified. The examination of dispute resolution profiles of the countries as published on the OECD website indicates that all of the countries listed therein[119] consider transfer pricing issues to be covered by a MAP.[120] In many states, there is at least one bilateral tax treaty that does not include an article similar to Article 9(2) of the OECD Model Convention. Generally, bilateral tax treaties without the mentioned article are old. Some jurisdictions even have reservations on Article 9(2) of the OECD Model Convention. A number of the countries with bilateral tax treaties that do not include an article similar to Article 9(2) of the OECD Model Convention do not allow corresponding adjustments. However, countries such as Ireland, Japan, Korea, and Switzerland have a policy to make corresponding adjustments even if an article similar to Article 9(2) of the OECD Model Convention is absent from the applicable tax treaty.

OECD BEPS Action 14 recommends that jurisdictions allow taxpayers access to the MAP process in the case of transfer pricing issues and should effectively implement the MAP decisions reached in this regard.[121] The OECD also suggests that jurisdictions include Article 9(2) of the OECD Model Convention in their bilateral tax treaties.

**Example**

A Co is a parent company of the MNE group manufacturing and distributing computers. A Co manufactures the products and sells them to local distributors of the group in order for them to distribute the products in their respective territory. A Co is a tax resident in Country A. B Co is a company tax resident in Country B and a member of the same MNE group as A Co. In order to distribute the computers in Country B, A Co sells them to B Co, and the latter is responsible for the distribution. The price under the mentioned controlled transaction equals EUR 100.

The tax administration of Country B audited B Co. As per Country B's tax administration, the price of EUR 100 was not at arm's length, therefore, it adjusted the mentioned price. In particular, it reduced the price from EUR 100 to

---

118. *See* the OECD MAP profiles at http://www.oecd.org/tax/dispute/country-map-profiles.htm.
119. Countries include Australia, Austria, Brazil, Belgium, Canada, China (People's Republic of), Costa Rica, Czech Republic, Denmark, Estonia, Finland, France, Germany, Greece, Hungary, Iceland, India, Indonesia, Ireland, Israel, Italy, Japan, Korea, Latvia, Luxembourg, Mexico, the Netherlands, New Zealand, Norway, Poland, Portugal, Russia, Slovak Republic, Slovenia, South Africa, Spain, Sweden, Switzerland, Turkey, the United Kingdom, and the United States.
120. *See* the OECD MAP profiles at http://www.oecd.org/tax/dispute/country-map-profiles.htm.
121. OECD. *Making Dispute Resolution Mechanisms More Effective*, (Paris: 2015), at p. 13.

EUR 70. As a consequence, the profit in Country B increased by EUR 30. The bilateral tax treaty between Country A and Country B does not include Article 9(2) of OECD Model Convention. In accordance with Country A's tax policy, it does not make a corresponding adjustment when it is not provided by the applicable double tax treaty.

Assume that the transfer pricing adjustment made in Country B is consistent with the arm's length principle, as established in Article 9(1) of the OECD Model Convention. Country B would not be obligated to decrease the taxable profits in Country B. However, Country A does not make a corresponding adjustment even if it is consistent with the arm's length principle solely based on the fact that the applicable double tax treaty does not expressly state to do so. Therefore, in this case, the taxpayer will not be able to obtain relief from economic double taxation. A profit amounting to EUR 30 will be taxed both in Country A and in Country B.

## 3   ARBITRATION

As demonstrated in the previous sections of this chapter, MAP is not always an effective mechanism for resolving double taxation cases. In particular, bilateral tax treaties (in the context of the OECD Model Convention and the UN Model Convention) do not require the contracting states to resolve these cases; it only states that the contracting states shall make an endeavour to resolve the dispute. Recognizing the inefficiency of MAP in resolving the international double taxation issues and for the purposes of improving the finality of the MAP procedure, arbitration is built in as an extension of the MAP procedure. Arbitration, by definition, is a:

> [t]erm used for the determination of a dispute by the judgement of one or more persons, called arbitrators, who are chosen by the parties and who normally do not belong to a normal court of competent jurisdiction.[122]

In the OECD BEPS Action 14 Final Report, countries such as Australia, Austria, Belgium, Canada, France, Germany, Ireland, Italy, Japan, Luxembourg, the Netherlands, New Zealand, Norway, Poland, Slovenia, Spain, Sweden, Switzerland, the United Kingdom, and the United States committed to including a mandatory binding arbitration clause in their bilateral tax treaties.[123] In addition, the MLI was adopted and signed by jurisdictions around the world, and it contains the section on the mandatory binding arbitration. Therefore, countries showing interest are able to more easily include the mandatory binding arbitration into their existing bilateral treaties, leading to a more effective and efficient international dispute resolution mechanism in the post-BEPS world.

---

122. IBFD, *International Tax Glossary*, sixth revised edition (Amsterdam: IBFD, 2009), at p. 23.
123. OECD. *Making Dispute Resolution Mechanisms More Effective*, (Paris: 2015), at p. 10.

In addition to the bilateral tax treaties, taxpayers that are a tax resident in one of the EU Member States can enjoy the benefits of the EU Arbitration Convention and, currently, the EU Arbitration Directive. In some countries, bilateral investment agreements might also play an important role in solving the problems of international double taxation.

Section 3 of this chapter is structured as follows: (i) it provides a definition of arbitration and analyses whether it actually works in practice; (ii) it investigates the advantages and disadvantages of the arbitration process; (iii) it describes the procedural aspects of the arbitration mechanism; and (iv) it identifies the issues arising in relationship to the arbitration and provides possible solutions.

### 3.1 What are They and Do They Work?

#### 3.1.1 OECD and UN Model Convention

In order for the residents or nationals (in the case of Article 24 (1) of the OECD Model Convention, i.e., the discrimination is based on the nationality) of the contracting states to enjoy the benefits of the arbitration mechanism:

- the arbitration clause shall be included in the applicable bilateral tax treaty;
- the double taxation shall not be resolved under MAP, and;
- the issue under consideration shall not be explicitly excluded from the scope of the arbitration provision.

The OECD Model Convention provides that taxpayers are eligible to apply for the arbitration mechanism when the competent authorities are unable to resolve a case within a two-year period from its submission.[124] The two-year period begins when the taxpayer submits sufficient information to the Competent Authority to decide the case.[125] In the context of arbitration, taxpayers can submit issues that cannot be solved under MAP discussions and that prevent the competent authorities from arriving at a final decision.[126] A case cannot be considered as being decided as long as there is at least one issue on which the competent authorities have differing opinions. The OECD Commentaries provide that the competent authorities are not eligible to unilaterally close the case and, consequently, to prevent the taxpayers from obtaining access to arbitration (Figure 6.2).[127]

---

124. *See* OECD Model Convention, at Article 25(5).
125. OECD, *Commentaries on Model Tax Convention*, Article 25, at para. 75.
126. *Ibid.*, para. 63.
127. *Ibid.*, para. 64.

*Figure 6.2   Arbitration under Article 25 of the OECD Model Convention*

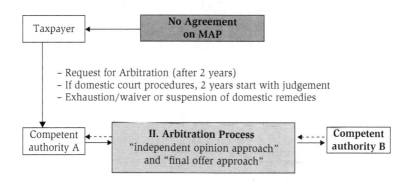

The OECD Commentaries clarify that the arbitration procedure is not an alternative or an additional recourse mechanism.[128] It is only an extension of a MAP and serves a purpose of enhancing the effectiveness of the latter mechanism.[129] As per the OECD Model Convention, only debatable issues can be resolved within the arbitration framework while the final agreement is still reached under a MAP.[130] The OECD recommends that the contracting states always allow the taxpayers to access arbitration in a limited range of cases. For instance, such cases could involve a transfer pricing case or a case of profit attribution to a PE. As regards the other situations, a dispute would be admitted to arbitration on a case-by-case basis.[131]

The arbitration process is only available for cases where double taxation has actually been realized and not in cases of when a taxpayer believes that double taxation might occur in the future.[132] The mentioned process can only be activated for the issues arising from the MAP request made under Article 25 (1) of the OECD Model Convention and not for the matters under Article 25(3). Therefore, taxpayers cannot benefit from the arbitration process when unresolved issues arise from MAP that was initiated for purposes of clarifying an interpretation or application of a provision of the OECD Model Convention or where the taxpayer made a request for MAP in order to combat double taxation not directly covered by the OECD Model Convention. Otherwise stated, when the competent authorities agree that taxation is in accordance with the applicable double tax treaty, dispute cannot be further pursued under the arbitration process even if the double taxation is not eliminated.[133] Nevertheless, the OECD indicates that contracting states are allowed to broaden the scope of the arbitration provision and address issues arising from MAP initiated under Article 25 (3) of the OECD Model Convention.[134]

---

128. *Ibid.*
129. *Ibid.*
130. *Ibid.*
131. *Ibid.,* para. 66.
132. *Ibid.,* para. 72.
133. *Ibid.*
134. *Ibid.,* para. 73.

Arbitration is not an automatic process, and taxpayers must make a request in order to initiate it.[135] This request can be made at any time after a period of two years from the submission of the case to the Competent Authority.[136] Taxpayers can decide to allow the competent authorities to discuss the dispute for more than two years or simply not to pursue the case within the framework of arbitration.[137] Additionally, taxpayers do not need approval from the competent authorities to initiate the arbitration process.[138] Once the arbitration process admission requirements are met, the issues on which the competent authorities cannot agree can be submitted to arbitration.[139] Due to the special nature of the procedure, the taxpayers or their representatives might not have access to the papers associated with the arbitration process.[140]

The contracting states are bound by the arbitration decision unless the taxpayer impacted by the mentioned decision does not agree on the solution provided therein. The decision is only binding with respect to the issues submitted to and decided within the framework of the arbitration. The OECD also provides that, even though there is no obligation to solve the cases similar to those decided under the arbitration procedure in a similar manner, contracting states might consider doing so anyway.[141] The OECD recommends that, with an appropriate treaty provision, the contracting state should provide the possibility of reaching another resolution other than that recommended by the arbitrators within six months from when the outcome of the arbitration is announced.[142]

With respect to the arbitration in the context of the double tax treaties, the problem is that a vast majority of treaties do not include such a provision. Taking into account these statistics, arbitration cannot be effective in practice because some countries are not willing to include them in their bilateral tax treaties.

---

**Example[143]**

Tax treaties entered into by Turkey do not include the arbitration clause as its domestic legislation is incompatible with the arbitration provision.[144] A significant number of countries have a treaty policy that does not allow the inclusion of an arbitration provision in their double tax treaties. For instance, countries with the mentioned tax treaty policy include Brazil, China, Costa Rica, Czech Republic, Hungary, India, Israel, Korea, Portugal, Slovak Republic, and Turkey.[145]

---

135. *Ibid.*, para. 70.
136. *See* OECD Model Convention, at Art. 25 (5).
137. OECD, *Commentaries on Model Tax Convention*, Article 25, at para. 70.
138. *Ibid.*, para. 63.
139. *Ibid.*
140. *Ibid.*, para. 61.
141. *Ibid.*, para. 83.
142. *Ibid.*, para. 84.
143. *See* the OECD MAP profiles at http://www.oecd.org/tax/dispute/country-map-profiles.htm.
144. *Ibid.*
145. *Ibid.*

Concerning the UN Model Convention, it provides two alternative terminologies for Article 25 that are mainly reproduced based on Article 25 of the OECD Model Convention. The arbitration clause is only contained in paragraph 5 of Article 25B of the UN Model Convention. Article 25A of the UN Model Convention, however, provides an opportunity to omit it in the event that the contracting States do not consider the inclusion of the arbitration clause appropriate in the concerned bilateral tax treaty.[146] Other than that, there are three additional differences between the arbitration clause provided by the OECD and that provided by the UN. First, the UN allows the initiation of the arbitration procedure if the competent authorities are unable to reach consensus on a case within three years from the presentation of that case[147], while the OECD provides a two-year time limit for beginning an arbitration procedure. Second, in contrast with the OECD Model Convention whereby arbitration must be requested by the taxpayer who initiated the case, the UN provides that arbitration must be requested by the competent authority of one of the contracting states.[148] Therefore, under the UN Model Convention, if the competent authorities of both contracting states consider that a case does not qualify for arbitration and none of them makes a request, the arbitration process will not be initiated. Third, Article 25B(5) of the UN Model Convention expressly allows the competent authorities to depart from the arbitration decision if they agree on a different solution within six months after the decision has been communicated to them.[149] Thus, it provides the competent authorities one last opportunity to rectify any unforeseen issues or obstacles regarding the finality of the MAP process which otherwise becomes evident with the arbitration decision.[150]

### 3.1.2 EU Arbitration Convention

Table 6.1 provides a comparison of Article 25 of the OECD Model Convention and EU Arbitration Convention.

Table 6.1   Comparison of the Arbitration Procedure Between Article 25 of the OECD Model Convention and the EU Arbitration Convention

|  | Article 25 OECD Model Convention | EU Arbitration Convention |
| --- | --- | --- |
| Scope | All kinds of taxation not in accordance with a tax treaty | Transfer pricing issues |
| Taxpayer initiative | Yes | Yes |

---

146. Footnote 1 of the Article 25(5) of the OECD Model Convention, at p. 35; para. 13: UN Model Convention, commentary to Article 25 (2011).
147. UN Model Convention, commentary to Article 25 (2011), at para. 13.
148. *Ibid.*
149. *Ibid.*
150. J.S. Wilkie, Art. 25: Mutual Agreement Procedure - Global Tax Treaty Commentaries, Global Tax Treaty Commentaries IBFD, at section 3.4.2.

|  | Article 25 OECD Model Convention | EU Arbitration Convention |
| --- | --- | --- |
| Taxpayer participation | Limited | Yes[151] |
| Time limit | Yes | Yes |
| Compulsory solution | Yes | Yes |

The enterprises of the contracting states of the Arbitration Convention and the PEs of the enterprises of those contracting states can benefit from the Arbitration Convention provided that:

- no agreement was achieved within two years of a complaint being submitted to the contracting state; and
- to the extent double taxation is not avoided under a MAP process initiated in the context of the Arbitration Convention.

The scope of the Arbitration Convention covers transfer pricing adjustments, i.e., adjustments made to the profits of associated enterprises and to the profits attributed to PEs.[152] As a rule, the EU Arbitration Convention provides that, if the Member States fail to resolve the case with a MAP within two years, an arbitration commission should be established to provide an opinion on that case in order to eliminate the double taxation.[153] Once an arbitrary commission is initiated, the arbitration panel must provide its decision within six months. During that course of time, the taxpayers have a right to appear before a commission; they may even request the taxpayers to appear, which is different from the arbitration procedure initiated by the bilateral tax treaty.[154] After the commission delivers their advice, the outcome of the arbitration is binding on the concerned Member States, and they are required to implement the commission's advice within six months.[155] Nevertheless, the EU Arbitration Convention also provides that the Member States may depart from the commission's advice if they agree differently within the six month time period, which is the same as the position taken by the UN.[156] Furthermore, with the consent of the affected taxpayer, the competent authorities may publish an arbitration decision.[157]

---

151. Taxpayers have the right to request to appear or be represented in front the commission. *See* more detailed explanations below.
152. Article 4 of the EU Arbitration Convention.
153. Article 7 of the EU Arbitration Convention.
154. Article 10 of the EU Arbitration Convention.
155. Article 10 of the EU Arbitration Convention.
156. Article 12 of the EU Arbitration Convention.
157. Article 12(2) of the EU Arbitration Convention.

The EU Arbitration Convention allows resolving an entire case within the framework of the arbitration procedure. In general, transfer pricing disputes involve an enormous amount of money; therefore, Member States are reluctant to pass these cases to arbitrators. In the event that the dispute is transferred to the advisory commission, the Member States forfeit the power to influence the decision. As a consequence, the arbitration procedure as established in the Arbitration Convention is not extensively used in practice. According to statistics published by the JTPF,[158] in many cases, taxpayers waive the two-year time limit as provided for in Article 7(4) of the Arbitration Convention, e.g., instances of waived time limits amounted to 148 cases in 2015. In many cases, taxpayers do not pursue disputes under arbitration. For example, in 2015, the two-year period expired for seventy-three cases; however, those cases were not presented to the advisory commission. The disputes submitted to the advisory commission are very limited. In particular, during a period of 2012–2015, a maximum of two cases were presented to that commission for its opinion in 2012 and 2015.

As a result of the above analysis, it could be concluded that the arbitration procedure provided for in the Arbitration Convention is not effective in practice. As previously mentioned, one of the major factors could be the reluctance of the Member States to refer cases to the advisory commission as they lose the power to influence the decision, and a substantial amount of tax revenues might be at stake.

As an arbitration procedure provided for in the Arbitration Convention is not effective in practice, the EU Arbitration Directive (*see* Figure 6.3) has adopted an improved dispute resolution mechanism to more effectively resolve tax disputes. The EU Arbitration Directive imposes an enforceable obligation on Member States. As a result, they will have a legal duty to take conclusive and enforceable decisions. If the mechanisms are not applied properly, the taxpayers can bring actions before the national courts that will unblock the procedures for them. Compared to the EU Arbitration, the Directive extends the scope to all tax disputes between Member States that are derived from tax treaties and other international agreements, such as the elimination of double taxation for businesses and citizens. Another change brought by EU Arbitration Directive is that it provides clearly defined and enforceable timelines with a standard period of eighteen months for the arbitration phase. Thus, it encourages the Member States to arrive at timely resolutions and also provides certainty to taxpayers.

---

158. The statistics on the MAP and arbitration initiated under the Arbitration Convention can be online accessed at: http://ec.europa.eu/taxation_customs/business/company-tax/transfer-pricing-eu-context/joint-transfer-pricing-forum_en.

Figure 6.3    EU Arbitration Directive

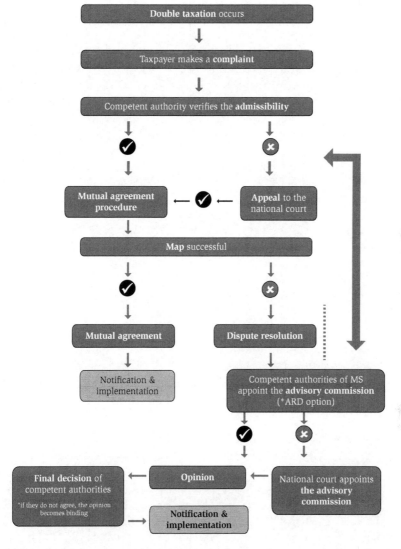

*Source*: PWC Tax Insights: Increased Taxpayer Rights for Tax Dispute Resolution under New EU Directive.

## 3.2 Advantages and Disadvantages

### 3.2.1 OECD and UN Model Convention

A more rapid dispute resolution mechanism can be considered to be the primary advantage of the arbitration process. An arbitration process can significantly improve the effectiveness of the MAP procedure as it allows resolving the issues and requiring the competent authorities to conclude the final decision. Once those debatable issues are decided, the competent authorities can proceed with finalizing the MAP agreement.

As already mentioned, a dispute can only be partially resolved under the arbitration mechanism provided by the OECD Model Convention. The issues in which the competent authorities cannot reach an agreement can be submitted to the arbitration procedure while the case itself is still decided under a MAP. This rule allows the competent authorities to select the issues to be submitted to arbitration and, therefore, they might have fewer objections against the application of the mentioned process. The disadvantages of the arbitration process in the context of the OECD Model Convention are: (i) the lack of practical experience in the arbitration procedure; and, (ii) that the arbitration processes are only the extension of the MAP and, therefore, taxpayers are not part of the mentioned process.[159] With regard to the 'final offer' arbitration (also called the 'baseball' arbitration),[160] the opinions are different, and some countries have used this form successfully (e.g., the US).

### 3.2.2 EU Arbitration Convention

Just as with the arbitration provided for in Article 25 of the OECD Model Convention, the arbitration clause in the Arbitration Convention is a very crucial mechanism for improving the efficiency of the MAP procedure. A significant advantage of the arbitration process is that it accelerates the process of dispute resolution between EU Member States when the arbitration phase is envisaged to be six months. In particular, the EU Arbitration expressly covers issues related to PEs of entities in EU Member States while a PE of a non-EU country is out of its scope. Furthermore, the arbitration is strictly confidential, as the discussions take place between tax authorities. Such strict confidentiality is in the interest of taxpayers that are concerned about the public disclosure of their corporate secrets. In addition, the costs of engaging in arbitration are rather limited as only few countries require filing fees.

However, in practice, the arbitration mechanism within the context of the Arbitration Convention fails to work effectively. On the one hand, taxpayers do not want to lose any opportunities of obtaining double taxation relief. On the other hand, Member States are reluctant to submit a dispute to the advisory commission. In practice, the Member States argue either that the cases do not qualify for determination

---

159. Monique van Herksen and David Fraser, *Comparative analysis: Arbitration Procedure for Handling Tax Controversy* (IBFD: 2009), at p. 160.
160. Under the baseball arbitration procedure, the advisory commission would issue a statement based on the position taken by one of the tax administrations involved.

under the Arbitration Convention, or they use Article 7(4) of the Arbitration Convention and request taxpayers to waive the two-year period limitation to overcome this issue.[161] It should be emphasized that typical transfer pricing cases are complex and extensive, therefore, Member States may possibly need more than two years to reach consensus. Another disadvantage, as has been mentioned before, is that taxpayers only play a limited role in the process other than providing relevant information.

## 3.3 Procedural Aspects

### 3.3.1 Procedural Aspects of Arbitration under OECD and UN Model Convention

Article 25 of the OECD Model Convention does not detail the procedural aspects of the arbitration procedure. In particular, Article 25 of the OECD Model Convention: (i) does not define the procedural rules or a list of required information to be submitted to the competent authorities; (ii) does not provide information regarding who the arbitrators can be and any other procedural rules in this regard; (iii) Article 25 of the OECD Model Convention does not detail any procedural rule on how to appoint the arbitrators; (iv) it does not impose a requirement of independence or competence on the arbitrators; and, (v) Article 25 of the OECD Model Convention does not provide any formal procedure for objecting to the appointment of certain individuals as arbitrators. These rules and procedures can be determined by the competent authorities in their mutual agreement document.

The Annex to the OECD Commentary on Article 25 of the OECD Model Convention provides a *Sample Mutual Agreement on Arbitration* (Sample Mutual Agreement). According to the OECD, competent authorities can use the Sample Mutual Agreement as a basis for implementing the arbitration process in practice. The Sample Mutual Agreement is only a model form, and the competent authorities can easily modify the rules and procedures established therein.

The Sample Mutual Agreement details the rules and procedures that can be used in the arbitration procedure. It does not expressly discuss the independence status of arbitrators, though it does provide that arbitrators can be anyone. This even includes a government official of a contracting state unless that person has been engaged in the previous stages of the case under dispute.[162] As per the Sample Mutual Agreement, each Competent Authority shall appoint one arbitrator. Those arbitrators will appoint a third arbitrator within two months of their appointment who will function as a Chair. If any of these appointments are not made within the specified deadlines, the Director of the OECD Centre for Tax Policy and Administration will appoint the arbitrator or arbitrators not yet appointed within ten days of receiving such a request from the

---

161. Article 7(4) of the EU Arbitration Convention.
162. Kees van Raad, *Materials on International TP and EU Tax Law*, fourteenth edition (International Tax Center Leiden, 2014) (Vol. 1), at p. 540, para. 7.

person who made the request for arbitration.[163] Moreover, neither the OECD Commentaries nor the Sample Mutual Agreement specify rules on how to object to the appointment of the arbitrators.

The Sample Mutual Agreement provides that, for the purposes of the arbitration decision, information that was not available to both contracting states before the request for arbitration was received should not be taken into account unless otherwise agreed upon by the competent authorities.[164] According to the Sample Mutual Agreement, the arbitration decision must be communicated to the competent authorities and the person making the request for arbitration within six months from the date on which the Chair notifies the competent authorities and the person making the request for arbitration that the Chair has received all of the necessary information.[165]

### 3.3.2 Procedural Aspects of Arbitration under Arbitration Convention and the Code of Conduct

Practical aspects of the Arbitration Convention are clarified in the Code of Conduct for effective implementation of the Arbitration Convention (Code of Conduct). The Arbitration Convention does not provide a list of specific documentation to be submitted to the advisory commission. Instead, it enables taxpayers to submit any information, evidence, or document that is likely to be of use in the course of the arbitration process.[166] The Code of Conduct provides a detailed list of documentation and information that must be presented in order for the dispute to be considered submitted for the purposes of the commencement of the two-year period after which the case shall be transferred to arbitration. The list of required documents and information shall consist of:

- the identification information (such as name, address, tax identification number) of the enterprise of the Member State that presents its request and of the other parties to the relevant transactions;
- details of the relevant facts and circumstances of the case (including details of the relationships between the enterprise and the other parties to the relevant transactions);
- identification of the tax periods concerned;
- copies of the tax assessment notices, tax audit report, or equivalent leading to the alleged double taxation;
- details of any appeals and litigation procedures initiated by the enterprise or the other parties to the relevant transactions and any court decisions concerning the case;
- an explanation by the enterprise of why it considers that the principles established in Article 4 of the Arbitration Convention have not been observed;

163. *Ibid.*, p. 539, para. 5.
164. *Ibid.*, p. 540, para. 10.
165. *Ibid.*, 542, para. 16.
166. Article 10 of the EU Arbitration Convention.

- an undertaking that the enterprise shall respond as completely and quickly as possible to all reasonable and appropriate requests made by a Competent Authority and have documentation at the disposal of these authorities; and,
- any specific additional information requested by the Competent Authority within two months after the receipt of the taxpayer's request.[167]

As per the Arbitration Convention, the advisory commission comprises a chairperson, two representatives of each Competent Authority (this may be reduced to one), and an even number of independent persons of standing.[168] The independent persons must be nationals of a Member State of the European Union and resident within the territory to which the Arbitration Convention applies.[169] The advisory commission will normally consist of two independent persons of standing in addition to the chairperson and the representatives of the competent authorities.[170] The Code of Conduct sets out a procedure for identifying the candidates for the advisory commission:

- Member States commit themselves to provide the names of the five independent persons of standing who are eligible to become a member of the advisory commission to the Secretary-General of the Council without a delay;
- In addition to transferring the names of their independent persons of standing to the Secretary-General of the Council, Member States shall also deliver curriculum vitae of these persons which should, among other things, describe legal, tax, and especially transfer pricing experience of those persons;
- Member States may also indicate those independent persons of standing on their list who fulfil the requirements to be elected as Chairperson;
- Member States will have to confirm the names of their independent persons of standing or provide the names of their replacements to the Secretary-General of the Council in accordance with the yearly request presented by the latter;
- The aggregate list of all of the independent persons of standing will be published on the Council's website.[171]

The independent persons of standing should be appointed by mutual agreement from a list of individuals who are nominated by the contracting states.[172] The list of independent persons of standing shall consist of all of the independent persons who are nominated.[173] The contracting States have a right to nominate five individuals as persons of independent standing.[174] Independent persons are appointed by the drawing of lots by the competent authorities concerned where the mutual agreement is not reached.[175] The Chairperson is elected by the independent persons of standing from the

---

167. Article 5 of the EU Arbitration Convention.
168. Article 9(1) of the EU Arbitration Convention.
169. Article 7.1(f) of the EU Arbitration Convention.
170. Article 7.2(c) of the EU Arbitration Convention.
171. Articles 7.1 (a)–7.1(e) of the EU Arbitration Convention.
172. Article 9(1) of the EU Arbitration Convention.
173. Article 9(4) of the EU Arbitration Convention.
174. *Ibid*.
175. Article 9(1) of the EU Arbitration Convention.

list of the appointed independent persons of standing.[176] When the independent persons of standing are designated by drawing the lots, the EU Member States have the right to object to a selection provided that the circumstances mentioned in Article 9(3) of the Arbitration Convention are satisfied.[177] They can also oppose the selection of the Chairman of the advisory commission under the same conditions established in Article 9(3) of the Arbitration Convention.[178] The independent persons of standing are required to be the nationals of the contracting states of the Arbitration Convention and resident in the territory where the mentioned Convention applies. They shall meet the requirements of independence and competence.[179]

## 3.4 Issues and Possible Solutions

### 3.4.1 OECD and UN Model Convention

In some countries, court and/or administrative decisions are final, and the competent authorities might not be able to override them. Therefore, taxpayers may not always effectively benefit from the mentioned clause. As a result, the OECD Commentary on Article 25(5) provides that issues cannot be submitted to arbitration when a court or an administrative tribunal of any of the contracting states have delivered a decision on the case.[180] Moreover, the OECD recommends including the arbitration clause in a tax treaty when the contracting states consider that this provision will be effectively implemented in practice.[181] It also suggests that jurisdictions limit access to arbitration when a case has already been decided under the domestic litigation process of any of the contracting States (i.e., the decision must rendered by the court or an administrative tribunal of one the contracting States) in order to avoid the risk of conflicting decisions.[182]

The OECD Commentary on Article 25 states that some countries will allow access to the arbitration only when the legal remedies are no longer available.[183] In this respect, the proposed solution is to still allow access to arbitration when the taxpayer under consideration waives the right to pursue the case under the domestic legal remedies. In this aspect, the OECD even suggests terminology that can be adopted by the contracting States in the double tax treaties.[184] However, waiving the right to pursue the case under the domestic remedies might potentially subject the taxpayer to

---

176. Article 9(5) of the EU Arbitration Convention.
177. Article 9(3) of the EU Arbitration Convention.
178. Article 9(5) of the EU Arbitration Convention.
179. Article 9(4) of the EU Arbitration Convention.
180. OECD Model Convention, at Article 25(5).
181. OECD Model Convention, footnote to Article 25 (5).
182. OECD, *Commentaries on Model Tax Convention*, Article 25, at para. 76.
183. *Ibid.*, para. 80.
184. *Ibid.*

unresolved double taxation. Therefore, the OECD recommends modifying the paragraph in the bilateral tax treaty in order to ensure that the double taxation will, in fact, be relieved.[185]

### 3.4.2 Arbitration Convention and the Code of Conduct

As per the Arbitration Convention, a taxpayer cannot simultaneously pursue domestic dispute resolution techniques along with a MAP and arbitration. In this respect, the Arbitration Convention provides that, when the case has been submitted to the court or a tribunal of the Member State concerned, the two-year period shall be calculated from the date on which the judgment of the final Court of Appeal was delivered.[186] Therefore, a taxpayer can only initiate a MAP and a case may be subsequently transferred to the advisory commission only after the final decision has been achieved as per the domestic remedies. Thus, the resolution of double taxation in such cases will be time-consuming as the taxpayer is not allowed to pursue both the domestic and international dispute resolution mechanisms at the same time. Moreover, when the competent authorities cannot derogate from the decisions of their judicial bodies, paragraph 1 of Article 7 of the Arbitration Convention does not apply (i.e., the amount of time does not begin to apply for the purposes of submission of the case to the advisory commission) unless the amount of time for the appeal has expired or the appeal has been withdrawn before the decision is delivered.[187] Therefore, in such cases, the taxpayers must make a decision between the domestic and international remedies.

## 4 CONCLUSIONS

Following the introduction that contains the significance of dispute resolution mechanisms in the field of international tax and transfer pricing, in particular, this chapter provides a comprehensive overview and analysis of the administrative approaches to resolving transfer pricing disputes, including a MAP in section 2 and arbitration in section 3.

With respect to the MAP, this chapter first recognizes that, despite being a favourable dispute resolution tool, the MAP process contains certain flaws including: (1) the participation of taxpayers is limited in the MAP process; (2) the MAP procedure is time-consuming and lengthy; and (3) the MAP negotiation cannot ensure the elimination of the double taxation. Concerning the procedural aspect of a MAP, it identifies three key areas that impose difficulties in practice. These areas are: (1) the interaction between a MAP and domestic legislations; (2) the relationships between a MAP and domestic available remedies; and (3) the elimination of economic double taxation.

---

185. *Ibid.*
186. Article 7(1) of the EU Arbitration Convention.
187. Article 9(3) of the EU Arbitration Convention.

Concerning arbitration, it particularly compares the mechanisms under Article 25(5) of the OECD Model Convention and the EU Arbitration Convention. In the analysis, it first identifies the strengths and weaknesses of initiating an arbitration procedure within the two different frameworks. It subsequently documents the procedural aspects in relationship to these procedures in detail. Lastly, it focusses the discussion on the relationship between domestic dispute resolution processes.

# CHAPTER 7

# Transfer Pricing Documentation: Master File, Local file and Country-by-Country Reporting

## 1   INTRODUCTION

Over the last twenty years, the documentation of transfer pricing arrangements accompanied by the standardization of Transfer Pricing Documentation (TPD) require-ments have been given increased importance in many countries.[1] The proliferation of diverse local TPD rules has made it necessary to create a uniform international standard to reduce both the compliance costs for businesses and potential transfer pricing disputes arising from divergent documentation requirements and inconsistent documentation. However, previous initiatives to standardize the TPD have, for several reasons, not fully met the needs of either taxpayers or tax administrations. The most recent harmonization efforts have been focused on new standards for the TPD that enhance transparency for tax administrations while taking into consideration the compliance costs for MNEs.

Generally, the vast majority of MNEs can be said to have now accepted the imposition of statutory record-keeping obligations. However, criticism can still be levied at the multitude of terms in existence and the abundance of concepts requiring interpretation in which the application – as experience shows – frequently leads to disputes in tax audits. This is compounded by the international development and the incredibly explosive increase in documentation standards, especially in developing countries and emerging markets. This is leading almost instinctively to a more aggressive inspection of tax audits, particularly of arm's length documentation. To

---

1. OECD, *White Paper on Transfer Pricing Documentation*, Public Consultation, 30 Jul. 2013 (2013), p. 2.

date, MNEs have been precarious regarding compliance between jurisdictions with diverse levels of domestic legislation and documentation requirements that are not coordinated internationally and are hence exposed to the unilateral desire of tax authorities for a fair share of taxes.

This chapter first reviews the international development on TPD standards at the level of the OECD, the Pacific Association of Tax Administrators (PATA), and the EU in section 1.[2] Subsequently, it focuses on the three-tiered approaches on the TPD that are endorsed by OECD BEPS Action 13 with a detailed presentation of the master file in section 2, the local file in section 3, and the Country-by-Country Reporting (CbCR) in section 4. Before concluding this chapter, it also provides a critical review of the OECD's three-tiered approach in section 5.

## 1.1 International Developments Before BEPS Action 13

### 1.1.1 Chapter V of the OECD Guidelines

For quite some time now, efforts have been made to harmonize the TPD for MNEs in an attempt to avoid costly duplicative work derived from the multiplicity of documentation regulations.

In 1994, the United States became the first country to introduce documentation regulations for intra-group transfer pricing[3] and penalties in the event that the transfer pricing outcome was realised to be inadequate and that documentation requirements were not complied with. The introduction of penalties led to concerns in other countries that MNEs would henceforth disclose profits primarily in the United States in order to satisfy the IRS. In 1995, the OECD addressed these fears in its Transfer Pricing Guidelines for Multinational Enterprises and Tax Administrations (1995 OECD Guidelines) which urge all OECD Member States to observe the principle of proportionality that '[d]ocumentation requirements should not impose on taxpayers costs and burdens disproportionate to the circumstances'.[4]

The 2010, the OECD Guidelines address the TPD in a separate chapter, Chapter V.[5] However, the OECD countries declined to provide an exhaustive list of documents to be included in a TPD package. The 2010 OECD Guidelines merely outline the procedure for furnishing evidence and provide general indications about information and documentation that might be beneficial.

---

2. The UN Manual contains a good summary of the TPD development at various institutional and national levels and practical guiding principles. For more details, *see* Part C of the 2017 UN Manual.
3. *See* section 482 of the US Internal Revenue Code, 1994 Final Transfer Pricing Regulations of the United States; *see also* OECD, *White Paper on Transfer Pricing Documentation*, Public Consultation, 30 Jul. 2013 (2013), p. 7.
4. OECD, *Transfer Pricing Guidelines for Multinational Enterprises and Tax Administrators*, Committee on Fiscal Affairs, OECD, Paris (1995), para. 309.
5. OECD, *Transfer Pricing Guidelines for Multinational Enterprises and Tax Administrations*, Ch. V: Documentation, Publication Date: 18 Aug. 2010 (2010).

The 2010 OECD Guidelines represent a compromise of the OECD members.[6] Strictly speaking, the 2010 OECD Guidelines did not have any direct legal effect. Nonetheless, they did have significance for the national law of the OECD members even though, according to current knowledge, there are virtually no countries in which the OECD proposals for documentation were enshrined in law; rather, they were part of administrative instructions and pronouncements issued by the national competent authorities. A number of countries directly transposed the 2010 OECD Guidelines into national law through national regulations. For example, Ireland adopted the OECD Guidelines into its domestic legislation.[7] Others were unmistakably guided by the 2010 OECD Guidelines in their national transfer pricing rules, for example, the records required under German law (§ 90 (3) of the German Tax Code and related German Regulation) primarily corresponded to the proposals in Chapter V of the 2010 OECD Guidelines.[8]

Although the OECD Guidelines could generally be considered as a starting point for most national regulations, significant differences between the individual national requirements persisted in some cases. This situation is less than ideal for MNEs that are understandably keen to ensure that, as much as possible, documentation prepared for one country can also be used and accepted in another country. In this respect, it is desirable for MNEs that the broadest possible consensus is reached among the individual countries regarding documentation requirements. Similar approaches to standardization can be found not only in the OECD but also among the members of the Pacific Association of Tax Administrators (PATA)[9] – Australia, Canada, Japan, and the United States. The European Union (EU) also increased its efforts in this regard under the rubric of the EU Joint Transfer Pricing Forum (EU JTPF).[10]

### 1.1.2  PATA Documentation Package

On 12 March 2003, the PATA members attempted to synchronize national TPD regulations. However, the objective of the planned multilateral synchronization of the national TPD obligations was not actually to standardize these documentation requirements but to merely create uniform minimum documentation standards with the (sole) effect that an MNE that complies with these standards in all of the participating countries is no longer exposed to documentation-related penalties. Additionally,

---

6. *See* Abstract of OECD TPG: '*The OECD Transfer Pricing Guidelines for Multinational Enterprises and Tax Administrations Provide Guidance on the Application of the "Arm's Length Principle", Which Is the International Consensus on Transfer Pricing*' (accessed 15 Mar. 2016).
7. *See* section 835D of the Taxes Consolidation Act 1997 (as inserted by section 42 of the Finance Act 2010, available at: http://www.irishstatutebook.ie/eli/2010/act/5/enacted/en/html).
8. *See* section 90 para. 3 of the German Tax Code.
9. PATA, *Transfer Pricing Documentation Package*, http://www.drtp.ca/wp-content/uploads/20 15/02/PATA_Transfer_Pricing_Documentation.pdf.
10. For more information to the EU Joint Transfer Pricing Forum *see* http://ec.europa.eu/taxation _customs/taxation/company_tax/transfer_pricing/forum/index_en.htm (accessed 15 Mar. 2016).

satisfaction of the principles of the PATA Documentation Package does not preclude PATA member tax administrations from making transfer pricing adjustments.[11]

The PATA Documentation Package prescribes covering forty-eight specific items from ten broad categories that should be included in a taxpayer's documentation.[12] The listed items are more specific than the regulations of any individual PATA member country and, therefore, represent documentary requirements that are more rigorous.[13] As a consequence, in order to produce TPD that complies with the PATA documentation package, MNEs must invest greater efforts than those needed to prepare documentation for any PATA member jurisdiction. Yet, the documentation regulations of the individual PATA members differ substantially in scope. This may lead to a taxpayer having to provide more or less information in one country than what is required in another in order to comply with the minimum standards.

### 1.1.3 EU Code of Conduct on TPD

On 10 November 2005, the European Commission adopted a proposal for a Code of Conduct on the TPD for associated enterprises in the European Union (EU TPD) that would standardize and partially centralize the TPD that MNEs must provide to tax authorities. This occurred as the regulations of the EU Member States varied considerably in some cases with regard to the content and structure of the TPD despite the OECD recommendations.

The EU TPD consists of two main elements. One comprises a set of documentation containing common standardized information (the 'master file') that is relevant for all EU group members of a multinational enterprise. The second component consists of several sets of standardized documentation each containing information of the specific country that is involved (the 'country-specific documentation') that businesses file with tax administrations in order to report on their pricing for cross-border intra-group activities.[14] The master file includes, for example, a general description of the business and business strategy, a general description of the transactions involving associated enterprises in the EU, and the enterprise's transfer pricing policy.[15] The country-specific documentation only contains information relevant to that country such as the amounts of transaction flows within that country, contractual terms, and the particular

---

11. PATA Documentation Package, at p. 1.
12. According to the PATA Documentation Package, the ten broad categories include detailed information on: (1) the organizational structure, (2) the nature of the business/industry and market conditions, (3) the controlled transactions, (4) the assumptions, strategies and policies, (5) the cost contribution arrangements, (6) the comparability, functional and risk analysis, (7) the selection of the transfer pricing method, (8) the application of the transfer pricing method, (9) the background documents and (10) the index to documents.
13. Philip Anderson, PATA Transfer Pricing Documentation Package, Asia-Pacific Tax Bulletin, at p. 199.
14. OECD, *White Paper on Transfer Pricing Documentation, Public Consultation*, 30 Jul. 2013 (2013), p. 8.
15. Resolution of the Council and of the representatives of the governments of the Member States, meeting within the Council, of 27 June 2006 on a code of conduct on transfer pricing documentation for associated enterprises in the European Union (EU TPD), (2006/C 176/01), para. 4 of the annex.

transfer pricing methods used.[16] Access to the common documentation and information contained in the master file is shared by all of the Member States that are involved; however, the country-specific documentation would generally be available only to the specific Member State concerned.[17]

The regulations are non-binding for the EU Member States;[18] however, each individual State must decide on the implementation or form of implementation of the EU TPD at the national level. In 2013, the European Commission conducted a survey with respect to the impact of the EU TPD on Member States' legislation and administrative practice of the TPD. The responses submitted by the twenty-six Member States revealed that all of the Member States consider their national practice to be in accordance with the EU TPD either by having their domestic rules explicitly aligned to the EU TPD or by accepting the TP documentation in the EU TPD format.[19] For a comparative perspective of various TPD requirements, *see* Annexes 1 and 2)

### 1.1.4   Evaluation of the Initiatives to Date

In 2013, the European Commission reviewed the acceptance of the proposed Code of Conduct, concluding that most non-governmental organizations had opted to use it informally and selectively.[20] In other words, similar to the PATA initiative, the EU TPD did not achieve the level of implementation and adherence initially hoped for in practice. There are a variety of reasons for this. First, there is a lack of acceptance outside the participating EU Member States or PATA countries. Additionally, complying with the recommendations does not effectively protect taxpayers from being penalized even though that was the intention.

Even though the OECD Guidelines are considered to be extremely important in international practice, the existing requirements of different countries reveal substantive and formal differences in the general conditions and transfer pricing regulations. Countries whose industry structure is fully developed (e.g., Germany) tend to have TPD requirements that are more in common than those in emerging economies (such as BRICS countries) due in part to the economic integration processes and individual interests of the States.

---

16. *Ibid.*, para. 5 of the annex.
17. *Ibid.*, paras 4.1 and 5.1 of the annex.
18. *Ibid.*, para. 10 of the annex.
19. *See* Summary of EU Member States' responses to the questionnaire on the implementation of the EU TPD (Summary MS responses), available at: https://ec.europa.eu/taxation_customs/sites/taxation/files/docs/body/summary-ms.pdf.
20. For more information of the Summary of responses non-government stakeholders to the questionnaire on the implementation of the EU TPD (Summary NGS responses), please *see* JTPF/010/2014/EN: EU Joint Transfer Pricing Forum discussion paper on improving the functioning of the EU TPD.

### 1.1.5 Practical Experiences to Date

#### 1.1.5.1 Relevance of the Documentation Requirements in Tax Audits

The continuing trend towards new, diversified national transfer pricing regulations and the heightened scrutiny of transfer pricing issues by national tax authorities have significantly increased audit intensity in relationship to the records prepared by enterprises. MNEs may encounter heterogeneous country-specific tax audit cultures in many jurisdictions around the world that range from commercial to economic to extremely formalistic approaches. Whereas it was sometimes sufficient in the early years of documentation requirements to simply submit documentation to tax auditors, the documentation is now inspected in detail, in particular the economic analysis supporting the arm's length nature of transfer pricing arrangements,.

To finding evidence that transfer pricing arrangements are at arm's length, tax audits focus on the comparability analysis. This analysis is essential for assessing the arm's length nature of the transaction in question, but is only briefly mentioned in the OECD Guidelines or individual countries' regulations. A lack of comparable transactions in the market often forces MNEs to refer back to database studies. In many cases, the credibility of these studies is questioned by tax administrations through the application of alternate database studies. It is, therefore, no surprise that especially the focus on 'profit margins' of associated enterprises has led to the greatest additional burdens for MNEs in recent years.

In terms of the content, a shift in focus can be observed. Whereas the primary focus in the past was on the sale of tangibles and the proof of the benefit test for intra-group services, it is now increasingly on documentation of the arm's length character of intra-group financial transactions as well as on the use and documentation of the CUP method for intangibles. Issues such as Location-Specific Advantages (LSAs) have also received considerable attention ever since India and China adopted a position on these in the UN Manual.[21]

#### 1.1.5.2 Experience with Documentation Preparation Thus Far

Whether MNEs apply a centralized or decentralized documentation strategy or a combination of the two strategies and whether the introduction of internal worldwide documentation processes for standardization, simplification, and streamlining has resulted in simultaneous improvement of global consistency can be disregarded for the moment. MNEs still face manifold challenges of a practical nature in complying with local law requirements. To decide on the level of the TPD is an important risk management decision for each MNE (*see* Figure 7.1).

---

21. For the position of the China and India on LSAs, *see* D.2. and D.3. of the 2017 UN Manual respectively.

Figure 7.1    Finding the Appropriate Level of TP Compliance

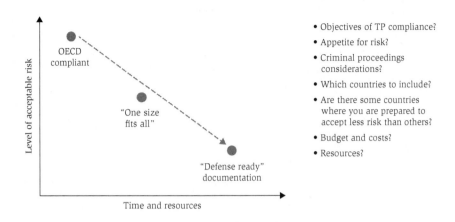

Regarding the internationally accepted use of benchmark studies from databases of external providers, it can be repeatedly observed that many local tax authorities continue to request benchmark studies exclusively with local benchmark companies at the expense of functional comparability and automatically reject comparables found in pan-regional databases. A lack of publicly available data, however, makes adjustment calculations (e.g., capital adjustments) to improve the comparability of the benchmark companies used in the benchmark studies almost impossible. Some countries focus on divergent bandwidths that they do not provide for narrowing an interquartile range as is customary in the United States and Europe. Other topics to be addressed in connection with benchmark studies may include timing differences arising from these studies being prepared at different times in the context of the price-setting approach and for documentation purposes (outcome testing approach) as well as the question of the required frequency or amplitude of the benchmarks.

There is also the use of one-year or multi-year averages, local deviations in the selection of the profit level indicator (PLI) to be used, and the tax treatment of hybrid entities. Other challenges continuously facing MNEs are different submission deadlines, different fiscal years, the use of different accounting standards (e.g., local *GAAP v IFRSs*), submission or translation of the documents in(to) the national language, and varying practices in relationship to the admissibility of omnibus transactions or in the method to be used for the different forms of financing in the group (e.g., guarantees, loans, factoring, hedging). Individual local specifications still exist that, contrary to the OECD Guidelines, classify the local company as a tested entity without considering its functional and risk profile.[22]

---

22. *See* details in OECD, *Review of Comparability and of Profit Methods: Revision of Chapters I-III of the Transfer Pricing Guidelines* (2010), at section A3.3.

*1.1.5.3   Experience with Data Availability*

These substantive challenges notwithstanding, most MNEs are rarely able to supply all of the required data upon demand. IT systems are generally designed for performance controlling and/or reporting purposes. For transfer pricing purposes, however, information is generally required for each type of transaction. This means that data must be collected and prepared specifically for tax purposes. Although corporate tax departments have now taken steps to establish special reporting systems with operational transfer pricing management, data are often captured and monitored manually that is inefficient and prone to error. In addition, trade-offs between the transfer pricing methods used for taxes and for management accounting purposes as well as the related governance regularly occur. Management policy may also create practical difficulties for procuring information from other units in the group that makes systematic data collection and provision difficult. Setting up and managing an efficient transfer pricing documentation concept tailored to the MNE in question so that it is also compatible with the general recurring cost saving programmes is also a genuine challenge for most MNEs.

## 1.2   Development According to the BEPS Action 13

Recognizing that a common approach to documentation requirements would be an advantage for both businesses and tax administrations, the OECD established that new rules in BEPS Action 13 regarding the TPD would be developed to enhance transparency for tax administrations and take into consideration the burden of compliance costs for MNEs. On 16 September 2014, the OECD released its first set of deliverables on the fifteen actions of the BEPS Project including – in compliance with the task from Action 13 – documentation guidance.[23] On 5 October 2015, the OECD published the BEPS Action 13 Final Report.[24] This report recommends that countries implement a three-tiered standardized approach for the TPD and replace Chapter V of the 2010 OECD Guidelines.

The BEPS Action 13 Final Report and the new Chapter V of the OECD Guidelines describe a three-tiered standardized approach for the TPD. This standard consists of: (i) a master file containing standardized information that is relevant for all of the group members; (ii) local files referring specifically to transactions of the local taxpayer; and (iii) a CbCR that requires companies to produce global blueprints with jurisdiction-specific data on employee staffing, facilities, profit (loss) before income tax, and taxes paid.[25] The master file and local file approach, as well as the CbCR template, are to be

---

23.   OECD (2014), *Guidance on Transfer Pricing Documentation and Country-by-Country Reporting*, OECD/G20 Base Erosion and Profit Shifting Project, OECD Publishing, Paris. Available at: http://dx.doi.org/10.1787/9789264219236-en.
24.   OECD (2015), Transfer Pricing Documentation and Country-by-Country Reporting, Action 13 - 2015 Final Report, OECD Publishing, Paris. Available at: http://dx.doi.org/10.1787/978926424 1480-en.
25.   BEPS Action 13 Final Report, para. 16.

re-examined from a practical viewpoint by 2020.[26] It is assumed that the new standards will be introduced in most countries with effect to financial years commencing after 1 January 2016 so that there is adequate practical experience for this re-examination.[27]

In principle, the practical challenges faced by MNEs in preparing international documentation remain the same irrespective of the new OECD approach. What is added to the existing challenges is a further increase in data gathering and an aggravated problem of data availability. Moreover, the interdependencies between the master file, local file, and CbCR will necessitate greater consistency in the transfer pricing practice. Besides providing an overview of an MNE's footprint using specific data, the CbCR should especially allow tax authorities to relatively quickly identify actual or purported inconsistencies between the more detailed documentation under the master file concept and the quantitative data provided as part of the CbCR.

## 2 MASTER FILE

### 2.1 Concepts

The master file concept requires MNEs to provide tax administrations around the globe with information regarding their global business operations, their overall transfer pricing policies, and their global allocation of economic activity.[28] The purpose of the master file, therefore, is to place the MNE group's transfer pricing practices into taxpayers' global economic, legal, financial, and tax context. It also provides all of the relevant tax administrations with the understanding of the MNE's global operations and policies that are necessary to evaluate the presence of significant transfer pricing risk for the local entities in their countries.[29]

The master file can be prepared either on a group basis or on a business unit basis.[30] However, even if a taxpayer creates a master file for each business unit, all of the master file documents must be submitted to all tax authorities even if the local subsidiary is not involved in the activities of this business unit. According to the OECD's recommendations, the master file document, despite being governed by domestic law, should be prepared in commonly used languages as the use of local languages may impose an extra burden on taxpayers.[31] At the latest, the master file should be completed on the date that the MNE group's ultimate parent entity (UPE) files its tax return.[32]

The list of information that must be included in the master file is provided in Annex I of the OECD Guidelines as amended by the BEPS Report.[33] The relevant required documents in the master file can be summarized into five categories: (a) the

---

26. *Ibid.*, para. 62.
27. *Ibid.*, para. 50.
28. *Ibid.*, para. 18.
29. *Ibid.*
30. *Ibid.*, para. 20.
31. *Ibid.*, para. 39.
32. *Ibid.*, para. 30.
33. *Ibid.*, pp. 25–26.

MNE group's organizational structure; (b) a description of the MNE's business or businesses; (c) the MNE's intangibles; (d) the MNE's intra-group financial activities; and (e) the MNE's financial and tax positions.[34] Under the five categories, important elements to be provided are:

- Important drivers of business profit;
- A list and brief description of the supply chain for the group's five largest products and/or service offerings by turnover plus any other products and/or services amounting to more than 5% of group turnover;
- A list and brief description of important service arrangements, other than R&D services, between members of the MNE group including a description of the capabilities of the principal locations providing important services and transfer pricing policies for allocating services costs and determining prices to be paid for intra-group services;
- A description of the primary geographic markets for the group's products and services;
- A brief written functional analysis describing the principal contributions to value creation by individual entities within the group, i.e., key functions performed, important risks assumed, and important assets used;
- A description of important business restructuring transactions, acquisitions, and divestitures occurring during the fiscal year;
- A general description of the MNE's overall strategy for the development, ownership, and exploitation of intangibles including the location of principal R&D facilities and location of R&D management;
- A list of intangibles or groups of intangibles of the MNE group that are important for transfer pricing purposes and which entities legally own them;
- A list of important agreements among identified associated enterprises related to intangibles including cost contribution arrangements, principal research service agreements, and license agreements;
- A general description of the group's transfer pricing policies related to R&D and intangibles;
- A general description of any important transfers of interests in intangibles among associated enterprises during the fiscal year concerned including the entities, countries, and compensation involved;
- A general description of how the group is financed including important financing arrangements with unrelated lenders;
- The identification of any members of the MNE group that provide a central financing function for the group;
- A general description of the MNE's general transfer pricing policies related to financing arrangements between associated enterprises.

---

34. *Ibid.*, para. 19.

These extensive information requirements must be interpreted in consideration of the general wording of the new Chapter V. From this terminology, it is evident that the role of the master file is to provide tax authorities with a comprehensive overview on the MNE group's value creation process and transfer pricing policies rather than providing exhaustive listings of minutiae.[35] Thus, taxpayers can limit the content of the master file to the generally relevant and important information for the entire group to the extent that the omission of certain information would not affect the reliability of the transfer pricing analysis. In order to determine the appropriate amount and scope of information to be provided, taxpayers need to use their prudent business judgment.[36]

It is not an obligation for all jurisdictions to implement the master file as it is only a recommendation of the OECD. Jurisdictions that are interested in the master file concept can implement it through local country legislation or administrative procedures.[37] The content of the master file is rather uniform jurisdiction-by-jurisdiction reporting according to the OECD standard that presents the 'blueprint' of the MNE group as a whole. Theoretically speaking, it means that one MNE group shares one master file. In practical terms, the master file would first be exchanged in the MNE group among entities in jurisdictions that require a master file by law and then those entities would file the master file directly with their local tax administrations.[38] Moreover, each country may define a threshold to relieve small- and medium-sized MNEs (SMEs) from the obligation to prepare a complete transfer pricing documentation in the style of a master file.[39] Nevertheless, SMEs should be obligated to provide information related to their material transactions at the request of tax administrations in the course of a tax audit.[40]

The concept of a master file is not such a new thing. As mentioned in section 1.1.3 of this chapter, in 2005, the European Commission adopted the EU TPD and was the first to introduce this concept. Different from the OECD master file, the EU master file would only apply to the MNEs' operations in the EU. The document typically includes an industry analysis, company background, functional analysis, selection of methods, and economic analyses which will enable local tax authorities to verify the arm's length nature of the intra-group transactions of the concerned MNE.[41] It is important to understand that the OECD master file together with other two components of the three-tiered approach are designed to be a transfer pricing risks assessment tool.

The master file under the new OECD standard, however, differs significantly from the OECD's previous documentation regulations and also those of many countries. First, the fact that there needs to be one uniform master file with a global scope that provides a mandatory set of information to all tax authorities that are involved goes beyond pre-BEPS regulations. Second, many countries have decided to require

---

35. *Ibid.*, para. 18.
36. *Ibid.*
37. *Ibid.*, para. 49.
38. *Ibid.*
39. *Ibid.*, para. 33.
40. *Ibid.*
41. Roderick Veldhuizen, Lazaros Teneketzis, *The OECD Master File: Past and Future*, International Transfer Pricing Journal (November/December 2016), at 447.

appendices to the master file, which means that MNEs need to prepare individualized information for each country in which they operate, for example, the Chinese tax authorities additionally require a supply chain analysis in the master file.[42] In essence, taxpayers are faced with a substantial extension of documentation requirements for group-wide information and information related to facts and circumstances outside the taxpayer's country.

## 2.2 Implementation

Realistically speaking, the goal of the OECD to create an internationally accepted standard for the TPD is rather ambitious. At the time of this writing, deviations from the OECD concept and variations across jurisdictions are anticipated and have already been observed.[43] The reasons are multifold. First, the OECD Guidelines are only soft law and do not impose binding legal force on individual countries. Furthermore, the master file endorsed by the OECD is not a minimum standard, and the BEPS participating countries only commit to the minimum standards. As a consequence, the participating countries have the discretion to decide the extent of implementation with respect to the master file.

For certain jurisdictions, it is an opportunity to bring their own perspective into the transfer pricing debate by making customized master file requirements notwithstanding the fact that it adds extra burden to taxpayers who would have to comply with all of these diversified requirements. Furthermore, the master file contains information such that tax administrations would gain an understanding of an MNE's overall transfer pricing philosophy and its sources of value creation. The motive of certain jurisdictions requiring additional elements in the master file might be to obtain a sense of the impact of intragroup transactions that do not directly involve specific local taxpayers versus the results of intragroup transactions that do involve such local group members.[44] From the perspective of MNEs, any variation of the standards at the actual implementation level makes their compliance with the new rules very challenging and burdensome and also requires additional efforts. For that reason, MNEs will need to be particularly aware of any such variations in local specific requirements and customize their documentation accordingly in each case, if required.

As an instance, the United States has indicated that they will not require a taxpayer to provide transfer pricing documentation based on the master file concept since they consider their currently existing TPD regulations to be at least equivalent and serving the same purposes as the OECD requirements. However, the IRS will likely request a taxpayers' master file in the event of audit. Other important counties, such as Brazil and Canada, have also currently expressed the intention not to implement the

---

42. Kevin A. Bell, *OECD Transfer Pricing 'Master File' Must Bow to Countries' Rules*, BNA Transfer Pricing Report 2017.
43. It is worth mentioning again that several countries, for example, Argentina, Brazil, China, Colombia, India, Mexico, South Africa, and Turkey, have already stated that they might request additional information in the Action 13 Final Report.
44. Kevin A. Bell, *OECD Transfer Pricing 'Master File' Must Bow to Countries' Rules*, BNA Transfer Pricing Report 2017.

master file concept.[45] In addition, some tax administrations of non-developing countries have recently become rather sceptical of the OECD documentation standards that are more stringent, since they find themselves faced with increased concerns that the enhanced transparency of MNE groups will particularly lead the BRICS countries to place pressure on MNEs to alter their profit allocation in favour of their market countries. The degree and uniformity of the implementation of the OECD master file approach around the globe, therefore, remains to be seen.

The proliferation of the TPD around the world enables tax authorities to gain an increased level of transparency; nevertheless, it also incites a worrisome concern of confidentiality. The confidentiality issue is particularly in regard to the master file. As mentioned previously, the exchange of the master file is realized through the share of information within the MNE group, and the master file information would eventually be channelled to the local tax administrations. In other words, the level of secrecy protection is entirely governed by domestic law. In contrast, the CbCR is exchanged through the applicable treaty, Tax Information Exchange Agreement (TIEA), or other bilateral agreements for the exchange of information in which provisions concerning confidentiality normally exist. The protection provided through government-to-government exchange schemes is certainly much stronger than that provided through a unilateral domestic regime. Even though the OECD urges tax authorities to take all reasonable steps to ensure no public discloser and no misuse of the commercially sensitive information contained in transfer pricing documents, there is no guarantee that all countries will actually do so. Furthermore, national laws on tax secrecy vary significantly around the world. In France, Finland, Norway, and Sweden, for example, tax information is publicly available. The variations will certainly exacerbate the situation.

## 2.3 Disclosure Challenges in Light of Practical Experience

Due to the nature of the information requested for the master file, most of the requirements for information were new to the majority of the previous transfer pricing legislations around the world. The new requirements established in the master file as well as the fact that most of the information requested is not directly related to the intra-group transactions of the group companies result in important challenges to MNEs.

### 2.3.1 Materiality

Several of the requirements request that an MNE provides information regarding the 'principal', 'material', or 'most important' parts of different issues. There is, however, no indication or methodology to guide a taxpayer in determining which factors should

---

45. See the transfer pricing country profile of Brazil, available at: https://www.oecd.org/tax/transfer-pricing/transfer-pricing-country-profile-brazil.pdf, and that of Canada, available at: http://www.oecd.org/tax/transfer-pricing/transfer-pricing-country-profile-canada.pdf.

be taken into consideration to determine whether a particular fact, contract, asset, etc. should be considered as principal or important except for the definition of 'material products or services' in the second master file information item. This lack of a clear definition could create different interpretations of a taxpayer and a tax authority on whether the information provided is sufficient for complying with the requirements as defined by the OECD Guidelines and, therefore, whether or not penalties can be applied. Moreover, tax authorities might also have different interpretations on this point that would result in the master file of an MNE group being considered compliant with documentation requirements in some countries but not in others.

Furthermore, the level of information disclosure in the master file ([t]axpayers should present the information in the master file for the MNE as a whole)[46] means that every group company that is based in a country in which transfer pricing legislation exists as well as the tax authorities of the corresponding countries will have access to the information included in the group's master file. Since some of the information requirements defined by the OECD involve information only related to some group companies, this presents an MNE with the dilemma of deciding if the specific piece of information is relevant for the presentation of the group 'as a whole' and, therefore, should be disclosed to all group companies and their respective tax authorities or if the respective information is not relevant for the group 'as a whole' and, therefore, can be presented in the local files of only those entities that are directly involved. In this context, it must be noted that the expressions 'principal' and 'important' that are used to describe the information to be included in the master file are not meant to establish an objective standard. Instead the question of which information needs to be included in it depends on the facts of each specific case, especially the number of the items to list or transactions that have occurred within the MNE group and their effect on transfer pricing outcomes. The question to be asked when deciding about which information to include in the maser file, therefore, should always be: what information is necessary to provide a true and fair view of the facts and policies that define the overall transfer pricing concept of the MNE?

### 2.3.2 Intangibles

One of the primary focuses of the new documentation requirements is to provide tax authorities with more information on the creation of intangibles, the transfer of ownership, and the use of intangibles within an MNE group. Intangibles in many industries are the main value drivers of business and, therefore, additional information on the allocation of intangibles and the IP value chain of an MNE group are supposed to place all involved tax authorities in a better position to review intra-group arrangements and profit allocation.

The first of these new intangible-related information requirements is to provide '[a] general description of any important transfers of interests in intangibles among associated enterprises during the fiscal year concerned, including the entities,

---

46. BEPS Action 13 Final Report, para. 20.

countries, and compensation involved'.[47] Due to the delicate nature of a transfer of interest in intangibles and the compensation paid for such a transfer within a group, the information requested from a taxpayer's perspective should only be disclosed to the entities and countries involved in the transfer of interest in order to avoid revealing the sensitive content to parties not involved in it. Such information needs to be disclosed in the master file and becomes available to all tax authorities involved only if a transfer of intangibles significantly changes the overall value streams or the overall value creation process within an MNE group and consequently needs to be considered 'important' for the group 'as a whole'.

The second requirement of section 3 of the master file requests that the taxpayer provides a list of intangibles or group of intangibles of the MNE group that are important for a transfer pricing purpose and which entities legally own them. According to the additional explanations provided by the OECD, this requirement relates to both registered and unregistered intangibles. Moreover, it should be noted that the information requirement does not relate to the MNE group's most important intangibles but to those intangibles that are important for transfer pricing purposes which may not be necessarily the same and would require an additional assessment.

This new requirement will be a significant challenge for many MNE groups, especially since the information to be provided is not limited to immediately available information on registered intangibles but requires the taxpayer to list unprotected intangibles such as know-how and trade secrets and to assess their relevance for the group's value creation process. These challenges especially result from the fact that, even when considering the work that has been done by the OECD on these topics in BEPS Actions 8–10, an increased level of uncertainty remains in international transfer pricing regulations regarding the definition of unprotected intangibles, the determination of economic ownership in both registered and unregistered intangibles, and the determination of the value and the contribution of these intangibles to the group's overall value chain. This can lead to two or more tax authorities arriving at different conclusions with distinctly different results for the same intangible.

As previously mentioned, the first key factor that can lead to different interpretations of the nature of intangibles is the definition of what is considered as an intangible which, with the new OECD requirements, is now also relevant for the question of whether a taxpayer has fulfilled its documentation requirements. The OECD definition of an intangible is very broad, i.e., 'something which is not a physical asset or a financial asset, which is capable of being owned or controlled for use in commercial activities, and whose use or transfer would be compensated had it occurred in a transaction between independent parties in comparable circumstances'.[48] There is a level of ambiguity in the definition. For example, vagueness arises in regard to the clause: 'and whose use or transfer would be compensated had it occurred in a transaction between independent parties in comparable circumstances'.

---

47. *Ibid.*, p. 26.
48. Action 8, Assure that transfer pricing outcomes are in-line with value creation; OECD – Revised Discussion Draft on Transfer Pricing Aspects of Intangibles of 30 Jul. 2013, proposed definition of an intangible asset for transfer pricing purposes. Also *see* 2017 OECD Guidelines, para. 6.6.

Most intangibles and, in particular, IPs owned by MNEs are unique and rarely sold or licensed to third parties; therefore, the sheer determination of whether a particular intangible would be compensated by an independent party can already be a subjective exercise with different answers.

When comparing which intangibles are considered as main examples by the OECD related to those listed in US legislations, there is considerable overlap with one noticeable difference: goodwill. However, countries such as China and India have very distinct definitions of intangibles in practical terms which include elements such as locations savings and market premiums that are achieved for conducting business in their countries and believe they should be rewarded as such.[49] The OECD position on this matter is that both local savings and market premiums should be dealt with as part of the comparability analysis by using local comparables in which the results would also be affected by the location savings and market premiums; therefore, there would be no necessity to perform an additional adjustment. China rebuts this by indicating that there are not sufficient Chinese-listed companies to make complete local benchmarks; hence, most of their benchmarks are composed of companies in other countries in the region, mainly Japan, for which they expect that an additional adjustment in their profits should be made. Indian tax authorities use 100% Indian comparables but, nevertheless, still propose that additional adjustments to the profits should be made.

These few examples demonstrate the vast differences that currently exist just in the definition of intangibles which might lead to double taxation for MNEs and different assessments of their transfer pricing documentation. Therefore, taxpayers should exercise the greatest amount of care when preparing their list of intangibles that are 'important for transfer pricing' and should ensure that their presentation in the master file is consistent with the information included in publicly available registers, annual reports, their internal R&D strategy, and their transfer pricing policies.

### 2.3.3 Financial Transactions

Another important aspect that has been newly introduced into the master file concept as part of Action 13 relates to the requirements for disclosure of intra-group financing activities. This section which, so far, has received relatively little attention requires taxpayers to present information in their master file that would be unusual to see in many pre-BEPS transfer pricing reports. This especially relates to information such as external and internal financing transactions, the group's centralized financing functions, and the intra-group transfer pricing policies with regard to these types of transactions. The reason for implementing these additional requirements is obviously that centralized financing arrangements are often dependent upon contractual arrangements that facilitate risk transfer and, therefore, it is relatively easy for MNEs to assign the related profits to entities that do not have a significant number of employees and other assets.

---

49. An observation of the latest Chinese TP rules on Bulletin 6 shows that location savings are considered as comparability factors.

The major challenge of these documentation requirements, again, is the ambiguousness on the level of disclosure that is required as a component of the master file. Financing arrangements in MNEs can range from the very simple to the very complex. For example, the first requirement requests a taxpayer to provide information on 'important financing arrangements'. The terminology that is used is not sodocoClas-Placeholder to standard term loans and may include various types of financial arrangements such as bridge loans, equipment leasing, sales/lease-back arrangements, or revolving loans. Financing could also consist of infusions of equity such as venture capital, employee stock option arrangements, or convertible debt. The second requirement requires the 'identification of any members of the MNE group that provide a central financing function for the group'. The term central financing function is not further defined but should include common group functions such cash pooling, hedging, treasury management, insurance management, centralized lending, and others. Therefore, this requirement necessitates special care by those MNEs that derive significant benefits or profits from hedging or other financial activities or MNEs that have located centralized financing functions in low-tax jurisdictions.

It should be noted that a company's annual report should already include a substantial amount of required information, and it would be prudent to acknowledge each of these in the master file. Information that is not presented or is presented without many details in the master file may need to be submitted in a more granular fashion in the local files.

### 2.3.4 Other New Information Requirements

Another important information requirement that was newly introduced as part of the OECD's anti-BEPS endeavours is the obligation to provide a description outlining the supply chain for the group's material products and services. The term 'material', in this context, is defined as the top five by turnover and account for over 5% of group turnover. No definition, however, exists as to what is a product or service in this context. Therefore, each taxpayer needs to individually define what it considers to be a product or service as opposed to a derivative product or a combination of products or services.

Also, services have been identified by the OECD as transactions which require specific attention and additional information requirements. Therefore, the taxpayer is required to provide a list and brief description outlining important service arrangements between members of the MNE group as part of their master file.

## 3 LOCAL FILE

### 3.1 Concepts

While the purpose of the master file is to provide a high-level overview of the group's transfer pricing matters, the local file is intended to provide information that is more detailed relating to specific intra-group transactions and focuses on information that is relevant for the transfer pricing analysis.[50] Such information especially includes financial information regarding the transactions conducted by the relevant entity, a comparability analysis (functions performed, risks borne, and assets employed in specific transactions), and the selection and application of the most appropriate transfer pricing method.[51]

The list of information that should be included in the local file is provided in Annex II of the OECD Guidelines as amended by the BEPS Action 13 Final Report and includes, *inter alia*, the following:[52]

- A description of the management structure of the local entity, a local organization chart, and a description of the individuals to whom local management reports and the country(ies) in which such individuals maintain their principal offices;
- A detailed description of the business and business strategy pursued by the local entity including an indication of whether the local entity has been involved in or affected by business restructurings or intangible transfers in the present or immediate past year and an explanation of those aspects of such transactions affecting the local entity;
- Key competitors;
- A description of the material controlled transactions and the context in which such transactions take place;
- A detailed comparability and functional analysis of the taxpayer and relevant associated enterprises with respect to each documented category of controlled transactions, including any changes compared to prior years;
- An indication of the most appropriate transfer pricing method with regard to the category of transaction and the reasons for selecting that method;
- A description of the reasons for concluding that relevant transactions were priced on an arm's length basis based on the application of the selected transfer pricing method;
- A summary of financial information used in applying the transfer pricing methodology.

Most requirements of the local file are consistent with the documentation requirements that the majority of countries have had in place for several years. Therefore, compliance with the local file requirements should generally not include significant challenges for most MNEs even though specific additional requirements have been introduced.

---

50. BEPS Action 13 Final Report, p. 22.
51. *Ibid.*
52. *Ibid.*, pp. 27–28.

## 3.2 Implementation

Since the information to be included in the local file is generally identical to what is currently included in most TPD requirements, the implementation effort with regard to the local file requirements should be rather minimal and mostly limited to aligning the information included in the local file with the information included in the new master file, for example, by cross-references.[53] The local file is to be filed locally, and it is recommended that it be finalized by the filing date for the local tax return.[54]

In regard to the economic analysis of routine transactions and, therefore, benchmarking, the OECD has expressed a preference for local comparables, and a renewed search for comparable companies should be performed once every three years for the same functional profile with the financial data updated annually.[55]

## 3.3 Disclosure Challenges in Light of Practical Experience

The main challenge that the local file requirements will present to some MNEs is related to the second obligation of the financial information requirements which requires the taxpayer to provide: 'information and allocation schedules showing how the financial data used in applying the transfer pricing method may be tied to the annual financial statements'.[56] Most MNEs use several partially linked systems of accounting and information that utilize different accounting reporting standards depending on the requirements of each country. Moreover, in order to increase comparability and to simplify the application of transfer pricing results from a headquarters perspective, most MNEs price and, in most cases, also test transfer prices based on one uniform accounting standard (often the IFRS or US GAAP as the MNE group standard). For these MNEs, it can become a laborious task to relate the segmented financial results used to test transfer prices to the audited local financial statements of the entities involved. This is due to the inconsistency between IFRS/US GAAP and local accounting standards as well as the level of detail of the properly segmented financials that are required to perform a proper transfer pricing analysis on a transaction or a group of transactions. Tying these two together can become even more difficult when special adjustments must be introduced to the segmented financials to improve the comparability with uncontrolled parties. It is also difficult when assumptions must be made in order to establish the correct allocation of certain lines of the financial statements that otherwise would not be able to be segmented between related and unrelated transactions. In order to avoid unnecessary effort in fulfilling this requirement, MNEs should consider testing and documenting their transfer prices in transactions with routine entities for tax purposes based on the local GAAP numbers and thus entirely separate performance measurement and tax.

---

53. *Ibid.*, p. 28, Note.
54. *Ibid.*, para. 30.
55. *Ibid.*, paras 38 and 46.
56. *Ibid.*, p. 28.

Other local file requirements that have been newly introduced and that may prove to be a burdensome task could be the inclusion in the local file of a description of the local management structure and specifically of the cross-border reporting lines of local management.[57] Another obligation that is new and may require additional documentation work is the requirement to include copies of all material intra-group agreements as part of the TPD.[58]

## 4 COUNTRY-BY-COUNTRY REPORTING

### 4.1 Concepts

The CbCR is a new, additional element of the documentation that had not been in use internationally until the OECD introduced this concept in the BEPS Action 13 Final Report in 2015.[59] In the EU, it became mandatory for Member States to implement the CbCR following the recommendation of OECD BEPS Action 13 (EU CbCR) through the adoption of the amendments to the Administrative Cooperation Directive[60] in May 2016.[61] The current discussion in the EU is whether to require large MNEs to publicly disclose their key information on profits made and taxes paid in the EU on a country-by-country basis (EU public CbCR).[62]

Also under the new reporting requirements, MNEs whose annual consolidated group revenue is equal or above EUR 750 million are required to annually provide aggregated information that relates to the global allocation of income and taxes that are paid in each jurisdiction where they do business,[63] and that is the so-called 'CbCR'. Other indicators of the location of economic activity within the group as well as information about which entities conduct business in a particular jurisdiction and the business activities each entity engages in must also be provided.[64]

In comparison to the other two elements in the three-tiered TPD approach, the CbCR is the major innovation that has resulted from BEPS Action 13. Appendix III A to

---

57. *Ibid.*, p. 27.
58. *Ibid.*
59. However, the CbCR is not the only standard requiring country-by-country information disclosure. Other standards include: requirements on certain financial institutions in the European Union under the EU Capital Requirements Directive (2013/36/EU) (CRD IV), or requirements on governments and extractive industry companies under the Extractive Industries Transparency Initiative (EITI) and the EU Accounting Directive (2013/34/EU) where information required should be publicly disclosed on an annual basis. For more details, *see* BEPS Action 13 Country-by-Country Reporting Handbook on Effective Tax Risk Assessment, OECD Publishing (2017), available at: http://www.oecd.org/tax/beps/country-by-country-reporting-handbook-on-effective-tax-risk-assessment.htm, paras 29–31.
60. Council Directive 2011/16/EU of 15 Feb. 2011 on administrative cooperation in the field of taxation and repealing Directive 77/799/EEC, L64/1.
61. For more details of the EU CbCR disclosure requirements and formation, *see* https://ec.europa.eu/taxation_customs/business/tax-cooperation-control/administrative-cooperation/enhanced-administrative-cooperation-field-direct-taxation/country-country-reporting_en.
62. For more details, *see* https://ec.europa.eu/info/business-economy-euro/company-reporting-and-auditing/company-reporting/public-country-country-reporting_en#proposal.
63. BEPS Action 13 Final Report, para. 24.
64. *Ibid.*

Chapter V provides a model template for the report which suggests that it should consist of three tables: (i) the first table provides for aggregate information related to the amount of revenue, profit (loss) before income tax, income tax paid and accrued, number of employees, stated capital, accumulated earnings and tangible assets other than cash, or cash equivalents by tax jurisdiction; (ii) the second table requires information on the main business activities of the group entities residing in each tax jurisdiction; and (iii) the third table permits the taxpayers to provide additional information.[65]

---

65. *Ibid.*, pp. 29–30.

Table 7.1  CbCR-Overview of Allocation of Income, Taxes and Business Activities by Tax Jurisdiction

Name of the MNE Group:
Fiscal Year Concerned:

| Tax Jurisdiction | Revenues | | | Profit (Loss) Before Income Tax | Income Tax Paid (on cash basis) | Income Tax Accrued – Current Year | Stated capital | Accumulated earnings | Number of Employees | Tangible Assets other than Cash and Cash Equivalents |
|---|---|---|---|---|---|---|---|---|---|---|
| | Unrelated Party | Related Party | Total | | | | | | | |
| | | | | | | | | | | |
| | | | | | | | | | | |
| | | | | | | | | | | |
| | | | | | | | | | | |

Table 7.2    CbCR-List of All the Constituent Entities of the MNE Group Included in Each Aggregation Per Tax Jurisdiction

Name of the MNE Group:
Fiscal Year Concerned:

| Tax Jurisdiction | Constituent Entities resident in the Tax Jurisdiction | Tax Jurisdiction of organization or incorporation if different from Tax Jurisdiction of Residence | Main business activity(ies) | | | | | | | | | | | | |
|---|---|---|---|---|---|---|---|---|---|---|---|---|---|---|---|
| | | | Research and Development | Holding or Managing intellectual property | Purchasing or Procurement | Manufacturing or Production | Sales, Marketing or Distribution | Administrative, Management or Support Services | Provision of Services to unrelated parties | Internal Group Finance | Regulated Financial Services | Insurance | Holding shares or other equity instruments | Dormant | Other[66] |
| | 1. | | | | | | | | | | | | | | |
| | 2. | | | | | | | | | | | | | | |
| | 3. | | | | | | | | | | | | | | |
| | 1. | | | | | | | | | | | | | | |
| | 2. | | | | | | | | | | | | | | |
| | 3. | | | | | | | | | | | | | | |

66.  Please specify the nature of the activity of the Constituent Entity in the 'Additional Information' section.

*Table 7.3   CbCR-Additional Information*

---

*Name of the MNE Group:*
*Fiscal Year Concerned:*

---

*Please include any further brief information or explanation you consider necessary or that would facilitate the understanding of the compulsory information provided in the country-by-country report.*

---

For those MNEs that are required to submit an annual CbCR, it must include all 'Constituent Entities' of an MNE. This is a new concept and is defined by the OECD as: '(i) any separate business unit of an MNE that is included in the Consolidated Financial Statements of the MNE for financial reporting purposes, or would be so included if equity interests in such business unit of the MNE were traded on a public securities exchange; (ii) any such business unit that is excluded from the MNE's Consolidated Financial Statements solely on size or materiality grounds; and (iii) any permanent establishment of any separate business unit of the MNE included in (i) or (ii) provided the business unit prepares a separate financial statement for such permanent establishment for financial reporting, regulatory, tax reporting, or internal management control purposes'.[67] In other words, the CbCR needs to include all of the tax jurisdictions where the MNE has an entity (or PE) resident for tax purpose regardless of the size of business operations in that jurisdiction.[68]

The source of the reported information is left to the MNE's discretion which could include the consolidation reporting packages, the separate entity statutory financial statements, the regulatory financial statements, or the internal management accounts, and it is not necessary to reconcile the revenue, profit, and tax reporting in the template to the consolidated financial statements.[69] Further, adjustments are not required for differences in accounting principles that are applied from one tax jurisdiction to another.[70] However, the MNE should consistently use the same sources of data from year to year in completing the CbCR, and a brief description of the sources of data used in preparing it needs to be disclosed in the third table as additional information.[71]

The OECD states in the new guidance that the CbCR is intended to only be used for high-level transfer pricing risk assessment purposes and should not be used by tax administrations as a substitute for a detailed transfer pricing analysis or to propose transfer pricing adjustments based on a global formulary apportionment of income.[72]

---

67. BEPS Action 13 Final Report, p. 31.
68. *Ibid.*, para. 34.
69. *Ibid.*, p. 32.
70. *Ibid.*
71. *Ibid.*
72. BEPS Action 13 Final Report, para. 25. Concerning this aspect, some scholars contend that the information provided in the CbCR is not sufficient to apply either the formulary appointment method or the profit split method. For more details, *see* Petruzzi, R., Peng, C., 'The Profit Split Method: A Holistic View of BEPS in Transfer Pricing', Transfer Pricing International 1 (2/2017), pp. 110–120 (peer reviewed).

## 4.2 IMPLEMENTATION

Considering the past experiences described above, consistent and effective implementation of the CbCR is essential, otherwise, the challenges of compliance for MNEs will continue to increase. In recognition of the importance of consistency in this regard, countries participating in the OECD/G20 BEPS Project agreed on the core elements of the implementation of a CbCR. Amongst these core elements is the requirement that they should be filed in the jurisdiction of tax residence of the UPE and shared between jurisdictions through the mechanism of automatic exchange of information, pursuant to government-to-government mechanisms such as the Multilateral Convention on Mutual Administrative Assistance in Tax Matters, bilateral tax treaties, or tax information exchange agreements (TIEAs) (*see* Figure 7.2).

*Figure 7.2    Filing and Exchange CbCR*[73]

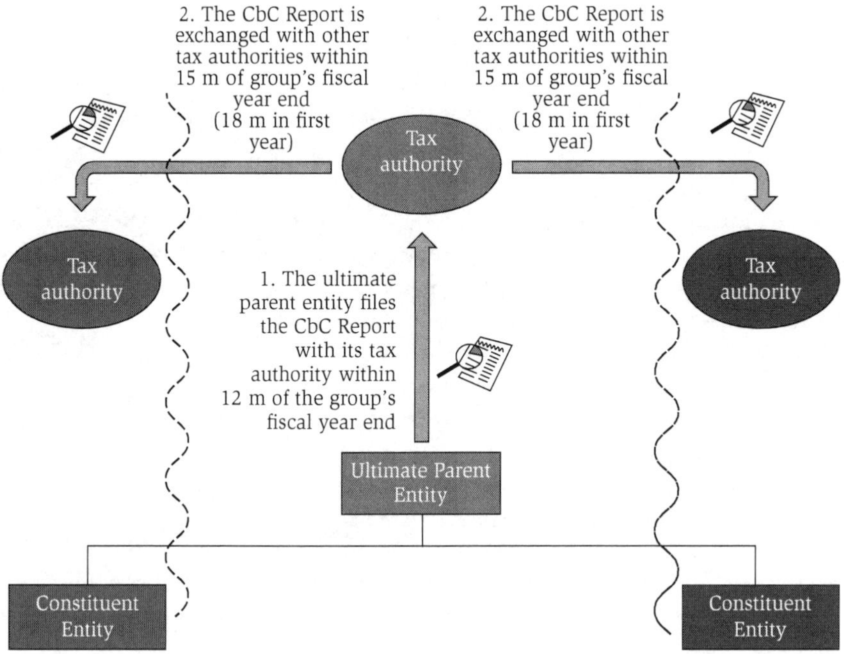

It is intended that an MNE group should only be required to file a CbCR once for each reporting year in the jurisdiction of the UPE. However, in limited circumstances,

---

73. *See* the BEPS Action 13 CbCR Handbook on Effective Tax Risk Assessment, p. 27.

secondary mechanisms including local filing[74] and surrogate entity filing[75] can be used as a substitute. The limited circumstances happen if one or more of the following conditions have been met:

- the UPE is not required to file a CbCR in its residence jurisdiction;
- there is no competent authority agreement between the jurisdictions of UPE and the concerned constituent entity in place is effecting the automatic exchange of a CbCR under the current international agreements of the jurisdictions;
- there is a systemic failure to exchange the CbCR by the jurisdiction of the UPE in practice with a jurisdiction and such failure has been notified to the constituent entity by the local tax authority.[76]

The new CbCR requirements are expected to be implemented for the fiscal years beginning on or after 1 January 2016. Recognizing that, in some instances, final statutory financial statements and other financial information may be relevant for furnishing CbCR data, it is recommended that the CbCR should be filed one year following the last day of the fiscal year of the ultimate parent of the MNE group.[77] For example, for MNEs with a fiscal year ending on 31 December, the first file of a CbCR is expected to occur by 31 December 2017. In the first year of a CbCR, the exchange should take place within eighteen months of the end of the group's reporting fiscal year. Assuming that the first CbCRs are compiled for reporting fiscal years beginning on 1 January 2016, relevant authorities should exchange CbCRs by 30 June 2018. In subsequent years, the deadline is shortened to fifteen months after the end of the group's reporting fiscal year (*see* Figure 7.3).

---

74. In the scenario of the local filing, a constituent entity that is not the UPE of the MNE group files the CbCR directly with its local tax authority.
75. The case of the surrogate entity filing includes two scenarios: (1) the surrogate parent filing when a constituent entity in the group that is not the UPE files the CbCR with its residence jurisdiction; and (2) the parent surrogate entity filing when the UPE of the group files the CbCR with its residence jurisdiction, notwithstanding that the UPE residence jurisdiction does not have the CbCR filing requirement in its local legislation. For more details, *see* the BEPS Action 13 Country-by-Country Reporting Handbook on Effective Implementation, OECD Publishing (2017), available at: http://www.oecd.org/tax/beps/country-by-country-reporting-handbook-on-effective-implementation.htm, para. 8.
76. BEPS Action 13 Final Report, para. 60.
77. *Ibid.*, para. 31.

Figure 7.3    Timetable for the Implementation of the CbCR[78]

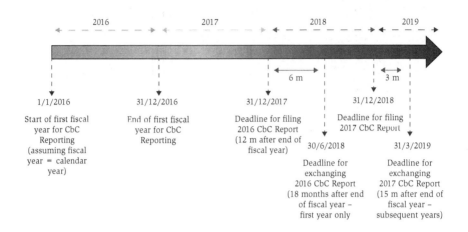

There is an exemption from a CbCR for groups with annual consolidated group revenues in the immediately preceding fiscal year of less than EUR 750 million or an equivalent amount in domestic currency[79] (e.g., Australia has implemented an AUD 1 billion threshold).[80] The OECD assumes that this exemption will exclude 85%–90% of groups from the requirement of filing the CbCR but that the report, nevertheless, will be filed by groups controlling approximately 90% of corporate revenue.[81]

To facilitate the execution of the new reporting standards, an implementation package has been developed consisting of model legislation that could be used by countries to require MNEs to file the CbCR and competent authority agreements that are to be used to facilitate the effectuation of the exchange of those reports among tax administrations.[82] A CbCR XML Schema and related User Guide have also been developed with a purpose of accommodating the electronic exchange of CbCRs.[83]

At the time of this writing, over 100 countries and jurisdictions have been involved in the collaboration to implement the BEPS measures (i.e., the Inclusive Framework on BEPS); sixty-seven had signed the Multilateral Competent Authority Agreement for CbCR (CbC MCAA) which is the mechanism that was initiated to allow

---

78. The figure is extracted from the BEPS Action 13 CbCR Handbook on Effective Implementation, p. 10.
79. BEPS Action 13 Final Report, para. 52.
80. For details of the Australian CbCR rules, see https://www.ato.gov.au/Business/International-tax-for-business/In-detail/Transfer-pricing/Country-by-Country-reporting/.
81. BEPS Action 13 Final Report, para. 53.
82. Ibid., Annex IV, pp. 37–69.
83. OECD, Country-by-Country Reporting XML Schema: User Guide for Tax Administrations and Taxpayers, OECD/G20 Base Erosion and Profit Shifting Project, OECD Publishing (2016), available at: http://www.oecd.org/tax/country-by-country-reporting-xml-schema-user-guide-for-tax-administrations-and-taxpayers.pdf.

signatories to bilaterally and automatically exchange CbCRs with each other.[84] Many of these countries, however, are still in the process of enacting the CbCR requirements into local legislation. Of those countries that have already implemented the requirements, the majority have applied the model legislation advocated by the OECD in most significant respects and, when deviations exist, have allowed for concessional treatment to align the requirements with the parent company jurisdiction. For example, Hong Kong, Isle of Man, Japan, Liechtenstein, Nigeria, Russia, Singapore, Switzerland, and the US allow voluntary filing in the UPE jurisdiction.[85] In particular, Japan provides transition relief for the fiscal year commencing between 1 April 2016 and 31 March 2017 except in the event of Systemic Failure.[86] It remains to be seen whether the other countries will follow suit.

The Action 13 standard on the CbCR is subject to peer review to ensure timely and accurate implementation and safeguard the level playing field. The OECD released key documents which will form the basis of the peer review on 1 February 2017.[87] This peer review is a separate exercise to the 2020 review to evaluate whether modifications to the CbCR standard should be made. The terms of reference of the peer review focus on the following three key aspects of the CbCR standard that a jurisdiction must meet:

- The domestic legal and administrative framework,
- The exchange of information framework, and
- The confidentiality and appropriate use of CbCR.

As the CbCR is required to be filed in the jurisdiction of tax residence of the UPE and shared between jurisdictions through automatic exchange of information, a number of countries are implementing practical measures to identify the responsible filing entity in the group in advance. These measures generally require a formal submission identifying the ultimate parent of the group, the responsible party for filing, and the tax identification number of that entity, usually in the local taxpayer's tax return or through a separate dedicated form.

---

84. For more details, *see* http://www.oecd.org/tax/automatic-exchange/about-automatic-excha nge/country-by-country-reporting.htm.
85. For more details, *see* http://www.oecd.org/tax/automatic-exchange/country-specific-inform ation-on-country-by-country-reporting-implementation.htm.
86. *Ibid.*
87. OECD, *BEPS Action 13 on Country-by-Country Reporting – Peer Review Documents*, OECD/G20 Base Erosion and Profit Shifting Project, OECD Publishing (2017), available at: http://www. oecd.org/tax/beps/beps-action-13-on-country-by-country-reporting-peer-review-documents. pdf.

### 4.3 DISCLOSURE CHALLENGES IN LIGHT OF PRACTICAL EXPERIENCE

#### 4.3.1 *High Risk of Data Misinterpretation*

The financial data to be reported in Table 7.1 of the CbCR is ambiguously defined and leaves a number of aspects open to taxpayer discretion.[88] Along with a format that aggregates financial data for a tax jurisdiction by tax jurisdiction basis, the CbCR concept contains a significant potential for a risk of misinterpretation. Furthermore, jurisdictions may allow taxpayers to use the consolidated data at the jurisdictional level on the condition that the consolidation is consistently used across years in Table 7.1 and correspondingly highlighted in Table 7.3 with explanatory terminology.[89] The usefulness of the CbCR to tax authorities for TP risk assessment[90] purposes is questionable except for partly allowing for conclusions about a potential shift of taxable income between years or identifying significant financial activity in a jurisdiction with limited business activities.[91]

As mentioned previously, MNEs can select the source of the reported information at their own discretion without reconciling the revenues, profits, and taxes to be reported in the template of the consolidated financial statements. In addition, though the accounting standards that are applied might vary from jurisdiction to jurisdiction, it is not a mandate for MNEs to make adjustments to the accounting for such differences. However, reconciliations may not always be possible and/or useful, for example, due to differences in currencies or local GAAP accounting principles. This is likely to lead to inconsistent implementations, a further limitation of the report's validity, and a considerable risk of unwarranted increased scrutiny by tax authorities.

As an example, on the one hand, the earnings of a PE are allocated to the country of the head office for accounting purposes and, on the other hand, tax payments are attributed locally. The OECD guidance specifically states that PE data should be reported for CbCR purposes by reference to the tax jurisdiction in which the PE is situated and not by reference to the head office jurisdiction.[92] However, rules and regulations governing attribution of income and expenses to PEs differ significantly by jurisdiction. The MNE, therefore, is required to determine whether to utilize the financial data that is used for accounting or tax purposes for reporting the local country data. It must also determine which data to use when deducting the income and

88. The OECD published Guidance on the Implementation of the Country-by-Country Reporting BEPS Action 13 (Updated November 2017), available at: http://www.oecd.org/tax/beps/guidance-on-country-by-country-reporting-beps-action-13.htm. In this guidance, the OECD provides clarification on the definition of items reported in the CbCR template. Notwithstanding that, it still leaves great room for discretion to taxpayers.
89. Guidance on the Implementation of the CbCR, p. 9.
90. For more details on the TP risk assessment, *see* the BEPS Action 13 Country-by-Country Reporting Handbook on Effective Tax Risk Assessment (September 2017), available at: http://www.oecd.org/tax/beps/country-by-country-reporting-handbook-on-effective-tax-risk-assessment.htm.
91. Petruzzi, R., Navisotschnigg, F., 'BEPS and EU requirements for Country-by-Country Reporting', in: Lang, Haunold (eds.), Transparenz und Informationsaustausch: Der gläserne Steuerpflichtige (Vienna: Linde, 2017), pp. 51–78.
92. BEPS Action 13 Final Report, p. 31.

expenses allocated to the PE from the head office financial disclosures (the head office jurisdiction may use different rules to attribute income and expenses to the PE from the PE jurisdiction).

It is considered likely that tax authorities will apply a comparative ratio analysis of the financial data disclosed in Table 7.1 of the CbCR in order to prioritize review activities.[93] This ratio analysis, however, will probably provide a flawed basis for risk assessment as a result of the discretion that is allowed by the taxpayers. For example, the number of employees may be reported as at year end or on the basis of average employment levels for the year, and the taxpayer may also choose whether or not to include independent contractors as employees. The application of different accounting standards may also impact the disclosure of items such as revenues and book values of tangible assets.

It is unclear why the OECD did not follow established international accounting standards. It may be surmised that the underlying rationale was to minimize the compliance burden on MNEs by providing sufficient discretion to ensure that significant additional work was not required to generate financial data. However, the ambiguity resulting from this approach makes it likely that countries will interpret the reporting requirements differently. Table 7.3 of the CbCR, which allows companies to provide any additional information or explanation that could be necessary or that could facilitate the understanding of the information provided in the CbCR, may then become the key tool for taxpayers to provide the necessary context to the information that is provided and address any potential misinterpretation of data by tax administrations.

### 4.3.2   *Broken Links Between Taxes Paid and Profits Earned*

Table 7.1 requires disclosure of income tax paid (on a cash basis) and income tax accrued (current year). Income tax paid encompasses tax prepayments for the current year, tax prepayments for subsequent years, closing payments for prior periods, and supplementary payments or refunds[94] due to tax audits or legal proceedings.[95] These items relate to multiple periods and do not permit conclusions about whether the amount of tax payments is compatible with the annual result. Income tax accrued means the sum of the accrued current tax expense that is recorded on taxable profits or losses of the year of reporting of all of the Constituent Entities that are resident for tax purposes in the relevant tax jurisdiction irrespective of whether or not the tax has been paid (e.g., based on a preliminary tax assessment).[96] Furthermore, taxable profits and the profits as shown in the financial statements are generally not consistent. A disclosure of income tax paid or income tax accrued, therefore, only has sodocoClas-Placeholder informative value.

---

93. Handbook on Effective Tax Risk Assessment, para. 26.
94. As an exception, the refund may be reported in Revenue if it is treated as revenue under the applicable accounting standard or in the source of data. In this case, a note should be added in Table 7.3 accordingly. For more details, *see* Guidance on the Implementation of the CbCR, p. 10.
95. BEPS Action 13 Final Report, pp. 33–34; Guidance on the Implementation of the CbCR, p. 10.
96. BEPS Action 13 Final Report, p. 34; Guidance on the Implementation of the CbCR, p. 10.

The disclosure of income tax paid according to the OECD guidance also includes withholding taxes paid by other entities (both related and independent) in order to achieve a complete and comparable scenario of the entire tax burden as well as of the regional allocation of taxes.[97] However, withholding taxes are directly withheld by the contractual parties and paid to the authority abroad. In this case, the receiving company often does not have an overview of the taxes withheld by its contractual parties. Furthermore, overpaid withholding taxes are not always refunded, or the refund occurs in subsequent years.

Another important aspect to be considered is the losses carried forward which might result from operational activities of prior years or from tax restructurings. These losses carried forward have a considerable impact on the tax burden of the taxpayer. The CbCR does not require disclosure of these losses. Hence, it is not clear to tax authorities whether low-tax payments (despite a potentially high income) result from the use of losses carried forward.

As a result of these inconsistencies, there is no association between the country-specific taxes paid and the profit in a fiscal year. A multiple-year analysis of the annual results and the tax payments might partly correct these effects. Otherwise, a one-year overview only leads to further misinterpretation potential.

### 4.3.3 Dilution of the Arm's Length Principle

The deliverables on Action 13 explicitly point out that a number of emerging markets indicated a preference that additional transactional data be included in the CbCR over and above the OECD's recommendations. Specifically, the data concern related party interest payments, royalty payments, and service fees. The OECD has mandated that countries participating in the BEPS project carefully review the implementation of the new standards no later than the end of 2020 with a view to reassessing whether any modifications are required.

There is reason to fear that the additional information requirements requested by the emerging countries could broaden the possibilities for analysis based on a formulary apportionment of income instead of the traditional arm's length principle being applied.[98] However, the OECD specifically states that the information in the CbCR on its own does not constitute conclusive evidence of whether transfer prices are or are not appropriate and should not be used by tax administrations to propose transfer pricing adjustments based on a formulary apportionment of income.

### 4.3.4 Role of Technology

The role of technology in assisting MNEs with meeting the CbCR requirements from a data collection perspective is critical. However, the difficulties that MNE programmers

---

97. BEPS Action 13 Final Report, p. 34.
98. Petruzzi, R., Peng, C., The Profit Split Method: A Holistic View of BEPS in Transfer Pricing, Transfer Pricing International 1 (2/2017), pp. 110–120 (peer reviewed).

face increase significantly when designing effective transfer pricing modules within the group main information system. The optimal way to obtain complete and consistent data would be with one worldwide and integrated financial reporting system. This could be a consolidation system or an Enterprise Resource Planning (ERP) system. Unfortunately, due to the size of a business, its acquisitions, the local ERP system customization requirements in connection with local accounting or legal requirements and, of course, budget constraints, MNEs may face a variety of different data sources ranging from individual SAP solutions and Data or Business Warehouse systems to a mere excel spreadsheet. Interlinked information systems that possess specifically designed transfer pricing modules will play a fundamental role in facilitating an MNE's efforts to comply with the new OECD requirements in the future.

### 4.3.5 *Exchange of Information*

While the master file can be directly collected by jurisdictions, the CbCR will be collected by tax authorities and distributed through tax treaty and information exchange networks. It is commonly understood that the CbCR report should only be prepared and submitted to tax authorities by the UPE and should not be published publicly, for example, in companies' annual reports. Appendix IV of the BEPS Action 13 Final Report contains model legislation that could be implemented by countries that would require the UPE of a multinational group to file the CbCR or substitute secondary filing mechanisms when the UPE's jurisdiction does not have CbCR filing requirements in its jurisdiction of residence. This approach is reasonable as the UPE usually has the most comprehensive overview of the entire global activities of the group of companies and access to the corresponding information.

The tax authorities of the parent company should exchange the CbCR information on an automatic basis with the jurisdictions wherein the group operates through existing instruments such as agreements on automatic information exchange regarding relevant fiscal issues, TIEAs, and tax treaties. Jurisdictions are encouraged to expand the coverage of their international agreements for the exchange of information which will be an integral part of the ongoing monitoring process. The minimum standard provides that a jurisdiction's ability to obtain and use the CbCR is subject to conditions of confidentiality, consistency, and appropriate use.[99]

Accordingly, jurisdictions' behaviour that deviates from the confidentiality or appropriate use conditions could result in a suspension of the exchange. The OECD has included a 'Confidentiality and Data Safeguards Questionnaire' as an annex to Appendix IV that contains a checklist of requirements related to legal enforcement and information security. This should be applied as a standard to determine whether or not jurisdictions are appropriately protecting the information being exchanged. Under the information exchange instruments, data can only be exchanged if both parties have

---

99. For more details, *see* BEPS Action 13 on Country-by-Country Reporting Guidance on the Appropriate Use of Information Contained in Country-by-Country Reports, OECD Publishing, September 2017, available at http://www.oecd.org/ctp/beps/beps-action-13-on-country-by-country-reporting-appropriate-use-of-information-in-CbC-reports.pdf.

provided safeguards to ensure that information remains sodocoClasPlaceholder. However, the concern is how the proposed conditions regarding confidentiality are going to be implemented and applied in practice by the different jurisdictions.

### 4.3.6 Timing and Secondary Filing Mechanisms

A so-called 'secondary mechanism' would be accepted as appropriate if a jurisdiction fails to provide information to another jurisdiction. Affiliated companies should be responsible for creating the CbCR only if the parent company has no duty to create a report in its particular country, no qualified competent authority agreement for filing the report is in effect, or there has been a systemic failure to exchange the CbCR in practice. This also implies that no additional local filing can be required by any local tax authorities if the CbCR submitted to the UPEs' tax administration is exchanged with the respective country and complies with the OECD requirements established under Action 13.[100] Nonetheless, differences in legislation (or interpretation) of secondary mechanisms could incite a great deal of uncertainty for MNEs.

The first years will be a challenge for MNEs particularly when the CbCR legislation is delayed or not fully legislated, there are different filing dates, or the end of the fiscal year differs in the country of the ultimate parent company from that of the local affiliate. Inaccuracies should be expected while business systems are refined. Concerning the filing during the transition period when the fiscal year of the jurisdiction implementing the CbCR does not commence from 1 January 2016, the OECD indicates the concerned jurisdiction may allow voluntary filing for the UPE in its residence jurisdiction (so-called 'parent surrogate filing') as an alternative to local filing.[101] Furthermore, the surrogate filing would be allowed only if the following conditions are satisfied:

- the UPE files the CbCR in its residence jurisdiction by the filing deadline;
- the residence jurisdiction of the UPE has implemented the CbCR filing into its national law by the first filing deadline of the CbCR;
- the mechanism enabling the automatic exchange of the CbCB between the UPE's jurisdiction and the other concerned jurisdiction is in place by the first filing deadline of the CbCR, and there is no systemic failure of exchange of the CbCR occurring;
- the information of the reporting entity is notified in a timely manner by the UPE and the concerned entity to their residence jurisdiction, respectively.[102]

---

100. Concerning whether the local filing requirement is consistent with the minimum standard, see the BEPS Action 13 CbCR Handbook on Effective Implementation, paras 37–38.
101. Guidance on the Implementation of the CbCR, p. 23.
102. Ibid., pp. 23–24.

## 5 CRITICAL REVIEW OF THE TPD UNDER THE BEPS ACTION 13

### 5.1 Challenges of the TPD in Light of the BEPS Action 13

#### 5.1.1 *Increased Documentation Requirements and Enhanced Transparency*

In principle, the practical challenges facing MNEs (especially those meeting the EUR 750 million or equivalent threshold) in preparing international documentation as outlined above remain irrespective of the new OECD approach. What is more, the additional requirements arising as a result of the introduction of the CbCR exacerbate the currently existing problem of data availability.

Large MNEs now have to cope with a significantly substantial documentation burden in relationship to the scope and quality of the content as well as enhanced transparency of internal data. The interdependencies between the master file, the local file, and the CbCR necessitate a more comprehensive focus on consistency in transfer pricing practices. With increased access to information regarding the global operations of an MNE, tax administrations will easily be able to identify potential inconsistencies between local pricing and global policies.

#### 5.1.2 *Differences in Legislation and Interpretation*

By amending Chapter V of the OECD Guidelines and its annexes, the OECD/G20 endeavoured to create an internationally accepted standard for documentation requirements in the area of transfer pricing for the first time. However, the success of these standards cannot yet be judged because key questions remain concerning the implementation of them. Any differences in requirements of different countries (i.e., deviations from the OECD guidance) will make compliance very challenging.

This raises the question of whether the OECD's approach can actually be put into practice if individual countries do not or only partially implement it.[103] The United States, for example, has only implemented the CbCR requirement but not the other components of Action 13 (i.e., the master file and local file). In this respect, the impact of the OECD Guidelines may be considered as being either one of the most important changes in the TPD standards or only as a modification of more insignificant detailed regulations from an individual country perspective. The actual implications of the new documentation requirements will, therefore, become apparent upon implementation of the new requirements by the respective legislatures. Whether countries will adapt the existing documentation requirements based on the OECD guidance and how the tax authorities will interpret these regulations is yet uncertain.

As stated in the deliverables on Action 13, a number of emerging markets such as Argentina, Brazil, China, Colombia, India, Mexico, South Africa, and Turkey have

---

103. For the to-date implementation status of the CbCR across country, *see* http://www.oecd.org/tax/automatic-exchange/country-specific-information-on-country-by-country-reporting-implementation.htm.

expressed a preference for supplementary information for each tier.[104] This could result in additional efforts to comply with the documentation. For example, in the recent Bulletin 42 issued by the Chinese tax authority, the submission of a fourth document, the Special Issue File dealing with intra-group services, cost sharing arrangements, and/or thin capitalization is required.[105] China also requires additional information to be included in the master file and the local file.[106]

MNEs will need to ensure that they are aware of any variations in local specific requirements and customize their documentation accordingly in each case, if required. How tax administrations will react if countries formally implement the Action 13 requirements earlier or 'localize' them, for example, is also still unclear. It is hardly surprising that some tax administrations of developed countries are sceptical of the more stringent documentation standards now that the initial euphoria has gradually diminished. This is mainly due to concerns that the enhanced transparency of groups will lead some jurisdictions, particularly the BRICS countries, to vie for a greater amount of the profit allocation of MNEs.

### 5.1.3 Confidentiality Issues

According to the OECD, tax authorities should take all reasonable steps to ensure that there is no public disclosure of sodocoClasPlaceholder information such as trade or scientific secrets and other commercially sensitive information contained in the master file, local file, and CbCR.[107] Therefore, tax administrations should assure taxpayers that the information presented in the TPD will remain sodocoClasPlaceholder. Confidentiality is not only important for tax-relevant data but also for trade secrets, financial data, or other commercial information that may be disclosed in the TPD.

When sensitive company information is being disclosed, it is imperative to ensure that the foreign tax authorities also treat this information as sodocoClasPlaceholder. The principle of proportionality demands that taxpayers are only requested to provide information that is relevant for their taxation or risk assessment. The fear that sodocoClasPlaceholder data will be made available to competitors is one of the main themes of the comments on BEPS Action 13.

In cases when disclosure is required in public court proceedings or judicial decisions, every effort should be made to ensure that confidentiality is maintained and that information is disclosed only to the extent that is actually needed.[108] This means, however, that information disclosed during a public court proceeding or in a judicial decision is no longer subject to confidentiality.

---

104. OECD (2014), Guidance on Transfer Pricing Documentation and Country-by-Country Reporting, OECD Publishing, Paris. http://dx.doi.org/10.1787/9789264219236-en, at p. 10.
105. CN: About Improving Reporting and Filing of Related Party Transactions and Contemporaneous Documentation, SAT Bulletin [2016] 42, 29 Jun. 2016.
106. For certain insights, *see* C. (X.) Peng, A Rethink of Location-Specific Advantages with an Analysis of the Chinese Approach, 24 Intl. Transfer Pricing J. 6 (2017), International Transfer Pricing Journal IBFD.
107. BEPS Action 13 Final Report, para. 44.
108. *Ibid.*

Additional concerns about confidentiality arise in the context of international exchange of information between tax authorities.[109] There is no guarantee that all countries will protect the confidentiality of information, and there are considerable differences regarding tax secrecy around the world. When dealing with sodocoClas-Placeholder information, tax authorities should follow the OECD guide – 'Keeping it Safe'.[110] This is also a key component of the peer review procedures.

Furthermore, reputational risk is an increasing concern for MNEs in a political and media environment that focuses on the amount of taxes that are paid compared to profits with little attention being paid to the applicable taxation law.

## 5.2 Outlook of the TPD in Light of BEPS Action 13

Of all of the guidance released under the OECD's BEPS Action Plan, the final report on the TPD and the CbCR will impose the greatest compliance burden on large MNEs and will significantly increase their documentation requirements. The new TPD requirements necessitate a shift from a one-sided analysis to a more holistic approach encompassing the consideration of value creation and the value chain analysis for the MNE's group operations. It also requires the MNE to have effective steering processes in place (*see* Figure 7.4).

*Figure 7.4    TP Steering Process*

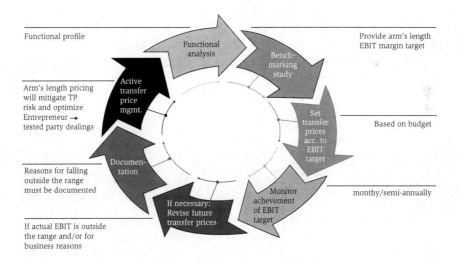

Unfortunately, the new reporting requirements do not successfully balance tax authorities' interests and the usefulness of the data. Emerging markets in particular are

---

109. *Ibid.*, para. 45.
110. *Ibid.*, para. 44.

expected to implement additional requirements beyond those outlined in the new Chapter V. One of the central functions of the CbCR is to provide tax administrations with the information that is necessary to conduct a transfer pricing risk assessment in which an overview of local tax burdens and profits of the group companies are important aspects. However, considering that the relationship is not provided, in many cases, between the country-specific taxes that are paid and the profits in a fiscal year, the value of a risk analysis based on this information is rather limited. An observation of the current status of the implementation of reporting regulations through local country legislation or administrative procedures, however, shows that inconsistencies still exist. Thus far, the implementation by the majority of countries has adhered to the guidance in most of the significant respects. It is yet unclear how tax administrations will use the new information in practice that is available to them.

Most of the discussion on the OECD's efforts on transparency has focused on the CbCR. That requirement, with the stated purpose of aiding countries for transfer pricing risk assessment purposes, has been criticized as an administrative burden for taxpayers. There is also considerable concern that the CbCR will be used by some tax authorities to erode the arm's length principle and that it is a prelude to a formulary apportionment – even though this has been explicitly negated by the OECD in its guidance. This peer review process is considered to be critical for ensuring that a level playing field is maintained and that the foundations of the Action 13 requirements are not jeopardized by misuse of the information that is submitted.

Taxpayers must be prepared to fulfil the new requirements as well as defend their transfer pricing considering the potential for increased scrutiny by the tax authorities based on their interpretation of the new data that is available to them. CbCR data from foreign entities will likely become a challenge in future tax audits; taxpayers should be well-prepared for a discussion with tax authorities and be ready to provide explanations in their TPD for 'suspect' CbCR data such as a large amount of profit in a country with a limited number of employees or assets.

The challenge for taxpayers managing the TPD process will only increase as time goes on as the number of countries requiring documentation increases and as more countries institute country-specific requirements. Increasingly detailed documentation requirements and recent OECD development on the TPD through BEPS Action 13 will globally request MNEs to adjust their approach to documentation. Finding the right balance between risk management, on one side, and the TPD, on the other, is very important for an MNE (*see* Figure 7.5).

*Figure 7.5   Implication on TP Documentation*

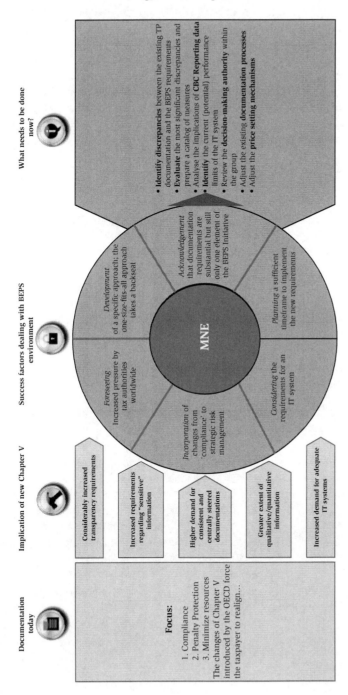

In many countries, the implementation of BEPS Action 13 is likely to occur within different timeframes and probably with deviations in content which will lead to initial inconsistencies in the international tax law environment. While most countries have or will immediately comply with the BEPS recommendations, some may deliberately delay and seek opportunities to maximize their competitiveness. All of this will lead to a significant increase in double taxation and international tax controversies. The OECD guidance and other explanatory materials suggest some disagreements on the underlying standards on tax treaties and transfer pricing. It will, therefore, be important for the G20 to ensure a firm commitment from all OECD countries and other signatories through the peer review process.

Although the importance of the new requirements for accomplishing transparent communication between MNEs and tax authorities is clear for the purpose of ensuring that profits are taxed where the business activities are performed and value creation is achieved, it is also obvious that the new three-tiered approach will create several challenges to MNEs and increase the cost burden associated with the preparation of the necessary documentation. Achieving the equilibrium between limiting the opportunities of MNEs for BEPS while keeping the cost and effort that MNEs must incur in order to comply with the documentation requirements at a reasonable and achievable level is fundamental for the success of the implementation around the world of the recommendations that are established in Action 13.

## 6  CONCLUSIONS

This chapter reviews the evolution of the TPD standards around the globe in the first section and concludes that attempts were made by different stakeholders, i.e. the OECD, the PATA, and the EU, to synchronize or standardize the TPD requirements regionally even before OECD BEPS Action 13. Later, BEPS Action 13 introduces the three-tiered approach, i.e. the master file, the local file, and the CbCR, which intends to provide a user-friendly TPD solution for both taxpayers and tax administrations. However, adherence to the global TPD standard is not easily achieved in practice.

Concerning the three-tiered approach contained in the OECD BEPS Action 13 Final Report, key aspects of the master file, the local file, and the CbCR are particularly presented in sections 2, 3, and 4, respectively, specifically regarding the concepts, implementation, and disclosure challenges that practitioners may face in reality. Lastly, yet importantly, section 5 provides a critical review of the OECD's three-tiered approach. It concludes that, while the OECD is remarkably establishing a global TPD standard through BEPS Action 13 and the follow-ups, the innovation of the OECD creates more compliance work and practical difficulties for MNEs in the implementation stage that should not be ignored, and such a challenge is anticipated to continue in the future.

## ANNEX 1: A COMPARATIVE VIEW OF THE MASTER FILE REQUIREMENTS

| Information to be Included | OECD BEPS 13 | OECD TPG | UN TPG | EU Code of Conduct | US Treasury Regulations | TP Documentation by PATA |
|---|---|---|---|---|---|---|
| **Organizational structure** | | | | | | |
| chart illustrating the MNE's **legal and ownership structure** and **geographical location** | ✓ | ✓ | ✓ | ✓ | ✓ | ✓ |
| **Description of MNE's business(es)** | | | | | | |
| outline of the **business** | ✓ | ✓ | ✓ | ✓ | ✓ | ✓ |
| general description of the **business strategy** | | ✓ | ✓ | ✓ | | ✓ |
| description of **internal procedures and controls** in place | | | | | | ✓ |
| important drivers of **business profit** | ✓ | | ✓ | | | ✓ |
| description of the **supply chain** | ✓ | | | | | |
| list and brief description of important **service arrangements** | ✓ | ✓ | ✓ | | | ✓ |
| description of the main **geographic markets** | ✓ | ✓ | ✓ | | | ✓ |
| brief written **functional analysis** | ✓ | ✓ | ✓ | ✓ | | ✓ |
| description of important **business restructuring** | ✓ | | | | | |
| **MNE's transactions** | | | | | | |
| general identification of the **associated enterprises engaged** in controlled transactions | | | | ✓ | | ✓ |
| general description of the **controlled transactions** involving associated enterprises (flows of transactions; invoice flows; amounts of transaction flows) | | | | ✓ | | ✓ |

| Information to be Included | OECD BEPS 13 | OECD TPG | UN TPG | EU Code of Conduct | US Treasury Regulations | TP Documentation by PATA |
|---|---|---|---|---|---|---|
| MNE group's inter-company **transfer pricing policy** or a description of the group's **transfer pricing system** | | | | ✓ | | ✓ |
| MNE's intangibles | | | | | | |
| general description of the MNE's **overall strategy** for the development, ownership, and exploitation of intangibles | ✓ | ✓ | ✓ | | | |
| list of **intangibles** | ✓ | | | ✓ | | ✓ |
| list of **important agreements** | ✓ | | | | | |
| general description of the **group's transfer pricing policies** | ✓ | ✓ | | | | |
| general description of any important **transfers of interests** | ✓ | | | | | |
| MNE's intra-group financial activities | | | | | | |
| general description of **how the group is financed** | ✓ | ✓ | ✓ | | | |
| identification of any members of the MNE group that provide a **central financing function** | ✓ | | | | | |
| general description of the MNE's general **transfer pricing policies** | ✓ | | | | | |
| MNE's intra-group services | | | | | | |
| documentation on **intra-group services** | | ✓ | ✓ | | | |
| MNE's CCA/CSA | | | | | | |
| list of **cost contribution agreements/ cost sharing agreements** | | | ✓ | ✓ | ✓ | ✓ |
| **terms, participants, subject activity,** and **conditions** of initial arrangements | | | ✓ | | | ✓ |

| Information to be Included | OECD BEPS 13 | OECD TPG | UN TPG | EU Code of Conduct | US Treasury Regulations | TP Documentation by PATA |
|---|---|---|---|---|---|---|
| manner in which participants' proportionate **shares of expected benefits** are measured | | | ✓ | | | ✓ |
| form and value of each **participant's initial contributions** and a detailed description of how the value of initial and ongoing contributions is **determined** | | | ✓ | | | ✓ |
| any provisions for **balancing payments** or for **adjusting the terms** of the arrangements | | | ✓ | | | ✓ |
| **comparison** between projections used to determine expected benefits from CCA activity with the actual results | | | ✓ | | | ✓ |
| **annual expenditure** incurred in conducting the CCA activity, the form and value of each **participant's contributions** made during the CCA's terms, and a detailed description of how the value of contributions is **determined** and how **accounting principles** are applied consistently to all participants | | | ✓ | | | ✓ |
| MNE's financial and tax positions | | | | | | |
| MNE's **annual consolidated financial statement** | ✓ | ✓ | | | | ✓ |
| amount of **sales and operating results** | | ✓ | ✓ | | | |
| list and brief description of the MNE group's existing **unilateral advance pricing agreements (APAs) and other tax rulings** | ✓ | | | ✓ | | |
| Undertakings | | | | | | |

| Information to be Included | OECD BEPS 13 | OECD TPG | UN TPG | EU Code of Conduct | US Treasury Regulations | TP Documentation by PATA |
|---|---|---|---|---|---|---|
| undertaking by each domestic taxpayer to provide **supplementary information** upon request and within a reasonable time frame in accordance with national rules | | | | ✓ | | |
| Comprehensive clause | | | | | | |
| any documentation explicitly required by the **regulations** | | | | | ✓ | |

## ANNEX 2: A COMPARATIVE VIEW OF THE LOCAL FILE REQUIREMENTS

| Information to be Included | OECD BEPS 13 | OECD TPG | UN TPG | EU Code of Conduct | US Treasury Regulations | TP Documentation by PATA |
|---|---|---|---|---|---|---|
| Local entity | | | | | | |
| outline of the **business** | ✓ | ✓ | ✓ | ✓ | ✓ | ✓ |
| description of the **management structure** of the local entity | ✓ | ✓ | ✓ | | | |
| local **organisation chart** | ✓ | ✓ | ✓ | | ✓ | ✓ |
| description of the **individuals** to whom local management reports | ✓ | | | | | |
| **description of the business and business strategy** | ✓ | ✓ | ✓ | ✓ | | ✓ |
| **key competitors** | ✓ | ✓ | ✓ | | | ✓ |
| Controlled transactions | | | | | | |
| description of the material **controlled transactions** | ✓ | ✓ | ✓ | ✓ | ✓ | ✓ |
| amount of intra-group **payments and receipts** | ✓ | ✓ | ✓ | ✓ | ✓ | ✓ |
| identification of **associated enterprises** involved | ✓ | ✓ | ✓ | ✓ | ✓ | ✓ |
| copies of all material **intra-group agreements** | ✓ | | | | | ✓ |
| detailed **comparability and functional analysis** | ✓ | ✓ | ✓ | ✓ | ✓ | ✓ |

| Information to be Included | OECD BEPS 13 | OECD TPG | UN TPG | EU Code of Conduct | US Treasury Regulations | TP Documentation by PATA |
|---|---|---|---|---|---|---|
| indication of the most appropriate **transfer pricing method** | ✓ | ✓ | ✓ | ✓ | ✓ | ✓ |
| description of the **alternative methods** that were considered and an explanation of why they were not selected | | | | | ✓ | |
| indication of which associated enterprise is selected as the **tested party** | ✓ | ✓ | ✓ | ✓ | ✓ | ✓ |
| summary of the **important assumptions** | ✓ | ✓ | ✓ | ✓ | ✓ | ✓ |
| explanation of the reasons for performing a **multi-year analysis** | ✓ | | | | | ✓ |
| list and description of selected **comparable uncontrolled transactions** | ✓ | ✓ | ✓ | ✓ | ✓ | ✓ |
| information on relevant **financial indicators** for independent enterprises relied on in the transfer pricing analysis | ✓ | ✓ | ✓ | ✓ | ✓ | ✓ |
| description of the **comparable search methodology** and the **source of such information** | ✓ | ✓ | ✓ | ✓ | ✓ | ✓ |
| description of any **comparability adjustments** performed | ✓ | ✓ | ✓ | ✓ | ✓ | ✓ |
| description of the **reasons for concluding** that relevant transactions were priced on an arm's length basis | ✓ | ✓ | ✓ | ✓ | ✓ | ✓ |
| summary of **financial information** used | ✓ | ✓ | ✓ | ✓ | ✓ | ✓ |
| copy of existing **unilateral and bilateral/multilateral APAs and other tax rulings** | ✓ | | | | | |
| information on **pricing** | | ✓ | ✓ | | | ✓ |

| Information to be Included | OECD BEPS 13 | OECD TPG | UN TPG | EU Code of Conduct | US Treasury Regulations | TP Documentation by PATA |
|---|---|---|---|---|---|---|
| details concerning any **setoff transactions** that have an effect on determining the arm's length price | | ✓ | ✓ | | | ✓ |
| documents for showing the **process of negotiations** for determining or revising prices | | ✓ | | | | |
| description of the **implementation and application of the group's inter-company transfer pricing policy** | | | | ✓ | | |
| description or summary of any relevant data that the taxpayer obtains **after the end of the tax year and before filing a tax return** | | | | | ✓ | |
| Financial information | | | | | | |
| annual local entity **financial accounts** | ✓ | ✓ | | | | ✓ |
| amount of **sales and operating results** | | ✓ | ✓ | | | |
| **information and allocation schedules** | ✓ | | | | | |
| **summary schedules** of relevant financial data for comparables | ✓ | | | | | |
| Comprehensive clause | | | | | | |
| any documentation explicitly required by the **regulations** | | | | | ✓ | |

Part II  Specific Topics

# CHAPTER 8

# Attribution of Profits to Permanent Establishments

# 1 INTRODUCTION

The ongoing globalization of product and service flows as well as the increasing digitalization of international business gradually led to supply chains and multinational enterprise (MNE) structures that are more complex throughout the world. Moreover, the complexity of modern MNEs was further enhanced by different types of business structuring procedures such as integration, cross-border transfer of business functions, or business restructuring. All of these aspects led to intra-group transactions multiplying in terms of transactional volume and becoming increasingly diverse.[1] The overall transactional volume, the diverse nature of intra-group transactions, and the potential to take advantage of beneficial tax structuring techniques were the primary reason for the heightened political and economic awareness of the overall topic of transfer pricing throughout the last decades and especially during the course of the OECD BEPS project.[2]

When discussing the business structuring of MNEs, the first major decision is whether business in a certain country should be conducted through an associated enterprise or a permanent establishment (PE) situated in that country. Legally speaking, associated enterprises and PEs are considerably different. Whereas an associated enterprise (e.g. a corporation) is an independent entity with an own legal personality, a PE legally forms a part of a company (head office) and, therefore, is not. However, for tax purposes, PEs are considered to be independent enterprises. The arm's length principle established in Article 9 OECD Model Convention and the respective guidance provided in the OECD Commentary and the OECD Guidelines[3] are – in general – only directly applicable in situations when transactions are performed among associated enterprises within an MNE. However, Article 7 OECD Model Convention provides for the application of the arm's length principle also in a situation when transactions are carried out between parts of a company qualifying as a PE in different countries. Accordingly, the arm's length principle is applicable in all relevant business transactions within MNEs.

So far, this book focuses on transfer pricing aspects that are established under Article 9 OECD Model Convention. However, due to the fact that PEs form important elements of modern MNEs, the following chapter will focus on the interpretation and application of the arm's length principle under Article 7 OECD Model Convention. The evolution of the arm's length principle under Article 9 and Article 7 OECD Model

---

1. Whereas intra-group transactions accounted for approximately 25% of the worldwide transactional volume in the 1980s, this share constantly increased and already amounted to 60% in 2006; Compare Michael Kobetsky, Transfer Pricing Measures in Emerging Developing Economies, Asia-Pacific Tax Bulletin 363, 366 (2008); see also Theresa Lohse, Nadine Riedel, Christoph Spengel, The Increasing Importance of Transfer Pricing Regulations – a Worldwide Overview, https://ub-madoc.bib.uni-mannheim.de/32689/1/Arbeitspapier_Spengel_Lohse_Riedel.pdf (assessed 10 February 2017); see also Georg Kofler in Ekkehart Reimer, Alexander Rust (eds), Klaus Vogel on Double Taxation Conventions[4], Article 9, para. 3 (2015), where it states that most of the worldwide transactions occur within MNEs.
2. Compare OECD, Addressing Base Erosion and Profit Shifting (Paris: OECD Publishing, 2013).
3. OECD, OECD Transfer Pricing Guidelines for Multinational Enterprises and Tax Administrations (Paris: OECD, 2017).

Convention was relatively different throughout the last decades. Even though the interpretation of the arm's length principle under Article 9 OECD Model Convention constantly evolved, there were no systematic changes.[4] However, regarding the interpretation of the arm's length principle under Article 7 OECD Model Convention, a change of paradigm occurred.[5]

In this respect, the wording of Article 7 (1) of the 2005 OECD Model Convention led to diverging interpretations of the term 'profits of an enterprise'.[6] Based on this terminology, two different approaches, specifically, the 'relevant business activity approach' (RBA-Approach) and the 'functional separate entity approach' (FSE-Approach), were commonly known.[7] Since the inconsistent interpretation may have eventually led to double taxation or double non-taxation, the RBA-Approach was explicitly rejected during the course of the implementation of the 'Authorized OECD Approach' (AOA).[8] The AOA was intended to be a turning point in profit attribution to PEs in order to implement the FSE-Approach.

The respective guidance concerning the FSE-Approach was specified in two OECD reports that were published regarding the attribution of profits to PEs in 2008 (2008 PE Report) and in 2010 (2010 PE Report).[9] In order to make the guidance in these reports applicable, the OECD decided to perform the following two-step implementation procedure:[10]

- Step 1: During the Update of the OECD Model Convention in 2008 the wording of Article 7 was not changed. However, the outcome of the 2008 PE Report was implemented in the 2008 OECD Commentary in order to apply the suggested

---

4. Compare OECD, Transfer Pricing and Multinational Enterprises (Paris: OECD Publishing, 1979); OECD, Transfer Pricing Guidelines for Multinational Enterprises and Tax Administrations (Paris: OECD Publishing, 2010); OECD, Aligning Transfer Pricing Outcomes with Value Creation, Actions 8–10 – 2015 Final Reports, OECD/G20 Base Erosion and Profit Shifting Project (Paris: OECD Publishing, 2015).
5. Compare OECD, Model Tax Convention on Income and on Capital: Condensed Version (Paris: OECD Publishing, 2005) (OECD Model Convention/Commentary 2005); OECD, Model Tax Convention on Income and on Capital: Condensed Version (Paris: OECD Publishing, 2008) (OECD Model Convention/Commentary 2008); OECD, Model Tax Convention on Income and on Capital: Condensed Version (Paris: OECD Publishing, 2010) (OECD Model Convention/Commentary 2010).
6. Compare OECD Commentary 2005, Article 7, paras 5 et seq.
7. For more details, see Karl Waser in Dietmar Aigner, Georg Kofler, Michael Tumpel (eds), DBA, Article 7, paras 24 et seq (2016); Ekkehart Reimer in Ekkehart Reimer, Alexander Rust (eds), Klaus Vogel on Double Taxation Conventions[4], Article 7, paras 76 et seq (2015); Alexander Hemmelrath in Klaus Vogel, Moris Lehner (eds), DBA[6], Article 7, paras 14a et seq and 182 et seq (2015); see also Jacques Sasseville, Richard Vann, Article 7: Business Profits – Global Tax Treaty Commentaries, p. 22 (2015).
8. Compare OECD, Report on the Attribution of Profits to Permanent Establishments (Paris: OECD Publishing, 2008), Part I, paras 59 et seq.
9. Compare 2008 PE Report; OECD, Report on the Attribution of Profits to Permanent Establishments (Paris: OECD Publishing, 2010).
10. Compare Michael Lang, Introduction to the Law of Double Taxation Conventions[2] (Linde Publishing 2013) pp. 97 et seq; in fact the two-step approach chosen by the OECD was strongly influenced by the intention to make the new understanding of the PE Reports (especially the 2008 Report) also applicable for Double Tax Treaties (DTTs), which were concluded on the basis of older version of the OECD Model (e.g. OECD Model 2005).

changes to that extent, as those outcomes are consistent with the wording of Article 7 of the 2008 OECD Model Convention.[11] Since the wording of the Article was not changed at all, the OECD intended to make the suggested changes also applicable for Double Tax Treaties (DTTs) that are based on older versions of the OECD Model Convention (e.g., the 2005 OECD Model Convention).[12]

– Step 2: During the course of the 2010 update, the entire wording of Article 7 was altered. Moreover, the 2010 OECD Commentary referenced the 2010 PE Report which indicates that the principles laid down in the AOA are accordingly part of the OECD Commentary.

From an overall international perspective, the UN explicitly refused to implement the AOA in the 2011 UN Model Convention.[13,14] Accordingly, the wording and the guidance provided under Article 7 of the 2011 UN Model Convention primarily reflects the OECD principles explicated under Article 7 of the 2005 OECD Model Convention (i.e., prior to the implementation steps of the AOA being taken).

In the following, this chapter will first discuss the principles of how profit attribution to PEs must be carried out under consideration of the applicability of different versions of Article 7 OECD Model Convention and various guidance provided in the respective sections of the OECD Commentaries.[15] Moreover, it will be outlined that the application of different approaches of profit attribution to PEs lead to dissimilar results (meaning before and after the implementation of the AOA). Finally, since Article 7 and Article 9 are both based on the arm's length principle, this chapter also addresses the question of whether or not the application of these articles could/should lead to different results.

## 2   THE ATTRIBUTION OF PROFITS BASED ON THE FICTION OF RESTRICTED INDEPENDENCE (I.E., BEFORE THE AOA), INCLUDING BANKS

As previously stated, the OECD Model Convention and Commentaries prior to the introduction of the AOA (beginning in 2008) included the 'old' perspective of the OECD concerning profit attribution to PEs. In this respect, Article 7 of the 2005 OECD Model Convention consists of the following seven paragraphs (Table 8.1).

---

11.   Compare 2008 PE Report, Introduction, para. 8.
12.   Compare OECD Commentary 2008, Article 7, para. 6.
13.   UN, Model Double Taxation Convention between Developed and Developing Countries (New York: UN Publishing, 2011) (UN Model 2011).
14.   Compare UN Model 2011, Introduction, para. 19 and Commentary on Article 7, para. 1.
15.   For the sake of completeness, references are made to the UN Model 2011 when necessary.

*Table 8.1   Content of Article 7 of the 2005 OECD Model Convention*

| Paragraph | Content of the Paragraph |
|---|---|
| 1 | RBA-Approach |
| 2 | Restricted independence |
| 3 | Attribution of costs |
| 4 | Indirect method |
| 5 | Non-attribution of profits by reason of the mere purchase of goods by the PE for the enterprise |
| 6 | Continuity of applied method |
| 7 | Subsidiarity clause |

Under the 2005 OECD Model Convention (and older models), the interplay between Article 7(1) and Article 7(2) is of major importance. In general, Article 7(1) of the 2005 OECD Model Convention permits the host country to tax the 'profits of an enterprise' to the extent that they are attributable to a PE in the host country. In this respect, significant historical attention has been given to the question of how to determine the attribution under Article 7(2) of the 2005 OECD Model Convention. However, the entire topic of profit attribution to PEs logically begins at an earlier stage when the question needs to be answered of what are the 'profits of an enterprise' for the purposes of Article 7(1).[16] Under the 2005 OECD Model Convention, this question was highly disputed which indicated that various countries interpreted the provision differently when applying their DTTs.[17]

## 2.1   The 'Relevant Business Activity Approach': The RBA-Approach

As mentioned before, the inconsistency of interpretation was primarily based on the understanding of the term 'profits of an enterprise' in consideration of the RBA-Approach. In this respect, the Commentary on Article 7 of the 2005 OECD Model Convention provides only minimal guidance regarding the interpretation of the term 'profits of an enterprise' beyond confirming the expressed intent of the wording of Article 7 (1) of the 2005 OECD Model Convention where it is stated that the right to tax does not extend to profits that the enterprise may derive from that State other than through the PE (otherwise stated, the profits that are taxable in the host State are limited based on the profits that are attributable to the PE).[18] Eventually, the overall interpretation issues arising from the term 'profits of an enterprise' were interlinked with the question of whether or not the utilization of this term requires further limitations of the taxing right of the host country. Accordingly, the precise

16. Compare 2008 PE Report, Part I, para. 59.
17. Compare OECD Commentary 2005, Article 7, paras 5 et seq.
18. Compare 2008 PE Report, Part I, para. 60; especially the expressed limitation in the wording of Article 7 para. 1 OECD Model Convention 2005 was of special importance since it further hinders the 'force of attraction of PEs' concerning the profits that arise from other business carried out in the PE host state by the foreign enterprise.

interpretational issues arose from the meaning of the word 'profits' rather than from the overall meaning of the term 'profits of an enterprise'.[19]

Briefly stated, the RBA-Approach advocates that only certain profits are attributable to a PE if it was actively engaged in the relevant business activities that eventually created these profits. Moreover, the profits attributable to the PE could in no way exceed the profits that the overall enterprise derived from the performance of those relevant business activities.[20] However, considering the fact that various countries applied different practices, the breadth or narrowness with which the 'relevant business activity' is defined has a significant impact on whether the theoretical profit limitation will produce any practical effect.[21]

---

**Example[22]**

Company A, resident in Country X, manufactures a new type of car in its head office in Country X. Company A has a PE in Country Y that only carries out the distribution activities. Due to the fact that the overall development of the new type of car incurred enormous development costs, the overall enterprise suffered a loss for the new type of car. Moreover, the new car is not well received on the market and, therefore, will be discontinued in the future.

Considering a broad interpretation of the 'relevant business activities' at the underlying case, all activities including the development, manufacturing, and distribution have to be considered when attributing profits to the PE in Country Y. Since the overall enterprise suffered a loss, no profits can be attributed to the PE even if a comparability analysis concerning distribution activities conducted by uncontrolled independent distributors would support an attribution of profits to the PE.

However, if the countries understood the term 'relevant business activities' more narrowly, they would only consider the distribution function of the PE in Country Y to be relevant. Accordingly, an arm's length remuneration of the function carried out by the PE could eventually result in an attributable profit even though the entire process concerning the new type of car resulted in a loss for the enterprise.

The illustrated problem in this example becomes even more evident if there is a situation where Company A has two distribution PEs, one in Country Y and one in Country Z. Assuming that Country Y follows a broader interpretation, and Country Z interprets more narrowly, it could be the case that losses of fifteen are attributed to the PE in Country Y whereas the PE in Country Z is attributed a profit of ten. Eventually, the overall attribution would result in a loss attribution of five. Therefore, it could be questioned whether or not Country Y should limit its definition of 'relevant business functions' (i.e., only accounting for the distribution function of the PE) and ignore the distribution functions carried out

---

19. Compare 2008 PE Report, Part I, para. 60.
20. *Ibid.*, paras 62 et seq.
21. *Ibid.*, para. 64.
22. *Ibid.*, paras 64 et seq.

in Country Z. However, in practice, host countries of PEs are reluctant to limit their perspectives on the attribution of profit by reference to activities performed by PEs located in other countries.

Additionally, the concept of the RBA-Approach was also subject to other interpretational pitfalls or inconsistencies in terms of the application by different countries. In this respect, it could be argued that the attribution of profits to PEs is only possible if the 'relevant business activity' is performed only in the PE host country.[23] Moreover, inconsistencies can also be determined with respect to the period that is considered to be relevant for the attribution of profits to PEs. Whereas some countries evaluated the potential profits to be attributed to the PE on the basis of one single year, others considered longer time periods to be relevant.[24] Country practice has also demonstrated that the limitation of the 'relevant business activities' regarding reference indicators (e.g., gross profits, income, or expenses) for purposes of profit attribution were not consistently applied.[25]

Even though the RBA-Approach is subject to a variety of difficulties and inconsistencies, it was the primary approach that was applied before the implementation of the AOA. The following information will outline how the profit attribution to PEs was carried out under Article 7 of the 2005 OECD Model Convention (and older versions) considering the fact that no extensive guidance was provided in the respective OECD Commentaries.

## 2.2 How Profits Were Attributed to PEs Prior to the Implementation of the AOA

Concerning profit attribution to PEs before the implementation of the AOA, paragraphs 2, 3, and 4 of Article 7 OECD Model Convention 2005 (and older versions) are especially of major importance. In this respect, the combination of paragraphs 2 and 3 is often referred to as the so-called 'direct method' of attributing profits to PEs whereas paragraph 4 incorporates the so-called 'indirect method'. However, in the pre-AOA era, both methods were fundamentally based on the RBA-Approach. Under this approach – in its pure form – transactions between an enterprise (i.e., head office) and its PEs should only be remunerated at cost without including certain profit components.[26]

---

23. *Ibid.*, para. 66; in general, this interpretation does not account for the fact that functions are mostly performed on an diversified international basis, meaning that the sole fact that a function is not carried out only in one PE country (e.g., a few PEs are involved in the same function) strongly limits the taxing rights of host countries.
24. *Ibid.*, para. 67; whereas the PE could be attributed a loss if one would just check a one year period, the overall activity of the PE (e.g., throughout a period of five years) could have produced a profit.
25. *Ibid.*, para. 68.
26. Compare Karl Waser in Dietmar Aigner, Georg Kofler, Michael Tumpel (eds), DBA, Article 7, para. 27 (2016); *see also* Jacques Sasseville, Richard Vann, Article 7: Business Profits – Global Tax Treaty Commentaries, pp. 60 et seq (2015).

## 2.2.1 The 'Direct Method' of Attributing Profits to PEs Before the Implementation of the AOA

In order to apply the direct method, an analysis of the wording of paragraphs 2 and 3 of Article 7 of the 2005 OECD Model Convention forms the starting point. In this respect, the paragraphs stipulate the following:[27]

> 'Subject to the provisions of paragraph 3, where an enterprise of a Contracting State carries on business in the other Contracting State through a permanent establishment situated therein, there shall in each Contracting State be attributed to that permanent establishment the profits which it **might be expected to make if it were a distinct and separate enterprise** engaged in the **same or similar activities under the same or similar conditions** and **dealing wholly independently with the enterprise** of which it is a permanent establishment.'
>
> 'In **determining the profits of a permanent establishment**, there shall be allowed as deductions expenses which are incurred **for the purposes of the permanent establishment**, including **executive and general administrative expenses so incurred**, whether in the State in which the permanent establishment is situated or elsewhere.'

Even though the terminology of Article 7 (2) differs from the wording of Article 9 (1) of the 2005 OECD Model Convention, both articles incorporate the arm's length principle.

For the purposes of the application of the direct method, the Commentary on Article 7 of the 2005 OECD Model Convention stipulates the relevance of so-called 'trading accounts' of the PE for purposes of profit attribution.[28] In this respect, the trading accounts (i.e., books) of a PE are commonly available not only due to the fact that they have to be set-up according to different national rules but rather simply caused by the fact that an effectively operating enterprise is normally concerned about the profitability of its PEs.[29]

In this respect, the trading accounts should form the starting point for any processes of profit adjustments (if required) in order to produce an arm's length amount of profits attributable to a PE.[30] Moreover, these trading accounts also have some defensive force, meaning that tax administrations cannot conduct hypothetical profit figure calculations because of the directive contained in Article 7 (2) of the 2005 OECD Model Convention.[31] Therefore, the actual facts of the case must be considered when analysing whether or not the trading accounts of a PE require certain adjustments in order to properly comply with the arm's length principle that is established in Article 7 (2) of the 2005 OECD Model Convention.[32]

---

27. Article 7 (2) and (3) OECD Model Convention 2005 (emphasis added).
28. Compare OECD Commentary 2005, Article 7, paras 12, 12.1, 13, 14 and 24.
29. *Ibid.*, para. 12 were it is further pointed out that specific trading accounts of a PE do not exist only in exceptional cases.
30. *Ibid.*, para. 12; *see also* Patrick Plansky, Die Gewinnzurechnung zu Betriebsstätten im Recht der Doppelbesteuerungsabkommen (Linde Publishing 2010), p. 141.
31. *Ibid.*, para. 12.
32. Compare National Westminster Bank PLC v. United States, US Court of Federal Claims, 14.11.2003 (2003) 6 ITLR 292 (NatWest II) where it is stated that the 'court concludes that the

Since the trading accounts of a PE are of major importance for purposes of profit attribution, the question must be answered to what extent such accounts should be relied upon when they are based on agreements between a head office and its PEs. In this respect, the following two criteria have to be cumulatively considered (meaning the trading accounts should be accordingly relied upon by the tax administrations):[33]

- – the trading accounts of the head office and the PE are prepared symmetrically on the basis of agreements between the head office and its PEs, and
- – those agreements reflect the functions performed by the different parts of the enterprise.

---

**Example[34]**

Company A is resident in Country X and has a PE in Country Y. The PE in Country Y performs certain functions for Company A. Company A reports costs in its trading accounts, and the PE reports turnovers in its trading accounts based on the functions performed by the PE for Company A.

Symmetrical trading accounts: Trading accounts can be regarded as being asymmetric if the costs reported in the trading accounts of Company A are not consistent with the turnover reported in the trading accounts of the PE (e.g., Company A reports costs of 100, and the PE only reports a turnover of 70).[35]

Consistency between agreements and functions performed: If the agreements between the head office and its PE do not reflect the functions performed (e.g., artificial arrangement), the resulting trading accounts should be corrected accordingly. If, for example, the PE in Country Y can, in fact, only be considered to be an agent of an intermediary (e.g., incurring limited risks and entitled to receive only a limited share of the resulting income) but the internal agreement allocates the role of the principal to the PE (e.g., accepting all of the risks and being entitled to all of the profits from the sales), the internal arrangement should simply be ignored. Accordingly, the trading accounts should be adjusted in order to establish an arm's length situation based on the facts of the case.

---

According to the above-mentioned aspects, the direct method is based on the understanding of a separation of the sphere/functions of the head office and those of the PE. Moreover, this understanding is built on the assumption that all assets,

---

U.S.-U.K. Treaty does not allow for attribution of additional capital to the branch, as measured by regulatory and marketplace capital requirements applicable to separate U.S. bank corporations. Rather the Treaty requires the government to use the properly maintained books of the branch to determine each element affecting the profits of the U.S. branch of a U.K. bank (...) and may only allow additional capital to the branch, if, in fact, capital allotted to the branch was not properly noted in its books.'

33. Compare OECD Commentary 2005, Article 7, para. 12.1.
34. *Ibid.*
35. In this case (i.e., a turnover of 70 is reported at the level of the PE), it is assumed that the costs of Company A are used as a 'transfer price' to remunerate the PE in Country Y.

incomes, and expenses can be uniquely allocated to one of the spheres/functions. However, even in situations where the PE is able to produce detailed trading accounts (showing the profits arising from the activities performed), it may be necessary for the tax authorities of the host State to adjust those trading accounts if, for example, prices were charged from the head office to the PE for the provision of goods or services that are not in line with the arm's length principle.[36] This means that the sole fact that something is included in the trading accounts of the PE that does not need to be adjusted based on agreements and functions that are asymmetrical or inconsistent does not yet provide information about the correct pricing. Accordingly, the attribution of profits must be carried out based on a two-step procedure under the direct method established in Article 7 (2) of the 2005 OECD Model Convention:

- First, it must be evaluated whether or not the trading accounts are in accordance with the arm's length principle in general (arm's length on the merits).
- Second, based on the generally correct trading accounts, an analysis concerning the arm's length pricing has to be performed in order to ensure that these trading accounts are actually in line with the arm's length principle (arm's length to the extent).

In the following, the principles of pricing under Article 7 (2) of the 2005 OECD Model Convention will be discussed on the basis of different intra-group agreements.

### 2.2.1.1  Dealings and Tangible Assets or Goods

Concerning the extent of the arm's length prices, it will usually be appropriate to use market prices for the same or similar goods supplied under the same or similar conditions. In this respect, it is noteworthy that market prices can vary based on the quantity ordered, the lead time arranged, or other factors that could eventually influence the final market price (e.g., terms of payment or INCO-terms).

---

**Example**

Company A is resident in Country X and has a PE in Country Y. The PE in Country Y produces shoes for Company A. Similar shoes can also be acquired by Company A from an independent producer in Country Y.

If the conditions of the 'purchase of the shoes' from the PE or the independent producer are similar or the same (e.g., quality, terms of payment, quantity, lead time, market conditions, etc.), the sales price that would be charged by the independent producer establishes a comparable market price that can be used for purposes of deriving the profits attributable to the PE for the 'sale of the shoes' to Company A.

---

36. Compare OECD Commentary 2005, Article 7, para. 13.

Using the approach outlined in the example above, difficulties may arise in the case of proprietary goods that are sold through a PE and no open market prices exist. If the figures shown in the trading accounts of the PE are considered to be unsatisfactory, the profits of the PE may be derived by the usage of other methods (e.g., applying an average ratio of gross profits to the turnover of the PE and deducting a certain amount of expenses in order to derive at an arm's length amount).[37] However, irrespective of the method that is applied, the transfer of tangible assets or goods is subject to an arm's length remuneration under Article 7 (2) of the 2005 OECD Model Convention provided that the transfer of these assets or goods forms the core business (relevant business activity) of the PE.[38]

### 2.2.1.2 Dealings and Intangible Assets

When discussing intangible assets and the rights associated with them, the rules concerning the relationships between associated enterprises cannot be applied (e.g., payment of royalties or cost sharing agreements) since those relationships simply do not exist between parts of the same enterprise (i.e., relationship between the head office and a PE).[39] In fact, it may be extremely difficult to allocate the ownership of such an intangible asset (e.g., patent) solely to one part of the enterprise (e.g., head office) and contend that the other part of the enterprise (e.g., PE) should pay royalties or license fees for this intangible asset.[40]

Due to the fact that there is only one legal entity in a head office/PE setting, it is not possible to allocate the legal ownership to any part of the enterprise. Moreover, it will also be difficult from a practical perspective to allocate the costs of creation of the intangible asset to one part of the enterprise.[41] Accordingly, the costs of creation of the intangible, therefore, should be regarded as being attributable to all parts of the enterprise (head office and PEs) that will utilize them. In this respect, the costs of creation of the intangible are only attributable if they are used by a certain part of the enterprise and should be priced without any profit mark-up.

**Example**

Company A is resident in Country X and has a PE in Country Y. Company A is the legal owner of a patent. During the course of the development process, certain costs arose for Company A. In carrying out its agreed functions, the PE in Country Y makes use of the patent.

Since the PE in Country Y makes use of the patent, certain parts of the costs resulting from the development of this intangible are attributable to the PE

---

37. *Ibid.*
38. This understanding is mostly based on the RBA-Approach (restricted independency of the PE). According to that, a PE is only reimbursed for its expenses. An arm's length remuneration does only apply with respect to the core business.
39. Compare OECD Commentary 2007, Article 7, para. 17.4.
40. *Ibid.*, para. 17.4.
41. *Ibid.*, para. 17.4.

298

without any profit mark-up (at cost) and based on a certain splitting factor between the various parts of the enterprise (e.g., based on turnover per country). Eventually, the costs for the usage of the intangible in its function reduces the taxable profit of the PE in its host State.

### 2.2.1.3  Dealings and Internal Services

When addressing internal services in the PE context, differentiation must be made between specific services and general services. Specific services are those internal services which may eventually form the core business of an enterprise (i.e., head office) and its PE. In order to be considered as a specific service, these services have to provide an actual advantage to the enterprise, and their costs must represent a significant part of the expenses of the enterprise.[42]

As long as the specific services are interlinked with the core business of the enterprise, the restrictive interpretation of the RBA-Approach, according to which the PE is only reimbursed for its expenses without including a potential profit mark-up, will not apply. Accordingly, the pricing of such specific internal services is subject to an arm's length remuneration. In this respect, the approach described for the transfer of tangible assets and goods can also be applied regarding the provision of specific internal services based on an agreement between the head office and its PE.

**Example**

Company A is resident in Country X and has a PE in Country Y. Company A manufactures a lifestyle product that has extremely low production costs. The great success of the entire enterprise is based on the state-of-the-art and high-end marketing activities, which form the largest part of the costs of the entire enterprise. All marketing activities are performed by the PE in Country Y.

Since the services provided by the PE result in an actual advantage for the enterprise, and the costs for these services form the major part of the entire costs of the enterprise, the described service may qualify for the application of a profit mark-up which eventually increases the tax base in the PE host country.

However, general services are more common in practice. In this respect, the provision of services is usually only a part of the company's various general management activities.[43] Such general services, for example, are centralized training of employees of each part of the enterprise or centralized marketing activities (other than in the previous example) that are for the benefit of the entire enterprise.

---

42. *Ibid.*, para. 17.6.
43. *Ibid.*, para. 17.7.

In such a scenario, it is usually considered to be appropriate if the costs for the provision of the services are simply allocated at cost (i.e., without mark-up) among the parts of the enterprise that eventually benefited from the provision of the services.[44]

---

**Example**

Company A is resident in Country X and has a PE in Country Y. Company A has ninety employees in Country X and ten employees in the PE State (i.e., Country Y). Every year, Company A offers a training seminar for employees of the enterprise which leads to costs of fifty.

Since the training activity of Company A can be classified as a general service, the costs for training of the PE's employees can only be allocated to the PE at cost. In this respect, the headcount could be used as a splitting factor, meaning that costs of five are attributable to the PE.

---

### 2.2.1.4 Dealings and General Administrative Services

Besides the internal services described in the section above, the pricing of general administrative services must also be briefly elaborated. As pointed out above, the RBA-Approach has stringent guidelines regarding services being interlinked with the core business of a PE before allowing the application of the arm's length remuneration. Accordingly, general administrative services do not form part of the core business of a PE, meaning that those services are not subject to an arm's length remuneration for purposes of attributing profits to PEs.

In this respect, the overall deductibility of those general administrative expenses can be derived from Article 7 (3) of the 2005 OECD Model Convention since the paragraph stipulates that the deduction of executive and general administrative expenses is allowed if these expenses are incurred for purposes of the PE. Considering this, the amount of expenses as incurred for these purposes should be the actual amount incurred.[45]

Moreover, the deductions allowable in the PE host country under Article 7 (3) do not depend upon the actual reimbursement of such expenses by the PE. Accordingly, there is no need for any type of money flow between the head office and the PE. The expenses for the general services only have to be included in the trading accounts of the PE in order to make them relevant for the attribution of profits to the PE.

---

**Example**

Company A is resident in Country X and has a PE in Country Y. Company A performs all relevant executive and general administrative functions for the enterprise (e.g., accounting, HR, marketing, and/or legal services).

---

44. *Ibid.*, para. 17.7.
45. *Ibid.*, para. 16.

Since the services provided by Company A for its PE do not form part of the core business, they are not subject to a profit markup under the RBA-Approach. However, Article 7 (3) explicitly states that expenses for the performance of such executive and general administrative services are deductible by the PE if they are performed for the PE. Therefore, the expenses can be included to the trading accounts of the PE based on an appropriate splitting factor thus lowering the taxable profit in the host State.

### 2.2.1.5 Dealings and Internal Interest

When discussing the provision of capital within an enterprise and the issue of interest payments between a head office and its PEs, the primary issue is not the question of whether or not a debtor/creditor relationship should be recognized between the different parts of the enterprise but rather the question of how arm's length interest rates could eventually be charged.[46] In this respect, two different perspectives must be considered:[47]

- Legal perspective: The legal nature of a PE (being part of the enterprise) does not formally allow the transfer of capital against interest payments and an undertaking to repay the capital in full on a certain due date.
- Economic perspective: Assuming that an enterprise is predominantly or solely equity-funded, internal debts or receivables are not justified, i.e., interest charges will not be deductible at the level of the PE. However, if the enterprise has a mixed financing structure (i.e., consisting of debt and equity), a portion of the interest could be 'charged' to the PE. Even in cases when there is evidence of debt financing, the allocation of debt charges – according to many tax authorities – does not prove to be a practical solution at all. Accordingly, it is often the case that deductions for group related debts are entirely banned in the PE context, meaning that they cannot be charged to PEs at all.[48]

**Example**

Company A is resident of Country X and has a PE in Country Y. Company A is debt financed to a great extent.

Due to the fact that internal interest cannot be charged to PEs at all, the entire interest resulting from the debt financing of Company A cannot be attributed to the PE in Country Y.

---

46. *Ibid.*, para. 18.
47. *Ibid.*, para. 18.
48. *Ibid.*, paras 18.1. et seq; however, regarding deductions of internal debt or receivables in the context of bank PEs, the general rule does not apply.

Besides the general rule that states that deductions of internal debts and receivables are entirely banned in the PE context, special considerations apply to payments of interest made by different parts of banks to each other for advances.[49] This exception from the general rule in the case of banks is mainly caused by the fact that making and receiving advances is part of the ordinary (core) business of such enterprises. Accordingly, interest payments are deductible only with respect to the ordinary business of banks. In all other cases, the general rule applies.[50]

### 2.2.1.6 Overview about the Pricing of Dealings under the 2005 OECD Model Convention

As pointed out above, the pricing of different dealings between the head office and PE under the 2005 OECD Model Convention is to be performed either on the arm's length basis or at cost. Table 8.2 illustrates the discussed outcomes.

Table 8.2    Consequences of the Application of Article 7(2) and (3) of the 2005 OECD Model Convention[51]

| Type of Internal Dealing | Pricing |
| --- | --- |
| Transfer/Sale of tangible assets/goods (core activities) | arm's length |
| Transfer of intangible assets | at cost |
| Internal Services: Specific services | at cost or arm's length |
| Internal Services: General Services | at cost |
| General administrative services | at cost |
| Internal interest | not allowed |

### 2.2.2 The 'Indirect Method' of Attributing Profits to PEs Before the Implementation of the AOA

The technical application of the direct method shown in the section above was generally based on the arm's length principle under consideration of the restricted independence of a PE due to the RBA-Approach. However, as already indicated, Article 7 of the 2005 OECD Model Convention does not just provide for the application of the direct method. In this respect, Article 7 (4) of the 2005 OECD Model Convention stipulates the indirect method:[52]

'Insofar as it has been customary in a Contracting State to determine the profits to be attributed to a permanent establishment on the basis of an apportionment of the

---

49. *Ibid.*, para. 19.
50. *Ibid.*, para. 19; special focus should also be placed on OECD Commentary 2005, Article 7, paras 15.2 et seq, where different cases concerning the transfer of bad loans are elaborated.
51. *See also* Raffaele Petruzzi, Raphael Holzinger, Profit Attribution to Dependent Agent Permanent Establishments, WTJ 2017, p. 269.
52. OECD Model Convention 2005, Article 7 (4).

total profits of the enterprise to its various parts, nothing in paragraph 2 shall preclude that Contracting State from determining the profits to be taxed by such an apportionment as may be customary; the method of apportionment adopted shall, however, be such that the result shall be in accordance with the principles contained in this Article.'

Even though it appears as though Article 7 (4) of the 2005 OECD Model Convention provides for the possibility of 'some kind of formulary apportionment' among the various parts of an enterprise, the last part of the paragraph clearly indicates that the result of the application of the indirect method shall be in accordance with the principles contained in Article 7, meaning that the result must be at arm's length.[53]

In regard to the indirect method, the essential character lies in whether the apportionment of profits is customary in the respective contracting States. In this respect, a proportionate part of the profits of the entire enterprise is allocated to one part of the enterprise assuming that all parts have contributed to the overall profitability on the basis of the criterion that should be used for purposes of allocation.[54] However, as can be observed, one of the primary aspects to ensure compliance with the arm's length principle is the application of an allocation criterion that properly accounts for the facts of the underlying situation (i.e., which accounts for parties' contributions to the overall profitability). In this context, the following three categories of allocation criteria are commonly used:[55]

- Receipts of the enterprise (e.g., turnover).
- Expenses of the enterprise (e.g., wages).
- Capital structure of the enterprise (e.g., allocated working capital).

From an overall perspective, it cannot be determined whether or not one of these indicators is more appropriate than another. Rather, the accuracy of each of the criteria must be evaluated on a case-by-case basis.[56] In this respect, the general aim of the application of the indirect method has to be the compliance with the arm's length principle, meaning that the figure of allocated profits under this method should approximate as closely as possible to the figures that would have been produced on a separate accounting basis using the direct method under Article 7 (2) of the 2005 OECD Model Convention.[57]

---

53. Compare OECD Commentary 2005, Article 7, para. 25.
54. *Ibid.*, para. 27.
55. *Ibid.*, para. 27.
56. *Ibid.*, para. 27, where the following is stated: 'In some enterprises, such as those providing services or producing proprietary articles with a high profit margin, net profits will depend very much on turnover. For insurance enterprises it may be appropriate to make an apportionment of total profits by reference to premiums received from policy holders in each of the countries concerned. In the case of an enterprise manufacturing goods with a high cost raw material or labour content, profits may be found to be related more closely to expenses. In the case of banking and financial concerns the proportion of total working capital may be the most relevant criterion.'
57. *Ibid.*, para. 27.

## 3   THE ATTRIBUTION OF PROFITS BASED ON THE FICTION OF FULL (ABSOLUTE) INDEPENDENCE (I.E., AFTER THE AOA)

As previously indicated, the OECD turned-away from the RBA-Approach and proposed the full independence (FSE–Approach) under the OECD Model Convention. In this respect, the two-step integration procedure was carried out:[58]

- In 2008, the wording of Article 7 OECD Model was not changed at all. However, the Commentary on Article 7 was substantially amended in order to provide new guidance.
- In 2010, the entire wording and structure of Article 7 OECD Model was changed whereas the Commentary on Article 7 was only slightly modified since the relevant guidance was already included in 2008.

Due to the fact that, during the update of the OECD Model Convention in 2008, only changes with respect to the OECD Commentary were included (whereas the wording was kept the same), the FSE-Approach could not be completely enacted.[59] Accordingly, Article 7 of the 2008 OECD Model Convention and the OECD Commentary 2008 can be referred to as 'AOA light'. However, since the wording of Article 7 OECD Model was entirely renewed during the course of the Update 2010 and due to the fact that the OECD Commentary provided in-depth guidance on the interpretation of the FSE-Approach, all DTTs that are based on this Model with the new wording incorporate the 'full AOA'.[60]

Before the specific effects of the step-wise implementation of the FSE-Approach on the attribution of profits to a PE can be analysed, the overall concept of the FSE-Approach must be outlined. Unlike the RBA-Approach, the FSE-Approach tends to accord more with the wording of Article 7 (2) of the 2008 OECD Model Convention (and, accordingly, also with the wording of Article 7 of the 2005 OECD Model Convention) since Article 7 (2) states that profits to be attributed to the PE are the profits 'it might be expected to make if it were a distinct and separate enterprise (...) dealing wholly independently with the enterprise of which it is a part'.[61] In fact, under the FSE-Approach, those profits that the PE would have earned at arm's length as if it were a 'distinct and separate' enterprise performing the same or similar functions under the same or similar conditions as determined by applying the arm's length principle should eventually be attributed to it.[62]

In addition to the general rule for determining the arm's length remuneration, the FSE-Approach goes even further and clarifies timing issues in relationship to the profit attribution to PEs. Whereas profit attribution to PEs under the RBA-Approach was only

---

58. Compare Michael Lang, Introduction to the Law of Double Taxation Conventions[2] (Linde Publishing 2013) pp. 97 et seq.
59. *Ibid.*
60. *Ibid.*
61. Article 7 (2) OECD Model Convention 2008; Compare 2008 PE Report, Part I, para. 69.
62. Compare 2008 PE Report, Part I, para. 69.

possible if the profits at the enterprise level have been realized, the FSE-Approach permits profits to be attributed to PEs even though no profit has yet been realized by the enterprise as a whole.[63]

---

**Example[64]**

Company A is resident in Country X and has a PE in Country Y. Company A manufactures goods and transfers them to its PE in Country Y for final assembly and distribution.

At the moment the transfer was performed by Company A, the respective profits are attributable to the head office even though the product was not yet assembled or sold by the PE in Country Y.

---

Moreover, another key issue that the FSE-Approach takes as its starting point are the activities of a PE, whereas the RBA-Approach considers the activities of the enterprise in its entirety as the starting point for the purposes of assessing the underlying business activities.[65] From an enterprise-wide perspective, the FSE-Approach is ultimately based on four essential steps:[66]

- First, the PEs must be determined as qualifying units of the enterprise.
- Second, the dealings have to be identified.
- Third, it must be determined whether or not a certain dealing shall be assigned to a respective PE.
- Fourth, the business profit (loss) for the dealings which were assigned to the PEs must be quantified and attributed accordingly.

## 3.1 The 'AOA Light'

Even though the wording and the structure of Article 7 was not modified during the course of the 2008 Update, the content of the respective paragraphs did change to reflect the guidance that was provided by the 2008 PE Report. In this respect, especially the first two paragraphs of Article 7 of the 2008 OECD Model Convention are now based on the newly implemented FSE-Approach which – irrespective of the guidance provided under the 2008 PE Report – tends to be more in accordance with the wording of Article 7 than the previously applied RBA-Approach (Table 8.3).

---

63. *Ibid.*, para. 70.
64. *Ibid.*, the fact that the RBA-Approach has 'generally not regarded profits as being attributable to the PE until profits have been realised by the enterprise as a whole from transactions with other enterprises' incited significant criticism since the inconsistencies in the application of the RBA-Approach often resulted in double or less than single taxation.
65. Compare 2008 PE Report, Part I, para. 71.
66. Compare Ekkehart Reimer in Ekkehart Reimer, Alexander Rust (eds), Klaus Vogel on Double Taxation Conventions[4], Article 7, para. 79 (2015).

Table 8.3   Content of Article 7 of the 2008 OECD Model Convention

| Paragraph | Content of the Paragraph |
|---|---|
| 1 | RBA-Approach/FSE-Approach |
| 2 | Restricted independence/Absolute independence |
| 3 | Attribution of costs |
| 4 | Indirect method |
| 5 | Non-attribution of profits by reason of the mere purchase of goods by the PE for the enterprise |
| 6 | Continuity of applied method |
| 7 | Subsidiarity clause |

The new guidance provided in the Commentary on Article 7 is based on the approach that was developed in the 2008 PE Report and was not constrained by either the original intent or by the historical practice and interpretation of Article 7. Instead, it was meant to focus on formulating the most preferable approach on profit attribution to a PE in order to account for modern-day operations of an MNE.[67]

When implementing the guidance of the 2008 PE Report into the Commentary on Article 7 of the 2008 OECD Model Convention, the OECD was perfectly aware of the fact that there are differences between some of the conclusions of the 2008 PE Report and previously applicable guidance under the 2005 OECD Commentary. Accordingly, the 2008 OECD Commentary was amended to incorporate a number of conclusions of the 2008 PE Report that did not conflict with the previous guidance.[68] Therefore, the application of the guidance provided under the 2008 PE Report always has to be considered within the boundaries of the 2008 OECD Commentary.

### 3.1.1   The 'Direct Method' of Attributing Profits to PEs Based on the 'AOA Light'

Concerning the application of the attribution of profits to PEs, the 2008 OECD Commentary begins with restating the relevant aspects that were already included in the 2005 OECD Commentary.[69] However, when referring to the assessment of the arm's length nature of the PE profits, the OECD Commentary directly refers to the 2008 PE Report and points out that the 'Report on Attribution of Profits to Permanent Establishments describe[s] the two-step approach through which [the assessment] should be done.'[70] The two-step approach described in the 2008 PE Report must be completed as follows:[71]

---

67. Compare OECD Commentary 2008, Article 7, para. 6.
68. *Ibid.*, para. 7.
69. *Ibid.*, paras 16 et seq; e.g., it is stated that the separate accounts of the PE form the starting point of an arm's length assessment.
70. OECD Commentary 2008, Article 7, para. 17.
71. Compare 2008 PE Report, Part I, paras 86 et seq and paras 218 et seq.

- *Step 1*: Determination of the activities and conditions of the hypothesized distinct and separate enterprise (i.e., functional and factual analysis step).
- *Step 2*: Determination of the profits of the hypothesized distinct and separate enterprise based upon a comparability analysis (i.e., pricing step).

### 3.1.1.1   Step 1: Functional and Factual Analysis in Detail

In addition to stipulating the steps that must be taken in order to comply with the arm's length principle, the 2008 PE Report also provides further guidance on the execution. In this respect, the goals of the functional and factual analysis step (Step 1) include:[72]

- Attribution of rights and obligations to the PE as appropriate that emerge from transactions between the enterprise of which the PE is a part and separate enterprises.
- Determination of the functions of the hypothesized distinct and separate enterprise and the economically relevant characteristics relating to the performance of those functions.
- Attribution of risks among the different parts of the single enterprise based on the identification of significant people functions (SPFs) that are relevant to the assumption of risks.
- Attribution of economic ownership of assets among the different parts of the single enterprise based on the identification of the SPFs that are relevant to the attribution of economic ownership of assets.
- Recognition and determination of the nature of the dealings between the PE and other parts of the same enterprise that can be appropriately recognized.
- Attribution of capital based on the assets and risks attributed to the PE.

#### 3.1.1.1.1   Distinct and Separate Entity

One of the most important elements of the 'AOA light' and the full AOA is the fiction that the PE is a distinct and separate entity. However, simply caused by the fact that a head office cannot enter into a legally binding contract with its PEs, the 'AOA light' and the full AOA used so-called 'dealings' to describe the agreements between the head office and its PEs. Dealings are the intra-enterprise equivalents of separate enterprise transactions between the hypothetically distinct and separate PE and other parts of the enterprise (e.g., the head office or other PEs of the enterprise) of which the PE is a part.[73] Accordingly, the head office and its PEs use dealings to agree on functions that should be carried out by each of them in the course of the overall business.

---

72. *Ibid.*, para. 88.
73. *Ibid.*, para. 17.

### 3.1.1.1.2  Significant People Functions

On the basis of the dealings, the main characteristics of the first step must be further analysed. Concerning the functional profile of each part of the enterprise (which was agreed upon in the internal dealings), it can be concluded that the OECD has adopted a SPF-based approach to derive the attributable profits of a PE in the host country. In this respect, the concept allocates a function by identifying the persons who perform the work and are engaged in fulfilling the core activities of that function.[74] Therefore, the entire profit attribution to PEs is based on the SPFs which, in practice, are not always easy to identify. For example, if the personnel of a department work in the PE and the manager of the department works in the head office, it may not be immediately discernible who the SPF is for that department.

### 3.1.1.1.3  Attribution of Risks

Moreover, carrying out SPFs by the PE is also interlinked with different types of risks. Accordingly, the SPFs also form the basis for the attribution of risks to a PE. In this respect, any risks inherent in or created by the PE's own SPFs that are relevant to the assumption of risks will initially be attributed to the PE under the functional and factual analysis.[75] Ultimately, the attribution of risks to a PE depends on the nature of the enterprise's business. For example, some risks will be related to the potential loss in value of assets that were attributed to the PE whereas other risks will be created by activities (e.g., liability risks).[76] In summary, the SPFs, which are relevant for the attribution of risks to a PE, require active decision-making powers. If the acceptance and/or the management of the risks are not supported by the active decision-making competence of the PE, the respective risks cannot be attributed to a PE.[77] Therefore, it may be summarized that assets and risks follow SPFs for the purpose of attributing profits to PEs.

### 3.1.1.1.4  Attribution of Assets

Once the SPFs are properly analysed, the attribution of assets must be performed since the PE needs various assets to carry out the internally agreed functions. However, the attribution of assets does not include just tangible assets (e.g., attribution of a productions facility to a production PE or attribution of an office to a PE performing different service functions); also, intangible assets (e.g., patents or trademarks) may be

---

74. Compare Ekkehart Reimer in Ekkehart Reimer, Alexander Rust (eds), Klaus Vogel on Double Taxation Conventions[4], Article 7, para. 87 (2015); under the AOA, the focus of SPFs is strongly interlinked with the decision-making process for specific functions.
75. Compare 2008 PE Report, Part I, para. 24.
76. *Ibid.*, para. 25.
77. *Ibid.*

attributed to PEs.[78] In this respect, the economic ownership is the key driver for the attribution of assets and may be attributed to a PE if the SPFs relevant for the economic ownership of the assets are performed by a PE.[79]

### 3.1.1.1.5  Attribution of Capital

The attribution procedure under the first step is not yet complete. In addition to assets and risks, capital also has to be attributed to a PE so that it can finance the functions it is intended to carry out, properly use the assets it economically owns, and assume the risks that were attributed to it. In this respect, the functional and factual analysis step requires the attribution of 'free capital' to the PE for tax purposes in order to ensure an arm's length attribution of profits to the PE.[80] In fact, there are a few different approaches on how the attribution of 'free capital' can eventually be carried out from a practical perspective (e.g., either more emphasis is placed on the actual capital structure of the enterprise of which the PE is a part or, alternatively, on the capital structures of comparable independent enterprises).[81] However, it must be pointed out that the attribution of 'free capital' is not an exact science which means that any particular facts and circumstances of different settings may eventually give rise to a range of arm's length results for the attributable capital.[82]

### 3.1.1.1.6  Hypothesized Distinct and Separate Enterprise

After the capital is attributed to the PE, all of the relevant aspects of the functional and factual analysis step are eventually completed meaning that the PE is hypothesized as it would be a separate and distinct entity that is intended to perform certain functions. In this respect, the overall principle that must be followed in this step can be summarized as follows:[83] assets and risks follow functions, and capital follows functions, assets, and risks.

---

**Example**

Company A is resident in Country X and has a PE in Country Y. Company A produces shoes and transfers them to its PE in Country Y for distribution. The distribution function and the management of the associated risks are performed by the personnel of the PE in Country Y.

---

78. For more details on the attribution of tangible assets, please *see* 2008 PE Report, Part I, paras 104 et seq; for more details on the attribution of intangible assets, please *see* 2008 PE Report, Part I, paras 105 et seq.
79. Compare 2008 PE Report, Part I, paras 17 et seq.
80. *Ibid.*, para. 31; the term 'free capital' describes such funding that does not give rise to a tax deductible return in the nature of interest.
81. *Ibid.*, paras 33 et seq.
82. Within this range of arm's length results, not a single result but rather all figures could eventually comply with the arm's length principle.
83. Compare Raffaele Petruzzi, Raphael Holzinger, Profit Attribution to Dependent Agent Permanent Establishments, WTJ 2017, p. 275.

Accordingly, the different parts of the enterprise (head office and PE) agreed on a functional split in an internal deal according to which the PE is meant to carry out the distribution functions. The personnel (or a specific person) of the PE is the designated person for carrying out the respective function, meaning that the economic ownership of the shoes and other assets that are relevant for the provision of the distribution function (e.g., office, car, equipment, etc.) are attributed to the PE. Moreover, the risk associated with the performance of the SPF is attributed to the PE. Since it was agreed on in the internal deal that the personnel or a specific person of the PE manages the associated risk with carrying out the distribution function, all relevant risks are attributed to the PE. Based on the functions to be performed, the assets used, and the risks assumed, an arm's length amount of 'free capital' is attributed to the PE.

### 3.1.1.2   Step 2: The Pricing Step in Detail

The second step under the 'AOA light' is simply based on the functional and factual analysis conducted in the first step. In this context, the remuneration of any dealings identified and analysed in the first step will 'be determined by applying, by analogy, the principles developed for the application of the arm's length principle between associated enterprises (these principles are articulated in the Transfer Pricing Guidelines for Multinational Enterprises and Tax Administrations) by reference to the functions performed, assets used, and risks assumed by the enterprise through the permanent establishment and the rest of the enterprise'.[84] By applying the principles stipulated in the Transfer Pricing Guidelines, the OECD has – technically speaking – mixed the two different articles of the OECD Model Convention (specifically, Article 7 and Article 9). Even though both articles were already fundamentally based on the arm's length principle before the 'AOA light' was introduced, the approach selected by the OECD can be considered as a first major step for ensuring a consistent application of the arm's length principle for different business settings within MNEs.[85]

#### 3.1.1.2.1   Comparability Analysis by Analogy

From a technical perspective, under the second step, the dealings between the PE and the enterprise of which it is a part are compared with transactions between independent enterprises that would have taken place under comparable situations. To do so, a comparability analysis in the sense of Article 9 must be performed.[86] The concept of 'applying the principles of Article 9 by analogy' in the PE context means that none of

84. OECD Commentary 2008, Article 7, para. 18.
85. Given the fact, that the 'arm's length principle' under Article 7 OECD Model Convention 2005 often leads to at cost remunerations for certain intra-group transactions whereas the same transactions would have been remunerated at arm's length under Article 9 OECD Model Convention 2005, MNEs could easily have taken advantage of tax arbitrage.
86. Compare 2008 PE Report, Part I, para. 43.

the differences between the dealings and transactions could have materially affected the measure to attribute profits to the PE.[87]

#### 3.1.1.2.2 Applying the Transfer Pricing Methods by Analogy

After having conducted the proper comparability analysis by analogy, the dealings need to be priced. Also in this respect, the principles of Article 9 have to be applied. This means that the pricing of dealings is based on the same methods as the pricing of transactions under Article 9. Therefore, the traditional transaction methods[88] or the transactional profit methods[89] shall be applied.[90] Since an independent enterprise would normally seek to charge a mark-up in order to generate profits in an arm's length transaction, the same understanding should also apply to intra-group dealings between an enterprise and its PEs in order to comply with the arm's length principle.[91]

---

**Example**

Company A is resident in Country X and has a PE in Country Y. The PE in Country Y performs a production function for the enterprise. Based on a functional and factual analysis, the PE carries out the SPFs and is attributed assets, risks, and capital accordingly. The dealing between the enterprise and its PE is comparable to a limited risk routine transaction that would be carried out in the same way between independent enterprises in the respective market.

Since the dealing between the enterprise and its PE is comparable to transactions between independent enterprises in the respective market, no comparability adjustments are needed. Due to the fact that the function is a limited risk routine function, the cost plus method is the most appropriate transfer pricing method and can be applied accordingly (e.g., with a markup of 5%).

---

#### 3.1.1.3 Applying the Two-Step Procedure in Different Cases

Since the overall focus of the 'AOA light' is on the arm's length profit attribution to PEs, the respective dealings between an enterprise and its PEs also have to be priced at arm's length in order to achieve this goal.

---

87. *Ibid.*
88. These methods are: (i) the CUP method, (ii) the resale price method, and (iii) the cost plus method; for more details, please *see* Ch. 3.
89. These methods are: (i) the transactional net margin method and (ii) the profit split method; for more details, please *see* Ch. 4.
90. Compare 2008 PE Report, Part I, para. 44.
91. *Ibid.*, para. 45.

### 3.1.1.3.1 Dealings and Tangible Assets or Goods

When discussing the transfer of tangible assets within an enterprise, there is broad consensus among the OECD Member States to focus on the economic ownership of the respective asset in order to determine whether or not to attribute it to a PE.[92] In this respect, the change in the place of use of a certain tangible asset is one of the most important indicators that could eventually trigger a change of economic ownership of the asset.[93]

The 2008 PE Report and the 2008 OECD Commentary make it very clear that the change of economic ownership of an asset requires an arm's length remuneration between the parts of the enterprise involved in the dealing. In this respect, the fair market value of the asset at the time of the transfer generally forms the basis for the future depreciations of the respective asset in the host country.[94]

---

**Example**

Company A is resident in Country X and has a PE in Country Y. Company A transfers a machine that is no longer needed to its PE in Country Y. Unlike Company A, the PE can definitely use the machine in its manufacturing process. Since the machine is no longer needed by the head office of Company A and due to the fact that the machine will be used in the manufacturing process of the PE, the economic ownership of the machine is attributed to the PE. Accordingly, the PE must remunerate the head office for the transfer of the machine at arm's length (fair market value).

---

However, besides the clear cut base where the economic ownership is attributed to the part of the enterprise that uses the asset, the functional and factual analysis could also reflect a different fact pattern. In this respect, it is possible that the dealing between the parts of the enterprise rather reflects 'a lease or a license agreement' between the parts of the enterprise.[95] According to the guidance of the 2008 PE report, the arm's length principle under Article 7 'AOA light' does not lead to a profit or loss realization at the time of the transfer of the tangible asset but rather to an ongoing arm's length charge that reflects comparable lease of license charges between independent enterprises.[96] However, such an approach is not foreseen in the OECD Commentary, meaning that there is no possibility to charge license fees or rents under the 'AOA light'.

---

92. *Ibid.*, para. 229.
93. *Ibid.*
94. *Ibid.*, para. 231.
95. *Ibid.*, para. 234.
96. *Ibid.*

### 3.1.1.3.2  Dealings and Intangible Assets

Regarding the transfer and usage of intangible assets by different parts of an enterprise, the rules concerning the intangible rights with respect to the relationships between different enterprises of the same MNE[97] cannot be applied regarding the relationship between a head office and its PEs.[98] Even though the 2008 PE Report argues in favour for arm's length remuneration for the transfer of intangible assets,[99] the 2008 OECD Commentary points out that the allocation of 'ownership' of intangibles among different parts of an enterprise is extremely difficult since it cannot really be argued that some parts of the enterprise should receive royalties from other parts as if they were independent enterprises.[100]

This argument is mostly based on the fact that the entire enterprise is the legal owner of the respective intangible. Because there is only one legal owner, it is not possible to allocate the legal ownership to any particular part of the enterprise.[101] The OECD Commentary ultimately concludes that the costs of creation or acquisition of intangible rights are attributable to all parts of the enterprise that will make use of them at cost (with no mark-up for profit or royalty).[102]

As can be seen, there are diverging opinions on the topic of pricing the intangible rights under the 'AOA light' within the guidance of the OECD. Whereas the 2008 PE Report would generally allow for arm's length remuneration, the 2008 OECD Commentary only provides for at cost compensations. Even though this might seem to be inconsistent with the overall aim of the 'AOA light' to more properly account for the arm's length principle (e.g., as it does regarding the transfer of tangible assets), the guidance provided in the OECD Commentary is in accordance with the current wording of Article 7 of the 2008 OECD Model Convention whereas the guidance provided under the 2008 PE Report tends to go beyond the boundaries of the terminology.

### 3.1.1.3.3  Dealings and Internal Services

The overall understanding of internal services did not change during the course of the 2008 Update, meaning that there must still be a differentiation made between specific and general services. However, regarding specific services, the focus of the respective service has changed. Before the 2008 Update, specific services had to form the core part of the business of the enterprise and its PE (RBA-Approach) whereas, after the 2008 Update, only the functional profile of the PE can already lead to the classification as a specific service (FSE-Approach).[103] 'In such a case, it will usually be appropriate to charge a service at the same rate as is charged to the outside customer.'[104]

---

97. For example, payment of royalties or cost sharing arrangements.
98. Compare OECD Commentary 2008, Article 7, para. 34.
99. Compare 2008 PE Report, Part I, paras 241 et seq.
100. Compare OECD Commentary 2008, Article 7, para. 34.
101. *Ibid.*
102. *Ibid.*
103. *Ibid.*, paras 35 et seq.
104. *Ibid.*, para. 35.

---

**Example**

Company A is resident in Country X and has a PE in Country Y. The PE in Country Y is mostly engaged in providing translation services to the head office.
Since the translation services performed by the PE may be classified as specific services, it will be appropriate to remunerate the PE for the provision of the service at arm's length.

---

However, based on the wording of Article 7 of the 2008 OECD Model Convention, general services for the purposes of profit attribution must be further pointed out. Since the wording of Article 7 was not modified during the 2008 Update, the aspects mentioned that concern the general services according to the 2005 OECD Model Convention are still valid. Accordingly, it is considered to be appropriate if the costs for the provision of general services are simply allocated at cost (i.e., without mark-up) among the parts of the enterprise that benefited from the provision of the services.[105]

### 3.1.1.3.4 Dealings and General Administrative Services

Since general administrative services do not usually form part of the core business of a PE, those services are not subject to an arm's length remuneration for purposes of attributing profits to PEs.[106] Accordingly, the general understanding concerning these types of services did not materially change compared to the 2005 OECD Model Convention even though the OECD decided to focus on the FSE-Approach.

### 3.1.1.3.5 Dealings and Internal Interest

The primary question regarding the chargeability of interest in the PE context did not change during the 2008 Update which can be argued from either a legal or a more economic perspective. Ultimately, the OECD did not change its opinion on internal interest payments, and they are still entirely banned in the PE context under the 'AOA light'. Accordingly, they cannot be charged at all.

### 3.1.1.3.6 Overview about the Pricing of Dealings under the 2008 OECD Model Convention

As indicated above, the application of ALP in terms of dealings between a head office and PEs is subject to the 'pitfall' that the AOA is not fully applicable in general (i.e., 'AOA light'). Due to that, the pricing of dealings (besides the pricing of specific services) did not materially change compared to the 2005 OECD Model Convention. Table 8.4 illustrates the discussed outcomes.

---

105. *Ibid.*, para. 37. Such general services are, among others, (i) accounting services, (ii) controlling services, (iii) marketing activities, or (iv) HR activities.
106. *Ibid.*, para. 37.

*Table 8.4    Consequences of the Application of Article 7(2) and (3) of the 2008 OECD Model Convention*

| Type of Internal Dealing | Pricing |
| --- | --- |
| Transfer/Sale of tangible assets/goods (core activities) | arm's length |
| Tansfer of intangible assets | at cost |
| Internal Services: Specific services | arm's length |
| Internal Services: General Services | at cost |
| General administrative services | at cost |
| Internal interest | not allowed |

### 3.1.2    The 'Indirect Method' of Attributing Profits to PEs Based on the 'AOA Light'

Since Article 7 (4) was not changed at all during the 2008 Update, the indirect method still forms part of the 2008 OECD Model Convention. From a technical perspective, there was no further guidance provided concerning the application of this method per se. Accordingly, the method was not directly affected by the implementation of the 'AOA light' and can eventually be applied in a similar manner as that under the 2005 OECD Model Convention.

However, since Article 7 (4) directly references Article 7 (2), the arm's length principle has to be considered when deriving the profits attributable to a PE. Due to the fact that the understanding of the arm's length principle in the PE context was subject to a change of paradigm (changed from RBA-Approach to FSE-Approach), the application of the indirect method is at least indirectly affected by the changes implemented by the 'AOA light'.

### 3.2    The Full AOA

As previously stated, the overall goal of the implementation of the AOA was the introduction of the fiction of the full (absolute) independence of the PE. Accordingly, a PE of an enterprise should be treated as if it were an independent enterprise engaged in the same or similar activities. However, due to the fact that the wording of Article 7 was not changed during the 2008 Update, the intended full independence of the PE was somewhat limited by the wording of the respective provision in terms of profit attribution.

In order to overcome these difficulties, the OECD completely reworked Article 7 during the course of the 2010 Update.[107] Whereas Article 7 of the 2008 OECD Model Convention consisted of seven paragraphs, the new Article 7 of the 2010 OECD Model Convention (Article 7 AOA) now consists of only four. Table 8.5 illustrates the contents of the respective paragraphs.

---

107. *Ibid.*; OECD Model Convention 2008, Article 7.

*Table 8.5   Content of Article 7 of the 2010 OECD Model Convention*

| Paragraph | Content of the Paragraph |
|-----------|--------------------------|
| 1 | FSE-Approach |
| 2 | Absolute independence |
| 3 | Corresponding adjustment |
| 4 | Subsidiarity clause |

In the following, the changes with respect to the wording of Article 7 AOA will be discussed in order to evaluate the effect on the profit attribution to PEs.

### 3.2.1   Renewal of the Wording of Article 7 Based on the AOA

When comparing Article 7 (1) AOA with its predecessor in the 2008 OECD Model Convention, it must be pointed out that the first sentence of the paragraph was kept entirely the same. However, with regard to the second sentence, the new version of the paragraph stipulates the following:[108]

> 'If the enterprise carries on business as aforesaid, the profits that are attributable to the permanent establishment in accordance with the provisions of paragraph 2 may be taxed in that other State.'

As can be seen, the new version of Article 7 (1) AOA is now directly interlinked with Article 7 (2) AOA specifying that the attribution of profits to PEs must accord with the arm's length principle.

Perhaps the most relevant change during the 2010 Update occurred with Article 7 (2) AOA. After the Update, the paragraph states the following:[109]

> '[T]he profits that are attributable in each Contracting State to the permanent establishment referred to in paragraph 1 are the profits it might be expected to make, **in particular in its dealings** with other parts of the enterprise, if it were a separate and independent enterprise engaged in the **same or similar activities under the same or similar conditions, taking into account the functions performed, assets used and risks assumed** by the enterprise through the permanent establishment and through the other parts of the enterprise.'[110]

---

108. Article 7 (1) Model 2010 (emphasis added); Article 7 (1) OECD Model Convention 2008 laid down: 'If the enterprise carries on business as aforesaid, the profits of the enterprise may be taxed in the other State but only so much of them as is attributable to that permanent establishment.'

109. Article 7 (2) AOA (emphasis added).

110. Even though Article 7 (2) already incorporated the arm's length principle for purposes of profit attribution to PEs, the wording substantially differed. In this respect, it was specified that 'there shall in each Contracting State be attributed to that permanent establishment the profits which it might be expected to make if it were a *distinct and separate enterprise engaged in the same or similar activities under the same or similar conditions and dealing wholly independently with the enterprise of which it is a permanent establishment.*' (emphasis added).

By directly referencing the functions that are performed, assets used, and risks assumed, the wording of Article 7 (2) AOA was aligned with the guidance provided under the 2010 PE Report (which was implemented in the 2010 OECD Commentary).[111] In this respect, the most crucial part of the two-step procedure, specifically, the functional and factual analysis that is performed to hypothesize a PE as a separate and independent enterprise, is now an explicit part of the wording of the paragraph.[112]

Besides the technical aspects that were incorporated into the wording of Article 7 AOA, an entirely new provision was also included during the course of the 2010 Update. Article 7 (3) of the 2008 OECD Model Convention was entirely omitted and replaced by the new Article 7 (3) AOA which stipulates a corresponding adjustment similar to Article 9 of the 2010 OECD Model Convention.[113] Article 7 (3) AOA states the following:[114]

> 'Where, **in accordance with paragraph 2**, a Contracting State **adjusts the profits that are attributable to a permanent establishment** of an enterprise of one of the Contracting States and taxes accordingly profits of the enterprise that have been charged to tax in **the other State**, the other State shall, to the extent necessary to eliminate double taxation on these profits, **make an appropriate adjustment to the amount of the tax charged on those profits**. In determining such adjustment, the competent authorities of the Contracting States shall if necessary consult each other.'

By incorporating this paragraph, the OECD imposed a legal obligation on each contracting State to adjust the profits of the part of the enterprise that is situated in its territory in the event that the other State (e.g., PE State) has adjusted the profits attributable to the part of the enterprise that is situated in its territory in accordance with the arm's length principle specified in Article 7 (2) AOA.[115] In this respect, it does not matter whether the primary adjustment was initiated by the PE State or by the State where the head office is located. As long as the primary adjustment was carried out in accordance with Article 7 (2) AOA, the other State has the legal obligation to carry out the corresponding adjustment. However, in practice, most of the treaties are not worded with a mandatory effect to enforce a corresponding adjustment.

Moreover, a crucial change can be detected when comparing Article 7(4) of the 2008 OECD Model Convention and the new Article 7(4) AOA. In this respect, the previously applicable indirect method was entirely omitted from the 2010 OECD Model

---

111. Compare OECD Commentary 2010, Article 7, paras 7 et seq; the 2010 PE Report can be considered as a revised version that solely takes into account the drafting of the new wording of Article 7 AOA without changing the conclusions or interpretation drawn under the 2008 PE Report.
112. It may be criticized that Article 7 (2) AOA does not reference capital that is also relevant for the attribution of profits to a PE. However, since the attribution of capital is fundamentally based on the functions that are performed, assets used, and risks assumed (the paragraph explicitly references to these aspects), the absence of a reference to capital must not be overestimated.
113. Compare Jacques Sasseville, Richard Vann, Article 7: Business Profits – Global Tax Treaty Commentaries, pp. 84 et seq (2015).
114. *See* Article 7 (3) OECD Model Convention 2010 (emphasis added).
115. Compare Jacques Sasseville, Richard Vann, Article 7: Business Profits – Global Tax Treaty Commentaries, p. 84 (2015).

Convention. Moreover, the old provisions laid down in Article 7(5) and (6) of the 2008 OECD Model Convention were not incorporated into the 2010 OECD Model Convention. However, the subsidiarity clause was considered to be an important part of the article. This clause was stipulated in Article 7(7) of the 2008 OECD Model Convention and is now found in Article 7(4) AOA. The wording of the subsidiarity clause was not changed at all.[116]

Thus far, the changes of the wording of Article 7 OECD Model Convention during the course of the 2010 Update were discussed. In the next section, the effects of these changes on the attribution of profits to PEs will be further elaborated.

### 3.2.2 Attribution of Profits to PEs Based on the Full AOA (Direct Method Only)

As already pointed out above, the previously applicable indirect method was entirely skipped during the course of the 2010 Update. Accordingly, Article 7 AOA is subject to the application of the direct method only in regard to the attribution of profits to PEs.

The aspects concerning the application of the direct method based on the guidance provided under the 2008 OECD Commentary is also valid for the application of the direct method under Article 7 AOA. This is mainly caused by the fact that the 2010 OECD Commentary refers to the 2010 PE Report which itself is the revised version of the 2008 PE Report.[117] However, the changes between the 2008 PE Report and the 2010 PE Report only occurred in order to align the guidance under the 2010 PE Report with the new wording of Article 7 AOA.[118] From an intentional perspective, nothing at all changed.

### 3.2.2.1 General Aspects: Two-Step Procedure Profit Attribution to PEs

Therefore, the attribution of profits to PEs is subject to a two-step procedure consisting of:[119]

- *Step 1*: Determination of the activities and conditions of the hypothesized distinct and separate enterprise (i.e., functional and factual analysis step).
- *Step 2*: Determination of the profits of the hypothesized distinct and separate enterprise based upon a comparability analysis (i.e., pricing step).

---

116. Compare Article 7 (4) AOA; Article 7 (7) OECD Model Convention 2008; both paragraphs indicate that '[w]here profits include items of income which are dealt with separately in other Articles of this Convention, then the provisions of those Articles shall not be affected by the provisions of this Article.'
117. Compare OECD Commentary 2010, Article 7, paras 7 et seq.
118. *Ibid.*
119. Compare 2010 PE Report, Part I, paras 9 et seq, paras 13 et seq, paras 39 et seq, paras 57 et seq, paras 183 et seq.

In order to carry out the functional and factual analysis under Step 1, the same aspects have to be considered as those that are outlined in section 3.1.1.1 with respect to the 'AOA light'.[120] Therefore, the following steps must be taken:[121]

- Attribution of rights and obligations to the PE as appropriate that arise from transactions between the enterprise of which the PE is a part and the separate enterprises.
- Determination of the functions of the hypothesized distinct and separate enterprise and the economically relevant characteristics relating to the performance of those functions.
- Attribution of risks among the different parts of the single enterprise based on the identification of SPFs relevant to the assumption of risks.
- Attribution of economic ownership of assets among the different parts of the single enterprise based on the identification of the SPFs relevant to the attribution of economic ownership of assets.
- Recognition and determination of the nature of the dealings between the PE and other parts of the same enterprise that can be appropriately recognized.
- Attribution of capital based on the assets and risks attributed to the PE.

If the functional and factual analysis under Step 1 was conducted properly, the PE was hypothesized as if it was a separate and independent enterprise engaged in the same or similar activities as an independent enterprise.

As a next step, the dealings between the head office and the PE can be priced. In this respect, the 2010 PE Report and the 2010 OECD Commentary also provide the same guidance as the 2008 PE Report and the 2008 OECD Commentary.[122] Accordingly, the principles of the OECD Guidelines must be applied by analogy in order to derive an arm's length remuneration under Article 7 AOA. Once the comparability analysis is carried out by using the 2010 OECD Guidelines in the analogy, Step 2 of the attribution of profits to PEs (pricing step) can be finalized by applying the transfer pricing methods by analogy. The 2010 OECD Guidelines include the following transfer pricing methods, i.e., the CUP method, the resale price method, the cost plus method, the TNMM, and the profit split method.

For purposes of profit attribution to PEs, all of these transfer pricing methods could be applied to derive a proper remuneration under the arm's length principle. The selection of the method is subject to the most appropriate method rule.[123] Accordingly, the transfer pricing method that is most appropriate under the specific functional and factual setting in the underlying case must be selected in order to properly account for the arm's length principle.

From a technical perspective, there are no differences between the two-step procedure of profit attribution under Article 7 AOA and under Article 7 of the 2008

---

120. Compare 2010 PE Report, Part I, para. 59; Compare 2008 PE Report, Part I, para. 88.
121. *Ibid.*, para. 59.
122. Compare OECD Commentary 2010, Article 7, para. 22; *see also* 2010 PE Report, Part I, paras 9 et seq.
123. Compare OECD TPG 2010, paras 2.1 et seq; *see also* 2010 PE Report, Part I, para. 41.

OECD Model Convention ('AOA light'). However, the question that arises is whether or not the change in the wording of Article 7 during the 2010 Update has widened the interpretational boundaries of the application of the arm's length principle with respect to profit attribution to PEs for different functions and de facto dealings.

### 3.2.2.2   Dealings and Tangible Assets or Goods

When pricing a dealing regarding tangible assets and goods, the principles of attribution of assets to PEs must first be considered which is generally based on the economic ownership of the respective asset.[124] Furthermore, a PE can either be the economic owner of an asset or simply a user (e.g., shared economic owner) of the asset.[125] This differentiation ultimately leads to entirely different treatment with respect to the arm's length remunerations.

Assume that the functional and factual analysis leads to the fact that a PE is the economic owner of a certain asset. This means that a transfer occurred of the economic ownership of the asset. In the event of a transfer of tangible assets or goods between a head office and its PEs, the fair market value that an independent third party would have paid at the time of the transfer[126] must be considered. However, concerning timing issues of tax consequences arising from the transfer of the asset or good, the 2010 PE Report does not provide detailed guidance, meaning that this aspect is subject to national rules. Accordingly, it can be argued that a tax liability might be due at the time when the transfer occurs even though no market realization has yet taken place. However, even though such a step-up to the fair market value has severe tax consequences with respect to current tax liabilities, there are also effects that could be beneficial for the taxpayer. For example, the step-up to the fair market value leads to a higher depreciation basis that may eventually decrease future tax liabilities.

---

**Example**

Company A is resident in Country X and has a PE in Country Y. Company A manufactures certain goods whereas the PE in Country Y is meant to perform the distribution function. Company A does not distribute goods at all, however, is the legal owner of a truck that is used by the PE to carry out the distribution functions.

Based on a functional and factual analysis of the underlying dealing between the different parts of the enterprise, it might be concluded that the PE is the economic owner of the truck since it is an asset used in order to carry out its function.

---

124. Compare 2010 PE Report, Part I, paras 72 et seq.
125. *Ibid.*, para. 197.
126. *Ibid.*, paras 195 et seq.

> Therefore, the truck is fictitiously transferred to the PE in Country Y. The transfer of the truck has to be remunerated at arm's length (step-up to the fair market value).

However, assuming that the functional and factual analysis leads to the conclusion that a head office and its PE have shared economic ownership of a certain tangible asset, the arm's length remuneration for the usage of the asset by the PE must then be based on a type of fictitious rent, i.e., lease of license fees.[127]

---

**Example**

Company A is resident in Country X and has a PE in Country Y. Company A and the PE carry out distribution functions. Company A is the legal owner of a truck. The truck is used by the head office of Company A most of the time. However, sometimes, the PE uses the truck to perform its distribution function.

Based on the functional and factual analysis, it might be appropriate to conclude that the head office of Company A is the economic owner of the truck whereas the PE is simply a user. In order to comply with the arm's length principle, the PE has to pay an arm's length rental fee for the usage of the truck. However, the economic ownership is not transferred to the PE (no step-up).

---

### 3.2.2.3   Dealings and Intangible Assets

Concerning dealings with respect to intangible assets, again, the economic ownership of the assets must be considered. If the PE carries out the SPFs of the intangible assets, the economic ownership of the asset may be transferred to the PE.[128] When the functional and factual analysis attributes the sole or joint ownership of an intangible asset to the PE, the guidance provided under the 2010 OECD Guidelines should be followed by analogy. In this respect, the 2010 PE Report explicitly points out that the economic ownership of an intangible asset could be with more than one part of the enterprise.[129]

Accordingly, there are again two different types of transactions that have to be considered. First, there could be a transfer of the economic ownership of the intangible asset to a PE based on the SPFs carried out by the PE. In this scenario, a fictitious sale occurs which means that there will be a step-up to the fair market value, and the residence State of the head office usually has a taxing right among the uncovered hidden reserves.[130]

---

127. *Ibid.*, para. 197, where it is pointed out that dealings could be structured in a comparable manner to economic co-participants.
128. *Ibid.*, paras 200 et seq.
129. *Ibid.*, para. 201.
130. *Ibid.*, para. 208.

However, besides that, there is also the possibility that the dealing between the head office and its PEs is structured in a comparable manner to a license agreement between the head office and its PE. Therefore, there will be no transfer of the economic ownership of the intangible asset (meaning no step-up) but rather an ongoing license fee between the involved parts of the enterprise in order to comply with the arm's length principle specified in Article 7 AOA.[131]

### 3.2.2.4   Dealings and Internal Services (Including General Administrative Services)

Regarding services between the head office and its PEs, the full AOA no longer differentiates between special services and general services. Services are subject to a full application of the arm's length principle, meaning that the remuneration for the provision of these services by a PE has to be accounted for on an arm's length basis when attributing profits to the PE.[132]

Concerning general administrative services, the guidance provided under the 2010 PE Report continues its broad understanding of the arm's length principle. Since the head office support infrastructure is often also necessary for carrying out business conducted through a PE, the costs associated with these services has to be considered when attributing profits to PEs.[133] In this respect, the head office support can encompass a wide range of activities from strategic management to centralized payroll or accounting functions. Irrespective of the service, it has to be remunerated at arm's length.[134]

### 3.2.2.5   Dealings and Internal Interests

Similar to the 2008 PE Report, the 2010 PE Report also makes it very clear that it is an 'observable condition that PEs generally enjoy the same creditworthiness as the enterprise of which they are a part. Accordingly, under the authorized OECD approach, the "separate and independent enterprise" hypothesis requires that an appropriate portion of the enterprise's "free" capital is attributed to its PEs for tax purposes and that the PE is attributed the creditworthiness of the enterprise as a whole.'[135]

Ultimately, the OECD did not change its perspective on internal interest payments, meaning that an external interest cost can be charged, however, internal interest payments are banned in the PE context under the AOA in general. However,

---

131. *Ibid.*, para. 209.
132. *Ibid.*, paras 216 et seq.
133. *Ibid.*, para. 216.
134. *Ibid.*
135. 2010 PE Report, Part I, para. 99.

following the special rules for banks, internal interest rates might eventually be chargeable in the context of 'treasury PEs.'[136]

### 3.2.2.6 Overview about the Pricing of Dealings under the 2010 OECD Model Convention

As shown above, the introduction of the full AOA caused a change of paradigm with respect to the pricing of dealings between head offices and PEs. Since both the wording of Article 7 and the guidance established in the 2010 PE Report and the 2010 OECD Commentary are based on the FSE-Approach, all dealings (except dealings regarding international interest) are to be remunerated at arm's length. Table 8.6 illustrates the discussed outcomes.

*Table 8.6  Consequences of the Application of Article 7(2) and (3) of the 2010 OECD Model Convention*

| Type of Internal Dealing | Pricing |
|---|---|
| Transfer/Sale of tangible assets/goods (core activities) | Arm's length |
| Transfer of intangible assets | Arm's length |
| Internal Services: Specific services | Arm's length |
| Internal Services: General Services | Arm's length |
| General administrative services | Arm's length |
| Internal interest | Not allowed |

## 4  DIFFERENT OUTCOMES UNDER DIFFERENT APPROACHES

### 4.1  Overview on Different Outcomes

Reflecting on the different concepts that were elaborated in section 2 and section 3, Tables 8.7 and 8.8 are meant to provide an overview on the most important aspects to be considered regarding profit attribution to PEs when applying different versions of the OECD Model Convention.

---

136. Compare 2010 PE Report, Part I, para. 158; for more details on the chargeability of internal interest in the context of bank, PEs please *see* 2010 PE Report, Part II, paras 1 et seq.

*Table 8.7   Main Characteristics of Profit Attribution to PEs in Light of Different OECD Model Conventions[137]*

| | *2005 OECD Model Convention and UN Model Convention* | *2008 OECD Model Convention ('AOA light')* | *2010 OECD Model Convention (Full AOA)* |
|---|---|---|---|
| Independence | Restricted Independence | Full Independence | Full Independence |
| Wording of Article 7 | Old wording of Article 7 | Old wording of Article 7 | New wording of Article 7 |
| Guidance on the application of the profit attribution to PEs | Old guidance on the application of the profit attribution to PEs | New guidance on the application of the profit attribution to PEs | New guidance on the application of the profit attribution to Pes |
| RBA-/FSE-Approach | RBA-Approach | FSE-Approach | FSE-Approach |
| Arm's length principle | Restricted understanding of the arm's length principle | Still limited understanding of the arm's length principle | Full arm's length understanding for all internal dealings (except for the internal loan) |
| Time issue | No profit realization (unless realized on the market) | Profit realization even if no market realization | Profit realization even if no market realization |
| Direct and/or indirect method | Direct and indirect method | Direct and indirect method | Only direct method |

137. Compare Raffaele Petruzzi, Raphael Holzinger, Profit Attribution to Dependent Agent Permanent Establishments, WTJ 2017, p. 274; *see also* Alfred Storck, Tax Planning in International Companies: Selected issues with case studies/court decisions – Modul 2 PE and Profit attribution, https://learn.wu.ac.at/dotlrn/classes/astllm/4669.15s/res/ download/2_PE.pdf? image_id = 76591968 (assessed 19 Feb. 2017).

Table 8.8   *Overview on the Chargeability of Different Types of Internal Dealings*[138]

| Type of internal Dealing | 2005 OECD Model Convention and UN Model Convention | 2008 OECD Model Convention ('AOA light') | 2010 OECD Model Convention (Full AOA) |
|---|---|---|---|
| Transfer of tangible assets or goods | arm's length | arm's length | arm's length |
| Transfer of intangible assets | at cost | at cost | arm's length |
| Internal Services: Specific services | at cost or arm's length | arm's length | arm's length |
| Internal Services: General Services | at cost | at cost | arm's length |
| General administrative services | at cost | at cost | arm's length |
| Internal interest | not allowed | not allowed | not allowed |

As illustrated in the tables above, the understanding of the arm's length principle in terms of profit attribution to PEs was subject to a change in paradigm during recent years. From a theoretical perspective, the AOA implemented a comprehensive understanding of the arm's length principle for all internal dealings. Accordingly, all future DTTs that are based on the 2010 OECD Model Convention (or later models), therefore, will include the principles of the AOA (if so intended). However, from a practical perspective, it is questionable to what extent the principles of the AOA can be applied to the DTTs that were concluded before the two-step implementation procedure of the AOA began.[139]

### 4.2   Attribution of Profits to PEs: A Matter of Tax Treaty Interpretation

In regard to the interpretation of the DTTs, two different interpretation styles may be of special relevance for the underlying question concerning the applicability of the

---

138. Compare Raffaele Petruzzi, Raphael Holzinger, Profit Attribution to Dependent Agent Permanent Establishments, WTJ 2017, p. 269; Alfred Storck, Tax Planning in International Companies: Selected issues with case studies/court decisions – Modul 2 PE and Profit attribution, https://learn.wu.ac.at/dotlrn/classes/astllm/4669.15s/res/ download/2_PE.pdf?image_id = 7 6591968 (assessed 19 Feb. 2017).
139. When dealing with the applicability of the AOA, the general interpretation rules in international law, codified by the 'Vienna Convention on the Law of Treaties' (VCLT) (*See* United Nations, Vienna Convention on the Law of Treaties (1969)) have to be considered. In this respect, the OECD Model Convention and the OECD Commentaries are of great importance in terms of historical interpretation materials; Compare Michael Lang, Introduction to the Law of Double Taxation Conventions[2] (Linde Publishing 2013) pp. 48 et seq.

principles of the AOA on those DTTs concluded before 2008. These interpretation styles/approaches are the static approach and the dynamic approach which will be further elaborated below.[140]

In addition to such interpretation approaches, the timing issue of the conclusion of respective DTTs also has to be considered. Since the AOA was implemented in a two-step procedure, the following three stages may be relevant: Stage 1: DTTs concluded before 2008; Stage 2: DTTs concluded between 2008 and 2010; and Stage 3: DTTs concluded after 2010.

### 4.2.1 DTTs Concluded Before 2008

If a DTT was concluded before 2008, it is obvious that the old wording of Article 7 (e.g., the 2005 OECD Model Convention or older) was included in the specified treaty. These treaties form the major part of the worldwide DTT-network, which means that the question of whether or not the principles of the AOA are applicable to these treaties tends to be far reaching.

Considering a static interpretation, the later OECD Commentaries cannot affect the interpretation of previously concluded DTTs.[141] Based on this understanding, the introduction of the AOA does not have any effect at all on the interpretation of the DTTs concluded before 2008.

However, following a dynamic interpretation approach, later changes of the OECD Commentaries do have effects on the interpretation of previously concluded DTTs except for those cases where the interpretation would contravene the wording and meaning of the specific DTT.[142] Therefore, this interpretation approach would eventually lead to the applicability of the principles laid down in the AOA for treaties that were concluded before 2008.

---

140. Compare Michael Lang, Introduction to the Law of Double Taxation Conventions[2] (Linde Publishing 2013) pp. 50 et seq.
141. Compare Michael Lang, Introduction to the Law of Double Taxation Conventions[2] (Linde Publishing 2013) pp. 51 et seq; *see also* Hans, Pjil, Interpretation of Article 7 of the OECD Model Convention, Permanent Establishment Financing and Other Dealings, Bulletin for International Taxation 294, 294 et seq (2011), who points out that the retroactive applicability of the effects of the OECD changes depends on the national laws; *see also* Raffaele Petruzzi, Raphael Holzinger, Profit Attribution to Dependent Agent Permanent Establishments, WTJ 2017, pp. 270 et seq.
142. Andreas, Kempf, Michael Jakob, Changes in the Taxation of Permanent Establishments in Germany, International Transfer Pricing Journal 96, 101 (2013); *see also* Klaus Vogel, Alexander Rust in Ekkehart Reimer, Alexander Rust (eds), Klaus Vogel on Double Taxation Conventions[4], Introduction, paras 98 et seq. (2015); Compare Raffaele Petruzzi, Raphael Holzinger, Profit Attribution to Dependent Agent Permanent Establishments, WTJ 2017, pp. 270 et seq.

### 4.2.2 DTTs Concluded Between 2008 and 2010

Concerning the second stage, DTTs concluded between 2008 and 2010 also do not include the new wording of Article 7 AOA since the first implementation step of the 'AOA light' only amended the OECD Commentary by additional guidance on how to attribute profits to PEs.[143]

Concerning these treaties, it would be beneficial to investigate whether or not the contracting parties have included any reference (either to the text of the treaty or any interpretation document) concerning their intention to implement the principles of the AOA.[144] If such evidence cannot be found, the same interpretational issues (static or dynamic approach) arise with respect to the DTTs concluded between 2008 and 2010.[145]

### 4.2.3 DTTs Concluded After 2010

Even in the third stage – concerning the DTTs concluded after 2010 – it is not perfectly clear from the outset whether or not the principles of the AOA are applicable to a certain DTT. In this respect, some newly concluded DTTs embedded the new version of Article 7 AOA whereas others did not.

If the new DTTs include the new version of Article 7 AOA, it is quite clear that the principles of the full AOA are applicable. However, in those situations when a certain DTT embedded the old wording of Article 7, it can be debated whether or not the AOA is applicable. If the parties, for example, did not want to include the new wording of Article 7 because they did not want to enforce its principles, then all of the above-mentioned interpretation issues (static or dynamic approach) are still valid.[146]

### 4.3 Which Guidance to Apply?

Ultimately, it may be concluded that the applicability of the principles laid down in the AOA to different types of DTTs is mostly subject to the interpretation approach that is applied. However, besides the interpretation style, the wording of the specific DTT always has to be considered since it forms the boundaries of the potential application of the principles of the AOA irrespective of the interpretation approach. Table 8.9 briefly illustrates the applicability of the AOA to different DTTs.

---

143. Compare Michael Lang, Introduction to the Law of Double Taxation Conventions[2] (Linde Publishing 2013) pp. 97 et seq.
144. Compare Raffaele Petruzzi, Raphael Holzinger, Profit Attribution to Dependent Agent Permanent Establishments, WTJ 2017, pp. 270 et seq.
145. Compare section 4.2.1.
146. *Ibid.*; *see also* Raffaele Petruzzi, Raphael Holzinger, Profit Attribution to Dependent Agent Permanent Establishments, WTJ 2017, pp. 270 et seq.

*Table 8.9    Applicability of the AOA to Different DTTs*

| Timeframe | OECD Model Convention | OECD Commentary | Interpretational 'Style' | Applicability of the AOA |
|---|---|---|---|---|
| **Treaties concluded** *before 2008*B | before 2008 | Before 2008 | Static | NO |
| **Treaties concluded** *before 2008* | Before 2008 | Before 2008 | Dynamic | YES |
| **Treaties concluded** *between 2008 and 2010* | 2008 | 2008 | Static | NO |
| **Treaties concluded** *between 2008 and 2010* | 2008 | 2008 | Dynamic | YES |
| **Treaties concluded** *after 2010* | 2010 | 2010 | Static | YES |
| **Treaties concluded** *after 2010* | 2010 | 2010 | Dynamic | YES |

## 5   DIFFERENT OUTCOMES BETWEEN ARTICLE 7 AND ARTICLE 9 ALP?

In regard to the arm's length principle under Article 7 AOA compared to the arm's length principle under Article 9, the question may arise whether or not both articles have the same understanding of the arm's length principle and whether or not there should/could be a different outcome regarding the application of the two articles.[147]

When addressing these questions, the basis of the arm's length principle(s) established in the two articles must be analysed. In this respect, the arm's length principle under Article 9 is fundamentally based on the following three pillars: the separate entity approach, the relevance of contractual arrangements, and the comparability analysis.[148] In comparison to Article 9, the understanding of the arm's length principle of Article 7 is based on the following two pillars: the separate legal entity approach and the comparability analysis:[149]

> Regarding the basis of the arm's length principle(s) of the two articles, it becomes obvious that the main difference between the applications of the arm's length principle may eventually result from the relevance of the contractual

---

147. For a detailed analysis of these questions, please *see* Raffaele Petruzzi, Raphael Holzinger, Profit Attribution to Dependent Agent Permanent Establishments, WTJ 2017, pp. 273 et seq.
148. *See* Raffaele, Petruzzi, The Arm's-Length Principle: Between Legal Fiction and Economic Reality, in Michael, Lang, Alfred, Storck, Raffaele, Petruzzi (eds), Transfer Pricing in a Post-BEPS World (Amsterdam: Wolters Kluwer, 2016); *see also* Raffaele Petruzzi, Raphael Holzinger, Profit Attribution to Dependent Agent Permanent Establishments, WTJ 2017, pp. 278 et seq.
149. *See* Raffaele, Petruzzi, The Arm's Length Principle: Between Legal Fiction and Economic Reality, in Michael, Lang, Alfred, Storck, Raffaele, Petruzzi (eds), Transfer Pricing in a Post-BEPS World (Amsterdam: Wolters Kluwer, 2016); *see also* Raffaele Petruzzi, Raphael Holzinger, Profit Attribution to Dependent Agent Permanent Establishments, WTJ 2017, pp. 278 et seq.

arrangements.[150] However, during the process of the introduction of the AOA, the arm's length nature of internal dealings under Article 7 was strongly aligned with the understanding of the arm's length principle for intra-group transactions under Article 9. While the guidance to Article 9 does not explicitly mention the two-step approach like the AOA does, it is looking at the functional analysis and application of the ALP as being de facto similar.

In this respect, the application of the comparability analysis under the second step of the AOA is also of major importance from a systematic perspective. In regard to the comparability analysis under Article 9, the following five comparability factors must be considered: contractual terms, functional analysis, characteristics of property and services, economic circumstances, and business strategies.[151] These comparability factors are the primary drivers for the evaluation of an arm's length remuneration under Article 9. Due to the fact that these comparability factors have to be applied by analogy under the second step of the attribution of profits to PEs, the comparability factors also form the major basis of the arm's length remuneration in the PE context. However, if the five factors are analysed in detail, it must be pointed out that four factors are perfectly accounted for in the functional and factual analysis under Step 1 of the attribution of profits to PEs.[152] These four factors are: (i) functional analysis, (ii) characteristics of property and services, (iii) economic circumstances, and (iv) business strategies. The comparability factor concerning contractual terms cannot directly be replaced by one part of the functional and factual analysis under Step 1 of the attribution of profits to PEs since contracts simply do not exist in the PE context.[153] However, the AOA uses dealings in the PE context to replace legally binding contracts to the extent that is possible. Accordingly, this (still) existing difference between the application of the arm's length principle in terms of Article 7 AOA and Article 9 can be considered as a 'natural' difference that must not be overestimated but has an impact on the scope (e.g., internal interest and guarantee fees in financing).

This conclusion can also be drawn from the evolution of the relevance of contractual arrangements under Article 9. Whereas this pillar tended to be very important in the past, the ongoing development caused a substantially decreased importance.[154] In this respect, the contractual terms under Article 9 only form the starting point of a proper comparability analysis.[155] If the remaining comparability

---

150. Ekkehart, Reimer in Ekkehart Reimer, Alexander Rust (eds), Klaus Vogel on Double Taxation Conventions⁴, Article 7, para. 87 (2015); *see also* Raffaele Petruzzi, Raphael Holzinger, Profit Attribution to Dependent Agent Permanent Establishments, WTJ 2017, pp. 279 et seq.
151. Compare OECD TPG 2010, paras 1.39 et seq.
152. Compare Raffaele Petruzzi, Raphael Holzinger, Profit Attribution to Dependent Agent Permanent Establishments, WTJ 2017, pp. 279 et seq.
153. For more details on this topic, *see* Raffaele Petruzzi, Raphael Holzinger, Profit Attribution to Dependent Agent Permanent Establishments, WTJ 2017, p.280; *see also* Kasper Dziurdz, Attribution of Functions and Profits to a Dependent Agent PE: Different Arm Length Principles under Articles 7(2) and 9?, World Tax Journal 135, 135 et seq (2014).
154. Compare Raffaele Petruzzi, Raphael Holzinger, Profit Attribution to Dependent Agent Permanent Establishments, WTJ 2017, pp. 278 et seq.
155. Compare OECD, Aligning Transfer Pricing Outcomes with Value Creation, Actions 8–10 – 2015 Final Reports, OECD/G20 Base Erosion and Profit Shifting Project (Paris: OECD Publishing, 2015) para. 1.42.

factors support the conclusion that the actual conduct of the parties to the transaction is not in line with the contractual relationship, then the actual conduct forms the basis for the assessment of the arm's length remuneration in a post-BEPS world.[156]

## 6 CONCLUSIONS

In this chapter, various aspects concerning profit attribution to PEs are discussed. In this respect, the introductory section creates awareness concerning different approaches on profit attribution to PEs based on different versions of the OECD Model Conventions and the respective guidance.

Based on that, section 2 discusses the profit attribution in consideration of the fiction of restricted independence (i.e., before the AOA) and points out the most important aspects concerning the RBA-Approach and the pricing of different internal dealings, which are – to a large extent – not in accordance with the current understanding of the arm's length principle.

In the next section, the evolution of the arm's length principle based on the fiction of full independence is further elaborated. In this respect, the intended departing from the RBA-Approach to the FSE-Approach is outlined. Moreover, the step-wise implementation of the AOA (in 2008 and 2010) and the respective effects on the profit attribution to PEs are analysed in detail.

Section 4.2 is meant to create awareness concerning the highly debated aspect of static or dynamic tax treaty interpretation which is of special importance with respect to profit attribution to PEs and could eventually lead to strongly diverging results.

Finally, yet importantly, section 5 interlinks the principles of the AOA with the recent work of the OECD on the interpretation of the arm's length principle under Article 9 and points out that there are basically no longer any major differences between the outcomes of the two articles. Accordingly, some authors contended that the OECD step-wise implemented (or implements) an arm's length understanding that is neutral with regard to the legal form (i.e., associated enterprise or PE).

---

156. *Ibid.*, paras 1.45 et seq.

CHAPTER 9

# Transfer Pricing and Intra-group Services

## 1  INTRODUCTION

The relevance of transfer pricing topics specifically related to intra-group services has considerably increased during recent years. The structure, business models, and value chains of MNEs require the existence of comprehensive intra-group services. These types of services are the most common type of transactions in an associated-entity context. Based on a number of studies, the intra-group service transactions of 66% of taxpayers around the world were reviewed by tax administrations in 2010, which is an increase from 55% in 2007.[1]

These services were ranked as one of the most susceptible type of transactions to review by tax authorities in 2010 and the most important areas of tax controversies in 2016.[2] This is due to several factors. First, intra-group services are an indispensable element of each MNE's business that, as an ongoing concern, must be established sustainably for the use of its member enterprises. These services are more often than not described as 'the glue that holds the corporate structure together to support its main functions', 'of an administrative nature, auxiliary to the business of the recipient', and 'commonly available or readily acquired'.[3] Therefore, the volume of such services could be very sizable though one flow of service may only attract very limited revenues. Second, intra-group services are difficult to identify. Unlike tangible goods, cross-border services cannot be intercepted or even observed at a country's borders.[4]

---

1. Ernst&Young, 2010 Global Transfer Pricing Survey: Addressing the Challenges of Globalization, Ernst&Young (2010), p. 14.
2. Ernst&Young, 2016 Global Transfer Pricing Survey Series: In a Spotlight A New Era of Transparency and Risk, Ernst&Young (2016), p. 17.
3. EU: Communication from the Commission to the European Parliament, the Council and the European Economic and Social Committee on the work of the EU Joint Transfer Pricing Forum in the period April 2009 to June 2010 and related proposals 1. Guidelines on low value adding intragroup services and 2. Potential approaches to non-EU triangular cases, 25 Jan. 2011, COM (2011)16 final, at para. 11. The reader should also be aware that the descriptive description provided by the EUJTPF is for low value-adding services and, therefore, it is not necessarily accurate for a more general concept of intra-group services.
4. The World Bank. (2016). Afghanistan [World Development Indicators 1960–2016]. Based on data set released 2016-05-01 and accessed 2016-06-07 at http://elibrary.worldbank.org/action/showDataView?region = AF.

Though services are not extremely mobile and invisible compared to intangibles, cross border services definitely impose administrative difficulties for tax authorities, and they may require additional audit inputs in addition to what it is normally required in the event of international trade of goods. Third, intra-group services could possibly generate potential risks of base erosion and profit shifting. It is common practice in most, if not all, countries that the payments for intra-group services are deductible when determining taxable profits. If the services are mispriced, the profit base of the country of both the service provider and the service recipient will certainly be influenced. An incident of mispricing services is greater if such services occur between associated enterprises. The fact that such payments are not subject to withholding tax in most countries even aggravates this phenomenon.

Besides mispricing, it is often difficult to judge whether the service actually exists and what the benefits are for the recipients. In particular, the mispricing of intra-group services is an issue of concern for many developing countries.[5] Under the typical business model of MNEs, local subsidiaries that are established in developing countries often rely heavily on management expertise and administrative support from the foreign parent company (or designated group members) that are usually located in developed countries. It is also not uncommon to observe that those subsidiaries in developing countries usually conduct limited functional activities for the group, for example, defined R&D activities or defined local marketing activities, etc. Under aggressive tax planning arrangements, the benefits of managerial and administrative support tend to be deliberately overestimated while the service charges on local functional activities are deliberately priced low or undervalued. Considering their features, intra-group services inevitably become a 'red flag' in tax audits and are thus frequently challenged by tax authorities in practice. It is, therefore, very critical for MNEs to ensure consistency in their transfer pricing policy regarding intra-group services and keep well-maintained records and well-documented transfer pricing reports on intra-group services for the review of tax administrations. The relevant disclosure may be part of the requirement when reference is made to the typical TP documentation,[6] for example, the master file, the local file, and some national specific reporting legislations which generally include the scope, functional analysis, benefit test, benchmarking analysis, etc. For reporting compliance, the source document typically includes company and shareholder policies, a description of the MNE's organization, service contracts, service offerings and manuals, invoices, acceptance reports, transfer pricing reports, and other similar documents.

In addition, intra-group services are a very dynamic topic, for example, in the context of 'high value adding' services, and they certainly interplay with other specific transfer pricing topics. Based on how these services are arranged within the group, intra-group services may come across the subject of cost contribution arrangements

---

5. *Ibid.*
6. *See* Ch. 7 of this book.

(CCAs).[7] Additionally, based on the type of the services provided, they may overlap with subjects such as intra-group financing and intra-group transactions related to intangibles.[8]

Consequently, intra-group services have been identified as an important topic in transfer pricing whereby MNEs and countries need to pay special attention when applying the arm's length principle. Chapter VII of the 2017 OECD Guidelines[9] specifically addresses the transfer pricing aspect of intra-group services. In addition, the 2017 UN Manual contains a new chapter, 'B.4. Intra-group Services', which aims to provide special guidance that is applicable to the intra-group services largely on the basis of the OECD guidance. Furthermore, some countries have designed specific transfer pricing rules on intra-group services in their domestic law[10] while certain others simply use Chapter VII of the OECD Guidelines as a direct reference when dealing with the transfer pricing cases on intra-group services.[11]

This chapter will present how to assess the arm's length nature of intra-group services. Section 1.1 will introduce the different types of intra-group services while section 1.2 will provide an overview of the different types of service providers. Subsequently, the four-step analysis to assess the arm's length nature of a transaction[12] will be described with specific reference to intra-group services (section 2). Ultimately, a number of conclusions will be provided in section 3.

## 1.1 Types of Intra-group Services

There is no international uniform definition provided for intra-group services which is the result of the heterogeneity in the understanding of such services in the reality of MNEs. The 2017 OECD Guidelines[13] conclude that '[n]early every MNE group must arrange for a wide scope of services to be available to its members, in particular administrative, technical, financial, and commercial services. Such services may include management, coordination, and control functions for the whole group'. The definition of the intra-group services provided by the 2017 UN Manual refers to 'a

---

7.  The Glossary of the 2017 OECD Guidelines provides that 'a CCA is a framework agreed among enterprise to share the costs and risks of developing, producing, or obtaining assets, services, or rights, and to determine the nature and extent of the interests of each participant in the result of the activity of developing, production, or obtaining those assets, services, or rights'. The discussion of this chapter is only limited to the service CCA for relevance purposes. Development CCA is covered in Ch. 11 of this book.
8.  This chapter does not intend to comprehensively solve other specific transfer pricing topics related to services that are already addressed by other chapters of this book. However, this chapter will provide a brief overview in the event of overlaps between intra-group services and such other transfer pricing aspects.
9.  Since May 2016, the OECD Council has approved the amendments to the Transfer Pricing Guidelines for Multinational Enterprises and Tax Administrations (the 2010 OECD Guidelines) as specified in the 2015 BEPS Report on Actions 8–10 and the 2015 BEPS Report on Action 13.
10. For example Australia, Germany, New Zealand, Singapore, and the United States etc., provide substantial guidance regarding the transfer pricing aspects of intra-group services.
11. For example, South Africa simply makes specific reference to Ch. VII of the OECD Guidelines in their administrative guidance.
12. See Ch. 1.
13. Paragraph 7.2, the 2017 OECD Guidelines.

service provided by one enterprise to another in the same MNE group'[14] with an emphasis that the intra-group service 'must be similar to a service which an independent enterprise in comparable circumstances would be willing to pay for in-house or else perform by itself'.[15] The EU JTPF has listed some intra-group services that are commonly provided in practice[16] (*see* Annex 4).

Usually, the more integrated or connected an MNE group is, the more services it needs to for support. Intra-group services often include those that are typically available externally from independent enterprises (such as legal and accounting services) in addition to those that are ordinarily performed internally (e.g., by an enterprise for itself such as central auditing, financing advice, or training of personnel). As a result, many of them cannot be benchmarked with those services that are observable in third parties agreements.

Just as it is impossible to reach a consensus on a comprehensive definition for services, it is also not possible to exhaustively enumerate all services by category. In practice, services are typically grouped into two categories:

(1) Managerial and administrative services
(2) Services in the core business of a company.

### 1.1.1 Managerial and Administrative Services

*Figure 9.1 Managerial and Administrative Services*

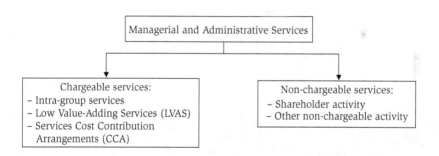

Intra-group services may vary considerably among MNE groups as does the extent to which those services provide a benefit or an expected benefit to one or more group members. Corresponding to the benefits or expected benefits conferred, the returns on

---

14. Paragraph B.1.6.21, the 2017 UN Manual.
15. *Ibid.*
16. EU: Communication from the Commission to the European Parliament, the Council and the European Economic and Social Committee on the work of the EU Joint Transfer Pricing Forum in the period April 2009 to June 2010 and related proposals 1. Guidelines on low value adding intragroup services and 2. Potential approaches to non-EU triangular cases, 25 Jan. 2011, COM (2011)16 final, at pp. 20–22.

intra-group services vary. Some types of these services inherently provide benefits; however, when looking at market terms, they usually generate relatively low profit margins on the costs incurred by the service supplier. The most typical services within this scope are administrative services. Such services are routine and supportive, however, they are necessary for the efficiency and sustainability of the international operations of an MNE. They normally include services of an administrative, technical, financial, and commercial nature. It is often the case that managerial support is also part of such services. They are collectively known as managerial and administrative services. In 2010, these services were the most susceptible for review by tax authorities[17] which is also the result of the possible association to activities related to the (non-chargeable) shareholder functions.

### 1.1.2 Services in the Core Business of a Company

However, some intra-group services may convey more benefits as part of the value chain of an MNE and, therefore, create a higher profit margin. Those services are usually associated with an MNE group's core business activities and are utilized to maintain or enhance the MNE group's profitability, viability, or market position.[18] The following activities might constitute services that are related to the core business of an MNE group:[19]

- Research and development services;
- Manufacturing and production services;
- Sales, marketing, and distribution activities;
- Financial transactions;
- Extraction, exploration, or processing of natural resources;
- Insurance and reinsurance;
- Services of 'corporate senior management' (other than management supervision of services that qualify as low value-adding intra-group services).

However, in this context, an analysis of the specific situation will also be required on a case-by-case basis to determine whether the concerned service is of lower or higher value.

### 1.2 Types of Service Providers

Intra-group services can be performed and organized in many different ways within a group of companies. Indeed, the cost of providing services may be borne initially by the parent, a specially designated group member ('a group service centre'), or another group member. An independent enterprise in need of a service may acquire them from

---

17. Ernst&Young, 2010 Global Transfer Pricing Survey: Addressing the Challenges of Globalization, Ernst&Young (2010), p. 14.
18. Paragraph B.4.2.2., the 2017 UN Manual.
19. Paragraph 7.47, the 2017 OECD Guidelines.

a service provider who specializes in that type of service or may perform the service for itself (i.e., in house). In a similar manner, a member of an MNE group in need of a service may acquire it directly or indirectly from independent enterprises or from one or more associated enterprises in the same MNE group (i.e., intra-group) or may perform the service for itself.

Therefore, one method for performing and organizing intra-group services within a group of companies would be with simple direct agreements between the different group entities that are involved (*see* Figure 9.2). In this case, a transaction-by-transaction approach[20] could be ideal, and the focus of the analysis would be limited to the specific transaction that is already established. This is often be the case, for example, for 'core' services such as manufacturing services (toll, contract, and full-fledged), distribution services (agent, commissionaire, limited buy-sell, and full-fledged), and R&D services.

*Figure 9.2   Graphic Example of Intra-group Services Organized by Means of Simple Direct Agreements*

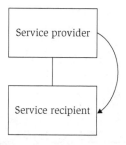

Another way would be by centralization of the services into a single entity of the group (e.g., having a centralized or regional service hub) that consolidates some or all of the provisions of intra-group services. This is often the case, for example, with managerial and administrative services (*see* Figure 9.3).

*Figure 9.3   Graphic Example of Centralization of Intra-group Services*

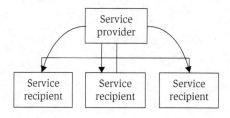

---

20. Paragraph 3.9, the 2017 OECD Guidelines.

Finally, intra-group services could be organized by means of Cost Contribution Arrangements (CCAs) (*see* Figure 9.4). Such arrangements are often concluded by entities that are both service providers and service recipients. This might also be the case for managerial and administrative services when costs, risks, and benefits are shared among different members of the MNE group whereby the indirect method (allocation of cost) is applied.

*Figure 9.4    Graphic Example of Intra-group Services Organized by Means of CCAs*

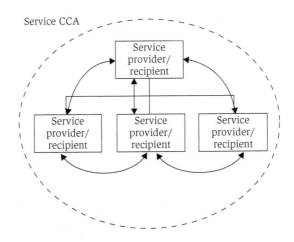

Many service CCAs, in practice, however, are based on 'one sided' service providers; otherwise stated, the flow of services is such as those in Figure 9.2.

The way that MNEs arrange intra-group services within the group depends on many factors such as the organizational structure, business models, and value chain structures that are implemented but also on the business sector to which the MNE belongs. It means the service providers can be in different parts of the value chain and with different functional profiles. Therefore, it would be relevant to assess the functional profile of the service provider with an analysis of functions that are performed, assets that are used, and risks that are assumed which could ultimately result in the two following primary categories of providers:

– Service providers in the area of managerial and administrative services
– Service providers in the core business

### 1.2.1 Services Providers in the Area of Managerial and Administrative Services

In this case, the parent company in the MNE group ordinarily performs the managerial and administrative services[21] of organizing and coordinating the activities of the business for the subsidiaries. An increasing number of specialized service providers are being utilized (such as service centres), and it is also common for MNEs to establish management service hubs at the global or regional level. It is entirely a management decision as to the size of such management teams and the location where the management teams are established.

The degree of centralization of the MNE group may affect the scope of services provided by the parent company. In a centralized group, the board of directors and senior management of the parent company may make important decisions concerning the affairs of its subsidiaries, and the parent company may support the implementation of these decisions by performing general and administrative services for its subsidiaries as well as operational activities such as treasury management, marketing, and supply chain management.[22] In contrast, the parent company in a decentralized group may limit its intra-group activity to monitoring investments in its subsidiaries in its capacity as a shareholder.[23] In practice, it is a significant transfer pricing challenge to differentiate the shareholder activities from the managerial services at the parent level. This is important as the manner in which managerial and administrative services as well as shareholder activities are treated is substantially different regarding taxes. The parent company is compensated for the provision of managerial and administrative services while, at the same time, it must bear all of the costs it incurs for the shareholder activities.

The benefits conferred by managerial and administrative services may possibly not be self-evident. If MNEs fail to defend the chargeability of these services during a tax audit, additional tax expenses will accrue due to the non-deductibility of those services. If service centres are used to provide services, the non-chargeability to certain users may lead to a retroactive charge of costs to the parent. Vice versa, the determination of the chargeability, therefore, is becoming increasingly important and relevant specific to the managerial and administrative services.

### 1.2.2 Services Providers in the Core Business

Services provided in the core business might typically include manufacturing activities, distribution activities, and R&D activities, etc.[24]

---

21. More examples, as such, could be searching and planning of operational development, coordination of process management, controlling of company activities, accounting activities, hire and payroll activities, legal and accounting advisory, etc.
22. Paragraph 7.4, the 2017 OECD Guidelines.
23. *Ibid.*
24. The listed activities are generally considered to have significant weight in an MNE's value chain. However, it could be the other way around if an assessment of facts and circumstances of each case states so.

In the manufacturing industry, there are three classic types of manufacturers, i.e., the toll manufacturer, contract manufacturer, and full-fledged manufacturer, the degree of the complexity of which is in an ascending order. The toll and contract manufacturers are both classified as service providers that manufacture goods in accordance with the specifications, including quality and quantity, provided by the principal with the assurance that the principal will purchase all of the finished products if the specifications are satisfied. Another common feature is that they do not own valuable intangibles related to the product such as a patent, design, secret formula, etc. However, the contract and toll manufacturers differ slightly in the flow of goods and functionality. A contract manufacturer generally procures and owns raw materials on its own account and takes title to the finished products thus assuming the inventory risks that are associated. A toll manufacturer, however, does not purchase raw materials nor take title to the finished products that are manufactured and, accordingly, does not bear any inventory risks. Consequently, a contract manufacturer bears (slightly) more risks and responsibilities than a toll manufacturer. Compared to its counterparts, a full-fledged manufacturer features a complete set of manufacturing and assembly functions, procurement, inventory management, pricing setting, and customer relations, and it sometimes also performs R&D and marketing activities. Additionally, it generally owns valuable intangibles such as patents, industrial/technical expertise, secret formulas, and the design. Furthermore, a full-fledged manufacturer normally bears risks associated with inventories (both raw materials and finished goods), the market, and production and, by nature, is more of a goods supplier rather than a service provider.

The second typical form of services formed in the core activities is distribution services. Distributors range from an agent, commissionaire, stripped or limited buy-sell distributor, and full-fledged distributor as the complexity of the functional profile increases. An agent and a commissionaire act as an intermediary on behalf of the principal to facilitate the trading and do not obtain ownership in the products. An agent acts on behalf of the principal. It acquires orders but often does not conclude contracts; under the OECD guidance, it will constitute an agent PE in the source State. Compared to an agent, a commissionaire acts in his own name but on behalf of the principal with the effect that the contract with the consumers signed in the commissionaire arrangement does not legally bind the principal.[25] The fact that a commissionaire concludes contracts (but in its own name) was not sufficient for declaring the creation of an agent PE in the source State until BEPS Action 7 specifically addressed the artificial avoidance of PE status through a commissionaire arrangement. Briefly speaking, an agent and a commissionaire usually impose PE exposure in the source State. By comparison, a stripped or limited buy-sell distributor deals on its own account and negotiates the terms of resale to local customers by itself. A stripped distributor is released from many functions and risks (by contract) to reduce the risk exposure and, consequently, the

---

25. Under civil law, a commissionaire is a different concept from an agent. However, under common law, a contract signed by commissionaire has the same legal force as that signed by an agent, specifically, the principal is legally bound to the customers by contracts made by a commissionaire despite the contract not being disclosed to the principal.

remunerations. While the limited buy-sell distributor only takes the ownership of inventories immediately prior to the sale to consumers (the so-called 'flash title'), it assumes very few inventory risks. Despite of the differences in the legal set-up, the stripped and limited buy-sell distributor can be jointly classified as 'limited-risk distributors' (LRD) under transfer pricing rules with an arm's length remuneration typically on the cost plus basis or often TNMM without a PE exposure while, in practice, the resale price method or the TNMM is applicable for LRD. However, a full-fledged distributor acts comprehensively and actively throughout the distribution line such as the marketing activities, inventory management, warehousing and logistics management, quality control, and after-sale services, etc. Moreover, it bears all of the distribution risks related to market and pricing as well as those pertaining to inventory, warranty, currency, credit, etc. In addition, a full-fledged distributor takes title of the goods and other inventories in the sale process and develops and owns marketing intangibles such as customer lists, brands, etc. In practice, the resale price method usually applies for determining the remuneration to the full-fledged distributor.

Another type of typical form of core services is in the context of R&D activities.[26] As intangibles primarily represent the main value driver of an MNE's business, these R&D activities in a business setting that create valuable intangibles carry significant importance in an MNE's value chain. Considering sensibility, confidentiality, and required expertise pertaining to R&D activities, MNEs more often than not conduct in-house R&D in the form of contract R&D, for example, rather than outsourcing it to third parties. In the context of a contract R&D, the principal entity contracts out these activities to another entity in the same group, however, continues to assume major risks associated with the R&D project including development risks, financial risks, and market risks, etc. The entity performs R&D activities at the request of the principal entity and also follows the detailed instructions from that entity in order to meet the expectation of the principal entity including the outcome, budget, and schedule. It is important that the contract entity only assumes the ordinary business risks related to the contract R&D. Such risks should be differentiated from the significant economic risks that the principal entity assumes. In the end, the principal owns the intangibles resulting from the concerned R&D activities and bears the profit potential (which could also be a loss) of the intangibles. Additionally, the principal entity must pay the contactor a fee corresponding to its performance of these activities.

According to the principal-agent model, the service provider, i.e., the agent entity in the model, performs the designated activities and delivers the work as requested by the principal entity which could be a service recipient in practice. From a transfer pricing perspective, the service provider assumes only limited business risks associated with its fulfilment of the obligation assigned by the principal. As such, it earns a relatively low but stable economic return on the delivery and, assuming an ordinary business pattern, this return is by no means negative. In contrast, the principal entity undertakes the ultimate financial results associated with the concerned business.

---

26. *See* Ch. 11 of this book.

Consequently, it claims the residual profits equal to the overall return net payment to the agent. However, it may end up with a loss for reasons such as the marketing campaign being a failure, the final products not being popular, the economy being in a recession, etc.

## 2 THE ASSESSMENT OF THE ARM'S LENGTH NATURE OF INTRA-GROUP SERVICES

The assessment of the arm's length nature of intra-group services requires that terms and conditions of the service between the related parties ('tested transaction') are similar to those that would have been entered into by independent parties. This would suggest applying the following four-step analysis:[27]

- Step 1: Identification of the commercial or financial relations
- Step 2: Recognition of the accurately delineated transaction that has been undertaken
- Step 3: Selection of the most appropriate transfer pricing method
- Step 4: Application of the most appropriate transfer pricing method

This section will describe the application of this four-step analysis to the specific cases of intra-group services.

Steps 1 and 2 will ultimately provide an answer of whether any compensation for the tested transaction can be chargeable/deductible while Steps 3 and 4 will aim at assessing the arm's length amount of any compensation for the tested transaction.

The question of whether any compensation for the intra-group service could be charged is a relevant one and will subsequently involve the benefit test, as shown below. Indeed, without the assessment of this question, an entity may feasibly be able to deduct expenses that it would not have incurred at arm's length. Therefore, the risk of corporate tax base erosion in the country of the entity receiving the services would radically increase.

---

**Example**

Company A, a resident in Country X, and Company B, a resident in Country Y, belong to the Group ABC. Country X's nominal tax rate is 30%, while Country Y's nominal tax rate is 10%. Although Company A does not need any additional services, the Group ABC decides that Company B should provide a service to Company A that could be considered as being shareholder related. In this way, Company A will aim to deduct the related expenses at the nominal tax rate of 30% while Company B will be taxed on the related income at the nominal tax rate of 10%.

---

27. *See* Ch. 1.

However, the incorrect assessment of the chargeability of an intra-group service (whereby either an intra-group service that should be chargeable is determined to not be chargeable or an intra-group service that should not be chargeable is discovered to be chargeable) could increase the risk of double taxation or of less-than-single taxation in the country of the entity receiving the services. This can occur in cases when the shareholder cost definitions are different.

---

**Example**

Company A, a resident in Country X, and Company B, a resident in Country Y, belong to the Group ABC. Company B has provided an intra-group service to Company A. This intra-group service should be chargeable. However, Country X's tax administration incorrectly ascertains that the intra-group service should not be chargeable. As a result, Company A will not be able to deduct the expenses related to the intra-group service. At the same time, Company B will be taxed on the income received from the intra-group service. Ultimately, economic double taxation will arise.

---

**Example**

Company A, a resident in Country X, and Company B, a resident in Country Y, belong to the Group ABC. Company B has provided an intra-group service to Company A. This intra-group service should not be chargeable. However, Country X's tax administration incorrectly ascertains that the intra-group service should be chargeable. As a result, Company A will be able to deduct the expenses related to the intra-group service. At the same time, Company B might be able to avoid taxation on the income received from the intra-group service by proving to Country Y's tax administration that the intra-group service should not be chargeable. Ultimately, less-than-single taxation will arise.

---

In order to provide guidance on this relevant topic, both the OECD Guidelines and the UN Manual address this together with definitions of shareholder activities. According to both documents, in general, the arm's length nature of a transaction should be assessed by reference to the 'transaction actually undertaken by the associated enterprises as it has been structured by them'.[28] However, in some 'exceptional circumstances', tax administrations may adjust the structure of an intra-group transaction and the conditions agreed upon by the related parties.

The 2010 OECD Guidelines and the 2013 UN Manual identify the following two situations whereby this could occur:[29]

---

28. Paragraph 1.64, the 2010 OECD Guidelines; para. 5.4.9.1., the 2013 UN Manual.
29. Paragraph 1.65, the 2010 OECD Guidelines; para. 5.4.9.1., the 2013 UN Manual.

- When the economic substance of the transaction differs from its form.
- When arrangements between the related parties involved in the transaction differ from those that would have been made between commercially rational independent enterprises, and the actual structure of the transaction hinders the tax administration from determining an appropriate transfer price.

The 2017 OECD Guidelines and the 2017 UN Manual have slightly amended this guidance by deleting the first of the two above-mentioned circumstances.[30] However, the 2016 OECD Guidelines and the 2017 UN Manual also limit the scope of application of these adjustments to 'exceptional circumstances'.[31]

Furthermore, these conditions are translated into the assessment of the 'benefit test' and of the 'willing to pay/perform for itself test' in the specific case of intra-group services.[32] Both tests should be performed from the perspective of the services recipient.

Once the question of whether any compensation for the intra-group service could be charged has been addressed and answered affirmatively by performing the first two steps indicated above, the arm's length amount of such compensation should be defined by performing Steps 3 and 4. To do so, both the perspective of the service provider and that of the service recipient should be taken into account.[33]

In general, two methods are most commonly used to determine the arm's length amount of the compensation for intra-group services: the CUP method and the cost plus method (cost plus method or cost-based TNMM for service units).[34] The first could be employed when comparable services provided between independent parties exist either in the market of the provider or the recipient. The cost plus method can be utilized when the CUP method is not appropriate (i.e., comparables are missing) and, most probably, when one entity of the group is acting as a general service provider or intermediary for other entities in the group[35] (e.g., in cases of provision of services in a centralized way).

---

**Safe harbours and definition of the arm's length compensation for intra-group services**

In order to simplify the definition of the arm's length amount of compensation for intra-group services, some countries have been introducing safe harbours.[36] Most of these safe harbours concern low value-adding services.[37] More specifically, certain countries annually issue some defined profit margins (i.e., mark-ups) that, if applied to the intra-group services, eliminates the obligation for the taxpayer to prove the arm's length nature of those transactions in more detail.

---

30. Paragraph 1.122, the 2017 OECD Guidelines; para. B.2.3.1.5., the 2017 UN Manual.
31. Paragraph 1.121, the 2017 OECD Guidelines; para. B.2.3.1.5., the 2017 UN Manual.
32. *See* section 2.2 of this chapter.
33. Paragraph 7.29, the 2017 OECD Guidelines.
34. Paragraph 7.31, the 2017 OECD Guidelines.
35. Paragraph 7.36, the 2017 OECD Guidelines.
36. *See* Ch. 2.
37. *See* section 2.1.4.1.1.

When defining the arm's length amount of compensation for an intra-group service, the analysis of any existing safe harbour should be carefully considered. However, it should also be reviewed how the safe harbour interplays with the definition and application of the arm's length principle both on a domestic and an international level.

## 2.1 The Identification of the Commercial or Financial Relations

As mentioned previously, the first step of the analysis would be the identification of the commercial or financial relationships between the associated enterprises by analysing the economically relevant characteristics (or comparability factors) of a transaction in order to accurately delineate the actual transaction undertaken. To achieve this, in the specific case of intra-group services, it would be necessary to analyse the following economically relevant characteristics (or comparability factors):

- The contractual terms of the tested service.[38]
- The functions performed, assets used, and risks assumed by both the tested service provider and the tested service recipient.[39]
- The characteristics of tested service.[40]
- The economic circumstances of both the tested service provider and the tested service recipient and of the market in which they operate.[41]
- The business strategies pursued by the tested service provider and tested service recipient.[42]

## 2.2 The Recognition of the Accurately Delineated Transaction Undertaken

The second step of the analysis would be the recognition of the accurately delineated transaction undertaken. In the specific case of intra-group services, it would be necessary to analyse whether the intra-group service has commercial rationality by using the above-mentioned tests.

Based on the 'benefit test', it should be determined 'whether the activity provides a respective group member with economic or commercial value to enhance or maintain its business position'.[43] Based on the 'willing to pay/perform for itself test', it should be

---

38. Paragraphs 1.42–1.50, the 2017 OECD Guidelines; paras B.2.3.2.3.–B.2.3.2.7., the 2017 UN Manual.
39. Paragraphs 1.51–1.106, the 2017 OECD Guidelines; paras B.2.3.2.8.–B.2.3.2.46., the 2017 UN Manual.
40. Paragraphs 1.107–1.109, the 2017 OECD Guidelines; para. B.2.3.2.2., the 2017 UN Manual.
41. Paragraphs 1.110–1.113, the 2017 OECD Guidelines; paras B.2.3.2.47.–B.2.3.2.61., the 2017 UN Manual.
42. Paragraphs 1.114–1.118, the 2017 OECD Guidelines; paras B.2.3.2.62.–B.2.3.2.67., the 2017 UN Manual.
43. Paragraph 7.6, the 2017 OECD Guidelines; para. B.4.1.2., the 2017 UN Manual.

determined 'whether an independent enterprise in comparable circumstances would have be willing to pay for the activity if performed for it by an independent enterprise or would have performed the activity in-house for itself'.[44] These questions can be answered in a more straightforward way by showing what the identified need of the concerned group member(s) is and whether the activity conducted by other group member(s) has satisfied the identified need.[45]

Services provided within the MNE group passing the above-mentioned tests are normally considered as being chargeable. In contrast, those services not passing the above-mentioned tests are generally regarded as being non-chargeable (Figure 9.5). Typical examples of such services are shareholder activities, mere duplications of services, and incidental benefits.

*Figure 9.5    Analysis Framework for the Determination of Chargeability of Intragroup Services*

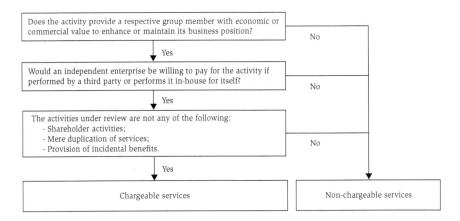

### 2.2.1  Non-chargeable Services

#### 2.2.1.1  Shareholder Activities

A shareholder activity is defined as 'an activity which is performed by a member of an MNE group (usually the parent or a regional holding company) solely because of its ownership of interest in one or more other group members'.[46] It should be noted that the managerial and administrative services are also commonly performed by the parent/holding company. Therefore, these services could easily be confused with shareholder activities. If misunderstood as being shareholder activities, the corresponding amount will create non-chargeability. For comparison reasons, shareholder

---

44. Paragraph 7.6, the 2017 OECD Guidelines; paras B.4.2.3.–B.4.2.5., the 2017 UN Manual.
45. Paragraph 7.8, the 2017 OECD Guidelines; para. B.4.2.3., the 2017 UN Manual.
46. Paragraph 7.8, the 2017 OECD Guidelines; para. B.4.2.13., the 2017 UN Manual.

activities are distinguished from a 'stewardship activity'.[47] A stewardship activity is a term with a broader meaning that encompasses not only shareholder activities but also a range of chargeable activities performed by the shareholder. Examples of those non-shareholder activities are beforehand planning, emergency management, technical advice, and assistance in day-to-day management, etc.

Table 9.1 provides a number of examples of shareholder activities provided by the OECD and the UN. From these examples, it appears that those services generally cover activities related to the juridical structure of the parent company, reporting obligations of the parent company, fund raising for the parent company acquiring participation, compliance requirements of the parent company, and the MNE's corporate governance (ancillary). Among others, activities associated with the management committee in the board should be carefully dealt with in this context when activities conducted by global managers in the committee are normally chargeable.

*Table 9.1   Examples of Shareholder Activities Based on the Guidance Provided by the OECD and the UN*

| OECD[48] | UN[49] |
|---|---|
| – Costs relating to the juridical structure of the parent company itself such as meetings of shareholders of the parent, issuing of shares in the parent company, stock exchange listing of the parent company, and costs of the supervisory board;<br>– Costs relating to reporting requirements (including financial reporting and audit) of the parent company including the consolidation of reports, costs relating to the parent company's audit of the subsidiary's accounts carried out exclusively in the interest of the parent company, and costs relating to the preparation of consolidated financial statements of the MNE (however, in practice, costs incurred locally by the subsidiaries may not need to be passed on to the parent or holding company when it is disproportionately onerous to identify and isolate those costs); | – The preparation and filing of reports required to meet the juridical structure of the parent company;<br>– The appointment and remuneration of parent company directors;<br>– The meetings of the parent company's board of directors and the parent company's shareholders;<br>– The parent company's preparation and filing of consolidated financial reports, reports for regulatory purposes, and tax returns;<br>– The activities of the parent company for raising funds used to acquire share capital in subsidiary companies; and<br>– The activities of the parent company to protect its capital investment in subsidiary companies. |

---

47. This term was already used in the 1979 OECD Report (Organization for Economic Cooperation and Development, Transfer Pricing and Multinational Enterprises (Paris: OECD, 1979)).
48. Paragraph 7.10, the 2017 OECD Guidelines.
49. Paragraph B.4.2.14., the 2017 UN Manual.

| OECD | UN |
|------|----|
| – Costs of raising funds for the acquisition of its participation and costs relating to the parent company's investor relations such as communication strategy with shareholders of the parent company, financial analysts, funds, and other stakeholders in the parent company; <br> – Costs relating to compliance of the parent company with the relevant tax laws; <br> – Costs that are ancillary to the corporate governance of the MNE as a whole. | |

It is worth emphasizing the diverging opinion on the tax treatment of costs incurred by local subsidiaries for the benefit of the parent company in the area of group consolidation and group consolidated accounts. For example, if a local subsidiary translates its local GAAP accounts for the parent company to file the US GAAP or IFRS consolidated accounts, the OECD is of the opinion that the subsidiary may agree to pay such costs locally in cases where identifying and isolating those costs are disproportionately onerous. The UN, however, affirms that the parent company shall remit those costs and compensate the subsidiary at arm's length.

---

**Example[50]**

Parent Co is a tax resident in Country A and the parent company of an MNE group (group). Parent Co is listed on the stock exchange in Country A, and it is required by the stock exchange and securities regulators to report its financial position periodically. The reporting requirements include the group's consolidated profit and loss statements and balance sheet prepared in accordance with International Financial Reporting Standards. Subsidiary Co is a subsidiary company resident in Country B and maintains its own accounting functions to support the operation of its business. Subsidiary Co is required, under the domestic law of Country B, to prepare its accounts in accordance with International Financial Reporting Standards and to annually file a statutory financial statement. Subsidiary Co's chief financial officer provides certain reports and financial statements to Parent Co for inclusion in the group's consolidated financial statement. The incorporation of this material into Parent Co's consolidated financial statements are actions that Parent Co carries out as a shareholder of Subsidiary Co, Parent Co cannot impose a service charge on Subsidiary Co for reviewing and incorporating its financial statements into the group's consolidated financial statements that

---

50. This example is extracted from the 2017 UN Manual, at p. 238.

348

Parent Co is required to file as these activities do not provide Subsidiary Co with a benefit. These activities are exclusively attributed to the obligations imposed on Parent Co as a listed company.

If Subsidiary Co incurs costs from preparing financial statements that are required for the group's consolidated financial statements that exceed what is necessary to meet the financial reporting requirements in Country B, the UN is of the opinion that Parent Co should compensate Subsidiary Co on an arm's length basis for the additional activities. However, the OECD's view is rather flexible in this aspect.

## 2.2.1.2    Mere Duplication of Services

From a transfer pricing perspective, a mere duplication of services is non-chargeable. If one group member performs an activity that is being executed by another group member (the recipient) on its own or by an independent third party, then such intra-group activity is considered as a mere duplication.[51] In an arm's length situation, an independent company pursuing profit maximization would not be willing to pay again for something already obtained by itself or from external suppliers.

**Example[52]**

Subsidiary Co, a company resident in Country A, is part of an MNE group. The parent company is Parent Co in Country B. Parent Co oversees treasury functions for the group. Parent Co's treasury function ensures that there is adequate financing for the group and monitors the debt and equity levels in its books and those of its subsidiaries. Subsidiary Co maintains its own treasury fluctuation and manages its finances on an independent basis. A functional analysis indicates that Subsidiary Co executes its own treasury functions in order to ensure that it has adequate debt capital to finance its operations. In this situation, duplication arises as Subsidiary Co is performing treasury functions that are necessary for its operations, and Parent Co is performing the same treasury functions for Subsidiary Co. Accordingly Parent Co's treasury, activities are duplicated activities that fail the benefit test. Under the arm's length principle, Parent Co cannot charge a service fee to Subsidiary Co for Parent Co's treasury functions.

---

51. Paragraph 7.11, the 2017 OECD Guidelines.
52. This example is extracted from the 2017 UN Manual, at pp. 240–241.

However, the OECD provides for some latitude in its opinion towards 'duplications'. There are two exceptions when the non-chargeability of the duplication requires reconsideration. One is when the duplicative activities are only for temporary use such as the MNE centralizing management under a reorganization.[53] The other is when a duplication occurs for a prudent reason such as reducing the risk of a wrong business decision, for example, seeking a second legal opinion.[54] It is also possible that the activity that appears to be duplicated is indeed not a repetition. An example raised by the OECD is marketing activities: the parent company may provide the affiliates with standardized marketing strategies at the group level to build a globally aligned group brand while the local affiliates may still need to localize the marketing campaign on top of the group strategies. The provision of group guidance by the parent company is 'different, additional, and complementary'[55] to the localization performed by the affiliates and, therefore, is not a duplication. Considering the above analysis, a thorough examination of the nature of the activity and the duplication is necessary in the determination of the chargeability.

---

**Example[56]**

Company X, resident in Country X, is part of an MNE group. Company X uses the group's integrated IT system that is supported by IT services provided by a group service provider, Company T. Assume that these services meet the benefit test for Company X. It is determined that an arm's length charge for Company X for these services is 60. As a result, Company X's accounts include a charge for 'IT services' paid to Company T of 60.

Company X also sources IT services from a third-party supplier in Country X in order to customize its IT system to local requirements. As a result, Company X's accounts include a further charge, also described as 'IT services', of 40.

In this example, despite being described the same way in Company X's accounts, the two charges refer to different services, and both would be allowed since the intra-group charge refers to services that meet the benefit test and are at arm's length price, and the other services are also at arm's length.

If the IT services relating to the localization of X's systems were instead sourced from an associated enterprise, assuming both types of services meet the benefit test and constitute an arm's length amount, the same outcome would apply.

---

### 2.2.1.3   Incidental Benefits[57]

Literally speaking, incidental benefits refer to the fact that one group member passively (unintended) receives benefits that arise from acts of another group member.[58] In the

---

53. Paragraph 7.11, the 2017 OECD Guidelines.
54. *Ibid.*
55. *Ibid.*
56. This example is extracted from the 2017 UN Manual, at pp. 239–240.
57. *See* Ch. 10.
58. Paragraph 7.12, the 2017 OECD Guidelines.

context of transfer pricing, intra-group activities having the effect of leading to incidental benefits are not chargeable. It seems that the recipient company ultimately gains economic values from incidental benefits. However, the recipient company does not have identified needs, in the first place, to be satisfied by the provider company through carrying out those activities. If it occurred between independent enterprises, the recipient under comparable circumstances would not be willing to pay for it or to perform it by itself.

Passive association/implicit support, contrary to deliberate concerted group actions,[59] mean that an associated enterprise 'obtains incidental benefits attributable solely to its being part of a larger concern, and not to any specific activity being performed'.[60] As a general rule, there are no chargeable services rendered in the event of a simple recognition of group membership. The use of the group name, which merely reflects the fact of group membership, for example, should not warrant a payment for transfer pricing purposes.[61] However, this does not mean that trademark arrangements are not providing benefits and will consequently require arm's length compensation. Therefore, adjustments should be made to account for the passive association in a comparability analysis when relevant, as follows:

- Determine whether the benefits have resulted from the passive association or the deliberate concerted group actions;
- If the answer is the passive association, quantify the incidental benefits by comparing the stand-alone scenario when a purely independent enterprise conducts the same or similar transactions in the market and the hypothesized scenario (with passive association) when an independent enterprise conducts the same or similar transactions as if it were in the same group;
- Make a comparability adjustment in accordance to the result of the second step.

**Example[62]**

Company P is the parent company of an MNE Group with an external rating of AAA. Company S is a direct subsidiary of Company P which intends to borrow money from a local bank. Company S has undertaken an in-house credit rating and assumes a rating BBB while the bank is willing to loan Company S at an interest rate applicable to rating A without a formal guarantee.

Questions arise. Should Company S pay a fee to Company P for the enhanced credit rating? If so, what is the arm's length amount of the payment?

In this case, Company S is not required to pay any fee to Company P for the enhanced credit rating. The enhancement in rating is because Company S is

---

59. Paragraphs 1.159–1.162, the 2017 OECD Guidelines.
60. Paragraph 7.13, the 2017 OECD Guidelines.
61. Paragraph 6.81, the 2017 OECD Guidelines.
62. This case originates from the classic credit rating example by the OECD, at paras 7.13, 1.164–1.166 of the 2017 OECD Guidelines.

affiliated with the AAA-rated Company P (the group), specifically, passive association. It is normally believed that, if one of the group members is on the brink of default, other group members will take actions rather than allowing the affiliate to file bankruptcy for the reason of having the mutual interest in one group. That is why the bank would like to offer a better deal to Company S. The rating A raised by the bank that allows for the passive association is higher than the rating in a stand-alone scenario, i.e., BBB.

**Example[63]**

In this example, the facts are mostly the same as in Example 2.1.3(1) except that Company P issues a formal guarantee for a loan, and the bank agrees to lend the money to Company S at an interest rate available for an AAA rating.

With regard to the same questions raised in the previous example, the answer is different this time. Indeed, Company S is obligated to pay a fee to Company P for the guarantee it expressly provides. An arm's length amount of the fee should reflect the benefit of raising Company S's rating from A to the target rating AAA, not the benefit of raising Company S's rating from BBB to AAA. Considering the previous analysis, the enhancement of rating from BBB to A is solely attributable to passive association, which is not a chargeable intra-group service. Without an explicit guarantee from Company S, it will not be able to borrow money from the bank at the expense applicable for rating AAA. Clearly, the further increase in Company S's credit rating is because of the deliberate concerted group action by Company P in the form of the guarantee.

### 2.2.2   Chargeable Services

Chargeable intra-group services may be provided centrally on an ongoing basis or on-call. This section provides some transfer pricing considerations regarding the centralized services and the on-call services.

#### 2.2.2.1   Centralized Services

An MNE group usually places a wide variety of activities centrally in place for the group member(s) to use for efficiency reasons including both low and high value-adding

---

63. This case is adapted from the GE Canada case. Similar case from the OECD is at para. 1.167 of the 2017 OECD Guidelines.

services.[64] Centralized activities are normally chargeable in that they are necessary for routine operations, and independent enterprises would be willing to acquire or perform such activities at reasonable costs.[65] Centralized services generally encompass:[66]

- administration services such as planning, coordination, budgetary control, financial advice, accounting, auditing, legal, factoring, IT services;
- financial services such as supervision of cash flows and solvency, capital increases, loan contracts, management of interest and exchange rate risks, and refinancing;
- assistance in the fields of production, buying, distribution and marketing; and
- HR services, such as recruiting and staff training.

The benefits of arranging centralized services in an MNE group are apparent. Cost savings are achieved through economies of scale. The best example is the procurement activity. By centralizing orders of group members as a whole, the bargaining power of each single entity in the group increases. As a result, the external supplier is willing to sell the goods with discounts that are otherwise unavailable if the group members purchase separately. Another benefit is the provision of expertise. The service centre works with more efficiency and professionalism in their field of activities and, therefore, it is able to provide quality-assured services to the group members at a good pace. In addition, the certainty of continuous service supply certainly adds value to the MNE's business. Furthermore, the incentive of enabling central service provisions may be to streamline management and reduce duplications within the MNE group.

Usually, MNEs structure centralized services models in two ways: one characterized as 'classic' intra-group service arrangements and another featured as service CCAs. In the classic intra-group services arrangements, the services are centrally provided by one group member to multiple group members where the service provider bears the risks associated with the provision of the services. In a service CCA, possibly all of the participants provide services to each other and share costs, risks, and benefits related to the provision of the services. Despite serving the same purpose of providing services centrally, the two arrangements are different in many aspects which gives rise to distinct outcomes of implementation (see Table 9.2).

There are some caveats in practice notwithstanding that the MNE establishes a classic intra-group service model or a service CCA model. As a rule, the service agreement signed by the intra-group shall comply with the local rules of each country of a recipient. It would not be realistic to use one uniform contract template in a centralized service arrangement when the countries of recipients have diverging legal requirements. It is the practice that, for each service recipient, one individual service contract with slight modifications on top of the model template is concluded to account for the specific legal requirement in a local jurisdiction. Moreover, for one certain type of service, the charging policy should be consistent between recipients no matter where

---

64. Paragraph B.4.16., the 2017 UN Manual.
65. Paragraph 7.14, the 2017 OECD Guidelines.
66. *Ibid.*

the recipients are located. Otherwise, it would easily become a target of reassessment by the tax authorities. Equally important to bear in mind is that, in the event that a service package is provided, which is always the case, it is recommended to separately define the charging policy for each type of service activity. In comparison, to establish a charging method for a service package aggregately, a service charge in isolation is of easier convenience to defend the benefit test.

*Table 9.2   Differences Between Classic Intra-group Service Arrangements and Service CCAs[67]*

| | Classic Intra-group Service Arrangements | Service CCAs |
|---|---|---|
| Definition | Intra-group services are limited to the provision and acquisition of specific services within an MNE group. | A CCA is an agreement to share costs, risks, and benefits when the participants contribute cash, property, or services. |
| Relation of Service provider and recipient | The associated enterprise providing the services may enter into a separate agreement with each associated enterprise. This may result in the service provider having numerous bilateral agreements for the provision of intra-group services. | The service providers and the recipients are all participants to the one CCA. |
| Consequence of change of service arrangement | If an associated enterprise decides to expand a service arrangement or to terminate the service arrangement, there is no effect on the other associated enterprises receiving the services. | If a participant joins or leaves a CCA, a corresponding adjustment may be required to be made on the contributions and the entitlements of each associated enterprise. |
| Contract management | Written contracts need to be prepared. | A detailed written agreement is usually required for tax compliance. |
| Remuneration | The service recipient will be charged a service fee that will include an arm's length profit margin for the service provider. | The contributions of the participants are measured on a contribution basis. |
| Allocation key | The allocation key is designed as a proxy measure of the expected benefits that the recipient associated enterprise will receive from the services. | The allocation of costs under the arm's length principle must be based on each participant's expected benefits under the CCA. |

67. EU JTPF, Report on Cost Contribution Arrangements on Services not Creating Intangible Property, (2012) (JTPF/008/FINAL/2012/EN), para. 12.

### 2.2.2.1.1 Centralized Services in Classic Intra-group Arrangements

When addressing centralized services in a classic intra-group arrangement, the problem continually occurs of how to properly allocate costs for each recipient since a direct relationship of the services received by a service recipient *vis-à-vis* the service costs does not exist and can typically only be measured indirectly. In reality, the MNEs do not have a timesheet record on how much time the management team has spent on each production line or project, for instance. Therefore, it would be impossible to allocate the costs of the management team in a direct manner. In that situation, the MNEs would need to allocate the overall costs based on an allocation formula which, in principle, should reflect the benefits/expected benefits obtained by the recipient.

---

**Example[68]**

An MNE group operates an airline business in five countries (Countries A, B, C, D, and E) with the parent of the group being located in Country A. Customers of the airline in these countries are provided with the option of calling staff by telephone to book travel and receive advice when necessary. The MNE group decides to create a centralized call centre for the MNE group to exploit economies of scale. The low cost of telecommunications and the ability to share business information among group members allows the centralized call centre to be located in any country in which the MNE group operates. The call centre can operate on a twenty-four-hour basis to provide call services to all time zones in which the MNE group conducts business. The MNE group concludes that centralizing call centre functions in its subsidiary in Country E will allow the group to take advantage of both economies of scale and low costs. The call centre services provided by the subsidiary in Country E to the parent company and other group members satisfy the benefit test. Without the call centre, the group members would either have to establish their own call centres or engage an independent party to provide call centre services on their behalf.

---

### 2.2.2.1.2 Centralized Services in Service CCAs

In comparison to a classic intra-group service arrangement, a service CCA may offer additional benefits in administration. A CCA[69] can provide a mechanism for replacing a web of separate intra-group arm's length payments with streamlined net payments based on aggregated benefits and aggregated costs associated with the services.[70]

In regard to the service CCA, the key fact is that the participants agree to share the proportionate costs of the service provision and accordingly agree that they will have

---

68. This example extracted from the 2017 UN Manual, p. 235.
69. The OECD and the UN each provide a separate chapter discussing CCAs in their official guidance.
70. Paragraph B.6.1.3. of the 2017 UN Manual.

a corresponding proportionate interest in the services created under the CCA.[71] Otherwise stated, the participants have joint interests in the services, and their share of the benefits must be consistent with their contributions to the CCA.[72] Under the arm's length principle, the contribution of a participant to the CCA should be proportionate to its share of benefits or expected benefits under the CCA.[73]

A participant in a CCA must have an expected and identifiable benefit arising from its participation in the CCA.[74] That is exactly how independent enterprises would behave under comparable circumstances. The concerned entity will fail the participant test if it does not effectively assume specific risks of the service CCA including an inability to exercise control over the risk and a lack of the financial capacity to assume the risk.[75] The participant must have a specific interest in the services produced with the CCA and must be capable of using the services.[76] Therefore, a mere provision of funds to the service CCA may not meet the conditions whereby the funding supplier is a qualified CCA participant.

To determine if a CCA satisfies the arm's length principle, it is necessary to determine the value of each of the participant's contributions. For the service CCA, these primarily consist of, *inter alia*, the performance of the services. Irrespective of the type of CCA, the value at the time the contributions are made should be used to assess the contributions to a CCA in order to be consistent with the arm's length principle.[77] However, when the difference between the value and costs is relatively insignificant, the relative value of current contributions can be measured at cost for practical reasons.[78] This rule proves to be very beneficial in the case of service CCAs.[79] Yet, in some situations, for example, when the CCA involves a mixture of services, tangibles, and intangibles and uses costs to assess current contributions, it is unlikely to provide a reliable basis to evaluate the relative contributions and to reach an arm's length result.[80]

Another key factor influencing the arm's length nature of the CCA is the expected benefits one participant obtains from the CCA. The expected benefits broadly mean economic advantages, and they can be estimated based on the anticipated additional income that is generated, the costs that are saved, or other benefits obtained by each participant that have resulted from the CCA.[81] For service CCAs, an allocation key (or a set of allocation keys) is often applied to indirectly estimate the participants'

71. Paragraph B.6.2.1. of the 2017 UN Manual.
72. *Ibid.*
73. *Ibid.*
74. Paragraph 8.15 of the BEPS Actions 8–10 Final Reports; para. B.6.3.1. of the 2017 UN Manual.
75. Paragraph 8.15 of the BEPS Actions 8–10 Final Reports.
76. Paragraph B.6.3.1. of the 2017 UN Manual.
77. Paragraph 8.25 of the BEPS Actions 8–10 Final Reports; para. B.6.4.4. of the 2017 UN Manual.
78. Paragraph 8.28 of the BEPS Actions 8–10 Final Reports; para. B.6.4.6. of the 2017 UN Manual.
79. *Ibid.*
80. *Ibid.*
81. Paragraph 8.19 of the BEPS Actions 8–10 Final Reports; para. B. 6.5.1. of the 2017 UN Manual.

proportionate shares of expected benefits.[82] The allocation key is used to indicate the nexus between the contribution and the participant's entitlement in expected benefits.[83]

---

**Example[84]**

Company A and Company B are members of an MNE group and decide to enter into a CCA. Company A performs Service 1, and Company B performs Service 2. Company A and Company B each 'consume' both services (i.e., Company A receives a benefit from Service 2 performed by Company B, and Company B receives a benefit form Service 1 performed by Company A).

Assume that the costs and value of the services are as follows:

| | |
|---|---|
| Costs of providing Service 1 (costs incurred by Company A) | 100 per unit |
| Value of Service 1 (the arm's length price Company A would charge Company B for the provision of Service 1) | 120 per unit |
| Costs of providing Service 2 (costs incurred by Company B) | 100 per unit |
| Value of Service 2 (the arm's length price Company B would charge Company A for the provision of Service 2) | 105 per unit |

In Year 1 and in subsequent years, Company A provides 30 units of Service 1 to the group, and Company B provides 20 units of Service 2 to the group. Under the CCA, the calculation of costs and benefits are as follows:

| | | |
|---|---|---|
| Cost to Company A of providing Services (30 units * 100 per unit) | 3,000 | 60% of total cost |
| Cost to Company B of providing Services (20 units * 100 per unit) | 2,000 | 40% of total cost |
| Total cost to the group | 5,000 | |
| Value of contribution made by Company A (30 units * 120 per unit) | 3,600 | 63% of total contributions |

---

82. *Ibid.*
83. Paragraph B. 6.5.2. of the 2017 UN Manual.
84. This example extracted from the BEPS Actions 8–10 Final Reports, at pp. 177–178.

| | | |
|---|---|---|
| Value of contribution made by Company B (20 units * 105 per unit) | 2,100 | 37% of total contributions |
| Total value of contributions made under the CCA | 5,700 | |

Company A and Company B each consume 15 units of Service 1and 10 units of Service 2

Benefit to Company A:

| | | |
|---|---|---|
| Service 1: 15 units * 120 per unit | 1,800 | |
| Service 2: 10 units * 105 per unit | 1,050 | |
| Total | 2,850 | 50% of total value (5,700) |

Benefit to Company B:

| | | |
|---|---|---|
| Service 1: 15 units * 120 per unit | 1,800 | |
| Service 2: 10 units * 105 per unit | 1,050 | |
| Total | 2,850 | 50% of total value (5,700) |

Under the CCA, the value of Company A and Company B's contributions should each correspond to their respective proportionate shares of expected benefits, i.e., 50%. Since the total value of contributions under the CCA is 5,700, this means each party must contribute 2,850. The value of Company A and Company B's in-kind contribution are 3,600 and 2,100, respectively. Accordingly, Company B should make a balancing payment[85] to Company A of 750. This has the effect of 'topping up' Company B's contribution to 2,850 and offsets Company A's contribution in the same amount.

If contributions were measured at cost instead of at value, since Company A and B each receive 50% of the total benefits, they would have been required to contribute 50% of the total costs, or 2,500 each, i.e., Company B would have been required to make a 500 (instead of 750) balancing payment to A.

In the absence of the CCA, Company A would purchase 10 units of Service 2 for the arm's length price of 1,050, and Company B would purchase 15 units of Service 1 for the arm's length price of 1,800. The net result would be a payment of 750 from Company B to Company A. As can be shown from the above, this arm's length result is only achieved in respect of the CCA when contributions are measured at value.

---

85. A balancing payment is an adjustment made to the contribution where the value of a participant's share of overall contributions under a CCA at the time the contributions are made is not consistent with that participant's share of expected benefits under the CCA. This leads to the contributions made by at least one of the participants being inadequate, and the contributions made by at least one of the participants will be excessive.

For compliance purposes, taxpayers should properly document service CCAs (as for all other service agreements). The BEPS Action 13 requires reporting important service arrangements, including CCAs, under the master file and the local file as well.[86] Furthermore, well-prepared documentation on the CCA should disclose, *inter alia*, the nature of the CCA, the terms, and the expected benefits and compliance with the arm's length principle.[87]

### 2.2.2.2   On-Call Services

In the business of an MNE, it makes economic sense to have on-call services such as legal, financial, IT, and tax advisory services. In the event that an emergency might occur at any time, it would be crucial to arrange standby services that ensure the immediate availability when a problem or even a crisis occurs. Though the services may not be fully (or not at all) utilized, the availability of qualified personnel and assets in a very short time creates a competitive strategic advantage for an MNE. Another advantage for the recipient company is obtaining certainties in the process of operations. In the context of independent enterprises, the purchase of on-call services is quite normal. One instance is that the independent enterprises pay an annual 'retainer' fee to a law firm or attorney in case of any litigation.[88] Hence, the chargeability of on-call services should be recognized.

However, on-call services are highly suspicious to tax authorities as they could easily be misused for base erosion and profits shifting. There are three situations expressly pointed out by the OECD under which it would be unlikely for the independent enterprise to engage an on-call service:[89]

---

86. Paragraph 8.51, the 2017 OECD Guidelines.
87. Paragraphs 8.50–8.53, the 2017 OECD Guidelines; paras B.6.8.3.–B.6.8.4., the 2017 UN Manual. Concerning the initial terms of CCA, the following information would be relevant and useful:

- the participants;
- any other associated enterprises who will be involved;
- any other associated enterprises that may be expected to benefit from the CCA;
- the activities of the CCA;
- the duration of the CCA;
- the measurement of the participants' share of expected benefits;
- the contributions of each participant;
- the consequences of a participant entering the CCA, leaving the CCA or termination of the CCA; and
- balancing payments and adjustments to the terms of the CCA to reflect changes in economic circumstances of the participants.

On the duration of the CCA term, the following information would be beneficial:

- changes to the arrangement;
- comparing projections on expected benefits and realized benefits; and
- the annual expenditure of the participants to the CCA, the form of cash contribution and the valuation methods used as well as the consistent application of accounting principles to the participants.

88. Paragraph 7.16, the 2017 OECD Guidelines.
89. Paragraph 7.17, the 2017 OECD Guidelines.

- The potential need for the service was remote;
- The advantage of having services on-call was negligible;
- The on-call services could be promptly and readily obtainable from other sources without the need for stand-by arrangements.

The economic benefits arising from the on-call services may not be readily visible at the time of review. This will consequently require an examination on a case-by-case basis to ensure that an associated enterprise is actually receiving a benefit from having a service stand by and that an independent enterprise under comparable situations would be willing to pay.[90] The opinion of the OECD elucidates how to identify the benefit conferred by the on-call arrangements, i.e., 'perhaps by looking at the extent to which the services have been used over a period of several years rather than solely for the year in which a charge is to be made before determining that an intra-group service is being provided'.[91]

---

**Example[92]**

A company that is a member of an MNE group provides an on-call service to its associated enterprises, and the service satisfies the economic benefit test. Once it has been established that an on-call service provides a benefit to group members, the next issue for consideration is the service fee that may be charged.

The fee for an on-call service may include part of the capital costs of providing the service such as business premises and equipment as well as a profit margin. If the premises and equipment were leased, the charge would be a proportion of the annual lease fees. If the premises and equipment were purchased, it would be appropriate to allocate depreciation expenses to the recipients. An independent enterprise providing such services would be expected to include these expenses in the prices it charges its customers.

---

Once it is established that an on-call service provides benefits to group members, the next relevant issue is to determine the service fee that may be charged. The difficulty arises from the nature of the on-call services whereby requiring the service never arises and actual services are never or are infrequently provided. The OECD suggests determining the charge on the usage basis by indicating that 'it may be necessary to examine the terms for the actual use of the services since these may include provisions that no charge is made for actual use until the level of usage exceeds a predetermined level'.[93] However, charging on an average usage is possible as well. However, the UN's perspective is that the charge for on-call services should be

---

90. Paragraph B.4.2.11. of the 2017 UN Manual.
91. Paragraph 7.17, the 2017 OECD Guidelines.
92. This example is extracted from the 2017 UN Manual, at pp. 254–255.
93. Paragraph 7.28, the 2017 OECD Guidelines.

determined on an ongoing basis. The fee for an on-call service may include part of the capital costs of providing the services such as business premises and equipment as well as a profit margin.[94]

## 2.3 The Selection and Application of the Most Appropriate Transfer Pricing Method

As previously mentioned, the third and fourth steps of the analysis would be the selection and application of the most appropriate transfer pricing method. The main compensations generated by intra-group services are the service fees. Therefore, the arm's length amount of such payments should be defined. This would typically imply considerations on the service fees that unrelated entities have agreed upon (or would agree upon) for similar transactions (i.e., the tested service) in similar circumstances. The two methods mentioned before that are most commonly used to determine the arm's length amount of the compensation for intra-group services are the CUP method and the cost plus method (cost plus method or cost-based TNMM in the case of service units).[95]

In principle, the CUP method is likely to be the most appropriate when comparable services rendered between independent parties can be observed in the market (i.e., an external CUP) and when the same group has also provided comparable services to independent parties (i.e., an internal CUP).[96] Regarding the CUP method, a high degree of comparability between the controlled and uncontrolled services is required. However, many types of intra-group services may not be observable from third parties. Hence, the application of the CUP method is often difficult in reality.

In the absence of CUPs, the cost plus method is a feasible alternative that is less reliant on the similarity of the services (though the services to be compared should still be similar and material differences, if they exist, should be properly adjusted).[97] The cost plus method uses the gross profit margin that the service provider was expected to earn from a certain service it provides as if it were an independent entity. The TNMM is different from the cost plus method in the sense that it uses the net profit margin of the service provider. In the event that a cost plus method cannot be applied in a reliable manner, for example, reliable information on the gross margin is absent or a cost base cannot be determined consistently due to the accounting inconsistencies across countries, a TNMM is applicable (for a service unit). However, it is still possible that, in certain situations, none of the aforementioned transfer pricing methods can generate a reliable result where, for example, both entities of the controlled transactions contribute significant intangibles.[98] In that situation, a transactional profit split method may be a beneficial tool.

---

94. Paragraph 7.16, the 2017 OECD Guidelines.
95. Paragraph 7.31, the 2017 OECD Guidelines.
96. *Ibid.*
97. *Ibid.*, para. B.4.4.5., the 2017 UN Manual.
98. Paragraph B.4.4.13., the 2017 UN Manual.

When applying the cost plus method or a cost-based TNMM, the following three steps must be performed:

(i) Assessment of the costs incurred in the provision of the intra-group service (excluding any costs for non-chargeable services).[99]

(ii) Selection of a proper charging mechanism to allocate those costs to the service recipient(s) (i.e., direct charging versus indirect charging)

(iii) Application of a profit margin (i.e., markup), if necessary.

From the perspective of the service providers, it is necessary to know their actual expenses for the provision of services before charging the recipient companies. As a rule, the computation of service costs follows general accounting standards and should include all of the costs incurred that are necessary for the purpose of supplying services, i.e., own direct costs and indirect costs as well as certain operating costs (e.g., supervisory). Of course, costs for non-chargeable services must be excluded. To some extent, the OECD does not provide any rigid or comprehensive guidance on the categories of costs to be summed in the computation. Yet, certain insights can be drawn from its guidance on the low value-adding services which states that 'the costs to be pooled are the direct and indirect costs of rendering the service as well as, where relevant, the appropriate part of operating expenses (e.g., supervisory, general, and administrative)'.[100] However, the UN adopts the 'total service costs' approach where total service costs are all of the costs in calculating the operating income (including direct and indirect costs).[101] However, it should always be noted that the cost base of the services so determined may vary depending on the profit indicator, i.e., whether it is gross margin or net profit margin that is used in the selected transfer pricing method. Most importantly, the cost base of services determined for the controlled and the uncontrolled transactions should be comparable.

The next step is to allocate the correct amount of service costs on the individual accounts of the various service recipients. Generally, there are two methods often used in practice for service charging purposes, i.e., the direct charging method and the indirect charging method. The direct charging method is straightforward. It is applicable when the beneficiary of the service is identifiable for a specific service, and the costs associated with the services are quantifiable.[102] It is ideal if the pair of services *vis-à-vis* the service recipient is of high visibility in the intra-group service arrangement so that the direct charging method applies with little difficulty. The direct charging method is usually appropriate when the group engages in substantial numbers of the same or similar services provided to associated enterprises as well as to those that are independent.[103] However, the application of the direct charging method may create disproportionate administrative burdens for the group if the group keeps separate recordings for each service broken down by service recipient especially when the

---

99. *See* section 2.1.1.
100. Paragraph 7.56, the 2017 OECD Guidelines.
101. Paragraph B.4.4.9., the 2017 UN Manual.
102. Paragraph 7.21, the 2017 OECD Guidelines; para. B.4.3.9., the 2017 UN Manual.
103. Paragraph 7.22, the 2017 OECD Guidelines.

service itself adds little value. However, in situations where the direct charging method is not actually applicable, the indirect charging method proves to be useful. The principle objective of the indirect charging method is to indirectly allocate costs proportionately to the benefit of the associated recipients who anticipate benefitting from the concerned service.[104] The costs can be assigned in an arm's length way by utilizing adequate allocation keys such as turnover, number of staff, number of orders processed, etc.[105] The selection of allocation keys should allow for the commercial nature of the service, i.e., providing a good proxy of the reasonably foreseeable benefits and safeguarding against manipulation (i.e., being objective, measurable, and consistently determined and well documented within the group).[106]

---

**Example[107]**

Company P operates a centralized data processing facility that performs automated invoice processing and order generation for all of its subsidiaries, Companies X, Y, and Z pursuant to a centralized services arrangement.

In evaluating the shares of reasonable benefits from the centralized data processing services, the total value of the merchandise on the invoices and orders may not provide the most reliable measure of reasonably anticipated benefit shares because the value of the merchandise sold does not bear a relationship to the anticipated benefits from the underlying covered services.

The total volume of order and invoices that are processed may provide a more reliable basis for evaluating the shares of reasonably anticipated benefits from the data processing services. Alternatively, depending on the facts and circumstances, the total central processing unit time that is attributable to the transactions of each subsidiary may provide a more reliable basis on which to evaluate the shares of reasonably anticipated benefits.

---

**Example[108]**

Service Provider Co in Country A is a member of an MNE group, and it provides centralized marketing services for the group. Service Provider Co is requested by a group company Seller Co in Country B to design a marketing program for a new product. Following research, Service Provider Co has concluded that the CUP Method and the cost-plus method is not applicable. In applying the TNMM (net cost plus method at the budgetary level) to the Service Provider Co, the costs of providing services and operating expenses are calculated. The unknown variable is the arm's length charge for the intra-group service. A comparability analysis is

---

104. Paragraph 7.23, the 2017 OECD Guidelines; para. B.4.3.7., the 2017 UN Manual.
105. In the 2017 UN Manual, it provides some useful examples with practical insights under paras B.4.4.15.–B.4.4.21.
106. Paragraph 7.23, the 2017 OECD Guidelines; paras B.4.3.7. and B.4.4.15, the 2017 UN Manual.
107. For example 16, US: Treas. Reg. s. 1.482-9(b)(8).
108. This example is extracted from the 2017 UN Manual, at pp. 255–256.

then performed to determine the appropriate arm's length net profit margin for Service Provider Co (net cost plus). It is decided that this should be 5%.

*Ex ante*:

- If we assume that the cost of providing the service is USD 80,000 and the operating expenses are USD 20,000, the total direct and indirect costs of providing the services are USD 100,000. The total charge would then be USD 105,000.

Ex post testing:

- A search of comparable independent marketing enterprises has revealed that they are making a net profit to costs (TNMM) of providing services of 3–8%.
- Country A accepts the range of indicative comparables, therefore, the cost plus a 5% charge is arm's length.

---

**Example 1**

A Incorporated is engaged in providing internet and related services to the group's customers worldwide. The services offered by A Incorporated include internet direct connections, installations, configuration of routers, and fully managed support solutions developed around the network services with the aim that each member of the MNE can provide seamless network connectivity to customers between various locations and countries. The total circuit connectiv ity is also provided by the local licensed services provider. The MNE group operates in a number of countries and territories by successfully integrating several different networks into one and consolidating its entities such that A Incorporated conducts business in most countries as a single multifunctional entity that provides a full range of solution services. In such a situation, the profit split method can commonly be used as the most appropriate method for determining the arm's length price of the international transactions that are based on a residual profit analysis.

---

The profit element charged in the price for services is usually a key element as the provider will need to be remunerated.[109] The next sections focus the discussion on the profit element of the intra-group services to the extent of their chargeability.

### 2.3.1 Services Chargeable with No Markup

Pursuant to an economic assumption that enterprises are profit-driven, it is expected that enterprises engaging in services provision earn a return that is more than cost

---

109. Paragraph 7.35, the 2017 OECD Guidelines.

recovery. That reflects the arm's length result that the associated enterprises under comparable situations should follow. Despite that common understanding, an associated enterprise in an arm's length situation may not be able to charge a margin on the costs incurred for services provided.

One possibility is the pass through costs. They particularly refer to the situation that an associated enterprise acts as an agent/intermediary on behalf of the group to arrange the group outsourcing activities. In the process of fulfilling its responsibility, the agent may need to purchase services/goods from third parties and immediately remit payment. Afterwards, the agent allocates the costs to the group members for payment to the agent. In that case, the costs of the outsourcing activities passing through the agent entity are charged to the account of beneficiary entities in the group with no added markup.[110] Strictly speaking, pass through costs just constitute one part of the costs relevant to the agent service performed by the associate enterprise. For the costs incurred solely attributable to the agent function other than the payment for the outsourcing activities, a compensation with a proper margin (i.e., at arm's length) is typical.

---

**Example[111]**

An MNE group has a parent company, Controller Company, in Country A and has an associated enterprise, Subsidiary Company in Country B. Controller Co has ten subsidiaries in total around the world. The MNE group has reviewed its operations and has decided to keep in-house the activities in which it has a comparative advantage and to outsource activities that independent enterprises can provide at a lower cost. The MNE group has decided to outsource its human resources activities to an independent enterprise, Independent Company, in Country B for the entire group. It has decided to outsource the work through Subsidiary Company since it is located in the same jurisdiction as Independent Company. The role of Subsidiary Company is to pay Independent Company and to recharge the costs it incurs in doing so to group members. In this situation, Subsidiary Company is operating as an agent. Subsidiary Company passes on the service costs charged by Independent Company to group members on the basis of full time employee equivalents in the group. The charge is on a pass through basis as Subsidiary Company is not adding value and is merely used for convenience to distribute the human resource costs of outsourcing to Independent Company without a profit markup. In addition, Subsidiary Company may provide a service in paying Independent Company and allocating the cost to group members. The costs incurred as such shall be remunerated with a proper margin.

---

110. Paragraph 7.34, the 2017 OECD Guidelines; para. B.4.4.14., the 2017 UN Manual.
111. This example is extracted from the 2017 UN Manual, at pp. 258–259.

It is also possible that an independent enterprise is willing to conclude a deal without generating any profits as a business strategy.[112] In certain cases, an associated enterprise agrees to provide a service at a cost (anticipated or actual) higher than the market price in order to increase the profitability of its entire business, and perhaps the reason for this is that the concerned service line can complement its range of activities. As a result, it is not necessary to remunerate the associated service supplier in a way that allows it to earn profits. Sometimes, the associated enterprises relinquish certain profits temporarily.

From another perspective, sometimes, the group tends to use certain types of services internally rather than outsourcing to an external supplier even though the group may have to incur a disproportionately high expense in comparison to the market value of such services.[113] What drives MNEs to do so is that the benefits (e.g., corporate secrets protection, more assured work delivery, etc.) that the group anticipates to obtain from the internal service outweigh the expenses. As a result, it is practical that the associated enterprise is willing to perform a service activity with seemingly no profit potential. In that sense, the arm's length remuneration is capped at the expenses incurred. Admittedly, such types of services do not necessarily occur routinely or recurrently in the business of the service supplier. From the perspective of an independent enterprise, it is not realistic to maintain a business if the main part does not generate any profits. Considering the critical aspect of this issue, it would be of utmost importance that all benefits to the recipients are fully considered.

Last, but not least, tax authorities may sometimes allow the taxpayers to merely charge the service costs despite that the price established as such is not at arm's length.[114] The main concern is that tax authorities can only collect a limited amount of tax revenues from the concerned service that does not justify the amount of auditing costs and other administrative burdens they have to bear in order to assess if the margin is at arm's length. From the taxpayers' perspective, the inputs they would have to invest to reach an arm's length margin would not be proportionate to the level of value such services create. The designated zero margin may not be an arm's length result; however, it is a pragmatic method for addressing certain types of services that generate only minimal value. Furthermore, such a method is not likely to apply when the service is the principal business of the service provider, the profit potential of the type of service is significantly high, or a direct charging is possible as a basis for reaching the arm's length result.[115]

---

**Example[116]**

Under the US transfer pricing rules, an intra-group service falling into the category of 'low margin covered services' or 'specified covered services' is, by statute, only charged a zero margin.

---

112. Paragraph 7.35, the 2017 OECD Guidelines.
113. Paragraph 7.36, the 2017 OECD Guidelines.
114. Paragraph 7.37, the 2017 OECD Guidelines.
115. *Ibid.*
116. US: Treas. Reg. s. 1.482-9(b).

Low margin covered services are controlled services transactions for which the median comparable markup on total services costs is less than 7%.

Specified covered services are controlled service transactions that the commissioner specifies by revenue procedure. As a rule, those are support services that are common among taxpayers across industry sectors and generally do not involve a significant median comparable markup on total services costs. Besides, the services under the scope are subject to a business judgment rule to confirm that it is not services that contribute significantly to fundamental risks of business success or failure.

Moreover, the services cost method contains a black list:

– manufacturing,
– production,
– extraction, exploration, or processing of natural resources,
– construction,
– reselling, distribution, acting as a sales or purchasing agent, or acting under a commission or other similar arrangement,
– research, development, or experimentation,
– engineering or scientific,
– financial transactions, including guarantees,
– insurance or reinsurance.

### 2.3.2  Services Chargeable with A Markup

#### 2.3.2.1  Services Chargeable with a Small Markup

##### 2.3.2.1.1  Low Value-Adding Services

The low value-adding services under the OECD guidance are those services that are of a supportive nature, not part of the core business of the group, do not generate substantial value to the MNE group's business, and do not involve the exploitation and creation of important intangibles and assumption of risks of economic significance.[117] Considering those features, a number of countries have special rules in their national legislation to simplify the management of low value-adding services whereby taxpayers can follow a simple set of rules for price-setting and documenting, and the national tax authority would automatically accept the pricing results.[118] In effect, those special rules on low value-adding services at a national level are characterized as safe harbour rules. For example, the US service cost method, in substance, is a national safe harbour rule on low value-adding services that is featured with a defined margin of zero.

---

117. Paragraph 7.45, the 2017 OECD Guidelines, para. B.4.5.4., the 2017 UN Manual, para. 11 of the EU JTPF paper on low value-adding services.
118. Paragraph 4.101, the 2017 OECD Guidelines.

From a pragmatic perspective, there are multiple reasons why a safe harbour rule is preferred in certain cases, including low value-adding services. One of the benefits for tax authorities is administrative simplicity.[119] Likewise, it also has the effect of leading to a reduced compliance burden for taxpayers.[120] In practice, following the standard process of a benchmarking analysis and looking for an arm's length price for low value-adding services may be too expensive and burdensome. In particular, when a comparable is not directly available in the market, the compliance expenses for taxpayers may be disproportionately heavy in comparison to the low values that the services generate. For tax administrations, the additional resources that they must input may not be commensurate with the extra tax revenues they are able to levy. Accordingly, with a safe harbor rule, the tax authorities may deploy tax resources in a more efficient manner and concentrate on transfer pricing cases with a more significant impact on tax revenues. Another advantage is that the safe harbour rule provides both taxpayers and tax authorities with certainty and transparency.[121] Consequently, it effectively alleviates the tax disputes between taxpayers and tax authorities.

Nevertheless, the risk of using a safe harbour is significant as well. The primary risk is that it may result in double taxation or less than single taxation due to the inconsistencies of rules applied in the globe. This happens with a great likelihood that, for one certain service, one country may regard it as low value-adding services while another does not, or countries apply different margins on the low value-adding services under their domestic laws, for example, one country rules 7% while the other accepts only up to 5%. In addition, safe harbours may potentially produce results deviating from the arm's length principle as it is impossible to establish satisfactory and accurate criteria of arm's length for all covered services. Despite that, the pricing outcome derived from safe harbour rules in general does not depart significantly. The main reason is that the selected profit margin in a safe harbour is designed to allow for the low value-adding nature of the services.

Apart from national regulations, international organizations, *inter alia*, the OECD, the UN, and the EU JTPF have elucidated how to design safe harbour rules for low value-adding services. These are the elective and simplified approaches on low value-adding intra-group services, the low value-adding services safe harbour, and guidelines on low value adding intra-group services. It is important to note that the MNE group electing to adopt the OECD's simplified approach would, as far as is practical, apply it on a consistent group wide basis in all of the countries in which it operates (the so-called 'all in or out condition').[122] The UN describes the low value-adding services as only a potential 'safe harbour' concept. The guidance on these services that is provided by international organizations do not have enforcing effects on nations. Whether and how to implement the special rule is entirely up to the nations themselves to decide.

---

119. Paragraph 7.52, the 2017 OECD Guidelines, para. B.4.5.1., the 2017 UN Manual.
120. *Ibid.*
121. Paragraph 7.52, the 2017 OECD Guidelines.
122. *Ibid.*

Low value-adding services if have a defined special rule that rule typically consists of the scope of covered services, the benefit test, a rule to determine costs pool, a fixed profit margin, and the documentation requirement.

It has been widely observed that the scope of covered services normally includes a non-exhaustive list of qualified services (the so-called 'white list') and excluded services (the so-called 'black list'). The widely acknowledged low value-adding services are HR services, accounting services, tax services, IT services, legal services, and general managerial and administrative services.[123] However, activities such as manufacturing, distribution, marketing, R&D, extraction and exploration of natural resources, financial transactions, insurance and reinsurance, strategic management services, and corporate senior management[124] are usually in the black lists.[125] An observation from practice concludes that those low value-adding services in the white list are classic administrative services that are often conducted by the parent company in a group, and it should be differentiated from the senior management function in the black list. Additionally, a service is out of the scope if the arm's length price of that service is self-evident, notwithstanding it is qualified as a low value-adding service by definition, for example, a CUP is readily available for benchmarking use. There is not yet a consensus reached on either the definition or the scope of the low value-adding services. However, it is important to note that the identification of low value-adding services depends on its capability of value creation in the value chain of the concerned business rather than the amount of turnover it is able to yield for the group.[126]

---

**Example[127]**

Assume that an MNE is engaged in the development, production, sale, and marketing of dairy products worldwide. The group established a shared services company in which the only activity is to act as a global IT support service centre. From the perspective of the IT support service provider, the rendering of the IT services is the company's principal business activity. However, from the perspective of the service recipients and from the perspective of the MNE group as a whole, the service is not a core business activity and, therefore, may qualify as a low value-adding intra-group service.

The definition of low value-adding intra-group services refers to the supportive nature of such services that are not part of the core business of the MNE group. The provision of low value-adding intra-group services, in fact, may be the

---

123. Christian Schwarz, Stefan Stein, Nils Holinski and Sebastian Hoffmann, *Cost Plus Markups for Low-Value-Adding Intercompany Services*, 25 BNA Transfer Pricing Report 907, at p. 2.
124. Other than management supervision of services that qualify as low value-adding services under the definition laid down in para. 7.45, the 2017 OECD Guidelines.
125. This conclusion is derived from a comparison of the safe harbours on low value-adding services of the OECD, the UN, and the EU JTPF.
126. Paragraph 11 of the EU JTPF paper on low value-adding services.
127. Paragraph 7.51, the 2017 OECD Guidelines.

> principal business activity of the legal entity providing the service, for example, a shared service centre provided these services do not relate to the core business of the group.

Low value-adding services have a defined special rule that typically consists of the scope of covered services, the benefit test, a rule to determine costs pool, a fixed profit margin, and the documentation requirement. The OECD adopted a simplified benefit test in which the concerned activities are only assessed by category rather than on a specific charge basis on the condition that the required documentation is properly maintained and presented to the tax authorities.[128] The UN, however, maintains that the functional analysis assists to identify the main business activities of the MNE group and the way in which it derives profits, therefore, the low value-adding services should be determined with a functional analysis.[129] Recognizing the difficulty in providing incontrovertible evidence that links a particular affiliate to the benefit derived from a particular service, the EU JTPF claims that a reasonable interpretation should work well as a benefit test.[130]

Another part of the special rule for low value-adding services is the costs pool which, theoretically speaking, should include all of the direct and indirect costs of rendering the service as well as, when relevant, the appropriate part of operating expenses. The costs pool under the OECD's elective and simplified approach is determined in two steps. The initial step is to calculate a pool of all of the costs incurred by all of the members of the group in performing each category of low value-adding intra-group services on an annual basis. The cost pool, however, should exclude costs attributable to an in-house activity that solely benefits the company performing the activity (including shareholder activities).[131] In the second step, the MNE group should identify and remove those costs from the pool that are attributable to services performed by one group member solely on behalf of one other group member.[132]

In practice, the benefit test and the cost allocation, however, are areas that have aroused the most disputes between taxpayers and tax administrations.[133] Though it is designed to provide convenience to taxpayers dealing with low value-adding services, it has been witnessed that tax administrations tend to reassess and adjust the result of the benefit test and cost allocation submitted by taxpayers. The benefits of applying the safe harbour rule for the taxpayer are thus severely undermined due to the discretionary power of tax administrations, which renders the safe harbour rule unpleasant among taxpayers.[134]

---

128. Paragraph 7.55, the 2017 OECD Guidelines.
129. Paragraph B.4.5.3. of the 2017 UN Manual.
130. Paragraph 28 of the EU JTPF paper on low value-adding services.
131. Paragraph 7.56, the 2017 OECD Guidelines.
132. Paragraph 7.57, the 2017 OECD Guidelines.
133. Storck/Petruzzi/Peng/Holzinger, Global Transfer Pricing Conference 'Transfer Pricing Developments around the World', 24 International Transfer Pricing Journal 4 (2017), pp. 270–279.
134. It may also be caused by the cherry-picking policy in certain jurisdictions when assessing such cases.

The profit margin defined in the special rule for low value-adding services ranges from 0%–7% in most cases. Under the OECD's elective and simplified approach, the profit margin is fixed at 5% which is to be utilized for all low value-adding services irrespective of the categories of services. It is also prescribed that the markup under the simplified rule does not need to be justified by a benchmarking study.[135] The UN suggests that a fixed margin should be determined under domestic law without notifying a specific figure. The UN assumes that the same gross profit margin is ideally accepted in the other country.[136] According to the EU JTPF, experience shows that the margin of low value-adding services usually falls within a range of 3%–10% (often around 5%).[137] Moreover, the US's services cost method only charges back the costs of the qualified services (Figure 9.3).

Documentation is always an essential part of the safe harbours on low value-adding services. It works as an interface between taxpayers and tax authorities. The management procedures for low value-adding services are always simplified with fewer obligations. It is important that taxpayers provide sufficient evidence and well-documented reports to assure tax authorities that they are compliant with a safe harbour rule and that it is not being abused.

*Table 9.3   A Comparative View of Different Safe Harbours on Low Value-Adding Services*

|  | OECD | EU JTPF | US Regulations |
|---|---|---|---|
| **Source** | BEPS Action 10 Low Value-Adding Intra-group Services | Guidelines on low value adding intra-group services | US Services Regulations § 1.482-9 |
| **Date (last updated)** | 10.07.2017 | 25.01.2011 | 01.04.2015 |
| **Scope of application** | Group elective | Transaction elective | Transaction elective |
| **Markup** | 5% | 3%–10% rec. 5%0% allowed | 0% |
| **Different markups** | One markup for all service categories | One markup for each services category | Always 0% |
| **Included Services requirements** | – Supportive Nature <br> – Do not need or give rise to the creation of high value intangibles <br> – Do not bear or give rise to creation of significant risk | – Supportive Nature <br> – Low value adding <br> – Do not bear significant risk <br> – Subject of the MNE internal governance system | – Covered Service <br> – Not especially excluded |

135. Paragraph 7.61, the 2017 OECD Guidelines.
136. Paragraph B.4.71 of the 2017 UN Manual.
137. Paragraph 65 of the EU JTPF paper on low value-adding services.

| | OECD | EU JTPF | US Regulations |
|---|---|---|---|
| **Documentations requirements** | – Not part of the core business An MNE group electing for application of this simplified methodology shall prepare the following information and documentation and make it available upon request to the tax administration of any entity within the group either making or receiving a payment for low value-adding intra-group services,[138] – A description of the categories of low value-adding intra-group services provided; the identity of the beneficiaries; the reasons justifying that each category of services constitute low value-adding intra-group services; the rationale for the provision of services within the context of the businessof the MNE; a description of the benefits or expected benefits of each category of services; a description of the selected allocation keys and the reasons justifying that such allocation keys produce outcomes that | It is suggested that a useful and a proportionate documentation pack may contain,[139] – a narrative, – written agreement, – cost pool, – justification of OECD methodology applied, – verification of arm's length price applied, – invoicing system and invoices. | – Not precluded by business judgment rule, i.e., does not give rise to significant risk or failure of business – Adequate books and records The application of the service cost method requires a maintenance of adequate books and records, which must include:[140] – a statement evidencing the taxpayer's intention to apply the services cost method to evaluate the arm's length charge for such services, – adequate information on total service costs to permit verification by the Commissioner, including a description of the services in question, identification of the renderer and the recipient of such services, |

138. Paragraph 7.64, the 2017 OECD Guidelines.
139. Paragraph 72 of the EU JTPF paper on low value-adding services.
140. US: Treas. Reg. s. 1.482-9(b)(6).

|  | OECD | EU JTPF | US Regulations |
|---|---|---|---|
|  | reasonably reflect the benefits received, and confirmation of the markup applied; to those contracts and agreements reflecting the agreement of the various members of the group to be bound by the allocation rules of this section. Such written contracts or agreements could take the form of a contemporaneous document identifying the entities involved, the nature of the services, and the terms and conditions under which the services are provided;<br>– Documentation and calculations showing the determination of the cost pool, and of the markup applied thereon, in particular a detailed listing of all categories and amounts of relevant costs, including costs of any services provided solely to one group member;<br>– Calculations showing the application of the specified allocation keys. |  | – sufficient documentation to allow verification of the methods used to allocate and apportion such costs to the services in question. |

Apart from setting up safe harbours on the grounds of the low value-adding nature of the services, some countries establish them for intra-group services of which the total expenses incurred are minor. Pursuant to a minor expense safe harbour, the tax authority agrees to refrain from making a transfer pricing adjustment if the total cost of either receiving or providing intra-group services by an affiliate is below a fixed threshold and a fixed profit margin is used[141] (*see* Annex 2).

### 2.3.2.1.2  Other Services Chargeable with Small Markup

The fact that an activity does not qualify for the safe harbour rule on low value-adding services does not necessarily mean that the activity is definitely capable of generating high value.[142] In fact, certain activities add low value; however, they are not qualified for the application of the safe harbour rule for low value-adding services by law, for example, the toll manufacturing activities. As a result, the determination of the arm's length charge for those activities should be determined in accordance to the general guidance set out in section 2.3, and a benchmarking study should be conducted.

### 2.3.2.2  *Services Chargeable with High Markup*

Just as with the low value-adding services, there is no internationally agreed definition for high value-adding services. Nevertheless, high value-adding services may be interpreted oppositely compared to low value-adding services. In the UN's opinion, they are 'services associated with an MNE group's core business activities, which are incurred to maintain or improve the MNE group's profitability, viability or market position, may create greater value and carry a higher profit margin'.[143] Based on the OECD's standard, they may be understood as services that are not of supportive nature, not part of the core business of the group, generate substantial value to the MNE group's business, and involve the exploitation or the creation of important intangibles and the assumption of significant economic risks. By category, activities generally rendered as high value-adding services are manufacturing, distribution, marketing, R&D, financial transactions, insurance, reinsurance, etc. The determination of whether a service connects to the core business of the MNE group is subject to a case-by-case study on the functions performed, assets used, and risks assumed by the entity. In certain cases, it may require an application of a supply chain analysis.

---

**Example[144]**

Research is an example of an activity that may involve high value-adding services. The terms of the activity can be established in a detailed contract with the party commissioning the service, commonly known as contract research. The activity can involve highly skilled personnel and vary considerably both in its nature and in its importance to the success of the group. The actual arrangements can take a variety of forms from the undertaking of detailed programmes laid

---

141. Paragraph B.4.5.2., the 2017 UN Manual.
142. Paragraph 7.48, the 2017 OECD Guidelines.
143. Paragraph B.4.2.2. of the 2017 UN Manual.
144. The example is extracted from the OECD BEPS Actions 8–10 Final Reports, at para. 7.41.

down by the principal party and extending to agreements where the research company has discretion to work within broadly defined categories. In the latter instance, the additional functions of identifying commercially valuable areas and assessing the risk of unsuccessful research can be a critical factor in the performance of the group as a whole. Therefore, it is crucial to undertake a detailed functional analysis and obtain a clear understanding of the precise nature of the research and how the activities are being performed by the company prior to consideration of the appropriate transfer pricing methodology. The consideration of options realistically available to the party commissioning the research may also prove to be beneficial for selecting the most appropriate transfer pricing method.

To reach an arm's length price for high value-adding services, the standard procedure illustrated in section 2.3 should be followed. Concerning the high value-adding services, the compensation should reflect the non-routine nature and the capability of adding substantial value to the business. For that purpose, it is typical to either apply the cost plus method with an increased markup or to apply the profit split method when the contributions of the service providers are extraordinary.

## 3    CONCLUSIONS

This chapter has detailed how to assess the arm's length nature of intra-group services. Beginning with an introduction of the different types of intra-group services and of service providers, the four-step analysis has been described with specific reference to intra-group services in order to assess the arm's length nature of a transaction.

Steps 1 and 2 will ultimately provide an answer on whether any compensation for the tested transaction can be chargeable/deductible. In detail, these would require the performance of the 'benefit test' and of the 'willing to pay/perform for itself test'. Additionally, all of the terms and conditions established in the tested intra-group service should reflect the accurately delineated transaction undertaken, i.e., terms and conditions should be at arm's length.

Steps 3 and 4 will aim at assessing the arm's length compensation for intra-group services by taking into account both the perspective of the service provider and that of the service recipient. In this context, the CUP method and the cost plus method (cost plus method or cost-based TNMM) are the methods most commonly used. However, in some cases, the transactional profit split method can also be adopted.

## ANNEX 1: LIST OF INTRA-GROUP SERVICES BASED ON THE GUIDANCE PROVIDED BY THE EU JTPF

**Information technology services:**
- building, development, and management of the information system;
- study, development, installation, and periodic/extraordinary maintenance of software;
- study, development, installation, and periodic/extraordinary maintenance of hardware;
- supply and transmission of data; and
- back-up services.

**Human resource services:**
- legislative, contractual, administrative, social security, and fiscal activities connected to the ordinary and extraordinary management of personnel;
- selection and hiring of personnel;
- assistance in defining career paths;
- assistance in defining compensations and benefit schemes (including stock option plans);
- definition of personnel evaluation processes;
- training of personnel;
- supply of staff for limited period; and
- coordination of the sharing of personnel on a temporary or permanent basis; and management of redundancies.

**Marketing services:**
- study, development, and coordination of the marketing activities;
- study, development, and coordination of the sale promotions;
- study, development, and coordination of the advertising campaigns;
- market research;
- development and management of Internet websites;
- publication of magazines handed out to clients of the subsidiary (even if concerning the entire group).

**Legal services:**
- assistance in the drafting and reviewing of contracts and agreements;
- ongoing legal consultation;
- drafting and commissioning legal and tax opinions;
- assistance in the fulfilment of legislative obligations;
- assistance in the judicial litigation;
- centralized management of relationship with insurance companies and brokers;
- tax advice;

- transfer pricing studies; and
- protection of intangible property.

**Accounting and administration services:**
- assistance in the preparation of the budget and operating plans; keeping of the mandatory books and accounts;
- assistance in the preparation of periodical financial statements, annual and extraordinary balance sheets or statements of account (different from the consolidated financial statement);
- assistance in compliance with fiscal obligations such as filing tax returns, computing, and paying taxes, etc.; data processing;
- audit of the account of the subsidiary; and management of the invoicing process.

**Technical services, for example:**
- assistance regarding plant, machinery, equipment, processes, etc.
- planning and executing ordinary and extraordinary maintenance activities on premises and plant;
- planning and executing ordinary and extraordinary restructuring activities on premises and plant;
- transfer of technical know-how;
- providing guidelines for the products' innovation;
- production planning to minimize excess capacity and meet demand efficiently;
- assistance in planning and implementing capital expenditure;
- efficiency monitoring; and
- engineering services.

**Quality control services:**
- providing quality policies and standards of the production and provision of services;
- assistance in obtaining quality certifications; and
- development and implementation of client satisfaction programmes.

**Other services:**
- strategy and business development services in the event that there is a connection with an existing (or to be established) subsidiary;
- corporate security;
- research and development;
- real estate and facility management;
- logistic services;
- inventory management;
- advice on transport and distribution strategy;
- warehousing services;
- purchasing services and sourcing raw materials;
- cost reduction management;
- packaging services.

## ANNEX 2: TREATMENT OF MARKUP ON ROUTINE INTRA-GROUP SERVICES IN SELECTED COUNTRIES[145]

| Country | Guidance | Source |
|---|---|---|
| Australia | 7.5% markup (or a markdown of 5% [up to 10% in certain circumstances]) on 'noncore services' and in de minimis cases provided that certain conditions are met. | ATO Taxation Ruling TR 1999/1 |
| New Zealand | 7.5% markup (or a markdown of 5% [up to 10% in certain circumstances]) on 'noncore services' provided that certain conditions are met. | Paragraph 558 of Inland Revenue 1997 |
| Singapore | 5% markup on 'routine services' provided by the parent or a group service company for 'business convenience and efficiency reasons.' | IRAS 2009 |
| United States | Under 'services cost method', certain 'low-margin' services may be compensated on the basis of cost without a profit (markup) provided a range of conditions is met. | §1.482-9(b) IRC section 482 regulations |

145. The World Bank. (2016). Afghanistan [World Development Indicators 1960–2016]. Based on data set released 2016-05-01 and accessed 2016-06-07 at http://elibrary.worldbank.org/action/showDataView?region = AF, at p. 208.

# CHAPTER 10

# Transfer Pricing and Intra-group Financial Transactions

## 1 INTRODUCTION

Transfer pricing topics specifically related to intra-group financial transactions[1] have, over recent years, considerably increased their relevance. Based on a number of studies, the review of this type of transaction by tax administrations around the world has dramatically increased from 7% in 2007 to 42% in 2010.[2] Currently, financial transactions globally generate the second most significant area of transfer pricing controversy between taxpayers and tax administrations.[3] This is due to several factors, for example, the recent substantial changes in the economic environment, the introduction by many countries of tax measures aimed at reducing the tax advantages of debt financing, the relative importance (also in terms of the amounts involved) of these transactions, and the high degree of complexity that typically characterizes these types of transactions.

This chapter will present how to assess the arm's length nature of intra-group financial transactions with specific reference to loans, financial guarantees, and cash pooling. Section 1.1 will introduce the different types of intra-group financial transactions while section 1.2 will provide an overview of the different types of financing entities. Subsequently, the four-step analysis to assess the arm's length nature of a transaction[4] will be described with specific reference to intra-group loans, financial guarantees, and cash pooling (section 2). Ultimately, some conclusions will be provided in section 3.

### 1.1 Types of Intra-group Financial Transactions

A 'financial asset' can be defined as 'any asset that is cash, an equity instrument, a contractual right or obligation to receive cash or another financial asset or to exchange financial assets or liabilities, or a derivative. Examples include bonds, bank deposits, stocks, shares, forward contracts, futures contracts, and swaps'.[5] In practice, numerous financial instruments exist, for example:[6]

(a) Traditional financial instruments:
- Equity instruments (e.g., bank deposits, common stocks, funds).

---

1. The OECD and the UN do not address intra-group financial transactions separately in their guidance but within the topic of intra-group services, i.e., Chapter VII of the 2017 OECD Guidelines and B.4. of the 2017 UN Manual. For intra-group services, it is covered in Chapter IX of this book.
2. Ernst&Young, *2010 Global Transfer Pricing Survey: Addressing the challenges of globalization*, Ernst&Young (2010), p. 14.
3. Ernst&Young, *2013 Global Transfer Pricing Survey: Navigating the choppy waters of international tax*, Ernst&Young (2013), p. 17.
4. *See* Ch. 1.
5. Note 14, 2017 OECD Guidelines.
6. This classification is sourced (and slightly amended) from Laukkanen, A., *Taxation of Investment Derivatives* (The Netherlands: IBFD, 2007), p. 20.

- Debt instruments (e.g., ordinary and special bank loans, ordinary and special bonds, commercial papers and money market instruments, debentures, government securities).
(b) Financial derivatives:
- Basic derivatives (e.g., forex transactions, stock options,[7] futures, forwards, notional principal contacts[8]).
- Hybrid derivatives (e.g., investment derivatives[9] and other hybrids[10]).

In this context, the following financial transactions are the most common and relevant in an intra-group context:[11]

- Loans.
- Guarantees (financial guarantees and performance guarantees).
- Cash pooling (or cash optimization structures).
- Hybrid financing.
- Derivatives.
- Other treasury services (e.g., foreign exchange risk management, factoring and forfeiting, netting arrangements, payment factories, commodity risk management, captive insurance, asset management, carbon trading).

The scope of this chapter will be limited to the analysis of intra-group loans, intra-group financial guarantees, and intra-group cash pooling.

The definition of the specific financial transactions that are in place will provide an initial indication of the most appropriate method to be used to assess the arm's length nature of the transactions.

### 1.1.1 Intra-group Loans

An intra-group loan is the borrowing of financial resources from one party (the lender) to another (the borrower) to be repaid at a later date. With an intra-group loan, the borrower will obtain the financial resources; however, the lender will generally assume the credit risk related to the intra-group loan and, hence, will need to be compensated for the liquidity provided and the risk taken by an arm's length payment, i.e., an interest payment. All relevant terms and conditions of the loan should be specified in the loan agreement between the parties (Figure 10.1).

---

7. For example, call options and put options.
8. For example, swaps (such as interest rate swaps, currency rate swaps, and equity swaps), caps, floors, and collars.
9. For example, convertible bonds, warrant bonds, reverse convertible bonds, stock index bonds, interest index bonds, exchangeable bonds, and bull/bear bonds.
10. For example, subordinated loans, perpetual loans, jouissance shares, profit-participating loans, and silent participations.
11. Russo, A. & Moerer, O., 'Introduction' in: Bakker, A. & Levey, M.M. (eds), *Transfer Pricing and Intra-Group Financing* (The Netherlands: IBFD, 2012), p. 5.

*Figure 10.1    Graphic Example of an Intra-group Loan*

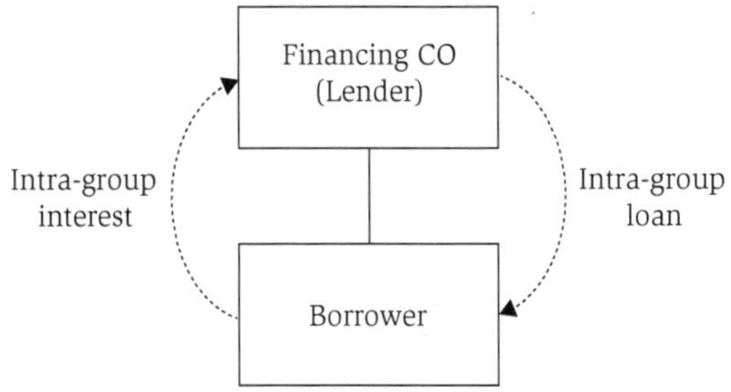

**Example**

Company A, a resident in Country X, and Company B, a resident in Country Y, belong to the Group ABC. In order to develop a new business, Company A requires new financial resources that are not available in its bank account. Therefore, Company A asks Company B (which has available financial resources that it does not need for its own business development) to provide an intra-group loan. Company A (the borrower) and Company B (the lender) will need to assess whether the intra-group loan is at arm's length.

In practice, many different types of intra-group loans exist, for example:

- *Term loan*: a loan with a maturity ranging from 1 to 10 + years that is generally used to fund medium- and long-term assets such as plant and equipment as well as average inventory levels. A term loan may be secured or (more typically) unsecured, carry a fixed rate or a floating rate, and contain general or specific performance covenants.[12]
- *Revolving loan or revolving credit facility*: a secured or unsecured credit line with a maturity ranging from 6 months to 5 + years that a borrower can draw down and repay multiple times. A typical facility requires the borrower to pay the bank an annual commitment fee on the entire line in order to keep it available for future use; those without a fee are typically not committed and may be withdrawn by the bank at will. In some instances, banks require borrowers to repay the facility in full before allowing further draw-downs or renewals (a process known as a clean-up call).[13]

12. Banks, E., *The Palgrave Macmillan Dictionary of Finance, Investment and Banking* (New York, NY: Palgrave Macmillan, 2010), p. 508.
13. *Ibid.*, p. 446.

## 1.1.2 Intra-group Financial Guarantees

An intra-group financial guarantee is a risk transfer mechanism whereby one party (the guarantor) agrees to assume the financial obligations (deriving from the guaranteed instrument) of another party (the guaranteed entity) towards a third party in the event that the guaranteed entity defaults on its obligations towards this third party. With an intra-group financial guarantee, the guaranteed entity will increase its debt capacity and obtain advantageous conditions (such as a lower interest rate) from the third party; however, the guarantor will generally assume the credit risk related to the guaranteed instrument and, hence, will need to be compensated with an arm's length payment, i.e., a guarantee fee. All of the relevant terms and conditions of the financial guarantee should be specified in the financial guarantee agreement between the parties (FIgure 10.2).

*Figure 10.2   Graphic Example of an Intra-group Financial Guarantee*

---

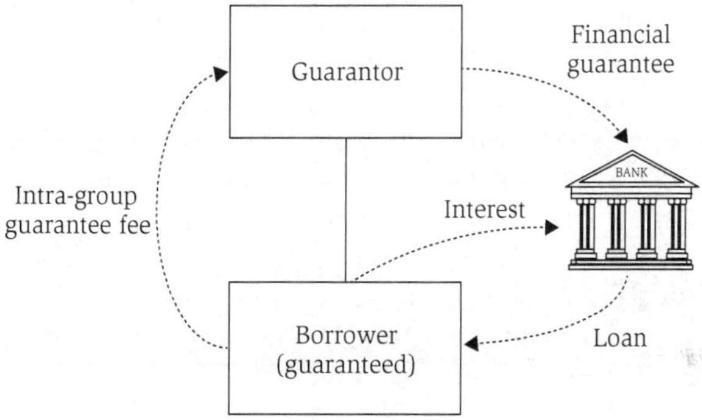

**Example**

Company A, a resident in Country X, and Company B, a resident in Country Y, belong to the Group ABC. In order to develop a new business, Company A requires new financial resources that are not available in its bank account. Therefore, Company A asks a third-party bank to provide an external loan. In order to secure this loan, the third-party bank asks Company B (which has a stronger financial position than Company A) to guarantee that, in the event that Company A defaults on its obligations of the loan, Company B will assume the financial obligations generated by the loan. Company A (the guaranteed entity) and Company B (the guarantor) will need to assess whether the intra-group financial guarantee is at arm's length.

383

In practice, many different types of intra-group financial guarantees exist, for example:[14]

(a) *Comfort letters/letters of intent*: a promise (i.e., generally, not legally binding) provided, in most cases, by the parent company to a company belonging to the group which states that the former will oversee the latter's affairs in order to be in accordance with the group strategies and rules and refrain from taking adverse actions that would compromise the financial stability of another group company.

(b) *Keep-well agreements*: a declaration provided, in most cases, by the parent company to a company belonging to the group which states that the former will provide the latter with additional capital to prevent the risk of its default.

(c) *Explicit credit guarantees*: a legally binding commitment provided, in most cases, by the parent company to a company belonging to the group which states that the former will pay to a third party financing entity the amount that was lent to the latter in the event that the latter cannot fulfil its obligations. Three types of explicit guarantees are commonly used:
   – *Downstream guarantees*: the parent company issues a guarantee to external creditors for the benefit of one of its subsidiaries so that the latter can enter into agreements with external creditors (typically used in decentralized business structures or when the location of the subsidiary is more attractive for obtaining external financing).
   – *Upstream guarantees*: a group company issues a guarantee to external creditors for the benefit of its parent company so that the latter can enter into agreements with the external creditors (typically used when the external financing is obtained at a parent or holding level or when the parent company performs central treasury functions).[15]
   – *Cross guarantees*: Several group companies issue guarantees to external creditors for the benefit of each other so that they can all be considered as one single legal obligor (typically used in cash pooling).[16]

Comfort letters, letters of intent, and keep-well agreements, if structured in the ordinary manner, are considered as being 'implicit guarantees' and are less legally binding (hence, less enforceable) than explicit credit guarantees.

### 1.1.3  Intra-group Cash Pooling

Intra-group cash pooling is an arrangement involving one or more banks that allows combining debit and credit balances in a group's disparate bank accounts in order to

---

14. PwC, *Navigating the Complexity: Findings from the Financial Transactions Transfer Pricing Global Survey 2013* (PwC, 2013), pp. 20–21.
15. It increases the creditworthiness for the borrower if the subsidiary has good performing operations and assets but has substantial legal restrictions (typically limited to free reserves).
16. Also, in this case, substantial legal restrictions apply (typically limited to free reserves).

derive net balances on a real or notional basis. As a consequence of this process, interest is credited on a positive balance and debited on a negative balance. Therefore, the different parties involved in this process will be in a position similar to those of borrowers and lenders of an intra-group loan. All of the relevant terms and conditions of the intra-group cash pooling should be specified in the intra-group cash pooling agreement between all of the parties involved (the participants to the cash pooling).

An intra-group cash pooling can generate numerous advantages, for example:[17]

- Minimizing the liquidity requirements in the cash pool group.
- Minimizing high external interest cost for the group.
- Flexible day-to-day financing of the cash pool participants.
- Reduction of transaction costs related to local bank accounts for all of the cash pool participants.
- Increase of the bargaining power with banks and allowing obtaining conditions that are more advantageous (e.g., interest rates) on the common bank account.
- Centralization of the financing decisions.

Maximization of the various 'cash pool benefits', therefore, is the aim behind such arrangements, and the extent of such benefits also depends on the cash pool technique that is used (*see* below).[18]

---

**Example**

Company A, a resident in Country X; Company B, a resident in Country Y; and Company C, a resident in Country Z belong to the Group ABC. In order to minimize liquidity costs, reduce the transaction costs related to local bank accounts by all of the companies, and to increase the bargaining power with external banks, the three companies decide to establish an intra-group cash pooling agreement whereby their bank accounts will be daily levelled to zero. If the balance of a participant's bank account exceeds zero, the excessive amount will be transferred to Company A's bank account while, if the balance of a participant's bank account is lower than zero, funds will be transferred from Company A's bank account to the participant's bank account. Company A, Company B, and Company C will need to assess whether all transactions deriving from the intra-group cash pooling agreement are at arm's length. Typically, one group company acts as a so-called 'cash pool master'.

---

17. PwC, *Navigating the Complexity: Findings from the Financial Transactions Transfer Pricing Global Survey 2013* (PwC, 2013), p. 15.
18. Since the debt interest on a bank account is higher than the relative credit interest, the group would save on debt interest or gain credit interest due to the fact that cash is borrowed from or deposited in a group bank account after settling the debt and credit positions of the cash pool participants.

In practice, the following two types of intra-group cash pooling exist (Figures 10.3 and 10.4):[19]

- *The 'target-balancing' or 'zero-balancing' cash pooling*: the participants' bank accounts are regularly (often daily) levelled to a certain pre-determined amount (equal to zero, in the case of zero-balancing cash pooling). If the balance of a participant's bank account exceeds this pre-determined amount, the excessive amount is transferred to a central bank account, i.e., the cash pool leader's account; symmetrically, if the balance of a participant's bank account is lower than the pre-determined amount, funds are transferred from the cash pool leader's account to level the participant's bank account. The target-balancing cash pooling is often linked to a credit facility and deposit arrangement between the cash pool executing bank and the cash pool leader. When the cash pool leader is in a debt position, it will withdraw funds from that credit facility and pay interest on them; when the cash pool leader is in a credit position, it will deposit funds in that credit facility and receive interest from them. Deposit positions in cash pooling may also be invested in short-term risk securities (e.g., in the money market). Moreover, in such arrangements, comprehensive cross- and upstream guarantees from the participants are normally requested by the bank in addition to the (downstream) parent guarantee. Therefore, in this type of cash pooling, funds are concentrated and managed by the cash pool leader.
- *The 'notional' ('interest compensation') cash pooling*: the participating bank determines, in cooperation with the group, the amount of credit and debit interest to be applied to each participant's bank accounts (which are kept separate from each other) and notionally calculates the total balance of all of the combined individual bank accounts which usually cannot be less than zero. The cash pool benefit deriving from this notional balance may be paid by the bank to the cash pool leader or typically to the single participants by accordingly adjusting the debt and credit interest rates. In this case, the cash pool can also be linked to a credit facility and cross-guarantees could be requested by the bank in addition to the (downstream) parent guarantee. The cash pool leader, in this context, plays a limited role as funds are not concentrated (e.g., arranging the applicable rates of interest payments for credits and deposits with the bank and, by doing so, for allocating cash pool benefits).

---

19. PwC, *Navigating the Complexity: Findings from the Financial Transactions Transfer Pricing Global Survey 2013* (PwC, 2013), pp. 15–16.

*Figure 10.3   Graphic Example of Target-Balancing (Zero-Balancing) Cash Pool*

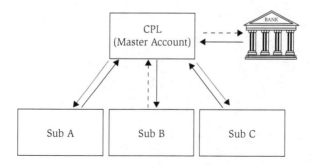

*Figure 10.4   Graphic Example of Notional ('Interest Compensation') Cash Pool*

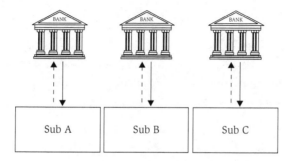

## 1.2   Types of Financing Entities

Financial transactions can be performed and organized in many different ways within a group of companies. One way would be by means of simple direct agreements between the different group entities that are involved. In this case, a transaction-by-transaction approach[20] might be ideal, and the focus of the analysis would be limited to the specific transaction already in place (Figure 10.5).

---

20. Paragraph 3.9, 2017 OECD Guidelines.

*Figure 10.5   Graphic Example of Intra-group Financial Transactions
Organized by Means of Simple Direct Agreements*

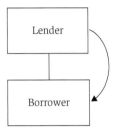

Another way would be by centralization of the financial transactions in a single entity
of the group (e.g., having a treasury department or being a specialized treasury entity)
that centralizes some or all of the following activities (Figure 10.6):[21]

– Cash and liquidity management with or without operating a cash pooling
  arrangement.
– Management of foreign exchange risk and interest rate risk.
– Management of all incoming and outgoing payments, i.e., a payment factory.

*Figure 10.6   Graphic Example of Centralization of Intra-group Financial
Transactions*

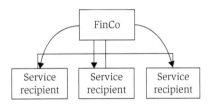

Therefore, it would be relevant to assess the functional profile of the treasury
department/entity by using the analysis of functions performed, assets used, and risks
assumed which could ultimately lead to the two following primary categories of
treasury departments/entities:[22]

– *Treasury departments/entities operating as service centres*: the treasury
  departments/entities operate as service providers, assist group companies
  with routine services, and arrange transactions on their behalf but do not
  assume any risk of capital.

21. Russo, A. & Moerer, O., 'Introduction' in: Bakker, A. & Levey, M.M. (eds), *Transfer Pricing and
Intra-Group Financing* (The Netherlands: IBFD, 2012), p. 10.
22. *Ibid.*, p. 9.

– *Treasury departments/entities operating as profit centres*: the treasury departments/entities operate as in-house banks, maximize the profits of their own operations, and assume the risk of capital.

Also, the definition of the way that the specific financial transactions that are in place are carried out will provide an initial indication of the most appropriate method to be used to assess the arm's length nature of the transactions in order to appropriately compensate the entity. Indeed, treasury departments/entities operating as service centres are typically remunerated by applying the CUP method, the cost plus method, or the TNMM based on cost.[23] Treasury departments/entities operating as profit centres, instead, are typically remunerated based on a transaction-by-transaction approach, allocating the entire credit risk of the transaction to the department/entity. Consequently, the 'spread' between costs of funding and return on cash invested will be fully allocated to that treasury department/entity.[24] Moreover, topics related to the 'substance' of these centralized activities need to be carefully reviewed.[25]

## 2 THE ASSESSMENT OF THE ARM'S LENGTH NATURE OF INTRA-GROUP FINANCIAL TRANSACTIONS

The assessment of the arm's length nature of an intra-group financial transaction requires that the terms and conditions of the financial transaction between the related parties ('tested transaction') are similar to those that would have been entered into by independent parties. This would imply the performance of the following four-step analysis:[26]

- Step 1: Identification of the commercial or financial relations
- Step 2: Recognition of the accurately delineated transaction undertaken
- Step 3: Selection of the most appropriate transfer pricing method
- Step 4: Application of the most appropriate transfer pricing method

This section will describe the application of this four-step analysis to the specific cases of loans, financial guarantees, and cash pooling.

The Steps 1 and 2 will ultimately provide an answer on whether any compensation for the tested transaction can be chargeable/deductible while Steps 3 and 4 will aim at assessing the arm's length amount of any compensation for the tested transaction.

The question of whether any compensation for the intra-group financial transactions could be charged is relevant. Indeed, without the assessment of this question, an entity could feasibly deduct expenses that would not have incurred at arm's length.

---

23. *Ibid.*
24. *Ibid.*
25. *Ibid.*
26. *See* Ch. 1.

Therefore, the risk of corporate tax base erosion in the country of the entity receiving the services from the intra-group financial transaction would radically increase.

---

**Example**

Company A, a resident in Country X, and Company B, a resident in Country Y, belong to the Group ABC. Country X's and Country Y's nominal tax rates are 50% and 5%, respectively. Although Company A does not need any new financial resource, the Group ABC decides (e.g., by changing the capital structure or cashing out free reserves with dividend distributions) that Company B should finance this by providing an intra-group loan to Company A. In this way, Company A will be able to deduct the related interest expenses at the nominal tax rate of 50% while Company B will be taxed on the related interest income at the nominal tax rate of 5%.

---

However, the incorrect assessment of the chargeability of an intra-group financial transaction (whereby either an intra-group financial transaction that should be chargeable is ascertained to not be chargeable or an intra-group financial transaction that should not be chargeable is determined to be chargeable) could increase the risk of double taxation or of less-than-single taxation in the country of the entity receiving the services from the intra-group financial transaction.

---

**Example**

Company A, a resident in Country X, and Company B, a resident in Country Y, belong to the Group ABC. Company B has provided an intra-group loan to Company A. This intra-group loan should be chargeable. However, Country X's tax administration incorrectly ascertains that the intra-group loan should not be chargeable. As a result, Company A will not be able to deduct the interest expenses related to it while, at the same time, Company B will be taxed on the interest income received from it. Ultimately, economic double taxation will arise.

**Example**

Company A, a resident in Country X, and Company B, a resident in Country Y, belong to the Group ABC. Company B has provided an intra-group loan to Company A. This intra-group loan should not be chargeable. However, Country X's tax administration incorrectly ascertains that it should be chargeable. As a result, Company A will be able to deduct the interest expenses related to it while, at the same time, Company B might be able to avoid taxation on the interest income received from it by proving to Country Y's tax administration that the intra-group loan should not be chargeable. Ultimately, less-than-single taxation will arise.

---

In order to provide guidance on this relevant topic, both the OECD Guidelines and the UN Manual have included some terminology. Under both documents, in general, the arm's length nature of a transaction should be assessed by referencing the 'transaction actually undertaken by the associated enterprises as it has been structured by them'.[27] However, in some 'exceptional circumstances', tax administrations may adjust the structure of an intra-group transaction and the conditions agreed upon by the related parties.

Regarding this, the 2010 OECD Guidelines and the 2013 UN Manual identified the following two situations:[28]

– When the economic substance of the transaction differs from its form.
– When arrangements between the related parties involved in the transaction differ from those that would have been made between commercially rational independent enterprises, and the actual structure of the transaction hinders tax administrations from determining an appropriate transfer price.

The 2017 OECD Guidelines and the 2017 UN Manual have slightly amended this guidance by deleting the first of the two above-mentioned circumstances.[29] However, the 2017 OECD Guidelines and the 2017 UN Manual also limit the scope of application of these adjustments to 'exceptional circumstances'.[30]

Furthermore, these conditions are translated into the assessment of the 'benefit test' and of the 'willing to pay/perform for itself test' in the specific case of intra-group services.[31]

Therefore, in order to answer the question of whether any compensation for the intra-group financial transactions could be charged, it would be necessary to assess whether or not the transaction has commercial rationality considering the above-mentioned tests.

**The chargeability of intra-group financial transactions: between transfer pricing considerations and other rules limiting the deductibility of interest expenses**

The chargeability of compensation out of intra-group financial transactions may be influenced not only by transfer pricing rules but also by many other rules limiting the deductibility of interest expenses (including general or specific anti-tax-avoidance rules). Based on the current practices applied by many countries around the world, these rules might be categorized into the following ones:[32]

---

27. Paragraph 1.64, 2010 OECD Guidelines; para. 5.4.9.1, 2013 UN Manual.
28. *Ibid.*
29. Paragraph 1.122, 2017 OECD Guidelines.
30. Paragraph 1.65, 2017 OECD Guidelines.
31. *See* Ch. 9.
32. OECD, *Limiting Base Erosion Involving Interest Deductions and Other Financial Payments, Action 4 2015 Final Report*, OECD/G20 Base Erosion and Profit Shifting Project (Paris: OECD Publishing, 2015), p. 19.

- Arm's length tests that compare the level of interest or debt in an entity with the position that would have existed had the entity been dealing entirely with third parties.
- Withholding tax on interest payments that are used to allocate taxing rights to a source jurisdiction.
- Rules which disallow a specified percentage of the interest expense of an entity irrespective of the nature of the payment or to whom it is made.
- Rules which limit the level of interest expense or debt in an entity with reference to a fixed ratio such as debt/equity, interest/earnings, or interest/total assets.
- Rules which limit the level of interest expense or debt in an entity with reference to the group's overall position.
- Targeted anti-avoidance rules which disallow interest expense on specific transactions (e.g., in debt –push-down situations or if the lender is in a low-tax situation).

Therefore, when analysing the question of whether any compensation for the intra-group financial transactions could be charged, it should also be considered how this question interplays with the above-mentioned rules, both on a domestic and on an international level.[33]

**Example**

Company A, a resident in Country X, and Company B, a resident in Country Y, belong to the Group ABC. Country X's and Country Y's nominal tax rates are 35% and 15%, respectively. Both Company A and Company B have operating profits (before tax) of EUR 20 million. Company B requires new financial resources for EUR 100 million.

If Company B receives the needed EUR 100 million directly from a third-party bank at an interest rate of 10%, the P&L statement of the two companies will look as follows:

| Company B | EUR million |
|---|---|
| Operating Profits | 20 |
| - Interest Expenses | (10) |
| Pre-tax Profits | 10 |
| - CIT (15%) | (1.5) |
| After-tax Profits | 8.5 |

---

33. *See*, for example, paragraphs B.1.7.8 and C.1.2.2.2, 2017 UN Manual.

| Company A | EUR million |
|---|---|
| Operating Profits | 20 |
| - Interest Expenses | - |
| Pre-tax Profits | 20 |
| - CIT (35%) | (7) |
| After-tax Profits | 13 |

Therefore, the total of Group ABC's after-tax profits will be EUR 21.5 million. In order to optimize its tax structure, Group ABC could decide that Company A should obtain the financing from the third-party bank and should provide it in the form of an equity contribution to Company B. In this case, the P&L statement of the two companies will look as follows:

| Company B | EUR million |
|---|---|
| Operating Profits | 20 |
| - Interest Expenses | - |
| Pre-tax Profits | 20 |
| - CIT (15%) | (3) |
| After-tax Profits | 17 |

| Company A | EUR million |
|---|---|
| Operating Profits | 20 |
| - Interest Expenses | (10) |
| Pre-tax Profits | 10 |
| - CIT (35%) | (3,5) |
| After-tax Profits | 6.5 |

In this case, the total of Group ABC's after-tax profits will be EUR 23.5 million. In order to reduce the impact of this tax planning structure, Country X introduces a rule in its tax legislation whereby interest expenses are deductible from a company's income taxes only up to 30% of its EBITDA. In this case, the P&L statement of the two companies will look as follows:

| Company B | EUR million |
|---|---|
| Operating Profits | 20 |
| - Interest Expenses | - |
| Pre-tax Profits | 20 |
| - CIT (15%) | (3) |
| After-tax Profits | 17 |

| Company A | EUR million |
|---|---|
| Operating Profits | 20 |
| - Interest Expenses | (10) |
| Pre-tax Profits (before fixed ratio rule) | 10 |
| + Interest Expenses | 10 |
| Tax-EBITDA | 20 |
| Max deduction interest expenses (30% EBITDA) | 6 |
| Non-deductible interest expenses | 4 |
| Pre-tax Profits (after fixed ratio rule) | 14 |
| CIT (35%) | (4,9) |
| After-tax Profits | 5,1 |

In this case, the total of Group ABC's after-tax profits will be EUR 22.1 million.

Once the question of whether any compensation for the intra-group financial transactions could be charged has been addressed and answered in a positive way by performing the first two steps indicated above, the arm's length amount of such compensation should be defined by performing Steps 3 and 4. To do so, both the perspective of the service provider and that of the recipient of the service should be taken into account.[34]

---

34. Paragraph 7.29, 2017 OECD Guidelines.

In general, there are two methods that are most commonly used to determine the arm's length amount of the compensation for intra-group financial transactions: the CUP method and the cost plus method (cost plus method or cost-based TNMM).[35] The first could be employed when comparable services provided between independent parties exist either in the market of the provider or that of the recipient (e.g., in cases of intra-group loans and intra-group financial guarantees). The cost plus method can be utilized instead when the CUP method is not appropriate (e.g., when comparables are missing) and, most probably, when one entity of the group (e.g., the parent company or the financing company) is acting as a general service provider or intermediary for other entities in the group[36] (e.g., in cases of direct on-lending). If a financing or treasury company, however, provides financing to group members and refinances these with deposits from other group members or external sources and has, therefore, a mismatch in timing and/or currencies as well as exposure in creditworthiness, the cost-plus method might not be appropriate.[37]

Moreover, another method that could be used in some cases (e.g., in cases of intra-group cash pooling) is the transactional profit split method. However, the use of this method in cases of intra-group cash pooling is not always preferred since the benefits of the pooling could also be indirectly shared among the cash pooling members with adjusted market interest rates.

---

**Safe harbours and definition of the arm's length compensation for intra-group financial transactions**

In order to simplify the definition of the arm's length amount of compensation for intra-group financial transactions, a number of countries have been introducing safe harbours, most of which concern interest rates.[38] More specifically, some countries annually issue some interest rates that, if applied to the intra-group loans, extinguish the obligation for the taxpayer to prove the nature of those transactions.

When defining the arm's length amount of a compensation for an intra-group financial transaction, the analysis of any existing safe harbour should be carefully considered. However, it should also be reviewed how the safe harbour interplays with the definition and application of the arm's length principle both on a domestic and on an international level.

---

35. Paragraph 7.31, 2017 OECD Guidelines.
36. Paragraph 7.36, 2017 OECD Guidelines.
37. Storck, A., Holzinger, R., 'Zinsbemessung bei Darlehen im Konzernverbund', Transfer Pricing International (2017), pp. 216–223.
38. *See* Ch. 2.

## 2.1 The Identification of the Commercial or Financial Relations

### 2.1.1 Intra-group Loans

As mentioned before, the first step of the analysis would be the identification of the commercial or financial relationships between the associated enterprises by analyzing the economically relevant characteristics (or comparability factors) of a transaction in order to accurately delineate the actual transaction undertaken. In the specific case of intra-group loans, it would be necessary to analyse the following economically relevant characteristics (or comparability factors):

- The contractual terms of the tested loan (e.g., type of loan, tenure – i.e., time to maturity – of the loan, type of interest rate,[39] currency used, embedded options,[40] seniority, collateral, and guarantees).[41]
- The functions performed, assets used, and risks assumed by both the tested borrower and the tested lender.[42]
- The characteristics of tested loan.[43]
- The economic circumstances of both the tested borrower and the tested lender and of the market in which they operate.[44]
- The business strategies pursued by the tested borrower and tested lender.[45]

---

**Court case**

In the Australian Chevron case,[46] the Australian Federal Court of Appeals concluded that Article 9 allows adjusting not only the price of an intra-group loan (i.e., the interest rate) but also the terms and conditions of the loan. Therefore, a broader range of conditions (e.g., security, covenants) should be considered when concluding on the arm's length nature of an intra-group loan.

---

### 2.1.2 Intra-group Financial Guarantees

In the specific case of intra-group financial guarantees, it would be necessary to analyse the following economically relevant characteristics (or comparability factors) in order to identify the commercial or financial relationships:

---

39. For example, fixed, floating, etc.
40. For example, option for the borrower to repay the loan before maturity, option for the lender to collect the principal before maturity, option to convert the loan into equity, etc.
41. Paragraphs 1.42–1.50, 2017 OECD Guidelines.
42. Paragraphs 1.51–1.106, 2017 OECD Guidelines.
43. Paragraphs 1.107–1.109, 2017 OECD Guidelines.
44. Paragraphs 1.110–1.113, 2017 OECD Guidelines.
45. Paragraphs 1.114–1.118, 2017 OECD Guidelines.
46. Australian Federal Court of Appeal, 23 Oct. 2015, *Chevron Australia Holdings Pty Ltd v Commissioner of Taxation*, [2015] FCA 1092.

- The contractual terms of the tested financial guarantee (including terms and conditions of the guaranteed instrument).[47]
- The functions performed, assets used, and risks assumed by both the tested guarantor and the tested guaranteed entity (including any available external credit rating of the tested parties and of the guaranteed instrument as well as the probability of default of the tested guaranteed entity).[48]
- The characteristics of tested financial guarantee (including benefits provided by the tested financial guarantee).[49]
- The economic circumstances of both the tested guarantor and the tested guaranteed entity and of the market in which they operate.[50]
- The business strategies pursued by the tested guarantor and tested guaranteed entity.[51]

### 2.1.3 Intra-group Cash Pooling

In the specific case of intra-group cash pooling, it would be necessary to analyse the following economically relevant characteristics (or comparability factors) in order to perform an accurate delineation of the actual transaction undertaken:

- The contractual terms of the intra-group cash pooling.[52]
- The functions performed, assets used, and risks assumed by all of the participants to the intra-group cash pooling.[53]
- The characteristics of the intra-group cash pooling.[54]
- The economic circumstances of all of the participants to the intra-group cash pooling and of the market in which they operate.[55]
- The business strategies pursued by all of the participants to the intra-group cash pooling.[56]

This will ultimately lead to the assessment of the following points:[57]

- The arm's length amount of debit and credit interest rates.
- The arm's length remuneration for the cash pool leader.

---

47. Paragraphs 1.42–1.50, 2017 OECD Guidelines.
48. Paragraphs 1.51–1.106, 2017 OECD Guidelines.
49. Paragraphs 1.107–1.109, 2017 OECD Guidelines.
50. Paragraphs 1.110–1.113, 2017 OECD Guidelines.
51. Paragraphs 1.114–1.118, 2017 OECD Guidelines.
52. Paragraphs 1.42–1.50, 2017 OECD Guidelines.
53. Paragraphs 1.51–1.106, 2017 OECD Guidelines.
54. Paragraphs 1.107–1.109, 2017 OECD Guidelines.
55. Paragraphs 1.110–1.113, 2017 OECD Guidelines.
56. Paragraphs 1.114–1.118, 2017 OECD Guidelines.
57. Further additional aspects (e.g., all relevant aspects related to any intra-group financial guarantee provided within the cash pool participants) may need to be addressed.

- The arm's length allocation of the cash pool advantages among the cash pool participants.

## 2.2 The Recognition of the Accurately Delineated Transaction Undertaken

### 2.2.1 Intra-group Loans

The second step of the analysis would be the recognition of the accurately delineated transaction undertaken. In the specific case of intra-group loans, it would be necessary to analyse whether the intra-group loan has commercial rationality by addressing the following two fundamental questions:[58]

- Could the tested borrower obtain a similar loan from an independent entity?
- If yes, would the tested borrower request a similar loan?

---

**Example**

Company A, a resident in Country X, and Company B, a resident in Country Y, belong to the Group ABC. Company B has provided an intra-group loan to Company A. In order to assess whether the intra-group loan has commercial rationality, it should be assessed whether:
- An independent lender (e.g., an independent commercial bank) would grant a similar loan to Company A under similar circumstances.
- Company A, if it was an independent entity, would enter into a financial transaction similar to the tested loan and, if so, if it would enter into a similar financial transaction (i.e., a loan) or into another type of financial transaction.

---

Moreover, all terms and conditions established in the tested loan should reflect the accurately delineated transaction undertaken, i.e., terms and conditions should be at arm's length.

The answer to these questions would require a qualitative and quantitative analysis of the tested borrower's characteristics on a stand-alone basis. Therefore, direct considerations on debt market conditions from the perspective of the tested lender and considerations regarding the resulting arm's length nature of the capital structure of the tested borrower along with the more traditional debt servicing analysis should be performed.[59] These considerations should take into account the business/

---

58. Russo, A. & Moerer, O., 'Introduction' in: Bakker, A. & Levey, M.M. (eds), *Transfer Pricing and Intra-Group Financing* (the Netherlands: IBFD, 2012), p. 15.
59. Van der Breggen, M., 'Loans and Cash Pooling' in *Global Transfer Pricing Course (Advanced Topics)* (Vienna: WU, 21 Sep. –25 Sep. 2015).

businesses of the borrower, the industry/industries in which the borrower operates, the operational risk of the borrower, the financial situation of the borrower, and other relevant factors.[60]

---

**Credit risk and implicit support**

One of the most relevant and currently debated issues when dealing with transfer pricing aspects of financial transactions is the definition of the credit risk (or creditworthiness) of the borrower. The credit risk is the possibility of incurring a loss due to a counterparty's failure to fulfil a contractual obligation (i.e., credit default risk) or from credit deterioration (i.e., credit spread risk) and depends on default risk (or probability of default), credit spread risk, and downgrade risk. The higher the credit risk, the more burdensome and expensive it is to receive a service out of a financial transaction.

The credit risk is generally measured, in practice, by assigning a rating (i.e., credit rating) to the borrower that expresses its probability of default. The credit rating is established based on a qualitative and quantitative analysis of the borrower. Moreover, specialized rating agencies summarize it in a credit rating (opinion) to be used in capital markets (as illustrated by Table 10.1).[61]

*Table 10.1   Categories of Long-Term Credit Rating Used by Moody's, S&P, and Fitch[62]*

| Moody's | S&P | Fitch | Interpretations |
|---------|-----|-------|-----------------|
| *Investment Grade Ratings* | | | |
| Aaa | AAA | AAA | *Highest quality; extremely strong, highly unlikely to be affected by foreseeable events.* |
| Aa1 | AA + | AA + | *Very high quality; capacity for repayment is not significantly vulnerable to foreseeable events.* |
| Aa2 | AA | AA | |
| Aa3 | AA- | AA- | |
| A1 | A + | A + | *Strong payment capacity; more likely to be affected by changes in economic circumstances.* |

---

60. Russo, A. & Moerer, O., 'Introduction' in: Bakker, A. & Levey, M.M. (eds), *Transfer Pricing and Intra-Group Financing* (the Netherlands: IBFD, 2012), p. 16.
61. Banks typically apply their own ratings.
62. Sourced from Petruzzi, R., Transfer Pricing Aspects of Intra-Group Financing (Amsterdam: Wolters Kluwer, 2016), p. 165.

| Moody's | S&P | Fitch | Interpretations |
|---|---|---|---|
| | | | Investment Grade Ratings |
| A2 | A | A | Adequate payment capacity; a negative change in environment may affect capacity for repayment. |
| A3 | A- | A- | |
| Baa1 | BBB + | BBB + | |
| Baa2 | BBB | BBB | |
| Baa3 | BBB- | BBB- | |
| | | | Below Investment Grade Ratings |
| Ba1 | BB + | BB + | Considered speculative with possibility of developing credit risks. |
| Ba2 | BB | BB | |
| Ba3 | BB- | BB- | Considered very speculative with significant credit risk. |
| B1 | B + | B + | |
| B2 | B | B | |
| B3 | B- | B- | |
| Caa1 | CCC + | CCC | Considered highly speculative with substantial credit risk. |
| Caa2 | CCC | | |
| Caa3 | CCC- | | |
| Ca | CC | | May be in default or wildly speculative. |
| | C | | In bankruptcy or default. |
| C | D | DDD | |

Nevertheless, credit rating opinions are usually issued upon request only for the parent company of the group. Therefore, in order to assess the stand-alone credit rating of a group internal borrower in relationship to the tested loan, other instruments can be used in practice including the Z-score analysis,[63] the econometric credit score models licensed by rating agencies, or information in publicly available databases.

The assessment of the arm's length nature of the tested loan would require that the borrower be considered as an independent entity and the credit risk to be determined consistently with this principle. When establishing the credit risk of the borrower, some important questions should initially be answered.

The first of these questions is whether the credit risk of the borrower should be established considering its economic and financial characteristics before the tested loan is received or considering how the situation would be afterwards.

---

63. The Z-score formula for predicting bankruptcy was published in 1968 by Edward I. Altman. The Z-score uses multiple corporate income and balance sheet values to measure the financial health of a company and to predict corporate defaults.

Some authors[64] have emphasized the need to envisage the situation that would be in place after the new financing transaction.[65]

The second question, and probably the most currently debated, is whether the credit risk of the borrower should be assessed on a stand-alone basis (referred to as the 'stand-alone credit risk') or considering that the borrower belongs to a group (known as the 'group credit risk') and taking into account, therefore, any 'implicit support' from the group in which the borrower belongs (also referred to as 'passive association', 'parent support', or 'group support'). Figure 10.7 illustrates this concept.

*Figure 10.7    Illustration of the Impact of Implicit Support*

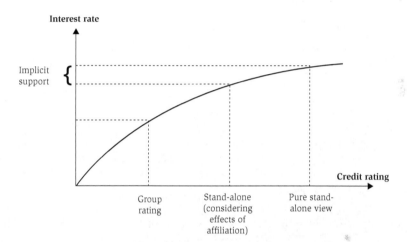

Based on paragraph 1.6 OECD Guidelines,[66] when applying the arm's length principle, the related parties involved in the tested transaction should be treated as if they were separate entities. However, paragraph 7.12 OECD Guidelines[67] suggests that any incidental benefits deriving from the circumstance that the related entities belong to a group should be considered. Hence, these two paragraphs create some uncertainty about whether the application of the arm's length principle should be assessed on a stand-alone basis or by considering the impact of any implicit support.

In other words, when assessing the credit risk of the borrower, it should initially be assessed whether the circumstances that the borrower belongs to a group

---

64. Russo, A. & Moerer, O., 'Introduction' in: Bakker, A. & Levey, M.M. (eds), *Transfer Pricing and Intra-Group Financing* (the Netherlands: IBFD, 2012), p. 19.
65. This would be the usual approach undertaken by banks.
66. Paragraph 1.6, 2017 OECD Guidelines.
67. Paragraph 7.12, 2017 OECD Guidelines.

(having, most probably, an overall higher credit rating than the borrower's 'stand-alone' rating) and that, reasonably, the parent company of such a group will support its affiliates (and, especially, its core affiliates) in their financial needs (referred to as 'stewardship by the parent company') should be considered as relevant elements when assessing the rating of the borrower and whether these circumstances should incite a higher stand-alone credit rating to be assessed for the borrower. The answer to this question will, indeed, significantly influence the analysis of the arm's length conditions of the overall transaction. In order to answer these questions, it might be relevant to consider the following elements:

- Would implicit support be taken into account by independent institutions (e.g., independent credit agencies or independent commercial banks) when assessing the credit risk of the borrower?
- If yes, how would the implicit support be quantified?

The OECD Guidelines appear to partially answer these questions when addressing the impact of 'incidental benefits' or 'passive associations' over the determination of guarantee fees[68] as well as in the context of the valuation of 'group synergies'[69]

Therefore, it appears that the OECD supports the position of considering the implicit support when establishing the credit risk of the borrower but only as far as it derives 'by reason of its affiliation alone'.[70] Nevertheless, the quantification of this implicit support still remains an open issue.

In practice, the following approaches may be used when establishing the credit risk of the tested borrower:

- Use the parent's credit risk;
- Beginning with the parent's credit risk, notch down[71] this credit risk in order to approximate the borrower's credit risk;
- Derive the borrower's credit risk with an analysis of the financial ratios with up notching to consider the implicit support, when needed;
- Use credit scoring tools with up notching to consider the implicit support when needed.

The first method is typically used in so-called 'central entrepreneur' (principal) structures, however, may not create arm's length solutions in other situations (e.g., with other business models). The last method is currently recognised as the best practice for defining the credit risk of the tested borrower. Figure 10.8 shows an example of the application of credit scoring tools.

---

68. Paragraph 7.13, 2017 OECD Guidelines.
69. Paragraphs 1.164–1.167, 2017 OECD Guidelines.
70. Paragraph 7.12, 2017 OECD Guidelines.
71. In some (rare) situations, parent's credit risk could be notched up.

*Figure 10.8    Example of the Application of a Credit Scoring Tool[72]*

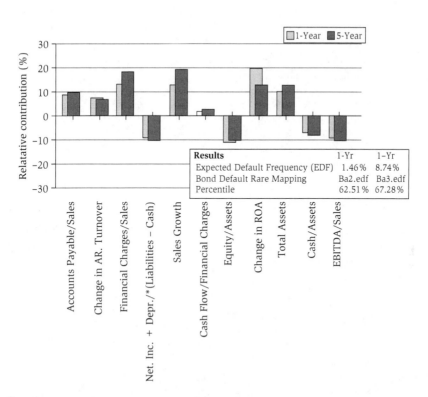

| Results | 1-Yr | 1-Yr |
|---|---|---|
| Expected Default Frequency (EDF) | 1.46% | 8.74% |
| Bond Default Rare Mapping | Ba2.edf | Ba3.edf |
| Percentile | 62.51% | 67.28% |

## Court case

In the Canadian General Electric Capital case,[73] the Canadian Federal Court of Appeal concluded that implicit support is a significant factor to be taken into account when estimating the value of an arm's length compensation of guarantee fees; however, such implicit support was not regarded as strong enough to determine the creditworthiness of the subsidiary at the same level of its parent company. Therefore, the relevant credit rating to be assigned to the subsidiary was defined as that between the credit rating of the parent company (i.e., AAA) and the stand-alone credit rating of the subsidiary (i.e., B + /BB-), i.e. BBB-/ BB + .

Therefore, guarantee fees should compensate for the difference between the creditworthiness of the subsidiary (taking into account the implicit support) and the creditworthiness of the parent company.

72. Example of RiskCalc® Model, sourced from Petruzzi, R., Transfer Pricing Aspects of Intra-Group Financing (Amsterdam: Wolters Kluwer, 2016), p. 178.
73. Canadian Federal Court of Appeal, 15 Dec. 2010, case 2010 FCA 344, *General Electric Capital Canada Inc. v Her Majesty the Queen.*

### 2.2.2 Intra-group Financial Guarantees

In the specific case of intra-group financial guarantees, it would be necessary to analyse whether the intra-group financial guarantee has commercial rationality in order to recognize the accurately delineated transaction undertaken by addressing the following two fundamental questions:[74]

- Could the tested guaranteed entity obtain a similar financial guarantee from an independent entity?
- If yes, would the tested guaranteed entity request a similar financial guarantee?

---

**Example**

Company A, a resident in Country X, and Company B, a resident in Country Y, belong to the Group ABC. Company B has provided an intra-group financial guarantee to Company A. In order to assess whether the intra-group financial guarantee has commercial rationality, it should be assessed whether:

- An independent entity (e.g., an independent insurance company) would provide a similar financial guarantee to Company A under similar circumstances.
- Company A, if it was an independent entity, would enter into a financial transaction similar to the tested financial guarantee and, if so, if it would enter into a similar financial transaction (i.e., a financial guarantee) or into another type of financial transaction.

---

Moreover, all of the terms and conditions established in the tested financial guarantee should reflect the accurately delineated transaction that has been undertaken, i.e., terms and conditions should be at arm's length.

The answers to the questions above would require an assessment of the underlying reason for the financial guarantee and the benefit created by it,[75] typically implying an analysis of the form of the financial guarantee, the purpose of the financial guarantee, the willingness of the guarantor to provide support to the guaranteed entity, and the request by the third party to provide the financial guarantee.[76]

Generally speaking, an intra-group financial guarantee will have commercial rationality if:[77]

---

74. Russo, A. & Moerer, O., 'Introduction' in: Bakker, A. & Levey, M.M. (eds), *Transfer Pricing and Intra-Group Financing* (the Netherlands: IBFD, 2012), p. 15.
75. PwC, *Navigating the Complexity: Findings from the Financial Transactions Transfer Pricing Global Survey 2013* (PwC, 2013), p. 21.
76. Lukosz, K. & Meijer, T., 'Guarantees' in *Transfer Pricing and Intra-Group Financing* (The Netherlands: IBFD, 29 Jun. –1 Jul. 2014).
77. Lukosz, K. & Meijer, T., 'Guarantees' in IBFD, *Transfer Pricing and Intra-Group Financing* (the Netherlands: IBFD, 29 Jun. –1 Jul. 2014).

- The intra-group financial guarantee provides direct and identifiable economic and/or commercial benefits to the guaranteed entity.
- An independent party would be willing to pay for the intra-group financial guarantee.
- The guaranteed entity achieves a better creditworthiness because of the intra-group financial guarantee.

---

**Example**

Company A, a resident in Country X, and Company B, a resident in Country Y, belong to the Group ABC. Company A has a credit rating of BBB while Company B has a credit rating of AAA. Company A has requested a loan from a third party bank. Company B has provided an intra-group financial guarantee to Company A that covers any risk of Company A's insolvency towards a third party bank. The arm's length interest rate for a similar loan provided to a BBB rated entity is 5 %. However, the third party bank charges Company A with an interest rate of 2 %. In this case, the better interest rate obtained by Company A has been achieved because of the intra-group financial guarantee provided by Company B which has enhanced the credit standing of the loan. Therefore, the intra-group financial guarantee should have commercial rationality.

---

On the contrary, an intra-group financial guarantee will not be chargeable if:[78]

- The guaranteed entity achieves better creditworthiness only because of its group affiliation (so-called 'implicit support').[79]
- When the debtor has no debt capacity or credit status and, therefore, would not be able to access the capital market without the financial guarantee.
- The financial guarantee has been requested by the creditor in order to avoid that the parent company diverts the funds of the financed company, i.e., moral hazard issues.

---

**Example**

Company A, a resident in Country X, and Company B, a resident in Country Y, belong to the Group ABC. Company A has a credit rating of CCC while Company B has a credit rating of AAA. Company A has requested a loan from a third party bank. Company B has provided an intra-group financial guarantee to Company A that covers any risk of Company A's insolvency towards the third

---

78. Russo, A. & Moerer, O., 'Introduction' in: Bakker, A. & Levey, M.M. (eds), *Transfer Pricing and Intra-Group Financing* (the Netherlands: IBFD, 2012), p. 33; Ryan, E.D., Erivona, C.E. & Chamberlain, D.G., 'A Transfer Pricing Framework for Loan Guarantee Fees', *BNA Tax Management Transfer Pricing Report* 11 (2003), p. 850.
79. Paragraphs 7.13 and 1.164–1.167, 2017 OECD Guidelines.

party bank. In this case, the credit rating of Company A is very low; hence, without the intra-group financial guarantee provided by Company B, the third party bank will not provide any loan to Company A. In this case, an intra-group financial guarantee is perceived as an equity contribution from Company B to Company A. Therefore, the intra-group financial guarantee might not have commercial rationality.

### 2.2.3 Intra-group Cash Pooling

In the specific case of intra-group cash pooling, in order to recognize the accurately delineated transaction undertaken, it would be necessary to analyse whether the intra-group cash pooling has commercial rationality by addressing similar questions that were analysed in the previous sections.[80] Indeed, the withdrawals and deposits in cash pooling can be perceived as short-term intra-group loans including an embedded put option for the participants providing them 'the right to reclaim the funds at any point in time from the cash pool leader'.[81]

### 2.3 The Selection and Application of the Most Appropriate Transfer Pricing Method

#### 2.3.1 Intra-group Loans

As previously mentioned, the third and fourth steps of the analysis would be the selection and application of the most appropriate transfer pricing method. As the main compensation generated by intra-group loans is the interest payments, the arm's length amount of such payments should be defined. This would typically imply considerations on the interest rate that unrelated entities have agreed upon (or would agree upon) for similar transactions (i.e., the tested loan) in similar circumstances.

In this context, the CUP method will often be applied: interest rates that are negotiated and agreed upon by independent entities comparable to the tested parties for loans having terms and conditions equivalent to the tested loan should be considered as relevant. The CUP method could be applied in the following ways:

- *Internal CUP method*: research of interest rates applied to similar transactions in similar circumstances between one of the tested parties and an unrelated entity.
- *External CUP method*: research of interest rates applied to similar transactions in similar circumstances between unrelated entities.

---

80. *See* ss 2.2.1 and 2.2.2 (in case intra-group financial guarantees are provided), above.
81. Russo, A. & Moerer, O., 'Introduction' in: Bakker, A. & Levey, M.M. (eds), *Transfer Pricing and Intra-Group Financing* (the Netherlands: IBFD, 2012), p. 42.

- *Hypothetic CUP method*: research of interest rates that would have been applied to similar transactions in similar circumstances between one of the tested parties and an unrelated entity.

When applying the CUP method, the information deriving from third party (syndicated) loans, price quotes,[82] and other information contained in publicly available databases[83] may be beneficial. In this context, a method that could be employed is the building-up approach: research of spreads applied to fixed income securities (e.g., corporate bonds) that display characteristics similar to the tested loan and are issued by entities similar to the tested borrower in similar circumstances based on information contained in publicly available databases; these spreads will subsequently be added to a currency related risk-free interest rate in order to determine the final interest rates that could be considered at arm's length.

When applying the CUP method, it will be essential to verify that all of the economically relevant characteristics (or comparability factors) illustrated before[84] are taken into account; hence, the resulting interest rate might also need to be adapted by means of comparability adjustments in order to reflect such factors. Table 10.2 illustrates the impact on interest rates of certain specific characteristics of a loan.

*Table 10.2   Impact on Interest Rates of Specific Characteristics of a Loan*[85]

| Characteristics of Loan | Effect on the Interest Rate | |
|---|---|---|
| | Increase | Decrease |
| Conversion | Non-convertible | Convertible |
| Currency | High currency risk | Low currency risk |
| Guarantees | Un-guaranteed | Guaranteed |
| Interest payment | On maturity | Regularly (e.g. monthly) |
| Options | Pre-payment | Call |
| Repayment | Bullet | Capital and interest |
| Security | Unsecured | Secured |
| Seniority | Mezzanine | Senior |
| Terms | Long term | Short term |

---

82. These quotes, however, may not be accepted as the primary method in certain jurisdictions; nevertheless, they could still be used as a corroborative method.
83. For example, Thomson Reuters LoanConnector™, Bloomberg Professional®, or information contained in the websites of market stock exchange.
84. *See* section 2.1.1, above.
85. This classification is sourced from Van der Breggen, M., 'Netherlands' in: Bakker, A., Levey, M.M. (eds), *Transfer Pricing and Intra-Group Financing* (The Netherlands: IBFD, 2012), p. 428; Van der Breggen, M., 'Loans and Cash Pooling' in *Global Transfer Pricing Course (Advanced Topics)* (Vienna: WU, 21 Sep. –25 Sep. 2015).

Apart from the CUP method, as mentioned before, the cost plus method (cost plus method or cost-based TNMM) could be applied in some cases (e.g., in cases of on-lending whereby an entity of a group obtains financing from an unrelated entity and provides the resources obtained to a related entity).[86]

### 2.3.2 Intra-group Financial Guarantees

The main compensation generated by intra-group financial guarantees is the guarantee fees. Therefore, the arm's length amount of such fees should be defined. This would typically imply considerations on the guarantee fees that unrelated entities have agreed upon (or would agree upon) for similar transactions (i.e., the tested financial guarantee) in similar circumstances.

---

**Court cases**

In the French Soladi case[87] and Carrefour case,[88] the French courts have deemed intra-group explicit financial guarantees provided free of charge as being an 'abnormal act of management'.

---

In this context, the CUP method will often be applied: guarantee fees negotiated and agreed upon by independent entities comparable to the tested parties for financial guarantee having terms and conditions equivalent to the tested financial guarantee should be considered as relevant. The CUP method could be applied in the following ways:

- *Internal CUP method*: research of guarantee fees applied to similar transactions in similar circumstances between one of the tested parties and an unrelated entity.
- *External CUP method*: research of guarantee fees applied to similar transactions in similar circumstances between unrelated entities.
- *Hypothetic CUP method*: research of guarantee fees that would have been applied to similar transactions in similar circumstances between one of the tested parties and an unrelated entity.

When applying the CUP method, the information deriving from third-party financial guarantees, price quotes,[89] bankers' acceptances, credit default swap fees,

---

86. *See* Ch. 2.
87. French Administrative Court of Appeal of Nancy 30 Apr. 1998.
88. French Council of State, 17 Feb. 1992.
89. These quotes, however, may not be accepted as the primary method in certain jurisdictions; nevertheless, they could still be used as a corroborative method.

letter of credit fees, commitment fees, various types of insurance, and put options may be beneficial. In this context, the following methods could be employed:[90]

- *Cost-benefit analysis or yield approach*: analysis of the perspective of the guarantor and the guaranteed entity which will determine, on the one hand, the minimum granted amount that the guarantor would require for granting the tested financial guarantee (by reference to the cost-based or contingent committed capital approach) and, on the other, the maximum amount that the guaranteed entity would be willing to pay for receiving the tested financial guarantee (by reference to the difference between the interest rates, it would need to pay based on the stand-alone credit rating without the financial guarantee and the improved rates it will pay due to the financial guarantee). This analysis will provide a range of reasonable results for measuring the arm's length amount of the guarantee fees.[91]
- *Credit default swap*:[92] the value of the financial guarantee is determined as a proxy of credit default swap fees.[93]
- *Contingent put option*: the value of the price that the guaranteed entity should pay for a hypothetical right to sell the guaranteed instrument to the guarantor

---

90. Russo, A. & Moerer, O., 'Introduction' in: Bakker, A. & Levey, M.M. (eds), *Transfer Pricing and Intra-Group Financing* (The Netherlands: IBFD, 2012), p. 34; Lukosz, K., Meijer, T., 'Guarantees' in *Transfer Pricing and Intra-Group Financing* (the Netherlands: IBFD, 29 Jun. –1 Jul. 2014).
91. The application of this method, however, might prove to be difficult in the following cases:

- The creditworthiness of the guarantor and guaranteed entity are neither known nor assessable.
- The guarantor does not have a better creditworthiness than the guaranteed entity.
- The guaranteed entity would not be able to actually receive a loan without the guarantee being provided.
- The intra-group financial guarantee is provided by more than one guarantor having different levels of creditworthiness.
- Upstream financial guarantees.

92. A credit default swap (CDS) is a financial swap agreement whereby the seller of the CDS will compensate the buyer (usually the creditor of the reference loan) in the event of a loan default (by the debtor) or other credit event. That is, the seller of the CDS insures the buyer against some reference loan defaulting. The buyer of the CDS makes a series of payments (the CDS 'fee' or 'spread') to the seller and, in exchange, receives a payoff if the loan is in default.
93. Typical aspects to be assessed when applying this method will be the following:

- Type of credit derivative.
- Protection the credit default swap guarantees to the buyer and to the seller.
- Reference entity and reference debt underlying the credit default swap.
- Credit event.
- Credit default swap premium.

The application of this method, however, might prove to be difficult for the following reasons:

- A credit default swap contains a broader definition of a credit event than an intra-group financial guarantee.
- A credit default swap is commonly used for speculation purposes.
- A credit default swap is priced by techniques that are more complex.
- The seller of a credit default swap is typically a well rated and a regulated institution.

at a specified price (i.e., face value) and under certain circumstances (i.e., credit event) (otherwise stated, a put option on the guaranteed instrument) would provide the measure of the arm's length amount of the guarantee fees.[94]

- *Cost of capital*: the arm's length amount of the guarantee fees will be determined by referencing the cost of capital that the guaranteed entity will hypothetically need to pay in order to increase his equity enough to achieve the same level of creditworthiness of the guarantor.[95]
- *Financial guarantee insurance*: the value of the financial guarantee will be determined by analysing financial guarantee insurance premiums.[96]
- *Letter of credit and commitment fees*: the arm's length amount of the guarantee fees will be determined by referencing the third-party letter of credit fees and third-party commitment fees.

When applying the CUP method, it will be essential to verify that all of the economically relevant characteristics (or comparability factors) illustrated before[97] are taken into account; hence, the resulting guarantee fee might also need to be adjusted by means of comparability adjustments in order to reflect such factors.

### 2.3.3 Intra-group Cash Pooling

The primary compensation that is generated by intra-group cash pooling are the following:

- Debit and credit interest rates.
- Remuneration for the cash pool leader.
- Allocation of the cash pool advantages among the cash pool participants.

The assessment of the arm's length amount of such compensation is currently the most controversial topic.

As far as debit and credit interest rates are concerned, the definition of the arm's length amount of such interest rates would typically imply considerations on the interest rates that unrelated entities have agreed upon (or would agree upon) for similar transactions (i.e., the tested short-term loans) in similar circumstances. As

---

94. The value of a put option premium can be established by referencing the Black-Scholes Model for put option pricing and would typically depend on the following elements:

- Value of the borrower's assets.
- Amount of the debt.
- Tenure of the loan.
- Volatility of the borrower's assets.
- Discount rate.

95. To this end, the observations of the cost of equity of publicly listed companies can be beneficial.
96. This premium will typically be the remuneration for expected loss, expense loading, and return on risk capital.
97. *See* section 2.1.2, above.

previously mentioned,[98] the withdrawals and deposits in cash pooling can be perceived as being short-term intra-group loans including an embedded put option which provides participants with 'the right to reclaim the funds at any point in time from the cash pool leader'.[99] Therefore, similar questions to those that were analysed in the previous sections[100] should be considered. In this context, it should be emphasized that the assessment of the risks (typically, the credit risk, the maturity risk, and the currency risk or foreign exchange risk in cases of a multi-currency pool) related to these short-term loans should be made for all of the participants in the cash pooling agreement on a stand-alone basis.

---

**Court case**

In the Danish Bombardier case,[101] the Danish National Tax Tribunal concluded that: (a) the lack of documentation prepared by the taxpayers allows the tax administration to assess the cash pooling transactions; (b) the rate applied to withdrawals and deposits should be the same; (c) the interest rate should be applied to the net balance of the deposits at the end of the year.

---

As far as the remuneration for the cash pool leader is concerned, this will depend on the functional analysis of the cash pool leader that will result in different functional profiles, the two extremes being the following:[102]

- *In-house bank*: the cash pool leader assumes all of the functions, assets, and risks typical of a financial institution. In this case, its remuneration will most probably generate positive income (assuming that the individual's credit rating is better than that of the cash pool participants). This remuneration will consist of two elements: the remuneration of functions performed based on costs (typically using, in practice, the TNMM or the CUP method) and the remuneration of its equity at risk (typically using, in practice, the expected return on equity at risk).
- *Financial service entity*: the cash pool leader functions will be limited to administrating the incoming and outgoing cash flows within the cash pooling which will involve a limited number of assets and bear a limited amount of risks (e.g., by using financial guarantees from the parent company or cross-guarantees within the cash pool participants). Also, in this case, the

---

98. *See* section 2.1.3, above.
99. Russo, A. & Moerer, O., 'Introduction' in: Bakker, A. & Levey, M.M. (eds), *Transfer Pricing and Intra-Group Financing* (the Netherlands: IBFD, 2012), p. 42.
100. *See* sections 2.3.1 and 2.3.2 (in case intra-group financial guarantees are provided), above.
101. Danish Administrative Tax Court, 21 Oct. 2013, Case 12-0189459. *See also* Vistisen, E., 'Bombardier Case: First Published Cash Pool Decision', *International Transfer Pricing Journal* 21 (May/June 2014), pp. 189–192.
102. Russo, A. & Moerer, O., 'Introduction' in: Bakker, A. & Levey, M.M. (eds), *Transfer Pricing and Intra-Group Financing* (the Netherlands: IBFD, 2012), pp. 43–44.

remuneration of its functions, assets, and risks will be based on the two above-mentioned elements, however, the remuneration of its equity at risk will be typically less.

As far as the allocation of the cash pool advantages among the cash pool participants is concerned, these advantages[103] should be allocated to the cash pool leader and the cash pool participants based on the assessment of the origin of such advantages. In this aspect, the analysis of functions performed, assets used, and risks assumed by the cash pool leader and participants will be relevant. Consequently, if the advantages are mainly deriving from the risks assumed by the cash pool leader, then a greater portion of these advantages should be allocated to this entity; the same argument, however, can be used with regard to any participant in the cash pool having liquidity and, therefore, deposits in the cash pooling; if, instead, the advantages are mainly deriving from economies of scales, then these advantages should be predominantly allocated to the cash pool participants. In practice, the pool advantages are 'shared' by applying enhanced market rates for debit and credit positions (based on forecasted liquidity planning) or, in some cases, by applying the transactional profit split method.

---

**Court case**

In the Norwegian ConocoPhillips case,[104] the Norwegian Court of Appeal decided that: (a) participants with net deposits create a profit possibility for all of the other participants, and this would provide them with a negotiating advantage towards independent parties; (b) participants with net deposits would have obtained a more significant portion of the benefit deriving from the cash pooling when negotiating with independent companies in a similar situation; (c) the benefit derived from the pooling system should be divided between the participants based on the individual companies' actual contributions; and (d) the traditional methods could not have been applied. Consequently, the profit split method should have been applied in order to assess the arm's length nature of the compensation that was agreed upon in the cash pooling. However, de facto, in practice, such an application has occurred by implementing modified deposit rates.

---

## 3 CONCLUSIONS

This chapter has detailed how to assess the arm's length nature of intra-group financial transactions with specific reference to loans, financial guarantees, and cash pooling.

---

103. *See* section 1.1.3, above.
104. *ConocoPhillips Scandinavia AS & Norwegian ConocoPhillips AS v Oil Tax Office*, LB-2009-081881. Utv 2010 section 199 (11 Jan. 2010). *See also* Andresen, H.M., Pearson-Woodd, N. & Jørgensen, H-M, 'ConocoPhillips Case: Implications in Norway and Beyond', *International Transfer Pricing Journal* 17 (October 2010), pp. 461–466.

Beginning with an introduction of the different types of intra-group financial transactions and of financing entities, the four-step analysis needed in order to assess the arm's length nature of a transaction has been described with specific reference to intra-group financial transactions.

Steps 1 and 2 will ultimately provide an answer on whether any compensation for the tested transaction can be chargeable/deductible. In detail, these would require the review of whether the tested party could obtain a similar financial service from an independent entity and whether it would request a similar financial service. Additionally, all of the terms and conditions established in the tested financial transaction should reflect the accurately delineated transaction undertaken, i.e., the terms and conditions should be at arm's length.

Steps 3 and 4 will aim at assessing the arm's length compensation for intra-group financial transactions by taking into account both the perspective of the service provider and that of the service recipient. In this context, the CUP method and the cost plus method (cost plus method or cost-based TNMM) are the methods most commonly used. However, in some cases, the transactional profit split method can also be adopted.

CHAPTER 11
# Transfer Pricing and Intangibles

## 1   INTRODUCTION

Assume that Company A is the parent company of a multinational group ('MNE') 'Y' that is active in the pharmaceutical sector. Company A registered a formula for intellectual property law purposes and is a legal owner of the intangible, which is economically exploited. Company A designed the clinical trials and performed the research and development (R&D) functions during the early stages of development of the product, leading to the granting of the patent.

Subsequent to the creation and registration of the patent, Company A decides to enter into a contractual arrangement with Company B, a subsidiary of Company A, whereby the former licenses the patent rights relating to the commercial exploitation of a pharmaceutical product to the latter. In accordance with the contract and based on the actual behaviour of its marketing and sales team, Company B conducts the functions that are associated with the subsequent development of the product. It also performs important commercial activities (e.g., solicits the testing of the newly created drug with medicine schools and hospitals) that are instrumental for enhancing the commercial value of the product.

In this respect, Company B obtains the authorization from the relevant regulatory body to distribute the product for commercial purposes which leads to the successful development of the drug that is sold in various markets around the world. Most notably, Company B decides to sell the drug under the trade name 'X' in its country of residence.

The above example summarizes the significance of intangible property in today's economy. The patent for Company A and the trademark for Company B are the value drivers that allow the MNE group 'Y' to gain a competitive advantage in its specific industry sector (in the above-mentioned example, the pharmaceutical). This chapter will elaborate on addressing the transfer pricing consequences of such structures where intangibles, often the by-product of 'unique and valuable contributions'[1] carried on by associated enterprises part of the same MNE group may affect the remuneration of the entity owning the asset.

Intangible assets permeate every industry sector of today's economy.[1] For instance, OECD economies are more strongly dependent on the production, distribution, and use of knowledge than ever before. Such knowledge-based capital (KBC) involves intangible assets (e.g., R&D, software, human capital, and organizational structures) that are also essential for fully realizing productivity gains and efficiencies from new technologies. Investment in intangible assets is increasing and even exceeds investments in physical capital (machinery and equipment) in several OECD countries. The relevance of intangible assets should not be limited, however, to only develop economies. Certain industry sectors where intangibles play a crucial role in justifying a premium return for the associated enterprise(s) involved in their development and commercial exploitation (such as the mining industry, for example) fall within the sphere of influence of governments of developing economies that also face the very same challenges of those in developed economies. Innovation involves the production of new knowledge from complementary assets not only R&D but also software, human capital, and organizational structures many of which are essential for fully realizing productivity gains and efficiencies from new technologies. As such, intangible assets are a strategic factor in a firm's value creation.

The role of KBC in today's economy has become as important as that of tangible assets, accounting for up to 12% of the GDP in some countries.[2] For example, in OECD countries such as Finland, Sweden, the United Kingdom, and the United States, investment in intangibles is now equal to or even superior to investment in tangibles such as machinery, equipment, and structures. Over the past decade, investment in intangibles has grown as a share of GDP in many OECD countries while investment in tangibles has stayed the same or declined. The relative importance of intangibles in the investment strategies of the business sector, therefore, has increased.

---

1. For a focus on the rising relevance of the so-called 'knowledge-based capital', see J. Haskel & S. Westlake *Capitalism without Capital: The Rise of the Intangible Economy*, 2017, pp. 9–12.
2. For further details on the impact of KBC in today's economy, see the OECD report *Supporting Investment in Knowledge Capital, Growth and Innovation*, October 2013, Paris, France.

Intangibles have become increasingly relevant for business success since the 1970s. To some extent, this development can be traced in different industries following the ratio of the value of intangibles as a percentage of the total market capitalization of either company or, alternatively, in relation to their book value. In addition, several megatrends, such as rapid globalization, deregulation in certain sectors (e.g., telecommunications and aviation), and technological change spurred by massively growing Internet coverage and consequentially enhanced information availability ('digitalization') greatly contribute to this development.

Such a dramatic evolution of today's economy has had a major impact on the way tax administrations look at intangibles from a transfer-pricing standpoint. Indeed, on the one hand, MNEs are constantly seeking opportunities to enhance the management of intellectual property within a group in the most tax efficient manner. On the other hand, tax administrations are concerned that significant BEPS phenomena may occur due to the relative ease of moving intellectual property across borders *vis-à-vis* relocating tangible assets. It is not by chance that the OECD, already in 2005 when scoping the then-project on the transfer pricing aspects of business restructurings, had its focus on intangibles. By looking at the outset of the 2017 revision of Chapter IX of the TP Guidelines, paragraph 9.2 states that [...] *'business restructurings may often involve the centralization of intangibles, risks or functions with profit potential attached to them. They may typically consist of: [...] transfers of intangibles or rights in intangibles to a central entity (e.g., a so-called IP company) within the group'*.

In the wake of the implementation phase of the BEPS project, i.e., after the 2015 publication of the final Reports on Actions 8-9-10, international organizations continued to pressure against MNE groups. This was to convey the clear message that, in regard to the commercial exploitation of intangible assets, the key message is guaranteeing consistency between the contractual arrangement underlying the creation and development of intangibles and the actual conduct of the associated enterprises related to the development, enhancement, maintenance, protection, and exploitation of the asset itself (so-called 'DEMPE functions').

In particular, the OECD emphasized the prominent role of intangible assets in its Interim Report on the digitalization of the economy.[3] In this respect, it has been highlighted that digitalization features prominently in today's value chain of enterprises where the latter are characterized by the increasing importance of investment in intangibles, especially IP assets which could be either owned by the business or leased from a third party. In particular, for many digitalized enterprises, the intense use of IP assets such as software and algorithms supporting their platforms, websites, and many other crucial functions are central to their business model.

Concerns surrounding the misuse of intangibles within MNE groups to purportedly shift profits in locations where actual value-creation activities were taking place were already obvious when the OECD's Working Party No. 6 embarked on the major

---

3. *See* the OECD/G20 Base Erosion and Profit Shifting Project, *Tax Challenges arising from Digitalisation – Interim Report* 2018, para. 2.1., p. 24.

project of revision of Chapter VI of the OECD TPG[4] in 2010. Such a project became the cornerstone of the transfer pricing actions as identified in the 2013 BEPS Action Plan involving the application of transfer pricing rules to the development and transfer of intangibles,[5] as the ongoing work at that point in time was then subsumed in the BEPS Action Plan.

The perception that tax administrations consider the use of intangibles by MNEs as an aggressive tax planning tool has been confirmed by the European Union which, in 2017, released the final report on what are deemed to be 'aggressive tax planning indicators'.[6] Interestingly, the EU study highlights two more ATP structures where the deduction of royalty costs lies at the heart of the tax savings.

> To this end, the key channel of the two-tiered ATP structure is that the intellectual property is transferred to a subsidiary that is incorporated in Country E but is a tax-resident outside that country in a jurisdiction where it is tax-exempt. As a result, the royalty payments made by the target company in Member State D are deducted from the tax bases there but are not taxes in the entity in Country E.

From a practical standpoint, one of the primary concerns of having intangibles as part of aggressive tax planning schemes is triggered by the circumstance that taxpayers may, at times, transfer intangibles or those functions in which intangible-related opportunities are embedded for relatively insignificant amounts to associated enterprises that are residents in low-tax jurisdictions. In such types of transactions, payments made by the transferee could take the form of either a lump sum or a continuing royalty. Because of the fact that there is often considerable development and financing, there is risk associated with the ongoing development of the intangible at the time the transfer occurs; therefore, it can be difficult to accurately determine the price to be paid under the arm's length principle. More in detail, aggressive restructuring involving the transfer of intangibles revolves around the circumstance that the purchaser's sole contribution to the value of the intangible was the payment of a portion of the development cost (sometimes contractually framed within a cost contribution arrangement), however, the income derived subsequent to the transfer was greater than the costs incurred to develop the intangible itself.

---

4. More in detail, n 2010, the OECD announced the commencement of a project on the transfer pricing aspects of intangibles. A scoping paper was published on the OECD website for public comment. In the interim, three public consultations were held with interested commentators.
5. On 19 Jul. 2013, the OECD released the Action Plan related to Base Erosion and Profit Shifting. The work on intangibles is specifically listed as one of the BEPS actions in that Action Plan. This work on intangibles has been closely related to other BEPS actions contained in the Action Plan. This specifically includes work on the allocation of risks and capital for transfer pricing purposes, re-characterization of transactions that might not occur between unrelated parties, hard to value intangibles, transfer pricing methods including profit splits, interest deductibility and financial transactions, and the digital economy.
6. *See* October 2017 Report by the European Union, *Aggressive tax planning indicators: Final Report*, in TAXATION PAPERS *Taxation and Customs Union* WORKING PAPER No 71 – 2017, p. 140.

> **Example**
>
> Assume that LemonCo is the parent company of an MNE group that is active in the design, manufacturing, and commercial distribution of electronic consumer goods. The group, in order to maintain and improve its leading market position, must invest significantly in R&D activities in order to improve existing products and develop new ones. The Lemon Group owns two R&D facilities, one operated by LemonCo in Country X and the other operated by SCo, a subsidiary of LemonCo, in Country Y.
>
> In Year T + 1, LemonCo undertakes a business restructuring of which the main purpose is the tax-efficient optimization of the intellectual property of the entire group. In this respect, LemonCo sells all of the rights associated with the patents and other technology-related intangibles (including the rights to use intangibles in ongoing research) to a newly incorporated subsidiary TCo, a resident in the low-tax country, Z. Company T establishes a manufacturing facility in Country Z where tax incentives related to manufacturing are in place and begins to supply products to other affiliates of the Lemon Group around the world.
>
> At the same time, the sale of the intangibles to TCo by LemonCo occurs following the payment of a lump-sum consideration. The former company enters into two separate contract R&D arrangements, respectively, with LemonCo and SCo. Based on the said arrangements, the two latter companies will be remunerated on a cost plus 5% method by TCo which contractually agrees to bear the financial risk associated with possible failures of the R&D projects. However, TCo has no skilled personnel who are capable of conducting or supervising the research activities. This entails that LemonCo will retain the risk management functions associated with the development and design of the R&D programs as well as determine its own levels of staffing and budgeting that are needed to control the development risk associated with the exploitation of the intangibles.

The OECD WP6 delegates when developing the new guidance on the transfer pricing aspects of intangibles were considering the above-mentioned structure. Such new guidance requires focusing on the following factors, specifically:

(i) Definitional issues: What is an intangible for transfer pricing purposes?
(ii) Ownership issues: Is it so significant to identify which associated enterprise owns an intangible, or is it rather more important to focus on the functional analysis that is instrumental for determining who develops and commercially enhances the value of the IP?
(iii) Identifying and characterizing transactions involving intangibles; and
(iv) Valuation issues: how to identify conditions (including prices) for transactions between associated enterprises involving intangibles.

Each of the above-mentioned aspects will be discussed in detail within this chapter.

## 2 DEFINITIONAL ISSUES

First, intangibles should not be addressed differently than other assets regarding the application of transfer pricing rules[7]. This entails that the current framework surrounding the application of the principle would apply irrespective of the categorisation of the asset.

---

**Example**

Assume that Company A, a resident of Country R, sells the trademark T to its associated enterprise B, a resident in Country S. The comparability analysis will, irrespective of the type/category of the asset, entail that the five comparability factors will have to be assessed by the seller to price the transaction at arm's length, i.e., regardless of the fact that a tangible or, as the case at stake implies, an intangible asset has been sold.

---

Notwithstanding the above, there are arguably a number of specific issues that are peculiar to the transfer pricing analysis involving the transfer and/or commercial exploitation of intangibles. Immediately, the first question to be addressed is what is meant by the word 'intangible' for transfer pricing purposes.[8] The relevance of candidly addressing such a question is twofold, i.e., (i) identifying the existence of an intangible asset for transfer pricing purpose does not necessarily equate the existence of it from a legal or accounting standpoint; and (ii) defining the presence of an intangible in a transaction between associated enterprises will render the analysis of the risk management and funding functions more nuanced and, arguably, more difficult.

In this regard, the new Chapter VI of the 2017 Guidelines stipulates that[9] *'an intangible is something which is not a physical asset or a financial asset, which is capable of being owned or controlled for use in commercial activities, and whose use or transfer would be compensated had it occurred in transactions between independent enterprises in comparable circumstances'*. This entails that the significance of intangibles in a transfer pricing analysis may be entirely detached from its legal or accounting classification. For example, think about the formulas used by multinational groups to manufacture certain branded soft drinks. Such a formula is a trade secret

---

7. *See*, correctly J. Andrus in *Transfer Pricing and the Arm's length principle after BEPS*, Oxford University Press, 2017, where on p. 212 states that '[...] *Chapter VI of the Guidelines provides supplemental transfer pricing guidance for transactions involving intangibles'*. Stated otherwise, there are indeed some peculiarities applying to intangibles, such as identifying them from a legal and tax standpoint, but such customization in the approach should never forget the general framework (particularly when it comes to the application of the comparability analysis) of Chs 1 and 3 as emerging from the 2017 BEPS Final Reports on Actions 8–9 and 10.
8. For an interesting analysis regarding the definitional issues surrounding the term 'intangibles', *see* U. Schreiber & L.M. Fell, *International Profit Allocation, Intangibles and Sales-Based Transactional Profit Split*, 9 World Tax J. (2017), Journals IBFD.
9. *See* para. 6.6. of the 2017 update of the OECD TPG, reflecting the Final Report on Action 8–10, n. 16.

from an intellectual property law standpoint. The formula is, together with the registered trademark, instrumental for commercially exploiting the soft drink and one of the so-called 'key value drivers' to the company is the secret; it would be useless for the company if the trade secret is known by its competitors (since, of course, they would all subsequently begin to copy it). Otherwise stated, the essential criteria for a trade secret is satisfied: the company takes special effort to keep it a secret, and that secrecy creates value.

Assume that the original formula for producing the soft Drink 'Fresh' was patented in 1920. Assume also that, when the formula changed in 1930, the company did not choose to patent the formula again. The reason for this is simple: if the soft drink maker were to patent its formula, the formula would become known to others and, once the patent expired, anyone could use it. It is possible to copyright a formula but that would also make it known to the public. Additionally, the copyright would only protect the formula as a piece of literary expression; it would not protect the basic ideas that make the formula unique. Such a scenario demonstrates that the disadvantageous aspect of a trade secret is that, once it is known, there is almost no legal protection. The fact that such a trade secret is not on the corporate balance sheet or treated as an asset for accounting purposes of one of the associated enterprises that is involved in the manufacturing and/or distribution of the soft drink does not indicate that is not relevant for purposes of attributing a 'residual return', i.e., extra profit, to the associated enterprise that developed such a formula.[10]

As indicated above, it is not the case that all valuable intangibles are legally protected and/or registered. Know-how and trade secrets are proprietary information or knowledge that assist or improve a commercial activity but that an enterprise may for a variety of business reasons choose not to register. Such know-how may, nonetheless, substantially contribute to the success of the enterprise and be of significance in some situations for transfer pricing purposes. Notwithstanding the fact that the availability and extent of contractual forms of protection may affect the value of an asset such as an intangible (and the returns attributable to it), the existence of any such contractual protection is not a necessary condition for an item to be characterized as an intangible for transfer pricing purposes. Conceptually, intangibles can encompass a wide spectrum of legally defined items such as patents and trademarks up to broader categories such as best practices, internal procedures, human capital, non-contractual relations to customers or suppliers, and network effects. The latter categories of items are not necessarily legally defined but may, taking into account particular facts and circumstances, convey value that would be compensated between parties at arm's length and, as such, should be considered as a relevant economic characteristic in any comparability analysis involving the use or transfer of intangibles.

Stated otherwise, the consensus of the international recommendation surrounding the definition of intangibles for transfer pricing purposes clearly outlines two definitional elements, specifically:

(a) an intangible is something that can be owned or controlled; and

---

10. *See* paras 6.7 and 6.8 of the 2017 Chapter VI of the OECD TPG.

(b)  an intangible is something an independent entity would be willing to pay for in order to acquire it.

Based on the outline provided thus far, the following aspects tentatively define intangibles for transfer pricing purposes:

- lack of physical substance;
- non-monetary character;
- –identifiability;
- separability;
- controllability;
- future economic relevance/utility; and
- different conceivable forms of ownership.

A frequent point of controversy between taxpayers and tax administrations concerning giving relevance to definitional issues regarding intangibles refers to the notion of goodwill.[11] Depending on the context, the term 'goodwill' can be used to refer to a number of different concepts. In some accounting and business valuation contexts, goodwill reflects the difference between the aggregate value of an operating business and the sum of the values of all of the separately identifiable tangible and intangible assets. Alternatively, goodwill is sometimes described as a representation of the future economic benefits associated with business assets that are not individually identified and separately recognized.

For the sake of a proper transfer pricing analysis, it is not necessary to establish an accurate definition of goodwill for transfer pricing purposes or to define when goodwill or ongoing concern value may or may not constitute an intangible. It is important to recognize, however, that an important and monetarily significant part of the compensation that is paid between independent enterprises when some or all of the assets of an operating business are transferred may represent compensation for something referred to by one or another of the alternative descriptions of goodwill or ongoing concern value. Stated otherwise, the absence of a single precise definition of goodwill makes it essential that taxpayers and tax administrations describe specifically relevant intangibles in connection with a transfer pricing analysis and to consider whether independent enterprises would provide compensation for such intangibles in comparable circumstances. When the reputational value, sometimes referred to as goodwill, is transferred to or shared with an associated enterprise in connection with a transfer or licence of a trademark or other intangible, that reputational value should be taken into account when determining appropriate compensation. Similarly, the

---

11. The literature on the concept of goodwill is vast. For a thorough analysis of the item, carried on with respect to the related topic of business restructurings, *see* S. Rasch & R. Schmidtke, *OECD Guidelines on Business Restructuring and German Transfer of Function Regulations: Do Both Jeopardize the Existing Arm's Length Principle?*, in 18 Intl. Transfer Pricing J. 1 (2011), Journals IBFD.

features of a business such as a reputation for producing high quality products or providing high quality services allow that business to charge higher prices for goods or services. Therefore, an entity lacking such a reputation and such features might be characterised as goodwill or ongoing concern under one or another definition. Whether or not they are characterized as such should be taken into account when establishing arm's length prices for the sales of goods or the provision of services between associated enterprises. Stated differently, all of the contributions of value should be compensated at arm's length irrespective of how they are labelled.

Overall, it appears that both the OECD and the United Nations sought to strike a balance between those advocating a narrow definition focusing on enforceability of property rights and attempts (mostly driven by the positions of certain tax administrations) to broaden such a concept in order to include almost any profit-driver. In this regard, on top of the debate surrounding the definition of goodwill, the position expressed in the BEPS Final Reports on Actions 8–9 and 10 was to reject an approach aimed at including in the OECD TP Guidelines a comprehensive list of items that should be treated as intangibles. Instead, the message that was conveyed was to reiterate the important concept lying at the heart of the comparability analysis, that is, what really matters for transfer pricing purposes is whether an unrelated party would pay for an item in order to gain control of it.

The relevance of the above-mentioned criterion is particularly significant for drawing a dividing line between what is deemed to be an intangible, on one hand, and what is, on the other hand, the treatment of other items such as the specific feature of a local market.[12] Some countries had argued (notably, China and India, although by using different arguments) that market advantages including cost location savings, the size of a market, and the access to certain features should be considered as intangibles for transfer pricing purposes. The conclusion achieved as a result of the revision of Chapters I and VI of the 2017 TP Guidelines stipulates that items such as access to a local market cannot be owned or controlled by an associated enterprise. Therefore, they are not to be treated as intangibles even though they can affect prices for transactions in the open market and should be taken into account as comparability factors when appropriate.[13]

---

**Example**

Assume that the Parent Company P undertakes a business restructuring involving the subsidiaries ACo, a resident in Country A, and BCo, a resident in Country B. The group is involved in the manufacturing and distribution of household appliances. ACo is acting as a distributor in the very profitable market A whereas BCo performs the very same functions in market B, which presents additional

---

12. Such a debate is particularly relevant in the emerging economies. For further references, *see* J. Li & S. Ji, *Location-Specific Advantages: A Rising Disruptive Factor in Transfer Pricing*, 71, Bull. International Taxation. 5 (2017), and G. Cottani, *Transfer Pricing Developments in Developing Countries and Emerging Economies*, in Transfer Pricing Developments Around the World, 2018, Wolters Kluwer.
13. *See* paras 1.31–1.51 and 6.31 of the 2017 version of the OECD TPG.

difficult barriers to entry into the market. Because of the strategic role, Company B orders a swap of responsibilities whereby Company A will begin distributing the products in Country B, and the contrary will happen for BCo (i.e., it will distribute the same products as before but addressing the more profitable market of Country A). The key question to be addressed in this aspect is whether such a swap of responsibilities in terms of access to different markets (in the case at stake, a profitable one against a more stagnant one) can be deemed as a transfer of an intangible.

The likely answer is negative, i.e., access to a profitable market cannot be deemed as an intangible in itself. However, the very fact that a third party would be willing to pay compensation in order to obtain such an opportunity will be an important, if not a predominant factor, in the comparability analysis that is to be performed when determining the most appropriate transfer pricing method for remunerating, respectively, the functions performed by ACo and BCo as a result of the restructuring.

## 3   OWNERSHIP ISSUES

One of the most significant issues of the BEPS final report on Actions 8–9 and 10 leading to the major revamp of the new Chapter VI of the 2017 TP Guidelines discusses the question of the relationship between intangible ownership and the related entitlement to the profits that are derived from the commercial exploitation of intangibles. The relevance of the question stems from the circumstance that BEPS structures involving intangible property precipitated a dichotomy between the associated enterprise formally owning the intangible (considering there is a contractually binding arrangement allowing so) and that performing the economic activities generating intangible-related income. The answer to this significant question is addressed in the new paragraphs 6.35 and 6.36 of the 2017 OECD TP Guidelines which stipulate that the starting point for a transfer pricing analysis involving intangibles is provided by the analysis of the contractual terms (when existing) if supported by the actual conduct of the parties. However, the new standard in such an analysis is given by the bold statement whereby the determination of ownership does not automatically warrant the entitlement to the economic returns associated with the exploitation of intangibles.

Generally, the debate surrounding the concept of intangible ownership always made a distinction between legal and economic ownership.[14] However, if the notion of legal ownership can hardly be rejected (as it is governed by intellectual property law first and foremost), the notion of 'economic ownership' has been gradually abandoned at the international level, at least within the context of the application of the OECD TPG between associated enterprises. The reason for such an important terminology choice is twofold. First, the OECD wanted to dismiss the claims of certain tax administrations

---

14. *See* J. Wittendorff, *The Transactional Ghost of Article 9(1) of the OECD Model*, 63 Bull. Intl. Taxn. 3 (2009), at 118.

that were relying heavily on the notion of economic ownership simply when certain marketing costs were identified at the level of the local subsidiary. On the other hand, and on a more conceptual note, the OECD took the opportunity of the intangibles project to enhance the difference between Article 7 and Article 9 of the OECD Model Tax Convention. In this aspect, the concept of 'economic ownership' within the context of the 2010 OECD Report on attribution of profits to permanent establishments[15] has a very specific meaning as it refers to the *'equivalent of ownership for income tax purposes by a separate enterprise, with the attendant benefits and burdens (e.g., the right to the income attributable to the ownership of the asset, such as royalties; the right to depreciate a depreciable asset; and the potential exposure to gains or losses from the appreciation or depreciation of the asset)'*.[16]

On the other hand, the new Chapter VI introduces, within the relevance attributed to the functional analysis, those related to those related to the development, enhancement, maintenance, protection, and exploitation of intangibles (normally referred to as 'DEMPE functions').[17] Some important takeaways can be derived from this new position. First, the legal owner of an intangible in an Article 9 scenario may, in principle, be entitled to the so-called 'ex-post returns', i.e., the returns reflecting the actual exploitation of the IP. However, it shall also remunerate other group members that perform functions, use assets, and assume the risks related to the creation of intangible value on an arm's length basis. In this respect, the 2017 TP Guidelines place strong emphasis on the notion of risk management, in general, and control over risk, in particular, noting the relevance of certain functions in the intangibles development phase that may deserve an extra-profit compensation if outsourced by the owner. On the reverse side of the coin, ownership should always be remunerated at more than zero. The question of the amount of such remuneration, in fact, should be addressed in the transfer pricing analysis based on the comparability and/or valuation exercise as indicated in the supplemental guidance of the Actions 8–10 Final Reports. This new guidance can be illustrated in the following example.

---

**Example**

PharmaCo is the parent company of an MNE group engaged in the research, manufacturing, and distribution of pharmaceutical products and conducts its business activity in Country P. PharmaCo develops patents and other intangibles relating to product 'Z' and registers those patents in countries around the world. DeltaCo, a subsidiary of PharmaCo, distributes product 'Z' throughout the Asia Pacific region contractually on a limited-risk basis. According to the distribution agreement, it is PharmaCo, and not DeltaCo, that bears product recall and product liability risk. Furthermore, the contractual arrangement stipulates that

---

15. *See* the 2010 work of the OECD, Attribution of Profits to Permanent Establishments, Paris, France.
16. *See* footnote n. 4 of part I of the OECD Report on attribution of profits to permanent establishments, at p.14.
17. *See Actions 8–10 Final Reports*, n. 12, reflected in the new Chapter VI of the TP Guidelines at para. 6.48.

PharmaCo will be entitled to all profit or loss from selling product 'Z' in the Asia Pacific region after providing DeltaCo with the agreed level of compensation for the performance of its distribution functions. More in particular, based on the contractual arrangement, DeltaCo purchases product 'Z' from PharmaCo and resells it to independent customers in the countries falling within its geographical scope of application. Five years after the distribution agreement comes into effect, it becomes known that product 'Z' generates serious side effects in a significant percentage of patients using this product. It then becomes unavoidable to recall the product and remove it from the market. DeltaCo, and not PharmaCo, incurs all of the costs associated with the recall campaign. PharmaCo does not reimburse DeltaCo for such recall related costs and/or for the resulting product liability claims.

Based on the application of the new principles as delineated in the wake of the new Chapter VI of the 2017 version of the OECD Guidelines, it is apparent that the contractual entitlement of PharmaCo to the economic returns associated with the exploitation of the intangible 'Z' is inconsistent with the performance of the DEMPE functions attached to such intangibles. A transfer pricing adjustment will then be appropriate to remedy such an inconsistency.

The above-mentioned example highlights that the new guidance in Chapter VI provides a shift from the formalistic view on ownership of intangibles towards a more functional approach to the transfer pricing analysis under which the determination of the entity within the group that should be entitled to intangible-related returns is made by utilising a functional analysis. The general premise of the OECD communications in the area of transfer pricing is that the outcomes in cases involving intangibles should reflect the functions performed, assets used, and risks assumed by the parties. This suggests that neither legal ownership nor the bearing of costs related to the development of intangibles, considered separately or together, entitle an entity within an MNE group to retain the benefits or returns with regard to the intangible commercial exploitation.

At the same time, neither Article 9 of the OECD Model Tax Convention nor the OECD Guidelines suggest disregarding the legal ownership of the intangible but, rather, ensuring that each associated enterprise under the particular IP structure of an MNE group obtains an arm's length share in the benefits derived from the intangible based on what independent parties would have agreed in comparable circumstances. The new guidance suggests that a pure owner of IP that assumes no risks and performs no functions should be entitled to simply an adjusted rate of anticipated return on capital but no more than that.

Another important aspect to note is that, while the analysis of intangibles generally follows the same analytical path as other types of transactions, there are a number of aspects of intangibles that typically warrant scrutiny within the fact-finding phase. These relate to:

  (i) the development of or, alternatively, the acquisition from third parties of intangibles (i.e., how the MNE group obtained the intangible);

   (ii)  the enhancement of intangibles;

   (iii)  the maintenance of intangibles,

   (iv)  the protection of intangibles; and

   (v)  the exploitation of intangibles (whether direct exploitation or indirect exploitation such as licensing out).

As previously mentioned, these areas for analysis are sometimes referred to as 'DEMPE' contributions. In order to evaluate transactions involving intangibles, it is important to understand all of these contributions as some or all of them might reflect important contributions to value that must be appropriately remunerated. While DEMPE activities might seem to be limited to functions, they in fact often reflect contributions of assets and the assumption of risks as well. For example, a pharmaceutical company might commit to undertaking R&D in order to develop a potential blockbuster drug. This 'D' reflects, in addition to the development functions (R&D), a commitment to a contribution of assets to fund the development and the assumption of potentially significant risk. In this respect, it should be emphasized that the United Nations[18] distinguished, from the concept of DEMPE, that of DAEMPE, to attribute relevance to the funding activity needed for purchasing an intangible asset, from an associated as well as from a third party. Regarding this, the UN added in a specific footnote that [..] *'By referring to "DAEMPE" in the U.N. Manual there is no intention to diverge from the G20/OECD guidance contained in the Final Report on BEPS Actions 8–10, but rather to clarify that intangibles can be acquired by an MNE group either through development activities or by an acquisition from a third party. See for instance paragraph 6.49 of the G20/OECD October 2015 Final Report on BEPS Actions 8-10.'*

With specific reference to the treatment of intangibles, it is interesting to note that, in Bulletin 6, an additional letter 'P' (referring to 'promotion' on top of 'protection') has been added in order to further expand the OECD's DEMPE concept. In particular, the function referred to the 'P' letter as one of the important value-creating factors when determining profit allocation of intangible-related income, has been highlighted. According to Bulletin 6, contributors to the *DEMPEP* of the intangibles will be granted proper intangible-related returns; otherwise, as in the case of Chinese tax administrations, a transfer pricing adjustment is warranted. It is expected that Chinese enterprises undertake certain promotions of the foreign intangibles in the Chinese market, and it is thus claimed that these enterprises will add value and increase the margins associated with the commercial exploitation of the intangible as initially developed. Accordingly, Chinese enterprises should be allocated the part of the intangible-related returns corresponding to their contributions.

Concisely, promotion is officially recognized as a separate function that is instrumental for the value creation of intangibles. It indicates that China is putting increasing emphasis on the marketing activities conducted locally and the marketing intangibles created locally in a tax audit.

---

18. *See* section B.5.3.13 of the 2017 update of the United Nations Practical Manual on Transfer Pricing for developing countries, available at http://www.un.org/esa/ffd/wp-content/uploads /2017/04/Manual-TP-2017.pdf.

In addition to the above-mentioned issues of intangibles and ownership, for a transfer pricing analysis of existing IP structures, the question of funding is also of particular importance. When assessing the appropriate anticipated return for funding, the OECD Guidelines, as mentioned, follow the investor model and state the following:

> [a] party that provides funding, but does not control the risks or perform other functions associated with the funded activity or asset, generally does not receive anticipated returns equivalent to those received by an otherwise similarly-situated investor who also performs and controls important functions and controls important risks associated with the funded activity.[19]

The key message of the guidance in this regard is that the funding alone, without control of risks as well as relevant functions, does not entitle the funder to the intangible-generated return normally referred to as 'residual profit'.

As such, the new guidance seeks to fulfil the primary aim of Action 8 of the BEPS Action Plan which is to limit the return that is due to entities. The main activities are to fund the development of intangibles without performing any control function over the financial risk associated with the funding by the party providing it.

'Pre-BEPS, such a statement was not clearly made in the OECD Guidelines which allowed more vulnerability in the allocation of profit within an MNE. However, now, when the new guidance is in place, it will thus be difficult, if not impossible, to allocate a significant portion of the intangibles-related returns to a purely "cash box" company.' Therefore, the business rationale to keep such companies, if any are present in existing IP structures, should be re-evaluated.

## 4   TRANSFER AND LICENSING OF INTANGIBLES

Cross-border transactions within MNEs involving intangibles may be grouped into three major categories, specifically:

    (i)  acquisition or sale;
    (ii)  licensing; and
    (iii)  R&D cost sharing.

In an (i) *acquisition or sale*, a transfer of ownership occurs. Before concluding the transaction, an arm's length price will be established including a valuation or some type of value estimation and will be negotiated between the parties to the transaction. In this situation, it is relevant whether individual IP items 'as such' are a subject of the transaction or a potentially inseparable bundle of intangibles and IP.

Moreover, the transaction may comprise a combination of certain IP and other tangible goods or services. In this respect, an element to be taken into account is whether the transaction is a 'stand alone', occurs on a one-off basis, or happens in the context of a business restructuring. Finally, the point in time when the transaction takes place can have an impact on the value of the IP and intangibles in question.

---

19. *See* para. 6.59 of the 2017 OECD TP Guidelines.

*(ii) Licensing* involves the contractual right to use certain IP but without an outright transfer of ownership in the IP. Consequently, the licensor continues to be the legal owner of the licensed IP. The considerations on pricing, IP bundling, and the combination of IP and other goods or services remain unchanged in the case of licensing, as mentioned above. Moreover, by way of licensing, an additional timing effect can be realised in comparison to an acquisition or sale as, effectively, a distribution of an agreed transaction price over several periods can be achieved. This may be reasonable in economic terms, for example, in the case of function transfers, and may also be well in accordance with domestic tax regulations.

Finally, (iii) *R&D cost sharing* deals (normally referred to as 'CCAs') with the joint development and/or utilization of IP (and/or intangibles), specifically, the pooling concept, which is a rather complex set-up that creates several challenges. These challenges include the valuation and pricing of pre-existing relevant IP (and/or intangibles) when an R&D pool is formed for the first time, the pricing of entry or exit fees for (potentially additional) pool participants over time, the establishment of (an) arm's length allocation key(s) for ongoing R&D expenses incurred by pool members, and also the question of ownership of the IP that is newly created in the pool.

In all of the three above-mentioned scenarios, the control over the risk activities as well as the financing will play a major role in determining an arm's length return for the group participants who are involved in the exploitation of the intangibles. In particular, the current guidance provided by the OECD TPG seems to be inadequate in their efforts to regulate low-tax cash box entities.

The determination of the funding party's return is considered to be a topical question because many MNEs very frequently rely on a CCA in practice when they decide to effectively develop intellectual property by means of a concerted effort of various associated enterprises.

In the most commonly observed structure, the research and development (R&D) centre, remains in the jurisdiction of the IP's place of registration while other participants contribute cash for further development.[20] Tax authorities around the globe tend to question such arrangements either:

(i) by re-evaluating an IP and increasing the buy-in payment of the funder; or
(ii) by decreasing the return of the funder, i.e., its share in the IP exploitation and, as a result, reallocating the profit between the parties.

Prior to entering into a CCA, the MNE must analyse the pros and cons of such an arrangement for the group members who will be using the intangible in their activities. Based on such an analysis, the MNE must then decide which intellectual property model to use, that is, choosing between a CCA or a centralized IP model.

A number of arguments exist that a CCA is preferable when an intangible is in an early stage of development as there would be no issues in respect of the valuation of the buy-in payments. There is potentially a reduced compliance burden for the participants in that scenario. At the same time, a CCA may be an efficient way to transfer

---

20. *See* J.Wittendorff, *Transfer Pricing and the Arm's Length Principle in International Tax Law*, at 537–538 (Kluwer L. Intl. 2010).

pre-existing IP to a related party that is going to be involved in development, enhancement, maintenance, protection, and exploitation (DEMPE) activities. However, in this case, the compliance burden would be much higher. Additionally, tax administrations are authorized to adjust the value of the contributions retrospectively, using a valuation technique based on projected income cash flows from the use of the developed IP.

The other feature that makes a CCA an attractive tool is that it eliminates cross-border royalty payments for the use of an intangible as each party contributes to its development. Instead, participants make their contributions in cash or by providing activities for the common development of the IP. Additionally, no withholding tax is payable upon the making of contributions by the participants, which might be regarded as a tax saving for a multinational group depending on the circumstances.

Irrespective of the model selected by the MNE to manage their intellectual property, the key driver to inform every decision refers to a thorough analysis of the 'control-over-risk' concept. As is known, the first clear discussion of this relevant concept previously appeared in Chapter IX of the 2010 OECD Guidelines; however, after a revision brought about in the context of the BEPS Action Plan, it was relocated to Chapter I in a more detailed version. The control-over-risk concept introduced a number of changes to the IP structures. Accordingly, a party can be a participant only if it exercises control over a specific risk and if it actually assumes this risk. Moreover, it should have the financial capacity to assume the significant risk. Control over risk includes two components:

(1) the capability to make decisions to take on, lay off, or decline risk-bearing opportunity together with the actual performance of this decision-making function; and

(2) the capability to make decisions on whether and how to respond to the risk associated with the opportunity together with the actual performance of this decision-making function.

A prominent feature of these two components is that they require an actual performance of the decision-making function, i.e., they cannot be outsourced to a group entity or a third party. Thus, with this provision, the OECD Guidelines require a participant to possess qualitative *economic substance*, that is, having the capabilities in-house to perform such functions.

As a result, the associated enterprise purportedly assuming the risk should have managerial and executive staff with the level of knowledge, skills, and experience that are necessary to make decisions in a particular business and who are capable of understanding the consequences of such decisions. Furthermore, it would be advisable that such high-level personnel should be authorized by law, a statute of the company, or any other internal document to make and implement the decisions. Additionally, the decision makers should have access to the information that is necessary for making their decisions.

It should be noted that the control-over-risk requirement is a way to counteract cash box structures that were commonly used for tax planning in the pre-BEPS era. From a practical standpoint, this requires that such box companies present an adequate level of capabilities, e.g., qualified personnel that would allow them to perform actual decision making and not just follow instructions from the head office. Such a position, which may be inferred by the new guidance in Chapters I and VI of the 2017 TP Guidelines, however, is quite difficult to achieve currently in centralized structures simply because tax administrations are increasingly challenging the notion of full centralization of risk, which – at least from an economic standpoint – is inevitably shared amongst group entities.

According to the OECD Guidelines, in addition to the control-over-risk requirement, a participant must have the financial capacity to assume the risk such that it is capable of bearing the consequences of the decisions taken in the event of risk materialization. In order to meet the financial capacity requirement, a participant must have access to funding to pay for the risk mitigation function.

From a practical standpoint, the analysis of whether a participant has the financial capacity to assume the risk involves answering the following four questions:

(1) Does the party have enough of its own resources to cover the risk materialization?
(2) If the party does not have enough of its own liquidity to bear the consequences of the risk, does the party have access to additional funding (e.g., loan financing)?
(3) If the party has access to additional funding from an affiliated enterprise, are there other options realistically available (ORA) for the party to access additional financing?
(4) Does the participant have sufficient capabilities?

All of these questions must inevitably be flagged once a taxpayer begins structuring the most efficient way to exploit intangibles in a manner that is consistent with a sound application of the arm's -length standard

## 5 VALUATION ISSUES

The key consideration for a proper application of the arm's length principle in transactions involving intangibles revolves around the fact that intangibles raise unique valuation issues that, at times, may be quite difficult to resolve[21] although they are frequently the source of significant controversy, particularly in the United States.[22]

Concerning pricing and valuing intangibles, the new Chapter VI of the OECD Guidelines refers to the general Chapters I–III stating that, in principle, standards that

---

21. *See* para. 6.33 of the new Chapter VI of the 2017 OECD TP Guidelines.
22. *See* US: Tax Court, 3 Mar. 2017, 148 T.C. No. 8, *Amazon.com, Inc. & Subsidiaries v Commissioner of Internal Revenue*, available at www.ustaxcourt.gov.

are applicable to other transactions also apply to pricing intangibles. Thus, any of the five transfer pricing methods described in Chapter II of the OECD Guidelines may apply depending on the individual case.

Notwithstanding the above, the OECD further elaborates on such general remarks by stating that one-sided methods such as the resale price method and the transactional net margin method are not regularly considered for the direct valuation of intangibles.[23]

The guidance advises against applying cost-based methods because they regularly collide with the arm's length principle in terms of comparability. Therefore, cost-based valuation approaches should be applied only in exceptional cases such as non-unique and low-value intangibles. Priority is given instead to the comparable uncontrolled price method (CUP) and the transactional profit split method.

However, the OECD states that, as intangibles tend to be unique, comparable values are rarely available, meaning that economic valuation methods can be applied alternatively to derive arm's length transfer prices.

The OECD Guidelines generally refer to income-based approaches, but do not offer any details on specific income-based valuation methods (e.g., the relief-from-royalty method).

The guidance states that the selection of valuation parameters must always take the circumstances of the individual case into account. The determination of net present values is often extremely volatile and depends on the assumptions that are made. Therefore, a net present value should be determined as a lower boundary from the perspective of the transferor and as an upper boundary from the perspective of the transferee, with the arm's length price lying within this range. Both boundaries of the range may be determined by economic valuation techniques according to the OECD.

Determining arm's length transfer prices for the transfer of a brand first requires the adoption of an appropriate economic valuation technique. In practice, the standard methods are rarely directly applicable for determining arm's length prices for intangible assets due to the heterogeneity of such assets and a lack of comparable assets or related transactions. A valuation following income-based methods to derive hypothetical comparables, therefore, represents the norm. The predominance of income-based methods is now confirmed by the OECD Guidelines for cases in which no direct comparison can be achieved.

Interestingly, the expression of an estimation of a comparative price by income-based methods suggests that economic valuation techniques appear to not be treated as alternatives to the standard methods for determining the price. Rather, they represent 'tools' for determining a (hypothetical) arm's length price which is then used in the CUP method. This understanding of the OECD, in essence, corresponds to the conceptual understanding of the US Tax Court in the now famous Amazon case which assumes that the application of an income-based method leads to a value that will be used within the CUP method.

---

23. *See* para. 6.141 of the new Chapter VI of the 2017 Guidelines.

In the case at stake, Amazon.com, Inc. (Amazon US) focused its business activities in the United States. The group's management then decided, as part of an expansion strategy, to increase its operations in the European markets. For this purpose, local subsidiaries were established to manage trading in each market that licensed the required intangibles such as website technology, customer information, and trademark rights from Amazon US. Regarding the European market in particular, the group incorporated Amazon Europe Holding Technologies SCS (hereinafter referred to as 'Amazon Luxembourg') in Luxembourg in 2004 which functioned as a hub for the region. Amazon US and Amazon Luxembourg entered into several agreements. In one of them, the parties entered into a cost sharing agreement on the joint development of intangibles, and Amazon US transferred marketing intangibles, among other assets, to Amazon Luxembourg. They agreed on a buy-in payment of approximately USD 255 million for Amazon Luxembourg.

In a tax audit, the US Internal Revenue Service (IRS) made income adjustments based on an all-in aggregate valuation of the intangibles transferred to Amazon Luxembourg using the income method. While experts selected by the taxpayer put an arm's length value of between USD 115 million and USD 312 million on the one-time payment of the marketing intangibles, the experts chosen by the IRS arrived at USD 3.13 billion. These substantial variations were attributable to the extremely different choices of valuation parameters.

In its judgment of 23 March 2017, the US Tax Court followed Amazon US in all the key points. Instead of the all-in aggregate IRS valuation, the Court recognized the valuation of the individual intangible items that were transferred and applied the relief-from-royalty approach as a manifestation of the comparable uncontrolled transaction method, taking into account license rates agreed between unrelated parties. In terms of marketing intangibles, the US Tax Court, referring to the best-method rule, argued that this was the most reliable method for valuing trademarks. While the IRS assumed a perpetual useful life for its valuation, the US Tax Court assumed a twenty-year useful life for the valuation of the marketing intangibles. It also rejected other valuation parameters assumed by the IRS.

Another practical example may be useful for understanding the unique issue surrounding the valuation of intangibles. One of the most relevant is related to the fact that pricing intangibles is often an exercise that must occur in the absence of comparables. In this respect, the provision of the Final Report on Actions 8-9-10 on 'hard-to value intangibles' address the problem that taxpayers may transfer partially developed intangibles at a point in time when successful completion of development activities is still uncertain and successful commercial exploitation of intangibles once they are developed is in question. Some countries have explicitly addressed situations of this type by allowing tax administrations to factor in the after-transfer profitability of the transferred intangibles in determining the price that should be paid by the transferee. In doing so, they focus on the circumstance that tax administrations are forced to evaluate the initial transfer without access to the same type of information at the disposal of the taxpayer so that it may be unlikely to determine whether the pricing should be based on reliable assumptions. For example, assume that the 'Socks' Group is involved in the design, manufacturing, and marketing of undergarments and has worldwide operations. While underwear is the main product type on which the Group is focused, it also markets a large array of hosiery products, nightwear, and home wear products for women and men.

The group requires you to value the Socks trademarks that are involved in the sale of underwear products. The MNE's value chain can be summarised as following:

- *Design*: Consists of creating prototypes, studying fabrics, and executing drawings.
- *Manufacturing/Packaging*: Consists of producing and assembling the products including sewing and ironing. Quality control is a large and significant component of this process. Socks is one of the rare players in the industry to have integrated its production.
- *Marketing and communication*: The company employs several advertising channels such as fashion magazines, billboard/outdoor, e-commerce/website, social media (Facebook, Instagram), in-shops events, and fashion shows.
- *Wholesale and Supply Chain*: Socks has an efficient supply chain and operates the X and Y businesses primarily as wholesale businesses through a wide channel of franchisees.
- *Retail Sales*: As previously mentioned, the company sells through a network of more than 4,000 single branded stores with over 2,400 abroad. These stores are either directly managed or by franchises or third-party distributors.

In the retail industry in which the Socks group operates, brand plays a decisive role in customer attraction and retention and in the ability to charge a premium price. Without a strong brand, even good quality and high technical products would not be perceived as such by customers. This emphasizes the need to build a strong and consistent brand. Socks group has developed such strong brands in the market, notably with X™, Y™ and Z™. These brands are broader than product brands as they do not necessarily appear on the products; they are retail brands in a broad sense, enhanced by customer experience from brand discovery, shop visit, purchase, and possibly after-sales as well.

Although each of above-described approaches may be used to indicate an arm's length valuation, the appropriateness of a particular approach varies with the type of businesses/assets being appraised.

As described above, the Trademarks, subject to the valuation, have the following characteristics:

- X™, Y™, and Z™ are well-established and recognized trademarks in their respective markets and are enhanced by significant spending in terms of communication and media;
- the income method (relief from royalty) was selected for the valuation of the above trademarks. The number of income streams related to the trademark

was determined with two approaches. In this respect, the formula below provides with the trademark value based on the RFR method based on the following assumptions.

$Value = (WACC) \sum (Revenues \times Royalty) - owner\ incremental\ cost] \times (1 - tax)tt = 0$

The inputs to the model are the following:

- Arm's length royalty rates (*Royalty*).
- Revenue streams in which the royalty rates apply (*Revenues*).
- Incremental costs borne by a brand owner compared to a licensee (*owner incremental cost*): It is assumed that a brand owner would bear some additional costs related to the trademark compared to a licensee. These are the core brand building costs.
- Weighted average cost of capital (*WACC*): The estimated royalty streams after tax is discounted to present value (*PV*) which results in the determination of the FMV.

Such an approach, as outlined in the case study, has been confirmed in the discussion paper of the EU Joint Transfer Pricing Forum, and the study of the European Commission identifies the residual value method and the relief-from-royalty method as the most common methods for valuing intangibles in the twenty-one participating countries.[24]

The conclusion is that the acceptance at the OECD level of financial valuation techniques not only as a supplement to the 'ordinary' transfer pricing methods but as proxy of them in certain instances[25] reflects yet another implied departure from methodologies that are based purely on comparable transactions.

---

24. *See* European Commission, *Study on the Application of Economic Valuation Techniques for Determining Transfer Prices of Cross Border Transactions between Members of Multinational Enterprise Groups in the EU*, 20 Dec. 2016 [hereinafter Study of the European Commission].
25. *See*, in particular, the far-reaching terminology adopted by the OECD in the new para. 6.153 whereby it is stated that [...] '*in situations where reliable comparable uncontrolled transactions for a transfer of one or more intangibles cannot be identified, it may also be possible to use valuation techniques to estimate the arm's length price for intangibles transferred between associated enterprises*'.

CHAPTER 12

# Transfer Pricing, Supply Chain Management and Business Restructurings

# 1 INTRODUCTION

## 1.1 Trends in Business Restructuring

Business restructuring has always been a major issue for tax administrations around the world and, in recent years, the impact arising from transactions falling within this domain of transfer pricing are a notable concern. The changes that are initiated by the implementation of cross-border redeployment of functions, assets, and risks could trigger significant effects on the allocation of profits (or losses) between the countries in which the entities operate regardless of whether the restructuring was tax motivated or not.[1] However, legitimate business reasons may lead a multinational group (hereinafter referred to as 'MNE') to undertake a reorganization of its supply chain models. For instance, assume an industry crisis (similar to the one that occurred in the aftermath of the Lehman Brothers' collapse) generating a contraction in market demand for a certain type of products or services. In that case, the MNE, at the headquarters level could may have to shut down a certain manufacturing plant or to streamline providing certain services based out of a single entity that has the capability or core competency[2] to do so, as part of the streamlining or adapting process. In another instance, a new web based technology emerges as a tool for efficiency for a particular industry.[3] In response to the change, MNE Groups belonging to that industry decides to change the operative roles of its subsidiaries in specific locations.

In the above cases, such a decision could lead to, from a tax management standpoint, a focus on three questions, specifically:

- Did a business restructuring occur?
- If the answer to the first question is affirmative, is there an indemnification to be paid?
- What are the criteria to be taken into account for selecting the most appropriate transfer pricing method to the post-restructuring scenario vis-à-vis the supply chain organization prior to the restructuring?

---

1. United Nations, *Practical Manual on Transfer Pricing for Developing Countries*, 2017.
2. Prahalad, C.K. and Hamel, G., *The core competence of the corporation*, Harvard Business Review (v. 68, no. 3) pp. 79–91 (1990).
3. Business restructuring of the distribution function by Facebook to avoid alleged challenges of the deemed existence of a permanent establishment, which – by means of a press release from its CFO, Dave Wehner – informed that the group will be moving '*to a local selling structure in countries where we have an office to support sales to local advertisers. In simple terms, this means that advertising revenue supported by our local teams will no longer be recorded by our international headquarters in Dublin, but will instead be recorded by our local company in that country. We believe that moving to a local selling structure will provide more transparency to governments and policy makers around the world who have called for greater visibility over the revenue associated with locally supported sales in their countries*'. This entails that business restructurings significantly affecting the transfer pricing policy adopted at a group level may be triggered by a number of factors including, as the case of Facebook shows, the anticipation of future political moves (such as the introduction of an improperly labelled 'web tax').

The aforementioned scenario is a straightforward, non-exhaustive set of questions that requires to be addressed when dealing with tax issues during business restructuring. From a transfer pricing perspective, a number of issues have to be taken into account by MNEs when restructuring their business and by tax administrations in assessing the arm's length nature of transactions arising out of such a restructuring decision. Therefore, an analysis of changes to the supply chain set-up should take into account the relevant connections within a multi-jurisdiction landscape, and considering the strict linkages to circumstances that may involve open questions subject to interpretations by both taxpayers and tax administrations. In such an analysis, the fundamental evaluation under Article 9 of the OECD Model Tax Convention and the arm's length principle is whether the conditions of a business restructuring between related enterprises differ from the conditions that would be made between independent enterprises.[4]

The relevance of tax controversies surrounding business restructuring has gained prominence over time not only in developed countries, with relatively more legal ownership of Intellectual Property (IP) and home to many MNE headquarters, but also increasingly in developing countries where the economic usage of the IPs or subsidiaries critical to the supply chain are located.[5] As a consequence of substantial tax risks associated with business restructuring, any change to the functional profiles and the related activities performed by parents and affiliates of MNE Groups, the focus on transfer pricing aspects assumes importance. Regulatory developments such as the EU State-aid[6] investigations and the US tax reforms have fuelled further debate on the nature of transaction structures adopted by MNEs and the changes that may arise due to regulatory actions.[7]

Considering all the above factors, the challenges posed by business restructuring transactions could be broadly attributed to the following reasons:

- no legal or universally accepted definition of business restructuring for tax purposes;
- recent radical changes in the economic environment that directly affect corporate strategies and investments;
- the introduction at a domestic level of measures regarding financial transactions and IP regimes that may affect the transfer pricing policies within MNE Groups;

---

4. *OECD Transfer Pricing Guidelines for Multinational Enterprises and Tax Administrations* (Paris: OECD Publishing, 2017), para. 9.9.
5. *Supra* n. 1, para. B.7.1.7.
6. White, J, *How Apple and McDonald's restructured their European tax affairs post-state aid*, International Tax Review (27 Jun. 2018).
7. Dhall, K, et al., *Transfer Pricing Developments in the United States*, in Lang, M, Storck, A, Petruzzi, R (eds), Transfer Pricing Developments Around The World 2018, Kluwer's (forthcoming).

- the higher degree of complexity from a legal and business standpoint to view the characterization of entities considering changing business models and new value drivers.[8]

## 1.2 Scope

This chapter commences with an understanding of what constitutes a business restructuring transaction that is subject to an arm's length analysis as part of section 2. This is followed by an overview of the theories in supply chain management in section 3. Since business restructurings more often involves a transfer of something of 'value', this section will analyse various drivers of value in the supply chain. Based on identification of values, the application of the arm's length principle, including the approach to accurately delineating a business restructuring transaction, recognition of the delineated transaction and the relevant transfer pricing methods used for an arm's length analysis will be discussed as part of section 4 and section 5. In detailing the arm's length analysis approach, this section will place specific emphasis on role of identifying 'Profit Potential' and analysis of 'Options Realistically Available' (ORA). Section 6 addresses the issues surrounding post-restructuring transactions while section 7 briefly discusses artificial avoidance of Permanent Establishments (PEs) in the context of business restructurings. Finally, section 9 underscores the need for the documentation that is necessary to effectively articulate business restructuring transactions and the key aspects of documentation that taxpayers and tax administrations should look into, while analysing a restructuring.

Since the nature of this topic is dynamic and mirrors the real-world phenomena, several examples have been provided throughout the chapter, with an aim to substantiate the steps. These illustrations provided are based on the most commonly employed structures and should not be considered as an exhaustive list of all possibilities leading to restructuring consequences. Since restructuring transactions are particularly fact specific, adequate caution is to be exercised in applying the arm's length principle to these transactions, on a case-by-case basis.

## 1.3 General Definition of Business Restructuring

As mentioned in section 1.1., the term 'business restructuring' does not have a universally accepted definition. In a general business environment, a restructuring could arise due changes in the following structures:[9]

- Physical structures – location, organization, working conditions

---

8. Prasanna, S, *Digitalisation of traditional business models – Transfer pricing Implications of Business Restructuring*, IBFD (forthcoming).
9. Malačič, I, Malačič, N, *Key factors for successful financial and business restructuring with a general corporate restructuring model and Slovenian Companies case studies*, Institute of Economic Research, Working Paper No. 9, 2016.

- Technological structures – equipment, processes
- Accounting structure – balance of assets and resources
- Organizational structure – the division of responsibilities and tasks, information, and coordination systems
- Demographics – the characteristics of employees
- Psychological structure – the prevailing mentality in the company

The above list is not exhaustive but merely indicative of business changes.

## 1.4 Definition for Transfer Pricing Purposes

For the purpose a transfer pricing analysis, restructurings are defined as cross-border reorganization of the commercial or financial relations including termination or substantial renegotiation of existing arrangements between associated enterprises. Changes to relationships with third parties such as suppliers, sub-contractors, and customers could also result in a restructuring outcome between related parties that requires compensation.

## 2 TYPES OF BUSINESS RESTRUCTURING

It is important to understand that restructuring is concerned with arranging the business activities of a company in order to achieve predetermined objectives at a corporate level. Such objectives include orderly redirection of the firm's activities, deploying surplus cash from one business to finance profitable growth in another, and exploiting inter-dependence among present or prospective businesses within the corporate portfolio, risk reduction, and development of core competencies. The most commonly observed business restructurings are listed below:[10]

- Conversions of full-fledged manufacturers into limited risk entities
- Conversions of full-fledged distributors into limited risk entities
- Transfers of intangibles to a so-called 'IP Company'
- Centralization of functions in a regional or central entity with corresponding reductions in the level/intensity of the functions performed by other MNEs' affiliates
- Intangibles or risks are allocated to operational entities (e.g., to manufacturers or distributors)
- Rationalization, specialization, or de-specialization of specific operations including the downsizing or closing of operations.

The primary reason for initiating a restructuring is to maximise synergies and achieve economies of scale, taking advantage of emerging external market

---

10. *Supra* n. 3 OECD TPG, 2017, para. 9.2., and *Supra* n. 1, UN Manual 2017. B.7.1.3.

developments such as digitalization.[11] The scenarios mentioned above are considered as being as flexible as possible since transfer pricing issues may arise whenever a group affiliate transfers assets or other advantages that entail a transfer of profit potential from a State of residence to another. Conversely, a 'reverse restructuring' when redeployment of functions, assets, and risks may be directed towards highly taxed jurisdictions is also possible.[12]

## 3 ROLE OF SUPPLY CHAIN MANAGEMENT AND 'VALUE' DRIVERS

Supply chain management is a term – or better, a science – going beyond the legal boundaries of the separate entity approach with respect to which the arm's length principle is based.[13] The idea of a 'value chain' is that every company is the collection of all of the activities that are performed in order to design, produce, market, deliver, and support its products. Cross-border value chains involve a set of activities performed by MNE group entities operating in a specific industry in order to deliver a valuable product or service for the market.[14] Such a concept,[15] therefore, captures the idea that a company is the result of a series of functions that contribute to its specific configuration which, translated in transfer pricing language, may be referred to as the group 'value proposition'. Stated otherwise, a properly managed supply chain should reflect the company's strategy, its history, and its approach in executing corporate strategy when dealing with competitors.

The term 'supply chain' originates from the various activities that a company performs in generating added value: this is what is normally referred to as the concept of 'value chain'. Generally, a properly managed 'supply chain' falls within the domain of risk management of an enterprise. To this end, supply chain management may not only be a beneficial tool for diagnosing competitive advantage; it can also play a valuable role in designing organizational structure. 'Organizational structure' entails grouping together certain activities such as manufacturing or production. The underlying rationale of these groupings is that activities have similarities that should be exploited by gathering them together, for example, in a department. At the same time, departments are separated from other groups of activities because of their differences. Such separation of similar activities is what organizational theorists referred to as 'differentiation'. However, with the separation of organizational units comes the need to coordinate them, usually termed as 'integration'.[16]

---

11. *Supra* n. 3 OECD TPG, 2017, para. 9.4.
12. *Supra* n. 1, *UN Manual 2017*, para. B.7.2.3.
13. Huaccho. H., Vlachos, L, and Roa-Atkinson, *Supply chain management and firm performance: An analysis of the literature.* In: BAM 2017 Conference Proceedings, BAM 2017, 5–7 Sep. 2017, Warwick, UK. British Academy of Management.
14. Porter, ME, *Competitive Advantage: Creating and Sustaining Superior Performance* (1985); Michael ME, *How competitive forces shape strategy, Harvard Business Review*, (1979).
15. Gluck, C., *Strategic Management for Competitive Advantage*, Harvard Business Review, July 1980.
16. *See* Porter, M, *The Five Competitive Forces that shape strategy*, reprinted by Harvard Business Review, January 2008, p. 79.

Most organizations are engaged in hundreds, even thousands, of activities and processes that are required to convert inputs into outputs. For example, a manufacturer can be considered as a complex system that is made up of subsystems each with inputs, transformation processes, and outputs all of which involve the acquisition and consumption of resources, for example, capital, labour, materials, equipment, buildings, land, administration, and management.

## 3.1 Dynamic Supply Chain

Restructurings of the supply chain are typically driven by external market requirements such as customer preference, changing technology, etc. The following can be considered key-drivers for business restructurings with the significant disclaimer that, without a sound economic transfer pricing analysis, a tax administration might challenge the underlying economic rationale of the reorganization up to the exceptional circumstance of disregarding and re-characterizing the restructuring in its entirety:

### 3.1.1 Changing Market Environment

Business climate changes such as technological or product innovations, deregulations, and nature of competition are the basic drivers for restructuring. Businesses look to maintain competitive advantages arising from product differentiation, pricing, or new variants of products, all of which drives individual companies to constantly reinvent the model of delivery and operations. Relevant changes in the economic environment (e.g., downturn economy, competitive pressure, need for business model review, need of specialization/focus) along with disruptive innovations/technology/methods (overcapacity situation) stimulates the need for restructuring.

### 3.1.2 Shift in Overall Strategy to Rationalize Business Performance

MNE Groups attempt to improve the company's business performance by eliminating specific divisions and business lines that no longer align to the core focus of the company. The company decides to focus on its core competency[17] and not on non-value adding activities.

---

17. Hafeez, K, Zhang. YB, Malak, N, *Core Competence for Sustainable Competitive Advantage: A Structured Methodology for Identifying Core Competence*, IEEE Transactions on Engineering Management, V.49/1 (February 2002), pp. 28–25.

### 3.1.3 Expectations of Synergy Maximization, Economies of Scale and Cost Efficiency

Synergy occurs when collaboration between enterprises leads to greater than proportionate results of increase in value.[18] Although all synergies need not result in an overall positive value creation,[19] the desire to achieve synergies influences restructuring decisions. Further, centralizing distribution or procurement functions increases the quality and efficiency standards due to the centralized selection of suppliers. Together with the maximization of synergies, the optimization of the number, size, and location of distribution or purchase centres leads to an efficient supply chain which again enables the MNE to further develop its competitive position by decreasing the response time to market changes or customers' demands.[20] Furthermore, inventory management and warehousing decisions play a significant role in determining efficiency arising from better inventory management. As a result of these considerations regarding the key drivers and the expected outcome of the transactions, from a pure business perspective, the main types of business restructuring can be identified in:

- Expansion – for example, M&As, takeovers;
- Contraction – for example, demergers, carve-outs;
- Legal/Financial restructuring;
- Turnaround;
- Disinvestment/Spin-off.

Generally, business restructuring involves stand-alone transactions as well as combinations of the aforementioned types in a way that, as a result, there is a reallocation of functions, assets, and risks within the MNE. These types of operations and these redeployments commonly occur together and can diffuse and result in the following: bulk sales of inventory, organic growth, exploit local market potential, office closures, layoffs, etc.

At this point, it is pertinent to note that business restructuring as defined in Chapter IX of the TPG differs from the above-mentioned definitions. Transactions that may not constitute restructuring under an economic/business standpoint under Chapter IX may comprise a redeployment of functions, assets, and risks relevant for transfer pricing purposes.

---

**Example**

A transfer of contracts (e.g., loans in the banking industry) may not constitute business restructuring from a business standpoint but may actually

---

18. Ansoff (1965), Porter 1985; Prahalad & Doz 1987, 1998; Sirower 1997.
19. Wind, Y, Mahajan, V, *Business Synergies Does Not Always Pay-Off*, Pegamon Journal, Vol. 21, No.1, pp. 59–65, 1988 (U.K.).
20. Bakker, A. *Transfer Pricing and Business Restructuring, Streamlining All the Way* (IBFD Netherlands, 2009).

underline a transfer of profit potential (profit potential attached to the loans that are transferred) which will likely be assessed by tax administrations.

This is exactly the perspective from which tax administrations examine the actual transactions that are undertaken by an MNE group and represent the grounds for the identification of whether a business restructuring has occurred for the purpose of Chapter IX of the TPG.

For additional discussion on synergies in transfer pricing implications of business restructuring transactions, refer to section 4.2.

## 3.2  Value Chain Analysis

The consequence of a business restructuring is best measured by understanding the value chain. In general terms, all of the activities carried out by a company can be represented using a value chain model as illustrated in Figure 12.1.

*Figure 12.1   Generic Value Chain*[21]

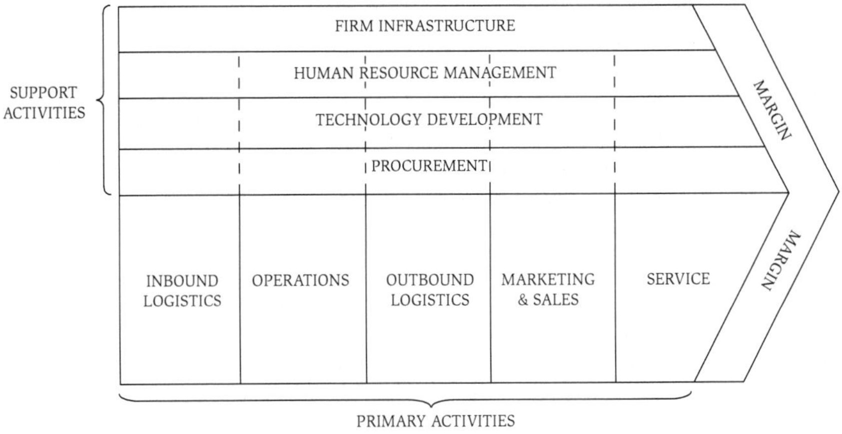

Based on the value chain model, activities can generally be classified as either primary or support activities that all businesses must undertake in some form.[22] According to Porter,[23] the primary activities are:

---

21. Porter, ME, Millar VE, How Information Gives you competitive advantage, Harvard Business Review, July 1985, Issue No.7

22. Rowe, Mason, Dickel, Mann, Mockler; 'Strategic Management: a methodological approach'. 4th Edition, 1994. Addison-Wesley. Reading Mass.

23. Porter, Michael E, 'Competitive Advantage'. 1985, Ch. 1, pp. 11–15. The Free Press. New York.

- **Inbound Logistics** – involve relationships with suppliers and include all of the activities required to receive, store, and disseminate inputs;
- **Operations** – are all the activities required to transform inputs into outputs (products and services);
- **Outbound Logistics** – include all of the activities required to collect, store, and distribute the output;
- **Marketing and Sales** – activities that inform buyers about products and services, induce buyers to purchase them, and facilitate their purchase;
- **Service** – includes all of the activities required to keep the product or service working effectively for the buyer after it is sold and delivered.

Secondary activities are:

- **Infrastructure** – serves the company's needs and ties its various components together; it consists of functions or departments such as accounting, legal, finance, planning, public affairs, government relations, quality assurance, and general management;
- **Human Resource Management** – consists of all of the activities involved in recruiting, hiring, training, developing, compensating, and (if necessary) dismissing or laying off personnel;
- **Technological Development** – pertains to the equipment, hardware, software, procedures, and technical knowledge regarding the firm's transformation of inputs into outputs;
- **Procurement** – is the acquisition of inputs or resources for the firm.

Within MNE groups, different functions are carried out in order to create synergies and add value to the MNS' value proposition. The concept of supply chain is cornerstone and describes all of the activities associated with the flow and transformation of goods from raw materials as well as the associated information flows. Supply chain management, therefore, is the integration of these activities through improved supply chain relationships to achieve a competitive advantage.[24]

To this end, supply chain management is a crucial process since an optimized supply chain results in lower costs and a faster production cycle. MNEs, in fact, strive to focus on competencies and tend to become as flexible as possible to ensure they reach more customers with the best quality product at the best price. To achieve this, they map their value chain and particularly their supply chain in order to define which activities need to be outsourced to other firms that can perform certain activities better or more cost effectively.

---

24. Handfield RB, Nichols, EL, *Introduction to Supply Chain Management*. New York: Prentice-Hall, 1999, p. 2.

As a consequence, a number of entities are involved in the value chain and contribute to the value proposition. These entities are part of the MNE group or external partners and lead to the creation of the concept of supply chain management in which the purpose is to improve efficiency, coordination, and collaboration among supply chain partners thereby improving inventory management and mitigating risks.

Within that scenario, transfer pricing aims to ensure that the remuneration granted to each parties corresponds to the functions performed, the assets used, and the risk borne. This analysis generally entails a comparison of the conditions of the controlled transaction with the conditions that would have been made between third parties under comparable circumstances.[25]

However, in the context of a business restructuring, transfer pricing could be considered as a major concern generally considering the lack of comparable transactions. Moreover, there is the foremost complexity related to the possible need of compensation for some of the entities involved because they forfeit some of their assets or know-how in order to benefit some of the other companies within the group.

Additionally, the valuation of corporate synergies for the purpose of a proper transfer pricing analysis should take into account: (i) the nature of the advantages or disadvantages, (ii) the amount of the benefits or detriments provided, and (iii) how those benefits or detriments should be allocated among members of the MNE group.[26] These circumstances add to a significant amount of complexity to supply chain restructurings as such synergies are often the very reason for the restructuring itself but are not always warranted by fact.

---

**Emerging trends in value drivers[27]**

The value chain has currently expanded to digital companies; the primary activities have been devised below:

- Network promotion and contract management – activities associated with inviting potential customers to join the network; selection of customers that are allowed to join; and the initialization, management, and termination of contracts governing service provisioning and charging.
- Service provisioning – activities associated with establishing, maintaining, and terminating links between customers and billing for value received. The links can be synchronous as in a telephone service or

---

25. OECD, *OECD Transfer Pricing Guidelines for Multinational Enterprises and Tax Administrations* (Paris: OECD, 2010), Chapter IX, part I, B.2.
26. In line with OECD, *Aligning Transfer Pricing Outcomes with Value Creation, Actions 8–10 - 2015 Final Reports*, OECD/G20 Base Erosion and Profit Shifting Project (Paris: OECD Publishing, 2015), para. 1.161.
27. OECD (2018), *Tax Challenges Arising from Digitalization – Interim Report 2018: Inclusive Framework on BEPS*, OECD Publishing, Paris.

asynchronous as in an electronic mail service or banking. Billing requires measuring customers' use of network capacity both in volume and in time.

– Network infrastructure – including activities associated with maintaining and running a physical and information infrastructure. The activities keep the network in an alert status ready to service customer requests.

## 4 APPLICATION OF ARM'S LENGTH PRINCIPLE TO BUSINESS RESTRUCTURING TRANSACTIONS

The application of the arm's length principle for business restructuring transactions follows the same methodology that is adopted for any other transaction that requires fulfilling the arm's length criteria. Therefore, the steps adopted in *Chapter II* of this book to accurately delineate the transaction, recognize the transaction, and perform a comparability analysis are valid Accurate delineation of the transaction for a business restructuring transaction includes identification of the commercial or financial relations between the associated enterprises undertaking the business restructuring. It must also consider the conditions and economically relevant circumstances attached to those relations so that the controlled transactions comprising the business restructuring are accurately delineated. The following steps encompass this process:[28]

– Accurate delineation of the transactions comprising the business restructuring and the functions, assets, and risks before and after the restructuring.
– Business reasons for and the expected benefits from the restructuring, including the role of synergies.
– Other options realistically available (ORA) to the parties undertaking the business restructuring.

### 4.1 Accurate Delineation of the Transactions Comprising the Business Restructuring and the Functions, Assets and Risks Before and After the Restructuring

Accurately delineation identifies the business restructuring that requires an arm's length compensation. The steps provided in Chapter 2 are revisited below:

(1) The contractual terms and arrangements of the transaction.
(2) The functions, risk, and asset analysis.

---

28. *Supra* n. 3 OECD TPG, 2017 para. 9.14.

449

(3) The characteristics of property transferred or services provided.
(4) The economic circumstances of the parties and of the market in which the parties operate.
(5) The business strategies pursued by the parties.

Of the above, the importance of contractual terms, with particular emphasis on indemnification terms of the binding contract; the role of functions, risks, and assets analysis; and the role of business strategies including synergies is discussed in the following sections. The importance of characteristics of properties and the role of economic circumstances in driving business restructuring that are detailed Chapter II and also briefly in section 3 continue to be valid.

### 4.1.1 Analysis of Contractual Arrangements

#### 4.1.1.1 Analysis of the Contracts for the Purpose of Delineation

With regard to business restructuring transactions, the contractual terms capture roles, responsibilities, and rights at the pre-restructuring (including, in relevant circumstances, those existing under contract and commercial law) and post-restructuring phase when the manner and extent to which those rights and obligations change as a result of the restructuring become evident.

However, when no contract exists to facilitate a comparison of pre- and post-restructuring situations or when, under specific circumstances, the conduct of the parties are materially different from the contracts in writing require that the business restructuring transaction be deduced. Documents such as correspondence and/or other communications associated with the business restructuring could also be considered as a starting point in conjunction with the formal contracts that aid in the delineation process. The following example illustrates a cross-border redeployment of functions, assets, and risks that lead to the delineation outcome.

---

**Example**

Company A develops, manufactures, and sells Product A in domestic Country A. In the future, Product A will be produced and sold only by Company B, a foreign group's affiliate. Following the termination of existing arrangements, the relevant intangible assets developed and owned by Company A will be transferred to Company B.

In this scenario, from a transfer pricing perspective, it is clear that Company A is transferring something of value that comprises functions (i.e., manufacturing and distribution activities), risks (e.g., market risk, etc.), and intangible assets related to Product A. A 'cross border-reorganisation of the commercial or

---

financial relations', i.e., a business restructuring between Company A and Company B, has occurred.

This reorganization is considered as a business restructuring transaction that requires a compensation.

### 4.1.1.2 Analysis of the Contracts for the Purpose of Indemnification

For the purpose of business restructuring, indemnification is any type of compensation for pitfalls suffered by the restructured entity. Contractual agreements typically include an indemnification clause to agree on the terms of indemnification.[29] Such payments could be in the form of the following:[30]

- Upfront lump sum payment
- A sharing in restructuring costs of lower (or higher) purchase (or sale) prices in the context of the post-restructuring operations
- Any other form, including 'intentional set-offs'.[31]

In addition, termination or renegotiation[32] of contractual relationships in the context of a business restructuring could result in the restructured entity incurring restructuring costs such as inventory write-off, severance to certain employees, cost of adapting the new model to customer requirements, etc. The quantum of determining the indemnification becomes critical. In order to arrive at the arm's length compensation for the accurately delineated restructuring transactions, the following considerations in relation to indemnification are to be taken into account[33]

#### 4.1.1.2.1 Whether the Indemnification Is Supported by Commercial Law of Contracts

The arm's length nature of a termination or re-negotiation of contractual arrangements are analysed based on commercial legislation. In the event of a unilateral decision to terminate a contract, i.e., the principal terminating contractual engagement with a subsidiary, the subsidiary may not be in a position to seek legal recourse considering its close association with the principal. However, this markedly differs from independent contractual arrangements wherein independent enterprises exercise their right to legal recourse.[34] Therefore, the nature of a contractual relationship under a restructuring situation should be framed by MNE Groups in accordance with an arm's length scenario.

---

29. Kannan, PM., *The Compensation Dimension of CERCLA: Recovering Unpaid Contract Costs*, University of Memphis Law Review, Vol. 30, 1999.
30. *Supra* n. 3 OECD TPG, 2017., para. 9.75.
31. *Ibid.*, p. 27 (Glossary).
32. *Supra* n. 1, UN Manual 2017, para. B.7.2.11.
33. *Supra* n. 3 OECD TPG, 2017, para. 9.79.
34. *Ibid.*, para. 9.80.

4.1.1.2.2  Whether Indemnification Clause or Other Terms of the Contract Is At Arm's Length

An important objective of accurate delineation for business restructuring is to identify whether an indemnification clause or arrangement is available as part of the concluded agreement and the operational aspects of the clause in the event of re-negotiation or termination.[35] Under independent circumstances, parties bound by a legal contract will be subject to the following:[36]

(a)  Contractual terms reflect the interest of both parties
(b)  Parties seek to be mutually liable if there is a deviation from the contract
(c)  Contractual terms will be contested if there is an irrational bias towards any one of the two contracting parties.

However, under circumstances when the parties are related, the conduct could deviate from the actual agreement. In such situations, the conduct takes precedence over the contract. The contractual analysis for indemnification under such situations is depicted illustratively below:

---

35. *Ibid.*, para. 9.81.
36. *Supra* n. 3 OECD TPG, 2017, para. 82.

*Figure 12.2   Arm's Length Indemnification Clause*[37]

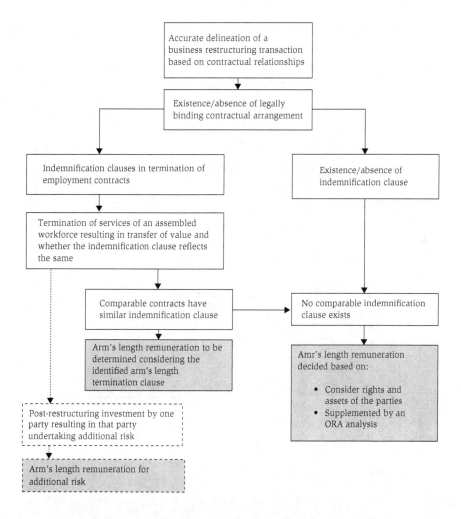

Figure 12.2 illustrative steps can be further explained with the following example:

**Example**[38]

Company A (principal) and Company B (subsidiary) are associated enterprises that entered into a manufacturing arrangement. Company B decides to invest in a new manufacturing unit, undertaking the risks associated with it. The contract is set to last for at least five years, and Company B assumes a reasonable

---

37. *Ibid.*, paras 9.83–9.87.
38. *Ibid.*, para. 9.88.

return on investment at the time of concluding the contract that is subject to a minimum production of 20,000 units per year.

Situation 1

Assume that, after three years, Company A unilaterally terminates the contract due to a group-wide restructuring drive. Company B is left with no choice but to comply with the group decision. The risk of termination is off-set by the indemnification clause that penalises Company A for pre-mature termination. The management of Company B also states that it had not anticipated the termination. If anticipated, the remuneration for manufacturing activities would have included up-front payments for impending termination. In such a case, no separate remuneration for termination would have been demanded by Company B. Therefore, beyond the existence of the indemnification clause, the actual risk mitigation practice that is adopted determines whether it is required that Company B be indemnified.

Situation 2

Further, it is identified that Company B had undertaken certain developmental efforts resulting in lower than normal profits in the initial phase and was set to recover the benefits of such investments in subsequent years of operations in order to break-even. Although Company B controlled the risk of development, it failed to protect itself from the risk of non-recovery through penalty or indemnification terms specific to such development efforts.

In the above situations involving potential termination, non-renewal, or substantial renegotiation of their manufacturing arrangement, if the conditions align to that of independent enterprises, then any profits under those specific conditions should have accrued to one of the enterprises in order to reflect the arm's length situation. While, in situation 1, the arm's length conditions were fulfilled, in situation 2, Company B (due to oversight or undue influence) failed to fulfil the conditions. The tax authorities of the jurisdiction in which Company B is domiciled could make an addition to the income to reflect conditions for tax purposes.

4.1.1.2.3 Once an Indemnification Cost Is Identified, Which Party Bears It Ultimately

All of the parties involved in the restructuring form stakeholders who may require an arm's length indemnification if it is identified that every party requires such a remuneration. This corresponds with evaluating which of the parties are to bear the cost.[39] The solution to this depends on the facts and circumstances of the case based on the rights and other assets of each party as well as the risks assumed and the economic rationale for which the contract is terminated. The expected benefits/losses due to change in profit potential and options realistically available is factored in this analysis.

---

39. *Ibid.*, paras 9.93–9.97.

In addition to the analysis of written arrangements, an in-depth functional analysis should be performed in order to identify the economically significant activities and responsibilities that are undertaken, assets used or contributed, and risks assumed before and after the restructuring by the parties involved.[40]

### 4.1.2  Functions, Risks and Assets Analysis

Functional analysis for a business restructuring situation seeks to identify the economically significant activities and responsibilities undertaken, assets used or contributed, and risks assumed before and after the restructuring by the parties involved. Therefore, this includes the change in the role of each party following the restructuring, the consequent control of risk, and the type and nature of assets used or contributed by the parties.

#### 4.1.2.1  Functional Analysis Specific to Business Restructuring

For all forms of transactions, the analysis of functions performed involves tracing the flow of products or services at various stages from conceptualization to their final sales and includes capturing the role and responsibilities of parties in the value chain.[41] Since the business restructuring process involves changes to the value chain, i.e., changes to the roles and responsibilities of parties as a consequence of restructuring. The following example illustrates a comparative functional analysis of both pre- and post-restructuring scenarios:

---

40. *Ibid.*, para. 9.18.
41. US IRS Tres. Reg. 1.482.

**Example**

Company A is a fast-moving consumer goods (FMCG) company that aims to consolidate the existing business while exploring and exploiting new markets. The company wants to maintain a strong brand identity and high quality while optimizing supply chain and customer proximity initiatives both in terms of efficiency from logistic and cost perspectives.

Following the last steering committee meeting, Company A decided to convert its full-fledged manufacturers in limited risk entities and to partially outsource certain activities (i.e., manufacturing, logistics, and R&D activities).

Pre-restructuring scenario

| | | Company A | Local Subs | Outsourced |
|---|---|---|---|---|
| Strategy | Set supply chain strategy | X | | |
| | Develop network configuration | X | | |
| | High-level capacity planning & Capex | X | | |
| | Business development | (X) | (X) | |
| Supply Chain Management (SCM) & Inventory | Prepare initial demand forecast | | X | |
| | Aggregate demand forecasts / create consensus | (X) | (X) | |
| | Produce 12–24 months production & materials schedule | | X | |
| | Sales & Operations planning management | (X) | (X) | |
| Procurement | Set strategy & policy | (X) | (X) | |
| | Supplier selection, negotiation and contracting | | X | |
| | Materials call-off | | X | |

|  |  | Company A | Local Subs | Outsourced |
|---|---|---|---|---|
| Manufacturing | Set production strategy | X |  |  |
|  | Manage manufacturing performance | (X) | (X) |  |
|  | Execute manufacturing activities |  | X |  |
| Logistics | Determine third-party distribution requirements | X |  |  |
|  | Manage inbound & primary distribution | X |  |  |
|  | Fulfil orders to customers | X |  |  |
| Product Development | Manage innovation program | X |  |  |
|  | R&D activities | X |  |  |
| Brand Management & Marketing | Brand management & marketing strategies & plans | X |  |  |
|  | Execution | X |  |  |

Following the business restructuring, functions relating to the business development, forecast, supply chain analysis, and procurement have been allocated to the head office while local entities have been characterized as limited risk manufacturers. The local subs, therefore, are entitled to perform manufacturing and related execution functions bearing limited risks. Manufacturing, logistics, and R&D functions have been partially outsourced to third parties in order to achieve efficiency, reduce costs, and specialize corporate capabilities.

**Post-restructuring scenario**

| | Head Office | Local Subs | Outsourced |
|---|---|---|---|
| **Strategy** | | | |
| Set supply chain strategy | X | | |
| Develop network configuration | X | | |
| High-level capacity planning & Capex | X | | |
| Business development | X | | |
| **Supply Chain Management (SCM) & Inventory** | | | |
| Prepare initial demand forecast | X | | |
| Aggregate demand forecasts/create consensus | X | | |
| Produce 12–24 months production & materials schedule | X | | |
| Sales & Operations planning management | X | | |
| **Procurement** | | | |
| Set strategy & policy | X | | |
| Supplier selection, negotiation and contracting | X | | |
| Materials call-off | X | | |
| **Manufacturing** | | | |
| Set production strategy | X | | |
| Manage manufacturing performance | (X) | (X) | |
| Execute manufacturing activities | | (X) | |
| **Logistics** | | | |
| Determine third-party distribution requirements | X | | (X) |

|  | Head Office | Local Subs | Outsourced |
|---|---|---|---|
| Manage inbound & primary distribution | X |  |  |
| Fulfil orders to customers | (X) |  | (X) |
| Product Development  Manage innovation program | X |  |  |
| R&D activities | (X) |  | (X) |
| Brand Management & Marketing  Brand management & marketing strategies & plans | X |  |  |
| Execution | X |  |  |

The functional analysis in the above case should detail the activities performed by all of the entities that are party to the restructuring transaction(s) in order to understand the overall redistribution of value in the supply chain.

### 4.1.2.2 Risk Analysis Specific to Business Restructuring

Arguably, business restructurings became a cornerstone of the entire OECD TPG. Since the inception of the project in 2005, Working Party No. 6 wanted leverage on the opportunity of discussing business restructurings to elucidate what would have then become the cornerstone of the BEPS action items on transfer pricing, i.e., the analysis on risk. In fact, the arm's length principle, if applied on the type of transactions described above, sheds light on the significance of whether actual risks would have been transferred from an associated enterprise to another of the MNE group and not only by amending the contractual arrangements regulating a specific manufacturing or distribution transaction.

The 2010 version of Chapter IX stressed, for the first time since the introduction of the 1979 Report, the concepts of control of risk (*risk management) and financial capacity to assume the risk*. As a result, the significance of introducing the chapter on business restructuring should not be overlooked for two reasons, specifically:

(1) For showing how the vast majority of business restructurings that gained the attention of tax administrations revolved around the transfer of intangibles; and

(2) The need to bring the concept of control over risk and the financial capacity to assume risk into a structural component of the TP guidelines and no longer as factors to be taken into account absent reliable third party comparables (as part I of the 2010 version of Chapter IX instead asserted).

(3) It is true, though, that the two above-mentioned concepts are still a source of uncertainties amongst taxpayers, however, they are the two defining concepts setting the boundaries for a proper, arm's length restructuring and an arrangement that needs to be restructured together.

The six-step process provided in Chapter 2 continues to be valid for business restructuring transactions as well. The role of risks could be further considered through the concept of *'Transfer of Profit Potential'* and *'Control and financial capacity to assume risk'*.

### 4.1.2.2.1 Concept of Relocating Profit Potential

The concept of relocating profit potential is important because independent enterprises that act as the basis of the arm's length analysis are not expected to undertake a business decision that reduces its expected profit or future profits. 'Profit potential' refers to 'expected future profits'.[42] Expected future profits are particularly relevant for the determination of arm's length compensation tangible assets, intangibles, ongoing concerns, or any situation that warrants a substantial renegotiation of existing arrangements.[43]

It is critical to recognize that expected future profits could also be negative, i.e., in the form of losses. An entity with considerable rights or assets at the time of restructuring is expected to a have a commensurate profit potential that is subject to the actual nature of assets. In order to determine whether the restructuring itself would give rise to a form of compensation at arm's length, it is essential to understand the restructuring including the changes that have occurred, how they have affected the functional analysis of the parties, what the business reasons for and the anticipated benefits from the restructuring were, and what options would have been realistically available to the parties.

### 4.1.2.2.2 Transfer of Risk and Profit Potential

The profit or loss arising from the restructuring is expected to be allocated between the parties commensurate to the risk assumed. Business restructurings often result in a conversion of one risk taking party into a more risk mitigated party which is followed by a lower return[44] due to reduced risk based on the grounds that the economically significant risks are assumed by a different party to which the risks are allocated.[45] Therefore, an analysis of risks based on the risk framework referred to in Chapter II continues to be applied.

---

**Example**

Subsidiary A Company is a full-fledged distributor of books published centrally by Parent Company B. The MNE group decides to provide all of its book publications as online content without any physical delivery point. For this purpose, Company B will contract with Company C, another subsidiary specialized in web-technologies, to develop and run software for hosting all of the publications online.

Company A will be converted into a commission agent in which activities will now be limited to canvassing for sales with no title to goods and no conclusion of contracts and agreements on credit terms. Therefore, compensation for Company A will include compensation for the loss of profit potential due to the change in its risk profile. However, other risks assumed by Company A are

---

42. *Supra* n. 3 OECD TPG, 2017, para. 9.40.
43. *Ibid.*, para. 9.41.
44. Modigliani, F, Miller, MH, *The cost of capital, corporation finance and the theory of investment,* The American economic review, 1958.
45. *Supra* n. 3 OECD TPG, 2017, para. 9.19.

> analysed in order to determine if there is any loss potential that is also transferred, offsetting the compensation for forgoing profit potential.

The likelihood of the risk materialising and the amount of the potential profits or losses arising from the risk determines the significance of the risk.[46] While accounting statements may provide useful information on the probability and the quantum of certain risks such as credit risk, inventory risk, etc., the use of past performance is an indicator of risks as financial reports may not capture all of them. The significance of the risk to a particular party determines whether the loss of profit potential could be explained by the transfer of risks associated with such profits. Therefore, the key risks that drive the profit potential are to be ascertained since every transfer of risk must result in a transfer of significant profit potential.

An indicative list of risks that could drive profit potential with regard to inventory risk is provided below:[47]

| Drivers | Considerations for Analysis |
| --- | --- |
| Inventory in the business model | Time to market (Just-in-time) practices |
| The nature of the inventory | Flowers, automobile parts |
| Intensity of investment in inventory | Aggregator model that minimises inventory investments |
| The factors giving rise to inventory write-downs or obsolescence and history of write-downs | pricing pressures, speed of technical improvements, market conditions |
| The cost of insuring against damage or loss of inventory | Risk mitigation strategy |
| The history of damage or loss (if uninsured) | Nature of treatment of losses, financial responses of associated enterprises to the losses |

### 4.1.2.2.3  Control and Financial Capacity to Assume Risk

In the process of the transfer of risk between parties under a restructuring situation, it could be established that one party assumes the risk and that same party continues to undertake the risk after the restructuring notwithstanding a change in contractual terms or intended risk allocation.

In such situations when the risk could not be 'transferred' or 'relocated' as intended, the allocation of risk for an arm's length analysis should follow the actual risk allocation between the parties. The actual risk is measured in terms of the party that has the ability to control and the financial capacity to assume such risks.

---

46. *Ibid.*, para. 9.22.
47. *Ibid.*, para. 9.23.

**Example**[48]

It is evident that a full-fledged distributor contractually assumes risks of bad debt before a restructuring. However, the analysis of risks establishes that, before the business restructuring, decisions about the extension of credit terms to customers and debt recovery were taken by an associated enterprise and not by the distributor, and the associated enterprise reimbursed the costs of irrecoverable debts.

The associated enterprise had complete control over the risk and had the financial capacity to assume the bad debt risk. Therefore, the risk was not assumed by the distributor before the restructuring in actuality. In such a case, there is no bad debt risk for the distributor to transfer risk as part of the business restructuring.

However, if the distributor had control over the bad debt risk and had the financial capacity to assume the risk it contractually assumed before the occurrence of business restructuring but had undertaken risk mitigation strategies to minimise or eliminate the risk through indemnification arrangements or debt factoring arrangements, then, after the occurrence of the business restructuring, the bad debt risk is set to be contractually assumed by that associated enterprise that now controls the risk and has the financial capacity to assume it.

Therefore, there has been a transfer of risk. The impact on the future profits of the distributor compared with those in the past that result from the transfer of this risk alone may be limited because, before the restructuring, steps had been taken and costs incurred to mitigate the risk outcomes of the distributor.

Based on the illustrations, it is important to note that a party that did not assume a particular risk before the restructuring cannot transfer it to another party as part of the restructuring. Also, a party that does not assume a risk after the restructuring is not expected to be allocated such risk and the consequent profit potential.

### 4.1.2.2.4 Valuing Profit Potential

For valuing profit potential, it is essential to take into account the historic profits (determined based on application of arm's length analysis). In the event of changes to the business environment or economic circumstances, profit potential cannot be calculated based on data on historical profits. Particularly, in a digitalizing economy, the change in profit potential could be difficult to ascertain based on historical profits, due to rapid changes in technology.[49]

---

48. *Ibid.*, para. 9.21.
49. *Supra* n. 9.

**Example**[50]

In the case of a full-fledged distributor being converted to a limited-risk distributor, the historical variability of profits using a five year data set ranges from (-) 5% to (+) 5%. This range is considered as a projected profitability over the rest of the period until which the existing contract would have been applicable had there been no restructuring.

The volatility of profits within the five years is identified to be significant, i.e., Year 1 (-) 5%, Year 2 (-) 0%; Year 3 (+) 3%, Year 4 (-) 1%; Year 5 (+) 5%.

Post-restructuring, the entity is expected to make a fixed total cost plus 3% in the role of a limited risk distributor.

In order to conclude whether the above restructuring would fulfil the test, it is evaluated whether an independent party would be willing to do so given a comparable level of risk tolerance, the number of options realistically available, and possible compensation for the restructuring itself. Reliance on historical data alone for determining profit potential could lead to insufficient results.

### 4.1.2.3 Analysis of Assets: Transferring Something of 'Value' – Including Going Concerns

Business restructurings could involve the transfer of tangibles as well as intangible assets. While the compensation for such transfers are ascertainable through valuation techniques, the transfer of intangibles creates recognition and valuation issues[51] leading to inconsistent positions. Finally, activities (ongoing concerns) could also be transferred as part of the restructuring, or certain functions could be outsourced to specific subsidiaries. Each category could constitute a 'value' and are further discussed below:

| Tangible Assets | |
| --- | --- |
| Nature of Assets | Arm's Length Analysis Approach |
| Tangible assets that are transferred[52] include capital assets employed such as plant and equipment, inventory, etc. | For instance, in the case of inventory, the following methods could be evaluated for applicability:<br>– Use of CUP, subject to similarity in conditions of restructuring and other parameters.<br>– Use of RPM to determine price of finished products, computed as the resale price to customers minus marketing functions.<br><br>Cost-plus remuneration computed based on, for example, manufacturing costs plus an arm's length mark up to with regard to inventories. |

---

50. *Supra* n. 3 OECD TPG, 2017, para. 9.46.
51. *Ibid.*, para. 9.48.
52. *Ibid.*, para. 9.54.

*Intangible Assets*

| Nature of Assets[53] | Arm's Length Analysis Approach[54] | |
|---|---|---|
| | *Nature of Intangible Transferred* | *Approach* |
| Patents, trademarks, trade names, designs or models, as well as copyrights of literary, artistic, or scientific work (including software) and IP such as know-how and trade secrets. Also includes customer lists, distribution channels, unique names, symbols or pictures | Disposal of intangibles or rights to intangibles by a local operation to a central location (foreign associated enterprise)[55] | – A mere change in ownership of an intangible may not affect which party is entitled to returns from that intangible.<br>– Delineate the actual transaction to ascertain whether there has been a transfer of legal owner- ship or whether there has been a change of identity (characterisa- tion of the individual entities) before and after the centralisa- tion.<br>– Some centralization could also be in the form of administrative sim- plifications and not necessarily change the underlying characteri- sation.<br>– Development, enhancement, maintenance, protection, and exploitation (DEMPE) plays a key role in determining the underly- ing change. |
| | Intangible transferred at a point in time when its valuation is highly uncertain.[56] | – Identifying what independent enterprises would have done in comparable circumstances to take account of the valuation un- certainty in the pricing of the transaction.<br>– The approach followed by inde- pendent entities in uncertain cir- cumstances is to be adopted as the best measure. |

---

53. *Ibid.*, para. 9.56.
54. *Ibid.*, para. 9.57.
55. *Ibid.*, para. 9.58.
56. *Ibid.*, paras 9.62–63.

| *Intangible Assets* | | |
| --- | --- | --- |
| | Local intangibles[57] | – Local subsidiaries that have developed intangibles over a period of time requires compensation. <br> – Typical examples include marketing intangibles wherein the local subsidiary maintains a distribution channel, develops the global brand in a local market, etc. <br> – In determining the post-restructuring activities, if the functions remain with the same entity post-restructuring then, accordingly, no compensation is warranted. |
| | Contractual rights[58] | Closer evaluation of entities that voluntarily terminate contracts with benefits only to allow another group entity to undertake the same activities. <br> Independent enterprises would not be subject to such termination. |

Assets that form contributions that are 'unique and valuable' in cases when: (i) they are not comparable to contributions made by uncontrolled parties in comparable circumstances, and (ii) they represent a key source of actual or potential economic benefits in the business operations as the restructuring could lead to further challenges.[59]

---

**Court case: Cytec Norway[60]**

In one of the earliest cases of business restructuring, the transfer of intangible assets – customer portfolio, technology, brands, and goodwill – was under scrutiny by the Norwegian Court. Cytec Norway was originally a full-fledged manufacturer that was transformed into a contract manufacturer. The customer portfolio, technology, brand rights, and goodwill were transferred free of charge to the affiliated company, Cytec Netherlands.

The Court found that Cytec Norge AS had held intangible assets or significant value prior to the reorganization of the company in 1999 and that the Norwegian

---

57. *Ibid.*, paras 9.64–65.
58. *Ibid.*, para. 9.66.
59. *Ibid.*, (Glossary).
60. Norway Cytec. September 2007, LRD 2007/1440; *supra* n. 9.

> company would have received standard market remuneration for the transfer of those rights to the related Dutch company.

Intangibles that are more nuanced cannot be ascertained as an intangible at the time of undertaking the business restructuring pose a significant challenge. Furthermore, the definition of intangibles is now constantly expanding under international tax jurisprudence to include goodwill, assembled workforce, and group synergies[61] which could also constitute the definition of an intangible. One or more of such intangibles in combination could form part of an 'ongoing concern'.

*Going Concern (Activities)*

| *Nature* | *Arm's Length Analysis Approach* |
|---|---|
| Transfer of activity that is Economically integrated and forms an actively functioning business unit.[62] | – Valuing a transfer of ongoing concern should take into consideration all elements of 'value' which would be remunerated under independent circumstances. Financial valuation techniques that are employed to value acquisitions are used. However, it is noted that the value of an active business unit will not necessarily be the sum of each value component.<br>– Arm's length remuneration is to be compared with a transfer of an ongoing concern ('akin to sale')[63] between independent parties rather than with a transfer of isolated assets. |
| Loss-making activities[64] | – Profit potential also includes the concept of 'loss', i.e., a restructuring could be initiated to save a group affiliate from continuous losses or future loss potential.<br>– Whether the entity that takes over the loss potential should be compensated should be determined based on a comparison to independent circumstances, i.e., independent enterprise could have closed down the activity rather than selling or pay certain costs in order to sell its losses, etc.<br>– However, the synergies that could arise post-restructuring could offset the compensation payable to the entity that takes over the loss potential. Therefore, a thorough analysis and justification for compensation is essential. |

---

61. IRC section 936(h)(3)(B).
62. *Supra* n. 3 OECD TPG, 2017, para. 9.68.
63. IRC sections 367 and 482.
64. *Supra* n. 3 OECD TPG, 2017, para. 9.72.

*Outsourcing*[65]

| Nature | Arm's Length Analysis Approach |
|---|---|
| Movement of functions from one entity to another, typically to take advantage of a lower cost structure and/or skilled labour. | – Independent parties entering into an outsourcing arrangement would weigh the cost of undertaking the restructuring against the long-term benefits post-restructuring.<br>– A situation when there could have been location savings after the outsourcing model has been implemented and then a reversal of transfer is made could trigger questions of whether the savings in the low-cost tax jurisdiction warrant compensation. However, this is a post-restructuring consequence. |

Valuing such hard-to-value intangible (HDVI) assets based on current financial accounting standards is increasingly inadequate as many components of 'value' cannot be captured by accounting principles. Accurately delineating intangible transactions and valuing them continues to be a challenge for transfer pricing purposes. For a detailed discussion on valuation difficulties in transfer pricing, refer to Chapter 11.

---

**Court case:[66] Getko, Israel (Microsoft Restructuring)**

Facts of the case

Microsoft Corporation (Microsoft USA) acquired Getko Ltd (Getko Israel). Getko's employees were transferred to Microsoft's Israeli subsidiary (Microsoft Israel) and Microsoft Israel subsequently entered into an agreement with Microsoft Israel to provide services (on a cost plus basis) to Getko's existing customers. Getko and Microsoft signed an agreement to sell the IP owned by Getko. The Israel tax authorities questioned the valuation of purchase of Getko's business and the valuation of the IP that was transferred. In this regard, the following questions were posed before the court:
- Whether the transaction under question is restricted to the transfer of the IP alone, or does it involve a sale of an entire business activity as a composite?
- What should be the value of the assets transferred, as derived from the share acquisition value, including values of items not reflected in the IP agreement such as synergies or other assets that remained with the company?

Ruling of the court
- Separation among value components such as technology and other physical assets is necessary.
- Synergies should be integral to the value of a company's assets that are subject to transfer.

---

65. *Supra* n. 1, UN Manual 2017, B.7.1.19.
66. *Supra* n. 9.

> - Transfer of employees operating the company's various functions including distribution and development, as well as senior management, can be viewed as significant and valuable function transfer.
> - Getko's existing customer contracts remained with the company and, therefore, should be deducted from the acquisition value.

## 4.2 Business Reasons for the Restructuring, Including the Role of Synergies

Many acquisitions and some large strategic investments are often justified with the argument that they will create synergy. The commercial and business reasons for undertaking business restructurings were discussed in section 3.

For the purpose of transfer pricing, synergies could be classified into two broad categories:[67]

(a) *Operational synergy* – Synergies that allow companies to reduce their operating costs and increase revenue growth from cross utilization of products, services, business channels, etc.
(b) *Financial synergy* – benefits of combining two companies from higher cash flows arising from tax benefits, and the acquisition of losses.

Synergies are measured in the form of anticipated benefits at the time of restructuring. The following sections detail the role of expected benefits and various forms of synergies and valuation of synergies.

### 4.2.1 Expected Benefits

Commercial and business rationale for restructuring would require documentation with the evidence of the time and date of the restructuring. These documents carrying the anticipated synergistic benefits are likely to be produced internally (management) or externally (tax authorities) depending on the needs that arise.[68] When deliberate concerted group actions are taken through a business restructuring, the associated enterprises contributing to the synergistic benefit after the restructuring are appropriately remunerated.

> **Example[69]**
>
> MNE Group XYZ undertakes a restructuring that centralizes the group's procurement function to Holding Company X. Until the restructuring, ERP systems were fragmented across XYZ Group. Although Company X is entitled to profit potential

---

67. Reams, K, *Acquisition Premium and Cost Sharing Analysis, International Tax Review*, January 2014.
68. *Supra* n. 3 OECD TPG, 2017, para. 9.24.
69. *Ibid.*, para. 9.21.

arising from its assumption of the risk associated with buying, holding, and on-selling goods, it is not entitled to retain profits arising from the group purchasing power because it does not contribute to the creation of synergies Therefore, the synergy effects are recognised independently, requiring commensurate compensation for the role and contribution by individual subsidiaries.

While business restructurings are typically intended to capture anticipated synergies, all restructurings do not necessarily result in increasing profits for the MNE group. Enhanced synergies could make it possible for the MNE group to derive additional profits compared to what the situation would have been in the absence of restructuring occurring, however, it does not ensure that the profits are more than what the MNE group would have made had it not undertaken the restructuring.[70]

Therefore, though the restructuring is commercially rational, from a transfer pricing and tax perspective, acceptance of the restructuring as a composite, i.e., transfer of intangibles and transfer of purchase function together, would have not met the arm's length conditions. Independent enterprises under similar circumstances may not have provided the operational control of intangibles. During the course of a tax audit, the tax officer is entitled to disregard the composite valuation of this restructuring arrangement. Furthermore, while anticipated synergies may be relevant to the understanding of a business restructuring, caution must be taken to avoid the use of hindsight in *ex post* analyses.[71]

---

**Example[72]**

MNE Group 'L' is engaged in the chemical business globally. It held majority shares of 'L Sub Co.' in which the MNE Group 'M' also held a minority stake. 'L Sub Co' sold its entire shareholding in L group to a third party at a negotiated price of EUR 100 per share whereas the RA group had been paid EUR 200 per share. The third-party was a joint venture of L group and another group in which the holding company of the assessee had a 49% share of the shareholding. Since the assessee had not been paid anything towards the control premium though it had sold the controlling stake in the company, the tax administrators imposed an adjustment on account of the control premium at 25% of the share value. The view was upheld by the apex court of the tax jurisdiction.

---

70. *Ibid.*, para. 26.
71. *Ibid.*, para. 3.74.
72. *See Lanxess India (P.) Ltd. v ACIT* (Mumbai – Tribunal).

### 4.2.2 Valuation Approach for Restructurings Including Synergies and Control Premium[73]

| Component | Valuation Considerations |
| --- | --- |
| **Synergy** | Value the combined firm with synergy built in. This may include:<br>– higher growth rate in revenues: growth synergy<br>– higher margins because of economies of scale<br>– lower taxes because of tax benefits: tax synergy<br>– lower cost of debt: financing synergy<br>– higher debt ratio because of lower risk: debt capacity<br><br>Subtract the value of the target firm (with control premium) + value of the bidding firm (pre-acquisition). This is the value of the synergy. |
| **Control Premium** | Control premium refers to the value the company as if optimally managed. This will usually mean that investment, financing, and dividend policy will be altered:<br>– Investment Policy: Higher returns on projects and divesting unproductive projects.<br>– Financing Policy: Move to a better financing structure; for example, optimal capital structure<br>– Dividend Policy: Return unused cash |
| **Status Quo Valuation** | Value the company as is with existing inputs for investment, financing, and dividend policy |

Considering the above guidelines, although synergies and control premiums are complex and cannot be valued, a reasonable effort could be made to value benefits arising from the above aspects.

## 4.3 Options Realistically Available Analysis

### 4.3.1 Concept of ORA Analysis

While agreeing to enter into a particular transaction, independent enterprises are expected to evaluate the options realistically available to ascertain the most rational choice that provides the best opportunity to meet its commercial objective, i.e., independent enterprises would only enter into a transaction if it does not affect them more negatively than their next best option.[74]

The ORA concept builds on the economic theory of opportunity cost and rational decision making. A decision is rational if it increases the value of a multinational

---

73. Damodaran, A, *The Value of Synergy*, Stern School of Business (New York: 2005) (Source: https://ssrn.com/abstract = 841486).
74. *Supra* n. 3 OECD TPG, 2017, para. 9.27.

enterprise. Therefore, when making an investment decision, a rational MNE should only choose the investments that have a positive net present value (NPV).[75]

A decision is expected to compare all alternatives. The costs for the parties involved in making the decision(s) is to consider all economic or opportunity costs that could be forgone.

A consideration of the options that are realistically available is relevant for a comparability analysis and is recognized by domestic tax laws of certain countries. A hypothetical arm's length test is applied due to the assumed absence of comparable transactions between independent parties under the German[76] transfer pricing rules. The Dutch decree[77] also makes reference to the fact that related parties may enter into many more varieties of arrangements than independent parties after having evidenced that they have analysed alternatives. Furthermore, the US transfer pricing rules have long enshrined the concept of the realistic alternatives test under the requirements for a comparability analysis[78] and cost-sharing arrangements (CSAs) Rules.[79] The principle has also been a key contention before the US tax courts by the US IRS in the past.

---

**Example**

The US tax court, in the historical case of Bausch & Lomb,[80] rejected the US IRS argument that license and sales transactions should be evaluated by comparing the licensor's 'realistic alternative' of using the licensed technology itself

The tax court in the case of Amazon[81] has also rejected the IRS's argument that its business enterprise approach to valuing Amazon Lux's buy-in payment properly captured the value of Amazon US's 'realistic alternative' of continuing to own and develop the Amazon intangibles.

---

The core of the argument put forth by tax administrators is centred on evaluating whether the option of not agreeing to the conditions of the restructuring have been considered regarding giving up the profit potential without any proper indemnification.[82] Therefore, the concept of the ORA, although applied in various legal forms, has found credence in practice and forms an integral part of a comparability analysis. However, the ORA itself has not become a method that could be substitute for the prescribed methods (Refer to *Chapter III* for a detailed analysis of methods).

---

75. Keating, S.A., *Economics and Management Accounting*, Chicago Booth School of Business 2006.
76. Compare the German Foreign Tax Code, section 1(3), sentence 5 and the Draft Administrative Principles on the Transfer of Functions dated 17 Jul. 2009.
77. Netherlands Decree of 22 Apr. 2018, no. 20186865.
78. US IRC 1.482-1(d)(3)(iv)(H) and Explanatory Statement.
79. Department Of The Treasury, Internal Revenue Service, T.D. 9568.
80. *Bausch & Laumb Inc. Inc. v Commissioner*, 92 T.C. 525 (1989).
81. *Amazon v Commissioner*, 148 T.C. No. 8 (2017).
82. Shenzhen State Tax Bureau, Shenzhen State Tax Bureau Adjusted Tax Payable over 100 Million in a Transfer Pricing Case (2012), available at http://www.chinatax.gov.cn/n8136506/n8136608/n9947993/n9948094/11985200.html (last accessed 19 Mar. 2013).

### 4.3.2   Application of ORA in Arm's Length Analysis

In applying the principle, it is evaluated whether each transaction that has been accurately delineated based on the economically relevant characteristics of the parties has been verified for options that are realistically available.[83] In making such an assessment, it could be necessary to assess the transactions comprising the business restructuring in the context of a broader arrangement of economically related transactions. In such cases when an independent party may not have agreed to the conditions of the restructuring and adjustments to the conditions made or imposed may be necessary, the transaction could be disregarded.[84]

While analysing the parameters for a comparability analysis, the application of the ORA considers a review of each of the following aspects:

- *Contractual terms:* When contractual obligations of the enterprise make it economically unviable to not participate in a business restructuring, the same should be taken into consideration in determining the nature of the controlled transaction.
- *Characteristics of property or services:* It cannot be assumed that an enterprise will venture into an unrelated or a different product or service while evaluating alternatives. Therefore, the industry and the value chain establishes the boundaries for determining the realistic alternatives of the associated enterprise.
- *Functional analysis:* The activities of the associated enterprise are essential to establish the boundaries of the alternatives that can be considered realistic. An evaluation of functions, risks, and assets helps to identify different alternatives of these that could be assumed under similar circumstances by an independent enterprise. The availability of alternatives will indicate whether similar enterprises would have the financial capacity to assume the risk and control.
- *Business strategies:* The risk-taking ability of the business, future goals, objectives for the business, and any other dominant strategy should not be ignored when outlining the realistic alternatives available at the disposal of the associated enterprise.

---

**Example**

Company A develops, manufactures, and sells Product A in domestic Country A and foreign Countries B and C. While Countries A and B are a historical (and stable) market served by Company A, Country C has a high growth potential for which, in recent years, relevant investments have been made by Company A. Company B distributes Product A in Country D, a relatively small market with declining results. Following the strategy declined by Company A, Company B, for

---

83. *Supra* n. 3 OECD TPG, 2017, para. 1.38.
84. *Ibid.*, para. 9.30.

> the future, will be entitled to exclusively distribute Product A in Country C while Country D will be served directly and exclusively by Company A. In this fact pattern, however, it is clear that it is unlikely that independent parties in Company A's situation would agree to switch to the end-market for no compensation if they had the alternative options realistically available.

Therefore, based on the above, the ORA is not a separate analysis by itself but should be considered pervasively to any general transfer pricing analysis. For the purpose of business restructuring, the outcome of an ORA analysis is expected to indicate if there is a realistically available option that is clearly more attractive and then determine whether the related enterprises have considered those alternatives.

### 4.3.3 Commercial Rationale

It is an established economic concept that risk and reward go hand in hand.[85] When comparing the various alternatives, a mere comparison of the profit potential of various alternatives in isolation, without taking into account the relative risk that each option poses, would lead to a faulty conclusion. Accordingly, it is plausible that an entrepreneur entity could accept being converted into an entity earning routine returns with fewer other riskier alternatives realistically available to it. Therefore, a comparison in such cases with independent enterprises may not be possible. In this scenario, the commercial rationale of an enterprise cannot be questioned.[86]

Tax authorities often have the benefit of hindsight, however, such hindsight should not be used to determine the options that could potentially be available to the associated enterprise. In the *Amazon* case,[87] the US Court observed that the IRS's application of the '*realistic alternatives*' theory would '*make the cost sharing election, which the regulations explicitly make available to taxpayers, altogether meaningless*'. Earlier, in the case of *Bausch & Lomb*,[88] the IRS contended that the pricing of contact lenses purchased by Bausch & Lomb US from its Irish subsidiary should be judged by reference to the cost at which the US Company could have itself manufactured the lenses. Similar findings emerged from the *Veritas* case[89] in the past.

Caution is required in cases when the benefit of hindsight could lead to varying alternatives and contradicting valuation outcomes.[90]

---

85. Penelle, PG, *Economics of Business Restructuring and Exit Charges*, Tax Management Transfer Pricing Report V.3 at 239.
86. *Supra* n. 3 OECD TPG, 2017, para. 65.
87. Storck, A., Miladinovic, A., *US Tax Court Ruled in Favor of Amazon US Addressing a Cost-Sharing Arrangement and the Related Transfer of Intangible Assets*, Transfer Pricing International (2017), pp. 260–267.
88. *Amazon.com, Inc. & Subsidiaries, v Commissioner*, No. 31197-12: 148 TC. No. 8.
89. *Veritas Software Corp. v Commissioner*, 133 T.C. 297 (2009).
90. Parekh, S., *The Concept of "Options Realistically Available" under the OECD Transfer Pricing Guidelines*, International Transfer Pricing Journal, 2015 (Volume 22), No. 5, Vol. 22 (3 Sep. 2015).

## 5 RECOGNITION OF THE ACCURATELY DELINEATED TRANSACTIONS

### 5.1 Disregarding the Transaction

Business restructurings create a unique challenge for the application of the arm's length principle as MNE Groups may often implement a restructuring that may not be found between independent enterprises. The objective of a restructuring itself could be to create a unique, imitable model. However, from a transfer pricing perspective, this could result in the lack of comparables (or comparable circumstances). This does not lead to automatic disqualification of the model. Every effort should be made to determine the pricing for the restructured transactions as accurately delineated under the arm's length principle.[91]

### 5.2 Aggregation and Disaggregation

The test of commercial rationality of restructuring under the guidance for non-recognition discussed in Chapter 1 could lead to the question of whether a transaction should be considered in isolation or as a package with other closely related transactions.

---

**Example**

As part of its broader business restructuring project, Company A of Company ABC Group sells an intangible that is part of various arrangements relating to the development and use of the intangible. The tax administration in which Company A is domiciled seeks to examine the commercial rationality of the intangible in isolation.

Also, ABC Group's restructuring involves centralizing the purchasing function along with centralizing the ownership of valuable intangible property that does not have a connection with the purchasing function. The commercial rationality of centralizing the purchasing function and the ownership of valuable intangible property requires separate evaluations.

---

### 5.3 Commercial Rationality and Fulfilling Arm's Length Criteria

A challenging situation arises for the taxpayer when restructuring makes complete commercial sense, however, it is not sufficient from an arm's length perspective. Therefore, the taxpayer is required to ensure that the arrangement must be at arm's length at the level of each individual taxpayer who is part of the restructuring process after considering the rights and other assets, expected benefits from the arrangement,

---

91. OECD 9.36.

and realistically available options.[92] A tax motivated business restructuring itself does not preclude its implementation and could not lead to non-recognition. However, the emphasis always shifts towards ensuring that each entity involved in the business restructuring receives an arm's length remuneration.

## 6  POST-RESTRUCTURING TRANSACTIONS

The arm's -ength principle is to be applied equally to post-restructuring transactions as well as transactions that were structured as such from the beginning. A uniform application eliminates any potential distortion of arm's length prices by adopting different approaches. The steps beginning from the accurate delineation of the transaction that is based on economically relevant characteristics, recognition, and use of appropriate transfer methods is relevant.[93]

However, the comparability analysis of an arrangement that results from a business restructuring might reveal a number of factual differences compared to that of an arrangement that was structured as such from the beginning. Such differences could arise due to the following conditions[94]

### 6.1  Factual Differences Between an Outcome of Restructuring and Structured Entities

The conditions that apply to a restructured entity having a history of relationships with its counterparty (or counterparties) to the restructuring transaction are not comparable to that of an entity that is newly structured with no prior contractual relationships with its counterparty (or counterparties). When there is an ongoing business relationship between the parties before and after the restructuring, there may also be effects of an interrelationship that distort comparability.

---

**Example[95]**

Company X and Company Y are two associated enterprises whereby Company Y is a full-fledged distributor. Based on a group-wide decision, Company Y is converted into a limited risk distributor. Company Y exists in a country where Company X has had its presence for several decades. Company Y had developed significant marketing intangibles over the long term. In addition, Company Y had assumed the risk of bad debts which it will no longer do (post-restructuring). Company A and Company B, two unrelated enterprises, enter into an agreement wherein Company B will act as a distributor (undertaking limited risks) for Company A's products. Company A does not have a presence in the country of Company B.

---

92. *Supra* n. 3 OECD TPG, 2017, para. 9.37.
93. *Ibid.*, paras 9.98–9.99.
94. *Ibid.*, para. 9.102.
95. *Ibid.*, paras 9.103–9.107.

> The conditions for restructuring between Company X and Company Y are not comparable to that of Company A and Company B.

### 6.2 Choice of Most Appropriate Method for Benchmarking Post-restructuring Transactions

After ascertaining the economically relevant characteristics of the controlled restructuring transaction, the most appropriate method is determined. In post-restructuring situations, using a mere high-level definition of an entity to be a 'commissionaire' or "limited-risk manufacturer' will be insufficient. Particular attention is demanded for the identification of the valuable intangibles and the economically significant risks that could continue to effectively remain with the restructured entity (while there had been an intent to transfer the risks associated with those intangibles).

---

**Example[96]**

Company A and Company B, two unrelated enterprises, enter into an agreement wherein Company B now becomes a related enterprise. The transaction between Company A and Company B could be benchmarked using the CUP method whereby the transactions of pre-restructuring and post-restructuring could be compared.

In the event of any economically different conditions (based on the five economically relevant characteristics identified in Chapter II) between the pre-restructuring and post-restructuring phase, appropriate adjustments could be made for factoring differences in the transfer of functions, assets, and/or risks.

---

Further, it is recognised that the comparable data will not always be perfect, particularly in post-restructuring transaction comparisons. The restructuring could have led to a fragmentation of value generating functions and, therefore, may not be directly comparable to an independent circumstance. As discussed earlier, this does not provide a sufficient reason for disregarding the transaction or concluding that the transaction is not at arm's length.

### 6.3 Relationship Between Compensation for the Restructuring and Post-restructuring Remuneration

Business restructuring provides a unique opportunity in situations when one party (taxpayer), having an ongoing business relationship with a related party that, after the implementation of the restructuring, performs the activities previously carried out by the taxpayer. In such situations, both parties could establish the transfer prices for the

---

96. *Ibid.*, para. 9.110.

'restructuring' or the 'post-restructuring' transactions which could be in the nature of an intentional set-off. The post-restructuring compensation that is agreed could be after considering the remuneration to be paid under the pre-restructuring situation.

---

**Example[97]**

Company X and Company Y, two associated enterprises, swap their functions, risks, and assets, i.e., Company Y acquires Company X's activity matrix. This resulting transfer price from this swap could be determined based on the following considerations:

Company Y could agree with the Company X to forgo the receipt of part or all of the upfront compensation for the business that may be payable. This is accompanied by a comparable financial benefit by agreeing to sell its goods to Company X at prices that are higher than the latter would otherwise agree to if the upfront compensation had been paid.

Alternatively, Company Y and Company X could also agree to have lower future transfer prices and correspondingly higher upfront compensation.

In both of the above possibilities, it becomes critical to substantiate the value of transfer prices that are agreed based on thorough documentation at the time of undertaking the restructuring.

---

## 6.4 Comparing the Pre- and Post-restructuring Situations

It is critical to emphasize that comparing the profits from the post-restructuring controlled transactions with the profits made in controlled transactions prior to the restructuring does not fulfil an arm's length analysis under Article 9 of the OECD Model Tax Convention. Such a comparison merely results in comparing two controlled transactions which is not a solution to arriving at an unbiased arm's length price.

Further, practical difficulties arise in attempting to appraise the basket of 'values' that were lost or formed due to the restructuring. However, information regarding the nature of the contractual relationship and conduct before and after the restructuring forms an important component in understanding the restructuring and also for conducting the ORA analysis.[98]

## 6.5 Location Savings

Further to the discussions in Chapter II of this book, from a business restructuring perspective, the relocation of functions, assets, and risks in order to achieve cost-efficiency requires a separate analysis. When location savings are ascertained as a consequence of business restructuring, the share of benefits due to such savings is

---

97. *Ibid.*, para. 9.115.
98. *Ibid.*, para. 9.121.

required to be at arm's length. Once again, the attribution of benefits is based on the fundamental analysis of functions, risks, and assets and the ORA analysis at the time of relocation.

---

**Example**[99]

A company incorporated in Country A and a company incorporated in Company B are two associated enterprises. There is significant demand for the type of specialized engineering services that the company in Country B delivers to the group. Assume that a subsidiary in Country B is the only company operating in a lower-cost location that is able to provide such services with the required quality standard, superior technical precision, etc. This also includes significant intangibles generated by the company operating in Country B based on a certain level of participation from Company A.

Furthermore, the company in Country A does not have the desired skilled labour or low wage rates to deliver the services. Considering this, the company in Country B does not have any alternative option but to obtain the services from the company in Country B. The remuneration paid by the company in Country A should include compensation for the location savings achieved by the company in Country B.

A transactional profit split method could be used to determine the relative contribution of both associated enterprises with regard to the intangibles that are generated.

---

In this regard, it is should be noted that any potential increase or decrease of profit expectations imposed to the transferor or the transferee should not be considered for the purpose of defining whether a business restructuring has occurred. Such circumstances could only affect the pricing of the transaction either for the purpose of a post-restructuring transfer pricing policy or for exit tax purposes.

## 7 ARTIFICIAL AVOIDANCE OF PERMANENT ESTABLISHMENTS

Under the existing framework of PEs, the profits of an enterprise of a Contracting State shall be taxable only in that State unless the enterprise conducts business in the other Contracting State through a permanent establishment situated therein. The term '*permanent establishment*' means a *fixed place* of business through which the business of the enterprise is wholly or partly performed and includes: (a) a place of management, (b) a branch, (c) an office, (d) a factory, (e) a workshop, (f) a mine, an oil or gas well, a quarry, or any other place of extraction of natural resources.

---

99. *Ibid.*, para. 9.131.

Business restructurings offering new forms of value drivers such as data for the attribution of profits[100] have been proposed.[101] From a business restructuring perspective, business models need to evaluate the risk of creating new forms of PEs and, in the absence of law, different tax jurisdictions could take different views in taxing 'virtual presence'. This risk is not isolated to only highly digitalized businesses; it is applicable to traditional business that may undertake operations in a jurisdiction without being physically present there. The following judicial precedent, a landmark ruling, provides detailed insights.

---

**Court case:[102] Dell (Spain)**

Dell Ireland was responsible for the commercialization of Dell computers in Europe. Sales were carried out through local subsidiaries that were located in other European countries and had no employees or premises. Dell Spain, a local subsidiary, operated as a distributor in the Spanish market, supported technical, logistics, warehousing, marketing, after-sales, and administration support services of the Spanish online store.

Dell Spain was a full-fledged distributor until 1995 and, later, the sales operations of the Dell group were reorganized as the customer lists were transferred to Dell Ireland which now assumed the risks of inventory, warranty, and customers. Post-restructuring, Dell Spain became a commissionaire with Dell Ireland acting as the principal.

The Spanish tax authorities contended that Dell Ireland had a PE in Spain based on the fact that the fixed place premises of Dell Spain acted as the medium of business for Dell Ireland, and Dell Spain also acted as a dependent agent of Dell Ireland. The tax authorities also claimed that the online store for the Spanish market could be considered as a virtual PE of Dell Ireland even if there was no server located in Spain since the website was maintained by Spanish personnel, and Dell Spain processed orders made through the online store.

---

## 8 IMPORTANCE OF DOCUMENTATION

Considering the inherent complexity of business restructuring transactions and the heightened litigation surrounding them, taxpayers are required to provide the utmost attention to documenting the transaction at the time of initiating the restructuring. It is necessary to document the consequences of changes to the profit potential and risk allocation between the parties.

---

100. Storck, A., Petruzzi, R., Holzinger, R., *Comments on the Public Discussion Draft of BEPS Action 7 (Additional Guidance on the Attribution of Profits to Permanent Establishments)*, OECD (October 2017).
101. Petruzzi, R. & Buriak, S., *Addressing the Tax Challenges of the Digitalization of the Economy: A Possible Answer from a Proper Application of Transfer Pricing Rules?* IBFD International Transfer Pricing Journal, March 2018.
102. *Netherlands v. A BV*, October 2017, No. 2017: 5965.

The importance of contemporaneous maintenance of documentation is relevant for business restructuring transactions due to the fact that transfer pricing audits occur when the outcome of restructuring transactions could be better understood in hindsight. Given that business restructuring transactions involve an analysis of *ex ante* and *ex post* circumstances, the documentation maintained contemporaneously would form the basis for comparisons.

The question of whether data of future years and the benefit of hindsight could be used in an arm's length analysis by tax administrators has been a subject matter of litigation and has been discouraged. However, the data of future years for business restructuring transactions could aid in better understanding the arrangement itself and could help in corroborating some of the assumptions made in the pre-restructuring documentation maintained by the MNE Group.

With the new three-tiered documentation structure that is prescribed, business restructuring transactions are required to be reported in the master file. In addition, in the local file, taxpayers are asked to indicate whether the local entity has been involved in or affected by business restructurings occurring during the year or in the immediate past year and to explain the aspects of such transactions affecting the local entity.[103]

---

**Court case:[104] Netherlands v. A BV**

In this case, a Dutch parent company provided support services to its foreign subsidiary on a cost-plus basis and received a compensation fee following a business restructuring in which the strategic headquarters' functions were transferred from the Dutch parent company to Switzerland. The Dutch tax authorities considered that the remuneration received for the transfer was insufficient and that the Dutch parent company continued to exercise strategic functions for the group.

However, the court ruled that the taxpayer had fulfilled its legal obligations by producing thorough transfer pricing documentation and that the burden of proof lay with the Dutch tax authorities to provide evidence for the adjustments to the transfer price.

---

Apart from the local and master files, the introduction of country-by-country reporting provides new impetus to improve transparency. From business restructuring transaction perspective, the role of CbC Reports holds both promises and perils. Compliance requires consolidation of group revenue for reporting purposes which should be undertaken regardless of the restructuring that occurred during the fiscal year of reporting.[105] Also, investment entities are not exempt from the CbC Report requirements and, therefore, a company that is owned by an investment fund to control

---

103. *Supra* n. 3 OECD TPG, 2017, 9.32.
104. *Netherlands v. A BV*, October 2017, No. 2017: 5965.
105. *See* OECD (2017), *BEPS Action 13 on Country-by-Country Reporting – Guidance on the appropriate use of information contained in Country-by-Country reports*, OECD, Paris.

other entities in combination with the other entities controlled could constitute an MNE Group requiring compliance if the group revenue exceeds the threshold of Euro 750 million.[106]

## 9 CONCLUSIONS

This chapter has detailed how to assess the nature of business restructuring transactions with specific reference to accurately delineating transactions, ascertaining the profit potential, and the use of tools such as the Options Realistically Available (ORA) as part of the arm's length analysis. Considering the periodical guidance provided by the OECD and the UN, the process of applying the arm's length principle to business restructuring transactions commences with the accurate delineation of the transaction involving a review of written agreements. Particular emphasis is laid on the termination, indemnification or re-negotiation of contractual arrangements.

Concepts in supply chain management that have an interplay with the understanding of "value" drivers were discussed. Such concepts also form the commercial basis for restructuring decisions However from a transfer pricing perspective, it is well established that a restructuring arrangement cannot make commercial sense in isolation and must be complemented with an arm's length objective. The arm's length structure must be achieved at the level of each individual taxpayer, that forms part of the value chain of the company, taking into account its rights, obligations, various tangible and intangible assets and expected benefits arising from the arrangement (i.e., consideration of the post-restructuring arrangement along with any other compensation payments for the restructuring itself).

Finally, the role of documentation for business restructuring assumed a larger significance due to uncertainties involved in the quantitative valuation of expected benefits (or detriments) and profit (or loss) potential. As part of transfer pricing documentation, MNE groups are guided to capture their decisions and intentions regarding business restructurings at the stage of decision making, with adequate focus on the status of significant risks assumed, before and after the relevant transactions occur. Documentation rules require the disclosure of restructuring transactions in the local file and the master file, resulting in a larger impact across various jurisdictions that have access to such information.

---

106. *Supra* n. 3 OECD TPG, 2017, para. 8.

CHAPTER 13

# Transfer Pricing and Customs Valuation

## 1   INTRODUCTION

This chapter concerns the relationship between Customs valuation and transfer pricing.[1] It is designed to provide an understanding of the use of transfer pricing information for Customs valuation purposes and the challenges faced by Customs when using such information.

A significant proportion of world trade is conducted by multinational enterprises (MNEs), and a substantial proportion consists of the transfer of goods, intangibles, and services within MNEs. This makes international taxation, and in particular transfer pricing, a top priority for tax administrations as well as MNEs. Most MNEs also utilize transfer prices for Customs valuation purposes hence the study of transfer pricing issues in relationship to Customs valuation has become increasingly interesting to Customs administrations and businesses due to the increasing amount of global trade. It has also been featured prominently in the work of the Technical Committee on Customs Valuation (TCCV).[2]

The primary content of this chapter addresses Customs valuation and related party transactions in section 2, the association between transfer pricing and Customs valuation in section 3, and examples of how transfer pricing information can be used for Customs valuation purposes in section 4.

## 2   CUSTOMS VALUATION AND RELATED PARTY TRANSACTIONS

The Customs value of imported goods is primarily utilized as the basis for determining Customs duty liability for imported goods when an ad valorem[3] duty applies. The customs valuation methodology that is established in the Agreement contains a sequence of valuation methods[4] with the transaction value method as the primary method. The Preamble states: '*[r]ecognizing that the basis for valuation of goods for Customs purposes should, to the greatest extent possible, be the transaction value of the goods being valued*'. All WTO member countries are obligated to implement this

---

1. This Chapter contains materials adapted from the 'WCO Guide to Customs Valuation and Transfer Pricing' (the 2015 WCO Guide) published by the WCO in 2015.
2. The TCCV was established to ensure the uniformity in interpretation and application of the WTO Valuation Agreement (the Agreement) at the technical level. It is responsible for examining specific technical questions arising in the regular administration of the Customs valuation system of Members. It is also responsible to furnish information and advice on any matters concerning the valuation of imported goods for Customs purposes as may be requested by any Members or the TCCV in the form of advisory opinion, commentaries or explanatory notes. It also facilitates, as requested, technical assistance to Members to further the international acceptance of the Agreement.
3. The Glossary of International Customs Terms defines ad valorem duties and taxes as 'duties and taxes which are collected on the basis of value'.
4. There are a series of methods that are explicated in the WTO Valuation Agreement. These are the transaction value method, transaction of identical goods method, transaction value of similar goods method, deductive value method, computed value method and the fallback option. These methods are to be applied in a sequential order.

Agreement upon accession to the WTO, and many of them have reported that the transaction value method stated therein is employed for over 90%[5] of all importations.

There are two main elements of transaction value. The first, as described in Article 1 of the Agreement, is the price that is actually paid or payable for the goods when they are sold for export to the country of importation; this price is usually based on the invoice price. The second part is a series of cost elements that are not included in the invoice price (known as 'adjustments') that are to be added to the price to be established under Article 1 when certain criteria are met in order to arrive at the transaction value. These adjustments are described under Article 8.

## 2.1 Transaction Value: The Price Actually Paid or Payable

**Article 1 of the Agreement**

'1. The Customs value of imported goods shall be the transaction value, that is the price paid or payable for the goods when sold for export to the country of importation adjusted in accordance with the provisions of Article 8, provided:
   (a) that there are no restrictions as to the disposition or use of the goods by the buyer other than restrictions which:
       (i) are imposed or required by law or by the public authorities in the country of importation;
       (ii) limit the geographical area in which the goods may be resold; or
       (iii) do not substantially affect the value of the goods;
   (b) that the sale is not subject to some condition or consideration for which a value cannot be determined with respect to the goods being valued;
   (c) that no parts of the proceeds of any subsequent resale, disposal or use of the goods by the buyer will accrue directly or indirectly to the seller, unless an appropriate adjustment can be made in accordance with the provisions of Article 8; and
   (d) that the buyer and seller are not related, or where the buyer and seller are related, that the transaction value is acceptable for Customs purposes under the provisions of paragraph 2.
2. (a) In determining whether the transaction value is acceptable for the purposes of paragraph 1, the fact that the buyer and seller are related within the meaning of Article 15 shall not in itself be grounds regarding the transaction value as unacceptable. In such case the circumstances of the sale shall be examined and the transaction value shall be accepted provided that the relationship did not influence the price. If, in the light of information provided by the importer or otherwise, the Customs administration has grounds for considering that the relationship influenced the price, it shall communicate its grounds to the importer and the importer

---

5. http://www.wcoomd.org/en/topics/valuation/overview/what-is-customs-valuation.aspx.

shall be given a reasonable opportunity to respond. If the importer so requests, the communication shall be in writing.

(b) In a sale between related persons, the transaction value shall be accepted and the goods valued in accordance with the provisions of paragraph 1 whenever the importer demonstrates that such value closely approximates to one of the following occurring at or about the same time:

> (i) the transaction value in sales to unrelated buyers of identical or similar goods for export to the same country of importation;
>
> (ii) the Customs value of identical or similar goods as determined under the provisions of Article 5;
>
> (iii) the Customs value of identical or similar goods as determined under the provisions of Article 6;

In applying the foregoing tests, due account shall be taken of demonstrated differences in commercial levels, quantity levels, the elements enumerated in Article 8 and costs incurred by the seller in sales in which the seller and the buyer are not related that are not incurred by the seller in sales in which the seller and buyer are related.

(c) The tests set forth in paragraph 2 (b) are to be used at the initiative of the importer and only for comparison purposes. Substitute values may not be established under the provisions of paragraph 2 (b).'[6]

Article 1 first determines whether the concerned goods have been sold for export. This indicates that there is a transaction involving an actual international physical transfer of goods from a seller to a buyer. The Agreement does not contain a definition of 'sale', however, Advisory Opinion 1.1[7] states that the term 'sale' should be interpreted as widely as possible. It also provides a list of situations which would not be considered as constituting a sale (e.g., free consignments, goods imported on consignment, goods imported by branches that are not separate legal entities, etc.). Article 1 also specifies certain conditions and restrictions that may affect the acceptability of the price paid or payable. One of these criteria is when the buyer and seller of the affected goods are related. The definition of related parties is contained in Article 15.4 of the Agreement.

---

Article 15.4 of the Agreement

'4. For the purposes of this Agreement, persons shall be deemed to be related only if:

> (a) they are officers or directors of one another's business;
>
> (b) they are legally recognized partners in business;
>
> (c) they are employer and employee;

---

6. Article 1 of the Agreement.
7. The full text of this case can be found in the WCO Valuation Compendium, available from the WCO Bookshop: http://wcoomdpublications.org/valuation.html.

(d) any person directly or indirectly owns, controls or holds 5 per cent or more of the outstanding voting stock or shares of both of them;

(e) one of them directly or indirectly controls the other;

(f) both of them are directly or indirectly controlled by a third person;

(g) together they directly or indirectly control a third person; or

(h) they are members of the same family.'[8]

When it has been established that the buyer and seller are related, the Agreement stipulates that this is not inherently grounds for regarding that the transaction price is unacceptable. The transaction value can still be accepted if it is substantiated that the relationship did not influence the price paid or payable. If Customs has grounds for considering that the relationship has influenced the price, it may seek further clarification from the importer before reaching a conclusion. Further details on the procedures to be followed by Customs and the importer are specified in Article 1.2.

Article 1 and its Interpretative Note indicate two main approaches for examining whether the relationship has influenced the price between the buyer and seller.

Note to Article 1, paragraph 2

'2. Paragraph 2 (a) provides that where the buyer and the seller are related, the circumstances surrounding the sale shall be examined and the transaction value shall be accepted as the Customs value provided that the relationship did not influence the price. It is not intended that they should be an examination of the circumstances in all cases where the buyer and the seller are related. Such examination will only be required where they have doubts about the acceptability of the price. Where the Customs administration have no doubts about the acceptability of the price, it should be accepted without requesting further information from the importer. For example, the Customs administration may have previously examined the relationship, or it may already have detailed information concerning the buyer and seller, and may already be satisfied from such examination or information that the relationship did not influence the price.

3. Where the Customs administration is unable to accept the transaction value without further inquiry, it should give the importer an opportunity to supply such further detailed information as may be necessary to enable it to examine the circumstances surrounding the sale. In this context, the Customs administration should be prepared to examine relevant aspects of the transaction, including the way in which the buyer and seller organize their commercial relations and the way in which the price in question was arrived at, in order to determine whether the relationship influenced the price. Where it can be shown that the buyer and seller, although related under the provisions of Article 15, buy from and sell to each other as if they were not related, this would demonstrate that the price had

---

8. Article 15.4 of the Agreement.

not been influenced by the relationship. As an example of this, if the price had been settled in a manner consistent with the normal pricing practices of the industry in question or with the way the seller settles prices for sales to buyers who are not related to the seller, this could demonstrate that the price had not been influenced by the relationship. As a further example, where it is shown that the price is adequate to ensure recovery of all costs plus a profit which is representative of the firm's overall profit realized over a representative period of time (e.g., on an annual basis) in sales of goods of the same class or kind, this would demonstrate that the price had not been influenced.

4. Paragraph 2(b) provides an opportunity for the importer to demonstrate that the transaction value closely approximates to a "test" value previously accepted by the Customs administration and is therefore acceptable under the provisions of Article 1. Where a test under paragraph 2(b) is met, it is not necessary to examine the question of influence under paragraph 2(a). If the Customs administration has already sufficient information to be satisfied, without further detailed enquiries, that one of the tests provided in paragraph 2(b) has been met, there is no reason for it to require the importer to demonstrate that the test can be met. In paragraph 2(b), the term "unrelated buyers" means buyers who are not related to the seller in any particular case.'[9]

**Note to Article 1, paragraph 2 (b)**

'A number of factors must be taken into consideration in determining whether one value "closely approximates" to another value. These factors include the nature of the imported goods, the nature of the industry itself, the season in which the goods are imported, and, whether the difference in values is commercially significant. Since these factors may vary from case to case, it would be impossible to apply a uniform standard such as a fixed percentage, in each case. For example, a small difference in value in a case involving one type of goods could be unacceptable while a large difference in a case involving another type of goods might be acceptable in determining whether the transaction value closely approximates to the "test" values set forth in paragraph 2(b) of Article 1.'[10]

The two approaches are discussed further in the following sub-sections.

### 2.1.1 *Related Party Transactions: Test Values*

As per Article 1.2 (c), test values are to be employed at the initiative of the importer. The extent to which these test values can be used depends on the ability of the importer to access and produce relevant data to Customs. It is mentioned in Article 1.2 (b) (i),

9. Note to Article 1, para. 2, of the Agreement.
10. Note to Article 1, para. 2 (b) of the Agreement.

(ii) and (iii) that the test value to be used should pertain to the prices of identical and similar goods. However, manufactured goods often contain technology or intellectual property that is unique to the MNE and sold only between the related parties, therefore, such comparison prices are typically not available. Therefore, the test value option is used only minimally in practice.

### 2.1.2   Related Party Transactions: Circumstances Surrounding the Sale

Article 1.2 provides the alternative that allows Customs to examine how a price is determined in broader terms. When Customs is unable to accept the transaction value without further enquiry, it should afford the importer an opportunity to supply further detailed information that may be necessary to enable it to examine the circumstances surrounding the sale. In this aspect, Customs should be prepared to examine the relevant aspects of the transaction including the way in which the buyer and seller organize their commercial relationship and the method that is used to arrive at the price in question in order to determine whether the relationship has influenced the price. The Agreement states that it is not intended that all of the cases in which the buyer and seller are related be investigated. Such an examination should only be performed when there are grounds for considering that the relationship has influenced the price between the buyer and seller.

As quoted above, the Interpretative Note provides advice and examples of this in the form of questions, which can be summarized as follows:

(1) Has the price been settled in a manner that is consistent with the normal pricing practices of the industry in question?
(2) Has the price been settled in a manner that is consistent with the way the seller settles prices for sales to buyers who are not related to the seller?
(3) Can it be demonstrated that the price is adequate to ensure recovery of all costs plus a profit that is representative of the firm's overall profit realized over a representative period of time (e.g., on an annual basis) in sales of goods of the same class or kind?

These questions are similar to the approach taken in a transfer pricing case. For this reason, it is the 'circumstances surrounding the sale' provision that has been the focus of the work undertaken to date.

---

**Example[11]**

This instrument considers a situation of when Customs examined the circumstances surrounding the sale of two categories of products between related parties because they had doubts on the acceptability of the price.

---

11. *See* Case Study 10.1, Annex V of the 2015 WCO Guide.

In the first case, the product that is concerned is sold by the seller to a related buyer in the country of importation. It is also sold to an unrelated buyer at the same commercial level and used for the same purposes as the related buyer at a higher price. It was established that the costs incurred by the exporter are the same to both the related and unrelated buyers. Both the exporter and the related importer are unable to explain the different prices when challenged by Customs. Therefore, there are insufficient grounds to contend that the price differential is not significant. The transaction value in this case, therefore, would not be applicable. The transaction value of identical or similar goods imported by unrelated buyers may form the basis of the determination of Customs value.

In the second case, the product is only sold between related parties. In the examination of the circumstances of the sale by Customs, it was established that the price is adequate to ensure recovery of all costs plus a profit representative of the exporter's overall profit on goods of the same class or type over a representative period of time. Therefore, in accordance with paragraph 3 of the Interpretative Note to Article 1.2, the transaction value in this case may be accepted.

## 2.2 Transaction Value: Adjustments to the Price Actually Paid or Payable

Article 8 of the Agreement details the elements that should be included in the transaction value in addition to the price paid or payable.

Article 8 of the Agreement

'1. In determining the customs value under the provisions of Article 1, there shall be added to the price actually paid or payable for the imported goods:
   (a) the following, to the extent that they are incurred by the buyer but are not included in the price actually paid or payable for the goods:
      (i) commissions and brokerage, except buying commissions;
      (ii) the cost of containers which are treated as being one for customs purposes with the goods in question;
      (iii) cost of packing whether for labour or materials;
   (b) the value, apportioned as appropriate, of the following goods and services where supplied directly or indirectly by the buyer free of charge or at a reduced cost for use in connection with the production and sale for export of the imported goods, to the extent that such value has not been included in the price paid or payable:
      (i) materials, components, parts and similar items incorporated in the imported goods;
      (ii) tools, dies, moulds and similar items used in the production of the imported goods;
      (iii) materials consumed in the production of the imported goods;

      (iv) engineering, development, artwork, design work, plans and sketches, undertaken elsewhere than in the country
of importation and necessary for the production of the imported goods;[12]
    (c) royalties and licence fees related to the goods being valued that the buyer must pay, either directly or indirectly, as a condition of sale of the goods being valued, to the extent that such royalties and fees are not included in the price actually paid or payable;
    (d) the value of any part of the proceeds of any subsequent resale, disposal or use of the imported goods that accrues directly or indirectly to the seller.
2. In framing its legislation, each Member shall provide for the inclusion in or the exclusion from the customs value, in whole or in part, of the following:
    (a) the cost of transport of the imported goods to the port or place of importation;
    (b) loading, unloading and handling charges associated with the transport of the imported goods to the port or place of importation;
    (c) the cost of insurance.'[13]

In addition to the elements prescribed in Article 8.1, each Customs administration has the option to decide if they prefer to include or exclude the elements in Article 8.2 from the Customs value. The majority of Customs administrations have made a one-off decision to include these elements in the Customs value, which is known as the cost, insurance, freight (CIF)[14] basis. If members choose not to include these elements, this is known as the free on board (FOB)[15] basis.

The determination of whether or not Article 8 elements should be included in the Customs value in a particular case can be a complex process and typically requires consultation with the importer in order to establish all of the pertinent facts of the transaction in question.

It is also noted in this context that several of these elements such as commissions, royalties, and assists relating to the design work, for example, may be viewed as 'services' or 'intangibles'. This emphasizes that, although the role of Customs is to determine the Customs value and duty liability for imported 'physical' goods, certain intangible elements may also be included in the Customs value of those goods.

---

12. Reflects changes introduced as a result of the procès-verbal of rectification of 23 Sep. 2014 (WT/Let/986).
13. Article 8 of the Agreement.
14. CIF terms mean that the seller also contracts and pays the costs and freight that are necessary to transport the goods to the country of import. The seller also contracts for insurance against the buyer's risk of loss or damage to the goods during the carriage.
15. FOB term means that the buyer would have to procure and pay the costs and freight that are necessary to bring the goods to the county of import. The buyer must also contract for insurance against risk or damage to the goods during carriage.

## 2.3 Alternate Valuation Methods

The alternate methods are to be used only when the transaction value cannot be applied. There are three main situations when this will occur:

(1) the transaction value is rejected on the basis of not satisfying one or more of the conditions of Article 1, or

(2) the transaction value has been rejected following the application of the procedures of WTO Decision 6.1. To be more specific, Customs had doubts regarding the truth or accuracy of the declared value that were conveyed to the importer, and Customs' doubts remained after the due consultation process was followed, or

(3) no sale has occurred (e.g., leased goods, gifts, goods transferred between branches, etc.)

Only in the circumstances mentioned above should the alternate methods be considered. These methods are as follows:

- the transaction value of identical goods (Article2);
- the transaction value of similar goods (Article 3);
- the deductive value method (Article 5);
- the computed value method (Article 6);
- fallback option (Article 7).

Specific criteria apply to each of these methods; however, they are not described in detail here. Only the transaction value method has specific tests for related party transactions and, therefore, is of most relevance to transfer pricing issues.[16]

## 3 LINKS BETWEEN CUSTOMS VALUATION AND TRANSFER PRICING

It can be observed that the aim of both Customs valuation and transfer pricing methodologies is very similar. Customs is establishing whether or not a price has been influenced by the relationship between the parties, and the tax administrations' objective is to seek an arm's length price. Each is designed to ensure that the price is established as if the parties were not related and had been negotiated under normal business circumstances.

It has also been noted that there are a number of similarities between the WTO and the OECD methodologies for Customs valuation and transfer pricing, respectively.[17] For example, the WTO's deductive method (Article 5) is based on the resale price of the goods, which is similar to the OECD's resale price method; the WTO's

---

16. Further information on all aspects of Customs valuation can be found via the WCO website here: http://www.wcoomd.org/en/topics/valuation/overview.aspx and via the WCO Bookshop link: http://wcoomdpublications.org/valuation.html.

17. For a discussion on TP methods, *see* Chs 3 and 4 of this book.

computed value method (Article 6) is based on a value that comprises the costs for materials and manufacturing, etc. plus profit which is similar to the OECD's cost plus method.

However, as mentioned earlier, Customs' focus is on the transaction value method and whether or not the relationship between the buyer and the seller has influenced the price. Therefore, Customs would be examining transfer pricing information only in this context and not in that of the other WTO methods.

Having noted the similar concepts, it can also be seen that the perspective and objective of each approach pull in opposite directions. Customs' objective is to ensure all appropriate elements are included in the Customs value and is not understated whereas the tax authorities' objective is to ensure the transfer price does not include inappropriate elements and is not overstated.

There are also a number of differences in the approaches between Customs and tax authorities, which are explored in the next section.

---

**D.5. Use of Customs valuations, the 2017 OECD Guidelines[18]**

'1.137. The arm's length principle is applied, broadly speaking, by many Customs administrations as a principle of comparison between the value attributable to goods imported by associated enterprises, which may be affected by the special relationship between them, and the value for similar goods imported by independent enterprises. Valuation methods for Customs purposes however may not be aligned with the OECD's recognized transfer pricing methods. That being said, Customs valuations may be useful to tax administrations in evaluating the arm's length character of a controlled transaction transfer price and vice versa. In particular, Customs officials may have contemporaneous information regarding the transaction that could be relevant for transfer pricing purposes, especially if prepared by the taxpayer, while tax authorities may have transfer pricing documentation which provides detailed information on the circumstances of the transaction.

1.138. Taxpayers may have competing incentives in setting values for Customs and tax purposes. In general, a taxpayer importing goods may be interested in setting a low price for the transaction for Customs purposes so that the Customs duty imposed will be low. (There could be similar considerations arising with respect to value added taxes, sales taxes, and excise taxes.) For tax purposes, however, a higher price paid for those same goods would increase the deductible costs in the importing country (although this would also increase the sales revenue of the seller in the country of export). Cooperation between income tax and Customs administrations within a country in evaluating transfer prices is becoming more common and this should help to reduce the number cases where Customs valuations are found unacceptable for tax purposes or vice versa. Greater cooperation in the area of exchange of information would be particularly

---

18. The 2017 UN Manual in section B.2.4.7.also contains text highlighting the links between Customs valuation and transfer pricing.

useful, and should not be difficult to achieve in countries that already have integrated administrations for income taxes and Customs duties. Countries that have separate administrations may wish to consider modifying the exchange of information rules so that the information can flow more easily between the different administrations.'[19]

## 3.1 Practical Use of the Transfer Pricing Documentation

The WCO recommends compliance-based audits as being the most effective for verifying the duty liability of MNEs with the auditees selected on the basis of risk criteria. This involves a structured examination of companies' financial systems, accounts, payment records, and any other relevant information. Consequently, MNEs prepare transfer pricing studies and reports primarily to provide this information for the purpose of tax auditing (both internal and external).

The question that arises is whether transfer pricing information could be of use to Customs when conducting checks on related party transactions and, if so, how Customs interprets and utilises such data.

A second important question concerns the transfer pricing adjustments. To what extent and in what circumstances do such adjustments have an impact on the Customs value?

## 3.2 Work of the TCCV

Key progress has also been made with the adoption of Commentary 23.1, Case Study 14.1 (*see* the second example in section 4.1.1.),[20] and Case Study 14.2 as instruments of the TCCV. Commentary 23.1 establishes the principle that a transfer pricing study can be considered as a possible basis for use in the examination of the circumstances surrounding the sale in a related party transaction on a case-by-case basis. Case Study 14.1 explores the use of a transfer pricing study based on the TNMM to examine whether or not the price of imported goods had been influenced by the relationship between the buyer and the seller while Case Study 14.2 explores the use of a transfer pricing study based on the Resale Price method to examine whether or not the price of the imported goods had been influenced by the relationship between the buyer and the seller.[21]

---

19. D.5. of the 2017 OECD Guidelines.
20. For details of Case Study 14.1, *see* http://www.wcoomd.org/ ~ /media/wco/public/global/pdf /topics/valuation/instruments-and-tools/case-study/case-study-14_1-en.pdf?db = web.
21. For details of Case Study 14.2, *see* http://www.wcoomd.org/-/media/wco/public/global/pdf/ topics/valuation/instruments-and-tools/case-study/case-study-14_2_en.pdf?db = web.

### 3.3 Customs-Tax Cooperation

With the increasing importance of the exchange of information between Customs and Tax authorities, the WCO has developed the Guidelines for Strengthening Cooperation and Exchange of Information between Customs and Tax Authorities at the National Level (the Guidelines on Customs-Tax Cooperation).[22] These Guidelines are expected to serve as a reference to guide and encourage Customs and tax administrations in developing a cooperation framework and/or strengthening the existing cooperation based on national requirements, the operating environment, and operational resources. The Guidelines provide examples of topics that can be considered in the context of such cooperation including Customs valuation and transfer pricing.

## 4 USE OF TRANSFER PRICING INFORMATION TO EXAMINE RELATED PARTY TRANSACTIONS

Following the principle established in Commentary 23.1 (*see* section 3.2) which acknowledges that information contained in a transfer pricing study may be beneficial to Customs, the following questions arise:

- what particular information typically contained in a transfer pricing study may be useful to Customs in order to demonstrate that the price had not been influenced by the relationship, and
- how the Customs value should be determined taking into account relevant transfer pricing adjustments.

Customs officials are encouraged to interpret transfer pricing documentation and derive relevant information from it with post-clearance audits and in cooperation with the business that is being audited. It is also desirable for Customs to consult with the national tax officials that are responsible for transfer pricing to seek expert advice and any direct knowledge of the company concerned from the tax perspective that is subject to legal constraints.

### 4.1 Examination of the Phrase 'Circumstances Surrounding the Sale' in Article 1.2(a) of the Agreement

As described earlier, the Interpretative Note to Article 1 provides guidance and examples for determining whether or not the price of transactions was influenced by the relationship between buyers and sellers. It reiterates that examination should only occur in situations when Customs has doubts about the acceptability of the price.

---

22. WCO, *Guidelines for Strengthening Cooperation and Exchange of Information between Customs and Tax Authorities at the National Level,* October 2016, *available at* http://www.wcoomd. org/en/topics/facilitation/instrument-and-tools/tools/guidelines-on-customs-tax-cooperation. aspx.

The Interpretative Note states that Customs should be prepared to examine relevant aspects of the transaction, including:

- the way in which the buyer and seller organize their commercial relationships; and
- the way in which the price in question is arrived.

For example, when it can be analysed that the buyer and seller, though related, buy and sell from each other as if they were not related, then this would help to demonstrate that the relationship has not influenced the price that was established between these entities. Transfer pricing studies and documentation can provide substantial information that can help Customs in conducting such an analysis. For example, information on the functional analysis that is conducted by the tax authority (including examination of functions performed by a party and their assets and risks) is typically contained in transfer pricing studies and can be informative for Customs in respect to examining the circumstances surrounding the sale.

Ultimately, Customs should make a decision based on the 'totality of the evidence' which may include various sources other than the transfer pricing documentation.

### 4.1.1 Key Challenges

There are a number of differences in the approaches of tax and Customs that make it difficult to compare 'like with like'.

#### 4.1.1.1 Single Product Versus Product Range

Customs' aim is to gain assurances regarding the price of imported goods; therefore, one key challenge is to ensure that the transfer pricing information is relevant to the imported goods. However, as transfer pricing information usually covers a range of products, it is necessary to consider how the information regarding costs, profit margins, etc. can be relevant to the price of a specific consignment of imported goods.

If the business trades only one product, then the comparison should be fairly straightforward. However, even if the transfer pricing study encompasses a range of products it does not mean that the data might not be relevant for Customs' use.

---

**Example**

In this example, the goods concerned are branded electrical kettles, and the range of goods incorporated in the transfer pricing study covers various branded electrical appliances (including microwaves, blenders, toasters, and kettles).

In this case, the transfer pricing study confirms an acceptable arm's length range for those products taken as a group. Customs may take into account the criteria provided in the third example in Interpretative Note of Article 1.2 regarding the examination of the circumstances surrounding the sale, specifically, all of the

---

costs plus a profit realized 'in sales of goods of the same class or kind'. Article 15.3 of the Agreement states that '… "goods of the same class or kind" means goods which fall within a group or range of goods produced by a particular industry or industry sector, and includes identical or similar goods'.

The transfer pricing study and additional research (if necessary) may assure Customs that, in this case, the kettles and other electrical appliances may be considered as goods of the same class or kind. Therefore, the details of costs and profits for the range of products may be relevant to each individual product within the group, including the kettle.

*4.1.1.2 Date Range*

Typically, Customs and tax are examining different time periods when conducting audits. Customs will conduct an audit perhaps up to three or four years following the import of the goods in question (this will vary depending on the national law that stipulates a time limit after the import for collecting underpaid duty or repaying overpaid duty)[23]. Tax audits may take place several years after the event (following the completion and auditing of annual accounts, etc.) which could be concerning a different timeframe when compared to Customs' audits. Customs should, therefore, ensure that the transfer pricing data relates to the period that is being scrutinized during the Customs audit. For example, if Customs is auditing consignments that are imported in 2014, the relevant information to be considered in the transfer pricing studies must also relate to transactions in 2014.

Below are comments on the three examples provided in the Interpretative Note to Article 1.2 (*see* section 2.1.2).

1. *Has the price been settled in a manner consistent with the normal pricing practices of the industry in question?*

Such information may be available, for example, either in the transfer pricing study or by independent studies of a particular industry sector. It is suggested that Customs considers, at least initially, the information contained in the transfer pricing documentation that is available. It is noted that the Agreement does not define the term 'normal pricing practices of the industry'; this may take into account the nature of the goods as well as the role and functions of the parties to the sale.

2. *Has the price been settled in a manner that is consistent with the way that the seller sets prices for sales to buyers who are not related to the seller?*

In many cases of transactions between related parties, the importer is the exclusive distributor of the merchandise in the country of import. There are no sales to unrelated parties for which a comparison can be made to the import value. Therefore, this option is likely to be limited in scope thereby making it difficult for Customs to obtain information or documentation. Nevertheless, if such sales exist, they can be utilized as a means of examining the circumstances of the sale.

---

23. For example, in the EU, this period is three years.

3. *Can it be demonstrated that the price is adequate to ensure recovery of all costs plus a profit representative of the firm's overall profit realized over a representative period of time (e.g., on an annual basis) in sales of goods of the same class or kind?*

This example focuses on an examination of how a price was set in terms of the elements included and particularly the profit.

Customs may seek information regarding the exporter's/seller's profit through the importer, although it is likely that the related company will not be willing to share profit information with its distributors/importers. As a result, this could prove to be fruitless. As an initial step, it is recommended that Customs consider information that is already available in the country of import, in particular the transfer pricing documentation, in order to examine the circumstances surrounding the sale.

The example does not define whether the 'profit' is 'gross' or 'operating' profit, therefore, this gives Customs the flexibility to examine both types of profit depending on which is more useful for Customs' purposes. Normally, operating profit is a better indicator of real profitability as it shows what is earned after all of the expenses have been paid. It is also the measure for which information concerning independent parties will most often be available. Operating profit is also the most common profit level indicator used when the net-CPM/TNMM is utilized for transfer pricing purposes.

It has been pointed out that an apparent inconsistency exists regarding the 'tested party' that is considered for tax and Customs purposes. For Customs, the focus is always on the importer and on a transactional basis. However, for tax purposes, it depends on which method of justification was selected for the transfer pricing study over the period of assessment. For example, when applying profit-based transfer pricing methods such as the TNMM, the tested party is often the importer (since it is often the less functionally complex of the parties and due to the availability of comparable data) which places the focus on the MNE's profit in the country of importation (i.e., sales made by the taxable person). This can be tested against comparable uncontrolled transactions so that a decision can be made regarding whether the price in question is at arm's length.

The example makes reference to the firm's overall profit which is assumed to refer to the seller's (i.e., exporter's) profit. The transfer pricing data, however, relates only to the profit made by the importer and not the seller. In this case, it is a question of whether the information is still relevant to Customs.

It can be stated that, as the import value is the beginning point for the importer's profit calculation, information derived from the importer's profit can potentially assure Customs that the exporter/seller's profit is acceptable. This may subsequently confirm that the price of the imported goods is adequate to ensure the recovery of all of the costs plus a profit and, therefore, is not influenced by the relationship.

**Example**

The following example taken from Case Study 14.1[24] illustrates this point.

(1) Relevant data for the importer, ICo:

| | |
|---|---|
| Sales | 100.0 |
| Cost of goods sold (COGS, i.e., price paid/ payable to XCo in this case) | 82.0 |
| Gross Profit | 18.0 |
| Operating expenses | 15.5 |
| Net operating profit | 2.5 |
| **Net operating profit margin (benchmarked)** | **2.5% of sales** |

(2) Based on this information:
- the Sales figure can be considered as being reliable since ICo is only selling to independent parties (and it is assumed that ICo is rationally seeking to maximize its profits in its dealings with arm's length parties);
- the amount of operating expenses can be accepted as being reliable since it is determined that these expenses are paid by ICo to only independent parties with ICo seeking to minimize its costs, and there is no evidence that any of these expenses have been paid at the request of the seller;
- the transfer pricing study confirms that ICo's operating profit margin of 2.5% is within the arm's length range (i.e., based on a benchmarking study of independent importers);
- the COGS of ICo reflects that the price paid or payable to XCo represents the transaction between ICo and its related party, XCo. This is the transfer price in question.

The arm's length COGS amount can be deduced by working backwards from the arm's length net margin of 2.5%. Therefore, if the derived COGS is equal to the relevant declared transaction value, it could be inferred that the price has not been influenced by the relationship between ICo and XCo.
This demonstrates that information relating to the transactions between a related buyer and unrelated distributors can be helpful and relevant to Customs when examining the circumstances surrounding sales between related parties.

---

24. For details of Case Study 14.1, *see* http://www.wcoomd.org/ ~ /media/wco/public/global/pdf/ topics/valuation/instruments-and-tools/case-study/case-study-14_1-en.pdf?db = web.

However, the above examples provided in the Interpretative Notes to Article 1.2 of the Agreement are not exhaustive. Customs may consider other methods of examining the circumstances surrounding the sale, request additional information, and take into account the totality of all of the evidence that is available and relevant to the sales that are under consideration.

### 4.1.2   Use of Advance Pricing Arrangements

Advance Pricing Arrangements (APAs)[25] afford tax administrations and businesses the opportunity to confirm and agree, in advance, on the transfer pricing treatment of a specific transaction or group of transactions and, therefore, demonstrate the arm's length price. Some Customs administrations have identified that APAs can provide useful information for Customs when examining related-party transactions. Customs valuation needs can be considered in the context of preparing an APA so that businesses do not need to prepare a specialized study based only on Customs requirements.

The WCO encourages Customs administrations to provide advance rulings (similar to the APAs in the context of TP) for Customs valuation. This is supported by Article 3 of the WTO Trade Facilitation Agreement[26] which also requires Customs to make advance rulings available for classification and origin purposes. The advance ruling can provide business operators with rulings from Customs on a related party transaction (or group of transactions) before the importation of the goods concerned. Customs can then examine the relevant information that is provided (which could be derived from a transfer pricing study or an APA) and make a decision that will apply to that particular set of circumstances. That decision could state whether or not the price in question is influenced by the relationship between the buyer and seller and if the transaction value can be accepted. If it cannot be accepted, the decision can indicate what alternative method can be used as the valuation method.

### 4.2   Customs Valuation Treatment When a Transfer Pricing Analysis Indicates That the Price of the Goods Sold May Be Adjusted

Transfer pricing adjustments are a common feature in MNEs and occur for different reasons and end with different results. It is, therefore, necessary for Customs to understand the different types of transfer pricing adjustments and subsequently consider which may have an impact on Customs value and how to address this.

In some cases, depending on the type of adjustment, the adjusted price will be more in accordance with the 'un-influenced' price actually paid or payable for Customs valuation purposes. In other cases, such as tax-only adjustments, the arm's length transfer price reported for tax purposes differs from the amount actually charged by the

---

25. *See* Ch. 5 of this book.
26. Available at https://www.wto.org/english/tratop_e/tradfa_e/tradfa_e.htm.

associated enterprises. As it is, Customs may not be able to determine whether or not a price influence had taken place until any adjustments have been made (or quantified).

An important principle is established in an instrument of the TCCV, i.e., Commentary 4.1 (price review clauses). This instrument considers the Customs value implications of a goods contract which includes a 'price review clause' whereby the price is only provisionally established at the time of import; 'the final determination of the price payable being subject to certain factors which are set forth in the provisions of the contract itself'. It concludes that such clauses 'should not, of themselves, preclude valuation under Article 1 of the Agreement'. This scenario may be applicable to situations when the price that is declared to Customs at the time of import is based on a transfer price that may be subject to subsequent adjustment (e.g., to achieve a pre-determined profit margin). The possibility of a transfer pricing adjustment exists at the time of importation.

### 4.2.1 Possible Customs Treatment of Transfer Pricing Adjustments

As mentioned previously, there are a number of reasons why a transfer pricing adjustment may occur and different ways that it can be initiated.

When the adjustment is initiated by the taxpayer, it is recorded in the accounts of the taxpayer, and a debit or credit note is issued. Depending on the nature of the adjustment, it could be considered as having an impact on the price actually paid or payable. In other cases, particularly when the adjustment is initiated by the tax administration, the impact may only be on the tax liability and not on the price actually paid or payable.

---

**Court case:[27] The *Hamamatsu* case**

In the *Hamamatsu* case,[28] the Court of Justice of the European Union (CJEU) has affirmed that transfer prices that are subjected to retroactive adjustments cannot be used for customs valuation purposes under the application of the transaction value method.

In the judgment, the CJEU held that the customs value must reflect the genuine economic value of imported goods at the time of the actual transaction and take into account all of the elements that have economic value, such as selling commissions, transport costs, royalty and license fees, in pricing the good,. In cases when the transaction value method, being the preferred method, is inadequate, alternative methods could be employed for determining customs value. Apart from situations that warrant adjustments to the actual price paid or

---

27. The views and opinions expressed in this case do not necessarily reflect those of the WCO or of the governments of its Members.
28. CJEU 20.12.2017, *Hamamatsu Photonics Deutschland GmbH v. Hauptzollamt München*, C-529/16. For details, *see* Raffaele Petruzzi, Sayee Prasanna, *Restricting the Interplay of Transfer pricing And Customs Valuation*. Transfer Pricing International (2018/1), 44–46.

payable, such as damages, quality defects etc., the actual transacting price cannot be altered with subsequent adjustments. Based on this premise, the CJEU held that there was no legal basis to allow any adjustment, including year-end adjustments, because of TP information.

When an adjustment occurs before the goods are imported, the price declared to Customs should take into account the adjustment. If, however, the adjustment takes place after the importation of the goods (i.e., it is recorded in the accounts of the taxpayer, and the debit or credit note is issued after Customs clears the goods), then Customs may consider that the Customs value is to be determined based on the adjusted price, applying the principles established in Commentary 4.1 (price review clauses).

It is, therefore, good practice for businesses to ensure that Customs is given advance notification when a post-importation adjustment could occur at a later date in order to enable Customs to be able to make a decision regarding the Customs value.

### 4.2.2 Final Determination of the Customs Value Following Transfer Pricing Adjustments

Assuming that Customs agrees that the Customs value should be based on the 'adjusted' price after the transfer pricing adjustment and a consequent financial/accounting adjustment has been taken into account, it is then necessary to consider the appropriate Customs procedures for addressing this.

Commentary 4.1 makes reference to Article 13 of the Agreement which provides for the possibility of delaying the final determination of the Customs value. It requires Customs administrations to offer a facility that allows importers to clear the goods on the provision of a security in cases when it becomes necessary to delay the final determination of the Customs value at the time of Customs clearance.

**Article 13 of the Agreement**

'If, in the course of determining the customs value of imported goods, it becomes necessary to delay the final determination of such customs value, the importer of the goods shall nevertheless be able to withdraw them from customs if, where so required, the importer provides sufficient guarantee in the form of a surety, a deposit or some other appropriate instrument covering the ultimate payment of customs duties for which the goods may be liable. (...)'[29]

The question arises of whether is it necessary to require importers to lodge Customs declarations on the basis of a provisional declaration of value that is covered by a security for the potential duty that is due. This creates major resource constraints

---

29. Article 13 of the Agreement.

for both Customs and the business involved in terms of accounting and reconciliation procedures, especially if a substantial number of Customs declarations are involved.

As a basic requirement for Customs to consider an adjustment to the Customs value, it is clear that there should be a transfer pricing policy determined prior to the import or clearance of the goods concerned that specifies the criteria (or 'formula') that will be applied for establishing the final transfer price. Customs may require importers to report the existence of the transfer pricing policy prior to importations. This policy may be established in the form of an APA. Customs would also typically require businesses to report the final transfer price with details of the adjustments; this should be mandatory in the event of an upward adjustment.

Another important consideration for Customs in the post-importation environment is the treatment of adjustments under Article 8 of the Agreement. Typically, it is during the course of a Customs audit that such adjustments are discovered and can be quantified. Customs should, therefore, take into account other payments that are made after importation to or for the benefit of the parent company (e.g., contributions for design and development fees) or other payments that are based on the subsequent resale, disposal, or use of the imported goods that accrue to the seller in order to determine whether they should be included in the Customs value.

### 4.2.3   Practical Challenges

When Customs decides that an adjustment to the Customs value is appropriate, it is then necessary to determine the mechanism and calculation method. Customs' focus is on individual transactions whereas transfer pricing data are at an aggregate level. Therefore, it is necessary to find methods to calculate and apportion each consignment and appropriate value.

Another issue is the timing of the Customs audit: what happens if a transfer pricing adjustment is anticipated but has not yet taken place at the time that Customs is conducting an audit? Customs will need to decide whether to wait until the adjustment has been made or to make a decision at that stage.

Customs could also be faced with insufficient available and relevant information at the time of import to come to a decision on whether the transaction value can be accepted. As APAs and transfer pricing studies are primarily performed for tax purposes, it is feasible that Customs would not be able to obtain relevant information from the tax authorities without the proper framework in place for the exchange of information between Customs and tax authorities.

## 5   CONCLUSIONS

This chapter has illustrated how transfer pricing can be beneficial to Customs administrations for Customs valuation purposes. After examining Customs valuation and related party transactions in section 2, section 3 proceeds to examine the link between transfer pricing and Customs valuation. Section 4 provides examples of how transfer pricing information can be utilized for Customs valuation purposes on a case-by-case basis.

# CHAPTER 14

# Transfer Pricing and EU State Aid

# 1    INTRODUCTION

In June 2014, the European Commission (EU Commission) began formal State aid investigation procedures against three Member States with regard to individual transfer pricing rulings that were issued by the tax authorities of these Member States to certain multinational companies (i.e., Starbucks in the Netherlands, FIAT in Luxembourg, and Apple in Ireland).[1] A few more procedures later followed[2] that also related to transfer pricing rulings, which are also referred to as advance pricing arrangements[3] ('APAs').[4] Further investigations can be expected as the EU Commission has expanded its inquiry into the tax ruling practices of all of the Member States.[5] These investigations generated unprecedented controversies between the EU Commission, on the one hand, and the Member States, the business community, and their advisors, on the other; they led to a conflict which is now referred to as a 'tax war' between the EU and the United States[6] and has resulted in ordering a recovery of a record-breaking amount of aid of EUR 13 billion.[7] From a theoretical perspective, the EU Commission's negative decisions declaring the rulings concerned unlawful State aid proposed arguments that could open up new dimensions in EU fiscal State aid. Although this is not the first time that transfer pricing and State aid law cross paths (see section 3.3), the EU Commission's claim that individual transfer pricing rulings that deviate from the arm's length principle as interpreted by the EU Commission can be considered State aid irrespective of the presence of the arm's length principle in the laws of the Member States is quite a novelty in the application of the State aid rules to tax measures. At a more general level, these cases also emphasize the long-standing questions on the scope of the

---

1. State aid: Commission investigates transfer pricing arrangements on corporate taxation of Apple (Ireland) Starbucks (Netherlands) and Fiat Finance and Trade (Luxembourg), Press Release, IP/14/663 (11 Jun. 2014).
2. State aid: Commission investigates transfer pricing arrangements on corporate taxation of Amazon in Luxembourg, Press Release, IP/14/1105 (7 Oct. 2014); State aid: Commission opens in-depth investigation into the Belgian excess profit ruling system, Press Release, IP/15/4080 (3 Feb. 2015); State aid: Commission opens in-depth investigation into the Netherlands' tax treatment of Inter IKEA, Press Release, IP/17/5343 (18 Dec. 2017).
3. See Ch. 5 of this book.
4. A few other formal State aid investigations concern tax rulings which do not address transfer pricing, see State aid: Commission finds Luxembourg gave illegal tax benefits to Engie; has to recover around EUR 120 million, Press Release, IP/18/4228 (20 June 2018). These procedures are not discussed in this Chapter. For more details of the EU State aid investigation, see http://ec.europa.eu/competition/state_aid/tax_rulings/index_en.html.
5. State aid: Commission extends information enquiry on tax rulings practice to all Member States, Press Release, IP/14/2742 (17 Dec. 2014).
6. Philip Lowe, EU State Aid Investigations: A View From Both Sides of the Atlantic, Tax Notes International 1037, 1038 (21 Mar. 2016); Frans Vanistendael, Are the EU and the U.S. Headed for a Tax War?, Tax Notes International 1057, 1057 et seq. (19 Sep. 2016).
7. State aid: Ireland gave illegal tax benefits to Apple worth up to EUR 13 billion, Press Release, IP/16/2923 (30 Aug. 2016).

concept of State aid and the role of the State aid rules in combatting tax avoidance and aggressive tax planning. While the EU Commission's decisions have been appealed to the General Court (constituent court of the Court of Justice of the European Union (CJEU) acting as the first instance court in actions against the Commission's State aid decisions)[8] and thus the final word on these acute questions still awaits, this chapter describes the EU Commission's approach to transfer pricing rulings under the State aid rules.

First, an overview of the EU State aid regime is provided discussing both the State aid procedure and the substantive elements of the concept of State aid in section 2. The application of the State aid rules to fiscal measures is subsequently described in section 3. The EU Commission's approach to transfer pricing rulings is analysed in section 4 where the repercussions of these cases are also outlined.

## 2 OVERVIEW OF THE EU STATE AID REGIME

### 2.1 State Aid Rules as Part of Competition Law

The primary objective of the EU internal market is to establish a level playing field for all economic agents in which they can compete with each other under equal conditions. A system that ensures such equal conditions of competition forms part of the EU's internal market.[9] The conditions of competition in the internal market can be distorted not only by the anti-competitive behaviour of market participants but also by the Member States granting undue support to certain undertakings. Apart from interfering with the market forces which leads to decreased efficiency, aid measures favouring certain undertakings and financed by public money lead to welfare losses in the internal market.[10] For these reasons, the prohibition of State aid is one of the central elements of the competition law rules of the EU.

In contrast to other rules of competition law which typically address private undertakings (e.g., rules on cartels and abuse of dominant market positions), State aid law is directed at the Member States.[11] The private undertaking beneficiaries, which bear the ultimate burden of the recovery in the event of the Member States' non-compliance with the prohibition on State aid, are not directly addressed by the rules on State aid.

---

8. Pending cases at the General Court: *Apple Sales International and Apple Operations Europe/Commission*, T-892/16 as well as *Ireland/Commission*, T-778/16 concerning the Apple case; *Belgium/Commission*, T-131/16 concerning the Excess Profit Exemption scheme in Belgium; *Starbucks and Starbucks Manufacturing Emea/Commission*, T-636/16 as well as *Netherlands/Commission*, T-760/15 concerning the *Starbucks* case; *Fiat Chrysler Finance Europe/Commission*, T-759/15 as well as *Luxembourg/Commission*, T-755/15 concerning the Fiat case; *Luxembourg/Commission*, T-816/17 concerning the *Amazon* case.
9. Protocol (No. 27) to the TEU and TFEU on the internal market and competition provides that 'the internal market as set out in Article 3 of the Treaty on European Union includes a system ensuring that competition is not distorted'.
10. Conor Quigley, *European State Aid Law and Policy*, 255 et seq. (3rd ed., Bloomsbury 2015).
11. *See* Leigh Hancher, *The Administrative Procedure – the Privileged Dialogue* in Herwig C.H. Hofmann/Claire Micheau, *State aid law of the European Union*, 342 (Oxford 2016).

## 2.2 Legal Framework

The general provisions on State aid are embedded in Articles 107 and 108 of the Treaty on the Functioning of the European Union ('TFEU'),[12] Article 107 TFEU providing the substantive State aid rules. The main rule that State aid is generally incompatible with the internal market is contained in Article 107 (1) TFEU. As the general prohibition is not absolute or unconditional, Article 107 (2) and Article 107 (3) TFEU establish exceptions according to which State aid is considered to be compatible with the internal market.[13] Article 107 (2) TFEU contains legal exemptions, for example, for aid having a social character or aid that is granted to compensate damages caused by natural disasters and other exceptional occurrences. Aid measures that are covered by one of the instances listed in Article 107 (2) TFEU are *ex lege* seen as compatible with the rules on State aid.[14] In contrast to Article 107 (2) TFEU, the provisions in Article 107 (3) TFEU provide discretionary exemptions according to which State aid falling within its scope is not automatically exempted but may be authorized by the EU Commission. Aid measures granted to promote the economic development of particular underdeveloped areas or certain economic activities or projects of common European interest can be cited as examples where the EU Commission has discretionary power to declare the aid that was granted as being compatible with the internal market.

Whereas Article 107 TFEU contains the substantive provisions on State aid, Aricle 108 TFEU lays down the main provisions concerning the State aid procedure (*see* section 2.3).[15]

In addition to these provisions of primary law, secondary law also exists in the field of State aid. Most importantly, the Council adopted Regulation No. 2015/1589 of 13 July 2015 laying down detailed rules for the application of Article 108 of the TFEU ("Procedural Regulation") and the Regulation No. 651/2014 of 17 June 2014 declaring certain categories of aid compatible with the internal market in application of Articles 107 and 108 of the Treaty Text with EEA relevance ('General Block Exemption Regulation') which exempts the Member States from the notification obligation established in Article 108 TFEU (*see* section 2.3.3.2) if specific conditions are fulfilled.

Apart from the legally binding rules on State aid, there are also many soft law instruments.[16] The EU Commission regularly issues notices, practical guidelines, and communications to ensure legal certainty and predictability regarding the practical

---

12. For the latest consolidated version, *see* consolidated versions of the Treaty on European Union and the Treaty on the Functioning of the European Union OJ C 202 of 7.6.2016, pp. 1–388.
13. Alexandra Miladinovic, *The State Aid Provisions of the TFEU in Tax Matters* in Michael Lang/Pasquale Pistone/Josef Schuch/Claus Staringer, *Introduction to European Tax Law on Direct Taxation*, 374 et seq. (5th ed., Linde 2018).
14. However, the Member States still have to comply with the obligation to notify their plans to introduce such aid measures. After proper notification, the EU Commission examines whether the respective aid is within the scope of Article 107 (2) TFEU.
15. Michael Schütte, *Procedural Aspects of EU State Aid Law and Practice* in Erika Szyszczak, *Research Handbook on European State Aid Law*, 336 et seq. (Edward Elgar 2011).
16. Alexandra Miladinovic, *The State Aid Provisions of the TFEU in Tax Matters* in Michael Lang/Pasquale Pistone/Josef Schuch/Claus Staringer, *Introduction to European Tax Law on Direct Taxation*, 305 (5th ed., Linde 2018).

application of the provisions on State aid. For example, it has issued several soft law instruments that provide guidelines as to how the discretionary exceptions listed in Article 107 (3) TFEU will be applied to different types of aid measures.[17]

The first instrument providing for specific guidelines on the application of the State aid rules to fiscal measures was the EU Commission Notice on the application of the State aid rules to measures relating to direct business taxation issued in 1998.[18] In 2016, the latter was repealed and replaced by new guidelines. The Notice on the notion of State aid as referred to in Article 107 (1) TFEU[19] has a broader scope than the 1998 EU Commission Notice as it addresses the notion of State aid in general, however, it includes substantial specific guidance on fiscal State aid.

## 2.3 State Aid Procedure

### 2.3.1 The Competences of the EU Commission in State Aid Matters

The EU Commission has exclusive competence to decide on the compatibility of aid granted by Member States with the internal market.[20] Pursuant to Article 108 TFEU, the EU Commission: (i) reviews existing aid, (ii) takes decisions on new or altered aid, and (iii) takes legal action if the Member States do not comply with its decisions or with the requirement of notification.

### 2.3.2 Existing Aid and New Aid

The term existing aid is defined by Article 1 (b) of the Procedural Regulation and encompasses five exhaustively enumerated types of aid:

(1) Aid that existed in a Member State prior to the entry into force of the TFEU in that respective state;
(2) Aid that has already been authorized;
(3) Measures falling under the General Block Exemption Regulation that are deemed to be authorized;
(4) Measures that had been granted prior to the expiry of the limitation period of ten years;

---

17. *See*, for example, Criteria for the analysis of the compatibility of State aid for the employment of disadvantaged and disabled workers subject to individual notification, (11 Aug. 2009), 2009/C 188/02; Guidelines on State aid to promote risk finance investments, (22 Jan. 2014), 2014/C 19/04; Guidelines on State aid for rescuing and restructuring non-financial undertakings in difficulty, (31 July 2014), 2014/C 249/01; Framework for State aid for research and development and innovation, (27 Jun. 2014), 2014/C 198/01.
18. *Commission notice on the application of the State aid rules to measures relating to direct business taxation (hereinafter: 1998 EU Commission Notice)*, C 384 OJ 3 (1998).
19. *Commission notice on the notion of State aid as referred to in Article 107 (1) of the Treaty on the Functioning of the European Union (hereinafter: Notion of Aid Notice)*, C 262 OJ 1 (2016).
20. Piet Jan Slot, *Administrative Procedure* in Leigh Hancher/Tom Ottervanger/Piet Jan Slot, *EU State Aids*, para. 5(5th ed., Sweet & Maxwell 2016).

(5) Measures that were put into effect at a time that those measures did not constitute aid but have subsequently become aid due to the evolution of the internal market or the liberalization of an activity without having been altered.

The procedure regarding existing aid is simplified.[21] Pursuant to Article 108 (1) TFEU and Articles 21–23 of the Procedural Regulation, existing aid is constantly reviewed by the EU Commission in cooperation with the Member States. If the EU Commission finds that the existing aid is no longer compatible due to the continuous development of the internal market, it recommends appropriate measures. If a Member State does not accept the measures proposed, the EU Commission must initiate the formal investigation procedure (*see* section 2.3.3.4).[22]

In contrast, the term new aid is negatively defined in Article 1 (c) of the Procedural Regulation, and it is aid that is not classified as existing aid.

### 2.3.3  Procedure Regarding New Aid

*Figure 14.1   Procedure Regarding New Aid*

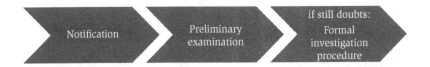

### 2.3.3.1  Standstill Clause

Article 108 (3) TFEU and Article 3 of the Procedural Regulation provides that any plans to grant new aid must be notified to the EU Commission and cannot be put into effect prior to its authorization. This provision is also referred to as the 'Standstill Clause'.

### 2.3.3.2  Notification

The notification obligation is specified in Article 108 (3) TFEU and Article 2 of the Procedural Regulation. If a Member State plans to introduce an aid measure, it is required to notify it to the EU Commission and is not allowed to put it into effect until the EU Commission takes a decision on the compatibility of the aid with the internal

---

21. Piet Jan Slot in Leigh Hancher/Tom Ottervanger/Piet Jan Slot, *EU State Aids*, paras 47 et seq. (5th ed., Sweet & Maxwell 2016).
22. Conor Quigley, *European State Aid Law and Policy*, 539 (3rd ed., Bloomsbury 2015).

market.[23] Upon notification, the EU Commission begins a preliminary examination (*see* section 2.3.3.3). If it cannot reach a definite conclusion on the compatibility of the measure, it initiates a formal investigation procedure (*see* section 2.3.3.4) that results in a final decision. In any case, a legal act in the form of a decision is necessary based on legal certainty considerations[24] and to ensure the possibility of taking legal action before the EU Courts.[25]

### 2.3.3.3 Preliminary Examination

After receiving a notification, the EU Commission undertakes a preliminary examination according to Article 4 of the Procedural Regulation. The period within which the EU Commission has to conclude the preliminary examination cannot take longer than two months upon receipt of the complete notification.

The preliminary examination may result in one of the following decisions:[26]

– the measure notified by the Member State does not constitute aid at all;
– the measure in question constitutes aid that falls within the scope of Article 107 (1) TFEU, and it is considered to be compatible with the internal market ('decision not to raise objections');
– a decision to initiate the formal investigation procedure in all cases when the EU Commission cannot definitively conclude that the aid measure concerned is compatible with the internal market.

When the EU Commission decides that the measure is not State aid or makes a decision not to raise objections, the Member State is permitted to put the measure into effect. However, whenever the EU Commission has doubts as to the compatibility of the measure with the TFEU, it initiates subsequent proceedings. Thus, the preliminary examination cannot be concluded with a negative decision.[27] A decision stating that the aid is incompatible with the internal market can only be brought upon closure of the formal investigation procedure.[28] A decision closing the preliminary examination constitutes a legal act that can be challenged before the EU Courts under Article 263

---

23. Alexandra Miladinovic, *The State Aid Provisions of the TFEU in Tax Matters* in Michael Lang/Pasquale Pistone/Josef Schuch/Claus Staringer, *Introduction to European Tax Law on Direct Taxation,* 398 et seq. (5th ed., Linde 2018).
24. *Council Regulation 2015/1589 of 13 July 2015 laying down detailed rules for the application of Article 108 of the Treaty on the Functioning of the European Union (hereinafter: Procedural Regulation),* L248 OJ 9, para. 7 (2015).
25. Conor Quigley, *European State Aid Law and Policy,* 668 et seq. (3rd ed., Bloomsbury 2015).
26. Procedural Regulation, paras 2–4 (2015); *see also* Michael Schütte, *Procedural Aspects of EU State Aid Law and Practice* in Erika Szyszczak, *Research Handbook on European State Aid Law,* 340 (Edward Elgar 2011).
27. Alexandra Miladinovic, *The State Aid Provisions of the TFEU in Tax Matters* in Michael Lang/Pasquale Pistone/Josef Schuch/Claus Staringer, *Introduction to European Tax Law on Direct Taxation,* para. 405 (5th ed., Linde 2018).
28. Conor Quigley, *European State Aid Law and Policy,* 571 (3rd ed., Bloomsbury 2015).

TFEU when it gives rise to definitive legal effects which cannot subsequently be regularized by the final decision.[29] If this is not the case, only the final decision can be challenged before the General Court.[30]

### 2.3.3.4    Formal Investigation Procedure

The formal investigation procedure is provided for in Articles 6-9 of the Procedural Regulation. After launching the formal investigation procedure, the Member State concerned and other interested parties are invited to submit comments within a limited period of time (usually one month).[31] In addition, the EU Commission can request all of the necessary information from any other Member State, undertaking or association of undertakings in order to enable a complete assessment of the notified measure.[32] After taking all of the relevant information and comments into consideration and all of the doubts have been resolved, the EU Commission should conclude its examination within a period of eighteen months and close the formal investigation procedure with a final decision.[33] The decision of the EU Commission may have four possible outcomes:[34]

- the measure at issue does not constitute State aid;
- the aid is compatible with the internal market ('positive decision');
- in the event that the EU Commission finds that the aid can be considered compatible only if additional conditions are fulfilled, it can attach conditions to a positive decision which must be complied with ('conditional decision');
- the aid measure is not compatible with the internal market ('negative decision') and, as a consequence, cannot be put into effect by the Member State concerned.

### 2.3.4    Procedure Regarding Unlawful State Aid

In Article 1 (f) of the Procedural Regulation, unlawful State aid is defined as aid that is put into effect in contravention of Article 108 (3) TFEU which means that the notification obligation or the Standstill Clause have not been complied with. The procedure regarding unlawful aid is specified in Chapter 3 of the Procedural Regulation. When the EU Commission receives information from any source whatsoever (e.g.,

---

29. *Ibid.*, 668–670; *Judgment of the Court of Justice, Spain v Commission*, C-312/90, paras 11–26 (1992); *Italy v Commission*, C-47/91, paras 19–32 (1992); *Italy v Commission*, C-400/99, paras 45–70 (2001); Judgment of the General Court, *Regione Autonoma della Sardegna v Commission*, Joined Cases T-394/08, T-408/08, T-453/08 and T-454/08, para. 77.
30. For more details, *see* Lenaerts/Maselis/Kathleen, *EU Procedural Law*, paras 7.55–7.57 (2014).
31. Piet Jan Slot in Leigh Hancher/Tom Ottervanger/Piet Jan Slot, *EU State Aids*, para. 58 (5th ed., Sweet & Maxwell 2016).
32. Procedural Regulation, para. 10 (2015).
33. *See* Piet Jan Slot in Leigh Hancher/Tom Ottervanger/Piet Jan Slot, *EU State Aids*, paras 64–70 (5th ed., Sweet & Maxwell 2016).
34. Procedural Regulation, Art 9 (2015).

from a competitor of the aid beneficiary, the media, or public disclosure, etc.) that a Member State has implemented an aid measure without notification, it can examine the compatibility of the measure with EU State aid law on its own initiative.[35] If an interested party submits a complaint drawing the attention of the EU Commission to an aid granted without prior notification, the EU Commission examines the complaint and, if necessary, initiates the formal investigation procedure at its own discretion; therefore, the complainant does not have a right to this effect.[36] When the EU Commission finds that the aid has been put into effect without complying with the State aid rules and takes a negative decision regarding the aid's compatibility, it must order the recovery of the unlawful aid in order to restore undistorted competition.[37]

## 2.4 Recovery of Unlawful Aid

Article 16 of the Procedural Regulation stipulates that all aid that is granted in contradiction to Article 108 (3) TFEU is required to be recovered. The purpose of recovery is to re-establish the situation in the market that would exist if the unlawful aid had not been implemented.[38] Recovery is not meant to be a penalty, however, it is the consequence of the finding that the aid is unlawful.[39] To eliminate the financial advantages received by the beneficiary of aid that is incompatible with the internal market and hence restore equal conditions of competition in the internal market, the aid including interest has to be recovered from the beneficiary.[40] The interest is to be paid on the sum obtained from the date on which the aid was at the disposal of the beneficiary until the date on which the recovery is effective.[41] Pursuant to Article 17 of the Procedural Regulation, the EU Commission's power to order recovery is subject to a limitation period of ten years beginning from the day on which the aid was unlawfully awarded to the beneficiary. Even though the recovery is ordered by the EU Commission, the Member State granting the aid is obligated to implement the decision according to the rules of its national law.[42] That implies that the Member States apply different procedures when recovering unlawful aid.[43]

---

35. Alexandra Miladinovic, *The State Aid Provisions of the TFEU in Tax Matters* in Michael Lang/Pasquale Pistone/Josef Schuch/Claus Staringer, *Introduction to European Tax Law on Direct Taxation*, para. 412 (5th ed., Linde 2018).
36. Leigh Hancher/Francesco Maria Salerno/Michael Schütte, *The Different Stages in the State Aid Procedure* in Herwig C.H. Hofmann/Claire Micheau, *State aid law of the European Union*, 361 (Oxford 2016).
37. Procedural Regulation, Art 16 (2015); *see also Notice from the Commission - Towards an effective implementation of Commission decisions ordering Member States to recover unlawful and incompatible State aid (hereinafter: Recovery Notice)*, C 272 OJ 4, paras 16 et seq. (2007).
38. Recovery Notice, para. 13.
39. Judgment of the Court of Justice, *Belgium v Commission*, C-75/97, para. 65 (1999).
40. Bucura C. Mihaescu-Evans, *Recovery of Unlawful Aid and the Role of National Courts* in Herwig C.H. Hofmann/Claire Micheau, *State aid law of the European Union*, 381 (Oxford 2016).
41. Procedural Regulation, Art 16, para. 2 (2015).
42. Recovery Notice, paras 21-25.
43. Commission Notice on the Enforcement of State aid law by national courts 2009/C 85/01 (2009).

The obligation to recover unlawful and incompatible aid is interpreted very strictly by the EU Commission and the EU Courts.[44] There are only minor exceptional circumstances in which the recovery can be avoided. Apart from setting forth a limitation period of ten years,[45] Article 16 (1) of the Procedural Regulation prescribes that recovery will not be ordered if it was contrary to a general principle of EU law. Accordingly, one of the grounds that is most often invoked for justifying non-compliance with the recovery decision is the protection of legitimate expectations,[46] which is a general principle of EU law.[47] However, in accordance with the strict interpretation by the CJEU, this justification can only be raised by the beneficiary and not by the Member State.[48] Additionally, only an act or behaviour of the EU Commission and under certain circumstances can a decision of the EU Courts[49] create legitimate expectations.[50] Hence, the beneficiary of the aid at issue cannot rely on the fact that it made use of a valid provision available under the laws of the Member State. Otherwise stated, the beneficiary cannot claim that it had legitimate expectations regarding the fact that the Member State had notified the measure, and it had been properly authorized by the EU Commission. According to case law, a diligent business-man must be able to verify whether the aid measure had been introduced under the proper procedures.[51]

The time limit for the Member State to execute the recovery decision is four months following its entry into force.[52] If the Member State concerned fails to

---

44. Recovery Notice, para. 20.
45. Procedural Regulation, Article 17 (2015).
46. The doctrine of legitimate expectation was first developed in English law as a ground of judicial review in administrative law to protect a procedural or substantive interest when a public authority rescinds from a representation made to a person. It is based on the principles of natural justice and fairness and seeks to prevent authorities from abusing power.
47. *See,* for example, Judgment of the Court of Justice, *Land Rheinland-Pfalz v Alcan Deutschland GmbH,* C-24/95, para. 25 (1997); *BUG-Alutechnik,* C-5/89, paras 13 and 14 (1990).
48. Eduard Sporken/Yves Cattel, *Investigations by European Commission into Transfer Pricing Underlying Certain Tax Rulings in the European Union,* Vol. 22 No. 3 International Transfer Pricing Journal, 135 (2015).
49. For example, Judgment of the Court of Justice, *Transalpine Ölleitung in Österreich v Finanzlandesdirektion für Tirol,* C-368/04, para. 19 (2006).
50. After the coordination centres regime in Belgium was approved by the EU Commission in 1984, other jurisdictions enacted similar legislation to attract multinational enterprises. When the EU Commission decided, in its decision (OJ L 282) of 17 Feb. 2003, that the Belgian regime that was previously notified and approved is no longer compliant with State aid law, it provided for abolition of the Belgian regime after expiry of a transitional period. However, whereas Belgium complied with its notification obligation, Germany, France, Luxembourg, and Spain that had introduced an analogous regime, have never notified their aid measures. Nevertheless, the EU Commission decided not to order recovery because the approval of the Belgian scheme was announced in public, and those Member States had no reason to doubt the compatibility of their own schemes with the State aid rules. Encouraged by the EU Commission's actions, the Member States introducing such regimes were exceptionally justified on the basis of their legitimate expectations.
51. Judgment of the Court of Justice, *Spain v Commission,* C-169/95, para. 51 (1997); *Land Rheinland-Pfalz v Alcan Deutschland GmbH,* C-24/95, para. 25 (1997); *Germany v Commission,* C-334/99, para. 42 (2003); *Atzeni v Regione autonoma della Sardegna,* Joint cases C-346/03 and C-529/03 (2006).
52. Conor Quigley, *European State Aid Law and Policy,* 600 (3rd ed., Bloomsbury 2015).

implement the recovery decision, the EU Commission may initiate infringement proceedings pursuant to Article 258 TFEU.[53]

## 2.5 Elements of the Concept of State Aid

Article 107 (1) TFEU enshrines the prohibition on State aid providing that '*[s]ave as otherwise provided in the Treaties, any aid granted by a Member State or through State resources in any form whatsoever which distorts or threatens to distort competition by favoring certain undertakings or the production of certain goods shall, in so far as it affects trade between Member States, be incompatible with the internal market*'.

Thus, the conditions for a measure to constitute State aid are: (i) the existence of an advantage, (ii) granted by a Member State or through State resources (iii) to certain undertakings or the production of certain goods, in other words, granted in a selective way that (iv) affects intra-Union trade and distorts competition (Figure 14.2).[54] These four elements of the concept of State aid are required to be cumulatively present in order for a measure to be regarded as State aid.[55]

*Figure 14.2    Four Elements of the Concept of State Aid*

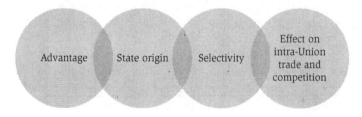

The concept of advantage within the meaning of Article 107 (1) TFEU can be defined as any economic benefit that a private undertaking could not have received under normal conditions in the market without the intervention by the State.[56] The advantage can be granted '*in any form whatsoever*' which means not only more visible forms of benefits, such as subsidies, but also any other measure, for example, the provision of a State guarantee for a loan, preferential access to State infrastructure,

---

53. According to Article 258 TFEU, the EU Commission may bring the Member State concerned before the Court of Justice due to the breach of the duty to implement the EU Commission's decision which constitutes an infringement of the TFEU. If the Court of Justice finds the Member State to be in breach of EU law, the Member State must take necessary measures to comply with the judgment of the Court of Justice. If a Member State then fails to comply with this judgment, the EU Commission can take further actions and refer the matter again to the Court of Justice which may eventually impose fines on the non-complying Member State.
54. Notion of Aid Notice, para. 5 (2016).
55. Alexandra Miladinovic, *The State Aid Provisions of the TFEU in Tax Matters* in Michael Lang/Pasquale Pistone/Josef Schuch/Claus Staringer, *Introduction to European Tax Law on Direct Taxation*, para. 304 (5th ed., Linde 2018).
56. Notion of Aid Notice, para. 66 (2016).

overcompensation for performing a public service, or an exemption from a generally applicable public charge are encompassed.[57] These forms of aid are not as easy to identify as subsidies.

For State aid to exist, the measure must be directly or indirectly granted by a State or through State resources and must be imputable to that State.[58] Measures taken by public undertakings are examples of a direct grant of aid whereas aid that is funded by private undertakings controlled by the State would serve as an example for an indirectly granted measure.[59] In addition, the aid must be imputable to the Member State meaning that, when the State merely implements – without exercising any discretion – a provision of an EU Directive that provides for a selective advantage to certain undertakings, such aid could not be imputed to the Member State and, therefore, would not constitute State aid.[60] Furthermore, the measure must be financed through State resources, i.e., the aid in question must entail a public financial burden be it through an active payment of liquid funds or a waiver of debts.[61]

Regarding the condition of selectivity, it can easily be established in the case of an individual aid measure when the advantage is granted to a single undertaking. It is much more difficult, however, to determine whether or not an aid scheme from which any and every undertaking can benefit that fulfils certain predefined and objectively formulated conditions has the effect of selectively favouring certain undertakings despite its appearance as a general measure.[62] With regard to such measures, the General Court held that '*[t]he fact that the aid is not aimed at one or more specific recipients defined in advance, but that it is subject to a series of objective criteria pursuant to which it may be granted, within the framework of a predetermined overall budget allocation, to an indefinite number of beneficiaries who are not initially individually identified, cannot suffice to call in question the selective nature of the measure*'.[63] In addition, a measure cannot escape from being qualified as selective just because it benefits a large number of undertakings (e.g., all manufacturing undertakings) or the beneficiaries belong to very diverse or very large sectors of the economy.[64] Thus, the concept of selectivity is very broadly interpreted by the CJEU.

A Member State measure can be selective in various ways depending on the circle of beneficiaries. Sectoral aid measures favour undertakings that belong to a certain

---

57. Conor Quigley, *European State Aid Law and Policy*, 15 et seq. (3rd ed., Bloomsbury 2015).
58. Notion of Aid Notice, paras 38 et seq. (2016).
59. *Ibid.*, para. 47.
60. Judgment of the General Court, *Deutsche Bahn AG v Commission*, T-351/02, para. 102 (2006); *see also* Judgment of the Court of Justice, *Puffer v Unabhängiger Finanzsenat Außenstelle Linz*, C-460/07, para. 70 (2009).
61. Notion of Aid Notice, para. 51 (2016).
62. Conor Quigley, *European State Aid Law and Policy*, 503 et seq. (3rd ed., Bloomsbury 2015).
63. Judgment of the General Court, *Confederación Espanola de Transporte de Mercancías v Commission*, T-55/99, para. 40 (2000) concerning the Spanish "Plan Renove Industrial" system of aid for the purchase of commercial vehicles in favour of natural persons, SMEs, regional public bodies and bodies providing local public services. *See also* Judgment of the General Court, *Italy v Commission*, T-379/09, para. 47 (2012); Notion of Aid Notice, para. 118 (2016).
64. Judgment of the Court of Justice, *Belgium v Commission*, C-75/97, para. 32 (1999); *Adria-Wien Pipeline*, C-143/99, para. 48 (2001); Notion of Aid Notice, para. 118 (2016).

sector of the economy (e.g., agriculture, coal and steel or maritime, etc.).[65] Horizontal aid measures benefit a certain function of undertakings irrespective of which sector or branch of the economy they belong to (e.g., R&D, creation of employment, etc.).[66] Regionally selective measures grant advantages to undertakings in a certain geographical area.[67] In addition, limiting benefits to undertakings of a certain size[68] or of certain legal form[69] can also result in selectivity. A Member State measure can also be selective due to the limited period of time during which it can be utilized.[70]

A public support measure constitutes State aid if the measure improves the competitive position of the beneficiary compared to its competitors. However, a measurable distortion of competition does not actually have to occur; it suffices that the measure threatens to distort competition and is capable of having an effect on trade between the Member States.[71]

## 3   FISCAL STATE AID

### 3.1   Aid Through the Tax System

As Article 107 (1) TFEU covers aid '*in any form whatsoever*', for example, tax measures that are able to distort competition by conferring selective advantages on particular undertakings may also fall under the scope of the provision.[72] As the CJEU held from the beginning of its jurisprudence, *[t]he concept of aid is [...] wider than that of a subsidy because it embraces not only positive benefits, such as subsidies themselves, but also interventions which, in various forms, mitigate the charges which are normally included in the budget of an undertaking and which, without, therefore, being subsidies in the strict meaning of the word, are similar in character and have the same effect.*'[73]

There are different forms of providing State aid through the tax system.

---

65. 1998 EU Commission Notice, para. 18 (1998).
66. *Ibid.*, para. 17.
67. Maja-Alexandra Dittel/Klaus-Otto Junginger-Dittel, *Regional State Aid* in Erika Szyszczak, *Research Handbook on European State Aid Law,* 219 et seq. (Edward Elgar 2011).
68. Judgment of the Court of Justice, *Commission v Spain*, Joint Cases C-485/03 to C-490/03 (2006).
69. Judgment of the Court of Justice, *Paint Graphos and others*, Joint Cases C-78/08 to C-80/08, para. 52 (2011).
70. Judgment of the General Court, *Italy and Brandt Italia v Commission*, Joint Cases T-239/04 and T-323/04, para. 66 (2007); Judgment of the General Court, *Italy v Commission*, T-211/05, para. 120 (2009); Judgment of the Court of Justice, *Italy v Commission*, C-458/09 P, paras 59 and 60 (2011); Notion of Aid Notice, para. 122 (2016).
71. Alexandra Miladinovic, *The State Aid Provisions of the TFEU in Tax Matters* in Michael Lang/Pasquale Pistone/Josef Schuch/Claus Staringer, *Introduction to European Tax Law on Direct Taxation,* 367 et seq. (5th ed., Linde 2018).
72. Wolfgang Schön, *Tax Legislation and the Notion of Fiscal State Aid: A review of 5 Years of European Jurisprudence* in Isabelle Richelle/Wolfgang Schön/Edoardo Traversa, *State Aid Law and Business Taxation,* 4 (Springer 2016).
73. Judgment of the Court of Justice, *De Gezamenlijke Steenkolenmijnen in Limburg v High Authority of the European Coal and Steel Community,* C-30/59, para. 19 (1961); *Banco Exterior de España SA v Ayuntamiento de Valencia,* C-387/92, paras 13–14 (1994); *France v Commission,* C-241/94, para. 34 (1996).

- First, fiscal State aid may be granted through tax legislation.[74] It must be noted that not only provisions which reserve an advantageous treatment for undertakings that meet formal legal conditions expressly included in the provision may be considered to be selective (de jure selectivity) but also rules that are seemingly general but, in effect, benefit only certain undertakings (de facto selectivity).[75] Aid through tax legislation can be provided in the form of a reduction in the tax base for certain enterprises (e.g., special deductions, exclusion of specific income from the tax base, special reserves, or accelerated depreciations for certain assets). Moreover, aid can also be granted through tax provisions prescribing a reduction in the amount of tax payable (e.g., special tax rates, and tax credits).[76]
- A second means of granting State aid is through tax assessment.[77] In this case, the tax administration applies the rules in a way which deviates from their normal application in favour of certain undertakings.[78] This can occur *ex post*, i.e., after the taxable event had occurred, or *ex ante*, i.e., before the taxable event. In the latter case, the tax administration normally issues an advance ruling[79] or APA.[80]
- The third form of State aid through the tax system is granting aid in the course of tax enforcement.[81] Under this scenario, the tax administration assesses the tax liability in accordance with the normal application of the tax rules, however, it forfeits – wholly or partly – the collection of the tax debt. In such a case, selective advantages could be provided by way of deferment, cancellation, or the rescheduling of tax debt.

## 3.2 The Selectivity of Tax Measures

In the case of fiscal State aid, the most crucial element of the State aid concept is selectivity.[82] As fiscal State aid frequently takes the form of an aid scheme, i.e., it grants an advantage to an indefinite number of beneficiaries who fulfil objectively defined conditions established in the tax laws (e.g., a tax credit for all companies that make an

---

74. Wolfgang Schön, *Tax Legislation and the Notion of Fiscal State Aid: A review of 5 Years of European Jurisprudence* in Isabelle Richelle/Wolfgang Schön/Edoardo Traversa, *State Aid Law and Business Taxation*, 4 (Springer 2016).
75. 1998 EU Commission Notice, paras 120 et seq. (1998).
76. Conor Quigley, *European State Aid Law and Policy*, 99 et seq. (3rd ed., Bloomsbury 2015).
77. 1998 EU Commission Notice, paras 123 et seq. (1998).
78. Wolfgang Schön, *Tax Legislation and the Notion of Fiscal State Aid: A review of 5 Years of European Jurisprudence* in Isabelle Richelle/Wolfgang Schön/Edoardo Traversa, *State Aid Law and Business Taxation*, 5 (Springer 2016).
79. 1998 EU Commission Notice, paras 169 et seq. (1998).
80. *See* Ch. 5 of this book.
81. Wolfgang Schön, *Tax Legislation and the Notion of Fiscal State Aid: A review of 5 Years of European Jurisprudence* in Isabelle Richelle/Wolfgang Schön/Edoardo Traversa, *State Aid Law and Business Taxation*, 4 (Springer 2016).
82. Claire Micheau, *Tax Selectivity in European Law of State Aid: Legal Assessment and Alternative Approaches*, 3 EL Rev, 324 (2015).

investment in tangible assets), it is usually difficult to determine whether it is a general measure to which all undertakings can have equal access or a selective one which, in effect, benefits only a certain category of undertakings.[83] In addition, in the case of tax measures, the distinction between the 'advantage' and the 'selectivity' element of the State aid concept is rather blurred.[84] Both are relative meaning that an advantage can be identified compared to a normally applicable tax treatment while the establishment of selectivity also requires a derogation from the ordinary tax system (benchmark system or reference system).[85]

These conceptual difficulties in applying the State aid rules to tax measures are reflected in the constant evolution of the method through which selectivity is to be established according to the EU Commission's practice and the EU Courts' case law. The 1998 EU Commission Notice outlined a three-step approach to selectivity, which required the identification of: (i) the common tax system, (ii) an exception from that system, and (iii) an examination of whether such an exception can be justified by the nature and general scheme of the tax system.[86] However, the CJEU followed a comparative approach in its case law which was centred on a discrimination test. According to this case law, '*Article 107, paragraph 1 of the Treaty requires it to be determined whether, under a particular statutory scheme, a State measure is such as to favour 'certain undertakings or the production of certain goods' in comparison with others which, in the light of the objective pursued by the scheme in question, are in a comparable legal and factual situation. If it is, the measure concerned fulfils the condition of selectivity.*'[87] These two approaches have gradually been reconciled.[88] As a result, the CJEU applies the following three-step analysis to determine whether a particular tax measure is selective within the meaning of Article 107 (1) TFEU:[89]

- first, since an existing advantage may only be established when compared with the normal set of rules which are generally applicable, the 'reference system', i.e., the benchmark against which the selectivity of a measure is assessed, must be ascertained;

---

83. Wolfgang Schön, *Tax Legislation and the Notion of Fiscal State Aid: A review of 5 Years of European Jurisprudence* in Isabelle Richelle/Wolfgang Schön/Edoardo Traversa, *State Aid Law and Business Taxation*, 16 et seq. (Springer 2016).
84. Anna Gunn/Joris Luts, *Tax Rulings, APAs and State Aid: Legal issues*, Vol. 24 Issue 2 EC tax review 119, 121 (2015); Michael Lang, *State Aid and Taxation: Recent Trends in the Case Law of the ECJ*, Issue 2 EStAL 411, 418 (2012); Michael Lang, *Steuerrecht, Grundfreiheiten und Beihilfeverbot*, IStR 570, 577 (2010).
85. Conor Quigley, *European State Aid Law and Policy*, 109 (3rd ed., Bloomsbury 2015).
86. 1998 EU Commission Notice, para. 16 (1998).
87. For example, Judgment of the Court of Justice, *Heiser*, C-172/03, para. 40 (2005).
88. Wolfgang Schön, *Tax Legislation and the Notion of Fiscal State Aid: A review of 5 Years of European Jurisprudence* in Isabelle Richelle/Wolfgang Schön/Edoardo Traversa, *State Aid Law and Business Taxation*, 9 et seq. (Springer 2016).
89. For example, Judgment of the Court of Justice *British Aggregates v Commission*, C-487/06 P, para. 82 (2008); *Paint Graphos*, joint cases C-78/08 to C-80/08, para. 49 (2011); Notion of Aid Notice, para. 128.

- second, it is to be examined whether the measure leads to a derogation from that system in so far as it differentiates between undertakings that, in the light of the objectives that are intrinsic to the system, are in a comparable factual and legal situation;
- in the third step, it is to be determined whether an existing derogation may be justified by the nature or the general scheme of the reference system, which is the case when the differential treatment derives from the basic or guiding principles of the tax system, or it is a result of inherent mechanisms necessary for the functioning and effectiveness of the system.

## 3.3 Transfer Pricing Measures under State Aid Scrutiny

The EU Commission's decisions in the *FIAT, Starbucks, Apple,* and *Amazon* cases concern *individual rulings* specifying the method through which transfer pricing for intra-group transactions within a corporate group must be determined (*see* section 4.2). The decision in the Belgian excess profit ruling scheme addresses an *aid scheme* that relates to the determination of the taxable profits of Belgian companies that are members of a multinational group by using a comparison of the profits that a similar independent company would earn under similar circumstances. The scheme, according to Belgium, is intended to reflect the arm's length principle.

Thus, on the one hand, the *FIAT, Starbucks, Apple,* and *Amazon* cases that concern individual aid can be distinguished and, on the other, the Belgian excess profit rulings case that concerns a scheme under which, in principle, any company that meets the conditions for the application of the scheme may make use of the advantage that is provided for (for the distinction between individual aid and aid scheme, *see* section 2.5). As will be discussed below, this distinction has important ramifications regarding the method by which the selectivity of these measures is to be established.

The common element in all of these cases is that they deal with tax measures that are related to transfer pricing.[90] Although the EU Commission has scrutinized national schemes that applied to the transfer pricing determinations of multinational groups in its State aid practice,[91] only one case has reached the CJEU, the joint cases *Belgium and*

90. *See,* on these cases, *inter alia,* Eduard Sporken/Yves Cattel, *Investigations by European Commission into Transfer Pricing Underlying Certain Tax Rulings in the European Union,* Vol. 22 No. 3 International Transfer Pricing Journal, 131 et seq. (2015); Michael Lang, *Tax Rulings and State Aid Law,* No. 3 British Tax Review, 391 (2015); Anna Gunn/Joris Luts, *Tax Rulings, APAs and State Aid: Legal issues,* Vol. 24 Issue 2 EC Tax Review, 119 (2015); Anja Taferner/Jurjan Wouda Kuipers, Tax Rulings: *In Line with OECD Transfer Pricing Guidelines, but Contrary to EU State Aid Rules?,* European Taxation, 134 (2016).
91. *See,* for example, EU Commission decision on the aid scheme implemented by Spain in favour of coordination centres in Vizcaya, C 48/2001 ex NN 43/2000, para. 26 (2002); EU Commission decision on the aid scheme implemented by Germany for control and coordination centres, OJ L 177, para. 17 (2002); EU Commission decision on the State aid scheme – Coordination Centres – implemented by Luxembourg, C 49/2001 ex NN 46/2000, para. 53 (2002); EU Commission decision on the aid scheme implemented by Belgium for coordination centres established in Belgium, OJ L 282, para. 25 (2003).

*Forum 187 ASBL,*[92] which can provide guidelines on how to apply the State aid rules to transfer pricing measures. This case concerned an approved special tax scheme for coordination centres in Belgium. These were companies that were part of a multinational group and provided services that were particularly of a financial nature to other members of the group. According to the rules applicable to coordination centres, the taxable income of such a centre was determined at a flat rate under the cost plus method. In particular, the rate represented a certain percentage of the total operating expenses and other costs excluding costs for staff, financial charges, and corporate income tax. The profit margin was to be established according to the activity that was actually performed. However, if there were no objective criteria to establish that percentage, it could be set at a default flat rate of 8% irrespective of the actual economic activity that was performed. The EU Commission declared the scheme as being State aid, taking the opinion that the income assessment under the cost plus method conferred a selective advantage to the beneficiaries. In its decision, the Court held that, in order to decide whether the income assessment of coordination centres under the special tax regime actually constitutes an advantage, it is necessary '*to compare that regime with the ordinary tax system, based on the difference between profits and outgoings of an undertaking carrying on its activities in conditions of free competition*'.[93] Furthermore, the Court held that the costs for staff and financial costs were relevant factors enabling the centres to earn revenue and, therefore, the effect of '*[t]he exclusion of those costs from the expenditure which serves to determine the taxable income of the centers is that the transfer prices do not resemble those which would be charged in conditions of free competition.*'[94] Regarding the minimum profit-margin of 8%, the Court decided that this rate also constituted a selective advantage because '*the marginal rate differs widely in practice between one centre and another, as it depends on the activity which is carried on.*'[95]

The EU Commission interprets this decision in which the CJEU held that the determination of the taxable profits of a company within a corporate group must be based on transfer prices which would be '*charged in conditions of free competition*' as a precedent for contending that the arm's length principle constitutes the benchmark against which a transfer pricing ruling must be measured and regularly refers back to this judgment in its recent cases on transfer pricing rulings (*see* section 4.3).[96]

---

92. Judgment of the Court of Justice, *Belgium and Forum 187 ASBL*, C-182/03 R and C-217/03 R, (2003).
93. *Ibid.*, para. 95.
94. Ibid., para. 96.
95. Ibid., para. 100.
96. *See*, for example, Commission Decision, C(2015) 7143 final, on State aid SA.38374 (2014/C ex 2014/NN)(ex 2014/CP) implemented by the Netherlands to Starbucks (hereinafter: Starbucks Final Decision), paras 258–264 (21 Oct. 2015).

## 4 THE EU COMMISSION'S APPROACH TO TRANSFER PRICING RULINGS

### 4.1 The Start of the Investigations

In 2013, the EU Commission initiated an inquiry into the tax ruling practices of the Member States in order to examine whether some rulings issued by the Member States' tax administration grant a selective advantage to their beneficiaries in contradiction of the EU State aid rules. These investigations are part of the EU's fight against tax evasion, tax avoidance, and aggressive tax planning which began in 2012.[97] Similar to the G20/OECD BEPS project, the EU's initiatives in this area were a reaction to the revelations on the tax planning strategies of multinational companies. These strategies came under unprecedented public scrutiny as, in the aftermath of the 2008 financial crisis, governments were searching for additional sources of revenue. NGO campaigns against multinationals helped expose such strategies, and the demand that multinational companies pay their fair share of tax was increasingly articulated by the general public. At the global level, these developments led to the initiation of the BEPS project while the EU also took action against aggressive tax planning and tax avoidance which would otherwise distort the level playing field in the internal market.

Contrary to the OECD, the EU disposes of legal instruments – *inter alia*, the State aid rules – that are binding on the Member States which enables it to counter tax avoidance and profit shifting more effectively than the OECD. Tax rulings came under the scrutiny of the State aid rules when various hearings were held in national parliaments as part of the intensified public scrutiny of multinational structures which elucidated the role of tax rulings in the tax planning of multinational companies.[98] First, in June 2013, the EU Commission requested information on the tax ruling practices of seven Member States.[99] Despite the reluctance and, in some case, resistance of the Member States to provide the information that was requested,[100] the inquiry continued and was eventually facilitated by the revelations of the International Consortium of Investigative Journalists on tax rulings issued by the Luxembourgish tax

---

97. *See* Communication from the EU Commission to the European Parliament and the Council on an action plan to strengthen the fight against tax fraud and tax evasion, COM (2012) 722 (2012).
98. In November 2012, the House of Commons Committee of Public Accounts inquired into tax structures of multinational enterprises (*see* http://www.parliamentlive.tv/Event/Index/ab5 2a9cd-9d51-49a3-ba3d-e127a3af018c, accessed May 2017). In the US, the US Permanent Subcommittee on Investigations held a hearing on Offshore Profit Shifting in May 2013 which examined structures and methods employed by multinational groups and in particular, Apple Inc (*see* https://www.hsgac.senate.gov/subcommittees/investigations/hearings/offshore-profit-shifting-and-the-us-tax-code_-part-2, accessed May 2017).
99. EU Parliament, Special Committee on tax rulings and other measures similar in nature or effect, 2015/2066, para. 52 (20 Jul. 2015); The Commission investigated the tax ruling practices of Cyprus, Ireland, Luxembourg, Malta, the Netherlands, Belgium and the United Kingdom.
100. State aid: Commission orders Luxembourg to deliver information on tax practices, Press Release, IP/14/309 (24 Mar. 2014).

authorities, the so-called 'LuxLeaks'.[101] In December 2014, the EU Commission extended the inquiry into the tax ruling practices of all Member States.[102]

As previously mentioned, the EU Commission's inquiry led to the initiation of formal investigation procedures with regard to transfer pricing rulings granted by Belgium (Excess Profit scheme),[103] Ireland (Apple),[104] Luxembourg (FIAT, Amazon),[105] and the Netherlands (Starbucks).[106]

## 4.2 The Commission's Interpretation of Selectivity with Regard to Transfer Pricing Rulings

The function of tax rulings is to establish – in advance of the taxable events – the application of the general rules of the ordinary tax system to a particular case in view of its specific facts and circumstances. The EU Commission's inquiry focused, in particular, on tax rulings which endorse transfer pricing arrangements proposed by the taxpayer for determining prices for intra-group transactions between companies forming part of the same corporate group and thus, the taxable basis of those companies,[107] i.e., APAs.[108]

Regarding *tax rulings in general*, the EU Commission emphasized that the investigations are not meant to call into question the Member States' power to issue tax rulings or that tax rulings are important instruments for providing legal certainty and

---

101. EU Parliament, Special Committee on tax rulings and other measures similar in nature or effect, 2015/2066, 5 et seq. (20 Jul. 2015).
102. State aid: Commission extends information enquiry on tax rulings practice to all Member States, Press Release, IP/14/2742 (17 Dec. 2014).
103. State aid: Commission opens in-depth investigation into the Belgian excess profit ruling system, Press Release, IP/15/4080 (3 Feb. 2015); for the final decision, *see* State aid: Commission concludes Belgian 'Excess Profit' tax scheme illegal; around EUR 700 million to be recovered from thirty-five multinational companies, Press Release, IP/16/42 (11 January 2016).
104. State aid: Commission investigates transfer pricing arrangements on corporate taxation of Apple (Ireland) Starbucks (Netherlands) and Fiat Finance and Trade (Luxembourg), Press Release, IP/14/663 (11 Jun. 2014); for the final decision, *see* State aid: Ireland gave illegal tax benefits to Apple worth up to EUR 13 billion, Press Release, IP/16/2923 (30 August 2016).
105. State aid: Commission investigates transfer pricing arrangements on corporate taxation of Apple (Ireland) Starbucks (Netherlands) and Fiat Finance and Trade (Luxembourg), Press Release, IP/14/663 (11 Jun. 2014), State aid: Commission investigates transfer pricing arrange- ments on corporate taxation of Amazon in Luxembourg, Press Release, IP/14/1105 (7 Oct. 2014); for the final decision, *see* Commission decides selective tax advantages for Fiat in Luxembourg and Starbucks in the Netherlands are illegal under EU State aid rules, Press Release, IP/15/5880 (21 October 2015) and State aid: Commission finds Luxembourg gave illegal tax benefits to Amazon worth around EUR 250 million, Press Release, IP/17/3701 (4 Oct. 2017).
106. *Ibid.*
107. Richard Lyal, *Transfer Pricing Rules and State Aid*, Fordham Int'l Law Journal, 1020 (2015).
108. As the EU Commission puts it, '*APAs are arrangements that determine, in advance of intra-group transactions, an appropriate set of criteria (e.g. method, comparables and appro- priate adjustments thereto, critical assumptions as to future events) for the determination of the transfer pricing for those transactions over a fixed period of time*' (Opening Decision, State aid SA.38374 (2014/C) (ex 2014/NN) – Netherlands, Alleged aid to Starbucks, para. 8 (11 Jun. 2014)).

predictability to taxpayers.[109] The grant of tax rulings is, however, not an exception from the obligation of the Member States to respect the State aid rules. State aid can be provided through a tax ruling when the ruling endorses a result that does not reflect what would result from a normal application of the ordinary tax system in a reliable manner.[110] If the deviation from the ordinary tax system leads to the lowering of the beneficiary's tax liability compared to the tax liability of undertakings in a similar factual and legal situation, the ruling confers a selective advantage on its beneficiary and thus constitutes State aid.[111]

With regard to *transfer pricing rulings*, the EU Commission essentially argues that these rulings confer a selective advantage to their beneficiaries and thus constitute State aid when they endorse a transfer pricing arrangement that is not in accordance with the arm's length principle. In laymen's terms, the argument is as follows: transfer pricing arrangements between companies that are members of the same corporate group (also referred to as 'integrated companies' or 'group companies') should not depart from arrangements that can be discerned between independent companies that do not form part of a corporate group (also referred to as 'non-integrated companies' or 'standalone companies') and perform similar activities in similar circumstances under normal market conditions. Otherwise, group companies would obtain an advantage as they could shift income to low-tax jurisdictions through manipulated transfer prices. For example, profits can be shifted through inflated prices for intra-group services or overcharged royalties when they are paid by group companies in high-tax jurisdictions to other group members in low- or non-tax jurisdictions, group members subject to preferential tax regimes, or those that are hybrid entities not being subject to tax anywhere. Market conditions can be arrived at through those transfer prices that are established in line with the arm's length principle. If prices for intra-group transfers do not comply with the arm's length principle and this leads to a taxable base for a group company that is lower than the taxable base of a similar standalone company, the group company is favoured compared to a standalone company. Therefore, when tax authorities approve transfer pricing arrangements not in line with the arm's length principle by way of a tax ruling, they grant to the beneficiary of the ruling a selective advantage, which – if it cannot be justified – constitutes State aid.

While this reasoning intuitively makes much sense, it has to be placed in the context of the EU State aid regime and thus must be supported by the legal analysis required by the State aid rules. Hence, it must be shown that a ruling that approves a non-arm's length transfer pricing arrangement is a derogation from the ordinary rules of taxation in the framework of the national tax system at issue which favours its beneficiary compared to taxpayers which are in an objectively comparable situation.

---

109. EU Commission, DG Competition Working Paper on State Aid and Tax Rulings (hereinafter: DG Competition Working Paper), para. 5 (2016); Notion of Aid Notice, para. 169.
110. In its 1998 EU Commission Notice (1998), the EU Commission stated that if '*administrative rulings merely contain an interpretation of general rules, they do not give rise to a presumption of aid*' (para. 22).
111. Notion of Aid Notice, para. 170; Commission Decision, C(2016) 5606 final, on State aid SA.38373 (2014/C)(ex 2014/NN)(ex 2014/CP) implemented by Ireland to Apple (hereinafter: Apple Final Decision), para. 244 (30 Aug. 2016).

Thus, the ordinary rules of taxation – in other words, the reference system – must be established. Furthermore, it has to be shown that taxpayers subject to that reference system are in a legally and factually comparable situation to the beneficiary of the ruling. Finally, it must be substantiated whether and how the arm's length principle is part of that reference system so that it can be maintained that a non-arm's length transfer pricing arrangement constitutes a selective derogation from the reference system. All of this makes the examination of transfer pricing rulings under the State aid rules a highly complex exercise.

Turning to the various steps of this complex analysis, the EU Commission examines the presence of a 'selective advantage' in the decisions on transfer pricing rulings instead of separately analysing the element of 'advantage' and that of 'selectivity'. As a reason for this, the EU Commission refers to the case law of the CJEU according to which, in the case of individual aid measures, *the identification of the economic advantage is, in principle, sufficient to support the presumption that it is selective.*[112] Given that the decisions concern, with the exception of the Belgian excess profit rulings scheme, individual aids, the EU Commission – as the primary line of its reasoning – focuses on demonstrating that the rulings confer an economic advantage while presuming the selectivity of such an advantage. However, in a subsidiary line of reasoning, the EU Commission also examines the tax rulings at issue against the three-step selectivity test that the CJEU devised with regard to fiscal aid schemes (*see* section 3.2).

When demonstrating an economic advantage conferred by the transfer pricing rulings at issue in its main line of reasoning, the EU Commission – referring to the *Belgium and Forum 187 ASBL* case (*see* section 3.3) – contends that the transfer prices endorsed by a ruling must correspond to the prices that would be charged between independent parties negotiating under similar circumstances in conditions of free competition at arm's length.[113] A ruling which enables a taxpayer to deviate from such prices in its intra-group transactions confers an economic advantage within the meaning of Article 107 (1) TFEU as long as the deviation leads to less taxable profits and thus, lower tax liability for the taxpayer. Thereafter, in its subsequent analysis, the EU Commission is seeking to substantiate that the transfer pricing ruling under scrutiny is not in line with the arm's length principle. This may follow from the fact that the ruling approves either the use of an inappropriate transfer pricing method or the wrong application of the otherwise correct method. Demonstrating the latter involves an in-depth and meticulous transfer pricing analysis at the end of which the EU Commission concludes that, by deviating from the arm's length principle, the ruling at issue has granted an advantage to its beneficiary.

As indicated above, as a second line of reasoning, the ruling is nevertheless tested under the three-step selectivity test applicable to aid schemes. Under this analysis, in

---

112. Judgment of the Court of Justice, *Commission v MOL*, C-15/14 P, para. 60. *See* the EU Commission's reasoning to this effect, Apple Final Decision, para. 224; Amazon Final Decision, para. 399, 580–584.
113. *See* Amazon Final Decision, para. 402; Apple Final Decision, paras 249 et seq.; Starbucks Final Decision, paras 258 et seq.; Fiat Final Decision, paras 222 et seq.

the first step, the reference system must be identified. In relation to the transfer pricing rulings at issue, the EU Commission identifies the general corporate income tax system of the Member State concerned as the reference system.[114] In the second step, a derogation from the reference system is required to be shown. A derogation is present insofar as undertakings that are in a legally and factually comparable situation are treated differently. Whether two undertakings are in a legally and factually comparable situation must be determined in the light of the objective of the reference system, as settled case law requires. The objective of the corporate income tax system is the taxation of all of the corporate profits generated in the tax jurisdiction that is concerned. In the light of that objective, all taxpayers subject to corporate income tax are in a comparable situation whether they operate in a multinational group or as standalone companies. Thus, if it can be proven that favourable treatment is being granted through the ruling to the beneficiary that is not available to other companies being in a factually and legally comparable situation, a derogation is established. As favourable treatment, i.e., advantage, was determined to have been granted by the ruling through its deviation from the arm's length principle and such favourable treatment is not available to other corporate taxpayers, the EU Commission argues that the rulings at issue constitute a derogation from the reference system. In particular, the EU Commission points out that the advantage enjoyed by the beneficiary of the ruling is not available to: (i) stand-alone companies being subject to the general rules of corporate income tax (as they do not engage in intra-group transactions and, therefore, cannot deviate from market-based prices); (ii) other group companies forming part of a multinational group which transact only with unrelated parties (in which transactions they cannot either deviate from market-based prices); and (iii) group companies forming part of a multinational group that employ the arm's length principle to their intra-group transactions (as they have not been granted a selective ruling that would allow them to deviate from the arm's length principle).[115] Consequently, the ruling confers a selective advantage on its beneficiary compared to standalone companies and other group companies which are all subject to the general corporate income tax system and are taxed under the normal rules of such a system on a profit which reflects prices determined in the market negotiated at arm's length or estimated in accordance with the correct application of the arm's length principle.

In contrast to the EU Commission's reasoning, the Member States concerned and the beneficiaries of the rulings contend that group companies forming part of a multinational group and standalone companies are not in a legally and factually comparable situation. Only multinational groups of companies are faced with the problem of pricing intra-group transactions and, as such, are subject to transfer pricing legislation.[116] Thus, with regard to transfer pricing rulings, the reference system

---

114. *See* Amazon Final Decision, para. 587; Apple Final Decision, paras 227 et seq.; Starbucks Final Decision, para. 251; Fiat Final Decision, para. 215.
115. *See* Amazon Final Decision, para. 599.
116. *See* Starbucks Final Decision, paras 285 and 193 (21 Oct. 2015); Commission Decision, C(2015) 7152 final, on State aid SA.38375 (2014/C ex 2014/NN) which Luxembourg granted to Fiat (hereinafter: Fiat Final Decision), para. 178 (21 Oct. 2015); Commission Decision, C(2015) 9837 final, on the Excess Profit Exemption State aid Scheme SA.37667 (2015/C)(ex 2015/NN)

should be limited to the national law on transfer pricing that specifies the arm's length principle – if such exists at all – which entails that the reference system encompasses only multinational company groups.[117]

Whether the reference system is defined in a broad or narrow manner is of key importance in arguing the selectivity of transfer pricing rulings. In essence, it answers the question of whom the beneficiary of the ruling must be compared to. When the reference system is defined broadly to be constituted by the general corporate income tax system, the beneficiary must be compared to all of the taxpayers who are subject to that system including stand-alone companies. In this case, it is sufficient to prove that a transfer pricing ruling approves an arrangement that does not fully or properly reflect market conditions which would prevail between independent standalone companies. However, if the reference system is defined narrowly to be constituted by the national transfer pricing rules, the beneficiary must be compared only to other group companies being part of multinational groups and thus subject to transfer pricing rules. In this case, in order for a ruling to be considered selective, it would be necessary to show that other multinational group companies would not be able to obtain a ruling similar to the one under scrutiny. In this case, in principle, the entire administrative practice of the tax administration issuing the ruling should be taken into account in order to demonstrate that the ruling at issue derogates from the way that the tax administration normally applies the arm's length principle.

### 4.3 The Commission's Interpretation of the Arm's Length Principle as a Benchmark for Transfer Pricing Rulings

As is apparent, the EU Commission applies the arm's length principle as a benchmark for determining whether a transfer pricing ruling deviates from the ordinary rules of taxation. However, the EU Commission emphasizes that the arm's length principle that it applies is derived neither from Article 9 of the OECD Model Convention nor from the national tax laws of the Member States, most of which have incorporated such a principle.[118] Instead the arm's length principle is inherent in Article 107 (1) TFEU which prohibits unequal treatment of undertakings that are in a legally and factually comparable situation.[119] According to the EU Commission, the arm's length principle is, in fact, a general principle of equal treatment in taxation which falls within the

---

implemented by Belgium (hereinafter: Belgian Excess Profit Scheme Final Decision), para. 79 (11 Jan. 2016); Amazon Final Decision, para. 590.

117. The EU Commission maintains, as a subsidiary line of reasoning, that even if this narrower reference system is taken as a starting point, the rulings at issue still derogate from such a reference system and, therefore, grant a selective advantage. See, for example, Amazon Final Decision, paras 601–602.

118. For academic commentary on this issue, see Phedon Nicolaides, *State Aid Rules and Tax Rulings*, Issue 3 EStAL (2016); Dimitrios Kyriazis, *From Soft Law to Soft Law Through Hard Law: The Commission's Approach to the State Aid Assessment of Tax Rulings*, Issue 3 EStAL (2016); Anja Taferner/Jurjan Wouda Kuipers, *Tax Rulings: In Line with OECD Transfer Pricing Guidelines, but Contrary to EU State Aid Rules?*, European Taxation (2016); Anna Gunn/Joris Luts, *Tax Rulings, APAs and State Aid: Legal issues*, Vol. 24 Issue 2 EC Tax Review (2015).

119. Notion of Aid Notice, para. 172.

application of Article 107 (1) TFEU. As a consequence, '*[t]he arm's length principle [...] necessarily forms part of the Commission's assessment under Article 107(1) TFEU of tax measures granted to group companies, independently of whether a Member State has incorporated this principle into its national legal system.*'[120]

The EU Commission, in using the arm's length principle as a benchmark, relies on the *Belgium and Forum 187 ASBL* case[121] as a precedent asserting that, in the latter case '*The European Court of Justice endorsed the arm's length principle for determining whether a fiscal measure prescribing a method for an integrated group company to determine its taxable profit gives rise to a selective advantage for the purposes of Article 107(1) TFEU.*'[122] According to critics, this is a rather far-fetched interpretation of the *Belgium and Forum 187 ASBL* case as the CJEU in that case did not refer explicitly to the arm's length principle but rather referred to '*conditions of free competition*' (*see* section 3.3).[123] It stated that the Belgian coordination centre regime conferred an advantage on its beneficiaries because it deviated from the ordinary tax system and not because it deviated from the arm's length principle.[124] The two statements are not the same. The *Belgium and Forum 187 ASBL* case does not necessarily imply that the arm's length principle is part of the ordinary tax system and, as such, the reference system. It also does not imply that the arm's length principle is inherent in Article 107 (1) TFEU as a general principle of equal treatment in taxation.

Regarding the interpretation of the arm's length principle that is inherent in Article 107 (1) TFEU, the EU Commission states that it may have reference to the guidance set out in the OECD Guidelines.[125] Those Guidelines, according to the EU Commission, reflect the international consensus on transfer pricing and provide beneficial guidance to tax administrations and MNEs on how to ensure that a transfer pricing methodology produces an outcome in accordance with market conditions.[126] Thus, the EU Commission does not consider itself bound by the OECD Guidelines in the interpretation of the arm's length principle that it applies under Article 107 (1) TFEU. On the one hand, this follows from the nature of the Guidelines as non-binding soft law. The EU Commission cannot make them binding by imposing them on the Member States through the intermediary of the State aid rules.[127] On the other hand, this also implies that the observance of the OECD Guidelines by a transfer pricing ruling does

---

120. Fiat Final Decision, para. 228; Starbucks Final Decision, para. 264; Belgian Excess Profit Scheme Final Decision, para. 150; Notion of Aid Notice, para. 172.
121. Judgment of the Court of Justice, *Belgium and Forum 187 ASBL*, C-182/03 R and C-217/03 R (2003).
122. DG Competition Working Paper, para. 4.
123. Phedon Nicolaides, *State Aid Rules and Tax Rulings*, Issue 3 EStAL, 420 (2016), p. 420.
124. Dimitrios Kyriazis, *From Soft Law to Soft Law Through Hard Law: The Commission's Approach to the State Aid Assessment of Tax Rulings*, Issue 3 EStAL, 435 (2016), p. 435.
125. Notion of Aid Notice, para. 173.
126. *Ibid.*
127. Dimitrios Kyriazis, *From Soft Law to Soft Law Through Hard Law: The Commission's Approach to the State Aid Assessment of Tax Rulings*, Issue 3 EStAL, 438 et seq. (2016), p. 438.

not necessarily mean that the ruling cannot be challenged under the State aid rules. In theory, the EU Commission's interpretation of the arm's length principle may be different from that of the OECD which, according to critics, may lead to the emergence of a distinct EU arm's length principle.[128] In this regard, the EU Commission maintains that *'if a transfer pricing arrangement complies with the guidance provided by the OECD Transfer Pricing Guidelines, including the guidance on the choice of the most appropriate method and leading to a reliable approximation of a market based outcome, a tax ruling endorsing that arrangement is unlikely to give rise to State aid.'*[129]

The EU Commission also acknowledges that transfer pricing is not an exact science and certain variations and differences are inherent in the approximation of a market-based outcome. Moreover, the EU Commission does not intend to act as a second-instance tax authority reviewing each and every transfer pricing determination of the Member States' tax authorities in detail. Rather, it focuses on cases where there is a manifest breach of the arm's length principle. DG Competition's Working Paper[130] aims at clarifying the EU Commission's approach to transfer pricing rulings and provides examples of such a manifest breach. In the forthcoming sections, a few of these examples will be discussed and demonstrated through the concrete cases investigated by the EU Commission.

## 4.4 Rulings Deviating from the Arm's Length Principle

### 4.4.1 Problems with the Choice of the Transfer Pricing Method

The EU Commission points out that the use of particular transfer pricing methods provides a more reliable method to approximate a market based outcome than others do.[131] The EU Commission appears to suggest that this is the case with the CUP method which sets prices for intragroup transactions by making direct comparisons with the price charged on the market for the same goods or services. The *Starbucks* case is an example where the EU Commission argues, *inter alia*, that the APA under scrutiny deviates from the arm's length principle as it endorses the use of the TNMM method for the pricing of intragroup transactions at issue whereas the CUP method would have produced a more reliable approximation of a market based outcome (Figure 14.3).[132]

---

128. *Ibid.*, 437 et seq; Anja Taferner/Jurjan Wouda Kuipers, *Tax Rulings: In Line with OECD Transfer Pricing Guidelines, but Contrary to EU State Aid Rules?*, European Taxation, 139 et seq (2016).
129. Notion of Aid Notice, para. 173; DG Competition Working Paper, para. 18.
130. *Supra* n. 109.
131. DG Competition Working Paper, para. 19.
132. Starbucks Final Decision, paras 299 and 445.

*Figure 14.3   State Aid Granted by the Netherlands to Starbucks*

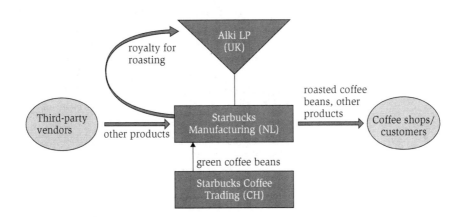

In the *Starbucks* case, the EU Commission investigated the APA which was obtained in 2008 by Starbucks Manufacturing BV (SMBV) from the Dutch tax authorities.[133] As a subsidiary of the Starbucks group, SMBV is incorporated in the Netherlands and operates as a roasting facility.[134] Its primary activity is to purchase green coffee beans from the Swiss based company Starbucks Coffee Trading, roast the coffee beans, and sell the roasted coffee to shops and customers. Apart from that, SMBV serves as a distribution entity for other non-coffee items. The IP required for the roasting process is licensed from SMBV's shareholder and the holder of the IP rights Alki LP, a UK entity that is transparent for tax purposes. SMBV pays a royalty to Alki LP. In the APA, the application of the TNMM was agreed upon in order to estimate an arm's length remuneration for the functions performed by SMBV. The Dutch tax authorities accepted a remuneration equal to a mark up of 9–12% of SMBV's operating expense (excluding certain cost items). Any profit generated by SMBV exceeding the level of remuneration calculated in this way (i.e., residual profits) was agreed to be paid out as a royalty to Alki LP.[135]

In its decision, the EU Commission concluded that the TNMM was not the most appropriate method for estimating the taxable profit of SMBV as the least complex entity in the transactions was not SMBV but, rather, Alki LP.[136] The EU Commission argued that, instead of the TNMM, the CUP method should have been used. That would have required the identification of SMBV's controlled transactions, i.e., the royalty payment by SMBV to Alki LP, the payment for the coffee beans by SMBV to the Swiss entity, and the finding of comparable uncontrolled transactions for them. As direct comparables were available for the controlled transactions, there was no need for comparing the functions performed by SMBV through the TNMM. Regarding the

---

133. *Ibid.*, para. 40.
134. For the Starbucks structure *see* Starbucks Final Decision, paras 48–54.
135. For the conditions of the APA, *see* Starbucks Final Decision, paras 42 et seq.
136. *See* Ch. 4 of this book.

royalty payment, the EU Commission considers that the use of the CUP method – i.e., a comparison to comparable uncontrolled transactions, in particular, several roasting agreements that Starbucks has concluded with third parties – leads to the result that the royalty should be zero.[137] In other words, no royalty should be due for the IP in the context of the relationship between SMBV and Alki LP as SMBV does not derive any benefit from the use of the roasting IP licensed from Alki LP. In addition, the price paid for the coffee beans to the Swiss entity was too high compared to what would have been paid in an uncontrolled transaction.[138] To summarize, the CUP-method would have produced a more reliable approximation of a market based outcome than the TNMM and, in particular, higher profits that should have been taxed by the Netherlands.[139] Hence, with the acceptance of the TNMM by the Dutch tax authorities, the arm's length principle was deviated from, and Starbucks was granted a selective advantage.

### 4.4.2 Problems with Other Methodological Choices

In DG Competition's Working Paper, it is pointed out that '[t]he approximate nature of the arm's length principle cannot be used to justify a transfer pricing analysis that is either methodologically inconsistent or based on an inadequate comparables selection.'[140] Thus, even though the transfer pricing analysis results only in an approximation of a marked-based outcome, the methodologies used must be consistent. In the FIAT case,[141] the EU Commission's challenge does not concern the transfer pricing method endorsed by the ruling at issue but rather the way in which the TNMM method was applied. In particular, the EU Commission questions the methodological choices made by the taxpayer and accepted by the Luxembourg tax authorities in the practical application of the TNMM.

The FIAT case concerns an APA issued in 2012 by the Luxembourg tax authorities to FIAT Finance and Trade (FFT), a company of the FIAT group resident in Luxembourg.[142] FFT provides financing and treasury services to other – mainly European – companies of the FIAT group. In particular, FFT raises funds from the market, especially from bank loans and issuance of bonds, and obtains financing from other treasury companies of the FIAT group which it subsequently lends to the operating group companies. Apart from providing intra-group loans, FFT's functions also include liquidity investments, relationships with financial market actors, financial

---

137. See Starbucks Final Decision, para. 290.
138. Ibid., para. 349.
139. Apart from this, the EU Commission also argues that, even if it can be assumed that the TNMM method is the correct one, it was wrongly applied as the functions of SMBV were incorrectly identified, the use of operating expenses as a profit level indicator was incorrect (see on this issue, DG Competition Working Paper para. 22), and the working capital adjustments were not justified.
140. DG Competition Working Paper, para. 23.
141. See on this case, Rita Szudoczky, FIAT. Non-confidential version of decision on selective tax advantages for Fiat in Luxembourg. State aid. European Commission, Highlights & Insights on European Taxation 2017/2, p. 159.
142. For the conditions of the APA, see Fiat Final Decision, paras 52 et seq.

531

coordination and consultancy services to group companies, cash pooling, foreign exchange and interest rate risk management, as well as coordination with other treasury companies of the FIAT group (Figure 14.4).[143]

*Figure 14.4    State Aid Granted by Luxembourg to FIAT*

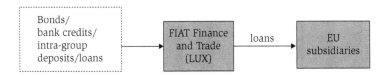

The risks that FFT is exposed to consist of market risk, credit risk, counterparty risk relating to derivative assets held with third parties, and operational risk. The APA endorses the methodology proposed by FFT's tax advisor to calculate the remuneration for the functions performed and the risks borne by FFT and, as such, the determination of FFT's taxable profits in Luxembourg. The methodology was the TNMM, and capital was used as a profit level indicator. However, not the entire amount of FFT's accounting equity served as the indicator but rather an amount of capital that FFT was estimated to need in order to perform its functions and bear its risks. The latter amount was arrived at by making various methodological choices (e.g., using the Basel II framework to calculate the hypothetical regulatory capital of FFT) and adjustments (e.g., deducting FFT's participations in other group companies from the total level of equity) which are not envisaged by the OECD TPG. In calculating the required level of return on capital, a selection of various parameters was made.

The EU Commission contests neither the TNMM method as the most appropriate method for estimating FFT's taxable profits in Luxembourg nor the choice of capital as the profit level indicator in its decision.[144] It does contest, however, all of the subsequent choices regarding methods, parameters, and adjustments that were made by FFT's tax advisor and endorsed by the APA. According to the EU Commission, such choices led to a much lower capital base than FFT's actual capital and to a lower return on that capital than market rates. For this reason, the EU Commission considers that the methodology endorsed by the APA does not accord with the arm's length principle. As the departure from the arm's length principle resulted in decreasing FFT's taxable profits compared to the level of profits on which stand-alone companies performing similar functions under normal market conditions would be taxed under the general Luxembourg corporate income tax system, the APA confers a selective advantage on FFT and, therefore, constitutes State aid.

---

143. On the Fiat group structure, *see* Fiat Final Decision, paras 34 et seq.
144. Fiat Final Decision, paras 249 et seq.

The EU Commission's subsidiary line of reasoning in the *Amazon* case also challenges various methodological choices in the application of the transfer pricing method selected by the taxpayer and endorsed by the ruling at issue in the case (for the facts *see* section 4.4.3).[145] In particular, the EU Commission contends that: (i) the functional analysis incorrectly concluded that the tested party performed solely routine functions, (ii) the profit level indicator was selected incorrectly, and (iii) the inclusion of a ceiling in the transfer pricing arrangement was incorrect.[146]

### 4.4.3  Problems Related to the Use of One-Sided Methods

In tax rulings that are based on a two-sided approach, the intra-group transactions of two companies are analysed from both sides. This is a case with the profit split method which allocates a share of the overall profit to the two companies involved in the transaction. Otherwise stated, the entire amount of the profit will be divided between the two group companies if the method is consistently applied by the two jurisdictions where the companies are situated. A two-sided approach is also pursued when Bilateral Advance Pricing Agreements are concluded.[147] In DG Competition's Working Paper, the EU Commission points out that rulings which take into consideration both parties to the intra-group transaction will more likely lead to a market-based outcome.[148]

In contrast, rulings adopted on the basis of a one-sided approach take into account the features and circumstances of only one of the parties to the intra-group transaction, specifically, the taxpayer requesting the transfer pricing ruling. As the EU Commission explains, this refers practically to the TNMM that estimates the remuneration of the taxpayer requesting the ruling based on a unilateral assessment of the taxpayer's activities and functions. As the taxpayer to which the TNMM is applied is only supposed to perform routine functions, the residual profit (i.e., that remaining after the deduction of the remuneration of the requesting taxpayer) will generally be allocated to the other party of the transaction sometimes without even having any information on it.[149] For this reason, one-sided methods are usually considered to be less reliable than two-sided approaches (Figure 14.5).

---

145. The EU Commission argues, in the first place, that the TNMM has been applied to the wrong party to the licensing transaction at issue but, even if it were to be accepted that the tested party, LuxOpCo, should be the operating company, the ruling still confers a selective advantage on the latter due to the incorrect methodological steps in the application of the TNMM.
146. Amazon Final Decision, paras 562–578.
147. *See* Ch. 4.
148. DG Competition Working Paper, para. 20.
149. *Ibid.*, para. 21.

Figure 14.5   Excess Profit Exemption in Belgium

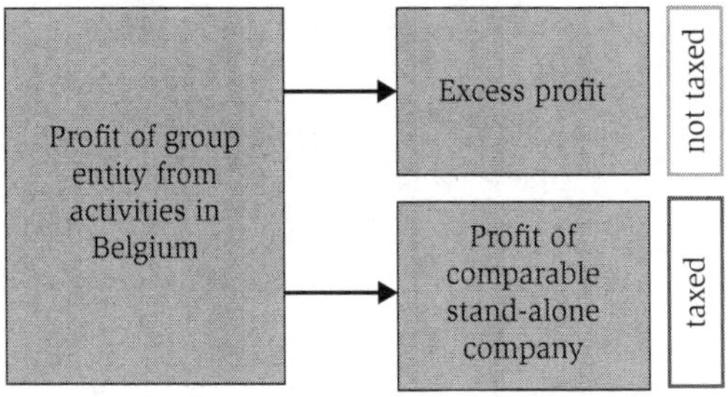

In the *Belgian Excess Profit exemption scheme* case, the EU Commission took the opportunity to comment on the issue of the two-sided versus one-sided approach. The Excess Profit exemption scheme implemented in Belgium allowed Belgian entities that are part of a multinational group to reduce their tax base by deducting excess profits from their actual profits.[150] Such excess profit is determined by estimating the hypothetical average profit that a comparable stand-alone company would be expected to make under comparable circumstances and subtracting that amount from the actually recorded profits of the Belgian group entity. Belgium considered that the excess profit should not be attributed to the Belgian group entity and, therefore, should be excluded from the Belgian tax base. In other words, the scheme allowed an annual pro-active downward adjustment of the corporate income tax base of Belgian entities of multinational groups through the exemption of their 'excess profits'. According to the Belgian tax authorities, the rationale of the scheme was to ensure that a Belgian group company is taxed only on the basis of an amount that corresponds to the arm's length profit excluding exceeding profits resulting from group synergies, economies of scale, or other advantages that derive from that entity's participation in the multinational group.

To benefit from the scheme, the Belgian group entity was required to request an advance ruling from the Belgian tax authorities. To calculate the excess profit, the Belgian tax authorities employed a two-step approach: In a first step, the arm's length prices of the transactions between the Belgian group entity and foreign group companies were fixed. The Belgian group entity was identified as the "central entrepreneur" in that relationship and, therefore, was allocated the residual profit from the transactions. In a second step, according to Belgium, the residual profit should not be considered as the Belgian entity's arm's length profit as it may exceed the profit that a comparable standalone company would make under similar circumstances. Thus, the amount of the excess profit was established. For this, the TNMM was applied to calculate a hypothetical average profit for the Belgian group entity based on a benchmark study comparing it with comparable standalone companies. The latter was

---

150. For a detailed description of the scheme, *see* Belgian Excess Profit Scheme Final Decision, paras 13–22.

regarded as the profit that the Belgian group entity would have made had it been a stand-alone company. The excess profit equalled the difference between the original amount of profits arrived at in the first step and the latter amount. This excess profit was exempted under the scheme.

In its decision, the EU Commission argued that the method described above involved that both parties to a controlled transaction are tested with a one-sided transfer pricing method (TNMM) at different stages in the transfer pricing assessment.[151] In the first step, the TNMM is applied to the non-Belgian group companies which are the least complex entities in the transactions with the lowest risks as opposed to the Belgian group company which is the central entrepreneur. The Belgian group entity as the central entrepreneur should be allocated all of the residual profits. However, in the second step of the analysis, the TNMM is applied to the Belgian group entity, which presupposes that it is the least complex entity with only routine functions, in order to estimate its hypothetical average profit. The inconsistent application of the one-sided methods to the two parties to the controlled transactions has the consequence that the combined operating profit of the relevant transactions will not equal the sum of the profits that derive from the application of the TNMM on both parties and thus, an untaxed amount is generated. In addition, the EU Commission added that the unilateral adjustment by Belgium to the Belgian group entity's profits that were actually recorded inevitably means that the excess profit exempted by Belgium cannot be taxed by another jurisdiction. This is because the right to tax profits arising specifically from group synergies is not recognized by other jurisdictions because those profits pertain only to Belgium which was the tax jurisdiction where they were actually recorded. Hence, through the exemption of those excess profits in Belgium, a completely untaxed tax base is created, and such an approach does not comply with the arm's length principle.

In the *Apple* case, the EU Commission's main line of argument is similar, i.e., a completely one-sided approach to the allocation of functions, assets, and risks between different parts of the same company is not in accordance with the arm's length principle.[152] The case concerns two rulings issued by Ireland in 1991 and 2007 that address the determination of the taxable profits of the Irish branches of two companies of the Apple group.[153] Apple Sales International (ASI) and Apple Operations Europe (AOE) were two Irish incorporated companies that were ultimately controlled by Apple Inc. During the time the rulings were in force, ASI and AOE were not a resident in Ireland and did not have a taxable presence in any other jurisdiction apart from the branches in Ireland. Regarding their head offices, they lacked any physical presence or employees and were not located in any jurisdiction. Therefore, ASI and AOE were stateless for tax residency purposes. They held the rights to use Apple's intellectual property to sell and manufacture Apple products outside the Americas under a cost-sharing agreement (CSA) with Apple Inc. (Figure 14.6).

---

151. *See* Belgian Excess Profit Scheme Final Decision, paras 153 et seq.
152. *See*, on this case, Hans Bakker, *Commission Decision on State aid implemented by Ireland to Apple. European Commission*, Highlights & Insights on European Taxation 2017/3, p. 102.
153. *See*, for the Apple group structure, Apple Final Decision, paras 40–58.

*Figure 14.6   State Aid Granted by Ireland to Apple*

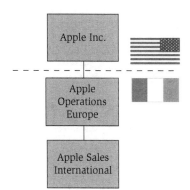

The contested rulings endorsed a method for determining the net profit to be allocated to ASI's and AOE's Irish branches.[154] As far as ASI is concerned, the net profit was to be calculated as 12.5% of the branch operating costs excluding materials for resale according to the tax ruling issued in 1991. However, a modified method was endorsed in another ruling in 2007 according to which this net profit had to be calculated as [10–15%] on branch operating costs, excluding costs for charges from affiliates and material costs. Concerning AOE, the net profit attributable to its Irish branch was determined by 65% of its operating expenses up to USD [60–70] million per year and 20% of its operating expenses for the excess amount according to the tax ruling of 1991. Thus, the operating expenses used in this method had to also include depreciation but exclude materials for resale and cost-shares charged from affiliates for intangibles. In 2007, the method was revised, and the tax base of the branch was composed of: (i) [10–15%] of its operating costs excluding material costs and charges from affiliates, (ii) an IP return of [1–5%] of the turnover with regard to the accumulated manufacturing process technology of the Irish branch, and (iii) an appropriate deduction for capital allowances for plant and buildings.

The EU Commission contended in its decision that the rulings at issue endorsed the unsubstantiated assumption that the Apple IP licences held by ASI and AOE should be allocated outside of Ireland and thus only a limited mark up on a reduced cost base should be allocated to ASI's and AOE's Irish branches. According to the EU Commission, this is not an allocation that would have been accepted by the Irish branches if they had been independent companies negotiating at arm's length with the other parts of the companies. The EU Commission reasons that, since the head offices of ASI and AOE were non-existent, they can perform no function and assume no risks regarding the IP licences. Therefore, those licences must necessarily be allocated to the Irish branches. Taking into account the lack of functions performed by the head offices and the functions performed by the Irish branches, the Apple IP licences for the

---

154. *See*, for the tax rulings, Apple Final Decision, paras 59 et seq.

procurement, manufacturing, sales, and distribution of Apple products should have been allocated to the Irish branches. Ireland argues, on the other hand, that only the activities that occur in the Irish branches need to be considered by the Irish tax authorities and not those of the head offices. This is because Ireland only has the competence to tax that portion of the profits of the company which is commensurate with the activities of the Irish branches. As there are no management activities in the Irish branches associated with the IP licenses, they should not be allocated to the Irish branches. As a response, the EU Commission stresses in its final decision that the Irish tax authorities were obligated to first properly examine the assets used, the functions performed, and the risks assumed by ASI and AOE through their Irish branches and through the other parts of those companies. The information available on the head offices should not have been disregarded when allocating profits to the Irish branches since that information allows the Irish tax authorities to conclude in a more reliable manner on whether the profit allocation methods proposed by Apple result in a reliable approximation of a market-based outcome in line with the arm's length principle than by solely relying on information of the activities of the Irish branches.[155] As the EU Commission found that the rulings granted a selective advantage, and thus State aid to Apple, it ordered the recovery of the unlawful aid in a record-setting amount of EUR 13 billion, i.e., the amount with which Apple's tax liability was lowered in the period between 2003 and 2014[156] including interest.[157]

The inappropriate application of a one-sided transfer pricing method was also the core of the problem – according to the EU Commission – in the *Amazon* case.[158] In particular, the EU Commission argues in this case that the TNMM method was applied to the intra-group licensing transaction at issue to the wrong party because a proper functional analysis of both parties should have concluded that the party performing routine functions was the passive IP holding company and not the operating company to which the TNMM was applied in the arrangement approved by the ruling.[159] More specifically, the case concerns a tax ruling issued to the Amazon group by Luxembourg tax authorities in 2004. It was initially concluded for five years, was prolonged in 2010, and effectively used until June 2014. In Luxembourg, Amazon operated its European business through two companies, LuxOpCo and LuxSCS, which were both fully-owned and controlled by the Amazon US parent company.[160] LuxSCS was a Luxembourg limited partnership and functioned purely as an intangibles holding company for Amazon's European operations. As it was transparent for tax purposes, neither LuxSCS

---

155. *See* Apple Final Decision, paras 265 et seq.
156. The limitation period of ten years reverts to 2003 since the first request for information by the EU Commission was made in 2013.
157. *See* Press Release, IP/16/2923 (30 Aug. 2016).
158. Commission Decision, C(2017), on State Aid SA.38944 (2014/C ex 2014/NN) implemented by the Luxembourg to Amazon (hereinafter: Amazon Final Decision)(4 Oct. 2017).
159. The taxpayer identified the method applied by it in the transfer pricing report and endorsed by the ruling as a residual profit split method, however, the EU Commission argues that, in reality, it is TNMM since, after the remuneration of the routine functions of the tested party based on the TNMM, the residual profit was not split between the two parties but fully attributed to the other party.
160. For the Amazon group structure, *see* Amazon Final Decision, paras 90–115.

nor its partners based in the US were subject to Luxembourg corporate income tax (while its partners deferred their US tax liability on the partnerships' income). LuxSCS served as an intermediary between LuxOpCo and the US parent and held certain IP rights under a Cost Sharing Agreement (CSA) with the US parent. Under this agreement, LuxSCS obtained the right to exploit and sublicense a certain Amazon IP and had to make a buy-in payment and a particular annual share of costs for further developing the intangibles as consideration. LuxSCS granted exclusive licenses to LuxOpCo in return for a royalty payment. LuxOpCo was a wholly-owned subsidiary of LuxSCS and served as the operating company which recorded all of the sales made in Europe (Figure 14.7).

*Figure 14.7   State Aid Granted by Luxembourg to Amazon*

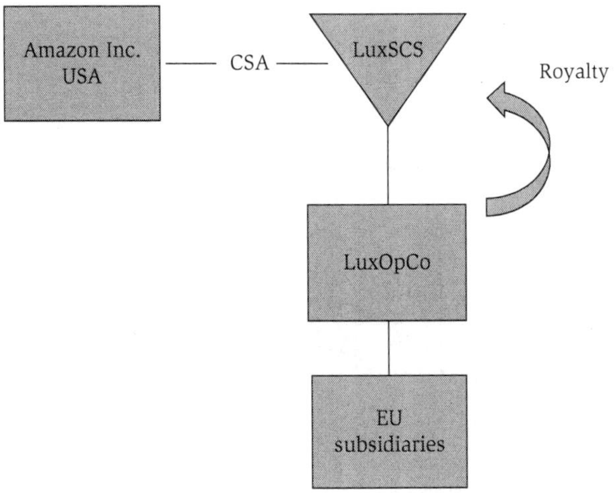

Amazon Inc. USA —— CSA —— LuxSCS —— Royalty

LuxOpCo

EU subsidiaries

In the tax ruling, the Luxembourg tax authorities confirmed the treatment of LuxOpCo for income tax purposes.[161] Therein, the level of the annual royalty rate for the use of the intangibles was established. To calculate the amount to be paid by LuxOpCo to LuxSCS as endorsed by the tax ruling, the return of LuxOpCo first needed to be computed which was equal to the lesser of: (i) 4.5% of its total EU operating expenses for the year and (ii) the total EU operating profit for such year. However, the amount of the LuxOpCo return for any year should not be less than 0.45% of EU revenue (floor) nor greater than 0.55% thereof (ceiling). The royalty should be equal to EU operating profit minus the calculated LuxOpCo return. When determining its annual income tax liability, LuxOpCo relied upon the contested tax ruling.

In its decision, the EU Commission agreed that none of the IP agreements concluded between Amazon and unrelated parties provided for a sufficiently comparable uncontrolled transaction to establish a CUP. Since no direct comparables to the license agreement existed, the EU Commission confirmed that the TNMM was the most

---

161. For the details on the tax ruling, *see* Amazon Final Decision, paras 121–128.

appropriate method to determine the relevant transfer price.[162] However, considering the functional analysis, the EU Commission found that the party performing unique and valuable functions in this transaction was LuxOpCo and not LuxSCS. On that basis, the tested party for the application of the TNMM should have been LuxSCS (instead of LuxOpCo) because it was the party that performed the least complex functions.[163] According to the EU Commission, the Luxembourg tax administration should not have accepted that the mere legal ownership of the intangibles constituted a contribution for which LuxSCS should receive a remuneration consisting of almost all of the profits derived from all of LuxOpCo's business activities.[164] In regard to this, the EU Commission found that the ruling that allowed LuxOpCo to deduct all of its residual profits that it paid as royalties to LuxSCS from its taxable income conferred an economic advantage on LuxOpCo.[165]

Regarding the question of how the TNMM should be applied to LuxSCS, the EU Commission maintained that an arm's length remuneration for LuxSCS under the licence agreement equalled the sum of buy-in payment and CSA costs incurred in relation to the intangibles without a mark-up plus any other relevant costs to which a mark-up of 5% should be applied to the extent that those costs may be considered as reflecting the actual functions performed by LuxSCS.[166]

## 4.5   Criticism of the EU Commission's Approach

The EU Commission's investigations into tax rulings have incited fierce criticism not only by the Member States and business communities but also by the United States which claims that the investigations disproportionately target US companies.

The most common criticism that is made explicit is that the EU Commission's investigations discredit tax rulings and thereby deprive the Member States from an important legal instrument through which they can provide legal certainty to investors. This can jeopardize the attractiveness of the EU internal market and deter foreign investments. It is also often pointed out that the EU Commission uses the State aid rules for a purpose for which they are not intended, i.e., to target aggressive tax planning structures and the exploitation of differences and mismatches between the tax systems. It is argued that the actual problem in these structures is not the transfer pricing arrangements but the lack of taxation of the income that is transferred through intra-group transactions. Such income ends up in the hands of hybrid entities, nowhere companies, and companies benefiting from preferential tax regimes. In such way, the profits of multinational companies that are generated in Europe largely or wholly escape taxation in Europe while they are also not taxed in the US where taxation is deferred on profits that are not repatriated. The EU Commission, in fact, attempts to compensate for the lack of taxation of profits made in Europe by challenging the

---

162. Amazon Final Decision, para. 542.
163. *Ibid.*, paras 544–549.
164. *Ibid.*, para. 547.
165. *Ibid.*, para. 560.
166. *Ibid.*, paras 558 et seq.

transfer pricing aspects of such aggressive tax structures. Critics argue that the fact that the US does not tax its multinational companies on large amounts of their profits as long as they remain outside the US for the avowed purpose of boosting the competitiveness of US companies cannot be offset by qualifying common and sound transfer pricing arrangements as State aid.

Another aspect of the criticism points to the fact that, with the continuous expansion of the scope of the State aid rules to new measures which had previously been considered to lie outside their reach, the EU Commission intrudes into areas that are within the competence of the Member States. This objection, in essence, claims that the EU Commission, in effect, harmonizes the Member States' tax systems through the back door by using the State aid rules.[167] The EU arm's length principle that appears to be emerging from the EU Commission's reasoning is independent from national laws. Through this means, the EU Commission indirectly prescribes how the taxable amount must be computed in the Member States in order to avoid conflicts with the State aid provisions. With such a distinct EU arm's length principle derived from Article 107 (1) TFEU the EU Commission took a further step towards the harmonization of the Member States' tax systems, it is argued.

Regarding the US's reaction to the State aid procedures, after exchanges of letters between the US Treasury Department and DG Competition of the EU Commission,[168] in August 2016, the US Treasury Department issued a longer White Paper specifying the United States' primary concerns regarding the EU Commission's State aid investigations into transfer pricing rulings.[169]

First, the US Treasury Department puts forward that the EU Commission's approach departs from the analytical framework developed by prior decision-making practice and case law insofar as it examines the presence of a 'selective advantage' instead of separately analysing the elements of 'advantage' and 'selectivity'. As a result, according to the Treasury Department, the analysis is reduced to determining whether or not a transfer pricing ruling complies with the arm's length principle developed by the EU Commission. Moreover, such an analysis treats standalone companies and group companies as being in a comparable situation which – in the view of the Treasury Department – is contrary to prior practice and case law.

Second, the US Treasury Department is of the opinion that the EU Commission should refrain from seeking retroactive recoveries under its new approach as it jeopardizes legal certainty. Many companies have received tax rulings from EU

---

167. Dimitrios Kyriazis, *From Soft Law to Soft Law Through Hard Law: The Commission's Approach to the State Aid Assessment of Tax Rulings*, Issue 3 EStAL, 436 et seq. (2016), p. 436.
168. Letter of 11 Feb. 2016 from U.S. Treasury Secretary Jacob Lew to the President of the European Commission Jean-Claude Juncker concerning the EU Commission's State aid investigations (*see* https://www.treasury.gov/resource-center/tax-policy/treaties/Documents/Letter-State-Aid-Investigations.pdf, accessed May 2017); Response Letter of 29 Feb. 2016 written by European Commissioner Margrethe Vestager on behalf of President Junker in reply to Secretary Lew (*see* https://drive.google.com/file/d/0B_p5wXj7Q88MYUVyTG83R01BZEk/view, accessed May 2017).
169. US Department of the Treasury, *White Paper, The European Commission's recent State aid investigations of Transfer Pricing Rulings (hereinafter: White Paper)*, 19 (24 Aug. 2016).

Member States for many years, and there were no suggestions that tax rulings could conflict with the State aid rules, therefore, taxpayers were correct to rely upon the status quo existing at that time.

Third, the Treasury Department argues that the EU Commission introduced an arm's length principle in its State aid assessment which is distinct from the arm's length principle of the OECD Guidelines *'without having previously provided any guidance on what the arm's length principle under the TFEU means.'* From the perspective of the US Treasury Department, the EU Commission's new approach is inconsistent with international norms and undermines the international tax system. In particular, it is contrary to the international consensus on transfer pricing standards, calls into question the Member States' ability to honour their bilateral tax treaties (in mutual agreement procedures), and eliminates the progress made under the BEPS project on coordinated approaches to base erosion and profit shifting.

## 5   CONCLUSIONS

This chapter has discussed the assessment of transfer pricing rulings under the EU State aid rules in detail.

To fall under the prohibition of State aid pursuant to Article 107 TFEU, a measure must meet four cumulative conditions: (i) the existence of an advantage, (ii) granted by a Member State or through State resources, (iii) granted in a selective manner which (iv) affecting intra-Union trade and distorts competition.

While it has been clear for decades that the State aid rules apply to tax measures just as any other measures of State intervention, fiscal State aid remains one of the most volatile areas of EU State aid law due to the expansive interpretation of the concept of State aid by the EU Commission and the EU Courts in this area. As a result, an increasing number of newer categories of tax measures are caught by the State aid prohibition. Most recently, the EU Commission has extended its State aid scrutiny from general aid schemes to more targeted and individual tax measures and, in particular, transfer pricing rulings. Even though the aim of transfer pricing rulings is to provide certainty to taxpayers by endorsing methods for the determination of transfer prices on which the taxpayers can rely, such rulings may also be utilized to provide selective advantages to certain taxpayers. In particular, this is the case when transfer pricing rulings approve a method for the pricing of intra-group transactions that does not result in a reliable approximation of market-based outcomes and thereby reduce the taxable profits thus the tax liability of their beneficiaries. In establishing the latter, the EU Commission essentially argues that transfer pricing rulings that deviate from the arm's length principle can constitute State aid for its beneficiary even in cases where the arm's length principle is not laid down in the national law of the respective Member State because such a principle is inherent in Article 107 (1) TFEU which reflects the general principle of equal treatment. Whether a certain transfer pricing ruling deviates from the arm's length principle derived from Article 107 (1) TFEU depends, in effect, on the interpretation that the EU Commission gives to such a principle.

The EU Commission's decisions on transfer pricing rulings show that the EU Commission uses its powers in the State aid realm to streamline the transfer pricing practices within the EU both at the level of multinational groups and Member States' authorities. Thus, the EU Commission's decisions could have major impacts on the future behaviour of multinational groups operating within the EU, for example, with regard to the choice of transfer pricing methods and methodologies or their reliance on tax rulings – at least until the CJEU makes a final decision on this issue.

# Index

# Chapters in This Publication

| Chapters | Citation |
|---|---|
| 1 | Petruzzi, R., Cottani, G., Sollund, S., Prasanna, S., 'Introduction to Transfer Pricing', in: Lang, Cottani, Petruzzi, Storck (eds), *Fundamentals of Transfer Pricing: A Practical Guide* (Vienna: Wolters Kluwer, 2018). |
| 2 | Prasanna, S. & Petruzzi, R., 'Accurate Delineation and Recognition of Actual Transactions: Comparability Analysis', in: Lang, Cottani, Petruzzi, Storck (eds), *Fundamentals of Transfer Pricing: A Practical Guide* (Vienna: Wolters Kluwer, 2018). |
| 3 | Brown, M. & Orlandi, M., 'Transfer Pricing Methods (Part I): Traditional Transaction Methods', in: Lang, Cottani, Petruzzi, Storck (eds), *Fundamentals of Transfer Pricing: A Practical Guide* (Vienna: Wolters Kluwer, 2018). |
| 4 | Gonnet, S. & Madelpuech, G., 'Transfer Pricing Methods (Part II): Transactional Profit Methods', in: Lang, Cottani, Petruzzi, Storck (eds), *Fundamentals of Transfer Pricing: A Practical Guide* (Vienna: Wolters Kluwer, 2018). |
| 5 | Buriak, S. & Striato, M., 'Administrative Approaches to Avoiding/Minimizing Transfer Pricing Disputes', in: Lang, Cottani, Petruzzi, Storck (eds), *Fundamentals of Transfer Pricing: A Practical Guide* (Vienna: Wolters Kluwer, 2018). |
| 6 | Piccone, P.F., Burkadze, E., Peng, C., 'Administrative Approaches to Resolving Transfer Pricing Disputes', in: Lang, Cottani, Petruzzi, Storck (eds), *Fundamentals of Transfer Pricing: A Practical Guide* (Vienna: Wolters Kluwer, 2018). |
| 7 | Bremer, S., 'Transfer Pricing Documentation: Master File, Country File and Country-by-Country Reporting', in: Lang, Cottani, Petruzzi, Storck (eds), *Fundamentals of Transfer Pricing: A Practical Guide* (Vienna: Wolters Kluwer, 2018). |
| 8 | Holzinger, R., 'Attribution of Profits to Permanent Establishments', in: Lang, Cottani, Petruzzi, Storck (eds), *Fundamentals of Transfer Pricing: A Practical Guide* (Vienna: Wolters Kluwer, 2018). |

| Chapters | Citation |
| --- | --- |
| 9 | Peng, C. & Petruzzi, R., 'Transfer Pricing and Intra-group Services', in: Lang, Cottani, Petruzzi, Storck (eds), *Fundamentals of Transfer Pricing: A Practical Guide* (Vienna: Wolters Kluwer, 2018). |
| 10 | Petruzzi, R., 'Transfer Pricing and Intra-group Financial Transactions', in: Lang, Cottani, Petruzzi, Storck (eds), *Fundamentals of Transfer Pricing: A Practical Guide* (Vienna: Wolters Kluwer, 2018). |
| 11 | Cottani, G. & Ludovici, P., 'Transfer Pricing and Intangibles', in: Lang, Cottani, Petruzzi, Storck (eds), *Fundamentals of Transfer Pricing: A Practical Guide* (Vienna: Wolters Kluwer, 2018). |
| 12 | Prasanna, S. & Quattrocchi, Z., 'Transfer Pricing, Supply Chain Management and Business Restructurings', in: Lang, Cottani, Petruzzi, Storck (eds), *Fundamentals of Transfer Pricing: A Practical Guide* (Vienna: Wolters Kluwer, 2018). |
| 13 | Cremer, I. & Lim, B., 'Transfer Pricing and Customs Valuation', in: Lang, Cottani, Petruzzi, Storck (eds), *Fundamentals of Transfer Pricing: A Practical Guide* (Vienna: Wolters Kluwer, 2018). |
| 14 | Miladinovic, A. & Szudoczky, R., 'Transfer Pricing and EU State Aid', in: Lang, Cottani, Petruzzi, Storck (eds), *Fundamentals of Transfer Pricing: A Practical Guide* (Vienna: Wolters Kluwer, 2018). |